Praxis
On Acting and Knowing

Praxis investigates both the existing practices of international politics and relations during and after the Cold War, and the issue of whether problems of praxis (individual and collective choices) can be subjected to a "theoretical treatment." The book comes in two parts: the first deals with the constitution of international relations and the role of theoretical norms in guiding decisions, in areas such as sanctions, the punishment of international crimes, governance, and "constitutional" concern. The second part is devoted to "theory building." While a "theorization" of praxis has often been attempted, Kratochwil argues that such endeavors do not attend to certain important elements characteristic of practical choices. *Praxis* presents a shift from the accepted International Relations standard of theorizing, by arguing for the analysis of policy decisions made in non-ideal conditions within a broader framework of practical choices, emphasizing both historicity and contingency.

FRIEDRICH KRATOCHWIL has taught at the universities of Maryland, Columbia, Denver and Pennsylvania, prior to becoming chair of international relations at the Ludwig-Maximilians-Universität, Munich, and later at the European University Institute in Florence (2003–2011). He was editor of the *European Journal of International Relations* and has served as a member of the editorial boards for several leading European, American, and Asian journals. He is the author of *Rules, Norms and Decisions* (Cambridge, 1989), *The Puzzles of Politics* (2011), and *The Status of Law in World Society* (Cambridge, 2014).

Praxis

On Acting and Knowing

Friedrich Kratochwil

European University Institute, Florence

CAMBRIDGE
UNIVERSITY PRESS

Shaftesbury Road, Cambridge CB2 8EA, United Kingdom

One Liberty Plaza, 20th Floor, New York, NY 10006, USA

477 Williamstown Road, Port Melbourne, VIC 3207, Australia

314–321, 3rd Floor, Plot 3, Splendor Forum, Jasola District Centre, New Delhi – 110025, India

103 Penang Road, #05–06/07, Visioncrest Commercial, Singapore 238467

Cambridge University Press is part of Cambridge University Press & Assessment, a department of the University of Cambridge.

We share the University's mission to contribute to society through the pursuit of education, learning and research at the highest international levels of excellence.

www.cambridge.org
Information on this title: www.cambridge.org/9781108457385

DOI: 10.1017/9781108557979

© Friedrich Kratochwil 2018

First published 2018
First paperback edition 2022

A catalogue record for this publication is available from the British Library

ISBN   978-1-108-47125-1   Hardback
ISBN   978-1-108-47125-1   Paperback

Civi ignoto

[T]he word "good" is used in as many senses as the word "is" . . . Using technical language we may predicate "good" in the categories of a) substance, b) quality, c) quantity, d) relation, e) time, f) space. Clearly then "good" is something that can be said in one and the same sense of everything called "good" . . .

Next, what do they mean by the "thing as it really is"? For in their own terminology "man as he really is" is just another way of saying "man" . . . If we are allowed to argue on these lines we shall find no difference either between the really good and the good, in so far as both are good. Nor will the really good be any more good by being eternal. You might as well say that a white thing, which lasts a long time, is whiter than one which lasts only one day . . .

The thought that a knowledge of the absolute good might be desirable as a means of attaining those goods which a man may acquire and realize in practice . . . The argument has a certain plausibility but it manifestly does not accord with the procedure followed by the sciences. For all these aim at some *particular* good and seek to fill up the gaps in their knowledge of how to attain it. They do not think it any business of theirs to learn the nature of the *absolute* good . . . Or how shall a doctor or a general who has had a vision of the Very Form [of the good] become thereby a better doctor or general?

Aristotle, *Nicomachean Ethics*,
Bk. I, iv (1096a 19–1097a 15)

In all incidents of life we ought still to preserve our skepticism . . . Nay if we are philosophers, it ought only to be upon skeptical principles and from inclination we feel employing ourselves in that manner . . .

While warm imagination is allowed to enter into philosophy, and the hypotheses embraced merely for being specious and agreeable, but were these hypotheses once removed, we might hope to establish a system or set of opinions, which if not true (for that perhaps it is too much to be hoped for) might at least be satisfactory to the human mind, and might stand the test of the most critical examination . . .

Generally speaking, the errors in religion are dangerous, those in philosophy only ridiculous.

David Hume, *A Treatise of Human Nature*,
Bk. I, part 4, sec. 7

A rule stands there like a sign post. Does the sign post leave no doubt about the way I have to go?

If I have exhausted all justifications I have reached bedrock and my spade is turned. Then I am inclined to say: This is simply what I do.

Ludwig Wittgenstein,
Philosophical Investigations, paras. 85 and 217

Contents

Acknowledgments

I wish to mention with gratitude the persons and institutions that have contributed to this book. Above all, my wife patiently put up with my mental absence and more than usual grumpiness while taking care of running a hospitable home and attending her project on language acquisition and integration of migrants.

The Institute CEDIN at Belo Horizonte and the Papal University of Minas Gerais offered me a congenial working environment as a guest professor, which allowed me to write several chapters during my stay in 2015.

Oliver Kessler and Hannes Peltonen pestered me again and again to make a manuscript out of the sketches they had seen, and thereby provided important impulses – the latter even at peril to his own work, as he consistently provided the needed IT assistance and had taken on the yeoman's job of compiling the humongous first draft, and valuable detailed criticism. I also owe a special thanks to Guilherme Vasconcelos who provided important feedback, with detailed comments on the first draft of several chapters and also on the book as a whole.

I also profited from a brief stay at the Forschungskolleg Humanwissenschaften and the Werner Reimers Stiftung at the University of Frankfurt and from discussion with the colleagues there, as well as from the comments of Gunther Hellmann and Jens Steffek of the Excellenz-Cluster "Normative Ordnungen" on the last few chapters.

Nicholas Rengger and Jan Klabbers at St Andrews University and the University of Helsinki, respectively, both provided generous support by organizing workshops which gave me an opportunity to try out my ideas and provided much-needed feedback.

John Haslam of Cambridge University was, as always, very supportive of the project despite its unusual length. In choosing two anonymous referees he was also instrumental for the much streamlined second version, as both reviewers had made excellent and detailed suggestions on how to strengthen the argument.

I also owe a special debt of gratitude to Abigail Neale, who managed the production process, and Ken Moxham, the copy-editor, who both did an excellent job in seeing this project through. It was a real pleasure working with them.

Finally, I gratefully acknowledge the reprint permission of several publishers and journals, which are listed separately, as they made it possible to use parts – often in quite altered form – of earlier arguments that had been published over the years.

Parts of Chapter 1 appeared in my chapter, "Constructivism as an Approach to Interdisciplinary Study," in Karen Fierke and Knud-Erik Joergensen (eds.), *Constructivism and International Relations: The Next Generation* (Armonk, NY, London: M.E. Sharpe, 2001): 13–35.

The discussion of "Two Transformative Moments" in Chapter 3 drew on an earlier article, "Politics, Norms and Peaceful Change," *Review of International Studies*, vol. 24 (1998): 193–218.

Chapter 5 (Guiding) incorporated some of the arguments made in my chapter, "How Do Norms Matter?" in Michael Byers (ed.), *The Role of Law in International Politics* (Oxford: Oxford University Press, 2000): 35–68.

Parts of Chapter 8 (Remembering and Forgetting) appeared as "History, Action and Identity," *European Journal of International Relations*, vol. 12, No. 1 (2006): 3–29.

Chapter 9 (Knowing and Doubting) made use of my earlier discussion of Hume: "Re-thinking Inter-disciplinarity by Re-reading Hume" in Nikolas Rajkovic, Tanja Aalberts, and Thomas Gammeltoft (eds.), *The Power of Legality* (Cambridge: Cambridge University Press, 2016): 29–74.

Some of the analysis presented in Chapter 11 (Judging and Communicating) relies on an article that Joerg Friedrichs and I co-authored: "On Acting and Knowing," *International Organization*, vol. 63, No. 4 (2009): 701–731.

All of the publishers have graciously granted reprint permission.

I also gratefully acknowledge the permission of the Alte Pinakothek in Munich Germany who allowed me to use the painting by Albrecht Altdorfer, "Die Alexanderschlacht," and Andres Gonzales's help in preparing the initial cover.

To all a heartfelt "thank you"! Errors of fact and judgment are, of course, exclusively mine.

Introduction

The Problem of Praxis and its "Theoretical" Implications

This book has been long in the making, perhaps too long. Thus, it is not surprising that its first conception was overtaken by events in the scientific debate and by practical political problems. Both circumstances made a rethinking of the problems addressed in such a treatise necessary, but also significantly altered its problematique. Originally this book was planned as a sequel to *Rules, Norms and Decisions*,[1] The first order of business was therefore the clarification of the original constructivist challenge to the dominant mode of "theorizing" in the field, even though issues and arguments have significantly changed over time, as e.g. the recent turn to practice demonstrates. To that extent, the familiar gambits become of limited usefulness, such as distinguishing between strong and soft constructivism, identifying constructivism with post-modernism, holding it compatible with traditional social science, or doubting its compatibility. Instead, a closer engagement with the *substantive issues characterizing political action*, and the realm of praxis seemed required, instead of limiting oneself to the debates on International Relations (IR) "theory."

The most important implication of those preliminary reflections was the idea which I plan to defend throughout this book: in the social sciences we are concerned with action, namely with accounts of what actors have done and said, believed, and desired, since also institutions "are" only because they are reproduced through the actors' actions. An analogy to nature and its "facts" is, therefore, misleading, since for action the temporal dimension of irreversible time matters. This irreversibility of time, calling attention to the performative aspect of actions, requires some finalistic explanation schemes that are quite different from accounts in terms of efficient causes. In short my argument is that because a characteristic of praxis is the problem of action taking place

---

[1] Friedrich Kratochwil, *Rules, Norms and Decisions: On the Conditions of Practical and Legal Reasoning in International Relations and Domestic Affairs*, Cambridge: Cambridge University Press, 1989.

in irreversible time, different epistemological and methodological tools are required than those of "theory" as understood by the unity of science position.

Against my espoused position several objections can be raised. One is to cast doubt on the alleged indispensability of emphasizing the actors and their intentions, which relies on Weber's famous argument for the "subjective" point of view. One could argue that certain important social phenomena are characterized precisely by their apparent lack of intentionality, of which the run on the bank is the best example. After all, it is a phenomenon of unintended consequences, which Waltz uses as a proof for his claim that some "structures" must be at work.[2] I think that such a conclusion is unwarranted. A run on the bank certainly cannot be explained in terms of intentions of *each single actor*, since it is the result of strategic interaction leading to undesired outcomes, but unintended consequences – as the word suggests – are simply *parasitic* on intentional accounts. In other words, we understand that the failure of accounting for the result consists in the mistaken assumption that the outcome must have been *intended* by each actor instead of being the perverse result of strategic interaction and aggregation. But this does not mean that we have to abandon the action perspective altogether.[3]

Similarly, we could object that by taking a purely subjective point of view we give up the ideal of scientific objectivity, and exchange it for the rather dubious procedures of empathy and trying to get into the "mind" of an actor. But Weber's operation called *Verstehen* has nothing to do with empathy, with reading an actor's mind, or with having a privileged access to her desires and psychological states,[4] as even a cursory reading of his writing shows. Admittedly, part of the confusion results from Weber's poor choice of words. However, the feelings, thoughts, and intentions, which we usually adduce in order to explain an action, are hardly ever "private" in the sense of the Cartesian model of the mental states of an actor. In other words, the feelings referred to are not simply the inaccessible internal dispositions of the mind or states of the individual psyche. The same can even be said about the most private of feelings, i.e. pain, as Wittgenstein suggested.[5] Even here we can and *do* communicate about it, even though we can never really feel somebody else's pain.

In sum, taking an action perspective does not mean that we need access to the psychology of the actor, but that we make an attribution that actor X

---

[2] Kenneth N. Waltz, *Theory of International Politics*, Reading, MA: Addison Wesley, 1979.

[3] For a fundamental discussion of the problems involved in intentional explanations, see G.E.M Anscombe, *Intention*, 2nd edn., Ithaca, NY: Cornell University Press, 1957.

[4] Max Weber, *Aufsätze zur Wissenschaftslehre*, 5th edn., Tübingen: J.C.B. Mohr, 1985. See especially the controversies with Roscher, Knies, and Stammler.

[5] See Ludwig Wittgenstein, *Philosophical Investigations*, trans. Elizabeth Anscombe, Oxford: Basil Blackwell, 1968, paras. 243–315 (discussed within the argument against a "private language").

chooses *a* in order to get *b* on the basis of typifying a situation and choosing the practices that provide the templates for reaching the goal (without assuming that what "works" is an optimizing choice). Here personal accounts concerning the motives are certainly important, but they need not be privileged in the explanation we accept as true. After all, the actors might have an incentive to misrepresent their true intentions or they might simply be confused, either about the situation or about the means of reaching the goal (or both). Thus, disclaimers by an actor who signed a form with the heading "Contract" will hardly be convincing to us – even if the actor avers that he simply exercised his penmanship and denies having actually signed a contract – unless we have evidence that this person is delusional or was incapacitated at the signing.

Another objection to my espoused position could be that the proposed action accounts violate in important respects the logical requirements of true causal explanations. To the extent that in finalistic or teleological accounts (Aristotle's famous *hou heneka*[6]) the goals of the action (effect) and the motive for action antedating the actual choice (cause) *are not independently* defined – as in the case of explanations utilizing efficient causes – this objection is true, but irrelevant for the following reasons. First, if we rejected all intentional accounts because of this epistemological belief, we would end up with an incredibly impoverished research agenda and with virtually no access to the social world, as I argue below. Second, if we attempted instead to recast intentional accounts in efficient cause language, the results are equally problematic. Indeed, an incredible amount of time and effort has been spent on this project, of which structuralist reports are good examples. Here agents are often treated simply as throughputs for "objective factors" that are then supposed to do all the explaining, but then the ominous agent/structure problem arises.[7]

Given these reflections I see no reason to follow the first two objections instead of critically reflecting upon the implications of the last argument. In other words, one realizes that "causality" is a cluster term, which exhibits some "family resemblances" among different notions of cause but the latter are not entirely of one cloth. To that extent, a "reductionist" urge to favor "efficient causes" is missing the point.

---

[6] Aristotle, *Nicomachean Ethics*, trans. J.A.K. Thompson, Harmondsworth: Penguin, 1955, at 25.
[7] For the agent/structure problem, see David Dessler, "What Is at Stake in the Agent/Structure Debate," *International Organization*, 43:3 (1989): 441–473; Alexander Wendt, "Anarchy Is What States Make of It," *International Organization*, 46:2 (1992): 391–425; Heikki Patomäki, "How to Tell Better Stories about World Politics," *European Journal of International Relations*, 2:1 (1996): 105–133; Roxanne Lynn Doty, "Aporia: A Critical Explanation of the Agent/ Structure Problem," *European Journal of International Relations*, 3:3 (1997): 365–392; Patrick Jackson and Daniel Nexon, "Relations before States: Substance, Process and the Study of World Politics," *European Journal of International Relations*, 5:3 (1999): 291–327.

The Plan(s) of the Book

For the above-mentioned reasons, I began to analyze social life through the prism of norms leading sometimes to a common misperception of what constructivists do. While "constructivists," among whom I am usually counted, have sometimes been accused of having some particular political project, be it peace, emancipation, or some notion of the good life, I think such a link to a specific political project is neither necessary – even if some type of elective affinity could be established for instance between advocates of human rights and their constructivist orientation – nor is it even useful for social analysis to begin with an overarching project or some ultimate values.

Another misunderstanding concerns the loose language often used to explore the role of norms. When we say that norms enable or prohibit certain actions, it should be clear that they are neither causes nor actors. It would be indeed fatal if the clarification that norms are not efficient causes led to the equally mistaken notion that they are "actors" or represent some agential matter that, like miasmatic pathogens, "get into" the actors and "make them" act in a certain fashion. Much of the norm diffusion literature is misleading if read with this metaphor in mind. But even if we want to avoid this pitfall and focus on "what norms do" (instead of what they "make us do"), we are prone to make a similar mistake, as norms do not act and thus cannot be "actors," even if the "life cycle" of norms suggests as much. Interestingly enough, although norms increase and decrease in their valence, the "death" of norms (as part of their "life") is hardly ever discussed in the social science literature, while in law "desuetude" or new supervening or abridging norms are supposed to take care of this problem. Here the discussions in IR could have profited from both more detailed historical investigations and from exposure to jurisprudence and legal theory.

It is therefore unsurprising that I sought help from those disciplines. The crucial question was to what extent insights from other disciplines can be "transported" to our field and still do good work instead of having to be declared dead on arrival. The "operationalization" of law as behavioral regularities, or as an "intervening variable" in the early regime debate, is an obvious example of dangers of the first kind, while the anemic discussion of the role of ideas that has been limping along in IR journals for the last two decades or so[8] was directly the result of apparent ignorance of the parallel debates in political theory, history, and sociology.

Given this predicament, the overall aim for this book – or rather its first conception – was pretty straightforward, even though its scope was already rather daunting. Two main tasks needed to be mapped out: an organizing

---

[8] Judith Goldstein and Robert O. Keohane (eds.), *Ideas and Foreign Policy: Beliefs, Institutions, and Political Change*, Ithaca, NY: Cornell University Press, 1993.

scheme for presenting my argument, and a more principled engagement with questions of interdisciplinary research, as otherwise the attempt at contributing to a social theory of IR had to remain fanciful indeed. Here an invitation to give a series of lectures on law and interdisciplinarity at an international law forum in 2011 at Belo Horizonte (Brazil) forced me into a critical engagement with interdisciplinarity, translatability, and intertextuality which was – with several additional chapters – published as a book in 2014.[9]

Yet, having written that book, and having identified some fruitful strategies for research, it became all the more important to tie the position elaborated there to a better-articulated analysis of action. Here again two focal points emerged after prolonged reflection: one, an inventory of the ongoing practices in contemporary politics and two, a more critical engagement with social action. In other words, it seemed imperative to examine praxis more explicitly as it was first outlined by Aristotle, only to resurface later in Hume's philosophy of common life and in his historical work, or in the "pragmatist" critique of the last century. It identified the "quest for certainty," i.e. a social "theory" informed by Cartesian ideas and the epistemological project, as the main reason for misunderstanding ourselves and the "world of our making."

Weaving together all these strands resulted – when judged with hindsight – more in a *tour d'horizon* of contemporary politics and its discourses than in a traditional book that is written from a "central perspective" and where one "problem" or one storyline carries the reader through the entire presentation. Instead, we have here a form of presentation that antedates such a central perspective, which Ruggie has so nicely identified with modernity,[10] and which perhaps is most visible for example in the painting of Piero della Francesca[11] and later representational styles. In other words, this opus follows a mode of presentation that comes closer to a painting in which the picture includes also elements which are not directly part of the central "theme." For, example, the sponsors are placed at the sides or below, or heavenly onlookers hover above the scene. Similarly, sometimes even actions and events which occurred before and could not have been observed at the time or point at which the picture "cuts in" are part of the oeuvre.

Sometimes a painter also tried to construe the meaning of the painting by using a heavy dose of anachronisms and allegories. Here for instance

---

[9] See Friedrich Kratochwil, *The Status of Law in World Society: Meditations on the Role and Rule of Law*, Cambridge: Cambridge University Press, 2014; Friedrich Kratochwil, "A Guide for the Perplexed? Critical Reflections on Doing Interdisiplinary Legal Research," *Transnational Legal Theory* 5:4 (2014): 541–556.

[10] See e.g. the reworked articles on territoriality, transformative change and post-modern forms of analysis by John Ruggie, *Constructing the World Polity: Essays on International Institutionalization*, London–New York: Routledge, 1998.

[11] Here both the portrait of Federico Montefeltro and the view of an "ideal city" come to mind.

Altdorfer's depiction of Alexander's battle with Darius at Issos (333 BC) comes to mind, which I chose as the book cover. This picture was painted in 1529 for William IV, Duke of Bavaria, who joined the Emperor Maximilian in battling the Turks who threatened Vienna. In order to show the "significance," the painter gives this battle a contemporary as well as a "cosmic" meaning by placing it in a European landscape – but also showing its transformative implications by depicting the Nile delta at the edges. Furthermore, the armies wear Renaissance armor, and the center of the painting represents the moment when Alexander faces Darius himself – here symbolizing the "East" – and puts him to flight. Still other parts of the painting tell the story of different tactical moves of the troops that must have occurred before. The artist also uses eschatological symbols such as the sun and moon (Christianity v. Islam's half-moon) to show that this battle had existential dimensions. It makes its message appear timeless, as the painting joins the history of the *civitas terrena* with that of the "end of times," namely the Last Judgment and the final redemption beyond time. Thus, different stories are told and represented here, so that this picture cannot be reduced to the familiar genre of a battle painting.

Perhaps another analogy, taken this time from music, is also helpful for how to "use" this present treatise. Think of polyphonic compositions in which the different "voices" are not only independent but come together and fade out, and new themes are introduced that are repeated in the form of a canon or lead against each other (as in double or triple fugues). All of this creates a different "music" and requires a different form of "listening" than following a single melody accompanied by supporting accords. Here the difference between Tallis's *Spem in alium* (composed for forty voices) and Beethoven's "breakthrough" Fifth Symphony (in C minor) can serve as an illustration.

Given the contemporary conventions of presenting arguments, my mode of exposition might be a problem, but it also could be an advantage, as it "trips up" the reader and makes her/him perhaps more critical and attentive, precisely because it does not provide for a smooth sailing over the intellectual ocean. Besides, such a "decentered" mode of presentation was put to good use in the treatise of the early international lawyers, such as Grotius, or moral philosophers, such as Montaigne, or even later by Hume (in his *Treatise*). Consequently, it is not a foregone conclusion that what we want to know can only be transmitted by following the present canonical (and largely Anglo-Saxon) form. What does, however, become obvious, is that this work cannot be "read" by skimming the Introduction and the Conclusion. "Reading" it requires a more dialogical engagement with the text than just taking note of some "results" in the conclusion. To that extent, a "user's" manual for such a text would suggest that – if a reader has neither time nor gusto to work through the "whole thing" – s/he could concentrate on certain themes, which are elaborated in subsections and for which the extensive index is helpful. For that purpose, a listing of the various "themes," that intertwine and disengage at different points rather than being dealt with in separate chapters, might be helpful.

The Themes

The *first* "theme" is that this book should not be considered as a work of traditional IR "theory." In its intention and execution, it is rather more at home – in terms of the current taxonomy – in international studies for the reasons outlined above. The transformative changes we are witnessing touch, after all, on comparative politics, on international law, on economics, on political theory and they also raise issues of culture and identity, thereby "redrawing" the boundaries of the established disciplines.

That leads me to a *second* theme that runs through the entire work: the emphasis on language and on conceptual analysis for analyzing social reproduction. The latter emerged from ordinary language analysis pioneered originally by Wittgenstein and was later further developed by Austin, Searle, and others. This mode of inquiry not only shows the importance of ordinary language in mediating between different disciplinary understandings but also has important epistemological implications. It serves as a powerful criticism of traditional taxonomies and "truth" theories and derives our understandings not from the traditional notion of a meeting of a concept with a preexisting "reality out there" – i.e. not from reference or essentialist properties – *but from the use of concepts* and our ability to "go on" with our individual and collective projects. To that extent, it remains "critical" as questions cannot be decided either by "fiat," as in Hobbes or "decisionist" approaches, or by the "things themselves" that show us their "fit" (world to mind). Instead this analysis calls attention to the fact that especially in the social world the question of what "is" ("this note is legal tender") runs from the mind to the world (mind-dependence), instead of the other way around as conceptualized by positivist "theories." The analysis remains critical since it tries to establish "criteria" for the "right" or problematic use of concepts and their embeddedness in the semantic field informing the practices of the actors.

From these considerations, the importance of a familiarity with the philosophical issues that establish our practices of arguing – both about nature and the social world – emerges as a *third* theme. It cannot be left unattended or reduced to issues of methodology, based on the unreflected borrowing of bits and pieces gleaned from the Cliff notes on philosophical writings. But it also does not allow for the killer argument that philosophy (epistemology) or "nature" (physics) provides the ultimate answer, since they are able to decide what "is" or "is not." Such a take on the problematique of knowledge is dogmatic, since it asserts what has to be proven in the first place. i.e. that there exists one and only one way to decide what is the right answer to a (any?)

question. But this assumption is obviously mistaken, since we can describe the world in various ways and ask different questions. What "is" a crime or a trespass in law can obviously not be answered by providing a coroner's account of a gunshot wound, or by showing that the physical laws and necessary factual conditions of a jump over a fence are all that there is to a "trespass." After all, the concept implies a lack of authorization for the act of jumping and thus does not get its meaning from the laws of motion, but from other norms to which it is linked.

The implication of these considerations is not only an argument against reductionism but a plea for taking the philosophical issues seriously that our ways of acting in the social world and of reproducing it by words and deeds entail. This is a *fourth* theme that informs my argumentation. It cannot be dismissed as just "gnawing on the little bones of Kant," as a leading political scientist during the "behavioral revolution" once suggested – and which recently was repeated again in the cause of exorcising "isms" in the field.[12] For me the obvious remedy lies in a more thorough engagement with the philosophical issues, not in their dismissal or bowdlerization.[13]

A *fifth* theme is that the absence of a "theory" providing the absolute "view from nowhere" means espousing a form of perspectivism, i.e. the recognition of the partiality of all of our knowledge and the need for "internalizing" such a recognition within our inquiries. But this requires also the recognition that we have to translate from one "theory" to the "other." instead of believing that we are testing "against nature." This gives rise to the anxiety that with such a stance we end up in "relativism" and with an attitude of "anything goes." Of course, nothing like that follows, particularly if we realize that the traditional true/false dichotomy with its principle of the excluded middle might be a poor philosopher's stone. Something might neither be true nor false but simply be irrelevant to a problem, as we all know, so that a "third" does exist and we had better examine the nature of the warrants which we attach to our statements in order to buttress our validity claims. Validity again has various sources, which all have to be subjected to criticism in particular cases. Thus, we might appeal to "evidence" (empiricism), to moral intuitions, to nature and its laws, to ontology, to authoritative prescriptions, or to overall plausibility, or (quite problematically) we (un)consciously rely on prophecy (unconditional

---

[12] See e.g. David Lake, "Why 'isms' are Evil: Theory, Epistemology and Academic Sects as Impediments to Understanding and Progress," *International Studies Quarterly*, 55:2 (2011): 465–480.

[13] Here I have to ask the reader for some patience since I insist on actually going to some key passages and interpreting them instead of relying on "Cliff notes" or uncritical acceptance of widely shared opinions. This might seem like digressions that disturb the flow of the argument, making it lengthier and less elegant. But as the discussion of the distortions of Humeanism, or the pedigree of "sovereignty," shows, such an engagement is indispensable.

predictions) because some events – which are treated as signs of the "things to come" – have already materialized.

While this enumeration of validity claims appears to constitute a rather checkered list – particularly since some "theological" criteria (prophecy) have been included – it will be the task of this book to show that much of what masquerades as IR "theory" relies for its explanatory power on a highly problematic philosophy of history which represents little more than a secularized version of a redemptory history. This recognition introduces three further themes that are central to this treatise: the appeal to authority and the importance of law for the study of the social world, the issue of prophecy and prediction (rehearsed in various "theories" of mapping the "stages of development" of the "end of history"), and the issue of "historicity." The latter distinguishes the realm of praxis, which makes its subjection to criteria of "theory" – conceived as a set of universal and ahistorical "true" statements of what is the case – an inappropriate yardstick, a problem which is taken up from different angles in the last three chapters of the book.

Let us begin with the appeal to authority and the importance of (positive) law for the study of the social world, which represents the *sixth* theme. While everybody probably agrees that law plays an important role in the reproduction of the social world, most interest is devoted to law as a technique of social engineering, i.e. the reproduction and orderly change in a society, whereby "compliance" problem takes pride of place. But this represents a rather reductive approach since law has special relevance to praxis as it deals (a) with situations and deeds (i.e. with conjunctions rather than with events in homogeneous time), (b) with the constitution of a social order (which could be conceptualized as a problem of parts and whole) and (c) with ascriptions of responsibility, which is unknown in nature (aside from using the term "causation" metaphorically).

To that extent my interest in (international) law had little to do with issues of "enforcement" or with the cosmopolitan project of substituting law for force – since after all, law might play a role in persuasion, but that observation does not dispense with law's own presumption that it is authorized to use coercive means, if persuasion fails. If we, however, jump to the conclusion that therefore "coercion" forms the "core" of law (à la Derrida) we should be careful, as the experiences neither with domestic nor international criminal law support this inference, a problem I address in Chapter 7. To that extent, I have always been rather agnostic towards much of the discussion about normative "boomerangs" or norm-cascades, or even the Kantian a priori duty to bring about a cosmopolitan order (which most of the time looks awfully like an imperial project). Here my Humean skepticism was always greater than the enthusiasm for trying to establish the "kingdom of ends." Judging by the results, such efforts frequently lead to highly problematic choices in which the political ideologies of idealism and realism become co-dependent enablers. To them I gladly leave the disputes of which orientation is then to blame for the policy disasters we are witnessing.

My interest in law originally centered on epistemological problems since it was the only discipline which has been able to maintain an alternative approach to analyzing choices without resorting to "ideal assumptions" and which provided for a resolution of conflict in the absence of a clear algorithm that could muster assent because of its (logically) compelling nature. This seemed particularly interesting to me as a student of politics since here we have to deal with choices which have to be binding on all but which cannot claim the compelling assent universal "reason" supplies for "true" theoretical propositions. Thus, the literature on "prudence" from Aristotle to Hume's common sense, to the pragmatists' criticism of the "quest for certainty" underlying our efforts to build a "theory" seemed to me of particular importance for social analysis. First it debunked the idea of the primacy of the epistemological project, and second, it called attention to the importance (of the power) of judgment – Kant's *Urteilskraft* – that provides the validation of "reflective" choices.[14] Finally, it provides us with an escape from the traps that since the Enlightenment have plagued social analysis by interpreting the emergence of "humanity" as a "plan of nature" that works itself out behind the back of the actors.

The criticism of this notion of "development" and the "end of history" which are indebted to the prophetic tradition – and thus pretend to possess the power of unconditional prediction! – on the basis of recognizing the identification of alleged "signs" that have been disclosed to the illuminated, represents the *seventh* important theme. I try to elaborate on the differences between a genuine historical understanding and prophetic understandings. The former uses the past as a guide for realizing the political projects whereby "history" provides important "lessons." The other sees the past as "gone" and done with, and orients itself, as far as action is concerned, solely by a pre-ordained "end" of history. Both strategies fail, however, in coming to terms with the problem of the "historicity" of action, i.e. its conjunctural and "constructed" dimension. The first strategy tends to treat "history" as a storehouse of data in order to derive from them some "theories"; it also calls attention to the constructed nature of any "history" that is always a "selection" or record of "things worth remembering" (*recordari*), in which not only cognition but emotions and "identities" of the historical individual are involved and the peculiarities of historical reflection, transmitted in narratives, come to the fore. The second strategy is the flipside of this misrecognition. It is blind to the fact

---

[14] "Reflective" choices concern decisions that cannot be buttressed by compelling but only by plausible or persuasive reasons. See the discussion below in Chapter 11.

that the meaning conveyed by such narratives requires critical reflection since the "data" of history might not be "facts" analogous to those of the natural world, but they are treated rather as "signs" that attain their importance from a hidden teleology that works itself out "behind" the backs of the actors. As Kant put it, the "cunning of nature" (*List der Natur*)[15] does virtually all the explaining but also provides the justification of action. Such a stance sits, of course, uneasily with his own argument about human freedom and responsibility, which are intrinsic to our understanding of "praxis" and of "making" our social world. This represents my *eighth* theme.

The dissatisfaction with this solution leads me to the *ninth* theme that emerged from a re-reading of Hume's argument about the conventional nature of the social world and the appropriate knowledge of things social. This knowledge is not founded on an "absolute foundation" as the epistemological project suggests, but is acquired through participation in – and not in withdrawal or abstraction from – an existing historical society. It is through "commerce and conversation" that we develop the competences for social life and the "know-how" that lets us function in the social world. This theme relates to the conventionalist account of the first part of the book but also places the problem of knowledge and the role of "philosophy" in the realm of *praxis* in a different light. Philosophy can no longer occupy the place of a last "court" of appeals that stands outside of society as a source of universal reason, but is an institution that is part of a society and has to defer to its conventions and traditions and ways of "doing business" that depend more on experience and some know-how than on demonstrations and principles which are so dear to "theorists." It nevertheless shapes the "civil" life of a society by deciding cases and offering precedents that can become points of orientation.

The *tenth* theme concerns the problems and limitations of "ideal theorizing" that follow from reducing the problem of individual and collective choice to either some individual maximization criteria or the "felicific calculus" à la Bentham, or the clarification of principles which are then "applied" to concrete cases. Here I try to show that inevitably some reduction occurs by limiting choices to a selection of means or taking the monetarily mediated exchange as the paradigm for virtually all "important" choices (idiosyncrasies excluded). I then develop an alternative for analyzing choices that takes "praxis" seriously instead of subordinating it to "theoretical" criteria and simplification (Chapter 11), and explore its implications for politics. As to the first part I follow here largely Charles Taylor:

---

[15] See Immanuel Kant, "Perpetual Peace" in H.S Reiss (ed.), *Kant's Political Writings*, 2nd edn., Cambridge: Cambridge University Press, 1991, First Supplement, at 112.

We can see how the understanding of what we are doing right now (without which we could not be doing this action) makes the sense it does because of our grasp on the wider predicament: how we continuously stand or have stood in relations to others and to power. This, in turn, opens out wider perspectives on where we stand in space and time: our relations to other nations and peoples ... and also where we stand in our history, in the narrative of our becoming.

The understanding implicit in practice stands to social theory in the same relation that my ability to get around a familiar environment stands to a (literal) map of this area ... for most of human history and for most of social life, we function through the grasp we have on the common repertory, without the benefit of theoretical overview. Humans operated with a social imaginary well before they ever got into the business of theorizing about themselves.[16]

When I turn to an assessment of the transformative changes we are experiencing for politics my analysis becomes somewhat gloomy. I am fully aware that my concept of politics is based on certain notions of a subject entitled and wanting to make free choices and being part of a community to which s/he has particular obligations that do not issue from transcendental first principles of reason or humanity. But such a form of politics is increasingly endangered, given the disappearance of the public sphere and the technological advances which are more designed to take away from the actors this freedom by offering to make choices on their behalf in order to insure general "happiness."

Having outlined the themes and provided at least indirectly a brief overview of some of the chapters, let me also address some bibliographical problems, particularly the different editions of the works of Hume, or Aristotle, which I have been using. Since I have worked on this Praxis text for quite some time and I had to use the libraries at different universities (Munich, Florence, Seoul, Budapest, St Andrews, Belo Horizonte), I could not always find the editions I was looking for. Since, as of yet, no standard edition exists for Hume – to compare with the Stephanus edition for Aristotle or Plato, or the Preussische Akademie Ausgabe for Kant – I did my best to identify as far as possible the passages to which I referred. But since I had to rely on different editions, I had to contend with all the inconveniences that come with this, since often not even the volume coincided, not to speak of the pagination. A case in point is Hume's *History of England* volume 5 in the recent Liberty Fund edition, which does not coincide with volume 5 of the same work edited by Smollett in 1834, or with the different editions of Hume's *Essays*. The reader will therefore frequently find several editions of the same work in the Bibliography.

---

[16] Charles Taylor, *Modern Social Imaginaries*, Durham, NC: Duke University Press, 2004: 26f.

1 Constructivism and the Practices of (International) Politics: The Case for a Humean Approach

1.1   Introduction

The Setting

Periods of rapid change engender crises of action and of thought. Not only do the familiar strategies for addressing problems no longer work, there is also the problem that we move in an increasingly unfamiliar environment. This is most obvious in the area of deterrence, which for a long time dominated IR analysis, but which was odd in the new world order, characterized by terrorist threats, and fundamentalist opposition to the Western political project which links the subject to the state and the state to an (anarchical) society among states. To that extent Zaki Laidie's early analysis in1994 (in the French edition) that the end of the Cold War was above all a "crisis in meaning" was apt, even if it was hardly noticed due either to the predominant triumphalism, or to the pre-occupations with the legacies of the Soviet Empire. Oddly enough, this crisis impacted not only the "successor states" and their attempts to return to the past and invent a political project based on the reproduction of a "tradition." It also forced those states, which had defined their identity largely in opposition to the dominant "block" template of post-World War II politics, to redefine their role, as we could see in the case of India, Algeria, or most notably Yugoslavia.[1]

In addition, the present crisis is not only the result of the "revolt against the West," of which we witness now the most spectacular episode. It arose also from significant changes within the West. These changes may lack the shock value of the 9/11 attack or the execution and abductions perpetrated by ISIS and Boko Haram – although the drone strikes and extrajudicial killings are on the way to becoming a close runner-up. Nevertheless, the less noticeable changes fundamentally transformed international practices.[2] Thus, after the

---

[1] Zaki Laidi, *A World without Meaning: The Crisis of Meaning in International Politics*, London: Routledge, 1998.

[2] See e.g. the Symposium of the journal *Cooperation and Conflict* organized around the article of Georg Sørensen, "What Kind of World Order?" *Cooperation and Conflict*, 41:4 (2006): 343–363.

end of the Cold War and the triumphalism of the "end of history," which quickly gave way to "Wilsonianism in boots," the US administrations no longer seemed to be very interested in the institutions of multilateralism or of "arms control" which once governed superpower relations. Relations between America and its allies were put under strain by the hypertrophic public and private data-search instigated by the National Security Agency (NSA), by the proprietary claims to information made by some American IT corporations, and by announcements of NATO's obsolescence. Similarly, Europe, while at first ignoring the latter threats, was increasingly enamored of its role as a "civilian power,"[3] which over the years morphed into a project of becoming a "normative power."[4] The EU neither registered the wake-up call that issued from Moscow in the war in Georgia[5] nor did it engage in a critical assessment of its own policy in the Balkans and beyond, which was bound to engender Russian opposition. Rather it engaged in a policy of expansion, euphemistically called a "neighborhood policy," that – similar to the American plans for "regime change" – was tantamount to creating a non-territorial form of empire. In it power would be exerted by the capillary control of social and political institutions subjected to "good governance" standards, even though no formal incorporation of those countries was envisaged for a later stage.

The unease occasioned by these political projects is heightened when we see that "protecting people" is given another twist by Russia's new vision, taking its cues from the "best practice" book on human rights, but bending them to new goals. As in the French Revolution, the rights of man are now again (or now primarily?) those of the citizen. This "fact" in turn legitimizes "Mother Russia's" intervention whenever the rights of her "children abroad" are infringed upon.[6] It needs no further discussion that such a conception is hardly attractive for outsiders, and that the margins for maneuver between Western and Eastern versions of a "global order"[7] have shrunk considerably. There seems no longer to exist a political language that could mediate these

---

[3] This concept was first floated by François Duchêne, "Europe's Role in World Peace" in Richard Mayne (ed.), *Europe Tomorrow: Sixteen Europeans Look Ahead*, London: Fontana, 1972, 32–47.

[4] Ian Manners, "Normative Power Europe: A Contradiction in Terms?" *Journal of Common Market Studies*, 40:2 (2002): 235–258. For a critique of this conception, see Robert Kagan, *Paradise and Power: America and Europe in a New World Order*, London: Atlantic Books, 2003.

[5] See the analysis of Syuzanna Vasilyan, "Moral Power as Objectification of the Civilian/Normative EUlogy: The European Union as a Conflict-Dealer in the South Caucasus," *Journal of International Relations and Development*, 17:3 (2014): 397–424.

[6] Samuel Layton, "Reframing European Security: Russia's Proposal of a New European Security Architecture," *International Relations*, 28:1 (2014): 25–48.

[7] For a general discussion of Russian foreign policy thinking, see Bobo Lo, *Russian Foreign Policy in the Post-Soviet Era: Reality, Illusion, and Mythmaking*, Houndmills: Palgrave Macmillan, 2002.

differences, since "values" and "rights" have replaced "interests" in the West, while "interests" were also replaced by "nature" and the "nation" in the East. All that bodes ill for politics since values cannot be compromised, and "nature" must not be fooled with (even if it stands for little more than a revulsion against unorthodox lifestyles).

Not surprisingly, calls for supplying a new "picture of the whole" can be heard everywhere. There are the visions of a cosmopolitan order based on the reform of existing institutions, which have captured the imagination of some international bureaucrats, academics, and "mission junkies" (public or private). Networks and global civil society also invent new projects for the political agenda. Finally, there are the attempts to capture our present predicament by means of the familiar grand narrative of realism concerning the "rise and decline" of states, nations, civilizations, or whatever.

I do not want to engage here these different speculations, which, as I show in the last chapters, often rely more on seductive but highly problematic metaphors of a *telos* promising emancipation and redemption, rather than on actual analysis. Instead, I want to call attention to another flaw in those interpretations, which is even more striking. Virtually all the "visions" take for granted that the Western conceptual baggage is appropriate for providing orientation, even though it clearly prevents us from even seeing, or "naming," some of the fundamental ruptures or transformations that are occurring before our eyes. The lack of interest in the "messy details" is often shocking, such as when we are appalled by the seizure of the Crimean Peninsula, although there had been large-scale military exercises the year before in Russia that provided a dry run for the later operation.[8] An American administration which always knows your whereabouts just as long as you have a cellphone is suddenly surprised and hapless when confronted with the invasion. But even if one wants to set one's sights on the higher concerns of being a force for good and promoting human rights instead of getting bogged down "estimating" power by various indicators, one should be aware that phrasing policy virtually exclusively in terms of "rights" leaves little room for maneuver.

After all, rights in general seem not only to have a "dark side" – even if they are endowed with the "double" trump of being "Human" rights supervening on on merely "positive rights"[9] – but make appropriate policy responses next to

---

[8] This is, of course, not to argue for some form of causal necessity between the earlier and the later event. See the Russian major "Zapad (West) 2013" exercises near the Baltics, on September 20–26, 2013; see Stratfor Enterprises, LLC of September 20, 2013, "In Zapad Exercises Russia Flexes its Military Strength." Available at https://worldview.stratfor.com/article/zapad-exercises-russia-flexes-its-military-strength.
[9] See Onora O'Neill, "The Dark Side of Human Rights" in Thomas Christiano and John Christman (eds.), *Contemporary Debates in Political Philosophy*, Chichester: Blackwell-Wiley, 2009, 425–436.

impossible. This can be seen even in the simple case of property rights in the information age. For years we hardly seemed to have noticed that private companies under contract with governments and their security apparatuses – another victory for public–private partnerships! – have been dismantling the fundamental normative underpinnings of our political order: the right to privacy, the presumption of probable cause, the prohibition of torture, the distinction between war and peace, the status of a combatant versus a civilian . . . you name it. Having successfully broadened the notion of "intellectual property rights," whereby even a collector of telephone numbers can claim copyright protection for that list,[10] information has nearly automatically become the property of the collector, and attempts of courts to sequester such information, protecting the person whose data are circulating through the World Wide Web, have hardly made a dent. The implications of this misstep dating back to the World Trade Organization (WTO) negotiations, are beginning to show themselves in full living color only now. Consider in this context the report on Google's plan to make a small electronic pill wandering through your body and analyzing your biological processes by making them into global information commodities.[11]

Things become even worse when we consider our "surprise" regarding the emergence of other forms of "meaning," such as ISIS, which not only has made barbarism its political program, but which lets "messages" percolate freely through the "social media" which are increasingly mobilizing youths in both, the downtrodden and traumatized societies, and in our very own countries. Obviously, the persons susceptible to these messages are struggling with their existential questions and try to escape from insignificance by submitting to the allure of brute power by becoming executors of "something big." There is, of course, no way in which these problems can be reduced to a simple diagnosis of what went wrong, save to realize that we do not even have a language – certainly not a political one – to probe these "breaks" in our understanding of the social world. Perhaps psychology, sociology, or religion can provide, if not answers, at least some tools for analysis, as our common understandings informed by liberalism, secularism, and the idea of progress seem woefully inadequate.

---

[10] European Parliament and European Council, *Directive 96/9/EC of 11 March 1996 on the Legal Protection of Databases*, 1996.

[11] See David B. Samadi, "Forget Self-Driving Cars: Here's How Google Plans to Change How We Live Forever," *The Observer* (Style & Design), May 14, 2015. Actually there were two interrelated missteps: one which was the dismantling of the public domain by its rigorous privatization, arguing on the basis of a labor theory of value that such an arrangement would increase public welfare. The other was that thereby someone could become an "author" not by some invention or creative activity but by collecting information on people without their consent and then involve the "public" power in the enforcement of his "rights" even against the objections of the very people who served as guinea pigs.

These observations have further ramifications for our quest for approaching these problems via a "theory." Although our hopes in a comprehensive "theory" of international relations have been disappointed, perhaps interdisciplinary research is able to provide a new map that would enable us to orient ourselves more successfully in this turbulent world. Thus we could perhaps be true to our conviction that all true knowledge has to be theoretical, while letting go – for the moment – of the idea of a general theory of international relations.

The Scientific Responses

In this way we can then at least face the serious paradox, even if we cannot resolve it: since the success of science results from the *disciplinary character* of the inquiry, the often incompatible fundamental assumptions underlying the various disciplines make a simple "addition" of the knowledge, generated in different fields, impossible. Thus, an economist is not helped by the suggestion that the question of justice, or even that of the "just price," should be included in economic analysis – even if philosophers and historians of economic thought might point to some interesting issues that arise in that context. Although disciplinary boundaries are certainly not immutable, they are usually not examined in the course of ordinary research, nor can they be. To that extent, different questions, even disconfirming evidence, are often simply discarded as an unimportant anomaly that, at best, gives rise to defensive gambits.

If this characterization is true, then the dangers of interdisciplinary research become apparent. Unless extreme care is taken, the distinctive contributions various disciplines make to our understanding might get lost, and behind the phrases of integration and bridge-building could stand an impoverished, rather than an original and fecund, new research agenda.[12]

Perhaps this is the reason why many attempts at interdisciplinary research are less based on a set of substantive problems or puzzles, but rather on the application of a new *methodology*. While the fruitfulness of the latter strategy is, of course, an open question, there exists the twin danger of imperialism and of degenerative problem shifts,[13] as when all the problems that do not fit a particular methodology are eliminated. After all, the "law of the hammer" perhaps not only implies that we will find things to nail down – even if the problems we encounter would call for the use of a screwdriver or a saw – it

[12] Here Morgenthau's six principles of realism are actually in agreement with Waltz's conception of the autonomy of international politics. See Hans Morgenthau, *Politics among Nations*, 4th edn., New York: Knopf, 1967.
[13] For the issue of degenerative problem shifts, see Imre Lakatos, "Falsification and the Methodology of Scientific Research Programmes" in I. Lakatos and A. Musgrave (eds.), *Criticism and the Growth of Knowledge*, Cambridge: Cambridge University Press, 1970, 91–196.

also hints at the possibility that the need for other instruments – be they drills, planes, or even wrenches – could be denied.

The insistence on substantive problems in interdisciplinary work rather than on methods could be objected to since it seems a curious stance, particularly for a constructivist. Given that constructivists are supposed to be "reflexivists,"[14] "idealists," and so on, who are engaged in "understanding" rather than "explaining,"[15] and, given that most of the discussion among the different schools in the field has centered on methodological issues, the espoused position seems rather odd. Yet, it is odd only if we accept what needs to be proven in the first place: that the issue can indeed be reduced to one of tests or methodology, and that outside of one specific method – called the "scientific method" – there can be no warranted knowledge. In other words, I claim that were constructivism simply a "theory," or only some methodological orientation, it could neither avoid the pitfalls of methodological imperialism, nor could it help us in our quest for interdisciplinary research.

Fortunately, I do not consider the relevant question as one of methodology. Rather, I believe that what is at stake is a systematic reflection on the observations of various disciplines. Through this critical reflection, a "translation" of disciplinary understandings becomes possible, and "blind-spots" and the exclusions of questions become visible. In short, I shall argue below that constructivism is such a meta-theoretical stance that is characterized by certain "ontological" assumptions concerning human action – or *praxis* to use the classical concept – as well as by (some) methodological assumptions that flow from this commitment.

The Potential of Constructivism

In making my case, I have to meet a preliminary objection and then satisfy more substantive criteria in order to establish my thesis. The preliminary objection concerns the usefulness of reviving those old issues of "theory" and "disciplinarity," particularly since the discussion in the field has moved to something else, to eclecticism,[16] or it has taken a practice turn,[17] or has even

---

[14] For a distinction along those lines, see Robert Keohane, "International Institutions: Two Approaches," *International Studies Quarterly*, 32:4 (1988): 379–396.

[15] Martin Hollis and Steve Smith, *Explaining and Understanding International Relations*, Oxford–New York: Oxford University Press, 1990.

[16] See Rudra Sil and Peter J. Katzenstein, "Analytic Eclecticism in the Study of World Politics: Reconfiguring Problems and Mechanisms across Research Traditions," *Perspectives on Politics*, 8:2 (2010): 411–431.

[17] See Emanuel Adler and Vincent Pouliot, *International Practices*, Cambridge: Cambridge University Press, 2011.

gone "quantum."[18] Since in all of these new debates former "constructivists" figured prominently, it may not seem to speak well of the former intellectual home that most if not all of the occupants have left the coop. While I cannot deny the observation, I think the inference from it is mistaken. On the contrary, it seems that some of the very same controversies are now carried on with often only slightly different vocabularies, suggesting that the issues are still with us and thus a new engagement with their "roots" could be highly informative.

For countering *the more substantive* reservations of old or new opponents of constructivism, I have to show that the rather motley crew of researchers who once became defined as the "out-group" by the hegemonic discourse shared indeed some substantive common ground – although not so much, as is usually assumed. Furthermore, without wanting to convert all of them to my particular position by assuming the role of a gatekeeper, I must make good on my claim that, given the substantive problems of political action, certain approaches have a better-articulated research program for dealing with issues of praxis[19] than others. Here, I admit to my biases by arguing that the linguistic turn in constructivism is more helpful than other forms that are sometimes described as "thin" constructivism. To that extent, "thick constructivism's" critical function,[20] as well as the new conceptual extensions suggested thereby, will be examined in greater detail. Third, I should demonstrate how the disciplinary understandings of law, sociology, and international politics can be bridged when viewed from the vantage point of praxis.

Conequently, my argument in this chapter will take the following steps. In the next section (Section 1.2) I outline the core position of constructivism and argue that a "thick" rather than a "thin" version of constructivism holds the greatest promise. It might come as a big surprise to some readers that this position comes very close to the classical Aristotelian teachings (*Politics, Nicomachean Ethics, Rhetoric*). Although I am aware that many "constructivists" have come to their particular approach without reading Aristotle, I shall, nevertheless, base my discussion on the Aristotelian texts. I do this not because I am interested in reviving one of the classics of politics (thereby preventing, or at least retarding, the "decline of the West") but because Aristotle makes his points particularly forcefully and clearly.

---

[18] See Alexander Wendt, *Quantum Mind and Social Science: Unifying Physical and Social Ontology*, Cambridge: Cambridge University Press, 2015.

[19] Here I use the old term for "practical choices" that goes back to Aristotle rather than to the recent "practice" turn. I do so for reasons I discuss systematically throughout out the book but especially in Chapters 8–10.

[20] For the distinction between "critical" and "problem-solving" theorizing, see Robert W. Cox, "Social Forces, States and World Order: Beyond International Relations Theory," *Millennium*, 10:2 (1981), 204–254.

In addition, it will become obvious from reading the subsequent chapters that there are productive links between the Aristotelian conception of praxis and ordinary language philosophy, as well as to Hume's work on conventions and historical reflection. These links allow us to develop a new and heuristically fruitful research agenda for the realm of praxis. Since practical reason differs from theoretical reason and from knowledge of producing things (*techne*), I also try to show how a reasoning based on types and resemblances rather than on assumptions – such as underlie non-cooperative game theory – or one based on generalizations or universal norms, can be used for a more fruitful analysis of "cooperation," which I develop by examining eight "cases," all of which raise different analytical issues. While this examination can hardly be more than a plausibility probe, it is intended to set the stage for the last few chapters of the book, which try to articulate a different approach to praxis than subjecting the analysis of action to theoretical standards.

Section 1.3 elaborates on the positive heuristics of a "thick" version of constructivism for the analysis of order. I develop my argument in two stages. First, by looking for a "hard case" and subjecting Hobbes's analysis (*Leviathan, Behemoth, Elements of Law*) to a subversive "constructivist reading," I argue that these works require a far more nuanced interpretation than is usually provided in the standard liberal and realist accounts. Thus, the Hobbesian sovereign is not only the mortal god – replacing the transcendental authorization for politics and law – he is also the new "fixer of signs."

From this vantage point I examine, in a second step, some of implications of this linguistic turn, foreshadowed, in a way, by Hobbes. I visit not only some of the well-known controversies about meaning and social action, showing that the present discussion is not merely a rehash of the *Methodenstreit* of Weber's time, but I also emphasize that significant new issues concerning reference and meaning have emerged during the last few decades. In particular, I shall focus on speech act theory, which was instrumental for a new understanding of institutions and their functioning.

In Section 1.4, I address the issue of a substantive set of problems that underlie political, social, and legal analysis and that provide us with a more fleshed-out account of the positive heuristics of constructivism. Here I take contractarian analysis, as it emerged in the seventeenth century, as my foil. Such a new conceptual founding had become necessary, since with the demise of a comprehensive ontological order that traditionally had provided standards of right rule, appeals to God and his established order had become problematic by escalating rather than assuaging social conflicts. The new conception of subjective rights and the establishment of order through the social contract provided a powerful antithesis to the older metaphysics.

In this context, however, I also address Kant's criticism against the construct of the social contract and I show that, indeed, a new "we" has to emerge among the members of a society, when they pass laws that are to govern their interaction. Kant's distinctions between legality and legitimacy point to the difficulties of the Hobbesian notion that the exercise of public power can be conceptualized as a single authorization in perpetuity. Instead, the creation of legitimate power, allowing the sovereign to utilize force, makes it necessary to legitimize *on a continual basis all of his actions*. In this way, important conceptual links between law and politics come into view which also cut across the Humean distinctions between is and ought. A short summary of the present argument follows in Section 1.5.

1.2   The Constructivist "Core" and the Need for a "Thick" Constructivism

The Hegemonic Discourse and the Constructivist Challenge

One characteristic of a hegemonic discourse is that the classification of the other approaches occurs on the basis of a simple exclusion.[21] To that extent, the "other" category usually gets filled with rather disparate alternatives. While the members of this cohort are critical of the orthodoxy, they often vary fundamentally as to their respective substantive and methodological assumptions. If one wants to claim, therefore, that constructivism is helpful in formulating a new approach to praxis, one has to point to some substantive assumptions and to a fuller articulation of their implications concerning the required methods, as e.g. Nicholas Onuf has done.[22] These epistemological corollaries can, in turn, serve as a criterion for evaluating the positive heuristics of the approach rather than simply indicate the points of disagreement with the hegemonic discourse. Let us therefore see what was new in the call for "constructivism."

Many of the contemporary controversies surrounding constructivism have their historical roots in nineteenth-century debates concerning the epistemology of the *Kulturwissenschaften*, as opposed to that of the natural sciences. There is no need to rehearse these arguments here, or to go back even further, namely to Vico's, Hume's, and Herder's opposition to the Cartesian program. Nevertheless, one should keep in mind that the most radical version of constructivism was formulated by the Chilean physiologist, Humberto Maturana, and by his sometime collaborator Varela, during the later decades of the last century.[23] Maturana's *Biology of Cognition* became a type of cult book that

---

[21] On the Gramscian notion of "hegemony," see Stephen Gill (ed.), *Gramsci, Historical Materialism and International Relations*, Cambridge: Cambridge University Press, 1993.

[22] Nicholas Onuf, *World of Our Making: Rules and Rule in Social Theory and International Relations*, Columbia: University of South Carolina Press, 1989.

[23] For a good introduction, see the volume of collected essays by Siegfried Schmidt (ed.), *Der Radikale Konstruktivismus*, Frankfurt: Suhrkamp, 1987.

engendered heated debates in the natural and social sciences as well as in philosophy (epistemology), particularly on the Continent.[24]

In the contemporary world, it remains to be seen whether a new consensus is emerging that re-establishes the "unity of science" position but on an entirely new basis. For my limited purposes here – dealing only with the constructivist-inspired approaches in the particular disciplines of international politics, sociology, and law – it seems to me that all constructivists in these fields base their research programs on the assumption that the human world is not simply given or natural, but that, on the contrary, it is one of artifice, "constructed" through the actions of the actors themselves. While such a stance rules out any form of naïve empiricism or naturalism, as well as most forms of structuralism, the specific contribution of constructivism consists in this heuristic and its corollaries.

In this context, I want to point out three things: (1) that it seems at least logically possible to agree to the "world as a construct" and still argue for an "empirically" based study of regularities based on some observationally oriented research program and/or the standard accounts of science, and (2) that this decision raises, however, some hoary meta-theoretical issues. (3) Given this problematique, constructivists *at a minimum* argue that those meta-theoretical issues have to be treated as an open question. *At a maximum*, they will contend that specific elements for explicating actions require methodological tools for which the traditional model of "science" is of little help, since what serves as an "explanation" for an action is extremely context-dependent and cannot be reduced to one form of "scientific" explanation. Thus, there are not always two stories to tell, as Hollis and Smith have maintained (against Wendt).[25] There also exists the possibility of telling several explanatory stories, as Heikki Patomäki has argued.[26] In short, causally efficient accounts are not only rivaled (or complemented) by constitutive explanations, as finalistic or teleological explanations will be paralleled by complex INUS accounts.[27]

The Aristotelian Heritage

Since I contend that teleological accounts remain an indispensable element for generating knowledge in practical contexts, it is necessary to examine this issue more closely. Questions of the purposiveness of an action (Aristotle's *hou heneka*) require not only an "internal point of view," as Hart has aptly

---

[24] Humberto R. Maturana, "Biology of Cognition," Biological Computer Laboratory Research Report BCL 9.0, Urbana: University of Illinois, 1970.

[25] Hollis and Smith, *Explaining and Understanding International Relations.*

[26] Patomäki, "How to Tell Better Stories about World Politics."

[27] See e.g. the INUS account (insufficient but non-redundant parts of a condition which is itself unnecessary but sufficient for the occurrence of the effect) in John Mackie, *The Cement of the Universe: A Study in Causation*, Oxford: Clarendon, 1988.

put it,[28] they also raise the problem of the role of intersubjective understandings that make the appraisal of the action possible. Aristotle addresses this issue with exemplary clarity in one of the key passages of his *Politics*:

It follows that ... man is by nature a political animal; it is in his nature to live in a state (polis). He who by his nature and not simply by ill luck has no city, no state is either too bad or too good, either sub-human or super-human – sub-human like the war-mad man condemned in Homer's words "having no family, no morals, no home"; for such a person is by his nature mad on war, he is a non-cooperator ... But it is not simply a matter of cooperation, for obviously man is a political animal in a sense in which a bee is not, or any gregarious animal. Nature, as we say, does nothing without some purpose; and for the purpose of making man a political animal she has endowed him alone of the animals with the power of reasoned speech. Speech is something different from voice, which is possessed by other animals also, and used by them to express pain or pleasure; for the natural powers of some animals do indeed enable them both to feel pleasure and pain and to communicate these to each other. Speech, on the other hand, serves to indicate what is useful and what is harmful, and also what is right and what is wrong. For the real difference between man and other animals is that humans alone have the perception of good and evil, right and wrong, just and unjust. And it is the sharing of a common view in these matters that makes a household or a city.[29]

Even if we no longer share with Aristotle the belief in the purposes of nature, the quote above remains an argument of considerable force concerning the social world. Fundamental for his analysis is the distinction of man's sociality from that of other "gregarious animals," which, in turn, is related to the opposition of "voice" and "speech." The latter pair is paralleled by the distinction between pain and pleasure on the one hand, and the intersubjectively shared notions of "right" and "wrong," on the other. Each oppositional pair deserves some brief comments.

The first distinction concerns the specific character of human sociality. While systems of gregarious animals also represent open, self-reproducing systems, their reproduction is regulated by genetically coded specialization, as the example of bees shows (workers, drones, and a queen). Yet, the further we ascend the ladder of evolution, the lesser the importance of genetically coded specializations becomes, as we see in a pack of wolves. Occupants of these positions have to be selected on the basis of individual properties, usually through fights. Nevertheless, in both types of biological system the signaling systems are of decisive importance. The biologist Karl von Frisch has demonstrated how bees communicate with other bees about food supplies, by "dancing."[30] Wolves must not

---

[28] See H.L.A. Hart, *Punishment and Responsibility*, Oxford: Clarendon Press, 1968.
[29] Aristotle, *The Politics*, trans. T.A. Sinclair, Harmondsworth: Penguin, 1962, bk. I, chap. 2, at 28.
[30] See Karl von Frisch, *The Dance Language and Orientation of Bees*, Cambridge, MA: Harvard University Press, 1993.

only recognize the other members by scent and through howls, they must also somehow learn *to act together*, to execute certain moves as part of a larger activity or plan. This has given rise to the speculation whether collective intentions form already on this pre-linguistic stage and are not necessarily tied to the capacity to conceptualize, as we traditionally have assumed. Whatever position we might take – and indeed newer research seems to indicate that many capacities, originally thought to be emerging only with the human species, reach much farther down the evolutionary ladder[31] – there is no dispute that an entirely new world emerges with speech.

Although already the world of signals – Aristotle's *voice (phone)* – contains the perception of "pain and pleasure," it is largely limited to the "here and now." Speech, on the other hand, frees us humans from the immediacy of the situation; it also allows us to make choices rather than merely respond to stimuli. With speech, an assessment of actions and events in terms of common values, and through recollection and comparison, becomes possible. In this way, we can also "learn" not only from our own experiences, but – through our conceptual grasp – even from those of others. In short, although the human world is one of artifice, it is not an idiosyncratic or subjective creation. Rather, it is through the intersubjectivity of language, and its shared meanings, that social order emerges. The person who does not participate in such a community constituted by common meanings, who utilizes a language of his own, is a person who lives in his own private world: he is the *idiotes* in the original sense of the term.

With the last remarks, we have reached the point of the *linguistic turn* of constructivism where some constructivists part company. Nevertheless, I plead for taking the linguistic turn seriously and argue for a "thick" rather than a "thin" version of the constructivist program, taking Aristotle's conception of cooperation as my point of departure.

The Issue of Cooperation

Aristotle's insistence that cooperation is not simply a human phenomenon, but is deeply rooted in and dependent upon certain biological capacities for communication, provides much food for thought. To that extent, we might not only throw away important information for understanding cooperation, when we begin our analysis with "interests." In the latter case, we might miss significant differences among different forms or types of cooperation.

For heuristic purposes I therefore do not want to start with the template of a constrained choice in strategic contexts, but I rather proceed via the examination

---

[31] See e.g. the account of "joint intentions" by Michael Bratman, *Shared Agency: A Planning Theory of Acting Together*, Oxford: Oxford University Press, 2014.

of several cases, which all illustrate some salient features of cooperative endeavors. Consider the following cases of cooperation: (1) the bee example above, (2) a hunting of a pack of wolves, (3) Wendt's minimal social situation (between extra-terrestrials and humans at first encounter), (4) a game of chess, (5) Vito, a Mafia enforcer, holding a gun to my head in order to induce me to cooperate, (6) "prepackaged cooperation" for which arm's-length transactions (spot contracts) serve as an example, (7) painting a house, and (8) playing a duet.

These admittedly odd examples, gathered from the voluminous literature in philosophy on intentionality and cooperative activity,[32] have the advantage that they range over a variety of domains, whose implications for IR analysis will emerge from the discussion. Let us begin with Example 1, the bees. The basic precondition for such a cooperative effort is intentionality, namely the capacity to represent aspects of the world "by which they are about something or directed at something."[33] In this technical sense, intentionality is a much wider concept than *intention*, which involves consciousness, i.e. a particular form of intentionality. Moreover, not all forms of consciousness are intentional either, as free-floating anxiety indicates. Furthermore, strategic interaction is not necessarily always involved in cooperative endeavors. The bees communicate on the basis of a reference to an external given (the sun) and they behave like independent actors vis-à-vis nature.

What makes Example 2 – the hunting of a pack of wolves – interesting is that it exhibits not only features of strategic interaction (e.g. in cutting off the deer's escape route by one part of the pack) but, as suggested above, the wolves have also somehow to arrange their actions in such a fashion that each of the animals is "doing its part." In other words, some are chasing, others are cutting off the escape route, and finally some attack (while the others have to keep their places, otherwise their chase would possibly end up in a Rousseauan stag hunt). Searle sees in such behavior the proof that social facts not only exist, but also that they are not reducible to an aggregation of individual actions. Social facts are not exclusive to the human species and to the human ability to communicate and conceptualize. Collective or "we-intentions," crucial for cooperative ventures among the more advanced species, are therefore

---

[32] See e.g. Anscombe, *Intention*; Wilfred Sellars, *Science and Metaphysics*, London: Routledge and Kegan Paul, 1968; Hector Castaneda, *Thinking and Doing*, Dordrecht: D. Riedel, 1975; Donald Davidson, *Essays on Actions and Events*, New York: Oxford University Press, 1980; John R. Searle, *Intentionality: An Essay in the Philosophy of Mind*, Cambridge: Cambridge University Press, 1983; Michael Bratman, *Intentions, Plans and Practical Reason*, Cambridge, MA: Harvard University Press, 1985; Raimo Tuomela and Kaarlo Miller, "We-Intentions," *Philosophical Studies*, 53:3 (1988): 367–389; Margaret Gilbert, *On Social Facts*, London: Routledge, 1989; Raimo Tuomela, "What Goals Are Joint Goals?" *Theory and Decision*, 28:1 (1990): 1–20; Michael Bratman, "Shared Cooperative Activity," *The Philosophical Review*, 101:2 (1992): 327–341.

[33] John Searle, *The Construction of Social Reality*, London: Penguin, 1995, at 7.

for him a biological "primitive" that reaches across species. The "critical element in collective intentionality is a sense of doing (wanting, believing, etc.) something together, and the individual intentionality that each person has, is derived from the collective intentionality that they share."[34]

Such a construction traditionally seemed problematic for two reasons: because it extended intentions as "plans" far down the evolutionary ladder to non-linguistic forms of behavior, and because it seemed to involve the rather implausible conception of a group-mind, which is one of the dearly loved bugbears of methodological individualists. Yet, the assumed dilemma of either having to postulate a collective mind or of reducing collective intentionality to an aggregate of individual intentionality might turn out, after all, to be false. It could be more the result of the fallacy of misplaced concreteness than of an epistemologically compelling reason. From the fact that, for instance, all thinking takes place in individual brains it does not follow that all mental life has to be expressed in individual terms, or in the form of a singular noun phrase referring to me. The intentionality that exists in each individual head has the form of "we intend,"[35] when my intention can only be formed and understood as part of "our" intending.

But it is also problematic to think that the collective "we-intentionality" can be reduced to individually held beliefs. As Wendt correctly pointed out in following Gilbert: "[W]e can ascribe beliefs to a group that are not held personally by any of its members, as long as members accept the legitimacy of the group's decision and the obligation to act in accordance with its results."[36] As Halbwachs has shown,[37] and as I discuss below in Chapter 8, individual memories are highly social and thus understandable only in terms of collectively shared meanings.

Consider in this context Example 3, i.e. Wendt's attempt of basing social order in an anarchical system on interactions in a minimal social situation. He chooses the imaginary first encounter between some space aliens and earthlings as his paradigm.[38] The purpose of this *Gedankenexperiment* is to show that it is not the structure of the encounter, but rather the subsequent interaction, that determines the future quality of the relations among the players. If they manage, e.g., to emphatically take the other's perspective, a virtuous, self-reinforcing cycle of cooperation ensues, rather than the usual lock-in of a mutual defect strategy typical of Prisoner's Dilemma situations. Therefore, anarchy is not only what the actors make of it, but Wendt derives through

---

[34] Ibid., 24f.   [35] Ibid., 25f.
[36] Alexander Wendt, *Social Theory of International Politics*, Cambridge: Cambridge University Press, 1999, at 162f.
[37] Maurice Halbwachs, *On Collective Memory*, trans. Lewis A. Coser, Chicago: University of Chicago Press, 1992.
[38] Wendt, "Anarchy Is What States Make of It."

extensions of his model some interesting further hypotheses of the importance of historical sequences for conflict management and for the stability of social systems. If rogue actors (states) emerge later rather than early on, and if they can be isolated, their deviant behavior need not upset the general expectations of the members of a system, and conflict is likely to be managed.

This interesting reconstruction is certainly correct in identifying expectations as the most important source of social (dis-)order. But two problems remain. First, the adherents of this perspective have to show that such a system of expectations is not only necessary for the maintenance of social order, but that it actually can arise out of the specified conditions. Second, they have to demonstrate how the experiences taken from bilateral interactions become ensconced in a general *system of expectations*.

Oddly enough, the emergence of a system of expectations depends, in a way, on the "suspension of the capacity to learn," as Luhmann has so aptly put it.[39] In other words, the members of a social system must continue to adhere to the expectation of a "normal" interaction even in the face of deep individual disappointments. If actors were simple calculators updating their expectations on the basis of actual experiences, social order would quickly disintegrate. Thus, even if we do not tie intentionality to language and the capacity to conceptualize, it is difficult to fathom how the actors in Wendt's minimal situation could arrive at a social relationship of any stability out of the sequence of interactions he depicts. In other words, even if the actors have learned to take each other's perspective, and even if they view themselves from the vantage point of the other, something else is required for a stable *system of expectations* to emerge. This "something else" need not necessarily be conceptual; instead it might be learned through habituation within a common life, as observed in the interaction and play of animals, or through a "convention" as suggested by Hume. But whatever it is, in the minimal social situation at least the meaning of gestures must be clear.

For example, a wave of the hand can be taken to mean "come here" (rather than "stay away"), and letting down a spacecraft's defensive shield presupposes first, a common knowledge of the function of such a device, and second, the notion that making oneself vulnerable signals peaceful intentions (rather than simple submission, as e.g. among the members in a wolf pack).[40] How individuals could, without such a shared "life world" or common cultural

---

[39] Niklas Luhmann, *Social Systems*, trans. J. Bednarz and D. Becker. Stanford: Stanford University Press, 1995.

[40] For this telling criticism, see Maja Zehfuss, "Sprachlosigkeit Schränkt Ein," *Zeitschrift für Internationale Beziehungen*, 5:1 (1998): 109–137.

templates, even go on in their interactions is not quite clear.[41] As soon as "culture" enters the picture, or an explicit set of symbolic understandings that is sufficiently separate in its meaning from the simple signals of the biological "world," the role of language and "translation" becomes the crucial issue. This has important implications for the contractarian solution of social order and for Wendt's further theoretical derivations or extensions of his model.

Consider also in this context Wendt's example of the "bad apple" which all the participants in an ongoing interaction must isolate. While the interaction context might be apt for establishing which of the actors is the bad apple, it is also apparent that such a judgment presupposes rather clear understandings of what constitutes "bad" behavior. Here, again, it is insufficient that the expectations of one or the other parties have been disappointed, since defections comprise difficult appraisals of intentions and meanings. Something more than mutual role-taking is required. Wendt seems to be aware of this problem, since he suggests that new identities emerge, which in turn create new interests for the actors. But strangely enough, Wendt neglects both the part played by the cultural system and of the internal sources of identity by staying at the level of interaction. Caught in a structuralist framework, he tries to solve complex problems of social theory without realizing that most of his conclusions follow only if additional and largely unarticulated assumptions are made.

This leads us to the second problem: the parties must also be able to view their interactions from the "social perspective" of the *first person plural*. Not the "I" or the "you," but the "we" is at issue. To that extent, the individuals have to distance themselves from their particularistic perspective and their strategic considerations and interests by forming collective intentions. Rousseau has seen this problem clearly by distinguishing the *will of all*, which is merely the aggregation of individual preferences, and the *general will*.[42] Furthermore, given that these collective intentions are now mediated by language, the naturalistic premises upon which Wendt's minimal social situation is founded are unlikely to carry the weight of explaining the subsequent results. Thus, Wendt's construct seems to suffer from similar shortcomings to Hobbes's theory, which cannot explain the emergence of order out of anarchy. As Habermas suggested:

Given the Hobbesian premises the actors cannot share the perspective from which every actor could assess whether the reciprocal force that limits the arbitrary natural freedom of every actor by general laws is in the common interest of all and thus can be willed by all actors. Hobbes recognized the kind of moral considerations, which come into play, in passing when he refers to the 'Golden rule' – *quod tibi fieri no vis, alteri non*

---

[41] Sujata Pasic-Chakrabarti, "Culturing International Relations Theory: A Call for Extension" in Yosef Lapid and Friedrich Kratochwil (eds.), *The Return of Culture and Identity in IR Theory*, Boulder, CO: Lynne Rienner, 1996, 85–104.

[42] This is not to say that his construction of the "general will" is already an explanation.

feceris – as a law of nature. But such a moral imbrication of the state of nature contradicts the naturalistic presuppositions of the proof, which Hobbes intends to provide, i.e. that a system can be founded solely on the enlightened self-interest of each member.[43]

Example 4, the chess game, seems to be at the other end of the spectrum of the social contract. Not only are the rules quite explicit according to which the players have to make their moves, but playing chess also seems to require some commitment to a common goal. After all, it is the purpose of this game that one party wins. If someone tried to cooperate with the other player – e.g. when a father is teaching his daughter the game, by letting her win – he is strictly speaking, not playing chess, but engaged in some form of (moral) training. Nevertheless, even for that purpose, he has to be careful what type of help he gives to the child. Deliberately overlooking an opportunity for a "check" is quite different from accepting the child's argument that her bishop can also move straight ahead, or that such exceptions are allowed on Tuesdays. To that extent, while the game allows for the meshing of individual (game) plans, and while it requires the cooperation of the players to play by the rules, it is not a cooperative endeavor like some other, far less specified activities.

Example 5, Vito and the gun, is easily disposed of. The use of force, or rather the threat of using force, clearly does not make it an instance of cooperation, since our understanding seems to be clearly interwoven with that of voluntary action. Only in an extended fashion do we speak of cooperation when threats or force are involved, e.g. when we want to stress that the actor (different from an object that can be moved only by actually applying force) still had a choice.[44] Thus, threats, different from the application of brute force, "work" via intentions, and to that extent we can speak of cooperation by the threatened. Our analysis focuses then on the conditions under which threats are effectively made (commitments, clear communications, resolve, credibility) and those that influence their per-locutionary effects.

Examples 6, 7, and 8 form a cluster of complex problems that are helpful in clarifying several other features. This is perhaps clearest in the case of playing a duet. But in order to show why this case is paradigmatic, I begin with the example of painting a house, since it lies between "prepackaged" cooperation and the ideal type of cooperative activity in Example 8. The first thing to note is that we can paint a house without really being engaged in cooperative activity. Assume that two persons, one living in the front, the other in the back, have noticed the shabby look of the house, and they both decide to do something about it. Each buys some paint from a hardware store. Luckily, they both decide on the same color: the original color of the house. One nice day

---

[43] Jürgen Habermas, *Faktizität und Geltung*, Frankfurt: Suhrkamp, 1993, at 120f. My translation.
[44] See e.g. Thomas Schelling, *Arms and Influence*, New Haven: Yale University Press, 1967.

they start scraping and painting, beginning at their respective entrance. But this does not entail that they are acting together or cooperatively. For that, it would be necessary that their *intentions and action plans mesh*, and that this fact is *common knowledge* among them. Furthermore, if the two persons had not just chanced on the right, same color, they would have to have some commitment to this joint activity; if one had decided on red and the other on white, they would have had to argue and agree on the color. In other words, this commitment manifests itself in the need for mutual responsiveness to the respective intentions, as otherwise cooperation will fail, despite the virtually identical "preferences" for painting the house

From this brief discussion the differences between Examples 6 and 8 become clear. In Example 6 – spot contracts – we have worked out in advance what roles we are to play in the realization of our cooperative endeavor. But then we can go off and do our "part" without much concern about how the activity shapes up. This would be odd, however, in Example 8. The non-interactive performance of these roles misses a crucial point in the cooperation, which requires mutual responsiveness in plans and in performance, not just the "prepacked" cooperation of *quid pro quo* exchanges, agreed *ex ante*. When you and I perform a duet, our performances require not only a common goal, the necessary common knowledge, and freely formed interlocking intentions (plans and their meshing), we must also commit ourselves to *mutual responsiveness in action*. If you miss your beat, or are playing faster, or come in at the wrong time, I have to try to accommodate your flawed performance by skipping a bar or by accelerating or retarding my playing. As Michael Bratman pointed out:

In this way each agent must treat the relevant intentions of the other as *end providing* for herself: for each intends that the relevant intentions of the other be successfully executed. And this system of intentions must also be *reflexive*: for each agent must have intentions concerning the efficacy of her own intentions. Shared cooperative activity involves appropriately interlocking reflexive systems of mutually un-coerced intentions concerning the joint activity.[45]

When we talk about social cooperation, most of the time we have this type of shared cooperative activity in mind. Other cases, however, do contain some of the same elements, as we saw in Example 5.

These distinctions are by no means of only academic interest. Rather, they systematically point to important elements of (non)compliance with agreements and of conflicts even when collective intentions have been formed and are part of common knowledge. Those problems are, however, insufficiently analyzed when we focus only on the condition of anarchy, the number of

---

[45] Bratman, "Shared Cooperative Activity," at 335.

players involved, and the shadow of the future, thereby reducing the problem of cooperation to issues of enforcement either through centralized means or through "self-help." Two examples, one from the domestic arena and one from international politics, show the problematic nature of this reductionism.

Consider in this context the problem of a "command economy." Certainly, neither the enforcement by the government nor the absence of clear rules is in doubt. Nevertheless, performance of such systems has been notoriously poor, precisely because neither the planners nor the managers have fostered shared cooperative activity. If such efforts occur, they are usually limited to some Stakhanov-type exertions by ideological zealots. Thus, cooperation is not simply "following orders," as the command theory of realism suggests, or being prevented from pursuing one's self-interest, because of the shadow of the sovereign, or of the future. Indeed, the above-described pathologies appear precisely because the orders *are followed all too well*, and because the fear of not fulfilling the plan prevents any type of reasonable adjustment. As Robert Jervis points out:

Having been told to maximize production, factories rationally turned out a high volume of shoddy goods with great waste; having given incentives for production with minimum waste, clothing factories produced nothing but large sizes. While at first glance the ability to direct behavior would seem to lead to perfect control, it is simply not possible to design incentives that can guide people through a multitude of unforeseen situations in a way that is desired by those who establish the rules.[46]

It was this recognition that led to new management techniques in "capitalist" enterprises, in which teamwork and *quality control by the workers themselves* were stressed, instead of leaving it to inspections by a supervisor. Thus, while the problems arising in the context of principal–agent relations, are, in a way, "enforcement" problems, their solution has very little to do with the conventional strategies suggested by the anarchy problematique. Instead of threats and exogenous enforcement, the formation of and socialization into a (corporate) culture provides the appropriate template.[47]

We also could cite an example from international politics that suggests that it is important to cast one's net wider than usual: one of the issues in arms limitations agreements concerned the question whether the SALT and START agreements were simply prepackaged forms of cooperation, or whether they also implied a farther-reaching shared cooperative activity. Not only was it important to conceive of these agreements as an iterative and incomplete

---

[46] Robert Jervis, *System Effects: Complexity in Political and Social Life*, Princeton: Princeton University Press, 1997, at 63.
[47] On this issue in general, see David Kreps, "Corporate Culture and Economic Theory" in James Alt and Kenneth Shepsle (eds.), *Rational Perspectives on Positive Political Economy*, Cambridge: Cambridge University Press, 1990, 90–143.

contracting problem,[48] it was also necessary to safeguard the cooperation *in action* and not only in plans. Here, for instance, one thinks of the distinction between "SALT as a treaty" and "SALT as a process," or of the distinction between "SALT as a one-shot deal," and as an attempt in "problem solving," as Antonia Handler Chayes and Abe Chayes have called it.[49] In addition, this perspective directs our attention to such institutions as the Standing Committee in Geneva, which played a crucial role in buttressing cooperative activity. In the face of possible deviations from the particular obligations, the parties assigned to this body the assessment of the infractions. In other words, this committee provided a forum in which problems could be discussed and the "meshing of plans" in the performative sense could be re-established.

With these preliminary analyses I have hopefully made at least a prima facie case for an approach informed by a "thick" form of constructivism. It is the task of the next two sections to elaborate on the positive heuristics of such an approach. For this purpose, my presentation will proceed in two steps. In the next section I attempt to show that, contrary to the prevalent interpretation of Hobbes, a constructivist reading of the Hobbesian text reveals some interesting new avenues for the analysis of social order. Second, my challenge also undermines the conventional notion that an understanding of social order requires a deductively formulated set of statements concerning trans-historical truths that are tested against the world "out there."

1.3   The Positive Heuristics of Constructivism

A "Subversive" Reading of Hobbes?

If Hobbes is truly the father of modern political theory, and if his "domestic analogy" has been constitutive of our understanding of internal order and external anarchy, a constructivist perspective can throw considerable light on the problem of order by taking the Hobbesian problematic as a point of departure, as Michael Williams suggested.[50]

Contrary to the vulgar interpretation of his work, Hobbes himself sees social order as depending on *expectations*, and not primarily on "power," (mis)conceptualized as capabilities. It is important to realize that for him it is not force pure and simple, but rather the *presumptions upon which people act* that are decisive, even though at times he suggests that force is the most

---

[48] On this point see my discussion in Friedrich Kratochwil, "The Limits of Contract," *European Journal of International Law*, 5:4 (1994): 465–491.

[49] Abram Chayes and Antonia Handler Chayes, *The New Sovereignty: Compliance with International Regulatory Agreements*, Cambridge, MA: Harvard University Press, 1995.

[50] See Michael C. Williams, *The Realist Tradition and the Limits of International Relations*, Cambridge: Cambridge University Press, 2005.

effective way of structuring expectations. Furthermore, the order problem he analyzes has more to do with problems of false and seditious beliefs than with conflicting interests.[51] To that extent Hobbes's problem of order – given the religious issues of his time – was much more radical than has been the case historically, as he himself suggests in his *Elements of Law*.[52]

What he had to address were the issues *concerning truth and salvation* that had rent the social fabric. This fundamental disagreement created a radically different situation, for which neither the examples of the Bible nor those of the classical *polis*, nor those of Christendom, provided any templates.

This difficulty hath not been of very great antiquity in the world. There was no such dilemma amongst the Jews: for their civil law, and divine law was one and the same law of Moses ... Nor is it a controversy that is ever taken notice of amongst the Grecians, Romans, or other Gentiles. Also those Christians that dwell under the temporal dominion of the bishop of Rome are free from this question. This difficulty, therefore, remained amongst and troubled those Christians only to whom it is allowed to take for the sense of the Scripture that which they make thereof, either by their own private interpretation, or by the interpretation of such as are not called thereunto by public authority.[53]

To that extent the "public order" had to ensure that the individual's conscience no longer interfered with the exercise of authority by the secular sovereign, or that "the danger of eternal damnation from simple obedience to human laws"[54] escalates conflicts. It had, therefore, to be an order in which individual beliefs can no longer be used for the de-legitimization of the public authority on the basis of conscientious objections.[55]

Different from the conventional reading, which stresses Hobbes's naturalism and the fundamental role of self-preservation and interest, we should realize that Hobbes's political psychology is far richer than that of a standard utilitarianism. In some of the most telling passages of his *Behemoth*, Hobbes deals explicitly with the power of imagination, prophecy, fantasy, and folly. Despite his alleged materialism, Hobbes pays particular attention to the role of ideas and emphasizes the powerful force of "names" (e.g. whom to call a "traitor") or to the success of sloganeering, which identified "ship money" with "tyranny"; he is also well aware that norms, such as traditional legitimacy, engender loyalty (towards the Stuarts), and that such beliefs have to be

---

[51] See his remarks in Thomas Hobbes, *Leviathan*, Baltimore: Penguin Books, 1968 [1651], chap. 29. See also Thomas Hobbes, *De Cive*, New York: Appleton-Century-Crofts, 1949 [1642], chap. 12.
[52] Thomas Hobbes, *Elements of Law*, Oxford: Oxford University Press, 1994.
[53] Ibid., II, 25, para. 22, 141f.   [54] Ibid., 152f.
[55] See the interpretation in Pasquale Pasquino, "Political Theory, Order, and Threat" in Ian Shapiro and Russell Hardin (eds.), *Political Order: Nomos XXXVIII*, New York: New York University Press, 1996, 19–41.

overcome by appeals to other legitimizing sources. In short, "equipped with imagination and language, human beings respond to the possible as well as to the actual, to the dreaded or anticipated future as well as to the experienced present."[56]

As a disciple of Bacon, and familiar with the code of honor and the folly of constantly endangering one's life by wanting to win recognition, Hobbes knew very well that the fear of violent death was not simply the *summum malum* for the politically relevant actors of his time. Modern interpretations of Hobbes, such as those of Holmes,[57] Johnston,[58] and Skinner,[59] have therefore suggested that Hobbes's writings should be seen as part of a rhetorical effort in promulgating a new personal "discipline," which would lead to a securer and more peaceful political order. Hobbes was very well aware that, far from designating natural conditions, interest and the fear of violent death are powerfully influenced by a variety of cultural factors.[60]

Hobbes reflected carefully on the impact of such passions as envy, revenge, love, honor, shame, and pity as they give rise to self-destructive courses of action. Even "boredom" leads, in the case of "seditious blockheads,"[61] to the mindless overthrow of political order for the sole purpose of wanting change for the sake of change. As Stephen Holmes puts it: "You cannot explain (much less foresee) social outcomes by reference to the postulate of universal self-interest. Human behavior, no matter how self-interested, remains unpredictable because it is guided partly by the assessment of the future – assessments that, in turn, result from irrational traits of the mind ... not from the calculations of a rational maximizer."[62]

When viewed from this perspective the perhaps at first rather strange interpretation of the *Leviathan* as a "rhetorical" piece attains not only considerable force, but it also shows us that interests are constructed, and that they become part of a "discipline" in the double sense of the meaning: as understanding and as a regime for leading one's life. Even our emotions are not simply natural but part of a specific cultural milieu whose influence becomes visible only when

---

[56] Stephen Holmes, "Political Psychology in Hobbes's Behemoth" in Mary G. Dietz (ed.), *Thomas Hobbes and Political Theory*, Lawrence: University of Kansas Press, 1990, at 122.

[57] See e.g. Stephen Holmes, *Passions and Constraint: On the Theory of Liberal Democracy*, Chicago: University of Chicago Press, 1995.

[58] David Johnston, *The Rhetoric of Leviathan: Thomas Hobbes and the Politics of Cultural Transformation*, Princeton: Princeton University Press, 1986.

[59] Quentin Skinner, *Reason and Rhetoric in the Philosophy of Leviathan: Thomas Hobbes and the Politics of Cultural Transformation*, Cambridge: Cambridge University Press, 2009.

[60] For a fundamental discussion, see Albert O. Hirschman, *The Passions and the Interests*, Princeton: Princeton University Press, 1977; Stephen Holmes, "The Secret History of Self-Interest" in Jane Mansbridge (ed.), *Beyond Self-Interest*, Chicago: University of Chicago Press, 1990, 267–286; Jane Mansbridge, "The Rise and Fall of Self-Interest in the Explanation of Political Life" in Mansbridge (ed.), *Beyond Self-Interest*, 1990, 3–22.

[61] Ibid., 113.   [62] Ibid., 122.

we reflect upon the particular political tradition and the contemporary controversies. Thus, in the case of the "fear of violent death," Hobbes obviously does not refer to something that is unproblematically given. Rather, he is engaged in a deeper political struggle concerning public authority and the effectiveness of its "secular" sanctions buttressing political order. After all, already St. Augustin remarked that it was *eternal damnation*, and not fear of violent death, that represented the *summum malum*. Such a belief, if accepted, tends to weaken the deterrent power of secular punishment, as Hobbes is quick to point out. In drawing the clear lessons from the English Civil War, Hobbes argues that, "[a]s much as eternal torture is more terrible than death, so much [the people] would fear the clergy more than the King."[63]

These brief remarks indicate that at least for Hobbes politics was not only about given "interests." For him, a viable theory of politics has also to deal with the question of where "interests" come from which, in turn, entails the endogenization of the interest problematique upon which contemporary constructivists insist. In this context, one important point for making our choices and selecting goals is not only the ranking of our preference, but also the regret or pride we feel in the *rankings themselves*. In other words, while we can be clear about our preferences, we also often know that they are actually problematic, and that we wished we had others. For example, while I might prefer smoking to abstention, I also might very well wish – without calling such a wish irrational – that I had different desires. To that extent, the "preferences" upon which we act can be shown not simply to be one-dimensional, to be treated as exogenously provided by the various tastes, which are no longer susceptible to analysis. Rather, we begin to realize that a theory that does not account for these meta-preferences is a theory of "rational fools," as Amartya Sen once called it.[64] This idea of meta-preferences indicates that humans as agents are strong evaluators, in Charles Taylor's parlance,[65] and that such evaluations are connected with our identities, which systematically link emotions to shared meanings expressed in a common language. This makes it possible for us to share, as Hume would have it, the "feelings" of approval and disapproval, which form the basis for our moral assessments

Two problems are flagged by the last remarks. First, moral assessments do not involve purely cognitive issues. Second, our feelings or sentiments, which we usually considered purely personal or private, as well as "separate" from our "rational" faculties, are not simply idiosyncratic indications of pleasure

---

[63] Ibid., 14f.
[64] Amartya Sen, "Rational Fools: On the Behavioral Foundations of Economic Theory" in Henry Harris (ed.), *Scientific Models and Men*, London: Oxford University Press, 1987, 317–344.
[65] See e.g. Charles Taylor, *Sources of the Self: The Making of Modern Identity*, Cambridge, MA: Harvard University Press, 1989.

and pain, as utilitarianism suggests. If our moral sense were nothing but the indication of private preferences, of just how I, or you, "feel" about something, no such common appraisals would be possible. In a way, we have returned to one of our core arguments about constructivism: Aristotle's distinction between the indication of pain and pleasure, which belong to mere "voice," and the sharing of common notions about right and wrong, of what is base and what is dignified, what we consider just or unjust, which are characteristic of language. Each of these issues deserves a further discussion.

First, how are emotions, or feelings, related to language, and how does such a perspective correct our standard account of motivation? After all, since Hume reason has been seen as the "slave" of passion. But there is certainly something amiss in this argument, especially since Hume's quote is taken out of context.[66] Not only is it on all fours with our own experience, it is also logically faulty. If this account were correct, and passion was indeed always "complete" and sufficient for motivating action, then no actor could maximize *expected* utility. The fact that I somehow can imagine other states of affairs, which promise me stronger delights in the future than the present desire, indicates that the classical utilitarian motivational account is untenable. Without my imagination, my conjuring up of alternatives, counteracting in this way the "completeness" of the present passion, no delay of gratification could occur. This is also why for Hume "imagination" and "sympathy," *and not reason*, are the decisive elements in the human *mind*. While these corrections of the common misinterpretation of Hume pertain only to the classical rigid separation of reason and passions and to the need to introduce second-order considerations into our calculus, one has thereby not yet shown the *inter-subjective character* of our assessments based on the "feelings of approbation and disapprobation." For this, something else becomes necessary explaining how language and feelings interact, and how they create a common or public space for their expression.

Here it is important to distinguish certain "language-dependent feelings" from emotions or drives. While certain feelings seem to correspond to our standard notions of immediacy – such as when we dread the person approaching us with a gun, or the fear that an overhanging rock might hit us while climbing – other feelings seem to be more complicated. Thus, in contrast to the experience of e.g. dread, feelings of remorse, shame, admiration, and dignity have to do with *who* and *what we are*. Put differently, their "reflexivity" involves "us" as persons with particular identities. As Taylor suggests:

---

[66] For a further discussion of this point that for Hume the mind and its imagination and not reason was the important issue, see the discussion below in Chapter 9.

To feel shame is related to an import ascription ... Beyond the question whether I feel ashamed is the question whether the situation is really shameful, whether I am rightly or wrongly, rationally or irrationally, ashamed.[67]

Precisely because we usually *can* provide reasons for the feelings of shame, dignity, or guilt the latter are not simply responses to situations, indicating pain or pleasure. They are in a way language-dependent in that the articulation of import is intrinsic to the *experience* of the emotion. When I realize that my action was a response to a provocation, my feelings of guilt are alleviated; when it becomes clear to me that my feelings of love were self-delusions, the emotions themselves – pathological cases aside – change.

These observations are by no means of only tangential interest as they expose the shortcoming of the classical liberal action theory that reduces everything to a pain/pleasure distinction and a maximization calculus. Here the recognition of not only cognitive limitations but also "motivated biases" is also making inroads into IR analysis. While it had been conventional wisdom during the sixties to assume that e.g. deterrence fails when either the threat is not communicated well or when the "commitment" of an actor is in doubt, Lebow and Stein's contribution[68] showed that many of the deductions of classical bargaining theory hold only when we assume that actors are *opportunistic maximizers*. Unfortunately, the measures adopted in order to increase the effectiveness of deterrence will fail, however, if actors are motivated *by fear*. In the latter case "talking" them out of their increasing hostility by reassuring them is the only promising strategy. Furthermore, James Davis has demonstrated how the need-disposition that initiates the escalatory cycles is crucially related to the initial assessment that the opponents must be invidious and hostile no matter what, since they attempted to deter "legitimate" demands.[69]

These observations suggest that our actions are based on complicated appraisals, not simply on simple descriptions of the world "out there,"[70] a reason why I advocated a "thick" form of constructivism. The next subsection elaborates further on this theme by probing the issue of whether "meaning" can be reduced to "reference," as the traditional "mirror" theory of language suggested and which was considered essential for an objectivist and "scientific" approach to action.

---

[67] Charles Taylor, "Self-Interpreting Animals" in Charles Taylor (ed.), *Human Agency and Language*, Cambridge: Cambridge University Press, 1985, 45–76, at 55.

[68] See e.g. Richard Ned Lebow and Janice Gross Stein, "Beyond Deterrence," *Journal of Social Issues*, 43:4 (1987): 5–71. See also Richard Ned Lebow and Janice Gross Stein, *We All Lost the Cold War*, Princeton: Princeton University Press, 1994.

[69] James W. Davis, *Threats and Promises*, Baltimore: Johns Hopkins University Press, 2000.

[70] For a critical discussion of this point, see Richard Rorty, *Philosophy and the Mirror of Nature*, Princeton: Princeton University Press, 1981.

The Linguistic Turn

The problem that the meaning of a sentence is not simply the sum of the correspondences of its various terms can be readily derived from the following observations. First, it is neither the correspondence of words nor the structure (syntax) alone that influence the meaning of a sentence since there are also certain important modifiers such as connectives and conditionals, which determine meaning. Thus it would be useless to search for the "correspondence" of the term "although." Furthermore, as soon as certain modalities are introduced, such as "may," "can," and "cannot," the traditional logic based on the dichotomy of "is / is not" is no longer adequate. Increasingly, it is the context that is determinative. If I enter a house and say "hello" what does it refer to? I use hello also when I meet a colleague in the corridor. In the first context "hello" is an abbreviated question, such as: "is anybody home?" In the second context, hello serves as a greeting. But "hello?" can also mean "why did you not get it" in a conversation, and is a request to the partner to pay attention.

At this point one further brief remark on truth and triviality is necessary. One of the constitutive assumptions of the constructivist program is the view that for understanding an action we need not only take the actual actors' perspective, but we must also be familiar with the *intersubjective* understandings that tell us something about the meaning of an act. For example, kicking a ball into a square of poles "means" something, given the background conditions of a game of soccer. If I provide only an account in terms of what the actor did and utilize as a "description" the physical movements I miss the mark. The meaning of "kicking a goal" is not only antecedent to the actor's intention and parasitic upon it, it is "understandable" only in terms of the "game" that is being played.

As the last example shows, what serves as an adequate "explanation" is context-dependent. Consequently, attempts to specify the logical conditions of *the* scientific explanation without considerations of context are problematic, as is an account which relies on equations "modeling" the physical actions of kicking a ball would show, even if it is "true" within another (physical) framework. Although the physical account provides a complete mathematical description of the action, its truth is at best trivial as far as the "game" is concerned. To that extent, something more than "truth" is required for a meaningful analysis (otherwise, the scribblers of tautologies would be the greatest theorists!) and one would indeed have to wonder what price strict adherence to such a scientific ideal would have. "Consistency" with such an ideal would be fatal, and it is hardly surprising that we would not want to embark on such an enterprise. Fortunately, there are also good reasons reinforcing our misgivings for following such an ideal, instead of leaving the criteria of "one scientific explanation" behind, since it is based on a faulty conception of language and of coming to an agreement of what is the case. Ultimately, it is tenable only if we accept the underlying premise that is based on a particular – and, as I might add, misinformed – interpretation of the Humean argument concerning the distinction between "facts" and "values" (norms).

According to the traditional interpretation of Humean epistemology, all sentences are then to be divided into "is" or "ought" statements. This division not only seemed to be exhaustive of all the possibilities, but there was also no way in which I could bridge the logical chasm that exists between the two. But this realization also implies that if we could find a type of sentence that was meaningful, but fitted neither category, our confidence in the initial division would have to be questioned. Even worse, the concomitant presumption that meaningful discourses are only possible about factual statements, while norms and values were beyond rational inquiry, would at least have to be re-thought. It is then not difficult to fathom that such revisions through various ad hoc adjustments will sooner or later necessitate a reconsideration of the entire epistemological project and its ideals.

While the exhaustiveness of the Humean fork was accepted for two centuries, J.L. Austin's William James Lectures in 1955 at Harvard demonstrated that there exists at least one class of sentences that are meaningful, but which fit neither of the two Humean sets.[71] When I say e.g. in a marriage ceremony "I do," I neither describe something, nor do I state a value or indicate a normative preference. As a matter of fact, here the notion of a description breaks down entirely, since I am "doing" something by the very act of making a statement. Different from "fishing," or "painting," this "doing" does not exist outside of the utterance, and its meaning does not lie in some descriptive accuracy, or in some indication of personal mental state, but in the utilization of a rule-governed practice underlying the utterance.

The discovery of speech acts has had revolutionary implications not only for linguistic theory but also for the social sciences in general. Since speech acts are incredibly numerous, ranging from demanding, to appointing, to apologizing, to asserting, and to threatening – to name just a few – their relevance for the analysis of social life is hardly controversial. The other point is that speech acts are constituted by norms, and they often come close to the model of "institutional facts." Finally, we can show that it is through such institutional arrangements that we, as members of a society, *constantly bridge the gap between the "is" and the "ought,"* even if such a bridging does not occur on the basis of *purely logical patterns of inference.*

---

[71] J.L. Austin, *How to Do Things with Words*, Cambridge, MA: Harvard University Press, 1962. See also John Searle, *Speech Acts*, Cambridge: Cambridge University Press, 1969.

The advantage of such institutions like promising or contracting lies precisely in our ability to draw normative conclusions from (seemingly) factual premises, thus tremendously simplifying our normative dilemmas. If e.g. I claimed that I do not owe Bill any money, and yet he can show me a paper, signed by me and with the heading of "Contract" on it, the conclusion that I have a prima facie obligation follows rather nicely from the fact that a contract exists. It "follows" even if the normative force of such a conclusion does not derive from a logical entailment but from the general (usually hidden) proposition that contracts are binding.

From this sketchy account of the importance of institutions, and their rule-based character we can also see where and how interdisciplinary research would be useful. Obviously, since lawyers have been arguing with rules all their lives, their styles of argument, as well as their methodologies, deserve far greater attention than they have received from social scientists. Beyond the legal argument, however, it would also be necessary to investigate further other types of discourses in which norms play a decisive role. Particularly the logical formalizations of the inferences in persuasive arguments, and the nature of what serves as a proof, ought to receive greater attention. Although constructivists as "reflexivists" (whatever that might mean) have been charged with the neglect of "empirical tests,"[72] the argument in this chapter should have demonstrated that this charge is rather scurrilous, given the fact that it is exactly the meta-theoretical issue of *what counts as a test* that is usually the crucial issue in the debates between constructivists and their opponents. For example, when we encounter the statement "This note is legal tender for all debts public and private," understanding the meaning of this statement does not involve checking this assertion against some natural facts of the "world out there." As Searle points out: "When the Treasury says it is legal tender, they are *declaring* it to be legal tender, not announcing an empirical fact that it is already legal tender."[73]

To that extent, the nature of social facts or objects is that they are not simply "there," and that the "materials" pointed to are only tokens for the ongoing practices. Thus, a dollar bill allows us to pay for something and settle debts, but the exchange or the settlement is neither simply describable from an external point of view in some neutral observational language, nor are we much helped by an internal phenomenological description. The reason is that focusing on the material factors or the psychological states of the actors misses the most important element in social facts: the underlying normative underpinnings that establish the practice in the first place, and that is not the result of any individual plans or subjective ideas but antecedent to any of them. Realizing

---

[72] See e.g. Keohane, "International Institutions: Two Approaches."
[73] Searle, *The Construction of Social Reality*, at 55.

this feature of social facts could considerably improve also the rather sterile debate on the role of "ideas" that has been limping along in the IR literature.[74] Finally, as the research focus is on institutions, it should also be clear that such a program will involve us in historical as well as in comparative research. As law students quickly learn in the first-year class on "property," there is not much sense in attempting to distill *the* concept of property out of the various historical forms, or even to test a general concept across history. This was, after all, Weber's argument in favor of "types" rather than universal generalizations.[75] That such a commitment does not inhibit serious historical research is evinced by Weber's own work.

With these considerations in mind, in the next section I examine a bit more closely the set of *substantive questions* that could form a constructivist research program. Such an examination involves us not only in uncovering the archeology of the disciplinary understandings of law and international politics, it has also to clarify the intrinsic link between law and politics that is badly misconstrued when we view both of them from the vantage point of the traditional interpretation of the Humean fork. In that case law has to do with norms, i.e. the "ought's," while "politics" deals with the "is," namely with behavior that can be described from a purely observational standpoint. This conceptual gambit gives rise to the antinomies between "power" and "validity," between "facts" and "values," but it misses important aspects of law and politics alike, as Paul Kahn has put it well:

The rule of law may be a fiction, but it is not merely fictional. It is a form of power – one that works from within the subject rather than as an external limit upon an already present subject. To explore the rule of law is to examine a creation of our collective imagination. The product of this imagining is not just our polity but ourselves as citizens.

To understand the rule of law requires, then, more than a specification of the elements of legal belief. It requires an examination of the rule of law in its continuing struggle with alternative appearances of the political.[76]

These remarks cast not only considerable doubt on the traditional disciplinary boundaries but also on the argument about the contractarian paradigm for explaining the existence of society and its institutions of governance.

---

[74] For a good critical review of some of the shortcomings of the predominant conceptualization, see Mark Laffey and Jutta Weldes, "Beyond Belief: Ideas and Symbolic Technologies in the Study of International Relations," *European Journal of International Relations*, 3:2 (1997): 193–237.
[75] See Max Weber, "Objectivity in the Social Sciences" in *The Methodology of the Social Sciences*, New York: Free Press, 1996, 49–112.
[76] Paul W. Kahn, *The Reign of Law: Marbury v. Madison and the Construction of America*, New Haven: Yale University Press, 1997, at 5.

1.4   The Set of Substantive Problems: Law, Politics, and Society

As we are accustomed to see law and politics as opposites, Judith Shklar suggests in her study *Legalism*,[77] that like a couple with dovetailing neuroses, realists and legalists depended on each other for their own validation. The result is that an increasingly anemic conception of law is paralleled by an equally implausible conception of politics. There is either "justice," or there is "anarchy." Lawyers are supposed to worry about the outlawing of war and later about human rights, but the dichotomy often also seems to suggest that unless all politics was transformed into the paradigm of "just" action, no stabilization of expectations, so crucial for social order, was possible. In case such stabilization occurred against all expectations, it did not deserve the name of "order." Political scientists, on the other hand, dealt with reality by maintaining that force in politics was no longer the *ultima ratio* but the "first and constant one."[78] This change entailed some not too subtle shifts in meaning of crucial terms, such as from anarchy in the technical sense, defined as the absence of central institutions, to that of anarchy in the sense of indicating the war of all against all. It is hardly surprising that given such disciplinary boundaries a dialogue across the different fields was hardly possible.

In painting these disciplinary developments with a broad brush, I do not want to imply that everything is thereby captured. But, even if we consider the above characterization as a "caricature," we should not forget that caricatures are not wrong in the sense that they depict something imaginary or non-existent. Rather they highlight and emphasize the most striking features that are characteristic while neglecting others. Nevertheless, constructivism as an approach could not provide a serious challenge to the very disciplinary understandings if its contribution were limited to this type of criticism only. Rather one needs to examine the co-constitution of law, politics, and society. One way of approaching this problem is via the social imaginary, as Taylor suggested,[79] since in it we find the origins of our disciplinary understandings. Both the notion of (civil) society and that of the establishment of political order via the social contract direct our attention to some important conceptual issues.

The construction of political authority on the basis of some authorization by the members of a society – either as in the corporatist notion of the heads of "houses" in antiquity and in the "founding" of new republics at the end of the Middle Ages, or as a contract among possessive individualists in the

---

[77] Judith Shklar, *Legalism: Law, Morals, and Political Trials*, Cambridge, MA: Harvard University Press, 1986.

[78] Waltz, *Theory of International Politics*, at 113.

[79] Charles Taylor, *Modern Social Imaginaries*; Taylor focuses especially on the economy, the public sphere, and the invention of "the people," which create the imaginary of an all-pervasive secular order that is disembedded from its theological or philosophical origins.

Hobbesian/Lockean construct[80] – signal a fundamental change in the concept
of social order. It occurs when politics and law emancipate themselves from
the sacred, or from a moral order that is based on tradition and its unproblematically accepted customs. Both Aristotle's argument about the *synoikismos*
and his celebration of law as the bond uniting all "citizens" by displacing the
customs of a heroic tribal society[81] show this rather vividly. Nevertheless, we
find the clearest expression of this notion in the contractarian treatises of
the seventeenth and eighteenth centuries in which individual subjective rights
are the central focus.

The notion of subjective rights seems at first a nearly antisocial conception.
Yet, precisely because rights delimit spheres of autonomous choice, i.e. of
Willkür in Kantian terms, the notion of subjective rights is nevertheless deeply
implicated in our sociality. As Michelman has so aptly put it:

A right, after all, is neither a gun nor a one man show. It is a relationship and a social
practice, and in both those essential aspects, it is an expression of connectedness.
Rights are public propositions, involving obligations to others, as well as entitlements
against them.[82]

Thus, something more than just abstention and the delimitation of a sphere of
autonomy is required for the functioning of rights. The members of a society
must take the perspective of the first-person plural rather than understand their
entitlements simply individually and privately. This perspective serves then
also as an important corrective to the notion that the social contract can be
a one-time authorization that is irrevocable, as Hobbes suggested, since the
emergence of a public authority points to the legislative activity, as well as to
its exercise of executive power, both of which have to be tied back to some
legitimizing notions of political autonomy and self-determination.

In criticizing Hobbes and recognizing that the social contract is actually
a rather special undertaking transcending the normal practice of contracts,
Kant elaborates some decisive differences of this act. Different from normal

[80] There is of course more continuity than at first appears since the modern social contract also is
only one among "men" who decide on behalf of their voiceless wives and children and the
slaves or "servants" who were part of the household. Although there were an increasing number
of masterless men in the seventeenth century and the "Levellers" pushed for a universal suffrage
of all men, the "contract" was still to be made among those holding property and who were
heads of a "house" or domain. C.B. Macpherson's argument is misleading, projecting back to
the seventeenth century the social conditions prevailing only in the midst of the nineteenth
century in England. See C.B. Macpherson, *The Political Theory of Possessive Individualism:
Hobbes to Locke*, Oxford: Clarendon Press, 1962.
[81] For that, see Aischylos, *The Orestean Trilogy*, trans. Philip Vellacott, Harmondsworth: Penguin, 1956.
[82] Frank I. Michelman, "Justification (and Justifiability) of Law in a Contradictory World" in
J. Roland Pennock and John W. Chapman (eds.), *Nomos XXVIII: Justification*, New York: New
York University Press, 1986, 71–99, at 91.

contracts, which concern exchanges of goods and specific services, the social contract has no temporal limits. There is, after all, no sunset provision for a constitution. Rather, this act re-describes who "the people" are in that it constitutes them, and makes their preservation an ongoing and trans-generational concern. Thus, as Kant aptly remarked, the social contract has no specific goal outside itself, but it is rather a device that brings a society into existence, in which the members are equally subject to a common self-prescribed norm.[83] As such, it not only guarantees individual subjective rights, but it also stipulates the performative conditions under which laws obtain validity. General laws have to be passed in a certain way, and administrative action has to be in accordance with the empowering legislation. To that extent, the issue of legality of an act, or of a law or statute, is more firmly anchored in an understanding of legitimacy and not solely derived from the auto-poietic capacity of law itself to create new norms.[84]

Historically, it is perhaps not surprising that the Hobbesian form of positivism was paralleled by a revival of natural law or a fallback to the ancient freedoms and customs. These controversies need not concern us at this point. For my purposes here it is rather the mutual co-conditioning of law, politics, and society that is the issue. As we saw, law constitutes not only "the people," but it also creates the "public power" vested in the government to decide all questions of common concern, thereby solving the collective action problem among the free and equal members of civil society. This specific power is not conceivable in a purely instrumental fashion. For one, public authority *does not exist outside* of the political legal context, and neither can it be reduced to the control of the means of violence, which are now entrusted to the enforcers. As law lends legitimacy to the acts of political authorities, political power helps to defend the integrity of the law by stabilizing expectations through the institutionalization of presumptions, through the ascription of specific responsibilities, and through the clarification of the norms and general principles that allow for prospective ordering. Finally, in making the law dependent on the consensus and the declarations of the legitimizing sovereign, the people and their particular interests and traditions are safeguarded and questions of membership (citizenship) – one of the most "political decisions" – are determined thereby.

From this brief sketch, it becomes obvious that the usual distinction between politics as the realm of simple "behavior," and that of law as being concerned

---

[83] Immanuel Kant, *On the Old Saw That Might Be Right in Theory but Won't Work in Practice*, trans. E.B. Ashton, Philadelphia: University of Pennsylvania Press, 1974.

[84] On the notion of law as an auto-poietic system, see Niklas Luhmann, *Rechtssoziologie*, vol. 2, Reinbeck: Rohwolt, 1972. See also Gunther Teubner, *Recht als Auto-Poietisches System*, Frankfurt: Suhrkamp, 1989.

with norms and the "oughts," is in dire need of revision. It is also obvious that the context of morals and law is much more complicated than the image of a hierarchy of norms topped by a final norm or by ultimate values suggests, precisely because in modern times one can no longer appeal to some secure foundation or intuition which is beyond debate. That these problems are not matters of purely academic interest is evidenced by the recent heated debates between universalists and communitarians, fundamentalists and modernists, and by the tangible implications of these debates on questions of citizenship, intervention, and the protection of human rights.[85]

Finally, issues of legitimacy become increasingly problematic when states are no longer the main actors and much of their activity has been delegated to corporate groups internally, or to international regimes and institutions externally. In addition, emerging networks make it increasingly possible to circumvent the traditional barriers that had established "publics" and created a common space within which the alternatives shaping our social lives are debated and legitimized. But while this proliferation of new actors, new agendas, and new organizational forms highlights the potential for a progressive development of a "world society" and of "law solutions," its downside also becomes obvious. The worldwide but uneven integration of "functional" systems from the fetters of law and processes of consensus formation of a public and its legitimization – as exemplified by the recent disorder created by the financial system – gives rise to rightful concern. It will be the task of the next chapters to elaborate on these themes.

1.5 Conclusion

This chapter was concerned with the elaboration of a constructivist perspective for social inquiry. It attempted to achieve this through criticism as well as through an outline of the positive heuristics of such an approach. In its *critical* part, I examined a particular understanding of social science and its implied imperatives concerning both the disciplinary boundaries and the concomitant methodological choices. Furthermore, given that knowledge presupposes disciplinary understandings, which often are based on incompatible presuppositions, I argued that calls for interdisciplinary work are as understandable as they are often misguided. Interdisciplinary work is not only difficult in a practical sense, it is conceptually challenging, as a new set of substantive puzzles has to be identified and their role in different disciplinary fields has to be analyzed.

[85] See also the argument by Christian Reus-Smith,"Human Rights in a Global Ecumene," *International Affairs*, 87:5 (2013): 1205–1218.

For that reason, I argued for an interdisciplinary research program based on a common "core" of problems (rather than method) that are crucial for the fields of law, society, and politics alike. This "core" is not only provided by the artificiality of the human world, but it is also given through the language dependence of social order, exemplified by Aristotle's remarks about man as a political and language-endowed animal. The constructivist move, however, was not only prepared by such classical understandings, but regained its impetus from ordinary language philosophy. Precisely because both classical and modern (Cartesian) epistemology had relied on the mirror quality of language, serious problems in the analysis of reference and meaning persisted. As soon as meaning was, however, no longer determined merely through representation, but was seen as part of the constitutive function of language itself, a new paradigm emerges that could provide us with a common set of puzzles.

This agenda then justified my plea for a "thick" rather than a thin version of constructivism. In order to further buttress my claim, I showed the fruitfulness of such a "thick" alternative by a "deconstruction" of Hobbes. Having subverted the dominant disciplinary understandings, I suggested that a set of substantive questions concerning the context of social order, law, and politics could fruitfully inform an interdisciplinary research program.

2   Constituting

2.1   Introduction

The previous chapter attempted to show why legal theory and sociological approaches are helpful in understanding the emergence and maintenance of social systems. In particular, law is helpful because it provides us with an authoritative map of the social whole, as in the case of a "constitution." Even in areas such as the international arena, where no such authoritative "document" exists, the institutional order can be grasped by looking at a variety of "sources," customary or codified, for an initial mapping. Although sovereignty remains the recognized organizational principle, new actors, such as intergovernmental organizations (IGOs) and nongovernmental organizations (NGOs), have emerged and have undermined the state's monopoly on determining sovereignty's meaning. In addition, new domains of politics, be it the environment, the international economy, or social movements, show entirely new organizational forms and patterns of interaction when compared to the classical practices of states, or the administrative routines of "functional" organizations.[1]

Tracing these changes will, by necessity, involve us in some historical reconstruction. Precisely because I do not assume an inherent teleology of social development, a careful analysis is required for examining the reasons for changes in the "principles of differentiation" that have marked off groups from one another, and for tracing the processes in which the new boundaries are being redefined in the present. Such an approach entails more a focus on the *drawing of the boundaries* than on the "units" that are thereby created. "Society," then, no longer coincides with the "integrated" inside of the unit, which is opposed to the external anarchy. Instead it becomes simply a shorthand for *drawing these boundaries* and for observing the subsequent interactions and interpenetration of the systems thus created.

---

[1] For an excellent historical analysis of the jurisdictional extensions of its authority over "money" by the state and by the eventual expression of "sovereignty" in a national currency, see Benjamin J. Cohen, *The Geography of Money*, Ithaca, NY: Cornell University Press, 1998. See also his discussion of different historical and contemporary regimes.

This approach owes much to Luhmann's Modern System Theory (MST), although I shall not simply adopt it, because important parts of the political problematique disappear if one makes that choice. Nevertheless, I find it useful as a first cut for analyzing transformative changes. Historically there have been only a limited number of differentiating principles, as Luhmann suggests. They range from the segmentation of a-cephalic "tribal" societies to the emergence of a center with its periphery – exemplified by the hierarchic centers of the ancient Middle East – to the stratification of a status society exemplified by late feudalism, to the functional differentiation prevalent in modernity.[2] There is no theoretical proposition from which this list of possibilities is derived; it seems, nevertheless, that this list (with subtypes to be introduced for heuristic purposes à la Weber) is indeed exhaustive of the forms of differentiation, which have occurred *historically*.

Interestingly enough, each of these forms has also been invoked as an appropriate heuristic template for the analysis of the international system. Segmentation speaks to the argument about the "primitive" nature of the international system as a social system,[3] as well as to the structuralist emphasis on the undifferentiated nature of the units in this system (Waltz).[4] Immanuel Wallerstein utilized the center–periphery model in his world systems approach.[5] Robert Gilpin's idea that international systems are products of hegemonic rule and of the establishment of at least weak hierarchies corresponds to the status model of society,[6] as do the arguments advanced by Ikenberry[7] and Lake.[8] Finally, the issue of functional differentiation and the emancipation of the "economy" from both the state and from society is explicitly one of the reasons why Susan Strange once called for a revised IR theory.[9] Investigating these forms of differentiation and their constitutive principles is therefore not peripheral to theorizing in the field of international politics. On the contrary, it provides us

---

[2] See Niklas Luhmann, *Die Gesellschaft der Gesellschaft*, vol. 2, Frankfurt am Main: Suhrkamp, 1997, chap. 4.

[3] See e.g. the argument by Roger D. Masters, "World Politics as a Primitive Political System," *World Politics*, 16:4 (1964): 595–619.

[4] Waltz, *Theory of International Politics*.

[5] Immanuel Maurice Wallerstein, *The Modern World System: Capitalist Agriculture and the Origins of the European World Economy in the Sixteenth Century*, New York: Academic Press, 1976.

[6] Robert Gilpin, *War and Change in World Politics*, Cambridge: Cambridge University Press, 1981.

[7] See John G. Ikenberry, *After Victory: Institutions, Strategic Restraint, and the Rebuilding of Order after Major Wars*, Princeton: Princeton University Press, 2001.

[8] David A. Lake, *Hierarchy in International Relations*, Ithaca, NY: Cornell University Press, 2009.

[9] Susan Strange, *States and Markets*, London: Pinter, 1998. See also Susan Strange, "Towards a Theory of Transnational Empire" in Ernst-Otto Czempiel and James N. Rosenau (eds.), *Global Changes and Theoretical Challenges: Approaches to World Politics for the 1990s*, Lexington, MA: Lexington Books, 1989, 161–176.

with important clues as to the changes, which nowadays we lump together under the rubric of "globalization."

In this chapter I elaborate on those problems by looking at the *constitutive function* of norms and their role in social reproduction. In this context, I have to address not only the problem of "order" as it arises in every social system, but also the question whether or not the international system can be conceived of as a "social" system.[10] Furthermore, I have to investigate the problem whether such a system can be a "system of action," namely result from the deliberate choices of the actors, or whether, at least for certain purposes, a different and more "systemic" perspective is required. Such a perspective would have to include the role of media of exchange and of codes which influence not only the choices of the actors but seem to do so often behind their backs. Adam Smith's metaphor of the unseen hand is the perfect example of this phenomenon, although the "market" model relies on a micro- rather than a macro-perspective.

In any case, much of system thinking in IR analysis begins with the issue of "unintended consequences." I argue below that while many systems' effects might indeed be characterized by a certain "perversity," it is not sufficient to point to the unintentional character of the observed consequences and leave it at that. For theoretical purposes the interesting question is that of the reasons underlying this perversity. Is it the result of simple aggregation problems, as in a stampede in a theater, when all try to reach the door and thereby block one another? Is it the outcome of strategic calculation that makes all rational actors in a generalized Prisoner's Dilemma worse off? Or is the observed perversity due to a lack of integration of various subsystems and thus the result of the boundary maintaining operations of systems? In the first two cases coordination norms or the threat of sanctions might suffice to impart some order to the system as a whole. In the latter case, no such design is available, and other means of integration – if any – have to be found.

Classical systems theory has attempted to deal with some of these problems in terms of the distinctions between open and closed systems, and by treating the issue of system integration in terms of the relations of parts to a whole. *Modern* systems theory suggests, however, that these root metaphors of "open versus closed" and the "part/whole" distinction might be insufficient for the analysis of complex social differentiation.[11] Social systems are not only open, but they are constantly engaged in boundary-spanning exchanges in order to

[10] For two recent contributions to this theme from different perspectives see Mathias Albert, Barry Buzan, and Michel Zuern (eds.), *Bringing Sociology to International Relations*, Cambridge: Cambridge University Press, 2013; Jonathan Joseph, *The Social in the Global: Social Theory, Governmentality and Global Politics*, Cambridge: Cambridge University Press, 2012.
[11] See the useful collection of essays in Mathias Albert, Lars-Erik Cedermann, and Alexander Wendt (eds.), *New Systems Theories of World Politics*, London: Palgrave, 2010.

reproduce themselves according to their own logic. Thus, paradoxically, they are open and closed at the same time. The "openness" of such systems consists in their ability to communicate with other systems, which form their environment. Their closure results then from the fact that each system can "recognize" the other system only in terms of its own "logic." In other words, every influence from the outside of the system is transformed (interpreted) by the operations of the system and thus becomes part of the system itself.

This self-referential character creates difficulties for traditional causal analysis as well as for the attempt at reducing the systemic approach to the interactions of concrete units or actors. These problems have important implications for standard IR analysis. There the actor designation problem is usually solved by a state-centric assumption. This makes states the only actors of consequence, and it also suggests that other phenomena, which often intrude into this neat picture, have to be analyzed in terms of access to, or influence via states. Yet, by this very move we prevent ourselves from analyzing what constitutes an actor in world politics in the first place, and why historically the boundaries constituting an "actor" are sometimes shifting and at times appear rather robust. In the absence of an explicit examination concerning the boundary construction we seem to fall back on some "we all know" presumption and eagerly embrace the fallacy of misplaced concreteness. This observation points to a more general problem. A theory that attempts to address the problem of systemic change cannot leave such issues somewhere "outside" by simply exogenizing them. Rather, it has to analyze the problem of differentiation by addressing the "inside" as well as the "outside," thus circumventing the fallacy.[12]

The upshot of this argument is that we can no longer begin with things or units and then explain systems through their aggregation or interactions. Instead, we have to draw analytical distinctions that "go through" the things and persons we encounter in the familiar world of everyday life. For purposes of analysis, "the world" understood as the sum of, or as the last horizon wherein things "stand" simply disappears. It disappears very much in the same way as the world of solid objects and the "fields" and "processes" in modern physics dissolve matter.[13] This makes it necessary to focus on boundaries and to view them as analytical constructs and as relational and process markers rather than as solid, material objects or their analogs.[14]

---

[12] For an interesting discussion along these lines, see Patrick Thaddeus Jackson, "On the Cultural Pre-Conditions of Political Actors" (paper presented at the Annual Meeting of the American Political Science Association, Boston, MA, September 3–6, 1998).

[13] For a recent attempt to make quantum physics a unifying frame for analysis of nature as well as the social world, see Wendt, *Quantum Mind and Social Science*.

[14] For a challenging discussion of the implications of these ideas, see Nicholas Rescher, *Process Metaphysics: An Introduction to Process Philosophy*, Albany, NY: SUNY Press, 1996.

In order to elaborate on these points my discussion takes the following steps. In the next section (Section 2.2) I examine the issue of society and the question of order, which is usually linked to it. In emphasizing the special role of law and its procedures to integrate society by resolving conflicts and by providing for the possibility of "prospective ordering," I take issue with the notion that a society requires some coherent value consensus and substantive widely shared normative commitments. Yet, I also show that stability of expectations, or cooperation by trial and error, is insufficient for explaining the emergence and reproduction of the international system. In short, I argue that there is good reason for following the English school tradition of choosing the "anarchical society" as a more appropriate metaphor, at least as a first cut.[15] On the other hand, given the increasing interdependencies among states, the emergence of global networks, and also a distinct broadening of the normative agenda in contemporary politics (vide the ecological concerns and human rights issues), it is nowadays hardly sensible to limit the inquiry to the concerns of a "society of states."[16]

Section 2.3 is devoted to an elaboration of different forms of differentiation. Here Luhmann's ideal types of segmented, hierarchical, and functional forms of differentiation serve as my foil. This discussion provides the analytical tools for examining the emergence of the state system from the universal order of feudal and estate society, to which I turn in the next chapter, before a short summary (Section 2.4) highlighting the main issues of differentiation concludes the chapter. The discussion here and in the next chapter prepares the ground for the discussion of the contested meanings of globalization and its implications for politics, to which I return in the last two chapters of the book.

2.2   The Problem of a "System," the Contested Meaning of "Society," and the Role of Law

The International System

That the interactions in the international arena show systemic character is one of the very few uncontroversial statements in our discipline. Fundamental disagreement arises when some sort of social character is ascribed to these

---

[15] In this context, see particularly Hedley Bull, *The Anarchical Society: A Study of Order in World Politics*, New York: Columbia University Press, 1977.

[16] See the lively debate between Nardin and representatives of schools of thought concerning the nature of international society in David Mapel and Terry Nardin (eds.), *International Society: Diverse Ethical Perspectives*, Cambridge: Cambridge University Press, 1998. For a concise statement of the notion of states as "practical associations" and a conception of international society as being constituted by the legal practices among states, see Terry Nardin, *Law, Morality, and the Relations of States*, Princeton: Princeton University Press, 1983.

relations. There are those who conceive of international politics as an anarchy, in which, supposedly, norms and values do not matter and in which anomic behavior of a Hobbesian war of all against all is to be expected. Nevertheless, even those theorists perceive an arrangement that is not only surprisingly stable, given its presuppositions, but self-reproducing throughout history. Nevertheless, a puzzle remains since the social element, or the orientation of action on the "other(s)," does not seem to be buttressed by common values in the sense of specifying a specific vision of the "good life" to be pursued.[17]

Traditionally this puzzle was "solved" by distinguishing social systems on the basis of their mode of integration, i.e. on Durkheim's or Tönnies's classical distinction between *Gesellschaft* and *Gemeinschaft*, both of which represent different forms of sociality. But there is something more to this. Even Hegel, certainly not a friend of any notion of community above the state, pointed in this context to the important element of social "recognition." He argues that rights and obligations, in short the capacity to act as a state, impart some form of sociality to the actors' actions in the international arena.

A state is as little an actual individual without relations to other states as an individual is actually a person without rapport with other persons ... [it] should receive its full and final legitimization through its recognition by other states although this recognition requires to be safeguarded by the proviso that where a state is recognized by others, it should likewise recognize them, respect their autonomy; and so it comes about that they cannot be indifferent to each other's domestic affairs.[18]

There is indeed a curious tension in Hegel, which also can be found in many "realists" after him. On the one hand there is the assertion about the need and importance of recognition, which constitutes a form of sociality, but on the other hand history has found for Hegel its end in the state, above which no further obligation or even meaning can be found.[19] Furthermore, as soon as we allow alliances or "poles" within our system, we have to admit that contracts, institutions, and norms exist, and it becomes difficult to argue that the outcomes in the international arena are simply shaped by the co-action of units in an anarchical environment.

---

[17] This is, of course, a contested issue. For example, Christian Reus-Smith has recently argued for a much more substantive understanding of international order than the former notion of a practical association introduced by Oakshott and Nardin implied. See Christian Reus-Smith, *Individual Rights and the Making of the International System*, Cambridge: Cambridge University Press, 2013; see also Terry Nardin, *Law, Morality, and the Relations of States*, Princeton: Princeton University Press, 1983.

[18] Georg Wilhelm Friedrich Hegel, *Philosophy of Right*, trans. T.M. Knox, Oxford: Oxford University Press, 1967, para. 331.

[19] For an attempt at providing a Hegelian justification for the existence of an international society and its relevance to ethics, see Mervyn Frost, *Ethics in International Relations: A Constitutive Theory*, Cambridge: Cambridge University Press, 1996.

"Society" as a Contested Concept

Obviously, a whole host of further distinctions are at least implicit in my first conceptual cut for liberating the notion of social action from the notion of society as a normatively or functionally integrated whole. It also seems necessary to examine more systematically the role of conflict in integrating groups and societies, which Lewis Coser had emphasized a long time ago.[20] To that extent, the notion that a society has to be a functionally or normatively integrated whole suffers from severe shortcomings. Furthermore, something additional has to be said regarding the problem of the stability of expectations, since a mutual defect strategy in an n-person Prisoner's Dilemma is also stable equilibrium. Obviously, the quality of stability matters, as I show below. For the moment, I take up the problem of order without, however, wanting to exhaustively rehearse the arguments among Parsonians (insisting on normative integration)[21] and their opponents, i.e. the members of the "conflict school" in sociology.[22] Two brief remarks shall suffice.

As to the functionalist version of integration that gained currency in the structural functionalism of the late 1960s, we should realize that "societies" are considerably less orderly than the functionalist argument seems to suggest. In tracing functionalism's intellectual roots to biology and to a rather influential philosophy of organism, Dennis Wrong points out: "Functionalism as an image of society that emphasized its similarity to an organism in the self-regulated interdependence of its parts contributing to the survival of the whole was entirely consistent with this prevailing intellectual *Zeitgeist*, affirming holism."[23] It is somewhat ironic that the organic metaphor, used until the sixteenth century for politics (the body politic), was later replaced by the concept of "contract," but attained a new life in the budding discipline of sociology. Together with this metaphor a further problematic assumption crept into sociological analysis. As in the case of a body, there had to be a controlling part (head) putting all these differentiated subsystems together again. Thus, society had to be conceived in terms of an overall design. Needless to say,

---

[20] Lewis A. Coser, *The Functions of Social Conflict*, New York: Free Press, 1956.

[21] See Talcott Parsons, *Social System*, Glencoe: Free Press, 1951. For Parsons's solution to the Hobbesian problem of order, see Talcott Parsons, *The Structure of Social Action*, New York: Free Press, 1949.

[22] For the "conflict school," see Ralf Dahrendorf, *Class and Class Conflict in Industrial Society*, Stanford: Stanford University Press, 1959. See also John Rex, *Key Problems of Sociological Theory*, London: Routledge & Kegan Paul, 1961. For the fundamental article that structured the later debate, see David Lockwood, "Social Integration and System Integration" in G.K. Zollschan and H.W. Hirsch (eds.), *Explorations in Social Change*, Boston: Houghton Mifflin, 1964, 244–257.

[23] Dennis Wrong, *Problem of Order: What Unites and Divides Society*, New York: Simon and Schuster, 1994, at 215.

this notion is, despite its popularity, not in tune with the concept of functional differentiation as it is used in biology.

Emphasizing common values and consensus, and relying on them rather than on some principle of functional design, provided an alternative explanation for the integration of societies (social integration). Unfortunately, it does not seem to fare much better than its predecessor. As mentioned above, common values do not prevent internecine warfare, as the frequency of violent conflicts among "true believers" amply demonstrates. On the other hand, even large-scale feuding or protracted conflict is not necessarily incompatible with the concept of a society, as tribal societies amply demonstrate. Far from disintegrating – as Hobbes avers with his "all or nothing" picture of order – a society might persist even if the stability of expectations consists largely in the experience of actors that the margins for cooperation are quite small.

In short, conflict, even violent conflict, is not incompatible with the notion of a society, although here we admittedly rather quickly might reach the limit. Nevertheless, there is a difference between an "anarchy" in Hobbesian terms, in which the only stable expectation is that of violence, and societies in which conflicts can be rampant but are *managed and do not escalate*, so that the society can reproduce itself. The discussion in the next section about the criteria for social coexistence – originally articulated by Hume and attaining prominence in Bull – shows why this is so. For the moment, I simply want to point out that I am not committing here the sin of conceptual over-stretching, since in everyday language we do seem to use the concept of society in this fashion. After all, we usually do not think that there is no Colombian society, despite the persistence of civil war there during the last half century,

Part of the problem is that society is entirely a symbolic construct and, this being so, no simple deictic procedure or observation will do. How do we know that a society exists, as no such "thing" can be observed (directly) in the world? The answer is simply that the meaning of a concept is not a function of its reference *but of its use*. Somehow, we feel justified in thinking about the continuity of the Colombian society despite the fact that the state has for long periods had difficulties in maintaining the rule of law. In other words, we have not only to take the self-referential nature of these concepts into account, we explicate their meaning by showing how they are nested in conceptual grids, and how the often-precarious stability of use of these contested concepts nevertheless allows for communication even if social reproduction is severely impaired.

In this context, it is worth remembering that the emergence of sociology as a discipline occurred after the establishment of full-blown states. Although not all states had been equally successful in transforming local differences and in eliminating elements of the old feudal order, there is no doubt that both state-building and nationalism fundamentally affected the shape of the respective societies. Society originally functioned as an oppositional concept to that of the court and later to the state, but it became in the nineteenth century increasingly identified with the nationalist project: nation and state had to coincide. Thus "society" ideal-typically had to show the same definite clear-cut boundaries as the territorial state. Consequently, people (and sociologists even more so) began to think about societies in the plural, not because we were facing widely isolated systems of interactions – which mostly anthropologists studied – but because the pluralities of states seemed to result in a plurality of societies. The meaning this concept carries discloses itself through its "archeology," not through a definitional exercise.

Recognizing this problem has an important further corollary. It frees us from *conceiving order as a result of an overall design in which various parts are harmoniously related to each other.* In focusing on processes, we see that norms provide for integration, not because of common values or because of some overall design, but because they let us "go on" with our interactions by providing for the resolution of inevitable conflicts. In short, integration occurs through controversies and through the decisions of authorized institutions. Both temporarily stabilize expectations and provide templates for certain types of problems without necessarily fitting smoothly an overall functional design or a well-ordered value system. To that extent even self-help involving force is not the end of "society," as long as it is recognized as a settled practice, and as long as it is capable of bounding conflicts and preventing their escalation, as we shall see below in the chapter on "sanctioning"

The upshot of the above argument is that to speak meaningfully about a society we need – aside from interdependent decision-making and the interlocking of actions (Weber's social action) – a certain kind of continuity. It is precisely this element that makes inferences from face-to-face encounters to society so problematic, unless they are framed and reinforced by the further ties of (mythical or "imagined") kinship or ancestral land. Here Simmel's sociology,[24] which focuses on processes of association (*Vergesellschaftung*) rather than on treating groups as existing entities that then engage in interactions, is of great importance. Such a shift in focus allows us to endogenize corporate identities,[25] which emerge from the interaction process and reconfigure the institutions of a group, whereby conflict with "others" plays a decisive role.[26] In any case, while pre-modern societies relied on face-to-face contacts and kinship systems, modern societies require more abstract categorizations

---

[24] Georg Simmel and Otthein Rammstedt, *Soziologie: Untersuchungen über die Formen der Vergesellschaftung*, Frankfurt am Main: Suhrkamp, 1992.

[25] For a further discussion, see Lars-Erik Cederman and Christopher Daase, "Endogenizing Corporate Identities: The Next Step in Constructivist IR Theory," *European Journal of International Relations*, 9:1 (2003): 5–35.

[26] Georg Simmel, *Conflict and the Web of Group Affiliations*, New York: Free Press, 1955.

and a different form of imagination in which written communications and legal frameworks take the pride of place.

Law and Integration

The considerations discussed above have several important corollaries. First, they show the distinct bases for individual and systems integration: the former functions mainly via identification with the group, the latter via codes of conflict resolution. Second, since functionally differentiated systems usually emerge later in the historical process, it is understandable that these new systems are usually considered as subsystems, thereby suggesting that the phenomenon is an instance of the part/whole logic. Although we have seen that such an attribution might be misleading – as systems might coexist quite incoherently – the need for measures of conflict resolution increases exponentially in that case. To that extent, "law" seems to be of special importance, because it plays a special role in providing not only for the punctual and temporary stabilization of expectations by deciding concrete cases, but – due to the precedent of the decision (or the legislative response to it) – also for prospective ordering. It is through law and its authority (not primarily through values) that the problem of both social and functional integration in a society is achieved, and that the transactions going beyond the boundaries of an established society can be managed. Both integrationist perspectives and rational choice approaches miss important parts of this story, because they are blind to the special role of norms antecedent to interactions and to the individual strategies. It is instructive to briefly review some common shortcomings of these approaches.

Among the integrationist approaches one can distinguish between more empirically oriented (ethnomethodological) studies, in which cultural nuances and the presentation of the self and the management of impressions are at the center of attention,[27] and some more theoretically oriented investigations. The latter often begin with a kind of minimal social situation (as exemplified e.g. by Wendt[28] or Axelrod[29]) and then attempt to derive in a second step far-reaching conclusions for social order from these encounters. While the normative ordering that results from these interactions seems to be rather straightforwardly based on the interactions and the particular experiences of the actors, several normative presuppositions have to be brought to the

---

[27] See e.g. Erving Goffman, *Behavior in Public Places: Notes on the Social Organization of Gatherings*, New York: Free Press of Glencoe, 1966. See also Erving Goffman, *Interaction Ritual: Essays in Face-to-Face-Behavior*, Chicago: Aldine, 1974.

[28] See Wendt's argument about "first encounters" in Wendt, *Social Theory of International Politics*, at 141f., 158, 187f.

[29] Robert Axelrod, *The Evolution of Cooperation*, New York: Basic Books, 1984.

interaction, so that it can "go on." These additional presuppositions seem to be antecedent to the sympathetic role-taking that occurs within the interaction. For instance, whether I can classify an interaction as an "exchange" hinges crucially on several implicit assumptions. The first and most important assumption is that the "other" is recognized as an autonomous or empowered actor, not someone lacking reason and therefore also the capacity to contract. To that extent, membership in a group at least answers to one part of the recognition problem, neglecting for the moment the conditions of a lack or loss of such capacities. Yet, despite the heartwarming story of exchanges among people in a state of nature, as reported by Locke,[30] the recognition of "outsiders" as equals often entails serious problems. It cannot simply be assumed away by starting with some "actors" in a first encounter, particularly if one wants to draw inferences from such a construct to international relations. After all, the killing of "savages," the enslavement of whole populations, the scandal of colonialism, unequal treaties, and so on, provide us with a rather sad testimony. Even sadder is that "law" – in that case "international law" – provided historically one of the main instruments for depriving the subjected "colonial people" of their possessions and identities, as Angie has so aptly shown.[31] Thus, the conferral of actor status at least establishes the *presumption* against the free resort to violence, and therefore fundamentally changes the expectations prevalent in a Hobbesian state of nature.

Second, each of the exchanging parties must accept that the other has a valid title to the things s/he is offering. Third, we must somehow understand that certain gestures or utterances count as promises, i.e. the promising-game has to be known to the actors, since a contract is based on mutual promises. It seems to me that these *criteria* are truly constitutive of social order, and thus they cannot be derived from some set of observable interactions, precisely because they are antecedent to any possibility of interacting and of knowing what is going on. At the same time the acceptance of these normative demands can hardly be construed as a "value-consensus," since it is also antecedent to particular notions of the common good, or a way of life. Finally, these norms are not necessarily *principles* in the sense that they are of higher order than the simple and clear rules, precisely because e.g. the injunction in the Ten Commandments against "shedding blood" has the form of a regulative rule, not of a principle. But since rules are supposed to be "stricter" and to provide

---

[30] John Locke, *The Second Treatise of Government*, Indianapolis: Bobbs-Merrill, 1960, at 10. "The promises and bargains for truck etc. between two men in the desert island, mentioned by Garcilaso de la Vega in his history of Peru, or between a Swiss and an Indian in the woods of America, are binding on them, though they are perfectly in a state of nature in reference to one another: for truth and keeping of faith belongs to men as men, and not as members of society."

[31] Anthony Angie, *Imperialism, Sovereignty and the Making of International Law*, Cambridge: Cambridge University Press, 2005.

firmer guidance, not all is clear because of the semantic open texture of rules. Is the killing of animals forbidden? Blood is shed, after all. What about the "enemy-exception"? Similarly, it would also be odd to argue that the stipulations of what counts as a promise are not simply constitutive of the practice of promising (or of contracts), but that they stand in a relationship of higher-order principles to the specific rule determining what counts as a promise. These reflections seem to indicate that attempts to "derive" the normative pull of norms from ultimate values or principles is highly problematic, a problem to which we will come back in the discussions of Hume's argument of "justice being an artificial virtue."

For the moment, I want to point out that the above argument contradicts in important respects (neo-)realist and rational choice approaches regarding cooperation under anarchy. To recapitulate one familiar idea: rational actors interacting in the absence of a sovereign face an n-person Prisoner's Dilemma. Cooperation, so the argument goes, might still be possible if certain conditions are met. Among other things, it is necessary that the same actors face each other multiple times, that no one round is decisive in the sense of leading to the elimination of the other actor, that the number of rounds is unknown, and that the players must adopt certain contingent strategies (tit for tat, or forgiving sinners) in "answering" the past choice of the other party. While such a conceptualization of cooperation requires several heroic assumptions, I want to focus only on two aspects: one, that a backward-looking iteration and the aggregation of dyadic interactions misses important constitutive elements of cooperation, and two, that the problem of sanctioning through changes in strategy is far too simplistic.

If one considers the objections in greater detail, the first thing to notice is that in rationalist approaches *commitments* – which have to be antecedent to the interaction – are excluded. The choice of strategy is solely determined by future expectations. On the other hand, the argument concerning the role of sanctions is backward-looking, despite its incorporation of the "shadow of the future." Does this not contradict the "logic" of the original argument that the past (and thus previous commitments) does not matter?

Furthermore, if we try to extend the game among two actors to the society at large, the implicit image of society is one that consists of numerous dyads, but obviously all players must then know all the choices in all dyads, or the victims must, at least, spread the news of who is the bad apple instead of being interested only in their own welfare. But this is an odd construction for several reasons.

First, sanctioning the defector by spreading the news is costly for the victim. It does not make much sense in terms of the stringent rationality requirements of non-cooperative game theory outside of a dyadic interaction with the same actor. This leads us to a *second* problem: i.e. the use of multiple dyads, which allegedly are the model for society.

When we act in a society, we do so because we have certain expectations, for instance that the bus will arrive, or that I can put out my garbage tonight because it will be collected in the morning. In other words, we presumably orient ourselves towards *future* actions of others, that is, count on something, which has not yet occurred and is "unknown." In a well-defined single shot game, this might not be a problem as all relevant information is supposedly contained in the matrices. But in the real world this would not make any sense if we had to exclude past experiences and assumed that this present instance would not be more or less a continuation of the past. True, if our expectations get consistently or frequently disappointed, we will eventually give up on that "trust." Nevertheless, our "normal" response in the case of disappointment will be to argue with those on whom we have relied, or to complain to the "higher ups." In short, we exercise "voice" and "loyalty," rather than simply opt for the exit strategy characteristic of the market and its rational actors.[32]

Third, the whole point of living in a society is not that the past is irrelevant but that we are held *not to learn* from certain past experiences, as Luhmann correctly pointed out. Even if we have been disappointed in a previous round, we have to start again from the expectation that the social norms structuring expectations are valid. In other words, a society is only possible if we are at least able to form *expectations about expectation* rather than being guided by purely "personal" experience. Moreover, if we imagine a society as a system in which everyone would only react to some previous action of someone else, we would end up with a kind of queue rather than the "meshing" of plans and expectations so important for joint cooperative activity.[33] To that extent even the aggregation of dyads as in the n-person Prisoner's Dilemma does not offer an apt analogy to what goes on in any social interaction of even minimal complexity.

Put in a nutshell, the emergence of *generalized expectation* needs to be explained in terms akin to "credit," which cannot be done by a simple relying on a tit-for-tat (stimulus–response) model.[34] Few of our actions can be interpreted as specific responses to accomplished facts, and it seems to be misleading to reduce all choices to an all-or-nothing choice of exit or continuation. But if this is true, then it is doubtful whether the addition of sanctions, of

---

[32] For a fundamental discussion of these three strategies for social life, see Albert O. Hirschman, *Exit, Voice, and Loyalty: Responses to Decline in Firms, Organizations, and States*, Cambridge, MA: Harvard University Press, 1970.

[33] This point is forcefully made by Heinrich Popitz, *Die Normative Konstruktion von Gesellschaft*, Tübingen: Mohr, 1980.

[34] Whether this feat can be achieved by more future-oriented process theories of decision-making, as e.g. in "prospect theory," is another matter. See the critical remarks in Jack S. Levy, "Prospect Theory, Rational Choice, and International Relations," *International Studies Quarterly*, 41:1 (1997): 87–112.

reputation, or even the relaxation of the common knowledge assumption can "fix" the shortcomings of this approach.[35]

My discussion so far suggests that the issue of reputation and the role of sanctions seem to be essentially mistaken. Virtually all the evidence from social psychology indicates that reputation is gained and lost in ways fundamentally different from those suggested by rational choice models.[36] Studies on compliance and deviance support our suspicions that sanctions cannot actually play the role assigned to them by rationalistic models,[37] precisely because *issues of interpretation* enter the picture and signals are hardly ever unambiguous because they can be misused. Equally misleading seems to be the assumption that coercion works in the same way irrespective of whether we deal with individuals or collectivities, and that therefore the absence of an enforcer is the main problem in the "anarchical" realm of international relations.

In short, my expectations in a social action are not simply describable as individual preferences plus probability wagers. Missing in such conceptualizations is exactly what is socially so important: the conception of constitutive rules that has to be antecedent to any notion of individual or strategic rationality. This is precisely why the Hobbesian original contract is unreachable for individuals operating in a Hobbesian world. The difficulty of getting the original contract off the ground is, first, that the contracting parties would have to act on an individually *irrational* assumption (given the absence of a sovereign in the state of nature). In other words, they must engage exactly in the above-described *generalized* wager on the future and act on the expectation of a change of state. The second, equally disabling, difficulty consists in the fact that, absent shared notions about rules constituting the contract, even the strongest (though irrational) motivations to make a contract will come to naught, if we are in the dark regarding which utterances or signs will "count" as a contract.

These shared expectations have to be normatively secured and must be reflected in the desires (or fears) of the socialized individual that transcend the "preferences" s/he might have in a particular case. Our reactions show this sometimes quite clearly. Take the following example. When I agree to meet

[35] For a discussion of some of the problems, see the German ZIB debate between Otto Keck and Harald Müller. Otto Keck, "Rationales Kommunikatives Handeln in den Internationalen Beziehungen: Ist eine Verbindung von Rational-Choice-Theorie und Habermas' Theorie des Kommunikativen Handelns möglich?" *Zeitschrift für Internationale Beziehungen*, 2:1 (1995): 5–48; Harald Müller, "Spielen Hilft Nicht Immer: Die Grenzen des Rational-Choice-Ansatzes und der Platz der Theorie Kommunikativen Handelns in der Analyse Internationaler Beziehungen," *Zeitschrift für Internationale Beziehungen*, 2:2 (1995): 371–391.
[36] For an excellent review of the social psychological literature and a sophisticated criticism of the economistic approaches to reputation, see especially chapters 1 and 2 in Jonathan Mercer, *Reputation and International Politics*, Ithaca, NY: Cornell University Press, 1996.
[37] See the discussion below in Chapter 3.

someone about whom I really do not care, but whom I have finally been talked into meeting, I want this expectation not to be thwarted, even if the encounter was not "my idea" (preference). If the other person does not show up at the appointed time, I might perhaps react with a certain relief, but it would be strange if I did not also feel considerable irritation, or even anger. What would irk me is not so much the other person's non-appearance, but rather that my relying on his coming has been frustrated. In our reactions, we clearly distinguish between our personal preferences and what "one" (can) expect(s) in such circumstances. It is because of this impersonal point of view that our individual resentment is not irrational.

Finally, with any type of social differentiation in a society, the expectations of the interacting parties need not be reciprocal in any substantive sense, as the rationalist model assumes, since different rights and duties for different classes of people can be explicitly created by law, as e.g. tax laws demonstrate.[38] Vital here is the development of social roles, particularly of those who enable someone to act for the group, for instance to authorize an actor to make binding decisions. In addition, authoritative decisions have to be backed by certain legitimizing beliefs among the members, so that they can rely on some form of trust and credit. It is, however, doubtful whether the establishment of authoritative structures can be explained in terms of simple "diffuse reciprocity," on which e.g. friendship relies as an institution. Nevertheless, social differentiation allowing for the unequal distribution of privileges and obligations allows us to understand why society does not fall apart when there is no single dominant motive or mood among its members. As Dennis Wrong put it in taking an organized group as the model for society:

An organized group consists of a plurality of roles, possesses a differential social structure ... and the roles are likely to activate different individual motives. Freud saw this – at least minimally – in imputing in Group Psychology markedly different constitutions to leaders and followers ... The members of milling crowds, rioting mobs, and fascinated audiences may be powerfully seized by a single purpose or emotion, but they are apt to be ephemeral and atypical collectivities for just that reason. Groups engaged in a regular activity on a routine basis are likely to develop a more complex structure and therefore draw on a range of individual motives to attract and keep members, or in the case of ascriptive groups, to activate them.[39]

Individuals might play their role not because they "benefit" in the sense of instrumental or strategic rationality, but because their "station in life" might

---

[38] This has nothing to do with the elimination of the correlativity of rights and duties, as this requirement is simply stating the conceptual relationship, but it does not deal with the concrete allocation of obligations and privileges.

[39] Wrong, *Problem of Order*, at 185.

not even make it possible for them to think in terms of a fundamentally different world. Both Gramsci and Weber have extensively written about this phenomenon. On the other hand, it is precisely because collective meanings and individual motivations can converge and do, in fact, overlap among the various members, that society as an ongoing concern is possible.

The above criticism of prominent approaches to social order was designed mainly as a ground-clearing exercise. The task of the next section, as part of the positive heuristics, is to investigate the emergence and function of historical principles of differentiation, which provide us with the necessary conceptual tools for analyzing transformative changes in the international system.

2.3   Forms of Differentiation

Considering that similarities abound among a variety of social formations it is not surprising that IR scholars have widely borrowed from other disciplines in order to describe the international system. Yet, relying on surface similarities does not entitle us to argue that such comparisons also establish reliable insights into the working of such a system. Analogies, which are useful for heuristic purposes, have to satisfy more exacting requirements. They must show e.g. that the similarities are not only "point" to "point," but that they concern similarities in *relations*. In other words, they should be of a structural kind rather than merely rely on object similarity. To the extent that we want to use societal categories for studying change of the international system, we should first identify via ideal types the principles according to which various societies are differentiated and then, in a second step, examine the generative grammar of these principles and their links to practice.

Segmentation

Without wanting to engage the voluminous literature on the so-called "primitive" societies, the most striking feature about their organization is their reliance on face-to-face interactions and their ability to reproduce themselves in identical segments. The latter principle prevents the differentiation of society into strata, while the boundary between who belongs in and who is out depends on kinship. In general, resistance to inequality by further differentiation is visible in the customs of communal distribution and consumption of surpluses (potlatch ceremonies).[40]

---

[40] See Michael Harkin, "Potlach in Anthropology" in Neil J. Smelser and Paul B. Baltes (eds.), *International Encyclopedia of the Social & Behavioral Sciences*, vol. 17, New York: Elsevier, 2001, 11885–11889.

This has two implications for the development of such societies. First, specialization, if it occurs, does not necessarily translate into status differentiation. Second, since the same organizational principle is invoked when building larger aggregates, the capacity of such societies to organize and regulate interactions decreases dramatically with distance. Lack of writing further reinforces this trend. Writing allows not only for an abstraction from the here and now, but also transcends the limited circle of those who must be present when they want to communicate. Attempts to go beyond the segments and to form larger aggregates are, therefore, usually not very successful in fulfilling their assigned functional task, such as defense or conflict resolution. Efforts at conflict resolution show this quite clearly. They occur, if at all, ad hoc and are geared to the concrete issue and *not to some "prospective ordering" via abstract norms* (precedent). Similarly, help in a conflict situation depends not so much on "the law" and its violation but on the ability to mobilize support. Here kinship rules limit interest on the part of those whose ox has not been gored.

Thus, self-help prevails, and the main limiting factor for preventing conflict escalation is precisely the lack of wider patterns of solidarity, not some primitive goodness or common values that have often been projected back into archaic times.[41] Primitive societies are rife with low-level, violent conflict and they also have considerable difficulties with variation and deviance.[42] Social order must continuously be monitored and re-established through public displays and rituals buttressing social conformity. Order is secured through taboos that cut off possible further explorations and questions, and by the recollection of and return to the origins. Social memory is thereby crucially dependent on "performances" rather than on concepts, and if the performances become tied to specific locations where "things happen," where the group meets for reinforcing rituals in trance and for the re-recitation and amplification of the "known." To that extent, a certain element of territoriality – determining the sacred places – is injected into the primitive social order. But it should be obvious that this is something entirely different from the homogeneity of space and of "jurisdiction" that characterizes territoriality in the European state-system. As one observer of the Australian Aranda aborigine put it: for the Aranda "the whole countryside was his living age-old family tree."[43] Similar

---

[41] For a useful corrective of the Rousseauan enthusiasm for natural goodness and its concomitant sentimentality concerning "golden times" of pristine societies, see Robert B. Edgerton, *Sick Societies: Challenging the Myth of Primitive Harmony*, New York: Free Press, 1992.

[42] Taboos and the exemption of certain areas of experience from further scrutiny by making them part of a secret (knowledge) belong here, as do "palavers," which have nothing to do with an exchange of information or providing reasons for certain decisions but with the re-establishment of conformity. Only after each member says the same thing has order been re-established.

[43] As quoted in Robert David Sack, *Human Territoriality: Its Theory and History*, Cambridge: Cambridge University Press, 1986, at 58.

notions are reported from Africa. Being part of a group means also having access to the land and thus becoming a participant in the order that unites the visible and the invisible, the living and the dead, and thus establishes a "cosmos" comprising both *physis* and *nomos*.

Segmented societies seem to be inhibited from developing into another social formation – at first blush rather strangely – by the *pervasiveness of reciprocity*. Precisely because it is so widely practiced and part of all types of specific expectations, it prevents the emergence of *generalized* expectations, which is necessary for hierarchical authority and for the translation of specialization into "rank." Some roles of pre-eminence might develop, but the transformation of such differences into a claim to authority is usually resisted. In fact, some leadership structures might develop, but they do not develop necessarily in the direction of clear hierarchies, or even towards the formation of a clear center, i.e. a multipurpose or multifunctional leadership. Rather, different functions are entrusted to different persons: shamans, priests, chieftains – one in charge in times of war, and one for peace – and so on.

Differentiation can take various paths, but each form seems dependent on certain innovations that either substitute for the old principle of differentiation or give the old principle of differentiation a new role,[44] though we cannot interpret this process as a single historical development with clear successive stages of progress, in which one form substitutes for the other. This is clearly evidenced by the fact that elements of segmentation are usually not simply abolished, but they become incorporated into other subsequent social formations. The best example is the family, which even in highly stratified societies has retained important functions. Such functions range from the determination of, for instance, who belongs in the "nobility" in a stratified society, to the trading "families" that facilitate exchanges in a highly complex and functionally differentiated global society.[45]

Centers and Hierarchies

Considerable disagreement exists about the historical development of hierarchic forms of organization. Either internal evolutionary forces, such as economic progress, an extension of trade, or external factors, such as conquest,

---

[44] For an illuminating discussion of the "stages" between "band" and "chiefdom" and the emergence of a "rank" society, which nevertheless has not become a principle of social organization, see Fried Morton, *The Evolution of Political Society*, New York: Random House, 1967.

[45] See e.g. the role of families in the traditional diamond trade, or the far-flung network of Chinese families influencing modern trading patterns, in Joel Kotkin, *Tribes: How Race, Religion, and Identity Determine Success in the New Global Economy*, New York: Random House, 1992.

have been adduced to account for it. Fortunately, one need not opt for any of these explanations when trying to understand hierarchy as a different constitutive principle of social order, since a different form of explanation (constitutive explanation) is required. But even if we are interested in causally efficient factors that brought about this result, several paths seem possible. We can imagine one path consisting in the small accretion of inequalities resulting in rank differences, and we can imagine another path involving some external factor, such as the catastrophe of subjugation of one society by another.

In whatever fashion such a transformation occurs, kinship no longer provides the template for social reproduction. Rather, a fundamental difference in rights and obligations becomes the distinguishing characteristic of such a social formation. Hierarchies not only allow for the making of binding decisions without the need to establish virtually universal consent, it also implies a different conception of the social system and its boundaries. This presupposes not only a different relationship with the outside, as the physical and the social worlds become increasingly distinct. With the institutionalization of power, adding its "second face" to the first of directly influencing another actor in a concrete situation,[46] the boundaries between "us" and "them" are now more or less a function of the authority under which one stands. Order is no longer conceived as repetition and sameness to be recreated by rituals but rather as a *conceptual* relationship among differences. As such, these differences have to be thought of as belonging to something that has a discernible identity. Here the notion of part and whole offers itself as a logical and perceptual category for orientation and understanding.

Without now engaging the arguments about archetypes, such as the meaning of the circle,[47] which systematically relates a center to the periphery, distinguishes the inside from the outside, and engenders the further distinction "within," it is historically significant that the establishment of hierarchies was connected with the creation of myths and the emergence of higher religions. The connection between the "sacred" and rule in the word "hierarchy" (*hieros* = holy, sacred; and *archein* = to rule) reflects this conceptual link and shows how the legitimization of inequality is tied to fundamental understandings of what "is." Indeed, so overwhelming is this new form of imagination that the tangible world – in which formerly the sacred had been diffused – is

[46] See the debates about decision and non-decision as indicators for power in Peter Bachrach and Morton S. Baratz, "Two Faces of Power," *American Political Science Review*, 56:4 (1962): 947–952. For a further discussion of the various "faces" of power, see Steven Lukes (ed.), *Power, Readings in Social and Political Theory*, New York: New York University Press, 1986.

[47] See e.g. Mircea Eliade, *Images and Symbols: Studies in Religious Symbolism*, trans. Philip Mairet, Princeton: Princeton University Press, 1961.

now stripped of its original character and facticity, and is viewed as the result of some conscious ordering (*kosmos*) or even as a *creatio ex nihilo*.

A variety of additional conceptual moves thereby become necessary. Luhmann suggests that two types are of particular importance for the new notion of society: differentiation according to spatial criteria, on the one hand, and of personal ones (nobility) on the other. For the former he suggests the model of center and periphery as the appropriate template; for the latter, notions of status and hierarchies. Although these conceptualizations are speculative, they serve some heuristic purpose, even if they are debatable.

If the asymmetries implied by rule can be institutionalized as belonging to a certain group, and if this group can successfully restrict exogamy to certain families, an upper and a lower stratum of society develop, and thus the society is no longer connected by kinship ties but by authority relations. In that case, stratified societies (status societies) are the likely result. When the distinction of authority is largely mediated by spatial patterns, the center–periphery differentiation develops. Luhmann considers the medieval estate society and the Mesopotamian temple cities as examples of the two models.[48] For the center–periphery form one could also use the example of the Chinese empire. But since space is in this context not a merely descriptive category of a homogeneous continuum, but rather a social construct, the differences among spatial types of differentiation seem as important as the similarities. In the Mesopotamian case, a system of city or temple states emerges, within which hegemonic struggles occurred between the cities. In the Chinese instance, however, the victory of Chin, ending the period of "warring states," insured not only the predominance of the center but also the suppression of the feudal nobility and instituted a direct link between the ruler and the ruled. Finally, the unusually strong role of the family in religious practices established a totally different social formation in China than we find in other areas.

Indeed, the Chinese construction of the world order perhaps best illustrates the use of the center–periphery template. It conceives the center not only as the middle but as the place where heaven and earth touch. From this center, the influence of law and virtue radiate until they come to an end somewhere in a frontier zone. This conception is quite different from the notion that a god dwells in a certain place and possesses the land, which is then administered

---

[48] Luhmann speaks here somewhat imprecisely about the "multifunctional" character or nature of a status position. Since medieval society is (not yet) a functionally differentiated society – the best example is the domain economy preventing the emergence of markets – and since the whole ethos of "nobility" consisted until well into the eighteenth century in the disdain for "wealth," sometimes even reinforced by the danger of losing the status through commercial activities, it is unclear what this argument is supposed to show. Luhmann, *Die Gesellschaft der Gesellschaft*, at 679.

for him (her) by priests and a ruler.[49] In the latter case (Mesopotamia), the relations among those territorially conceived units created by the submission under some ruler could be understood as an analog to the heavenly dispute among the gods for hegemony (*enlil-ship*).

Whatever the usefulness of these distinctions might be, two factors decisively influence the fate of the innovation of spatial or status differentiation, namely the emergence of writing and the organization of the material reproduction of life. Both factors seem also to interact. Thus, without the invention of writing, no territorial expansion of rule on any sustained basis seems possible, and neither could the organization of economic life have persisted,[50] in the sense of a temple economy or the "hydraulic despotism" à la Wittvogel. Indeed, aside from some religious uses, many of the earliest inscriptions concern bookkeeping operations. For example, the earliest documents of writing in Mesopotamia, datable to the beginning of the third millennium BCE, concern "lists" of things, utensils, animals, and so on. As a survey of the records suggests, writing at this time "was mostly limited to the production of administrative documents."[51] It is this context between administrative practice on the one hand, and the radically new legitimization of power through the sacred on the other hand, that explains the new potential but also the weakness of these ancient empires. A cursory look at the mode of communication in these imperial structures provides some suggestive insights.

We usually assume that writing simply developed when we wanted to record speech, but there are both analytical and historical reasons why such an assumption is problematic. Analytically the use of writing as a means of communication presupposes widespread literacy and a particular reflective use of texts (such as a knowledge of the audience for which something is written, the circumstances of opening the message, etc.). Oral communication solves all these questions through the face-to-face contact of the communicative situation. It is therefore not surprising that writing remained for thousands of years subordinate to various forms of oral modes of communication, and that it served largely as a mnemonic device for the person delivering a speech.[52] It did not (yet) address and have impact upon each subject, and it remained a

---

[49] The latter differentiation allows for a new determination of the "sacred" that is no longer diffused in nature or the land, but it is characterized by a special character of "separateness." Indeed, both the notion of the "temple" as the house of the god (derived from Indo-European *tem*, Greek *temein*) and the Hebrew concept of "kodesh" also emphasize this separateness.

[50] Karl August Wittfogel, *Oriental Despotism: A Comparative Study of Total Power*, New Haven: Yale University Press, 1957.

[51] Gerdien Jonker, *The Topography of Remembrance: The Dead, Tradition and Collective Memory in Mesopotamia*, Leiden: Brill, 1995, at 3.

[52] How difficult the road was to using writing as an imitation of speech can be seen in the development of an alphabet imitating the sounds of speech rather than serving as signs, something that can be seen from the development of writing in Egypt and Sumer. In pointing

means of recording great deeds, but it could not yet mobilize. By establishing, however, the first elements of rational administration, writing increased the power of the center, even if the form of communication was still largely wedded to the communicative structures of oral communication: personal presence, single topic, turn-taking, references to what was said before, reiteration, and amplification. Only with the emergence of wider literacy and of a "general audience," new forms of "making present" who or what is absent, but is made present by the reading of a "text," can a revolution in communication occur.

Since this is a problem that will occupy us in the last two chapters of this book I want to revert, for the moment, to the issue of the "other" possibility of institutionalizing hierarchical rule, the one which relies on personal relationships rather than spatial ones. The medieval period has usually been the example of such a personal order. But the existence of nobility, the attempted elaboration of a sacred kingship, and the development of various "estates" also clearly indicate the predominance of the hierarchical element as the main differentiating principle. Kinship was now subordinated to hierarchy. This is also exemplified by the fact that neither the individual qua individual nor even the nuclear family was the basic unit that constituted society. Instead, it was the "house." The house, however, comprised not only the kinship group, which in the parlance of those times would be called "blood line" or the "origin," but the "whole house," namely all the people attached to it and working in it.[53] As Bosl suggests, close to 90 percent of the population in England, France, Italy, and Germany lived during the Middle Ages in such a "house."[54] Most of them were indentured servants, who could not leave "their station" but were

to the political character of hieroglyphs that were to convey not only some information about things as exemplified in a "list" but also to tell a story, Jan Assman writes:

> Protodynastic pictorial narrative uses picture signs on two distinctly different physical scales. The large picture portrays a "scene," and the small pictures identify actors and places by including names. The small pictures therefore refer to language (names), the large pictures refer to the world (acts). It would be a mistake, however, to categorize only the small pictures as "writing" ... the entire complex picture "writes" a name, that is, the year named after that event ... Neither of the two media is self-sufficient in recording the intended or any other meaning. The small signs do not yet make up a writing system but are simply a constituent of a complex recording system.

Jan Assmann, "Ancient Egypt and the Materiality of the Sign" in Hans Ulrich Gumbrecht and K. Ludwig Pfeiffer (eds.), *Materialities of Communication*, Stanford: Stanford University Press, 1994, 15–31, at 19f.

[53] See the seminal study by Otto Brunner, *Neue Wege der Sozialgeschichte: Vorträge und Aufsätze*, Göttingen: Vandenhoeck & Ruprecht, 1956. See especially the chapter "Das 'ganze Haus' und die alteuropäische 'Oekonomik'."

[54] See Karl Bosl and Johannes von Elmenau, *Mensch und Gesellschaft in der Geschichte Europas*, München: Paul List, 1972, at 70.

required to perform certain services.[55] Focusing therefore on the crucial role of the house and the domain economy is not to submit to some economic determinism. Rather it allows us to see that the material reproduction of social life was part of "rule," even though the rule of the paterfamilias over his wife and servants (slaves) was in antiquity further subdivided and categorically distinguished by Aristotle from political power and its exercise among equals in the *polis*.[56] Thus we realize that it was precisely the egalitarian *polis* which was the innovation that broke the hierarchical template. Historically, the latter represented only two interludes, first in Greece and then, in a more attenuated form, in the Roman republic, only to be overwhelmed again by hierarchical social formations.

Functional Differentiation

At first blush functional differentiation and hierarchical forms of differentiation seem hardly distinguishable. A moment's reflection shows how these principles differ. Hierarchical orders are undifferentiated in that the upper sectors of a society usually have first call on goods, power, access to learning, and culture, even if some theorists of such a society tried to ascribe to each segment of a society a particular function. In this respect, Adalbert of Laon's (around 947–1030) speculation about the "three orders" and their naturalness served as an important legitimizing account for feudal society and its orders, based on praying, fighting, and working.[57]

Modern "functionally" differentiated societies, on the other hand, are not "functional" in this sense, since the term "functional" is used in an equivocal manner. Under modern conditions there is neither a predetermined function ascribed to any part without which the whole could no longer exist or maintain itself, nor can a modern functionally differentiated society be understood

---

[55] This touches, of course, also on the hotly contested Polanyi debate in classical history. Although Athens had developed both considerable literacy and a rudimentary manufacturing base, it was far from the development of a modern economy. For that, production for the market would have had to be emancipated from the *oikos* and from the connection with rule and its embeddedness in the conceptions of ethics. "Rule" is not absent from modern economic life, which is evidenced by the firm that substitutes imperative control for contractual exchange. Such a view, however, misses the point that the problem of rule is not only framed by modern notions of contract, subjective rights, the reliance on money (rather than provisions), and a functioning price mechanism that both sets the terms of exchange for existing goods and sends signals for production. See Karl Polanyi, *The Great Transformation*, Boston, MA: Beacon Press, 1957. For the debate in classics, see Moses I. Finley et al., *Economy and Society in Ancient Greece*, New York: Viking Press, 1982; Moses I. Finley, *The Ancient Economy*, London: Hogarth Press, 1985.

[56] See Aristotle, *Politics*, trans. H. Rackham, Cambridge, MA: Harvard University Press, 1972.

[57] See the discussion by Duby Georges, *Les Trois Ordres ou l'imaginaire du féodalisme*, Paris: Gallimard, 1978.

in terms of the part/whole problematic of hierarchical systems. But this was precisely how Aristotle originally used the term:

For in all things, which form a composite whole and which are made up of parts, whether continuous or discrete, a distinction between the ruling and the subject (ruled) element comes to light. Such a duality exists in living creatures, but not in them only; it originates in the constitution of the universe; even in things that have no life there is a ruling principle, as in the musical mode.[58]

From these brief remarks it is clear why functional differentiation is an ordering principle of quite a different sort than that of hierarchies. Fundamental to hierarchical orders is the notion that the *entire person* (or later also types of actions) can be attributed to one of the different parts, and that the society can be understood as a sum of these components, although the importance of emergent properties might be recognized (the whole is more than the sum of all parts). Functionally differentiated societies, on the other hand, are characterized by action systems operating separately from each other and by "going through" the concrete individuals or their actions. Thus, a payment might occur in the economy, but it also belongs to the political or the cultural system, if it concerns taxes or a contribution to the local symphony orchestra. No exclusive assignment or causal connection can be established, since the action occurs in all different systems at the same time.

Such a notion of society no longer provides the autonomous systems with some ready-made integrative design (as in the case of stratified hierarchies when each part derives its legitimacy from this whole and the contribution it makes to its maintenance). Instead, each system functions according to its own logic by perceiving other systems and reacting to them in terms of its own code. Thus, instead of some overall design, the theory of functionally differentiated systems developed by Luhmann stresses the processual and temporary character of mutual adjustments by the differentiated systems that interact and communicate with (or irritate) each other. Each system follows its own logic, and each has to "translate" the irritations from the outside (from other systems) into its own vocabulary in order to respond. For example, for the economy everything has to be translated into prices; when no prices exist for factors that are not traded on a market, the system has to invent "shadow prices" in order to go on.

It would take me too far afield to examine in greater detail the role of specialized codes, which enable differentiated systems to function and to recreate themselves (*autopoiesis*). While "money" as a medium and as a code has been extensively investigated, Luhmann's argument is that several other such codes exist in modern societies, such as "truth" as the code of science, or

---

[58] Aristotle, *Politics*, 1254a 28–34.

"power" which is that of politics.[59] These codes allow him then to study the autopoiesis of various systems and their mutual irritations and adjustments. In other words, the paradox of functional differentiation consists in the fact that specific functions are taken care of by autonomous systems, which are however allowed to claim universal validity for their particular perspective. This paradox can no longer be resolved by a parts/whole imagery. To that extent a new combination of universality and specificity has been reached, and it goes far beyond the traditional specification of "roles" in traditional, stratified societies.

For our purposes here, it is only important to notice that such an analysis has far-reaching implications for social analysis. The first implication is that, unlike in traditional systems analysis, no overall equilibrium is postulated or used in the explanatory account. Modern systems theory also transcends classical "open systems" analysis. In that case, systems were stabilized, because they selected from the environment certain inputs and, because of their "fit," they were believed to maintain themselves. The latter construction was compatible with notions of a dynamic equilibrium, in which feedback loops served to provide for the stabilizing selections. But such models presupposed the more or less unchanging nature of the environment in which the system existed. As soon as other autonomous systems are part of the "environment," in which a given system has to function – as is the case in modern systems theory – such an assumption becomes problematic. A system's survival depends then on its ability to select and innovate. In line with its own logic it has to generate operations that make it possible for it to "go on" without necessarily relying on negative feedback bringing it back to the old equilibrium.

These considerations lead to a second point. Precisely because a system's selections no longer consist in matching operations, its interactions with other systems become unpredictable and traditional notions of causality are no longer applicable. The new complexity consists in the simultaneity of reactions that an action or event calls forth in each system and to which each system has to react, thereby limiting the freedom of other systems. Since causality and our notion of control presuppose temporal distinctions between cause and effect, the simultaneity of reactions suggests that predictions of future states as well as traditional notions of (central) control have to be abandoned. The same cause might result in different states, and identical results might be reached through entirely different causal pathways.

---

[59] Here Luhmann clearly distinguishes between power and force, a crucial distinction which is, despite the "domestic analogy" being so entrenched in realist analysis, not made by most realists. Instead, all politics is seen as a struggle for power (Morgenthau), or power itself is reduced to mere "capabilities" (Waltz).

Consequently, third, we should realize that the overall integration of the social system can no longer be described in terms of the parts/whole, or in terms of cooperation, but in terms of the *"historical" i.e. temporal adjustments* of the systems vis-à-vis each other through coupling and decoupling. Different from traditional notions of a social system, which was supposed to be integrated by common values, the overall integration of various autonomous systems does not lie in their subordination to some normative design but in its "disintegration," namely in the weakening of such normative presuppositions. Again, the emancipation of the economy and the emergence of the "market" from social conventions and from normatively conceived ways of life provide striking examples.

The last remarks also show the importance of conflict resolution arising out of the operations of autonomous systems. Without some normative underpinnings, conflicts would soon destabilize the operations of autonomous systems. Luhmann suggests therefore that the analysis of the autonomy of functionally differentiated systems has to be supplemented by an analysis of "structural coupling" and a proper perspective on the evolution of complex systems. The former deals with the connections of functional systems with each other; the latter examines the dynamics of change without becoming victim to the myopia that evolution can be described as a process of greater and greater "adaptation."[60]

Structural coupling allows systems to interact by providing standard procedures for the recognition of and responses to the inputs of other systems. It therefore establishes the points of contact with other systems, but it also safeguards the system's identity and its continued *autopoiesis*. Luhmann mentions in particular the structural coupling of the political and economic system that is effected by taxes and transfers. The coupling of the political and the legal systems occurs by means of the constitution, the one between law and the economy through property and contract, and the one between science, the political, and economic systems through credentials. In addition, structural coupling sets the parameters for evolution. The operationally closed systems can innovate, or fail to do so, as long as their own reproduction remains possible. To that extent the occupation of niches and differentiation, not general homogenization or simple adaptation, are the results of evolution.

Two observations, or rather caveats, are in order at this point. First, from the mere enumeration of problems or "irritations" it becomes obvious that the

---

[60] See his remarks: "The old idea that evolution is a process from simplicity to complexity is untenable for the simple reason that there are no 'simple' matters and because nowadays simple and more complex systems co-exist and the former have not been replaced by the latter ... In any case evolutionary theory is entirely compatible with the observation that highly complex systems perish ... that they possess too few capacities for (further) evolution and that quite often evolution supplants highly complex systems with superior simplifications." Ibid., 446f.

autonomy of functional systems always presupposes the existence of law. Law protects the autonomy of the systems by "ruling out" certain challenges to the legitimacy of their operations. Law also provides means of resolving conflicts. It is the main means for "punctually" (rather than comprehensively) integrating various systems through decisions in a case and controversy, and through the prospective ordering that such decisions imply even if its impact is drastically reduced. While it might be true that justice in modern society can no longer be conceived of as an expression of a natural hierarchy of values, or some privileged notion of the good, an agreement, however, about the legitimacy of different "spheres of justice,"[61] and a strong commitment to the resolution of conflicts by procedural means, seems absolutely necessary. Precisely because modern (or rather post-modern) social orders can no longer rely on ontological foundations or moral intuitions concerning the naturalness of their constitution, procedural safeguards are increasingly important, and they explain why law plays a special role in our social life.

Second, since law remains largely bound to the territorial state, it might be premature to conclude that only the highly abstract notions of social systems and a world society provide the appropriate analytical tools. Luhmann's system theory, which seems to reify systems by rigorously abstracting from actors or even actions, still has to come to terms with the fact that some of the most important organizational features of our social life function on the basis of territorial limits, or according to membership criteria, and not only through impersonal codes. As a matter of fact, there remains a residual, but nevertheless important, part of our social reality that has to include the "entire" person: criminal law, as will be shown in Chapter 7. Although it punishes actions, not persons, its threats, as well as the infliction of actual punishments, are addressed to concrete actors. Admittedly, in modern societies there might exist a trend away from the classical means of social control,[62] since increasingly surveillance and information are being used – greetings from the NSA! – in both the public and private domains in order to insure compliance.[63] Nevertheless, both criminal responsibility and political activity seem to require more inclusionary notions of a person or actor than the argument of functionally differentiated systems suggests.

---

[61] See e.g. the argument in Michael Walzer, *Spheres of Justice: A Defense of Pluralism and Equality*, New York: Basic Books, 1983.

[62] See e.g. Stephen Gill, "The Global Panopticon? The Neoliberal State, Economic Life, and Democratic Surveillance," *Alternatives: Global, Local, Political*, 20:1 (1995): 1–49.

[63] See e.g. Didier Bigot's fascinating study of shifts in modern policing methods. Didier Bigo, "The Möbius Ribbon of Internal and External Security(ies)" in Mathias Albert, David Jacobson, and Yosef Lapid (eds.), *Identities, Borders, Orders: Rethinking International Relations Theory* (Minneapolis: University of Minnesota Press, 2001), 91–116.

2.4   Conclusion

The discussion of this chapter was devoted to the constitutive function of norms. In this context a sketch of the historical forms of differentiation became necessary. Its purpose was also to demonstrate the heuristic fruitfulness of a societal perspective in examining transformational change. Instead of assuming unproblematically given and ahistorically constituted units, and instead of construing the system out of the position of their units or their interaction, the perspective of modern systems theory of focusing on the processes of boundary construction allowed us to address the identity as well as the difference of such different organizational forms. Here segmentation, hierarchies, and functional differentiation served as organizing templates for the discussion of the observable historical modes of organizing societies, whereby the notion of "society" also was freed from the hidden or not so hidden premise to be a fully integrated whole in which conflicts become entirely externalized against the "others" in the environment.

What remains to be done is a more detailed examination of one hierarchical form of differentiation that became important in modernity, namely the emergence of the state, as it "solved" the problem of social order in a distinctive way. For that purpose I examine in greater detail the notion of sovereignty, its genealogy, and its transformations, leading to some of the paradoxes of modern politics. Here spatial metaphors such as the "indivisibility" of sovereignty – similar to the point in geometry – or of being "located at the apex" prove problematic since they are clearly at odds with the politics under conditions of complex interdependence. Nevertheless, sovereignty has not been displaced, neither in our vocabulary nor in the imaginary that links it to "the people," autonomy, and legitimacy. However it has fundamentally changed its meaning as the semantic field within which it is located and the concomitant practices have been reconfigured. To that extent sovereignty provides a nearly unique case for examining change in the social world not only in terms of the interstitial changes that come with contestations and interstitial lawmaking, but in terms of fundamental or transformative change. It is the task of the next chapter to address these issues.

3   Changing

3.1   Introduction

The above discussion of the concept of "society" has hopefully driven home the fact that transformative changes are part and parcel of our social world and that they cannot and should not be neglected in our analysis because we have been accustomed to think in terms of ahistorical "essences" and "equilibriums." Instead, recognizing patterns and bringing different forms of social organization under one concept by reflecting on their family resemblance provides us with the assurance of dealing with the actual world of praxis without necessarily wedding us to questionable essences or models. In this context it seems significant that Weber has no entry for "society" in his discussion of the basic concepts of sociology, contained in his monumental *Wirtschaft und Gesellschaft*, and focuses – as already mentioned – on two processes of association along the lines of Tönnies's distinction of *Gemeinschaft* and *Gesellschaft*.[1] What provides the conceptual anchor for those two different processes of association is "solidarity," i.e. the social bond that ties people together. Similar to Durkheim's later suggestion, the solidarity of pre-industrial social formations is characterized by a common conscience and repressive law – called in Durkheim "mechanical solidarity" – which, however gives way later to an "organic" form of solidarity, based on exchanges and the recognition of interdependencies. Nevertheless, something is still missing in these discussions for studying transformative social change, which Weber then supplies by his typology of different forms of authority.

Instead of beginning with the "state" or the original contract that creates the sovereign – as is the traditional starting point for IR analysis – Weber's more elaborate conceptual grid frees the analysis from a too state-centric view which has been the bane in the field of IR. After all, nearly everybody has become aware during the last few decades that the traditional map of the Westphalian

---

[1] Ferdinand Tönnies's work, entitled *Gemeinschaft und Gesellschaft*, appeared in 1887 and caused a lively discussion, as can be seen from Durkheim's first edition of his *The Division of Labor in Society* which was published in 1893.

system was not only historically inaccurate but hindered rather than helped IR analysis in a time of increasing interdependencies and "globalization." But despite the widely shared complaints against state-centrism, IR "theory" remained strangely static. Even in one of the leading works, which focused explicitly on interdependence, the "fundament" for the analysis was still provided by states and their power, which continued to serve as the "deep structure" that engendered the observable changes.[2] Similarly, even after two decades of castigating "state centrism," attempts, such as e.g. Ferguson and Mansbach's study on *Polities*[3] – which tried to cast the net wider by bringing the interactions of different processes of solidarity (identity), and of authority, and historical transformative change into focus – remained the exception.

Furthermore, while by the end of the century transformative change had been recognized as being important for politics, the analysis remained strangely apolitical and conventional, so that change was simply conceptualized as a displacement, such as the "prediction" of the demise of the state through "the market." Similarly, new forms of governing were often interpreted in terms of "functionalism," which had captured the imagination in the nineteenth century but did not quite fit our present observations. Even some anarchist hopes could sometimes be detected. Was perhaps a form of governing without government possible,[4] even if the new forms of rule-making beyond the traditional nation state still had to rely on governments and their "executive" capacities? In short, something was certainly amiss in many discussions about the demise of the state and its sovereignty, although the notion of an "unbound sovereignty" – which had always been a problematic notion – showed its limitations more clearly than ever before.

It is those problems which I want to address in this chapter. I begin in the next section (Section 3.2) with a conceptual history of "sovereignty" focusing first on the conceptual elaborations of Bodin and Hobbes. In Section 3.3, I examine issues of jurisdiction as they arose in the context of imperial expansions and increasing interdependencies in the late eighteenth and nineteenth centuries. This provides the background for a discussion of the general problem of social reproduction and transformative change, which will be illustrated here by reviewing briefly the settlements after World Wars I and II. Section 3.4 concludes the chapter with a brief summary.

---

[2] See e.g. Robert Keohane and Joseph Nye, *Power and Interdependence*, Boston: Little, Brown 1977.

[3] Yale H. Ferguson and Richard W. Mansbach, *Polities: Authority, Identities and Change*, Columbia, SC: University of South Carolina Press, 1996.

[4] See e.g. the influential analysis of James Rosenau and Ernst-Otto Czmepiel, *Governance without Government: Order and Change in World Politics*, Cambridge: Cambridge University Press, 1992.

3.2   On "Sovereign Authority"

Sovereignty is, strangely enough, one of the few concepts that have no precise counterpart in classical political theory,[5] even though "autonomy" (rather than primacy) captures perhaps its most salient dimension. The concept of "sovereignty" emerged in the medieval political discourse as a claim to superior authority. As such it did not originally mean absolute power. Since medieval authority relations were those of personal ties based on a feudal contract, which regulated the rights and duties of vassals and lords, an individual could have several sovereigns, depending on circumstances. Furthermore, the concept was also used by the end of the investiture controversy to delineate supreme authority "functionally," by distinguishing the sovereign in spiritual from the one in secular matters.

Despite the Concordat of Worms (1122), there still remained ample areas of contestation. Three issues proved difficult to settle once and for all. There was first the issue of order among the different autonomous functional realms. Thus, despite the fact that, different from Caesaropapism in the East (fusing spiritual and secular power), the "two swords" theory of power had won out in Western Christendom, this doctrinal distinction did not dispose of the question which power was higher or, put differently, how these different realms should stand in relation to each other. Given that the king as the protagonist of the worldly order was also increasingly deriving his legitimacy from the "sacred," and given the ontological basis for determining the "lower" and "higher" purposes of life claimed by the church, such conflicts seemed inevitable.[6] This difficulty was enhanced by frequent jurisdictional conflicts in practical politics, since many clergy held public office, or they were part of orders that claimed exceptions from the usual arrangements. Finally, religious dissenters challenged both the authority of the church and of secular rulers by recourse to the original meaning of the Christian message and by a claim to the freedom of individual conscience.

---

[5] See e.g. the discussion of the concept by Marcel David, *La Souveraineté et les limites juridiques du pouvoir monarchique: De IXe au XVe siècle*, Paris: Dalloz, 1954. One also should be careful not to read back into some of the records the later understanding of "sovereignty," when the context suggests rather simple "primacy" (instead of supremacy). Thus, a writer of the middle of the thirteenth century can say that each baron is *souverain* in his barony, but also say that the king is *souverain* among them without seeing a contradiction. "Chascuns baron est souverains en sa baronie ... Voir est que li rois est souverain par dessus tout" (p. 69). It seems that such a conceptualization is simply one establishing some rank order and indicating who is first, depending on the context and level which is being addressed.

[6] See the tensions between Christ's telling the Pharisees to give to God what is His and to Caesar what is his, and St Peter's admonition that one has to obey God more than secular authority.

For a long period of time, secular and church authorities succeeded in keeping these sectarian movements in check, as the example of the suppression of the Waldensians and Hussites showed. But with the Reformation, religious dissent was no longer limited to marginal groups or occasional radical converts from the privileges of a status society. The emerging "protestant" social movements could no longer be suppressed or reintegrated into the church by the creation of a new monastic branch, as had been the case in the earlier Franciscan or Dominican protests. The adoption of the reformed faith by leading strata of the estate society made it inevitable that constitutional questions about privileges and royal power, about duties and obligations, and about the legitimacy of resistance to a rule infringing on the "ancient freedoms," became intertwined with issues of religion and legitimization.[7] What characterizes the modern "state" and its order is that it established social order increasingly independently from God's commands, natural law, by making first "the sovereign" and later "the people" the lawgiver, until finally – after the popular will has led itself *ad absurdum* in the totalitarian excesses of the Nazi and Communist utopias – individuals and their subjective rights become the ultimate ground for the legitimate exercise of power.

This at first utterly secular conception of the "rule of law" leads, however, to a new form of foundationalism that despite its supposed secularism makes reference to the divine, the unfathomable, or to "humanity" (understood as a *telos* rather than as a collectivity of beings), a problem that will be taken up in later chapters of this book. For the moment, though, I want to devote some space to a brief textual exegesis of one of the key passages of Bodin's *Six Books of the Commonwealth* in order to contrast it then with the Hobbesian version of sovereignty stressing the "will" of the sovereign. Such an endeavor requires as a first step to place the concept in its larger semantic field and explore its relations to notions of legitimacy, law, and its "sources," and the traditional order from which at first the sovereign and later the "state" emancipates itself.

---

[7] We have to avoid reading back into the texts of the so-called *monarcomachi*, of both Protestant and Catholic background, a general right to resistance, which e.g. Locke's famous appeal to heaven seems to imply. The sixteenth-century French discussion remains firmly tied to the notion of an estate society in which only the highest magistrates have the right of sanctioning a king's violations of the "natural" order. In this context, see the doctrine of resistance expounded by Calvin's successor in Geneva: Theodorus Beza, *Du Droit des magistrats sur leurs subiets*, Saint-Julien-l'Ars: Imprimerie monastique, 1968 [1574]. Private persons as distinguished from the lower magistrates, who are "au dessus di souverain," have no right to resist even if the king is a tyrant, except they have a particular direct vocation from God about which Beza does not want to say anything. "Ie dy que sans extraordinaire vocation de Dieu, a laqueslle ie ne touche point, il n'est licite a aucun particulier d'opposer force a la force du Tyrann de son authorite privee," ibid., 190.

Bodin and Hobbes

That sovereignty and legitimacy have always been closely connected can be seen from the debates concerning the right of resistance and the permissibility of regicide that inflamed the sixteenth-century debates in France, and provided the background for Bodin's *Six Books of the Commonwealth*. Because Bodin's mode of exposition still owes much to traditional discussions about the ends of good government, and because the treatise related to the concrete issues of civil war in a society torn by internal conflict, the text is often contradictory. Nevertheless, several strands of innovative thought can be identified. There is first the transformation of the notion of personal rule into an abstract notion of authority providing through legislation for its own source of empowerment. Second, there is the attempt to distinguish this supreme power from the actual temporally limited exercise of unlimited power, such as the Roman institution of the dictator, or the *harmost* of Lacedaemon.[8]

The first strand represents a radical break with the medieval idea of rule as a personal relation and as a shared capacity among the nobles on the basis of traditional rights and privileges. The idea that law can be created through a volitional act (legislation) undermined the privileges of the past as the yardstick of order. It also emancipated the public realm from the fetters of social relations. The state became again a distinct sphere, and this innovation (or recovery of the old *res publica* idea) raised the question of how this power, now absolved from the restraints of a static estate society and increasingly also from ontological order speculations, could be legitimized. Given the complexities of these problems, especially the idea that the obligatory force of law now rested in the declaration of a will (first of the sovereign and later of "the people"), it is not surprising that many of the puzzles remain unresolved, as Bartelson's seminal study on the genealogy of sovereignty showed.[9] Such an extensive engagement with the rise of the modern state and of the knowledge which was productive of it, cannot be attempted here. Nevertheless, a brief discussion seems in order.

Although Bodin deals with sovereignty in several places in his *Six Books of the Commonwealth*, the most important part remains his treatment of sovereignty in the eighth chapter of the first book.

Majestie or Sovereigtie is the most high, absolute and perpetual power over citizens and subjects in a Commonweale: which the Latins cal Majestatem, the Greeks ... the Italians Segnoria and the Hebrews, that is to say: The greatest power to command ... For so it behovest first to define what majestie or Sovereigntie is, which neither lawyer

---

[8] See e.g. Bodin's remark in the eight chapter of the first book, Jean Bodin, *The Six Books of the Commonwealth*, Cambridge, MA: Harvard University Press, 1962, at 85.

[9] Jens Bartelson, *A Genealogy of Sovereignty*, Cambridge, Cambridge University Press, 1995.

nor political philosopher hath yet defined: although it be the principall and most neces-
sarie point for the understanding of the nature of a Commonweale. And foreasmuch as
we have before defined a Commonweale to be the right government of many families
and of things common among them, with most high and perpetual power: it resteth to be
declared, what is to be understood by the name of a most high and perpetuall power.
We have said that this power ought to be perpetuall, for that it may be, that it is absolute
power over the subjects and may be given to one or many for a short or certain time,
which expired, they are no more subjects themselves: so that whilst they are in their
puissant authoritie, they cannot call themselves Sovereign princes, seeing that they are
but men put in trust, and keepers of the sovereign power, until they shall please the
people or the prince that gave it them to recall it ... For as they which lend or pawne
into another man their goods, remaine still the lords and owners thereof: so it is also
with them, who give unto others power and authoritie to judge and command, be it for a
certaine limited time, or so great and long time, as all please them; they themselves
neverthelesse continuing still ceased of the power and jurisdiction, which the others
exercise but by way of loane or borrowing.[10]

Bodin's text gives rise to several important observations as to the content
and his style of arguing. First, one notices the elaboration of the autonomous
sphere of the state. It is still embodied in the personal sovereign, although the
admission of the possibility of "many" as the representatives of the highest
authority harks back to Aristotle's distinction of the different forms of government. Yet, his stress on the "new" character of this conception undermines
Bodin's own gambit of showing the necessity for such a power in every body
politic, for which he provided evidence that such an equivalent institution
existed in various historical societies. Finding a new vocabulary and marking
the breaks with the previous understandings, while showing that such an
innovation is actually in the "nature of things," provides, however, some
persuasive reasons for ultimately discarding the previous set of concepts, such
as the body politic.

   Second, it is interesting that Bodin does not employ the conventional terms
of Roman law for communicating his new conception of sovereignty. Thus,
sovereignty conceptually could be more clearly circumscribed as a fusion of
potestas (the power inherent in certain specific offices) and *imperium* (the
general capacity to issue commands to people transcending particular powers),
given originally to Roman military commanders in the field. Instead, he uses
the rather amorphous term *majesty*, which was classically used to denote a
claim to an intrinsic value that ought to be respected. Different from reputation
that has to be earned, and which can be given only by others to the actor (even
if its noun form misleads us into thinking that it is some type of possession),
majestas signifies something intrinsic that demands reverence or submission.
This is the case when we encounter the sacred. *Majesty* is, therefore, variously

---

[10] Bodin, *The Six Books of the Commonwealth*, bk. I, chap. 8, at 84.

ascribed to God, or to the Roman people, and – with the sacralization of the medieval king – to the king, who not only becomes untouchable, but to whom also some powers can be ascribed that nobody else possesses.[11] Later this dimension of the sacred or near sacred is ascribed to "the law" rather than to a person, and this ascription makes it possible for "sovereignty" to serve as the source of legitimacy enabling also its "move" from the king to "the people."

But those developments are still beyond the horizon. How much Bodin is still a child of his time is evidenced by the fact that the claim to this absolute power is still seen as being rooted in tradition, as succession is crucial for the legitimization of royal power. While a rightful heir to the throne of a sovereign also possesses the plenitude of powers, a monarch whose power originates in a delegation from the people cannot be a true sovereign.[12] Obviously, here two forms of legitimacy clash, and it remains for Hobbes to popularize a solution that preserves absolutism, while severing sovereignty from its last historical moorings in feudalism by starting with the analytical construct of a contract among individuals.

The function of this contract is to create both "the people" (subjects) and the "sovereign." The act of authorization constituting the sovereign becomes practically irrevocable for Hobbes and neither direct participation nor participation through representation in governmental decisions is possible. The sovereign's actions have to be understood by each person as his own act, while at the same time "the people" as a collectivity emerges *"not by the unity of the represented but by the unity of the representer."*[13] For Bodin, however, who starts with a model of society rather isomorphic with the "orders" of late feudalism, such a construction of extreme individualism is yet inconceivable.

Finally, the conception of law as creation, as an activity of making and breaking rather than merely of "finding" the law, raises the issue regarding the

---

[11] E.g. the medieval kings had the power to heal certain diseases by touching sick persons. For a general study of the sacred character of a king instantiating the sacred, see Ernst Hartwig Kantorowicz, *The King's Two Bodies: A Study in Mediaeval Political Theology*, Princeton: Princeton University Press, 1957. See also Ernst H. Kantorowicz and Manfred F. Bukofzer, *Laudes Regiae: A Study in Liturgical Acclamations and Medieval Ruler Worship*, Berkeley: University of California Press, 1946.

[12] "But let us grant an absolute power without appeal or controlment to be granted by the people to one or many to manage their estate or their entire government: Shall we therefore say him or them to have the state of Soverigntie, when a he onley is to be called absolute Sovereigne who next unto God acknowledges none greater than himself? Wherefore I say no sovereigntie to be in them, but in the people, of whom they have a borrowed power, or power for a certain time, which once expired, they are bound to yeeld up their authoritie." Bodin, *The Six Books of the Commonwealth*, bk. I, chap. 8 at 86. Only a transfer without any notion of "office," or eventual accountability, i.e. a "perfect donation," could establish a sovereign. The example Bodin gives is the "king of Tartarie," but even here traditional legitimacy, i.e. the royal bloodline, is mentioned as a necessary condition. Ibid., 88f.

[13] Hobbes, *Leviathan*, pt. I, chap. 16, at 220.

limits of this capacity, which self-referentially empowers itself. Strictly speaking, and in accordance with the spatial representation of sovereignty as a summit of a hierarchy, there should be only one limitation: self-limitation. Indeed, Bodin sees that as one of the limitations of sovereign power. Later, in much the same way, the nineteenth-century international lawyers explain the existence of law among sovereign states as an act of self-limitation by the states.[14] But it is highly significant that in Bodin this limitation is largely discussed in terms of obligations incurred through *contractual obligations* and not in terms of the "will problematic," familiar from the subsequent debates of self-limitation. For Bodin, the issue is vetted in terms of the existing institutional order, of whether a sovereign is bound by promises and oaths he once made.

Distinguishing mere declarations, even when done under oath, from contracts, Bodin holds that even the absolute sovereign is bound by promises and contractual undertakings, if the *"subjects ... have an interest"* in their observation,[15] namely if the instruments satisfy the formal conditions of a contract. Derogations from earlier guarantees, as e.g. those given to the estates by the King of Aragon, are explained away not by a generalized capacity to "break the law," but in terms of a fundamental change in circumstances that had defeated the original reason for the contract.[16] Bodin repeatedly asserts that even contractual obligations may be derogated from by the sovereign "without the consent of his subjects," if "the equity thereof has ceased."[17] But for us it seems rather strange that he adduces the principles of private law for the justification of such derogations instead of arguing with the automatic presumption of superiority of "public law." The superiority of public over private law, so familiar from Roman law and later from the *Staatslehre* of the nineteenth century, is here far from developed.[18] It makes in Bodin a nearly

---

[14] See e.g. Georg Jellinek, *Die Rechtliche Natur der Staatenverträge: Ein Beitrag zur Juristischen Construction des Völkerrechts*, Vienna: A. Hölder, 1880.

[15] The often quoted and I think generally misunderstood passage that a prince is not bound by "laws" deals with the obligatory character of promises and oaths of sovereigns. It basically elaborates on the distinction between promises and contracts "without considerations" (as the common lawyer would say). While Bodin rejects the binding force of promises even under oath, he *does* hold the sovereign accountable "as should a private man bee" for contracts with consideration (i.e. both parties having certain interests which they seek to advance through the mutual undertaking). The passage reads: "And so our maxim resteth: That the prince is not subject to his lawes, nor the lawes of his predecessors; but well to his own just and reasonable conventions, and the observation whereof the subjects in generall or particular have interest. Wherein we see many to be deceived, which *make confusion of lawes and of a princes contracts which they call also lawes*." Bodin, *The Six Books of the Commonwealth*, bk. I, chap. 8, at 92 (emphasis added).

[16] Ibid., 93.   [17] Ibid.

[18] See e.g. the fundamental distinction by Montesquieu that by political laws we acquire liberty and by civil law property. But since many of the social relations in the estate society are still mediated by property, Montesquieu argues that the protection of private property is the greatest public good. The decisive point, though, is that the protection of property is now a goal of

furtive appearance under the heading of "lawes which concerne the state of the realm ... insofar as they are annexed and united to the crown."[19] Yet, significantly, they are not mentioned in the context of creating a new public sphere and securing sovereignty by giving the sovereign a new license to act, by passing laws. Rather, they are introduced as a sort of law that a sovereign cannot change, and thus they run up squarely against the notion of an "unbound" will.

Bodin thereby gestures at the notion of a constitutional order, although it is not well articulated. But as long as the "rule of law" cannot be conceptualized as an abstract capacity of self-generation, certain traditions, or appeals to nature have to supply the limits. This leads to the ineluctable tension between the emphasis on will and command as a source of law, and the concept of law as "reason," or at least as a recognizable process that takes place according to certain rules.

Bodin seems somewhat aware of these conceptual issues without being able to articulate them. Undoubtedly, the decisive new element that sovereignty in Bodin entailed is the self-judging element in the exercise of power at the apex of the hierarchy of authority relations. It is this element that creates new opportunities for political action where formerly none existed or was perceived. Whatever criticisms we might have of Bodin's work, we should remember, however, that the discussion of sovereignty in Bodin is much more akin to the debates about the royal prerogatives during the Stuart period than to the rationalist reconstruction of law as a system of abstract powers. In the absence of a notion of subjective rights or an explicit constitution, social conventions and moral precepts (laws of nature) provide, despite all radically sounding pronouncements, quite important limits for political action through legislation.

After all, even the rulers of the *ancien régime* could never be absolute in the modern sense of the word, which suggests unlimited power in terms of scope and domain. As more recent historiography has shown, absolutist monarchs derived their strength from becoming arbiters among different sectors of society.[20] Even after the emasculation of the political ambitions of feudal society and the ascendancy of the court as the site for political action, the estates, even in France, were far from inconsequential. The absolute monarchs

---

public policy, and the power to enact laws and make public policy no longer *derived* from property. See Charles de Secondat Montesquieu, *The Spirit of the Laws*, trans. Thomas Nugent, New York: Haffner, 1966, bk. XXVI, chap. 14.

[19] Bodin, *The Six Books of the Commonwealth*, bk. I, chap. 8, at 95.

[20] For a discussion of the rather fragile rule of Louis, who tried to protect the nobility and its privileges by making himself arbiter of their intrigues, and popular resistance from the attacks of the first Fronde just before his reign (1648–1650) to the revolt of the Camisards (1702–1705) – not to speak of ubiquitous riots – see Roy L. McCullough, *Coercion, Conversion and Counterinsurgency in Louis XIV's France*, Leiden: Brill, 2007.

lacked, above all, direct access to their subjects, as the state machinery was woefully underdeveloped. One relevant reason for this underdevelopment was the absence of a conceptual space that would have legitimized the notion of the transformation of society through political action.

It is also worth remembering that even in centralized states, such as in the France of Louis XIV, where the king's law is supposed have supplanted local laws, it took the French Revolution and the subsequent codification by Napoleon to establish the supremacy of national law over local law.[21] Similarly in Prussia, it was only with the freeing of the peasants in the aftermath of the Jena debacle that those important remnants of feudalism, and thus of the predominance of society over the political sphere, were swept away. To that extent, the prevailing conceptions of legitimacy were quite different from the transvaluation of all values that emerged with the French Revolution. Only then did truly everything become possible, as long as it was "willed" by the sovereign.

In Bodin's case such a radicalization was yet unthinkable, because he understood – despite his hierarchical speculations – the sovereign's power to be limited by God the ultimate lawgiver and by social conventions. The latter provided in the analogy to property, a way out of the conceptual conundrum. Taking *dominium* as the template for understanding the powers of the sovereign avoids most of the conceptual problems of the will-problematic, and such a move provides a far more useful heuristic tool for tracing the changes in this institution. Precisely because the issues of authority and power are not reduced to one of location (where does sovereignty "rest"?), and because sovereignty is viewed as being embedded within the wider network of other institutions and background understandings, it can more systematically account for transformative change

Since the institution of property allows for a variety of social arrangements with attendant right and duties, sovereignty could then be understood as a bundle of rights rather than as an expression of a will. With such a conceptual move, sovereignty can now be much more variable than is suggested by the spatially inspired supremacy argument. Two examples might suffice. Despite ideas that sovereign states had to possess the entire panoply of powers, "neutrality" – even if imposed on a state (such as on Switzerland or Belgium) rather than autonomously chosen as its policy (Sweden) – was never considered an abrogation of sovereignty. Similarly, the change from a personal sovereign to constitutional systems of popular sovereignty could be easily accommodated within this semantics, despite the fact that the guiding idea of an absolute sovereign sitting at the apex of a hierarchy becomes then inapt, and

---

[21] See Fernand Braudel, *The Identity of France*, vol. 1, New York: Harper and Row, 1989, at 78–84.

that the introduction of the separation of powers in constitutional thought directly militates against a conception of a single locus of supreme power. Moreover, the recent emergence of "quasi-sovereignty" and the decay of the state in many parts of the world have not led to the revocation of their sovereignty,[22] despite the fact that in many cases any semblance of political order seems to have disappeared. To that extent the new conception of a *Responsibility to Protect* fits neatly into this institutional conception of sovereignty, although it does not resolve the practical issues of who can and shall act, and at which point, given the largely dysfunctional nature of the UN Security Council and the self-serving interests of a "coalition of the willing."

These examples point to the continued importance of the concept of sovereignty, but they also emphasize a need to understand its function in constituting (and thereby also regulating) political practices in a historical context.[23] The concept of sovereignty originated in domestic politics, but it was soon predominantly used to demarcate the outside of a political order, called the state, and its relations to other such entities. In the last two decades sovereignty has become again largely a problem of "internal" politics. The twin attacks of self-determination and human rights have undermined even further the notion of an authority placed beyond appeal. The emergences of boundary-spanning networks, ranging from markets to "telematics" (digital information networks linked to computers), have also clearly affected practices of inclusion and exclusion. They have also reshaped opportunities to create order through the traditional methods of territorial boundaries or the internationalization of the state.[24] Thus, we cannot be satisfied with registering simply the mounting deviations from the allegedly fixed historical norms.[25] Rather, we have to

---

[22] See Robert H. Jackson, *Quasi-States: Sovereignty, International Relations, and the Third World*, Cambridge: Cambridge University Press, 1990.

[23] Although I still believe that the distinction between regulative and institutional rules is important and should be carefully made, other theorists such as Onuf and Giddens have pointed out that all rules are constitutive as well as regulative. See Onuf, *World of Our Making*. Although the above example appears to buttress this claim, it seems, however, that this approach proves too much. First, the logical distinction between these two types of rules still holds. Second, I fail to perceive a constitutive function in regulative rules. Third, even if we emphasize the regulative functions of constitutive rules, there is a difference in the regulation which is attempted. These are the well-known distinctions between sanctions on the one hand and "invalidity" of acts (or engaging in nonsense rather than a game) on the other. For a further elaboration, see below, Chapter 6.

[24] The term internationalization of the state was used by Wendt and Duvall to denote the ever expanding role of regimes under conditions of complex interdependence. See Alexander Wendt and Raymond Duvall, "Institutions and International Order" in Ernst-Otto Czempiel and James N. Rosenau (eds.), *Global Changes and Theoretical Challenges: Approaches to World Politics for the 1990s*, Lexington, MA: Lexington Books, 1989, 51–73.

[25] This leads then to the rather unsurprising assertion that sovereignty never functioned as one imagined it and that "therefore" it just must be an instance of "hypocrisy." See Stephen D. Krasner, *Sovereignty: Organized Hypocrisy*, Princeton: Princeton University Press, 1999.

investigate whether we are not only seeing exceptions or deviance but a new form allowing for different practices. As the next subsection hopefully demonstrates, relying on "property" as a heuristic device proves to be quite useful for this purpose.

Sovereignty as "Dominium"

Irrespective of which definition of property we prefer, and the discussion up to now has shown that we are dealing here with a cluster of different ways of bundling rights,

we must recognize that a property right is a relation not between an owner and a thing but between the owner and other individuals in reference to a thing ... The classical view of property as a right over things resolves it into component rights such as *ius utendi, ius disponendi* etc. But the essence of private property is always the right to exclude others.[26]

It is in this context that the Roman law's conception of *dominium* and its emergence as a template for organizing social relations become important. Thus, while real property in Roman law is rather exclusive – servitudes and limitations such as the *sic utere tuo* principle, or adverse possession remain exceptions – Germanic customary legal orders contained various use-rights which did not clearly "come with the land." A brief discussion is in order.

As to the use-rights: for instance the possession of a forest in England did not necessarily bar others from using the same piece of land, namely for herding their swine or for collecting wood in it. As a matter of fact, the old English saying "by hook or by crook" is a reminder of the privilege allowing the poor to pull down branches from the trees for firewood. On the other hand, even important public functions often "went with the land." So, Maitland could argue by the end of the nineteenth century that the whole of English constitutional history seems but an appendix to the laws of real property[27] as e.g. the administration of justice in a baron's court resulted from his land ownership.[28]

Roman real property, on the other hand, was more exclusive and made a categorical distinction between public and private law. Virtually all rights belonged to the owner of the land and he alone could decide how to make

---

[26] Morris Cohen, "Property and Sovereignty" in C.B. MacPherson (ed.), *Property: Mainstream and Critical Positions*, Toronto: University of Toronto Press, 1978, 153–176, at 159.

[27] Frederic William Maitland, *The Constitutional History of England: A Course of Lectures Delivered*, Union, NJ: The Lawbook Exchange, 2013 [1908], at 538.

[28] This necessitated, on the other hand, in distinctions in the descent of real and personal property, distinctions that in England only the Property Act of 1925 abolished. The effect was to make land similarly salable as any other commodity and strip it from the last feudal remnant.

use of it. One of the implications of *dominium* in Roman real property was that originally apparently only a vertical division of property was possible, and that no rights e.g. in a second story of a house, could be acquired. *Dominium*, the capacity to exclude others from use, could then be nicely put in the formula *cujus est solum ejus est usque ad coelum et ad inferos* (to whom the land belongs, belongs everything up to heaven and down to hell).[29]

It is clear that in such a system of exclusive rights, boundaries attained a new meaning. The owner in this legal order was thus largely exempted from the traditional conventions that had regulated use-rights in Germanic customary systems. Limits to the exercise of property rights in Roman law were reduced to background conditions e.g. that one could not use one's property to infringe on the rights of others, as mentioned above (the *sic utere tuo* principle that in modern days is invoked for the resolution of transborder pollution disputes).[30]

Dominium, when applied to ordering external relations, also settled the issue of resource rights, and proved quite flexible in accommodating new problem areas, such as the extension of national sovereignty to the air space.[31] Permanent sovereignty over natural resources has been explicitly endorsed even by newcomers to the international legal order, although they often objected to the rules of traditional international law, frequently in the name of distributive justice.[32] Whatever the merits of other principles for assigning entitlements might be, exclusivity avoids, probably best, conflicts and stabilizes expectations in the absence of wider patterns of solidarity. While "need" might be, at first blush, an attractive alternative, it fails to provide a stable rule as to who can actually own anything, since needs constantly shift and "more deserving" claimants can usually be identified.

Of course, in focusing on land, which ceased to be the main source of wealth under modern conditions, adherence to the territorial principle, creates considerable tensions in a modern economy without necessarily providing many benefits. Here, consider the wealth which know-how and information can

---

[29] This formulation goes back to Accursius, a glossator of Roman law in the thirteenth century, whose son introduced it to England under Edward I.

[30] See the transborder pollution *Trail Smelter Case (United States, Canada)*, Reports of International Arbitral Awards, Volume III, 1905–1982 (1938 and 1941).

[31] See the discussion of the development of the law of air space in Arnold Duncan McNair, Michael R.E. Kerr, and Robert A. MacCrindle, *The Law of the Air*, London: Stevens & Sons, 1953. For the reasons for not relying on the Roman law analogy in regulating space law, see M.J. Peterson, "The Use of Analogies in Developing Outer Space Law," *International Organization*, 51:2 (1997): 245–274.

[32] United Nations General Assembly, *Permanent Sovereignty over Natural Resources, Resolution 1803 (XVII)*, (1962, UN Doc. A/5217).

deliver, exactly because of their boundary-crossing capacities.[33] Nevertheless, territorial exclusivity still carries with it important restrictions of access and thus represents structural power, even though the digitalization of information and the development of telematics have also undermined this potential of control.[34] However, as we will see below, it is difficult to imagine how modern property rights can be secured other than in a territorial fashion. But let us first return to the political consequences of the conception of sovereignty as "property."

Internally, *dominium* gave the prince the *Landeshoheit*, or exclusive jurisdictional authority on the basis of the sovereign's "possession." The scope and domain of this authority were now secure from certain challenges by subordinate vassals or estates as well as from outsiders. Here, the emergent notion of an abstract state served well to eliminate any notions of a shared rule, characteristic of feudal times. The change is clearly expressed in Louis XIV's famous (but probably apocryphal) dictum, *l'Etat c'est moi*, or in Frederick II's notion of the king being the "first servant of the state." Both link the right to exclusive rule with the notion of the state. The absolutist monarch no longer relied on the liberties and privileges of a feudal magnate, but claimed his powers as the representative of the state. Yet, basing claims on *dominium*, of course, did not immunize the sovereigns from challenges that derived their legitimacy from the laws of succession. It is therefore not surprising that monarchs had to construct complicated genealogies in order to buttress their claims to rule.

In other words, despite the territorial principle embodied in sovereignty conceived as *dominium*, the developing internal and external systems of relations still resembled very much those of dynastic feudal orders, as a recent discussion about the Westphalian founding myth has re-emphasized.[35] Instead of a sharp break, continuities abound. Not surprisingly even the first historian of the state system writes his history as one of the "ruling houses" rather than of

---

[33] See e.g. the critical remarks by Knieper based on these considerations and his experiences as an official for development aid in Rolf Knieper, *Nationale Souveränität: Versuch über Ende und Anfang einer Weltordnung*, Frankfurt: Fischer, 1991, particularly Teil IV. More generally for the discussion during the period of the New International Economic Order (NIEO), see Hans Reinhard, *Rechtsgleichheit und Selbstbestimmung der Völker in Wirtschaftlicher Hinsicht: die Praxis der Vereinten Nationen*, Berlin: Springer, 1980.

[34] See William J. Drake (ed.), *The New Information Infrastructure: Strategies for U.S. Policy*, New York: Twentieth Century Fund Press, 1995; William J. Drake and Ernest J. Wilson III (eds.), *Governing Global Electronic Networks: International Perspectives on Policy and Power*, Cambridge, MA: MIT Press, 2008.

[35] See e.g. Andreas Osiander, *The States System of Europe, 1640–1990: Peacemaking and the Conditions of International Stability*, Oxford: Oxford University Press, 1994; Benno Teschke, *The Myth of 1648: Class, Geopolitics, and the Making of Modern International Relations*, London: Verso, 2003.

states.[36] The famous *ius armorum*, that is, the capacity of contract alliances, which the *estates* of the German realm possessed – which in Krasner's account of the Westphalian order have simply become "states"[37] – is of feudal origin. This right, antedating the advent of the state system, remained after Westphalia but was now limited by the presumption that alliances against the emperor were illegal, and the decisive change of the freedom to contract alliances occurred only at the end of the eighteenth century.

Given these important remnants of the feudal order, most of the wars until late into the eighteenth century were wars of succession. Even alliances were often controlled by proprietary interest and not by the interests of the state.[38] Thus, in a way it is true that from the Westphalian settlement emerged a "state system," but it was certainly not one in the form assumed by neo-realists. The order that came into existence did not consist of homogeneous units facing each other in an anarchical arena. Rather, the *res publica Christiana* was highly heterogeneous and showed some interesting overlaps. At its core it consisted of a reconstituted loose association of entities of various degrees of independence, the Empire. In one of its decision-making bodies, the Diet, outside members such as Sweden and later – through the accession of the House of Hanover to the British throne – even the English sovereign played an important role. Some of the members of this association "contracted out" their defense, quite contrary to the assumed generative logic of anarchy, but even *de jure* questions of sovereign equality remained highly contested. Here, Leibniz's futile attempt to convince his contemporaries of a right of all sovereigns to send and receive ambassadors is highly instructive.[39] Contrary to the logic of his argument, this position was not even accepted by the most statist member: France.

This core of the system, which Pufendorf found hard to comprehend within the categories of the *ius publicum Europaeum* (which he called, therefore, a

[36] See e.g. the employment of this categorization instead of the one announced in the title in Samuel von Pufendorf, *An Introduction to the History of the Principal Kingdoms and States of Europe*, London: 1702.
[37] Stephen D. Krasner, "Westphalia and All That" in Judith Goldstein and Robert O. Keohane (eds.), *Ideas and Foreign Policy: Beliefs, Institutions, and Political Change*, Ithaca, NY: Cornell University Press, 1993, 235–264, at 246.
[38] The most famous example is the alliance of Great Britain before (Westminster Convention between Prussia and Great Britain) and during the Seven Years War (First and Second Treaty of Versailles of 1756, which made Austria and France allies), since it was the dynastic interest of the English monarch, who was also the ruler of Hanover, that decided the choice of alliance partner. See Charles W. Ingrao, *The Habsburg Monarchy, 1618–1815*, Cambridge: Cambridge University Press, 2000, 151–177. On the Seven Years War, see Daniel A. Baugh, *The Global Seven Years War 1754–1763: Britain and France in a Great Power Contest*, London: Pearson, 2011.
[39] See Gottfried Wilhelm Leibniz, "Caesarinus Fuerstenerius (1677)" in *Philosophische Schriften und Briefe, 1683–1687*, Berlin: Akademie, 1880.

"kind of monster"),[40] was surrounded by a ring of more or less modern states: England, France, and Sweden. But the Dutch Republic, with its federal structure, on the one side, and the disintegrating kingdom of Poland on the other side, proved notable exceptions. Finally, there were some players who remained outsiders even though they had played an important part in bringing about this system in two ways: through political practice and as an important element in defining the system as a *European* system with a particular identity.[41] The Ottoman Empire provides here the striking example After all, the Sublime Porte had contracted a formal alliance with France against the Habsburgs before their attempts to take Vienna (1683), but it did not become a member of the club until after the Peace of Paris (1856), as both sides originally had reservations about accepting the other as a bona fide member.

Unfortunately, this is not the place to examine in detail the various defining moments of the international system, but fortunately this has been ably done by Rodney Hall's impressive study.[42] Nevertheless, a cursory review of the historical stages and their specific dilemmas is in order. Conceptually, a variety of issues had a bearing on the question of how sovereignty could be asserted. Problems of territoriality, representation, identity, and legitimacy had to be mediated, and thus provided temporary stabilizations but no compelling "solutions" to the dilemmas.

Historically, three stages are discernible. First, there is the devolution of the bundle of sovereign rights to the "people" that raised issues of representation. Second, there is the emergence of nationalism as a political program to establish the congruence between nation and state. Third, we encounter the introduction of self-determination and human rights as constitutive principles which compete with territorial sovereignty in the international game. These principles, oddly enough, sometimes work in conjunction, as e.g. when human rights reinforce conceptions of a representative democracy. Similarly, self-determination is not a priori incompatible with notions of nationalism. Yet, historical experiences show us also that because these concepts rely on different principles of exclusion and inclusion, denying their potential for conflict would require heroic optimism.

Only in the American case, the legitimization of public authority, the assertion of individual rights, and the establishment of a new identity happily coincided. Indeed, it was only in the New World, where the territory had

---

[40] Samuel von Pufendorf, *Die Verfassung des Deutschen Reiches*, Stuttgart: H. Denzer, 1976, Vorwort.

[41] This point is well made by Iver B. Neumann and Jennifer M. Welsh, "The Other in European Self-Definition: An Addendum to the Literature on International Society," *Review of International Studies*, 17:4 (1991): 327–346.

[42] See Rodney Bruce Hall, *National Collective Identity: Social Constructs and International Systems*, New York: Columbia University Press, 1999.

served as the container to mold the "nation," that the fiction of a common ancestry played only a minor role after the great immigrations in the nineteenth century, even though "Americanization" was clearly an assimilation project. As can be seen from the original charters given to the founders of various colonies, they were the first ones in which *territoriality had the abstract quality of pure jurisdiction over an uncharted space.* The representation of the grants in the old maps consisted in delineating basically empty spaces – neglecting, significantly, any sign of native settlements – even though some topographical feature such as rivers or mountain ranges could be found. Thus, although the interior of the marked territory was often left blank since it was unexplored and considered "uninhabited" – nobly ignoring the "natives" – the grid relying on the homogeneity of space suggests the independence of jurisdiction exercised in this territory.[43]

It is highly significant in this context that colonial charters for North American colonies often also contained exact provisos as to the establishment of jurisdictional subdivisions, and by the mid-eighteenth century also some detailed prescriptions about proportional representation and periodic reapportionment.[44] To that extent, individual interest representation, which became an important program of federalists and anti-federalists alike, had its deep historical roots in pre-revolutionary history.

Clearly these conditions were entirely different from the developments in European societies. There, nationalism and self-determination played out quite differently. People in Europe, who had been captured by the national myth of the nineteenth century, and who engaged in the project of nationalism in order to receive *public recognition of their distinctiveness*, were often not satisfied with some democratic form of participation in government. The usual participatory rituals in a state, which a part of the population felt was not their own, were not attractive to them, particularly when previous historical experiences had created scores. To conceptualize self-determination as an individual human right to political participation is thus not only seriously misleading, it also blinds us to the competing and often incompatible goods that are subsumed under this heading. As Yael Tamir reminds us:

(democratic) self rule and national self determination are two distinct concepts. They differ in their individualistic and their communal aspects, represent two distinct human goods, and derive their value from two separate human interests ... The individualistic aspect of both these rights celebrates personal autonomy and the right of people to make constitutive choices. Whereas in the right to self rule this aspect points to the right of

[43] For a further development, see the important discussion by Sack, *Human Territoriality.*
[44] Ibid., 142.

individuals to govern their lives without being subject to external dictates, in the case of self-determination it concerns the way in which individuals define their personal and national identity.[45]

Obviously, the political project of creating a community thus transcends the notion of a society and "politicizes" at the same time certain concerns (identity) that previously were mainly part of the private realm. In this context we see, as the century goes on, the preoccupation with a people's uniqueness that becomes so pronounced as to overpower any meaningful participatory or civic dimension. It is this form of nationalism that e.g. Bismarck so masterfully used in order to establish Prussian hegemony and German nationalism, while at the same time subverting the liberal notion of consent of the governed through participation.

At this point it is useful to tie together some of my arguments so far and to deal with a serious objection. After all, the above interpretation of sovereignty as *dominium* might be considered only as *one possible* version of reading the historical record. A Hobbesian interpretation will lead to a certain type of law and politics, and an institutional account to some other. But precisely because social theories are therefore always at least partly political projects, one cannot rely on simple matching operations with a pre-given reality to ascertain their truth-value. This establishes, second, that counter-interpretations are always possible but that they cannot claim either that *they* somehow represent reality. They gain their standing not by some unproblematic null hypothesis but by the very same operations that any conceptual approach illuminating political praxis has to satisfy. Third, these considerations imply that we have to pay particular attention to concepts that serve not only as bridges between different vocabularies but whose generative capacity involves spin-offs so that the transformations give rise to new practices.

In this context, I pointed out that the notion of a contract as a root metaphor was important, because it linked to old conceptions of the feudal order but was also able to fundamentally reconstitute our understanding of politics by becoming foundational for the discourse of modernity. In a similar fashion, I claimed that "property" is such a generative concept, for it gave rise to the notion of subjective rights and of interest, which replaced the discourse on virtue as the central theme of politics. It thus created the modern "individual," conceived of as a rational actor; it allowed for a conception of politics as an exchange whose terms needed enforcement, thereby showing an important link to the prevalent theory of law and to the notion of sanction as its defining characteristic; and finally it prepared the way for utilizing the "market" as a template for the understanding of society.

---

[45] Yael Tamir, *Liberal Nationalism*, Princeton: Princeton University Press, 1993, 70.

3.3   Jurisdiction and Organizations

The discussion in the previous section, concerned with the generative grammar of sovereignty as property, has led to the point where the various strands of the argument can be brought together for the analysis of transformative change in the international system. It is the task of this section to elaborate on this problem.

The emergence of autonomous systems of action, such as the economy, the growth of interdependencies and their institutionalization, seems in no fundamental way to challenge sovereignty as a constitutive principle, although the map based on sovereignty seems more and more inadequate. But how are we to find a new vocabulary that lets us "go on" by avoiding some of the traps of the old semantics? This requires first of all a clear determination of where and how the contemporary puzzles arise which impair our orientation. Hence, I begin with the problem of jurisdiction, which directly links to the above discussion of *dominium*, and examine the fundamental changes that have occurred. Some of them have been quite "interstitial," as the extension of jurisdiction by virtually all states demonstrates. Others have been explicitly part of a reformist design, as the emergence of international organizations and of freestanding regimes suggests, which, in turn, might have problematic side effects, as the debate about the fragmentation of the international legal order suggested.[46]

Although we usually conceive of the international arena as a system in which states claim exclusive jurisdiction over their territory, even a cursory look at the historical practice shows the problems of such a conception. States have historically asserted jurisdiction on a variety of bases, of which territoriality is only one. Most notable among them is the claim to jurisdiction on the basis of the so-called "universality principle" with regard to perpetrators of international crimes, such as piracy. Furthermore, states have traditionally extended their "protection" to citizens abroad (passive nationality principle), and increasingly they have also asserted jurisdictional claims on the basis of the "active nationality principle," namely by subjecting their nationals to the extraterritorial reach of domestic legislation, for instance the tax laws.[47]

---

[46] For a further discussion of these points, see Kratochwil, *The Status of Law in World Society*, chap. 3.

[47] The passive nationality principle even gives rise to claims to a right of intervention in a state where public order has disintegrated and the home state undertakes a rescue mission for its citizens. Most recently, this type of "humanitarian intervention" has been expanded as it also covers acts of intervention against gross violations of human rights perpetrated even against non-citizens. For a further discussion see, Fernando R. Tesón, *Humanitarian Intervention: An Inquiry into Law and Morality*, Dobbs Ferry, NY: Transnational Publishers, 1988; Janet Chopra and Thomas G. Weiss, "Sovereignty Is No Longer Sacrosanct: Codifying Humanitarian Intervention," *Ethics and International Affairs*, 6:1 (1992): 95–117; Robert H. Jackson, "Armed

States have also asserted jurisdiction over *foreign nationals acting abroad* when their actions have an "intended and actual" or a "substantial or foreseeable effect" on the claiming state.[48] Since not even doctrinally is there any agreement on whether states have to establish a valid basis for their assertion of jurisdiction,[49] or whether such claims are legitimate implications of sovereignty, as the Permanent Court of International Justice had argued in the *Lotus* case,[50] conflicts seem rather endemic.

When such issues reach the courts because private rights are impinged, private international law provides for rules of conflict which allow settling some issues. Furthermore, there are some principles such as *forum non conveniens* and *comity* which resolve some controversies. Invoking, however, the principle of comity or some balancing test between the conflicting interests at stake is also becoming increasingly difficult.[51] As one baffled judge once remarked: "When one state exercises its jurisdiction and another in protection of its interests attempts to quash the first exercise of jurisdiction, it is simply

---

Humanitarianism," *International Journal*, 48:4 (1993): 579–606; Caroline Thomas, "The Pragmatic Case against Intervention" in Ian Forbes and Mark Hoffman (eds.), *International Relations, Political Theory, and the Ethics of Intervention*, London: Macmillan, 1993, 91–103; Friedrich Kratochwil, "Sovereignty as 'Dominium': Is There a Right of Humanitarian Intervention?" in Gene Martin Lyons and Michael Mastanduno (eds.), *Beyond Westphalia? State Sovereignty and International Intervention*, Baltimore: Johns Hopkins University Press, 1995, 21–42; Sean D. Murphy, *Humanitarian Intervention: The United Nations in an Evolving World Order*, Philadelphia: University of Pennsylvania Press, 1996; Oliver Ramsbotham and Tom Woodhouse, *Humanitarian Intervention in Contemporary Conflict: A Reconceptualization*, Cambridge: Polity, 1996; Nicholas Wheeler and Justin Morris, "Humanitarian Intervention and State Practice" in Rick Fawn and Jeremy Larkins (eds.), *International Society after the Cold War: Anarchy and Order Reconsidered*, New York: St. Martin's Press, 1996, 135–171; International Commission on Intervention and State Sovereignty, *The Responsibility to Protect*, Ottawa: International Development Research Centre, 2001; Jennifer M. Welsh (ed.), *Humanitarian Intervention and International Relations*, Oxford: Oxford University Press, 2004; Gareth J. Evans, *The Responsibility to Protect: Ending Mass Atrocity Crimes Once and for All*, Washington, DC: Brookings Institution Press, 2008; Alex Bellamy, *The Responsibility to Protect: The Global Effort to End Mass Atrocities*, Cambridge: Polity, 2009; Cristina G. Badescu, *Humanitarian Intervention and the Responsibility to Protect: Security and Human Rights*, Abingdon: Routledge, 2011; Hannes Peltonen, *International Responsibility and Grave Humanitarian Crises: Collective Provision for Human Security*, Abingdon: Routledge, 2013.

[48] See e.g. *United States v. Aluminum Co. of America et al.*, Circuit Court of Appeals, Second Circuit, 148 F.2d 416 (1945).

[49] See in this context the argument about "reasonableness" in Oscar Schachter, "International Law in Theory and Practice: General Course in Public International Law," *Recueil des Cours*, 178:5 (1982): 1–395, at 240f.

[50] In this the Court held that the burden of proof rests entirely with the party alleging a violation of international law. See *The Case of the S.S. "Lotus" (France v. Turkey)*, Permanent Court of International Justice, Ser. A, No. 10 (1927), at 20.

[51] See Joel R. Raul, "Comity in International Law," *Harvard International Law Journal*, 32:1 (1991): 1–80.

impossible to judicially balance these totally contradictory and mutually negating actions."[52] In a defensive move US courts have held that Congressional
statutes must be given effect – even if an exercise by the US Congress to
prescribe exceeds the limitations imposed by international law[53] – but one has
to ask, nevertheless, what remains of the image of the sovereign state and its
exclusive sphere of jurisdiction and lawmaking.

These last remarks turn our attention to the emergence of regimes and
organizations, because they represent another way of coping with the conflicts that arise out of unilateral measures. Institutionalizing a certain issue area
and providing for a more particularized and more coherent form of conflict
resolution – outside of the traditional state-to-state relations – seems an
appropriate response to the "demand for regimes." If these regimes also
possess dispute resolution mechanisms they become "freestanding" but their
proliferation creates distinct problems for the international order as they have
different jurisdictional domains and stand in no clear relationship defined by a
legal process.

Thus several trends are noticeable over the last century: first the phenomenal increase in treaties and special regimes in "functional" areas;[54] second,
the increase of multilateral frameworks, either created by successive extension
of originally bilaterally granted advantages (most-favored-nation status) or by
explicit design;[55] and third, the growth of intergovernmental and nongovernmental international organizations concerned with governance issues.[56] Below
I want to focus on two specific moments that transformed traditional elements
of sovereignty: the Versailles and the San Francisco settlements on the one
hand, and on the other hand, the less deliberate but nevertheless equally significant structural changes of the international system that were induced by growing interdependencies and the emergence of new actors. Both of them seem to
have completed the process of globalization, which in turn has redefined the
international game.

---

[52] *Laker Airways Ltd. v. Sabena, Belgian World Airlines*, D.C. Circuit, 731 F.2d 909 (1984),
at 951f.

[53] *Federal Trade Commission v. Compagnie De Saint-Gobain-Pont-a-Mousson*, US Court of
Appeals, D.C. Circuit, 636 F.2d 1300 (1980).

[54] See e.g. the analysis in Craig Murphy, *International Organization and Industrial Change:
Global Governance Since 1850*, New York: Oxford University Press, 1994.

[55] See John Gerard Ruggie (ed.), *Multilateralism Matters: The Theory and Praxis of an Institutional Form*, New York: Columbia University Press, 1993.

[56] Elinor Ostrom, *Governing the Commons*, Cambridge: Cambridge University Press, 1990; Oran
Young, *International Governance*, Ithaca, NY: Cornell University Press, 1994; Oran Young
(ed.), *Global Governance: Drawing Insights from the Environmental Experience*, Cambridge,
MA: MIT Press, 1997.

Two Transformative Moments

Whatever differences there might be among realists, idealists, peace advocates, or analysts of a coming world society, there is near-universal consensus that the two world wars and their subsequent settlements represent a sharp break. One could make the argument that these two wars actually are probably best understood as two episodes in a fundamental transformation of the international system from a European state system to a global system. The new beginnings invoked at Versailles, and even more so, at San Francisco, came in response to changing external and internal conditions. Externally, the Tocquevillian vision of the US and Russia (Soviet Union) determining the future course of events had gained more and more plausibility as time went by. Internally, the bankruptcy of the old elites, no longer able to provide the necessary leadership, had been demonstrated by the annihilative battles of World War I. The popularity of Wilson's Fourteen Points having convinced the publics of Europe that a new beginning was necessary clearly indicated that a return to business as usual was no longer possible

Somehow most of the official and social actors agreed – even though sometimes quite reluctantly – that new formal institutions were necessary to meet the challenges ahead. To that extent, this "move to institutions,"[57] which David Kennedy has so painstakingly documented,[58] appears to have transcended liberal, syndicalist, and even radical feminist movements. This belief in the effectiveness of formal organizations seems to have been buttressed by two converging notions, namely that political problems could be solved by bringing to bear some technical know-how – an idea that had been gaining currency since Saint-Simon – and that formal organizations represented the "solution" due to their greater efficiency. Bureaucracies would, as Weber suggested and Michels repeated, crowd out other forms of organizing precisely because of their efficiency. But the move to institutions might actually have been a bit subtler than the wholesale adoption of the technical bureaucratic perspective suggested.

Liberal statesmen, even the idealist Woodrow Wilson, like Kant before him, seem to have been less enamored with the prospects of some inchoate world governmental structures. Rather, they hoped that the spread of democracy[59] and the preponderance of the economic and military potential of democratic

---

[57] It might be useful here to distinguish between "institutions" that represent a settled practice and "organizations" that are a particular form of institutions characterized by hierarchies, headquarters, and a largely bureaucratic form of administration. Thus defined, "institution" is the wider term as e.g. "friendship" or even "greeting" is an institution.

[58] David Kennedy, "The Move to Institutions," *Cardozo Law Review*, 8:5 (1987): 841–988.

[59] For a good discussion of this point, see Andrew Moravcsik, "Taking Preferences Seriously: A Liberal Theory of International Politics," *International Organization*, 51:4 (1997): 513–553.

states in the aftermath of the Great War would make peace possible. Instead of decisive internal institutional reform and compulsory settlement of international disputes, the statist lawyers who dominated the last period of post-World War I planning envisaged a political assembly for the resolution of international disputes, a collective security arrangement, and some institutionalized sanctions. In other words, the order that was emerging was much more *reformist in regard to the international political process* than transformative, when compared with the radical social reforms and pacifistic prescriptions that had been advocated by social movements.

Nevertheless, by identifying war with chaos, and peace with systematic organization, the move to institutions created the *topos* that peace was synonymous with organization. Violence and disintegration were thoroughly externalized from international relations and projected upon actors beyond the pale, such as aggressors and terrorists (a move which was repeated recently in the "war on terror"). Nothing could show this change from the conventions of the traditional European state system more clearly than the subsequent efforts to renounce war as a means of politics (Kellogg–Briand Pact), or the attempt to hold the German Kaiser personally responsible for the outbreak of World War I. Thus, the transformative effect of this move to institutions was contained in the suggestion that the cycles of war and peace, as the only means of ordering the international system, had been transcended by a new organizational answer to the problem of international change.[60]

As important as the emphasis on the break with the past might have been, the narratives dealing with this defining moment had, however, also to establish a sense of coherence between the past and the present. In this way an understanding emerged, in which different organizational efforts of the past were shown to be the "forerunners" of the present system, without thereby challenging the state system and its operation. The Concert was viewed as the forerunner of the League's Council, the former river commissions became antecedents to the functional agencies, and in the efforts at arbitration one discovered the roots of the Permanent (and later International) Court of Justice.

To that extent the narrative also easily accommodated the creation of the UN system after World War II, since it incorporated the successor organization neatly, suggesting that it represented a response to the "lessons learned" in the interwar period. Two points were of particular importance in this context: the conviction that only a formal organization and an organization "with teeth" was able to solve the twin problems of securing peace and overcoming the collective action problem posed by the enforcement issue that had been left

---

[60] See e.g. Gilpin, *War and Change in World Politics*.

unattended by the League; and the fact that the traditional ordering devices of the balance of power and the gold standard could no longer fulfill their mission. The idea that the economy could be left to its own devices, hidden away from public scrutiny, while the "high politics" of security could be addressed by a collective security arrangement, had come to naught. After all, fascist leaders had used the "low politics" of the economic crisis to topple the "high politics" of the security arrangements of the interwar political order. In short, what was necessary was a multilateral economic arrangement that prevented races to the bottom, as well as beggar-thy-neighbor policies. Equally necessary was the institutionalization of a new understanding of the boundaries of the public and private realms in *conjunction* with a new conceptualization of the domestic and international arena.

It might be useful to reflect a bit further on the connection between these two issues, since the historical experiences suggested that one had to find a *simultaneous solution* to both problems if one wanted to create a stable international order.[61] While the political nature of this problem was disguised in the late nineteenth century by ideology (liberalism) and the relatively benign British hegemony, the outbreak of World War I had made it clear that the claims of different powers to a "place in the sun" would require far-reaching changes in future institutional arrangements. In a way, the German challenge and the outbreak of World War I brought things to a head. Different from imperialist adventures and accommodations, which formerly allowed for expansion into allegedly empty spaces, those spaces no longer existed. Instead, the dynamic interaction between the economy and the political system confronted European decision-makers with three fundamental problems.

First, by the end of the nineteenth century it had become clear to all foreign offices that a dynamic economy required far greater territorial units than even the largest European nation state provided. Second, the classical nostrums for dealing with change through territorial adjustments to the balance of power had also become highly problematic. Territorial acquisitions were, if not directly unavailable, nevertheless, rather costly. In Europe itself such adjustments created scores, which considerably curtailed a state's freedom in seeking alliance partners (vide Alsace-Lorraine and Bismarck's *cauchemar*). Because of nationalism no self-respecting government could conceive the treason of transferring part of its territory in the same way as sovereigns had once done with few qualms.

---

[61] For an imaginative "Marxist" reconstruction of the order problems created by the emergence of the "state" and the "economy" within European "society" and for the role of the "balance of power" and of the "unseen hand" as ordering devices, see Justin Rosenberg, *The Empire of Civil Society: A Critique of the Realist Theory of International Relations*, London: Verso, 1994.

But even more importantly, and sometimes only dimly perceived, there was a third problem: a change in the nature of power, which made the traditional strategies of dealing with change ineffective. Power increasingly depended more on industrial capacity and innovation than on territory per se. This made the task of balancing even harder, since one had to control the economic growth and innovative capacity of one's competitors. Only under the condition that key economic areas were adjacent to one's territory could one even consider incorporation, as France tried with the Saar and the Rhineland. Otherwise punitive discriminatory measures seemed to be the only means of reinsuring oneself against future challenges. Thus, it is not surprising that the post-war plans of all the major powers after World War I considered a mixture of territorial changes and discriminatory economic measures. This tendency was reinforced by the realization that the tremendous sacrifices of the war made a return to normalcy more unlikely the longer the hostilities continued. Consequently, when the war was not over as expected in a few weeks or months, most foreign offices engaged in speculations on how this quandary could be solved.

In Germany, Chancellor Bethmann-Hollweg's memorandum, written on September 9, 1914, and popularized by Fritz Fischer as the ominous *Septemberprogramm*, has become notorious.[62] In Fischer's view, this memorandum had "codified" German war goals. Although modern research suggests that Fischer's original thesis is open to serious challenge, these objections do not refute the wider logic underlying a variety of expansionist German designs.[63] In France, Etienne Clementel, the minister for industry and commerce, engaged in similar planning exercises in 1915. His proposal envisaged the return of Alsace-Lorraine to France, a regime of control over the Saar and Luxembourg, and a customs union with Belgium and Italy in order to cement France's economic hold on western Europe.[64] Encouraged by the Czar, who predicted the collapse and disintegration of the Reich,[65] the French position became increasingly punitive as the war went on.

In Britain, discussions about economic security took longer to shape up,[66] since here the conflict between the goals of economic security – through

---

[62] See Fritz Fischer, *Griff nach der Weltmacht: die Kriegszielpolitik des kaiserlichen Deutschland 1914/18*, Düsseldorf: Droste, 1961.

[63] See e.g. from a French perspective an even-handed assessment in Georges-Henri Soutou, *L'Or et le sang: Les buts de guerre économiques de la première guerre mondiale*, Paris: Fayard, 1989.

[64] See Georges-Henri Soutou, "Die Kriegsziele des Deutschen Reiches" in Wolfgang Michalka (ed.), *Der Erste Weltkrieg: Wirkung, Wahrnehmung, Analyse*, München: Piper, 1994, 28–53.

[65] Horst Günther Linke, "Russlands Weg in den Ersten Weltkrieg und Seine Kriegsziele 1914–1918" in Michalka, *Der Erste Weltkrieg*, 1994, 54–94.

[66] See Matthias Peter, "Britische Kriegsziele und Friedensvorstellungen" in Michalka (ed.), *Der Erste Weltkrieg*, 1994, 95–124.

control of and discrimination against Germany – and the aim of re-establishing British commercial and financial preponderance was painfully obvious. After all, reaching the latter goal depended on the revival of intra-European trade and on the maintenance of a liberal economic order. Only the Inter-Allied Conference on economic relations of June 1916 resolved this conflict, but it did so by giving precedence to security. Close economic cooperation among the Entente countries was linked to the continuation of discriminatory measures against Germany after the war. In April 1917, the Imperial War Committee, "having due regard to the interests of our Allies," pleaded for the introduction of an imperial preference system and thus laid the foundation for transforming the Empire into an economic bloc. When, in addition, in 1918 London finally accepted the policy that reparations from Germany should finance a revival of the British economy, ideas of European economic reconstruction and a return to a liberal trading order were doomed.

The rest of the story is well known. For a while, the informal recycling scheme let Germany pay its reparations with US loans, so that Great Britain and France could pay their debts to the US. But German failure to repay led to the occupation of the Rhineland, thereby creating new scores, as the pursuit of security had entirely subverted the idea that the economy was a self-regulating system of private exchanges. Besides, the structural issue of how a general recovery could be achieved was never faced. On the one hand, reparations could be extracted from the vanquished only if their economy performed, but security also made discrimination against that very country necessary, jeopardizing, in turn, Germany's capacity to earn the sums necessary to meet its bills.

The crash of 1929 ended all illusions. The radical delinking from the world economy and the erection of economic blocs were the result. The Schachtian system of bilateral economic relations based on barter and non-convertible currencies was one (exploitative) answer to the economic crisis, as was, in a different way, the Imperial Preference Tariff. Beggar-thy-neighbor policies, pursued by states in the absence of international cooperation, were designed to place the burden of unemployment on others, as states scrambled to find solutions for the realization of the new state goal: full employment.

Only during the planning phase for the post-World War II order did US decision-makers hit upon a solution that allowed for the welfare state, a liberal international economic order, and a security arrangement allowing for prosperity instead of a policing of economic strength.[67] Through the organizational

---

[67] For the seminal analysis of an order resulting in "embedded liberalism" after World War II see John Ruggie,"International Regimes, Transactions and Change: Embedded Liberalism in the Postwar Economic Order," *International Organization*, 36:2 (1982): 379–415.

implements of multilateralism, structures were created that made domestic and international structures compatible,[68] and they also solved the externalities that otherwise result from uncoordinated unilateral actions. Economies flowing from the complementary endowments in resources were also utilized through the encouragement of integration (rather than unilateral control of entire sectors), for which the High Authority of the European Coal and Steel Community was given special powers. Loans and grants, rather than reparations, provided the initial capital for putting war-torn countries back on track

It is not possible to provide here a comprehensive account of the historical developments in this area that led to a period of unprecedented peace and prosperity. For the present purposes it is sufficient to point out that the system functioned perhaps as much due to fortuitous circumstances as by design, but this happy coincidence did not last forever. Nevertheless, it entailed an unexpected bonus. Deterrence "worked" during the Cold War, and at its end notions that a "common security" and non-provocative military postures could replace it. Furthermore, there was even a short period in which hopes for a "New World" order were voiced and a new "constitutional moment" seemed around the corner.

Unfortunately, it did not happen for reasons briefly adumbrated in the previous chapter. It will be the task of the next few chapters to investigate further why the existing and invented practices have disappointed our hopes for such a new constitutional moment before we address in the last two chapters why instead we face now a world in which supposedly atavistic notions have "returned," ranging from nationalism to articulating common projects no longer in a political but in a religious vocabulary.

Obviously, this "evidence" does not imply that nothing has changed in politics, and that after some periods of random walks we are coming back to the "normalcy" of politics that realists have always "predicted." Rather, when viewed systemically, it raises precisely the question on the basis of which criteria the units or systems populating the global sphere are or should be differentiated, and which organizational forms between hierarchy and anarchy, between inclusions and exclusions, are going to develop in the future. That politics will increasingly revolve around membership questions is suggested by the force of mass migrations, and by the radical challenge posed by millenarian movements. We should therefore perhaps ponder more carefully Benedict Anderson's astute observation, made long before the disintegration of the

---

[68] On the link between the regulatory state emerging from the New Deal and the organizational design of the Bretton Woods system, see Anne-Marie Burley, "Regulating the World: Multilateralism, International Law, and the Projection of the New Deal Regulatory State" in Ruggie (ed.), *Multilateralism Matters*, 1993, 125–156.

Soviet Union, that in nearly every country there is a tomb of the Unknown Soldier, but none of the unknown Marxist,[69] or – one could add – of the "unnamed humanitarian." Nevertheless, what even these brief remarks also show is that there are too many sources of change at work that can no longer be pressed into the idyll of communitarianism or into a "realism" that is nostalgic about the Cold War and wants to go "back to the future." The failure to address issues of transformative change is therefore not a minor glitch, but rather calls into question the adequacy of our conceptual toolbox.

3.4   Conclusion

This chapter was concerned with the role of norms in constituting political life, in particular with the changing nature of sovereignty, which served me as a paradigm for transformative change.

I began with Bodin's classical text and showed two distinct strands in his (and also the subsequent) treatment of sovereignty. One strand emphasizes the "will" element, while the other focuses on the institutional framework within which sovereign powers must be exercised.

The following discussion explored the latter, for which the property/sovereignty analogy (*dominium*) served as my foil for both the development of the state and of the "system" conceived as an aggregate of exclusive zones of jurisdiction. This then set the stage for the discussion of transformative change that occurred when jurisdictional claims overlapped and territoriality was no longer the only, or even predominant, basis for claiming jurisdiction. This development not only made "rules of conflict" necessary (private international law), it also raised issues of the *ordre public* and of the (in)sufficiency of managing the international system through diplomacy, wars, and peace congresses. Increasingly, at some of the congresses after system-wide wars, "constitutional" issues came to the fore, which spawned new institutions. In this context I focused on two such transformative moments: the settlement at Versailles and the creation of the UN.

The last few remarks were devoted to raising the question of why such a new "constitutional moment" after the end of the Cold War could not be realized, particularly since both the capabilities for global solution seem better than ever before and also the information revolutions have created a probably unprecedented awareness throughout the world of "common problems" that require political solutions. Instead, we seem to observe the "return" of a politics of power that realists claim to have always "predicted," but which less

---

[69] Benedict Anderson, *Imagined Communities: Reflections on the Origin and Spread of Nationalism*, London: Verso, 1983, at 10.

committed observers fear might be an even further throwback to a fundamentalism familiar from religious war. However, before we are ready to place our bets – and agree with one or the other interpretation – it becomes necessary to further assess the state of existing practices and their functionality and shortcomings before we return, in the last two chapters, to an assessment of the changes for politics. It is the task of the next four chapters to do just that.

4 Showing

4.1 Introduction

In one of the most dramatic scenes of the tragedy *The Libation Bearers* (*Choephoroi*), Aeschylus lets the protagonist of this drama, Orestes, exit the palace, where he just has slain both his mother Clytemnestra and her lover Aegistos. This was in revenge for the murder of Agamemnon, Orestes' father, whom his mother had slain on his return from the Trojan War. Those events had been the subject of the first drama of the Aeschylean trilogy (*Agamemnon*). In the opening scene of the second drama, *The Libation Bearers*, Orestes had returned from exile to avenge his father, and now he confronts the audience, represented by the chorus, by trying to "name" what has just happened. In doing so he points to bloody pieces of clothing and entreats the chorus to become a witness. His attempts "to show" – instead of hiding the bloody deed which has taken place in the palace – are part of a wider framework in which what happens is related to deeds and events long before the present "deed" occurs and the protagonist's fate hangs in the balance. To that extent Orestes' compulsion to "show" is not accidental, since *dike*, the Greek word for "justice," derives from the verb "to show" (*deiknymi*).

ORESTES: Come all and see this sight. These two oppressed the land, murdered my father, plundered my inheritance.

In life they shared one dignity, one throne one love; Now with that dignity, that love, they share one death.

They swore one oath to kill my father miserably; likewise to die together. Both these oaths are kept.

Orestes points to a blood stained robe.

See too this evidence, your judges of my case: that neat device, the snare in which they trapped my father

Fettered and pinioned hand and foot *(To attendants)* Come spread it out! See this was used to truss a man . . .

104

Let the father see this thing – not mine but him whose eye beholds all deeds on earth:
Let the sun see this horror that was my mother's work! ...

CHORUS: No man may hope to spend his life untouched by pain and favored to the end.
Some grieves are with us now; others again time and the gods will send.

ORESTES: Now listen! At this moment I am like a man driving a team of horses and not
knowing where the gallop's going to end. My wits chafe at the rein under my weakened
grip, and carry me off the course.

Terror begins to sing at my heart and set it dancing with anger

Therefore, while I am still in my right mind,

To all who are loyal to me I solemnly proclaim: It was no sin to kill my mother, who
was herself

Marked with my father's blood ...

I offer in full warrant Apollo Loxias, who from his Pythean oracle revealed to me

That if I did this deed I should be clear of blame;

If I neglect it – I will not tell the penance

...

See what I do now. Framed with this branch this wreath

I will go as suppliant to Apollo's holy ground ...

As for this act

I call upon all the Argive men in time to come

To bear me witness, that the death she suffered here was not inflicted in mere
ruthlessness.[1]

The rest of the story unfolds in the third drama of the trilogy, the *Eumenides*.
Orestes goes to Delphi and is commanded by Apollo to go to Athens to submit
to a trial. On that occasion the Olympian Gods Apollo and Athena plead for
him, in the name of the *dike* of an all-seeing Zeus, while the Furies, the spirits
of revenge, make their case for retaliation. At the decisive moment – when the
popular assembly serving as a court votes on the verdict – Athena casts the
decisive vote absolving Orestes and thus also invalidating the old law of
blood revenge. But Athena through persuasion also accomplishes a change

---

[1] Aeschylus, *Choephori* in *The Oresteian Trilogy: Agamemnon, the Choephori, the Eumenides*,
trans. Philip Vellacott, Harmondsworth: Penguin Books, 1959, ll. 973–1019.

in the Furies. They now become servants of the new law of Zeus – *dike* – that supplants the old *themis* of self-help, requiring blood-revenge.

This transformation of law becomes perhaps clearest when we consider the changed role of the chorus in the three plays. It not only functions as an enunciator of traditional wisdom, but also as an interpreter of the deeds of the protagonists, or as a narrator who often provides the background context for the play.[2] Basic, however, is its function as a "witness." Already in the *Agamemnon* part of the trilogy Clytemnestra has triumphantly paraded before the chorus the net, which she had cast over Agamemnon to render him defenseless[3] in order to kill him, while justifying her action as the proper revenge for the death of their daughter whom Agamemnon had sacrificed before his departure to Troy. In *Agamemnon* the chorus just helplessly comments on Clytemnestra's repeated entreaties:

CHORUS: Where, where lies Right? Reason despairs her powers. Mind numbly ropes, her quick resources spent. Our throne endangered and disaster near: Where can I turn?[4]

In the *Eumenides* the chorus as the assembly of the people has, however, attained actor status as exemplified by its role in the trial before the popular assembly. Thus a new understanding of both law and politics becomes visible. As Christian Maier pointed out:

Orestes' acquittal is a victory for the polis as a whole over particularistic forces that are threatening to tear it apart – a triumph of justice over retribution, of freedom of decision over involvement in the vicious circle of vengeance . . .

What is effective here, in deliberate contrast with the archaic dispute that the Erinyes have conducted with Apollo and their primitive insistence on the upholding of their honor and their office, is the peaceful conciliation and the winning power of words, which the Greeks saw as the antithesis of violence . . .

According to Athena the success of *Peitho* (persuasion) represents a triumph of Zeus as the patron of the Agora: . . . the Zeus Agoraios has triumphed . . . The Agora that provided the citizen with a place and an opportunity to treat and argue with one another as citizens (that is politically) is presented here as instituted by Zeus; political controversy is presented as *agathon eris*, (the good quarrel) which ends in compromise.

Reconciliation with the dangerous defeated opponents not only brings peace; it also guarantees lasting blessings for the city, since the Erinyes by performing their new

---

[2] See e.g. Thomas G. Rosenmeyer, *The Art of Aeschylus*, Berkeley: University of California Press, 1982, especially chap. 6.

[3] For an interesting interpretation of the *Agamemnon* within the *Oresteia* see Mera J. Flaumenhaft, *The Civic Spectacle: Essays on Drama and Community*, Lanham, MD: Rowman & Littlefield, 1994.

[4] Aeschylus, *Agamemnon*, ll. 1530–1532.

office, will be able to ensure internal order. By assuming this task they become the Eumenides ("the well disposed").[5]

In a way the entire trilogy is then a story of the emergence of law, but it is not told as one of the emergence of centralized sanctions, or as one of the emancipation of the law from politics. True, the old order of blood feuds is overcome by the new *dike* of Zeus. But in the end stands not exclusion but incorporation, as the new law is not established through the effectiveness of sanctions but the new *dike* arises out of "showing" what is the case and by finding new procedures for it. Thus, there is more than an etymological link between this version of the rule of law and the nature of proofs.

To bring things out into the open seems not only to be a precondition of justice, there are also several other political benefits resulting from it, such as increased security, stability, and the empowerment of common people. It is therefore not surprising that high hopes are connected with higher transparency, as this is the precondition for both a sense of "security," as well as for holding someone accountable either for misdeeds or the improper use of discretion.

These points have been central to many of the contemporary debates within the field of IR. Given the absence of central law-enforcing institutions, "self-help" becomes possible if we can see what the "other" is up to, or perhaps we are also able to reconcile with one another if we have some form of proofs as to the benign nature of the other players' motivation.

This belief is not limited to trivial disputes: during the Cold War the effective use of "national means of verification," the various confidence-building measures, which often entailed notifications of troop movements and military exercises, led to successful arms control agreements, also easing the transitions after the demise of the Soviet Union.

Similarly, the reports of NGOs concerning blatant abuses of human rights have proved to be the bane of several dictatorial regimes, so much so that we seem almost to believe that "normative boomerangs" will hit those who deserve it and induce either a transformation of policy through naming and shaming, or bring obdurate perpetrators to justice. With the availability of better data and greater transparency, we are told, we could also manage our economies better and avoid financial crises. Finally, the commercial availability of an enormous amount of data,[6] which was not accessible to governments

---

[5] Christian Meier, *The Greek Discovery of Politics*, trans. David McLintock, Cambridge, MA: Harvard University Press, 1990, at 107f.

[6] For a discussion of the implications of the commercial availability of data from satellites, see John C. Baker, Kevin M. O'Connell, and Ray A. Williamson, *Commercial Observation Satellites: At the Leading Edge of Global Transparency*, Santa Monica, CA: Rand/ASPRS, 2001.

until recently,[7] will not only benefit the public by enabling more informed choices but – what most people seem to forget –will also decisively shift power from the "producers" of the data to the "owners."

The downside of these developments has been analyzed only recently. The earlier discussion was decidedly more optimistic, although different scholars emphasized different elements of the "transparency" problem. Oran Young focused more on the implications of the effectiveness of regimes,[8] while others, such as Picciotto[9] and van Ham,[10] placed more stress on the legitimacy aspect. Nevertheless, there seems to have been substantial agreement about the "virtues" of enhanced transparency, making the case for greater openness in the fight against governmental and private corruption and greater efficiency.[11]

Such assessments, however, usually overstate their case. Not only did the largest corruption scandals come after new accounting rules had been adopted by the US – i.e. they did little to stop the corruption – one could also immediately take issue with the argument that secrecy was characteristic of the old state order, which then is contrasted with the new "transparent order." After all, effective deterrence depended (even in the heyday of the Cold War) precisely *not* on secrecy because what you do not know and "see" cannot deter. To that extent, the present military posture, emphasizing again denial rather than deterrence, invites subterfuge and deception – such as the camouflaging of troops as "volunteers" and the use of surprise, as the Crimean conflict demonstrated despite the existing "transparency" created by the unprecedented use of electronic surveillance and data gathering by the NSA. Apparently, the "causal" chains linking transparency and secrecy to outcomes are a bit more complex than assumed.

The naïveté in regard to "transparency" derives less from the old liberal notion that more of a thing is always better, than from a misunderstanding of what data

---

7 Since the year 2000 there have been several commercial enterprises (around ten, ranging from Russian to French and Indian, Canadian American and joint Israeli–West Indian firms) that provide high-resolution, electronic-optical and radar imagery to private customers. For a discussion of the technologies and firms involved see Yahya A. Dehqanzada and Ann Florini, *Secrets for Sale: How Commercial Satellite Imagery Will Change the World*, Washington, DC: Carnegie Endowment for International Peace, 2000, 13–26.

8 Oran Young, "The Effectiveness of International Institutions: Hard Cases and Critical Variables" in James N. Rosenau and Ernst-Otto Czempiel (eds.), *Governance without Government: Order and Change in World Politics*, Cambridge: Cambridge University Press, 1992, 160–194.

9 Salomone Picciotto, "Democratizing Globalism" in Daniel Drache (ed.), *The Market of the Public Domain? Global Governance and the Asymmetry of Power*, London: Routledge, 2001, 335–359.

10 See The Hague Institute for Global Justice, and Netherlands Institute of International Relations Clingendael, "Special Report on Transnational Governance and Democratic Legitimacy," 2014. Available at www.clingendael.org.

11 See Ann Florini (ed.), *The Right to Know: Transparency for an Open World*, New York: Columbia University Press, 2007.

and facts are, and of how their constitution shapes their role in social life. Here a constructivist perspective and an inspiration taken from law are helpful. Constructivism suggests not focusing simply on what is being observed or given to the senses, but observing the observation, i.e. systematically inquiring *into the modi and procedures of transforming information (data) into knowledge* and of making it available for use. An empiricist understanding not only glosses over the problem of "interpretation" but also neglects the role of the scientific community in this process of knowledge generation and how the social processes of knowledge dissemination affects "trust" and "privacy," which are important elements for both social life and individual identity. Precisely because the data are not simply "there" but are "in the making," they are also vulnerable to misfires, attacks, and breakdowns.

In law, as we have seen, the discovery of facts – more precisely their "establishment" – involves appraisals, such as whether or not e.g. the famous *mens rea* principle has been satisfied. Such appraisals are the results of following certain procedures rather than relying on mere observations. However, given our common naïve understandings of the "world," we are mostly prone to identify law with enforcement, as the latter seems most germane for ordering. But such a view fails to realize that law's major function is its *prospective* ordering rather than its remedial aspect that follows *ex post* when a norm has been transgressed.

It speaks indeed to the genius of Aeschylus that he understood that especially in times of transitions the procedures for assessment necessarily become "political," requiring a politics that is informed by a special mode of deliberation. "Justice" can then no longer exhaust itself in simple retribution, in the exercise of power, or even in the permanent exclusion of those who have brought guilt upon themselves by breaking the law (wandering from city to city). It is this last problem which students of transitions, and of attempts at reintegrating societies rent by widespread horrendous crimes and civil wars, have come to appreciate.[12] Such a perspective on law reminds us of three things relevant to our topic: first, that a procedural understanding of "transparency" is necessary, second, that we must pay special attention to the close connections between law and politics, and third that transparency and accountability are only contingently related.

With these initial remarks in mind I want to develop my argument in the following way: In Section 4.2, I probe somewhat more deeply into the conceptual issues of transparency. The method I shall follow here is not to begin with a definition of what transparency "really" (essentially?) *is*, but rather with

---

[12] See the seminal contribution of Ruti G. Teitel, *Transitional Justice*, Oxford: Oxford University Press, 2000. See also her collection of essays Ruti G. Teitel, *Globalizing Transitional Justice: Contemporary Essays*, Oxford: Oxford University Press, 2014.

an examination of the web of neighboring concepts and practices in which transparency is enmeshed. This exploration then should also disabuse us of the notion that greater transparency involves just "casting more light" on the facts, which are "out there" anyway. Instead, I claim that it is more appropriate to examine those issues in the way of the "witness" conception of the Greek tragedy referred to above. This prevents us from also making a related mistake by believing that the only way of getting at the "truth" or rather to the bottom of things is to search for or discover universal laws, which "cover" our observations. Here, obviously, the call for more transparency is powerfully reinforced by the prejudice that "knowing" the social world requires procedures and criteria identical to those to which the sciences and their "theories" subject nature. Section 4.3 is a variation on this theme, examining issues of observation and inspection, focusing on the strategic aspects of disclosures that give rise to gross misperceptions on the part of the observer and the observed. This discussion is continued in Section 4.4 (ritual dances and self-fulfilling prophecies). In Section 4.5, I investigate the problems of "reports" propagated by the media in order to "inform" the public, with particular attention to the argument of the emergence of a "global public" as a means of control and legitimization. I argue that most discussions concerning "transparency" actually are speaking to issues of responsibility on which the "global public" cannot make good. A brief summary (Section 4.6) concludes the chapter.

4.2   The Issues of Transparency

Let us begin our discussion with the traditional argument for transparency. This will allow us to appreciate the notion that data are not just "out there" but are always in need of interpretation, and that often requires their assessment in the light of norms. While realists have focused on sanctions, adherents of the regime approach have emphasized that prior to the application of any sanction by an actor or institution, a "violation" of a relevant norm has to be discovered and established. This can lead to a variety of tradeoffs between these different parts of the compliance mechanism and thus establishes the need to interpret the data, and to assess the gravity of a violation. Thus, e.g., often the transgression of a norm has to be "material," in order to "count" as a violation (as e.g. in contract law, or in international law, where even in the case of an "attack" – which must be armed – an *animus belli gerendi* is required). These brief initial remarks have two implications for the interpretation of data and warrant a more detailed discussion.

First, both the pure theory of law and that of realism exaggerate the role of sanctions and depreciate the role that norms play in the wider social setting. Rather than "working" through making good on their threatened sanctions, norms are first of all important as benchmarks, since without marking some actions as a genuine "violation" no sanction could work, *as it could not be perceived as such*. Rather a sanctioning act would be indistinguishable from a random act of violent or hurtful behavior without much purpose.

A second issue within the penumbra of transparency concerns the role of the fear of being "found out" that might in itself often serve as a sufficient deterrent, even if the probability of becoming the target of explicit sanctions later on is rather low. Of course, one could argue that this fear of discovery already represents the "sanction." Although there is something to this argument, such an extension is, however, somewhat misleading. As already shown by Schelling a few decades ago, compelling someone by meting out punishment is something different from deterring him.[13] On the other hand seeing the two concepts in splendid isolation because of their analytical distinctiveness will not do either. As Kenneth Waltz once put it so bluntly, "In politics force is said to be the *ultima ratio*. In international politics force serves not only as the *ultima ratio*, but as the first and constant one."[14] The point here is not the hyperbole which characterizes so much of Waltz's writings but the probably unintended Freudian slip, i.e. the link to a "reason" (*ratio*), which indicates that a focus on force and coercion alone is likely to derail analysis and lead to an entirely unjustified overestimation of the effectiveness of force.

Consider in this context the *ultima ratio* argument. As Napoleon is said to have stated: "There are a lot of things you can do with bayonets, but only one thing you cannot do: you cannot sit on them." Similarly, Clausewitz's dictum that war is politics by other means suggests that force cannot be the "fundament" of politics. If it is supposed to serve any purpose at all and is not pursued for its own sake, it has to be a means to some political end. As the Palestinians and Israelis, or the American troops in Baghdad, have found out, it is certainly not the lack of force that has made for a disastrous situation in both those cases, and thus the distinction between "ultimate," and "first and foremost reason" seems beside the point. As Oran Young has pointed out:

The role of enforcement as a basis of compliance is regularly exaggerated ... any society compelled to rely on enforcement as the principal means of ensuring compliance would quickly find itself facing both financial and moral bankruptcy.[15]

The usual fallback is then to argue that sanctions work differently when they are applied to high politics issues (ineffective) as opposed to low politics issues (possibly effective) As a less ideological analysis discloses, the record is rather mixed. Contrary to our commonsense expectations we see that some tough

---

[13] See Thomas Schelling, *The Strategy of Conflict*, Cambridge, MA: Harvard University Press, 1980, chaps. 2 and 8.
[14] Waltz, *Theory of International Politics*, at 113.
[15] Young, "The Effectiveness of International Institutions," at 161.

issues involving high politics such as arms control, exemplified by the former SALT and START treaties, have led to institutionalized cooperation,[16] while welfare issues, such as sharing certain natural resources, have not only faltered because of distributional issues – as in the case of sharing the water of the big rivers in the Middle East – but because of intractable mistrust among the parties and the fragility of their political regimes. On the other hand, an agreement among some of the same mistrustful states was concluded establishing an environmental regime for the Mediterranean. However, it is also significant for our purposes that states have repeatedly insisted that e.g. "data" concerning pollution of the Mediterranean are reported only on an aggregate level,[17] obviously because in that way violations cannot directly be traced to a definitive actor and thus the opprobrium of a violation can be avoided. Finally, simple notifications ranging from the movement of dangerous chemicals[18] to twenty-four-hour advance notice for missile launches (as part of the SALT II and START agreements and arms control regimes),[19] or of troop movements and other military activities,[20] *were* – given certain circumstances – apparently sufficient to reassure others. In this way a change in the presumptions from

---

[16] See the Standing Consultative Commission created in 1972 by the Anti-Ballistic Missile Treaty (Art. VI) that was incorporated into the SALT I Treaty.

[17] See the "ten regions" created by the Barcelona Convention, which were used for a pollution assessment. Similarly only aggregate data are published under the reporting requirements of the Convention to protect the Rhine against Chemical Pollution, and the Montreal Convention reports only "consumption" data, not data on production, imports, and exports. For a further discussion see Chayes and Handler Chayes, *The New Sovereignty: Compliance with International Regulatory Agreements.*

[18] See Article 6 and Annex V of United Nations Environment Programme, *Basel Convention on the Control of Transboundary Movements of Hazardous Wastes and their Disposal* (22 March 1989). See also United Nations Environment Programme, *London Guidelines for the Exchange of Information on Chemicals in International Trade,* 15/30 (25 May 1989). It is interesting that the Rio declaration of the Earth Summit in 1992 included a notification consultation provision quasi as an "operationalization" of the good faith principle, thereby significantly modifying the ruling of the Lake Lanoux arbitration of 1957, which held that under international customary law no such obligation existed. For a general discussion of the notification problem in international environmental accords, see Elizabeth P. Barratt-Brown, "Building a Monitoring and Compliance Regime under the Montreal Protocol," *Yale Journal of International Law,* 16 (1991): 519.

[19] See Article XVI of United States and the Union of Soviet Socialist Republics *Treaty on the Limitation of Strategic Offensive Arms, together with Agreed Statements and Common Understanding Regarding the Treaty,* SALT II, Vienna, June 18, 1979. See also *Treaty on the Reduction and Limitation of Strategic Offensive Arms,* START I, Moscow, July 31,1991. See especially the Notifications Protocol, Sections VI–VII.

[20] See the CSBMS agreement 29-54, Document of the Stockholm Conference on Confidence and Security Building Measures and Disarmament in Europe, reprinted in United States Arms Control and Disarmament Agency, *Arms Control and Disarmament Agreements: Texts and Histories of the Negotiations,* Washington, DC: United States Arms Control and Disarmament Agency, 1990, 325–330.

which an actor makes his inferences (worst-case analysis) can prevent conflict escalation and perhaps even start a virtuous circle towards more cooperative solutions.

Since "showing" is supposed to lead to "knowing," the problem of transparency seems to presuppose some type of "common knowledge" that game theorists have identified as the crucial variable for cooperation. Similarly, contrary to the original *dystopic* vision popularized by Hardin in his "Tragedy of the Commons,"[21] Elinor Ostrom has shown that common resources can be managed satisfactorily – even when the assignment of exclusive property rights is not feasible, and frequently conditions of severe scarcity obtain – as long as the various actors can monitor each other's behavior. Her example is water use in the Central Basin of Los Angeles, where each party has to inform the water-master of his groundwater extraction and receives a report on the consumption of all other parties, which has been checked by several agencies.

Given the accuracy of the information and its ease of access, each pumper knows what everyone else is doing, and each knows that his or her own groundwater extractions will be known by all others. Thus the information available to the parties closely approximates the "common knowledge," so frequently necessary ... for solution to iterated dilemma games.[22]

Although I think that the last example is instructive of how institutions help overcome collective action problems I do not think that the alleged "solution," i.e. the creation of "common knowledge," is a useful shorthand for understanding all the issues that are bunched together in the concept of transparency. Some further discussion seems necessary.

Until now I have re-stated the traditional arguments for the importance of transparency: first, detecting the violation of a common norm is a precondition for influencing expectations and behavior via sanctions; second, the prospect of exposure, i.e. a transparent norm violation, can structure expectations independently of the retaliatory use of force (punishment).

This leads to a third point. The information sought by actors is usually something quite different from the data recorded from an objective position, which need only be checked and interpreted in accordance with some unproblematic background knowledge. Many "data" of the social world are embedded in a strategic context. This circumstance engenders two peculiar problems that go far beyond the difficulty of interpretation, or of simple checks against reality. Precisely because the significance of the data crucially depends on some unobservable intentions we connect with the observed behavior, we frequently need further clarification. This can be provided only if some form

---

[21] Garrett Hardin, "The Tragedy of the Commons," *Science*, 162 (1968): 1243–1248, at 1244.
[22] Ostrom, *Governing the Commons*, at 126.

of institutionalized dialogue is part of the regime. To that extent the above-mentioned Standing Consultative Committee (SCC) of the SALT I agreement was crucial for the survival of the regime, as it allowed the resolution of disputes concerning violations, such as the "camouflage" on US missile sites,[23] the suspected increase in Soviet Inter-continental Ballistic Missiles (ICBM) launching pads,[24] the use of encryption by the Soviets hampering verification, or the controversial Krasnoyarsk radar station.[25]

As the record shows, some disagreements could be resolved rather easily, while other issues, such as the Krasnoyarsk radar, had to wait for the surprising turn which US–Soviet relations took under Gorbachev. But even during the era of increased acrimony and hostility in the first Reagan administration – when the SCC became a rhetorical battleground – the delegates to these sessions were able to negotiate a series of understandings that prevented a regime breakdown. One such crucial element was the meaning of "testing in an ABM mode." Here, however, the argument can be made that it was ambiguity rather than clarification or increased transparency that "saved" the regime. The US chose to live with the lack of clarity, instead of falling back on a cumbersome amendment procedure by renegotiation. This leads to certain further paradoxes that call into question some of the alleged benefits that an increase in transparency promises, as the following examples show.

Consider in this context the issue of corruption, as it can – quite counter-intuitively – profit sometimes from greater transparency. The usual argument in favor of transparency is, of course, that it enhances the probability that wrongdoings are detected. But increased transparency frequently also improves outsiders' knowledge about the identity of key decision-makers and decision processes, thereby creating the incentives to establish special "connections" to the person who calls the shots. Instead of having e.g. to bribe several members of a committee under conditions of ignorance of the decision process, the briber might now have only one person to tempt. In other words, such a "connection-effect" might actually powerfully counteract the gains from increased transparency.[26]

Another paradox concerns the discrepancy which is common in appraising the nature of observed violations. As we know from the evolution of

---

[23] Raymond L. Garthoff, *Detente and Confrontation: American–Soviet Relations from Nixon to Reagan*, Washington, DC: Brookings Institution, 1994, at 513.

[24] United States Department of State, and Bureau of Public Affairs. *Compliance with SALT I Agreements*. Special Report no. 55, July 1979. See also Strobe Talbott, *Endgame: The Inside Story of Salt II*, New York: Harper & Row, 1980, at 143f.

[25] See e.g. Strobe Talbott, *Deadly Gambits: The Reagan Administration and the Stalemate in Nuclear Arms Control*, New York: Vintage Books, 1985.

[26] For an interesting discussion of this problem see Mehmet Bac, "Corruption, Connections and Transparency: Does a Better Screen Imply a Better Scene?" *Public Choice*, 107:1/2 (2001): 87–96.

cooperation literature, the establishment of self-reinforcing virtuous circles depends not only on the ability to detect but to isolate "bad apples" from the rest of the actors.[27] In spite of these arguments, in real life we do encounter the phenomenon that sometimes a single violation might be able to fundamentally alter the "normal" presumptions of the actors concerned (so to speak the violation has a benchmark or red line effect), although large-scale noncompliance might be compatible with interactions based on the presumption of "business as usual." Precisely because what something "is" depends in a strategic environment to a large extent on the appraisal of what the observations mean for the *pursuit of one's own plans*, even large-scale noncompliance by others need not necessarily lead to a breakdown of social interactions.

Similarly, the finding that most states have apparently a rather relaxed attitude towards their implementation of the reporting requirements (or even implementation of their obligations) under various regimes will perhaps come as no surprise, if we are aware that the failure to comply with reporting requirements does not usually lead to regime breakdowns. For example, a General Accounting Office (GAO) report on the implementation of the Montreal Protocol indicated that only sixty-five of the eighty-one members had filed the required reports of CFC consumption in 1990, and of those only twenty-nine were complete. The record of the inspection of vessels under the MARPOL regime seems hardly better and the same is true in the case of protecting wildlife[28] or human rights,[29] etc. Equally surprising is that even established and supposedly well-functioning states, such as Germany, are often laggard in implementing EU obligations,[30] which serves as a useful reminder that it is not only the environmental area – perhaps still considered by many a rather "exotic" sector – in which we notice such behavior. Here the "proxy nature" of transparency becomes obvious. What we are seeking is

[27] See e.g. Axelrod, *The Evolution of Cooperation*.
[28] The rate of reporting, however, rose significantly from a dismal 23 percent in 1985 to 38 percent in 1990 for MARPOL and OILPOL. See Ronald B. Mitchell, *Intentional Oil Pollution at Sea: Environmental Policy and Treaty Compliance*, Cambridge, MA: MIT Press, 1994, at 132. The corresponding figure for the Convention on International Trade in Endangered Species (CITES) is 24 percent.
[29] In a report by the UN Secretary General in 1992 concerning compliance with the reporting requirements of the seven human rights conventions a rather dismal record emerges. "Of the 164 states party to one or more of the treaties, substantially all were delinquent in at least one report, most were in arrears on several and 27 were behind on ten or more." Abram Chayes and Antonia Handler Chayes, *The New Sovereignty: Compliance with International Regulatory Agreements*, Cambridge, MA: Harvard University Press, 1995, at 161.
[30] Here the "infringement" cases in which the Commission institutes proceedings in the European Court for not implementing Community directives. See the two infringement cases of 2015 on failing to implement e-waste directives (May 28, 2015) and for violation in building a power plant (February 26, 2015), or failure to insure access to justice (in environmental disputes) Oct. 17, 2013. See also the recent failure (or rather suspension by Germany) of the Dublin rules in regard to migrants and refugees from outside the EU.

assurance, not necessarily information about the actual state of affairs. Consequently, as long as we do not feel that our individual or collective projects are threatened, we see no reason to take countermeasures or insist on greater "compliance." This is of course the reason for the inevitability of "intelligence failures" but also an antidote to vigilantism, which would make normal life all but impossible.

The important point here is that precisely because we are not entirely "transparent" even to ourselves – since we become what we are through the interaction with others – our plans and projects influence what we want to know and what we expect from others. But these expectations, in turn, are dependent on what we want to keep private or decide to disclose in varying degrees, or only after considerable time, depending on the nature of the connections we want to establish. For that reason we also need a protected space in which some things remain out of view. It is here that the potential totalitarianism of a certain form of liberalism becomes visible, which touts the ideal of "free knowledge" procured by indiscriminate access to all types of information. It is after all not accidental that our great liberal Bentham was also the inventor of the Panopticon! And it is furthermore cold comfort that such "transparency" fantasies were originally a domain reserved for the legislator, who as procurer of general happiness needed that information for his felicific calculus. In the meantime, such goals are, however, also eagerly pursued by private companies and (a-)social media, sometimes even by governments and corporations in partnership. If we had once believed that *la douce commerce* would refine people and give the civilizational project the necessary push, we have had to learn that the business with a "profile" of everybody's preferences might actually end civilization, since we all suspect instinctively that someone, who wants to know everything, no matter what, is likely to be up to no good.

The upshot of the discussion of these paradoxes is that they do not confirm the classical argument of "cheating" as the main obstacle to cooperation, and its flipside, that of transparency insuring it. As we can see, noncompliance per se does not automatically set off the alarm bells, leading to a change in decision premises. Rather than jumping the gun, states (like individual actors) are unlikely to be alarmed unless they feel threatened and unless their assurance is shaken by some "serious" incidence of noncompliance. This holds especially when they find out that often failure to report is simply due to other states' lack of capacity. Thus, states have even been willing to subsidize their noncompliant members, by helping those lacking the necessary staff to build up the necessary personnel and expertise.[31] Cases of willful, systematic, and persistent deception exist, but are, perhaps surprisingly, not that problematic.

[31] See e.g. United Nations Environment Programme, and the Ozone Secretariat, *The Montréal Protocol on Substances that Deplete the Ozone Layer* (September 16, 1987) and United

Although such cases occur, or certain actions and events might be considered alarming, the larger picture corrects the paranoia which some realists are taking as normal and base their "theory" on: because there is always a possibility that things might get out of hand, states allegedly prefer non-cooperation to cooperation in order to insure themselves. But this is just silly because whether I need insurance, or how much of it, cannot be read off from the existence of a "possibility" but has to be derived from an assessment of a "risk," which has something to do with actual experience, such as some knowledge about a distribution, as well as with my own risk propensity and that of others.

4.3   Observations and Inspections

The discussion above placed the transparency argument within a wider framework and examined some of the paradoxes that we encounter in enhancing compliance and providing assurances. One way of dealing with the resulting problems of getting the necessary data and of assessing their significance is to ask for specific inspections by a group of observers. "Observation" has been a time-honored institution in the European state system. Military attachés were part of the diplomatic corps, and special invitations to military exercises were designed to reassure or to warn other states by an *ad oculos* demonstration. The power of "inspection" was also often given to a neutral party, such as the Red Cross (to visit and monitor Prisoner of War (POW) camps), or a truce supervisory commission. But inspection attained perhaps the great saliency in the proposals for an Atomic Development Authority of the Baruch Plan (March 1946). The provisions would not only have vested this body with the general control of the nuclear stockpile and all nuclear energy activities, it also instituted a far-reaching (and according to US law, probably unconstitutional) intrusive inspection regime of civilian and military facilities connected with nuclear research and development.

While "observation" depends on the parameters set by the inviting state(s), "inspection" provides for more autonomy of the investigators, particularly when they are entitled to demand a "special" inspection, as e.g. the International Atomic Energy Agency (IAEA) regime allows. The Antarctica regime, e.g., also entitles the contracting parties to undertake such special inspections themselves. Unusually intrusive were the bilateral inspection regimes of the

Nations, *Convention on Biological Diversity*, Rio de Janeiro, June 5, 1992. Both provide for funds to "meet all agreed incremental costs of developing countries which are parties to the Protocol." See United Nations Environment Programme, *Amendment to the Montreal Protocol on Substances that Deplete the Ozone Layer* (London Amendment, June 29, 1990). See also chap. 37 of the United Nations Conference on Environment and Development, *Agenda 21, Rio Declaration, Forest Principles*, New York: United Nations, 1992.

118   Showing

Intermediate-Range Nuclear Forces (INF) and START treaties, or the "challenge" inspections[32] that have become part of the Chemical Weapons Convention.

It is, of course, not possible here to give a comprehensive account of all these different inspections, but a few numbers show that inspection has indeed become part of our international practice in both the "soft" as well as the "hard" areas. To get an idea one has only to realize that START I, which entered into force on December 5, 1994 (signed July 31, 1991), provided for eighty-two different notifications and twelve different kinds of on-site inspection, in order to accomplish the elimination of one-third of US nuclear forces and up to 40 percent of Russian strategic nuclear weapons systems. The regime was to remain in force until 2009.[33] Within the INF Treaty verification regime, 811 inspections (540 US in the former Soviet Union, and 311 Russian in the US and at US bases in England, Germany, and Italy) have been conducted over thirteen years.[34] In the US a special agency was created for these missions. The Cooperative Threat Reduction Program between the US and Russia (and some other successor states) ranges from quick fixes to help.

The Chemical Weapons Convention (in force since 1997) lists close to eighty thousand facilities around the world that have to be inspected.[35] It is clear that such an enormous task can be handled only with drastically reduced spot-checks. Here the often preferred method is to rely on sampling, assuming that the best way of finding out about the "state of the world" is to rely on a statistical technique. Such a short cut assumes, of course, that we are dealing here with a "normal distribution" of cases. But this leaves out precisely the one very important factor, i.e. that of intention. As the IAEA has to supervise all Nuclear Proliferation Treaty (NPT) states, much of the time of their inspectors is used up e.g. by the inspections of European countries – which are unlikely to engage in a secret nuclear weapons program – instead of focusing on the small number of problematic threshold powers with nuclear aspirations.

[32] A challenge-inspection was defined as a demand by a party "for an inspection solely for the purpose of resolving any questions concerning possible non-compliance" (Art. IX) The inspection must, however, be announced to the state where the inspection takes place twelve hours in advance and state authorities must get the inspectors within thirty-six hours to the perimeters of the facility to be inspected. The inspection team is provided by the Organization for the Prevention of Chemical Warfare.

[33] Avis Bohlen, "The Rise and Fall of Arms Control," *Survival*, 453 (2003):7–34, at 29.

[34] Part of the regime came to an end in 2002. The missions concern the destruction of INF missiles, i.e. Pershing I and II, as well as the BGM 109 (ground launch cruise missile on the US side totaling 846 US systems and SS-5, SS-12, SS-20, and SS-23 on the Russian side, totaling 1,846 Russian systems). See United States and the Union of Soviet Socialist Republics, *Treaty on the Elimination of their Intermediate-Range and Shorter-Range Missiles*, INF, Washington, DC, December 8, 1987.

[35] See Chayes and Handler Chayes, *The New Sovereignty: Compliance with International Regulatory Agreements*, at 190.

This leads me back to a third paradox mentioned only in passing above: "intelligence failures"[36] which can be induced by transparency and the perverse effects that "crying wolf" once too often may have. The best examples of the first side of the paradox are the Israeli intelligence failure in the Yom Kippur War[37] and Iraq's ability to hide its weapons program while inspectors roamed all over the country. The second part of the paradox is exemplified by the second "intelligence" failure in respect of the existence of weapons of mass destruction before the Second Gulf War.

Consider first the strategy of lulling the enemy, i.e. clouding the information by hiding it in a lot of "chaff" or by propagating demonstrably false information. Thus, Israeli military intelligence had very well registered the Egyptian mobilization in the Sinai several times during 1976. But they trusted the superiority of their air force, which made an Egyptian victory unlikely; having seen the same pattern of mobilization before, the general staff concluded that Egypt wanted once more to disrupt Israeli economic life through a costly mobilization.[38] Furthermore, because of the belief that an attack would only be made if Egypt had a chance of winning, Israeli decision-makers did not consider the possibility of a more limited objective, such as bringing some movement into a situation which President Sadat of Egypt considered an untenable stalemate.[39] Consequently, no dramatic countermeasures were taken when Egypt once more massed its troops on the borders, but this time for the purpose of an attack. Similarly, General Westmoreland discounted the Tet Offensive because such a move had been predicted in all the years before, but had never materialized.[40]

Two more recent intelligence failures concern Iraq, and each is actually the flipside of the other. While in the first case the lack of evidence was the result of a masterful deception program (the "weapons" were there right under the noses of the inspectors), the lack of evidence for the existence of such weapons in the second case assumed that – on the basis of past experience – those weapons *must have been* there but had not been found yet. The explanations not only of the Iraqi regime but also of the inspectors "proved" only that the

---

[36] On the general problem of intelligence failures, see Richard Betts, "Analysis, War, and Decision: Why Intelligence Failures Are Inevitable," *World Politics*, 31:2 (1978): 61–89; Gerald W. Hopple, "Intelligence and Warning: Implications and Lessons of the Falkland Islands War," *World Politics*, 36:3 (1984): 339–361.

[37] See the discussion in Lebow and Gross Stein, *We All Lost the Cold War*, especially chap. 7.

[38] Among the voluminous literature on the outbreak of the Yom Kippur War, see Avi Shlaim, "Failures in National Intelligence Estimates: The Case of the Yom Kippur War," *World Politics*, 28:3 (1976): 348–380; Michael I. Handel, "The Yom Kippur War and the Inevitability of Surprise," *International Studies Quarterly*, 21:3 (1977): 461–502.

[39] See the important analysis by Lebow and Gross Stein, *We All Lost the Cold War*, chaps. 7–11.

[40] William C. Westmoreland, *A Soldier Reports*, Garden City, NY: Doubleday, 1976, at 75.

opponent was devilishly clever in hiding them. Both cases show the pathologies in dealing with information in strategic contexts and they point at the same
time to the importance of historical experiences, which "frame" the data we
gather in the hope of enhancing our security by knowing what the opponent
is doing.

As is well known, the Iraqi concealment of a nuclear weapons program (the
first intelligence failure) came to light only in 1995 with the defection of
Saddam Hussein's son-in-law, Lt. General Hussein Kamal. His revelations
took not only the public but also even the experts and the respective national
intelligence organizations by surprise, and marked the beginning of a period of
increasing confrontation between UNSCOM and the Iraqi government. Iraq
had managed to hide three major uranium enrichment programs, had employed
a workforce of about twenty thousand in this clandestine program, had established a worldwide net for procuring the needed technologies, involving firms
in Brazil, Pakistan, the US, France, Switzerland, Germany, Italy, Japan, etc.,[41]
and was even testing weapons components and delivery systems – all while
remaining a member in good standing of the NPT regime, passing the twice-
yearly inspection by the IAEA with flying colors! As David Kay reports:

Contrary to assertions now made that IAEA inspectors were familiar with its declared
civilian program, the IAEA inspectors, who visited Iraq's Tuwaitha Nuclear Research
Center every six months, never looked beyond the narrow confines of the three "material balance areas," where declared nuclear materials were held, never even asked what
might be going on in one of the other seventy plus buildings, where declared nuclear
materials were held, lack of curiosity that we know emboldened the Iraqis to an
extraordinary level of brazenness.[42]

Three factors seem to account for most of the failure, of which two concern
the organizational culture which the IAEA had developed. On the one hand,
the mindset of the inspectors seems to have been formed by a highly legalistic
approach and an attempt at being scientific and objective. As Larry Scheinman
pointed out, the mindset "was based on the verification of what was declared
by the states as representing inspectable sites, which were specified by legal
agreement. Asking too many questions was said to lead to difficulty with the
state and ultimately at headquarters."[43] How problematic such a policy of
"cooperation" can be was evidenced by a visit of the IAEA team in Iran. Once

[41] See R. Jeffrey Smith and Glenn Frankel, "Saddam's Nuclear Weapons Dream: A Lingering
Nightmare," *Washington Post*, October 13, 1991, A1, A44–45.
[42] David Kay, "The IAEA: How Can It Be Strengthened?" in Mitchell Reiss and Robert Litwak
(eds.), *Nuclear Proliferation after the Cold War*, Washington, DC: Woodrow Wilson Center
Press, 1994, 309–334, at 314.
[43] Lawrence Scheinman and Atlantic Council of the United States, *Assuring the Nuclear
Non-Proliferation Safeguards System*, Washington, DC: Atlantic Council of the United States,
1992, at 27.

the inspectors declared after their return that they were "able to see everything they had wanted to" and that there had been "no limitation to access." As it turned out, the team had been led to a *totally different facility* instead of the one they had asked to visit. Having no GPS system as part of their inspection instruments – as the UNSCOM inspectors later had in Iraq – the team was apparently simply duped.[44]

On the other hand, the mindset seems to have been influenced by focusing virtually exclusively on the crucial "materials" which had to be accounted for, instead of putting things into a wider political context. This operationalization of the mission was a disastrous short cut, typical of bureaucratic tunnel vision. Despite the ever-increasing accuracy of the reports concerning the declared materials, the reports could not see the wood for the trees. Finally, as both the Iraqi and the North Korean cases,[45] but also the more recent Pakistani example, show, the decisive "breaks" in achieving some transparency came usually only after the defection of an official who turned whistleblower, or when a source of "human intelligence" put things in context. This, of course, does not mean that human intelligence, i.e. spies, etc., are simply superior – on the contrary they often are notoriously wrong or report only "chaff" – but it does mean that "getting it right" means more than just "seeing something," as the term transparency suggests. It means that one has to see the data as part of a whole gestalt and that requires operations going far beyond seeing, even seeing something clearly.

This circumstance also explains the second intelligence failure mentioned above, the "weapons of mass destruction" which could not be found after the US Forces had entered Baghdad.[46] While e.g. the Secretary of State was seeing decontamination vehicles in the satellite photos, some of the UN inspectors who had been at the sites saw only water trucks.[47] But given Baghdad's dismal record with inspections, virtually no evidence could now assure the US administration. After all, of almost two dozen "full, final, and complete disclosures" which the Saddam regime had filed over a decade, all of them subsequently

[44] Kay, "The IAEA: How Can It Be Strengthened?" at 318.
[45] Apparently the US became aware of North Korea's underground nuclear facility in Backchon county only after the defection of a North Korean diplomat in May 1991. See Jeffrey T. Ritchelson, "Can the Intelligence Community Keep Pace with the Threat?" in Mitchell Reiss and Robert Litwak (eds.), *Nuclear Proliferation after the Cold War*, Washington, DC: Woodrow Wilson Center Press, 1994, 291–308, at 300.
[46] For a critical assessment of the US policy to resort to force, questioning the official rationale and the National Intelligence Estimate (Oct. 2002) buttressing this policy, see Joseph Cirincione, Jessica T. Mathews, and George Perkovich, *WMD in Iraq: Evidence and Implications*, Washington, DC: Carnegie Endowment for International Peace, 2004.
[47] See Jessica T. Mathews, "Inspectors Had the Real WMD Clues," *Financial Times*, February 9, 2004, 15.

had turned out to be false! As Chantal de Jonge Oudraat suggests having reviewed the record:

In April 1991 Iraq declared that it had 11,500 chemical shells and 1000 tons of nerve and mustard gas. It declared 52 SCVUD missiles with 30 chemical and 23 conventional high-explosive warheads. It denied that it had any biological or nuclear materials that would fall under UN Sec Council Res. 687 (1991). Within three months inspectors found 46,000 chemical shells – four times the declared number. By October 1991 100,000 chemical shells had been discovered – ten times what Iraq had declared. Elements of a non-declared nuclear programme were discovered after two months. Most of Iraq's biological weapon programme was discovered only in 1995.[48]

The cat-and-mouse game, which began with declaring a thousand sites "presidential palaces" while claiming later, when UNSCOM inspections finally got tougher, that no one in Iraq even possessed adequate maps of them,[49] need not be rehearsed here again. Rather it is clear that inspection and transparency fail when the inspected party refuses to cooperate and is not interested in giving assurances. It is indeed cold comfort to realize that some of the denials by Saddam Hussein before the Second Gulf War were apparently mostly accurate.

4.4   Ritual Dances and Self-Fulfilling Prophecies

Although Saddam Hussein's regime was one of the most determined to obstruct the attempts at surveillance – in that it had set up a separate machinery to deceive the inspectors of UNSCOM[50] and had tried to intimidate them by launching grenades into their compound[51] – the problem of deliberately evading international surveillance is not restricted to some rogue states. Given the strategic incentives in such situations, substituting "other reporting" for "self-reporting" not only transforms inspectors into detectives, but inspection

---

[48] Chantal de Jonge Oudraat, "UNSCOM: Between Iraq and a Hard Place," *European Journal of International Law*, 13:1 (2002): 139–152.

[49] See Richard Butler, *The Greatest Threat: Iraq, Weapons of Mass Destruction and the Growing Crisis of Global Security*, New York: PublicAffairs, 2000, at 131. In one of the more absurd exercises the Secretary General asked a a senior UN official to undertake a survey mission to Baghdad. The maps produced by this mission – which turned out to be wrong! – were not given to UNSCOM but were entrusted to Vladimir Gratcheff, a Russian UN official, who served as a gatekeeper for a brief period of time in which the members of the Security Council could view the maps produced by this mission. Ibid., 132, 138.

[50] According to documents found later, Saddam charged Tariq Aziz with the concealment measures in 1991. See ibid., 52. Rolf Ekeus, the first head of UNSCOM, therefore created a countercapability, i.e. the Concealment Unit of six staffers charged with ferreting out the "truth" through a variety of methods including U2 reconnaissance, interviews with defectors, interviews with citizens, and the analysis of documents.

[51] Ibid., 3.

frequently takes on the features of hard bargaining.[52] Then politics raises its ugly head as different arguments – including competing notions of legitimacy – are mobilized in that e.g. obtrusive observations are rejected by shifting the blame;[53] or that specific measures are alleged to exceed the limits of the observation regime, thus representing a violation of sovereignty; or that some "preferred," or more "objective," inspectors are proposed who should be entrusted with the task. In a way, these arguments parallel notions of illegally obtained evidence in the domestic arena, although there is, of course, no court for deciding the issues, and no Miranda rule either. At best, some protracted discussions at the Security Council follow, in which the powers seldom show unanimity as soon as the collective action problem of sanctioning by force arises. Then the search for a more diplomatic approach, or some form of mediation by the Secretary General, perhaps provides an opening for the inspected state to bargain for more "reasonable" conditions, but such gambits also open the door for new deceptions.

In short, a whole host of new problems arises when we realize that the generative capacity of information creates problems for knowledge that exceed even classical expertise and risk assessment. To that extent the traditional measures of creating more transparency do not really work well. What instead is increasingly important are the practical problems that require local know-ledge, timing (emphasizing that the information we need is not only right but timely, providing us with possible fallbacks and alternatives), and finally issues of legitimacy, as they become important resources or trumps in the game. Let us begin with the seemingly simple problem of "reporting" before examining the "ritual dances" of the legitimacy game.

Consider in this context the problem of structural adjustments and the conditionality programs administered by international financial institutions (IFIs), which usually issue in specific proposals for greater liberalization and enhanced transparency.[54] Here the experiences with a variety of programs and

---

[52] I am relying here on the useful conceptual distinctions of Ronald B. Mitchell, "Sources of Transparency: Information Systems in International Regimes," *International Studies Quarterly*, 42:1 (1998): 109–130, at 116f.

[53] Thus, as if in an attempt to provide a tale for the *Thousand and One Nights*, an Iraqi spokesman "explained" the deliberate cutting of the wires of a surveillance camera in a chemical plant by saying that a "wandering psychopath" had done it because he had not received his medication due to the UN sanctions. Butler, *The Greatest Threat*, at 51.

[54] From the voluminous literature just a few examples, rich with case studies: Miles Kahler (ed.), *The Politics of International Debt*, Ithaca, NY: Cornell University Press, 1986; Joan M. Nelson (ed.), *Economic Crisis and Policy Choice: The Politics of Adjustment in the Third World*, Princeton: Princeton University Press, 1990; Stephen Haggard and Robert R. Kaufman (eds.), *The Politics of Economic Adjustment: International Constraints, Distributive Conflicts, and the State*, Princeton: Princeton University Press, 1992; Thomas J. Biersteker, *Dealing with Debt: International Financial Negotiations and Adjustment Bargaining*, Boulder, CO: Westview Press, 1993.

more than two decades of experimenting in getting it "right" provide us with fascinating materials, particularly since even some of the former success stories turn out to be problem cases.[55] The Chilean example is rather illustrative in this respect. Embarking vigorously on a liberalization policy from 1973 onwards in accordance with the reigning neoclassical orthodoxy, the country was near economic collapse in 1981/1982. Subsequent analysis showed that not all of the proposed policy measures for greater openness in the market worked as they were supposed to. While trade liberalization had more or less the intended effects, deregulation of the financial sector did not result in greater savings or investments. Instead of the expected near-automatic adjustment, bank failure, businesses insolvencies, and a general economic downturn forced the government to increase state intervention and protectionist measures, bail out large corporations and banks, and adopt special policies for agriculture and the construction sector.[56]

For our purposes what is at issue are not primarily the particular policy questions but rather the role data and increased transparency play in such reform proposals. As the example suggests, questions of economic development and adjustment raise complex issues of *competing values*, of *tradeoffs* and of *the sequencing* of policy measures, which cannot be mastered by simply increasing the transparency in a society. Recent claims of some proponents of "global governance" notwithstanding, such interventions touch upon three issues: first, of legitimacy or the appropriateness of the type of "knowledge" on which these policies are based; second on the embeddedness of the market in other social institutions; finally, on the role of "learning" and of "crisis" management by international institutions.

Let us begin with the hoary problem of *legitimacy*. Although we know that legitimacy is not a simple concept but rather a cluster term uniting several concepts with a certain family resemblance, we usually focus only on processes within the political system and distinguish between input and output legitimacy. It was the merit of legal theory to call attention to "coherence" among the norms, as another source of legitimacy[57] and of scholars working in

---

[55] See e.g. World Bank, *Adjustment Lending: An Evaluation of Ten Years of Experience*, Washington, DC: World Bank, 1988; Jeffrey Sachs, *Developing Country Debt and Economic Performance*, Chicago: University of Chicago Press, 1989. For an evaluation of the more recent policies, see Susan Park and Antje Vetterlein (eds.), *Owning Development: Creating Policy Norms in the IMF and the World Bank*, Cambridge: Cambridge University Press, 2012.

[56] See Robert R. Kaufman, "Stabilization and Adjustment in Argentina, Brazil, and Mexico" in Joan M. Nelson (ed.), *Economic Crisis and Policy Choice: The Politics of Adjustment in the Third World*, Princeton: Princeton University Press, 1990, 63–112; Barbara Stallings, "Politics and Economic Crisis: A Comparative Study of Chile, Peru, and Colombia" in Nelson (ed.), *Economic Crisis and Policy Choice*, 1990, 113–168.

[57] Thomas M. Franck, *The Power of Legitimacy among Nations*, Oxford: Oxford University Press, 1990.

the tradition of Ernst Haas[58] to emphasize the role of "science" or knowledge as a powerful legitimizing force. It is this latter claim, i.e. specialized knowledge and expertise, that allowed "economics" to become a bounded field of knowledge and to establish the legitimacy of the solutions put forward e.g. by international financial institutions.

However, the brief discussion above also suggested that policy recommendations, which require painful adjustments, often run up squarely against policies legitimated by other processes stressing e.g. input legitimacy. Since political office-holders usually want to stay in power, they can ill afford to alienate their constituency. The loss of legitimacy is for them the most serious political problem, irrespective of whether we are dealing here with a reasonably democratic government or a more oligarchic form of rule.[59] Three issues systematically raise problems of contestation. One is the question of "problem definition," the second one of the mix and the timing of reforms, and third, the benchmark for deciding on success and failure of a certain policy.

Obviously, these issues are interrelated. In deciding what worked, one has to have an idea what the problem was, even if the phenomenon of "solutions being in search of their problems" might be more frequent than assumed.[60] However, having sufficient data for describing and defining the problem or having good indicators for the impact of policies are then elemental requirements for a well-executed assessment. But in the absence of sufficient and reliable statistics, there is the tendency to utilize the "law of the hammer" and "assume" that all economies work alike. The same model is then useful for analyzing and conceiving of policy recommendations for widely diverging economic systems. This type of analysis has been (rightly) criticized by some developmental economists[61] and was part of an interesting debate in the 1960s between Alexander Gerschenkron,[62]

---

[58] See Ernst B. Haas, "Is There a Hole in the Whole? Knowledge, Technology, Interdependence, and the Construction of International Regimes," *International Organization*, 29:3 (1975): 827–876; Ernst B. Haas, *When Knowledge Is Power: Three Models of Change in International Organizations*, Berkeley: University of California Press.

[59] For a fundamental discussion placing the problem in the wider frame of democratic transitions and the chances for stable and democratic regime formation see Guillermo A. O'Donnell, Philippe C. Schmitter, and Laurence Whitehead, *Transitions from Authoritarian Rule*, Baltimore: Johns Hopkins University Press, 1986; Adam Przeworski, *Democracy and the Market: Political and Economic Reforms in Eastern Europe and Latin America*, Cambridge: Cambridge University Press, 1991.

[60] For this see e.g. the "garbage can model" of organization theory as developed by James G. March and Johan P. Olsen (eds.), *Ambiguity and Choice in Organizations*, Bergen: Universitetsforlaget, 1976.

[61] See e.g. W. Arthur Lewis, *Development Planning: The Essentials of Economic Policy*, London: Allen and Unwin, 1966; W. Arthur Lewis, *Growth and Fluctuations, 1870–1913*, London: Allen & Unwin, 1978.

[62] Alexander Gerschenkron, *Economic Backwardness in Historical Perspective: A Book of Essays*, Cambridge MA: The Belknap Press of Harvard University Press, 1962.

Walt Rostow,[63] and Albert Hirschman.[64] But the "Washington consensus," which served from the late 1970s as the basis of the International Monetary Fund (IMF) and World Bank policies, was based not only on Hirschman's criticized orthodoxy of "mono-economics,"[65] but also on a neoclassical synthesis that denied the importance of "local knowledge." This led to a curious misdiagnosis of the economic problems that several countries faced in the 1990s and to a strange discrepancy between theory and practice. But while an obvious failure should have led to correction in accordance with the epistemic requirement of refutation, expertise proved to be a sticky legitimizer and prevented some quick learning, substituting, instead, coercion for expertise.

Consider in this context also the Asian crisis, in which the IMF seems to have taken another leaf out of its "one size fits all" primer. As in the case of Latin America, the relevant problems were supposed to be inflated budgets resulting in inflation. Consequently, the orthodox prescriptions for Thailand, Indonesia, and South Korea entailed a rise in interest rates, and a tightening of fiscal policies, never mind that these countries had entered the crisis with *low inflation* and *balanced* or even surplus governmental budgets! It was indeed difficult to argue that expansionary fiscal policies and/or a too large public sector were at the root of the problem in these countries.[66] The suspicion that not science but a good deal of ideology (and US interests) was at work is heightened by the fact that in one case at least (South Korea) the crisis was used to push through some controversial "liberalization" measures in areas that were not even related to either the causes or the solutions for managing the crisis at hand. Critics have therefore pointed out that the IMF should only

provide the technical advice and the limited financial assistance necessary to deal with the funding crisis and to place a country in a situation that makes a relapse unlikely. It should not impose other economic changes however helpful.[67]

---

[63] W.W. Rostow, *The Stages of Economic Growth: A Non-Communist Manifesto*, Cambridge: Cambridge University Press, 1960.

[64] Albert O. Hirschman, "The Political Economy of Import-Substituting Industrialization in Latin America" in *A Bias for Hope: Essays on Development and Latin America*, New Haven: Yale University Press, 1971, 85–123.

[65] See Albert O. Hirschman, "The Rise and Decline of Development Economics" in *Essays in Trespassing: Economics to Politics and Beyond*, Cambridge: Cambridge University Press, 1981, 1–24.

[66] See Barry Eichengreen, "The International Monetary Fund in the Wake of the Asian Crisis" in Gregory W. Noble and John Ravenhill (eds.), *The Asian Financial Crisis and the Architecture of Global Finance*, Cambridge: Cambridge University Press, 2000, 170–191.

[67] Martin S. Feldstein, "Refocusing the IMF," *Foreign Affairs*, 77:2 (1998): 20–33, at 27. See also Thomas Willett, "For a Broader Public Choice Analysis of the International Monetary Fund" in David M. Andrews, C. Randall Henning, and Louis W. Pauly (eds.), *Governing the World's Money*, Ithaca, NY: Cornell University Press, 2002, 60–78.

But even if there is an agreement on the "problem," the various policy measures and mixes as well as their timing cannot be determined simply by theoretical or textbook knowledge, but depend for their effectiveness on a considerable amount of local knowledge. As Polanyi has shown, the establishment of the "economy" as a distinctive sphere of action was part and parcel of a larger social transformation that not only established the self-regulating market but also engendered a movement for protecting man and nature from some of the most egregious deleterious effects of the market.[68] Which form of "embedding" – to use Ruggie's felicitous formulation[69] – such a transformation took had to do with historical contingencies and particular policy choices in terms of certain social principles and purposes. Even if the "eventual" outcome seems somehow preordained, issues of policy mixes and of sequencing, of including and excluding particular areas, remain political questions of the highest order. An example would be the choice between proactive measures to alleviate poverty or chronic unemployment, vs. leaving these issues unattended to, trusting in "market" forces. But a viable strategy can only be one in which both the stability of the social and political institutions can be maintained while initiating reforms and taking the often painful adjustment measures.

Thus, both national decision-makers and economists have to face at this point problems that they would rather avoid. Examples of "failures" therefore abound. With balance of payments pressure removed (thanks to the help of international financial institutions), governments often reverse their course and fail to make the necessary adjustments. The economic experts, on the other hand, usually think that their task is done when they have provided an optimal policy approach as outlined in the initial agreement. As the experiences of the 1970s suggest, this leads to a strange phenomenon that Callaghy describes in the context of some African adjustment programs (but the same could be said e.g. of Poland or the Philippines[70]) as a "ritual dance."[71] Economists speak then of "slippage" – a euphemism for not reaching the agreed-upon targets – while the political authorities continue to make their bows to the "expertise" of

---

[68] Polanyi, *The Great Transformation*.
[69] John Gerard Ruggie, "International Regimes, Transactions, and Change: Embedded Liberalism in the Postwar Economic Order," *International Organization*, 36:2 (1982): 379–415.
[70] The case of the Philippines shows clear signs of a strategy of deception employed by the government. Ferdinand Marcos kept liberal technocrats in pivotal positions in order to attract foreign lenders while at the same time retaining a dualistic decision-making structure to insulate his crony capitalists from scrutiny and while manipulating the official statistics given to the IMF. See Stephen Haggard, "The Political Economy of the Philippine Debt Crisis" in Joan M. Nelson (ed.), *Economic Crisis and Policy Choice: The Politics of Adjustment in the Third World*, Princeton: Princeton University Press, 1990, 215–256.
[71] See Thomas Callaghy, "Toward State Capability and Embedded Liberalism in the Third World: Lessons for Adjustment" in Nelson, *Fragile Coalitions*, 1989, 115–138.

the officials of the IFIs, often even inviting or accepting "change-teams" into their national bureaucracies to "help" in the implementation of the renegotiated deals. But the "enforcement" of the negotiated terms is hardly straightforward even though open éclats are rather rare.[72] In short, each party knows that it needs the other for resources and/or validation and each, therefore, has a vested interest in continuing the policy "dialogue."

This leads me to "learning," my third point mentioned above. Without even wanting to enter the discussion of the complications that arise when transferring the concept of learning from individuals to organizations, there seem to exist two problems on the practical level. One is that the addition of "factors" leads to the above-noted difficulty of simply increasing the size of a laundry list to be monitored or, if further steps are taken, to micromanagement of an ever increasing set of policies. The second, and equally important, issue is that learning in the sense of the integration of local knowledge into the analysis and solution formulation runs counter to the identity of economists and has, therefore, frequently little chance to occur at all. As Thomas Willett observes:

> The External Surveillance Review reports a widespread, albeit not universal, perception among senior IMF staff that they "did not see it as their function to come up with policies that, while less than first best, moved the country in the right direction and were politically and institutionally acceptable." The report likewise notes that "IMF staffs . . . appear in general to be reluctant to give advice . . . that takes into account the political and institutional constraints within which policy makers need to cooperate." Given the training of most economists, such reluctance is quite understandable. Economists have no particular expertise in making such judgments. What is needed is additional capability at the Fund so that it can engage in the necessary political-economy analysis.[73]

While the IMF has in the aftermath of the criticism opened up its decision-making processes in order to allow for more "local knowledge," there remains the issue that such an opening undermines the self-understanding and disciplinary character of "economics" and their legitimacy based on expertise, as is quite rightly perceived by the professionals of the Fund. No longer primarily interested in understanding particular economic systems, their analysis is beholden to an ideal in which exogenously given preferences of rational actors, marginal utility and a general equilibrium fully specify the "economy." True, even in a fully specified system, rational actors might not know what exactly the case is, as there are risks and room for error. But basically these actors move in a world which is determinate and in which nothing new can appear, as

---

[72] One such notable exception is Zambia's open defiance of the IMF in 1987. See Thomas Callaghy, "Lost between the State and Market: The Politics of Economic Adjustment in Ghana, Zambia, and Nigeria" in Nelson, *Economic Crisis and Policy Choice*, 1990, 257–320.

[73] Thomas D. Willett, *Towards a Broader Public Choice Analysis of the International Monetary Fund*, Claremont, CA: Claremont Institute for Economic Policy Studies, 2002, at 75.

no radical uncertainty exists. We always know what we do not know and can update our expectations accordingly. In this way, the equilibrium in the neoclassical synthesis becomes something more that a simple heuristic tool; it "is" real and allows us to formulate policies because the present and the future are in principle reversible and we do not have to worry about the fact that we might not even know the things we do not know.

Although he narrowing of the economic analysis to a general equilibrium analysis and the discounting of "local" knowledge have been criticized by many economists as different in their outlook as von Hayek[74] and Stieglitz,[75] its intellectual hegemony leads to a strange inability to learn and to problematic policy advice in crisis situations.

As Stiglitz reports, the "IMF (and the US Treasury) reacted vehemently (though secretly) to a more thorough World Bank review," which had identified the "failure to be attentive to the microeconomic structures of the affected countries" as one of the reasons for the Asian crisis.[76] Even more ironic is the justification for the dismissal of criticism. The credo seems to be that "only if the market believes that the IMF is infallible will it be able to affect market psychology and restore confidence."[77] While this sentence might be true if taken as an analytical truth, it is hardly sensible if all indications suggest that we are in a different game, e.g. are now playing soccer rather than tennis.

The unreal character of such an analysis becomes even more evident when we examine the origins and subsequent dynamics of the crisis. As already mentioned, different from traditional crises and previous Latin American experiences, it was not the excess of imports that had caused the problem in the Asian crisis. Instead, much of the initial contagion effect was the result of a growing uneasiness with the "capitalist" cronyism with which, strangely enough, the US and others had lived quite well for a considerable time.[78] Now such a description (anticipating already the judgment of the market) was increasingly used as a watchword for "bringing about" the "liberalization" and the "restructuring" of the economies that had proved surprisingly resistant to external pressures. Thus, different from other countries, such as Australia, whose "fundamental data" were much more problematic than those of the

---

[74] Friedrich A. von Hayek, "The Use of Knowledge in Society," *American Economic Review*, 35:4 (1945): 519–530.

[75] Joseph E. Stiglitz, "Prize Lecture: Information and the Change in the Paradigm in Economics," Nobelprize.org, June 14, 2016, available at www.nobelprize.org/nobel_prizes/economic-sci ences/laureates/2001/stiglitz-lecture.html.

[76] See Joseph E. Stiglitz, "Democratizing the International Monetary Fund and the World Bank: Governance and Accountability," *Governance*, 16:1 (2003): 111–139, at 115.

[77] Ibid.

[78] This is one of the criticisms in Joseph E. Stiglitz, *Globalization and Its Discontents*, London: Allen Lane, Penguin, 2002, at 179f.

Asian countries,[79] the warnings that an "Asian" crisis was in the making showed all the tendencies of a self-fulfilling prophecy after its first episode, the crisis of the Thai Baht in July 1997. It became clear that we were dealing here with a contagion effect, induced by this characterization that then quickly mutated into a crisis of confidence and led to panicky capital outflows. As Louiz Pereira da Silva, a World Bank official assigned to Japan during the Asian crisis, remarks in a postmortem:

In sum the designers of the initial Asian stabilization programs quite correctly quickly saw that the crises were confidence crises related to the volatile behavior of capital account flows. But then they assembled and implemented a rather standard policy framework that works primarily in classical current account crises. In Asia such programs would either backfire or succeed but at the cost of a much more painful construction of the real economy ...

The IFIs, because of their internal bureaucratic rigidities and their modus operandi regarding economic analysis, were not capable of adapting to the new realities of capital account crises ... They use obsolete analytical tools that "most likely" worsened the problems.[80]

Although it is clear that the utilized orthodox model was inadequate, the issue remains whether the adjustments made in the subsequent second-generation models go far enough. Second-generation models agree that a crisis might develop due to the self-fulfilling prophecies,[81] familiar from bank runs, even if the "fundamental data" of an economy are in order. Although this family of models includes the self-generative element of information – as has been analyzed in the sociological literature on crowd behavior[82] – they still do not account for the links between the currency and the financial crises, which was important in the Asian crisis. In these models the government is no longer a simple "mechanism" but an actor which tries to minimize losses. Conflicts arise then mainly from efforts to defend the currency on the one hand, while keeping a critical eye on the tradeoffs between interest rates and unemployment. Raising the interest rate might help in fighting the currency crisis; counteracting a financial crisis implies, however, the adoption of an expansive monetary policy i.e. *low interest rates*. In addition, devaluing the currency in order to make the necessary "adjustments" puts considerable pressure on banks

---

[79] See e.g. Rodney Bruce Hall, "The Discursive Demolition of the Asian Development Model," *International Studies Quarterly*, 47:1 (2003): 71–99.

[80] Luiz A. Pereira da Silva, "The International Financial Institutions (IFIs) and the Political Lessons from the Asian Crises of 1997–1998," *International Social Science Journal*, 53:4 (2001): 551–568, at 562.

[81] See Maurice Obstfeld, "Models of Currency Crises with Self-Fulfilling Features," *European Economic Review*, 40:3 (1996): 1037–1047.

[82] See e.g. Mark Granovetter, "Threshold Models of Collective Behavior," *American Journal of Sociology*, 83:6 (1978): 1420–1443.

servicing their debts denominated in foreign currency. Still, as Drazen shows, models of the second generation leave the rapid spread of such crises somewhat mysterious.[83]

Third-generation models, therefore, focus increasingly on issues of a regulatory nature in banking, corporate governance, bankruptcy, and the "rule of law," particularly regarding the law of contracts. Instead of observing capital movements and analyzing disequilibria in the balance of payments, structural weaknesses of the institutional order are examined. The increasing interdependencies of a global economy require uniform or at least comparable standards in order to stabilize the expectations necessary for a functioning "free" market. But despite the very often invoked need for liberalization and the calls for deregulation and "private ordering," it is the *autonomous national regulation regimes* that are supposed to be dismantled in the name of a functioning "global" economic sphere.[84] Two questions are particularly important in this respect. One concerns the new knowledge that is generated by these models; the other addresses the more "political" issue, i.e. whether the identification of global regulatory needs, underlying much of the global governance discourse, adequately deals with the political problem of *cui bono*?

With regard to the first problem the seminal analysis of Oliver Kessler[85] strikes a rather skeptical tone. Although the third-generation models require greater transparency and regulatory intervention in national systems, even this broader focus on "governance" might be too narrow, for two interrelated reasons. One concerns the still problematic nature of dealing with crises in terms of traditional risk analysis, the other the denial of the need for "politics" in managing the economy, treating it as a self-contained autonomous system.

Thus, while it is true that *ceteris paribus* greater transparency and more information is better than less, the naming of a situation as a "crisis" clearly indicates that the actors are no longer convinced that they are operating on the assumption of "business as usual." Moreover, greater transparency is discounting the obvious cognitive limitations of real actors and the danger of

---

[83] See Allan Drazen, "Political Contagion in Currency Crises" in Paul Krugman (ed.), *Currency Crises*, Chicago: University of Chicago Press, 2000, 47–70. He argues that although there is asymmetric information among the speculators and the government of a country defending its currency there is a certain bonus recognized by all in being a member of a "club" that is successfully managing its currency. Crucial is now how the club members value their membership. If a speculative attack on one member succeeds, this move diminishes the incentives of others to take their own commitments seriously, which, in turn, encourages further aggressive attacks, etc.

[84] See the analysis of Ronnie D. Lipschutz and Cathleen Fogel, "'Regulation for the Rest of Us?' Global Civil Society and the Privatization of Transnational Regulation" in Rodney Bruce Hall and Thomas J. Biersteker (eds.), *The Emergence of Private Authority in Global Governance*, Oxford: Oxford University Press, 2002, 115–140.

[85] Oliver Kessler (ed.), *Die Internationale Politische Ökonomie der Weltfinanzkrise*, Wiesbaden: Springer, 2011.

facilitating collusion among potential "attackers." At this point, reliance on traditional risk analysis is an illusion. Consider in this context the "crash" of October 1987, which resulted in the loss of $1 trillion US stock values. The 20.5% loss of the Standard and Poor 500 index was an event that the Markowitz portfolio theory and the most sophisticated models of Merton and Scholes would have to treat as a 20 percent standard deviation event in a world of normal distributions and "random walks." Such an event "would not be expected during the lifetime of the universe – even allowing for holidays."[86] However, this is precisely what happened and what returned with a vengeance in the aftermath of the Russian crisis of 1998. One of the leading hedge funds, which relied on the expertise of two Nobel laureates in economics, lost $4.6 billion in one week! When order was restored it was not the result of self-equilibrating "frictionless" markets, but of political intervention and a bargain arrived at under "the shadow of the law."[87]

In short, what we face in crises is not a simple failure in the scope or reach of transparency, but the existential question of how to deal with the problems of radical uncertainty and the failure of "expertise" under such circumstances. As a former chief economist for the IMF admitted, "we sort of know what systemic risk is ... but to argue that it is a well-developed science ... is overstating the fact."[88] The fact that the European crisis of 1992 hit particularly hard the Scandinavian countries – well known for their clean and transparent regimes – and the fact that in the aftermath of Enron and World.com no comparable crisis developed in the US, all seem to demonstrate that a lack of transparency seems only contingently related to the outbreak of crises rather than being their cause. To that extent the new generations of models all try to "learn" from the previous crisis but they seem, like the military, to make plans for the last war, instead of realizing that the run after new data is somewhat quixotic since they are not simply there *ex ante*.

---

[86] For an excellent account of the financial crises of 1987 and the crash of the Long Term Capital Management corporation in 1998 despite, or rather because of, the "help" of mistaken assumptions underlying risk models, see Nicholas Dunbar, *Inventing Money: The Story of Long-Term Capital Management and the Legends Behind It*, Chichester: Wiley, 2000, at 95.

[87] The final deal brokered by the Federal Reserve included the removal of the LTC management and massive writeoffs by the institutions which had invested in the hedge fund. Thus the Swiss bank UBS marked down its investments from $766 million to $106 million, the Bank of America reported a loss of $1.4 billion, just slightly higher than Salomon Brothers (which lost $1.3 billion), all of which were topped by Merrill Lynch's $1.8 billions. Fortunately, the American public was nearly unaware of all of this, as it was enthralled by the Clinton sex scandal and the impending impeachment hearings. Again, more information (or rather the "processing" of the available information by larger segments of the public) most probably would have led to further panicky actions. For an account of the end of LTC see ibid., chaps. 8–9.

[88] As quoted in David Harvey, *The Enigma of Capital: And the Crises of Capitalism*, Oxford: Oxford University Press, 2011, at 261.

What we need in those contingencies is more an effective "fixer of signs," as Hobbes called the sovereign, instead of putting in an expert whose wisdom has just run out.

At this point, questions of "political" responsibility and accountability enter the picture. These are issues that go far beyond technical advice, transparency, and optimization. To that extent one can seriously doubt that even attempts to create further institutions for risk analysis and rely on their expertise are likely to solve the problem. Furthermore, the idea that credit rating agencies could somehow decide "what is the case" seems to be pernicious for several reasons. One is, such a proposal undercuts their own legitimization since it is thereby clear that neither the market nor economic expertise can vouch for their recommendations. What one hopes for is that these agencies know something (local knowledge?) which others do not. But how this know-how has been acquired – without specific language skills or deep familiarity with the countries in question – remains murky. Second, since the ratings of agencies have frequently been problematic (as they relied largely on the "information" of fund managers who were creating risky financial instruments against which they speculated), the only justification could be that despite these imperfections someone has to make a "judgment call" and that in the world of the blind the one-eyed person is king. But given this predicament the important question now is who should be entitled to make such a call, which provides a third reason. As Louis Pauly has pointed out:

When we speak of the authority of the market in other than an ultimate sense we appropriately mix private and public categories. The fact that actual governments obfuscate their final authority in financial markets is no accident. Blurring the boundary lines between public and private indeed is part of an intentional effort to render opaque political responsibility for the wrenching adjustments entailed in late capitalist development. Understanding this intentionality, its history and the deeper reasons behind it can provide a useful starting point for assessing such policies as those aimed at managing systemic risk or at redistributing adjustment burdens.[89]

The question is whether by enhancing transparency we are likely to create such new centers of responsibility or whether the emerging networks – be they of banks, IFIs, or professionals of various kinds – only continue to mystify their exercises (or abuses) of power. "Naturalizing" such a decision by making it appear that "this is the way the ball bounces" is tantamount to suggesting "this is also the only way in which the ball *can* bounce." The next section provides some further thought on these matters.

---

[89] Louis W. Pauly, "Global Finance, Political Authority, and the Problem of Legitimation" in Rodney Bruce Hall and Thomas J. Biersteker (eds.), *The Emergence of Private Authority in Global Governance*, Oxford: Oxford University Press, 2002, 76–90, at 77.

4.5   Transparency or Accountability: The Media and the Emergence of a Global Public Sphere?

In the present section I want to address the problem of whether or not the information revolution, which provides us with increasingly more data, is conducive to establishing new "fora" beyond the traditional ones, in which such political questions can be debated and decided. At least some "optimists" have suggested this with regard to the establishment of new "virtual" communities and the often decisive role of "social media" in solving coordination problems so that people can assemble for protests.[90]

Here I do not want to discount the importance of new networks and movements cutting across traditional boundaries and of the new spaces they have opened for new forms of "politics," as e.g. Wapner[91] and the social movement literature have pointed out. My skepticism is rather based on two interrelated arguments. One concerns the problem of the public agenda, which is heavily shaped by the "production" of the news with which the public is confronted. I argue that what is considered worth reporting is heavily influenced by the nature of the media and the commodification of information, which creates dilemmas about "what sells" instead of what ought to be an issue of public concern. My other concern has to do with the "transcendental conditions" of deliberation, which are supposed to inform political choices, insure their "quality," and establish loci for accountability. My preliminary assessment leads me to the at first counterintuitive conclusion that these two processes, singly and in conjunction, *are not conducive* to the development of a global "public," which could serve as the critical, encompassing forum for vetting issues of global concern.

The first process is likely to lead to some exclusionary practices – not in terms of the "admitted" audience but in terms of the range of topics, where the audience is flooded with chaff and gossip. News of the royals, or of the recent antics of celebrities, beats reports on "high politics" or on the economy any time, especially if the stock prices go up and we are told that is good for us all (despite the fact that many of the welfare gains of the middle class have or are in the process of becoming undone). In short, what we actually observe is the growth of apathy and escapism, and what is presented to us as "news" actually mostly appeals to emotions rather than raising critical questions. In this context the popularity of human interest stories rather than analysis is emblematic,

---

[90] For a fascinating account of the role of modern media for the "revolutions" in Egypt Tunisia, Iceland, Spain, and the Occupy movement, see Manuel Castells, *Networks of Outrage and Hope: Social Movements in the Internet Age*, Cambridge: Polity Press, 2012.

[91] Paul Wapner, "Politics Beyond the State: Environmental Activism and World Civic Politics," *World Politics*, 47:3 (1995): 311–340.

reducing complex problems to "Natasha standing in the breadline," or to reports "documenting" the plight of a victim of man-made or natural disasters. ("How do you feel, having lost your husband and child?") The second process concerns the opening up new fora on the Internet. One once hoped that these would be conducive to the development of a more critical "public" because there are no big entry costs and people with similar ideas can easily associate. Instead, the result is, oddly enough, a withdrawal from common concerns, the spreading of rumors, and the emergence of "shit-storms" familiar from the (a-)social media. If there is any political interest involved, we have to notice that most users of Internet chat rooms seek out "like-minded persons." The result is that over the years analysts have detected a radicalizing tendency among the users, as apparently people feel comfortable only with those who share the same preference and shy away from contro-versy, as one can easily "out" oneself.[92]

This tendency is precisely what counteracts the establishment of a genuine "public." In a real public discussion, for which free access is only one of the prerequisites, the participants would also have to deal not only with different opinions, but with several different interacting issues, i.e. dilemmas. However, since even the more politically active members of global civil society are "activists," i.e. usually concentrate on one issue only – even if it is as broad as "saving the globe" – questions of restructuring the labor markets, or actually reforming a corrupt banking system, or of rebuilding the badly damaged security architecture, is not "their thing." To that extent, discussions on the Internet usually lack the variety necessary for a vibrant discussion and for the development of solidarity among strangers, who are discovering that they are sitting in the same boat. But as one can check in and out of chat rooms and change one's preferences as easily as one's T-shirt, most of these encoun-ters lack, in addition, the necessary seriousness, save among fundamentalists and fanatics.

These findings are not just a pessimistic gloss on some of the aberrations with which we are all familiar. Instead, they point to a deep-seated change of the "public" and in the emancipatory role with which it was credited. The first thing we have to realize is that news is not just an agglomeration of facts, which are being communicated. Instead, it is a mediated communication, in that it no longer presupposes the co-presence of an addressee. But it is also, particularly in the case of electronic media, not a simple mediated communi-cation, directed to a particular person or audience through the use of a medium, be it writing (letters), wires (telephone conversation), or electronic means

---

[92] See the analysis of Cass Sunstein, *Republic.com*, Princeton: Princeton University Press, 2001; *On Rumors: How Falsehoods Spread*, New York: Farrar, Strauss, Giroux, 2009.

(e-mail). Rather it is in Thompson's[93] terms *"mediated quasi-interaction"* in that it is directed at an indefinite range of recipients. These rather straightforward observations have, however, important implications for communication and the way in which issues can be addressed.

Consider in this context different forms of communication. In a discussion (or speech) the interaction takes place in the context of co-presence; only one person can speak at a time, although others might chime in. What can be said and what is understood is governed by background conditions What is unclear can then be dealt with by requests for clarifications, elaborations, etc., or by "coming back to the point" later. *Mediated* interaction, such as writing a letter, alerts us already to the problem of selection, as we are no longer able to rely on a dialogue as the means of communicating. Now questions of what gets included and what need not be mentioned (perhaps mistakenly so) enter the picture. Most of the time, such considerations do not impair communications, since familiarity with the topic (family affairs, common remembrance, or projects) provides the "background." In telephone conversations, which establish a dialogical form of communication, such questions can be dealt with analogously to face-to-face interaction.

Reaching a "general audience," however, creates selection problems of a new kind in that this mode of communication is basically monological, and that for the effectiveness of the communication the communicator has to rely on common frames, which are supposed to provide the key and cues for the intelligibility of what is being reported. The first selection criterion has therefore to be that something is "unusual," as otherwise the perlocutionary effect of this type of communication, i.e. getting the attention of the anonymous audience, is difficult. It is therefore not surprising that the threatening, the odd, the unusual, even the lurid, shameful, and "criminal," has provided one of the important selection criteria for e.g. the handbills of yore that "informed" anonymous audiences. Natural disasters, wars, as well as the birth of a calf with two heads, court gossip, or egregious crimes were usually the topics of such publications. A further "selection" takes place when distinct "publics" emerge, e.g. one that focuses increasingly on "political" matters, which deals with issues of war and peace, court politics, and some "news" from abroad (colonies) and on "events" (such as births and deaths, feasts). These were originally the stuff of the (mainly) weeklies, such as *Corantos, Couriers, Intelligencers,* or whatever.

In the European context the Thirty Years War and the subsequent changes in in the domestic political order saw a withering away of representative political institutions – with the exception of England, which had a different trajectory.

---

[93] John B. Thompson, *The Media and Modernity: A Social Theory of the Media,* Stanford: Stanford University Press, 1995, at 82f.

But this change seems to have been the crystallization point for the emergence of the "news paper" and later for a "public" that claimed to represent the forum where matters of common concern could be subjected to critical reason. Thus, Amsterdam printers seem to have been pioneers in first servicing the salons and reading circles of an emerging public.

Of course their success enticed publishers to enter foreign markets, particularly when they had been "liberalized." It was again an Amsterdam printer, Pieter van der Keere, who exported the first "paper" in English to London[94] for the English audience. The English Revolution, and the abolition of the Star Chamber in 1641, which previously had subjected printers and engravers to a comprehensive licensing and censorship regime, led to the flourishing of "the press." In 1645 as many as fourteen newspapers appeared most weeks, and these papers also emerged as key players in the political struggles of the time.

Despite the reimposition of censorship during the Restoration, by the time of the Glorious Revolution and the War of Spanish Succession the first "dailies" had emerged and the media landscape showed considerable differentiation. Some publications focused on social and cultural events, some on commercial and financial news. But important for "politics" was the fact that some of them set themselves a mission to be an instrument of criticism in regard to social and political issues. Here Daniel Defoe's *Review*, or Jonathan Swift's *Examiner* have to be mentioned. They became part of the notion of the "public" whose genesis and function Habermas has charted.[95] Whatever criticism we might have of Habermas's interpretation, the emergence of the medium "news paper" simultaneously with a respective public bears out the idea that media are not simple observers but selectors and shapers of the news which are co-constitutive of the audience or public.

Furthermore, Benedict Anderson has shown how the emergence of the newspaper coincided with and powerfully shaped e.g. the Latin American independence movements. On the one hand it separated the former colonies from the mother country by inventing the modern form of the "nation" – as opposed to relying on notions of the status society inherited from Spain.[96]

---

[94] See Joseph Frank, *The Beginnings of the English Newspaper, 1620–1660*, Cambridge, MA: Harvard University Press, 1961, chap 1.

[95] See Jürgen Habermas, *Strukturwandel der Öffentlichkeit: Untersuchungen zu einer Kategorie der bürgerlichen Gesellschaft*, Berlin: Luchterhand, 1971.

[96] The reason why this became increasingly problematic for the creoles is that, as "natives" of the provinces, they were not admitted to any administrative offices either in Spain or their own country. All offices, even those of the church, were with rare exceptions filled by Spaniards, while after independence the small creole minority faced a large indigenous populace without the insurance of the Spanish coercive machinery. Thus San Martín's and Bolivar's solution was to declare that all inhabitants of the former colony were members of a "nation." Benedict Anderson, *Imagined Communities: Reflections on the Origin and Spread of Nationalism*, revised edn., London: Verso, 1991, chap. 4.

On the other hand it later reinforced the tendency of treating the former administrative districts of the Spanish empire as independent countries.

The fact that early Mexican nationalists wrote of themselves as "nosotros los Americanos" and of their country as "nuestra America" has been interpreted as revealing the vanity of the local creoles who, because Mexico was by far the most valuable of Spain's American possessions, saw themselves as the center of the New World. But, in fact, people all over Spanish America thought of themselves as "Americans," since the term denoted precisely the shared fatality of extra-Spanish birth.

At the same time, we have seen that the very conception of the newspaper implies a refraction of even "world events" into a specific imagined world of vernacular readers; and also how important to that imagined community is an idea of steady, solid simultaneity through time. Such a simultaneity the immense stretch of the Spanish American Empire, and the isolation of its components parts, made difficult to imagine. Mexican creoles might learn months later of developments in Buenos Aires, but it would be through Mexican newspapers, not those of the Río de la Plata; and the events would appear "similar to," rather than "part of events in Mexico."[97]

Here the "refraction" and the common center of concern, i.e. the imagined community, serve as powerful filters as well as constitutive elements for both the "news" and the "community."

But Anderson's reference to the role of "simultaneity" points to a further important element in such a mediated quasi-interaction, an element that becomes even more important in the medium of television. Since television is able to transcend both distance and time, or better, combines audiovisual presence with spatiotemporal absence, it creates the illusion of directness and participation. In this regard it seems like a form of face-to-face communication. But actually it is more akin to the mediated interaction of the print medium, as we cannot intervene or actually participate in what is being presented. Furthermore, the image overwhelms the spoken commentary; the vividness of footage makes it appear that what is being reported is what actually happens.

What does this mean for the selections by which our attention is supposed to be captured? First, it seems that this medium emphasizes immediacy. Rather than selecting the news through the reflective act of relating the reports to some notion of a forum of critique that was part of the concept of a "public," it again pays more attention to the "unusual," the gory, or lurid, or simply the entertaining. Suddenly the sexual peccadilloes of a president become much more important than "politics," i.e. matters that should concern us all are displaced by reports that pander to our curiosity by exposing the "all too human" side of our representatives. The ensuing "debates" degenerate quickly, as e.g. the

[97] Ibid., 62f.

president attempts to portray himself as the "victim" of some "conspiracy" of his enemies who are "out to get him," but also because of the near total erosion of the distinction between the public and the private and by the blurring of the boundary of "information" and "entertainment."

As a result the purported expansion of information in the name of "the public's right to know" is effectively a contraction of public discourse, because audience time is limited. Through a Darwinian mechanism, information about sexual scandal proliferates and drives out information that constitutes or could potentially constitute other elements of public discourse.[98]

Second, since the audience is not "present," there is a need for reassurance that the message will be accepted, i.e. is taken as intended. A variety of devices used by the televisual medium serve this purpose. The most obvious is the "heroization" of the reporter who appears in endless, nearly brainwashing spots of the media themselves. CNN and other stations following this format provide the perfect examples here. Their main task seems to be to advertise their own product, in the same way as the luxury items, such as overpriced watches or cosmetics, which pay for the "news" broadcast.

Significantly, the reporter is depicted as an inquiring person who can end-lessly and rapidly fire questions at the powerful, or s/he is the protagonist for delivering an endless sequence of human-interest stories, rapidly told and with proper "compassion." In case of actual interviews with members of "local publics," the clips frequently do not even record the answers, as most questions are only meant to be rhetorical. What the local decision-makers think is apparently irrelevant and can be passed over, and admittedly some of their declarations will indeed have the mantra-like quality familiar from American and EU politics. Interviewing ministers and heads of state serves then mainly as a demonstration that the hero-journalist has access to high places and is in the loop.

In this way the reporters are made into figures that can guarantee the truth of the news, since they are on the spot as eyewitnesses, even if their analysis of what they report operates at the depth of a puddle. Bad overacting, speaking at a high pitch – or in a pompous or ominous register of voice – using one's hands like a Neapolitan fishmonger, or displaying stereotypical facial expres-sions are now supposed to convey commitment, concern, and sincerity, which the verbal report is obviously unable to establish. Hands under the chin signal thoughtfulness and concern, the brisk walk of the hero – recorded in time-lapse – indicates determination. But it also conjures up associations with the chase of a cheetah or a hyena honing in on a victim. Other devices for

---

[98] J.M. Balkin, "How Mass Media Simulate Political Transparency," *Cultural Values*, 3:4 (1999): 393–413.

"massaging" the audience range from voiceovers of laughter on the appropriate spots similar to sitcoms (insuring that the passive viewer gets "the message"), to panels before a "studio audience" which usually remains just a prop for the "instant expert" or insider who explains to us in fifty words or less who is "winning" or "losing" or whether something is "good" or "bad" for us.[99]

Thus, in a way, television creates new forms of politics that are real only because they are seen on television. Oddly, it also recreates a focus on leaders that is even stronger than in absolute monarchies. While there the king and his court were usually recessed and had to display their power and aura through ceremony and occasional public spectacles, nowadays a new "need to know" what the leaders are "really like" has become part of our political reality. It has spurred a whole industry of image consultants and spin-doctors. To that extent the constraints of this new visibility, under which our political leaders have to operate, are quite different, despite some similarities to the former court practices and the showiness of present media politics. There are several reasons for this.

First, the audience is far greater and more heterogeneous than the restricted circle of nobles and court society to which the ruler was visible. Second, the intrusiveness of television cameras and the live aspect of reporting require a constant reflexive monitoring by the actors that was unknown before. The result is, oddly enough, the near-automatic responses of decision-makers utilizing uninformative prepackaged, but noncontroversial formulas of mantra-like quality, instead of conveying actual information. Third, and most importantly, the requirements of modern democracy do not allow for opting out of the media game, even if some of its downsides are well known to all. The aspiration of representing critical reason, which, in turn, insures proper deliberation about public choices, is thereby increasingly sacrificed on the altar of what sells. Since criticism might be disquieting for the general audience, it can easily be passed over as being "just negative," outmoded, or anti-progressive. This also has important repercussions on dissent since, given these "silencing constraints," it has to be presented in outrageous claims made in circus-like fashion. In this way the audience can relate to it, by "participating" through vicarious displays of their mood (shouting, gesturing to the cameras, throwing beer cans, etc.).

Whatever we might think about these developments, the preceding considerations explode the myth that media are just neutral instruments of observation that create transparency by providing us with more and better information. Instead, as we have seen, they are crucially *involved in the construction of*

[99] See Daniel Dayan and Elihu Katz, *Media Events: The Live Broadcasting of History*, Cambridge, MA: Harvard University Press, 1992.

social and political reality, bearing out one of the key points of "constructivism." This can best be seen when television broadcasts have unintended side
effects by serving as an informal coordination device, enabling people to
engage in spontaneous collective action.

Consider in this context the "silent revolution" in East Germany. People in
Leipzig could not only show up for their usual Monday protests, most of the
population of the GDR could also see on Western TV the crowding of the
West German embassy in Prague by East Germans who did not want to return
home, the dismantling of the Hungarian border, and finally on November 9,
the fall of the wall. The authorities, short of engaging in massive massacres,
had no option but to fold. Thompson calls this "concerted responsive action"
and observes:

the individuals involved in these events may be well aware of the constitutive role of the
media. They know that what they say on radio or television will be heard by thousands
or millions of others who may respond in concerted ways ... They know that, by
controlling the flow of images and information, the media can play a crucial role in
controlling the flow of events.[100]

A similarly successful story can be told of the Chiapas Indians (Zapatistas).
After their spectacular seizure of a town in southern Mexico (January 1994)
they were able to force concessions from the Mexican government through
the use of modern media, such as an internet website, fax campaigns, and
international television. However, since 140 NGOs took up the Zapatista cause
we have to realize that this case is quite different from the mere coordination of
spontaneous action in East Germany. But, before we jump to the conclusion
that this case proves that the media revolution has indeed created the means to
"publicize" local grievances globally – and thereby also created the necessary
mechanism to induce changes in policy – a word of caution is in order.

As Clifford Bob has suggested, it seems that for "every contemporary
conflict that arouses significant international action, dozens of others remain
obscure."[101] An action similar to the Zapatista seizure occurred around the
same time by the Popular Revolutionary Army in Mexico (August 1996), but
ended in total failure. While in two weeks 233 articles were written about the
Zapatistas, only forty-four publicized the success of the Revolutionary Army,
and the record worsened as time went on. In the following ten weeks, 553 stories appeared on the Zapatista case while only 69 dealt with the fate of the
Revolutionary Army insurrection. Crucial for the differential in support and
publicity were apparently the rhetoric and tactics which both movements used

---

[100] Thompson, *The Media and Modernity*, at 117.
[101] Clifford Bob, "Beyond Transparency: Visibility and Fit in the Internationalization of Internal
Conflict" in Bernard I. Finel and Kristin M. Lord (eds.), *Power and Conflict in the Age of
Transparency*, New York: Palgrave Macmillan, 2000, 287–314, at 288.

in justifying their attacks. While the Zapatistas held a town and shifted the initiative (and blame) to the government – should the latter decide to dislodge them by force in front of dozens of TV cameras? – the Revolutionary Army relied on the guerrilla tactics of hit-and-run actions. Even more important apparently was the ability of the Zapatistas to link their local grievances to global concerns, such as the North American Free Trade Agreement (NAFTA) and the dangers of globalization The Revolutionary Army, on the other hand, framed the grievance in terms of classical Marxist notions of class conflict, which elicited more yawns than sympathy.

In short, it was the immediate and strong support of many NGOs and their continued advice and commitment that made a coherent media strategy possible, since the themes resonated domestically as well as internationally. Margaret Keck[102] has documented nearly the same pattern in the case of the rubber tappers of Acre in Brazil. In that case a local fight against the enclosure of greater and greater chunks of the Brazilian rainforest became a struggle for social justice, and sustainable development. Again the crucial variable was the alignment of local grievances with frames salient in the international debate, rather than the transparency created by media coverage per se. Since the tappers' fight coincided with the campaign of Northern NGOs to hold multilateral banks accountable for the environmental damage caused by their projects abroad, both movements could link and establish important synergies.

In summarizing the experiences of media campaigns Clifford Bob aptly remarks:

First a focus on transparency alone neglects the significance of structural factors that play a large role in inhibiting or enhancing the visibility of conflicts. Second, transparency is inadequate for understanding third party responses to conflict because it neglects the role of agency in those processes. Insurgent groups take actions to raise their visibility and fit themselves into the agendas and interests of potential supporters, even as states take action to deflect or prevent such support.[103]

But if what matters is not transparency per se, but the link to larger networks or organizations of global civil society throughout the world, could not such a "transparency plus" approach deal with the above objections? Unfortunately, the answer is not straightforward, since it involves us in several conceptual issues. One has to do with the concept of a public sphere that arose in the peculiar circumstances of state-building in Europe and that is now applied by analogy to the global realm. Despite the striking similarity that the "global public" sphere seems to also emerge *next to, but outside* of the existing

---

[102] Margaret E. Keck, "Social Equity and Environmental Politics in Brazil: Lessons from the Rubber Tappers of Acre," *Comparative Politics*, 27:4 (1995): 409–424.
[103] Bob, "Beyond Transparency," at 297.

political structures, this parallelism provides at best a starting point for further analysis. However, important differences exist.

Above all, we have to remember that it was after all a *bourgeois* public sphere that emerged in Europe. It sequestered more than half of the population to the "private" household and kept them thereby practically invisible and voiceless, an important criticism made by various feminists. This raises a more principled point concerning the effectivess of this "public." While Habermas in his path-breaking study pointed to the importance of the print media for the constitution of the "public" as an institution of critique and reason, he failed to inquire more systematically into the role of media at this historical juncture. In the original version of his argument he quickly moved from the press to other parts of the "public" *which were deeply involved in and depended upon traditional modes of politics.* The negotiations and debates that took place in the salons, the coffee houses, and clubs remained beholden to a face-to-face dialogical model of communication that included the media only to the extent that articles in papers or pamphlets might have become the topic for discussion and debate. Thus the different ways in which publics are created and can be mobilized needs to be investigated further.

To what extent this historical case can then serve as a template for today's communication revolution remains an open question and could only be examined on the basis of a more explicit treatment of the media. As one critic argues:

we shall not arrive at a satisfactory understanding of the nature of public life in the modern world if we remain wedded to a conception of publicness which is essentially spatial and dialogical in character and which obliges us to interpret the ever growing role of mediated communication as a historical fall from grace ... With the development of the new media of communication ... the phenomenon of publicness has become detached from the idea of a dialogical conversation in a shared locale. It has become de-spatialized and non-dialogical, and it is increasingly linked to the distinctive kind of visibility produced by, and achievable through, the media.[104]

The important question though does not seem to be whether the new global public should or should not be considered a "fall from grace," but whether the links forged by such new media can do the job, e.g. become functional equivalents to the older forms of public communication. While it has been common to focus on information overload, "filtering" as an antidote might also have repercussions that are no less problematic.

As Cass Sunstein suggests, the possibility of just "tuning in" to those issues which are of idiosyncratic interest to an actor, and which are provided by programs that deliver "customized" news, music, or entertainment, might be the rational response of an individual who is being flooded by all types of

---

[104] Thompson, *The Media and Modernity*, at 132.

messages. However, collectively we are thereby in danger of losing a set of common experiences as well as the requisite variety of opinions which we perhaps had no idea existed, but upon which meaningful choices depend.[105] In other words, here some of the basic tenets of liberal thought are called into question: that more is better than less (whereby qualitative differences do not enter the calculus) and that political choices can or should be analyzed analogous to a "consumer's" choice. In the market we can simply refuse the offers and leave if we do not like the products. In the "forum" we have as an ongoing concern the maintenance of the community and, therefore, we emphasize voice and loyalty, rather than "exit."[106]

Consumer sovereignty means that the individual consumers are permitted to choose as they wish, subject to the constraints provided by the price system. Political sovereignty comes with its own distinctive preconditions, and these are violated if government (sic!) power is not backed by justification, and represents instead the product of force or simple majority will.[107]

Thus, while people might actually feel that they are part of a community when they use internet chat rooms, the question remains whether such self-ascriptions are apt. Are we just misusing words or are these new uses for old concepts indications of a new "practice"? Is there a different form of "politics" emerging that can replace the "old" notions, as suggested by e.g. by Beck?[108] Is politics with a small "p" replacing the notion of a politics written in capital letters?

There is indeed a new tendency to call any common interest shared by some people a "community." Thus the weather forecasters on American TV frequently speak of the "weather community" when a speaker tries to explain to the viewers what the best guess in a given situation is. Similarly, the nuclear scientists are frequently called a "community" and that not only in the epistemic sense (i.e. in that the persons falling under this description have a common expertise in a given subject matter), but also in a more extended, or "political" sense. After all, despite the fundamental differences resulting from membership in different political systems, there emerged during the Cold War – among quite a number of them – some notion of a common responsibility. This in turn even led to some form of institutionalization, such as the Pugwash meetings and the various efforts at arms control.

The upshot of this argument is that while the use of the term in the first example seems rather odd, the second one shows some family resemblance to our political practices. Thus, the extension of the term to such a phenomenon

---

[105] Sunstein, *Republic.com.*   [106] See Hirschman, *Exit, Voice, and Loyalty.*
[107] Sunstein, *Republic.com*, at 45.
[108] Ulrich Beck, *Risk Society: Towards a New Modernity*, London: Sage, 1992, at 183–236.

seems much less strained. A similar and perhaps even stronger case could be made for the "ecology" community, i.e. those international networks that not only try to influence state policy but to create new awareness and new practices at the grassroots, outflanking traditional political structures. Here again we see new forms of political practice emerging, but not in terms of the displacement of the old forms of "representative" decision-making through states (and its concomitant activity of lobbying), but by creating new forms of collaborative or conflictual practices. The role of NGOs in the agenda-setting[109] or even in the decision-making processes of "public" international organizations[110] and in the execution of certain policies, such as managing a country's debt[111] or engaging in joint development projects,[112] are striking examples of such

---

[109] Here the "greening" of the World Bank's agenda as well as the change from the Washington consensus to a post-Washington Consensus emphasizing poverty reduction as a policy goal for the World Bank and the IMF could be mentioned. For a general discussion, see Paul Nelson, "Agendas Accountability and Legitimacy among Transnational Networks Lobbying the Bank" in Sanjeev Khagram, Kathryn Sikkink, and James V. Riker (eds.), *Restructuring World Politics: Transnational Social Movements, Networks, and Norms*, Minneapolis: University of Minnesota Press, 2002, 131–154. See e.g. Philippe G. Le Prestre, "Environmental Learning at the World Bank" in Robert V. Bartlett, Priya A. Kurian, and Madhu Malik (eds.), *International Organizations and Environmental Policy*, Westport, CT: Greenwood Press, 1995, 83–101; Robert Wade, "Greening the Bank: The Struggle over the Environment, 1970–1995" in Devesh Kapur, John P. Lewis, and Richard Charles Webb (eds.), *The World Bank: Its First Half Century*, Washington, DC: Brookings Institution, 1997, 611–735. On "developmental" issues, see Paul J. Nelson, *The World Bank and Non-Governmental Organizations: The Limits of Apolitical Development*, New York: St. Martin's Press, 1995.

[110] Here the cases of two gigantic dams to be financed by the World Bank, whereby the Arun III Hydro Electric Dam in Nepal was finally cancelled by the Bank because of increasing pressures of NGOs, working at the grassroots level as well as through the US Congress and official political structures of several lender countries comes to mind. For an assessment, see Lori Udall, "The World Bank and Public Accountability: Has Anything Changed?" in Jonathan Fox and L. David Brown (eds.), *The Struggle for Accountability: The World Bank, NGOs, and Grassroots Movements*, Cambridge, MA: MIT Press, 1998, 391–436.

[111] For a comprehensive account of the evolution of the debt regime in which the Basle Committee on Banking Supervision, the Bank for International Settlement and the Paris Club of Creditor States cooperate on the basis of programs largely designed by NGOs and some insiders at the World Bank, see Thomas Callaghy, *Innovation in the Sovereign Debt Regime: From the Paris Club to Enhanced HIPC and Beyond*, Washington, DC: World Bank, 2004. Callaghy focuses here on the "Heavily Indebted Poor Country Debt Initiative" (HIPC) of the mid 1990s which included such initiatives as "Jubilee 2000," organized by a coalition of fifty NGOs mainly in Great Britain in order to press for debt relief by the year 2000, and the subsequent developments that led to the Enhanced HIPC Debt Initiative with its heavy focus on poverty reduction. Under the plan (labeled the Poverty Reduction Strategy paper, or PRSP), the proposals must be "nationally owned and must be produced in consultation with civil society." See www.imf.org/external/np/prsp/. See also Elizabeth A. Donnelly, "Proclaiming Jubilee: The Debt and Structural Adjustment Network" in Sanjeev Khagram, Kathryn Sikkink, and James V. Riker (eds.), *Restructuring World Politics: Transnational Social Movements, Networks, and Norms*, Minneapolis: University of Minnesota Press, 2002, 155–180.

[112] See e.g. John Farrington and Anthony Bebbington (eds.), *Reluctant Partners?: Non-Governmental Organizations, the State and Sustainable Agricultural Development*, London: Routledge, 1993.

changes. The "Working Group" of the World Bank, in which bank officials and NGOs examine the implications of existing policies, could also be mentioned in this context.[113]

With these important data in mind how shall we assess the changes? First, international organizations, as part of the "internationalization of the state,"[114] have created new structures for transnationally organized networks and movements to exert influence and hold international institutions accountable for their policies and rules. This can be seen in direct analogy to the case of the traditional "public" and the somewhat wider conception of "civil society,"[115] which articulated demands vis-à-vis the state. The "global governance" discourse correctly identifies the new forms of rule that develop beyond traditional state structures. While these new institutions have changed the "old" political game, even the most sympathetic assessments have to admit that these new forms of friendly or critical cooperation have not dislodged states from their dominant position (perhaps with the exception of certain sectors within the EU and its comitology).

Second, even if we agree with the argument that procedures are more legitimate when they are transparent and all the stakeholders have access to the relevant information, there remain two problems for the "politics" made in such arenas. One has to do with the legitimacy of those claiming to be stakeholders. From the corporatist literature we know that stakeholder arrangements are in danger of not only privileging well-organized interests but are also subject to capture impairing the legitimacy of the policies or rules. One might reply that the problem of the "voiceless," such as political prisoners or indigenous populations, can in a way be alleviated by the inclusion of various "stewards" or trustees of common but un- or under-represented interests. In the

---

[113] In addition, one could mention the campaigns of NGOs that led to the creation of an Inspection Panel by the World Bank in 1993 and the establishment in 1999 of an Ombudsman for International Finance Corporation (i.e. the part of the World Bank that deals with the private sector) and the Multilateral Investment Guarantee Agency. These structural changes created new transparency and a form of "horizontal accountability." See Ngaire Woods and Amrita Narlikar, "Governance and the Limits of Accountability: The WTO, the IMF, and the World Bank," *International Social Science Journal*, 53:170 (2001): 569–583.

[114] The term was first used by Cox in 1981 to emphasize the increasing rule-making capacity of institutions beyond the territorial State. See Robert Cox, "Social Forces, States and World Order: Beyond International Relations Theory," *Millennium*, 10:2 (1981): 204–254.

[115] Out of the vast literature on this topic I want to cite just three recent examples that engage this concept and the respective debates: Adam B. Seligman, *The Idea of Civil Society*, Princeton: Princeton University Press, 1992; Michael Edwards, *Civil Society*, Cambridge, MA: Polity Blackwell, 2004; Simone Chambers and Will Kymlicka, *Alternative Conceptions of Civil Society*, Princeton: Princeton University Press, 2002. A more sociological approach linking up with the social movement literature can be found in Sidney Tarrow, *Power in Movement: Social Movements and Contentious Politics*, Cambridge: Cambridge University Press, 1998; Donatella della Porta and Sidney Tarrow (eds.), *Transnational Protest and Global Activism*, Lanham, MD: Rowman & Littlefield, 2004.

international arena many NGOs have claimed to represent "the people,"[116] but the question of their legitimization cannot be taken at face value. If the question of "who elected the bankers" is legitimate, then the same can be asked about the IMF, the UN,[117] and probably also about Oxfam or Amnesty International, even if we like what they are doing.

The third problem concerns the inevitable conflicts that arise when two possibly equally legitimate policies conflict, or the jurisdictional question has to be decided, e.g. whether an issue is part of issue area A rather than B ("free trade" rather than "labor").[118] In the latter case, substantive understandings might fail us precisely because never before encountered problems arise, and the *ex ante* agreed-upon principles for resolving conflicts, such as the "principle of subsidiarity," might not be of much help either. Thus, an argument based on subsidiarity, that e.g. "safety" measures are best decided upon by the people at the workplace, seems to qualify as a clear candidate for "local" (or industry -wide) instead of national or even supranational regulation. But since such prescriptions might have effects on "competition," they also call for central regulation at the highest level, precisely because the effects of local regulations cannot be split neatly along the global (central) vs. the local (horizontal) axis.

It is for these reasons that we need some form of constitutional arrangement that provides not only for procedures to decide such conflicts of competence, but that also creates the presumption or the "prerogative" to act on a specific issue when it has been identified as a problem. It is, however, clear that such a power requires a legitimization that far exceeds that of a "stakeholder arrangement," or of some issue-oriented community, meeting occasionally in the virtual space of a chat room or even that of a network. Relying simply on some pragmatic notion of "output legitimacy,"[119] as is sometimes suggested, has an intuitive appeal but encounters two difficulties. On the one hand it does not answer to the democratic deficit objections,[120] and on the other hand it

---

[116] Thus at the 1999 Seattle Ministerial Conference of the WTO, 738 NGOs were accredited and also had some influence in the dispute resolution mechanism by being allowed to file *amicus curiae* briefs; see David Robertson, "Civil Society and the WTO," *The World Economy*, 23:9 (2000): 1119–1134.

[117] Jan Klabbers has articulated this question in his critique of the "functional ideology" on which the legitimacy of international organizations is built. See Jan Klabbers, "The EJIL Foreword: The Transformation of International Organizations Law," *European Journal of International Law*, 26:1 (2015): 9–82.

[118] See Kratochwil, *The Status of Law in World Society*, chaps. 3 and 4.

[119] Fritz Wilhelm Scharpf, *Demokratietheorie zwischen Utopie und Anpassung*, Konstanz: Universitätsverlag, 1970.

[120] Similar concerns are voiced in the present discussion about "fragmentation" in international law. The proliferation of courts, tribunals, and arbitration panels, not to speak of national courts in their function as institutions of the international legal order often coming to different conclusions in similar cases seems increasingly to require decision at levels of higher instance in order to reconcile the differences. In the national legal system, appellate and constitutional courts serve this purpose. No such clear-cut supraordination (aside from in some of the writings of legalists) is provided in the international arena.

neglects the fact that legitimacy is also deeply affected by considerations of the "coherence" of different arrangements.[121] Whatever position we might take on these issues,[122] one thing seems to be clear: Accountability raises a whole host of problems that go far beyond the issue of insuring transparency and the naïve underlying notion that "seeing" is "knowing" and that that is all there is. As Chapter 7 on international criminal justice will show, such a conclusion would hardly be justifiable.

4.6   Conclusion

This chapter was concerned with the function of norms by contributing to the establishment of "the facts." By linking this theme with the present discussions about transparency I tried in Section 4.2 to deal with the difficulties that the data we collect to make something more transparent are not simply "there" but always need interpretation. This was exemplified by first interpreting the records derived from remote sensing, and second by showing that the data most important to social issues concern facts, i.e. not simple events but "deeds" that necessitate their appraisal. Given that we, as participants and observers, are deeply implicated in the constitution of such facts, a critical awareness of this problem is required (Section 4.3). Section 4.4 examined the "slippage" that occurs between donors and debtors in international financial relations, which suggests that "transparency" is not enough since two different sources of legitimacy become an issue: "expertise" on the one hand and "popular" support on the other. Section 4.5 focused on the reports promulgated by the media, their effects on public debate and deliberation. In this context I examined the emergence of a "global public sphere" but noted that most discussions about transparency actually address the issue of "responsibility" on which especially the weakly articulated "global public sphere" cannot make good. This discussion brought us back to our previous theme of establishing "what is the case" by other means, such as by "sanctioning institutions" of various kinds, which will occupy us in the next three chapters.

It will be the task of the next chapter to elaborate on these points more fully.

---

[121] On the importance of this dimension of legitimacy, see Franck, *The Power of Legitimacy among Nations*.

[122] For a more optimistic reading of the transformative and democratic potential of international regimes on the basis of two case studies (WTO and Global Environment Facility), see Rodger A. Payne and Nayef H. Samhat, *Democratizing Global Politics: Discourse Norms, International Regimes, and Political Community*, Albany, NY: SUNY Press, 2004.

5   Guiding

5.1   Introduction

The purpose of this chapter is to probe the role of norms in guiding choices. While the interest in regimes has served as a bridge between law and international relations, the marriage has not necessarily been a happy one, for reasons suggested in my previous book on the difficulties of interdisciplinary research.[1] There is no reason to rehearse the argument here, save to note that the difficulties are of a historical and conceptual nature. In this context, the disciplinary understandings of "politics" and "law" as they emerged from the crisis of nineteenth-century philosophy and from the breakdown of the traditional order of the European state system in World War I were of particular importance.[2] As pointed out, the anemic conception of politics as "power politics" was paralleled by limiting the concerns of jurisprudence to issues of conceptual analysis and to the strict demarcation of the legal system, conceived as a hierarchy of norms. Oddly enough, these disciplinary understandings were, if not directly complementary, nevertheless parasitic upon each other.

It is my contention in this chapter that continuing these attempts is not very promising and that, therefore, a fundamental conceptual reorientation is necessary. In short, if we are interested in how norms matter, we had better begin with the problem of praxis and then proceed to draw out the implications of this turn for both political and legal analysis. Such an enterprise is obviously beyond the scope of this chapter alone and it reappears again and again in different sections of this book. I rely in that endeavor on some forerunners in sociology[3] and in

---

[1]   See Kratochwil, *The Status of Law in World Society.*
[2]   See e.g. E.H. Carr, *The Twenty Years' Crisis.* New York: Harper Torchbooks, 1981.
[3]   See Pierre Bourdieu, *Outline of a Theory of Practice*, Cambridge: Cambridge University Press, 1977.

practical philosophy,[4] and, as of late, on the debate on a turn to pragmatism in international relations.[5]

In this chapter, I want to focus on two conceptual problems that have played a decisive role in legal and political analysis: the conception of the indeterminacy of law with its corollary of extreme rule skepticism on the one hand, and the idea that the influence of norms on actual choices requires the discovery of some causal mechanism, on the other hand. Both positions are the result of considerable conceptual befuddlements. By showing this I also hope to make good on a wider claim: that our conceptions of explanation and justification both in law and in IR analysis are unduly restrictive and that the alleged indeterminacy of law, as well as the inadequacy of norms to "cause" a certain behavior, in no way justifies the conclusions usually drawn from such alleged failures of "theory." Rather, as I shall argue, they call into question the relevance and adequacy of the notion of "theory" itself for illuminating the realm of praxis, be it in law or in international relations.

These claims are admittedly rather heady, and in order to make good on them, my presentation takes the following steps. In the next section (Section 5.2), I investigate the defining moment of IR analysis and probe the repercussions that resulted from the emphasis on power as a defining criterion of a field of IR. Section 5.3 is then devoted to the problem of rule skepticism in general and to the notion that even if international law could be shown to be "true" law, it could not evade the weakness of this type of law, as it seems to aimlessly oscillate between "apology and utopia."[6] I proceed here in two steps. First I show that this position suffers from a semantic confusion about indeterminacy and second I demonstrate that the far-reaching conclusions derived from this alleged failure are unjustified on logical as well as on practical grounds. This argument in turn strengthens the normative pull of pluralism as a regulative idea for the analysis of the social world.

Section 5.4 takes up the contemporary debate in IR analysis concerning the status of norms as an explanatory "variable." In particular, I examine the dominant approaches, i.e. the rationalistic one and a more sociologically oriented one, which partially coincides with constructivism, and the emerging liberal

---

[4] Such an attempt is made e.g. by Joseph Raz (ed.), *Practical Reasoning*, Oxford: Oxford University Press, 1978; Frederick F. Schauer, *Playing by the Rules: A Philosophical Examination of Rule-Based Decision-Making in Law and in Life*, Oxford: Oxford University Press, 1991.

[5] Harry Bauer and Elisabetta Brighi (eds.), *Pragmatism in International Relations*, Abingdon: Routledge, 2009; Adler and Pouliot, *International Practices*; Christian Bueger and Frank Gadinger, *International Practice Theory: New Perspectives*, Houndsmill: Palgrave Macmillan, 2014.

[6] See e.g. the argument in Martti Koskenniemi, *From Apology to Utopia: The Structure of International Legal Argument*, Helsinki: Finnish Lawyers' Pub. Co., 1989.

theory of political action. In pointing to the respective strengths and weaknesses of these approaches, I prepare the way for a more principled discussion of the role of norms in explanatory schemes of social action in Section 5.5. There I argue that our preoccupation with identifying the efficient causes and the "mechanisms" by which norms are supposed to mold decisions prevents us from recognizing that explanatory schemes for actions serve different purposes and that therefore adhering to an unrealizable logical ideal of the uniqueness (and predictability) of outcomes has contributed to the derailment of social analysis. Similarly, given the characteristics of practical problems, "explanations" must satisfy different criteria and, on pain of irrelevance, we cannot pick one explanatory model and consider it the standard that all explanations have to satisfy. Far from suggesting that, therefore, "anything goes," the upshot of this argument is that pragmatic criteria play a much greater role in social science explanations than is usually assumed.

Section 5.6 is devoted to the discussion of stability and change, i.e. how rules allow us to "go on," but do so not by reproducing exactly the identical actions that are supposedly stored in the action repertoires, and become "causes." The interesting question then is not how the norms get "into the mind" of the actors and how we can insure that they will result in identical choices in the future in accordance with causal imputations. Instead I argue that considerable change is always part of praxis and of social reproduction, and thus not identity or "sameness" but the ability of going on is the important part of rule-following. Furthermore, since norms have to be "applied" to a problem at hand, interpretation and other modes of practical reasoning – ranging from exemplary to analogous reasoning to narrative "followability" – kick in. Consequently, our modes of using norms for orienting ourselves in choice situations cannot be fitted to the Procrustean bed of generalizing inferences, sub-sumptions, or efficient causal imputations. The focus on different ways of reasoning about practical problems allows us then to approach the problem of "precedent" in law and in political arguments. A brief summary (Section 5.7) concludes the chapter.

5.2   The Strange Symbiosis of Realism and Legalism

It has been the conventional wisdom that the emergence of IR as a field occurred when the utopian hopes that, with technical and economic progress, the rule of law would finally replace politics were disappointed in the bloodbaths of World Wars I and II. "Utopian thinking" had been clearly identified by E.H. Carr,[7] the "father" of the modern discipline of IR, as the culprit, by

---

[7] See Carr, *The Twenty Years' Crisis*.

reason of its belief in the natural harmony of interest, the perfectibility of the social order through the progressive development of law, and by the force of public opinion à la Bentham. The development of a new discipline called International Relations therefore required emancipation from the legal discourse and its concerns. Carr's cautious remarks on the impossibility of politics without a utopia, and his rather measured assessment of the role of moral principles in deliberations about the conduct of foreign affairs, were subsequently largely cast to the wind. The necessity of the new discipline legitimizing itself by claiming to be a science, as economics had done before, led to the rupture of the links that traditionally had connected prudential and pragmatic historical reflections with political praxis.

The allure of "science" explains the subsequent tendency to resort to the bag of methodological tricks, instead of addressing the underlying conceptual problems. It was this tendency which Hedley Bull with his advocacy for a "traditional approach" attempted to counteract,[8] but this move also explains a great deal of the curious mutual conditioning of the prevalent legal discourse and realism. As realism tried to cleanse itself of all normative conceptions (save power), so law had largely attempted to free itself from all social and moral contingencies.[9] Rules of law were either to be distinguished by their "character-tag" of sanctions, or they had to be members of a system and be traceable back to some source or rule of recognition.[10] In this fashion, law could establish its autonomy from morals, other social conventions, as well as any unprincipled form of bargaining.

We need not rehearse here the well-known arguments against such a conception of law, either in its Kelsenian version as a sanctioning order, or in the conception of law as a system of rules. What is interesting, though, is the fact that on the basis of these largely disciplinary considerations an entirely implausible conception of politics is paralleled by an equally problematic conception of law. Similar to the concern with the purity of law, the autonomy of politics, especially international politics, defined by the "national interest" in terms of power, must never be confused with other goals. The lesson seems clear: since war remains, in Hobbesian terms, the always-latent possibility, the core concern of international politics with power retains its prominence. But quite aside from the fact that such theory glosses over the important distinction between possibility and probability, the ideological character of this position becomes readily apparent.

---

[8] Hedley Bull, "International Theory: The Case for a Classical Approach," *World Politics*, 18:3 (1966): 361–377.

[9] See e.g. Hans Kelsen, *General Theory of Law and State*, trans. Anders Wedberg, Cambridge, MA: Harvard University Press, 1945.

[10] H.L.A. Hart, *The Concept of Law*, Clarendon Law Series, Oxford: Oxford University Press, 1961.

What the "national interest" can be except ideology is hard to say, but one thing is clear to realists – it must never be conceived in terms of moral or legalistic values. This was for instance, the great sin of Woodrow Wilson, the bête noire of realism ... its animus against Wilson goes well beyond a rejection of international law as the sole means to preserve peace. It is rather a direct dislike of liberal ideology, largely because the latter failed. The urge to debunk thus becomes a psychological response to disenchantment, a tough sneer at all "cant."[11]

Conversely, since the uncompromising character of justice, equated with strict rule application, militates against the unprincipled forms of accommodation, all politics must either be assimilated to the paradigm of "just action," or exorcised until the time finally comes when the orderly process of legal change prevails over violence, bargaining, and power. Thus, it is not surprising that for adherents of this position the lesson of World Wars I and II was not that legalism had failed because it relied on an unviable social theory, but rather that its failure was due to the fact that the pre- and interwar doctrines concerning the "rule of law" had not gone far enough.[12]

Inherent in the notion of law as a system of rules is a vision that only principled choice can be just and that, therefore, the successive development of law would provide the best prospects for a just and peaceful order. Forgetting that peace in the domestic arena has only partially to do with the "rule of law" but a great deal more with the successful *institutionalization of the political process*, the peaceful resolution of conflict at home seemed to provide the prescription for the international arena: codification and further development of international law. Oppenheim certainly was not alone in believing that the end of Machiavellianism was at hand, and although there would always be some bad men, in the meantime states themselves had become more and more civilized.[13] Law was not only independent of politics, it was held to be superior to it. After all, politics could not be understood without some constitutional rules, while law was "its own creation" and could freely generate new rules.

It needs only a moment's reflection to see that this entails a category mistake of considerable proportions. While rules might create other rules in that they validate them, it is obvious that this logical validation has little to do with historical creation or with the actual force which these rules will have in molding decisions. To believe that merely the membership in a system creates the action-guiding force is faulty for a number of reasons. One is that the idea

---

[11] Ibid., 124.
[12] See the well-taken critique of Martti Koskenniemi, "The Politics of International Law," *European Journal of International Law*, 1:1 (1990): 4–32.
[13] L. Oppenheim, *The Future of International Law*, Oxford: Clarendon Press, 1921, at 54f.

that law is a logically closed system is simply wrong, as higher-order principles are compatible with lower-order rules that contradict each other.[14] Closure occurs, if at all, only in the act of deciding a "case" in which a variety of factual as well as normative concerns play a role. Thus, not only do facts count, different fact descriptions may actually play a more decisive role in carrying the weight of a decision than the norms invoked.

Secondly, even explicitly formulated rules come with ambiguities, although we often do not realize how many implicit understandings we must invoke in order to establish the connection between the norms stated in the rule and the controversy the rule is supposed to resolve. Consider in this context Simmonds's simple example of the injunction: "No dogs on the escalator."[15] The prohibition seems pretty clear and unambiguous, but is so only because it is embedded in a whole host of at first unarticulated shared understandings. Thus, knowing something about the potential dangers of moving stairs and the panics of animals and people, seems as necessary for our "correct" understanding of the rule, as being able to link the rule with entirely unstated legal norms which stay in the background.

Suppose however, as Simmonds suggests, that the police's basset hound, Pluto, follows me with his keeper wherever I go since I am an alleged suspect. Unfortunately, Pluto somehow seems to like me, and seeks my contact. Do I have to kick him off the escalator? We probably fall back on the "understanding" that this injunction means only if the dog is *my* dog. But this again will not do, as I am clearly obliged to avoid the escalator when the dog does not belong to me, but I have taken him out for a walk. Thus, an adequate interpretation of the rule requires that we locate it within a complex body of assumptions and shared understandings of individual responsibility (the point being that the basset is not my responsibility, while Ulysse, the dog who is not "mine" but whose dog-sitter I am, is).

The upshot of the above argument is that, to the extent to which interpretation is an intrinsic part of a legal system, a theory of law which depicts law as a simple system of higher- and lower-order rules and which seems to suggest that only at the top (in the *Grundnorm*, or in an extralegal rule of recognition) does "the law" meet social reality is simply incomplete. Unable to account coherently for the differences among principles and rules, as well *soft law*,[16] a rule approach cannot defend consistently the rigorous exclusion of

---

[14] This point has been powerfully made by Dworkin criticizing the Hartian conception of law as a system of rules. See R.M. Dworkin, "Is Law a System of Rules?" in R.M. Dworkin (ed.), *The Philosophy of Law*, Oxford: Oxford University Press, 1977, 38–65.

[15] N.E. Simmonds, "Between Positivism and Idealism," *Cambridge Law Journal*, 50:2 (1991): 308–329.

[16] Ignaz Seidl-Hohenfeldern, "International Economic Soft Law," *Recueil des Cours*, 163 (1979): 165–246, at 169f.; Prosper Weil, "Towards Relative Normativity in International Law?" *The American Journal of International Law*, 77:3 (1983): 413–442.

considerations external to law, be they moral precepts, policy considerations, or contextual factors. It is therefore not surprising that modern legal theories have either radically challenged the notion of law as a system of rules, by emphasizing process and policy-consideration, or have introduced the problem of interpretation as the central conceptual puzzle. A brief discussion is in order.

The radical denial of the importance of rules, and the emphasis on policy, is characteristic of a process approach, perhaps best exemplified by the McDouglian inquiry.[17] Rules are devalued, as they are only indicators for past trends that may, or may no longer, further the present or future needs of the actors. The formality of rules representing their binding force is then a juristic illusion since their normative guidance derives from their effectiveness in furthering social goals, not from the validity conferred upon them by a source or other rule within a system.

The objections to such a radical reformulation of the legal problematique are legion and need not be rehearsed here at length. Above all, an approach that postulates a supreme "goal value," as e.g. McDougal's "human dignity," relies on a highly problematic naturalism, which together with the emphasis on the formative influence of the decision-making process on outcomes, is in constant danger of becoming just an apology for the policies and preferences of the most powerful.[18] To that extent, law is neither able to mediate between different conceptions of the good – a central tenet of liberal theory and of obvious relevance to international law – nor can it be said to shape the political process in a distinct way, as *it is* more or less the political process.

The other strategy for dealing with the difficulties resulting from the rules approach is to make legal theory explicitly a theory of interpretation. Law is no longer viewed from the outside as a system of rules, but as an argumentative practice, i.e. from the inside. What law means is then no longer simply ascertainable by the formal status of rules but by their use and the justifiability of the decisions arrived at. Legal theory is an interpretation of the practice of engaging in normative argument and arriving at justifiable positions. But different from morals, or from the process- or policy perspective, this justifiability is firmly tied to the conception of the integrity of law. This integrity requires that the rule-handlers – and here, particularly, appellate judges are adressed – are obliged to have regard to the established practices and must not simply invent them. To that extent, earlier decisions constrain later ones and deviations or reversals have to be justified in terms of principled arguments,

---

[17] Myres McDougal and Harold Laswell, "The Identification and Appraisal of Diverse Systems of Public Order" in Richard A. Falk and Saul H. Mendlovitz (eds.), *The Strategy of World Order*, New York: World Law Fund, 1966, 45–74.

[18] See James Boyle, "Ideals and Things: International Legal Scholarship and the Prison-House of Language," *Harvard International Law Journal*, 26:2 (1985): 327–360, at 349.

rather than by utility or policy considerations, particularly when rights are at stake.[19] Although Dworkin elaborated these ideas early on in his career, he defended such tenets against a mounting chorus of objections over the years, negating even that there is a conflict among values.[20]

In this context the issue of the discretion of the judge looms large and the justifiability of a decision depends virtually entirely on the problem whether the judge's discretion was exercised within the proper bounds. It is here that Dworkin attempts to demonstrate the virtually impossible, i.e. that even hard cases have, when all is said and done, one and only one "right" solution. Fortunately, for us, he charges a mythical figure (Hercules) with this task.[21] Hercules, although paradigmatic for the good judge, is obviously not of this world and need therefore not concern us any further here, particularly since neither a constitutional text nor a doctrine of *stare decisis* applies in international law. For our purposes two things are important: one, how this theory represents the latest attempt at upholding the tenets of legalism and thus reproduces once more the opposition and strange symbiosis of "law" and "politics"; two, how this symbiosis is disturbed by the internal criticism this particular legal theory has engendered. It is via the criticisms made by the critical legal studies movement[22] of this theory that I want to approach the issue of rule guidance in legal contexts in the next section.

5.3   Discretion and Uniqueness

The problem of the indeterminacy of rules has been one of the veritable chestnuts of jurisprudence. Already the legal realist had pointed out that due to the unclear boundaries of the legal concepts, judicial decisions could not simply be derived from rules and, therefore, they had to be largely the result of idiosyncratic factors. All the more important, therefore, was Dworkin's argument that such problems could be circumvented and that the correct solution could be found if the more general principles of a legal system, in conjunction with the proper standards of interpretation, were used.[23]

It is against this "one right answer" conception of law that the criticism of the critical legal studies movement was directed. Originating in a critical

---

[19] For a good exposition of these ideas, see e.g. the collection of essays by R.M. Dworkin, *A Matter of Principle*, Cambridge, MA: Harvard University Press, 1985.
[20] See Ronald Dworkin, *Justice for Hedgehogs*, Cambridge, MA: Belknap Press of Harvard University Press, 2011.
[21] Dworkin, *A Matter of Principle*, chap. 4.
[22] For an introduction to critical legal studies, see Kelman, *A Guide to Critical Legal Studies*.
[23] For a criticism of this position see the collection of essays by Marshall Cohen (ed.), *Ronald Dworkin and Contemporary Jurisprudence*, Totowa, NJ: Rowman & Allanheld, 1984.

assessment of contract law,[24] the critical legal school (CLS) soon branched out and subjected other parts of law to its criticism. For adherents of the CLS the existence of contradictions among rules and higher-order principles made both the notion of one correct decision and the idea of firm rule guidance for arriving at the "right" decision, rather fanciful.

Contradictions arise systematically on three distinct levels of the legal order. The first is the level of choice between specific rules and more general, but therefore vague, standards. The result of this contradiction is that in adjudicating any concrete dispute there remains the problem of how one is to justify the choice between strict rules and discretionary standards. The utilization of the former safeguards procedural uniformity; the invocation of the latter results in decisions that are more situation-sensitive, but carries with it with the danger of "ad hocery." Second, ambiguity also enters at the level of doctrines, which are designed to resolve first-level disputes. Doctrines, contrary to the hopes one might place in them, are only able to provide us with a list of counterpoised functional arguments for the applicability of rules and standards, without, however, being able to provide a solution to the new dilemma. Third, underneath this doctrinal ambiguity lies the hidden ambivalence concerning substantive ideals, particularly in the standard liberal vision of adjudication. While rules express the ideals of self-reliance and individualism, standards or principles favor substantive justice and possibly altruism.

The differences between the CLS arguments and those of legal realism now become clear. While maintaining the autonomy of law but locating indeterminacy deeply within the legal system itself, CLS adherents cast considerable doubt on the availability of the simple cure which realists had advocated: the "purposive" reading of legal prescriptions. In their trenchant criticism of the consequentialist yardstick used by the "law and economics" school, Duncan Kennedy pointed out that nothing in the principles of contract law is definite enough to allow a judge or legislator to calculate the costs that e.g. the insertion of implied warranties into contracts imposes on particular groups or interests. "Since on Kennedy's analysis law is too indeterminate to be a bearer of economic interest, it follows that it cannot be used in an instrumental fashion."[25] Thus, neither the economy nor society explains the development of law and its internal dynamic.

Similarly, international legal arguments exhibit, as Martti Koskenniemi suggests, the same structure.[26] They too are based on differing conceptions of law

---

[24] See Duncan Kennedy, "Form and Substance in Private Law Adjudication," *Harvard Law Review*, 89 (1976): 1685–1778.
[25] David Jabbari, "From Criticism to Construction in Modern Critical Legal Theory," *Oxford Journal of Legal Studies*, 12:4 (1992): 507–542, at 525.
[26] Koskenniemi, *From Apology to Utopia*.

(consent vs. justice), differing doctrines, and they have also to deal with the same dilemmas of rules vs. standards (concreteness vs. normativity). In criticizing the usual mainstream solutions, be they "middle of the road doctrines," or "balancing" facts with legal rules (as in the case of the emergence and recognition of statehood) – these strategies seem suspect and at odds with the notion of the rule of law. As Koskenniemi remarks:

> Mainstream doctrine retreats into general statements about the need to "combine" concreteness and normativity, realism and idealism, which bear no consequence to its normative conclusion. It then advances, emphasizing the contextuality of each solution – thus undermining its own emphasis on the general and impartial character of its system.
>
> A doctrine's own contradictions force it into an impoverished and unreflective pragmatism. On the one hand, the "idealist" illusion is preserved that law can and does play a role in the organization of social life among states. On the other hand, the "realist" criticisms have been accepted and the law is seen as distinctly secondary to power and politics. The style survives because we recognize in it the liberal doctrine within which we have been accustomed to press our political arguments.[27]

These are indeed serious dilemmas that could easily lead to nihilism and/or withdrawal, as no introduction of new values or purposes seems to be possible so as to resolve our quandary of the justifiability of our practical choices. True, there remains the position of an existential choice, but, by definition, such choices have to be private, and it is unclear how any coherent understanding of social order and its requirements can be based on such a footing. To that extent, the particular political agenda which many CLS members espouse seems even less justifiable than that which was connected with the old liberal conceptions of law, which the CLS so powerfully criticized. In this context a second dilemma arises: although we might now possess in law an at least powerful rhetorical tool, the critical attitude seems to rule out our using it justifiably for public purposes, on pain of inconsistency with our professed theoretical stance. Our predicament seems to be circumscribed by the Scylla of blind and unjustifiable activism and the Charybdis of existential withdrawal.

As with so many dilemmas, there is no solution as long as we accept the terms in which the dilemma is posed. Rather a solution becomes possible only after we have "deconstructed" the dilemma law and reworked some of the crucial conceptual issues that led to the impasse. The importance of such a gestalt shift for social theory has been pointed out by Rorty and is familiar to every student of the history of political thought.[28] For example, the conception of politics communicated by organic metaphors, such as the "body politic," was

---

[27] Koskenniemi, "The Politics of International Law," at 12.
[28] Richard Rorty, *Contingency, Irony, and Solidarity*, Cambridge: Cambridge University Press, 1989.

supplanted in the seventeenth century largely by the metaphor of "contract." The important point in this context is that the new conceptualizations can neither be reached from the old vocabularies and their logic, nor can the process of producing a new set of concepts and puzzles be interpreted as hitting upon or approximating a "correct" representation of reality, since a polity is neither a body nor a contract. Rorty's method, called "therapeutic re-description," provides us with the possibility of seeing the old in a new way and creating new opportunities for practices and experiences that sidestep the old vocabulary which is getting in the way.

Such creations are not the result of successfully fitting together pieces of a puzzle. They are not discoveries of a reality behind the appearances, of an undistorted view of the whole picture with which to replace myopic views of its parts. The proper analogy is with the invention of new tools to take the place of old tools. To come up with such a vocabulary is more like discarding the lever and the chock because one has envisaged the pulley.[29]

In other words, new ways of conceptualization presuppose two steps: one of unlearning by deconstructing the problem, and one of construction by utilizing in the analysis new conceptual tools.

In applying these insights to our problem, we have first to clear up some fundamental misunderstandings concerning issues of indeterminacy before we can examine various strategies dealing with this problem. Implicit in our understanding of how norms mold decisions seems to be the idea that the conclusion must not only follow from the legal premise contained in the major premise (in conjunction with the facts in the minor premise) via the standard patterns of inference, but that the solution has to be unique. To that extent, Dworkin's rather contorted argument about the availability of the "right" decision is only the flipside of the argument that in the absence of such determinacy everything has to end up in "relativism." The underlying idea is that logical consistency requires convergence on a unique result, since both together constitute "truth." Such a position has of course great appeal. After all, divergence of results is usually interpreted as an "error" or even refutation of the major premise, which necessitates corrective steps.

As persuasive as such arguments appear, a moment's reflection shows that matters are a bit more complicated. Let us take the prototypical case of determinacy: the mathematical problem, in which the complexities of the "real world" do not yet even play a part. Thus, the solution is entirely determined by logic. Nevertheless, we realize that "uniqueness" does not necessarily follow. It seems that uniqueness is an additional criterion that does not always go hand in glove with determination. One could not possibly argue that

---

[29] Rorty, "The Contingency of Language" in ibid., 3–23, at 12.

the solutions of quadratic equations, familiar from basic analytic geometry, are not "determined," despite the fact that two values for x and y satisfy the equations. Similarly, the Folke theorem of game theory has shown that generally multiple equilibria exist for a whole range of interdependent choices. Thus determinacy and uniqueness again do not coincide. It seems rather problematic then to require "uniqueness" as a criterion for judicial decisions, when it is frequently not even available in logic.

For whatever reasons we might believe that non-uniqueness condemns us to "relativism," adhering to this ideal seems more like chasing a rainbow than a rational attitude in respect to practical problems. Furthermore, taking the particular features of the practical realm into account, Sir Isaiah Berlin pointed out that the "right answer" thesis (uniqueness) and its flipside, "relativism," depend on a utopian claim concerning the metaphysics of values and of normative justification. They assume that all questions in the domain have one answer, that this is knowable, and that all answers in this entire realm are mutually compatible.[30] It needs no further elaboration that such assumptions are not only on all fours with our experience (ranging from "moral luck"[31] to "tragic choices"[32]), they also lead us to misdiagnose the nature of practical arguments as concerning mainly cognitive issues. Besides, we all know from practical experience that without a certain value opportunism, which allows us to make various tradeoffs in different situations, life would become pretty oppressive. Consistency is certainly a virtue but in practical questions it might be the virtue of small minds and/or fanatics.

Far from drawing us into the vortex of "relativism," the recognition of plural possibilities on the one hand, and the need to justify our particular choice on the other hand, is the basis for pluralism and orderly change, both of which are central goods a legal system is supposed to preserve. That these goals often conflict is hardly news. But this conflict in no ways implies the nihilistic or existential conclusion that anything goes and/or that because there is no single right answer, any answer is as good as any other. Rather what seems to be required is an investigation, first, of indeterminacy as it arises in legal reasoning, and second, of how particular choices (out of several "possible" ones) can be justified on non-idiosyncratic grounds. This emphasis on justification brings into play pragmatic considerations that relieve us of the problems of semantic indeterminacy. To that extent, the solution adumbrated here is similar to that proposed by the later Wittgenstein. Having tried to specify the rules of

[30] Isaiah Berlin, "The Pursuit of the Ideal" in Isaiah Berlin, *The Proper Study of Mankind: An Anthology of Essays*, edited by Henry Hardy and Roger Hausheer, New York: Farrar, Straus and Giroux, 1998, 1–17.
[31] See Bernard Arthur Owen Williams, *Moral Luck: Philosophical Papers, 1973–1980*, Cambridge: Cambridge University Press, 1981.
[32] Guido Calabresi and Philip Bobbitt, *Tragic Choices*, New York: W.W. Norton, 1978.

correspondence between a term and its object, in his *Tractatus*, Wittgenstein moved in his later work to a conception of language in which the meaning of a term was defined by its "use."[33] In other words, *criteria* define now the conditions for the assertibility of or justification for using a term, rather than its semantic "content."[34]

Without engaging in a comprehensive review of the sources of indeterminacy, some distinctions are in order. One type of indeterminacy concerns problems of *indifference* familiar both from deontological and utilitarian theories. Like Buridan's ass, there are certain situations in which not even explicit decision criteria, such as "utility" calculations (not to mention even general rules), can determine my choice, since the alternatives are all the same to me. To resolve my quandary I have to resort to some additional choice mechanism, such as the flipping of a coin, or just do what I did last time. Whatever I do, one thing is clear, the original criterion for guiding my choice is by itself not able to help. Similarly, the function of rules in deontological theories consists largely in determining the area of freedom for individual choice by demarcating first the duties of an actor.[35] Since specific actions within the area of freedom are morally equivalent, we can say that the system of rules is *indeterminate* at the level of individual choice, but *determinate* at the level of defining classes of actions. Thus, volunteering at a hospital is an act of charity, as is inviting a homeless person to Thanksgiving dinner, or giving some money to a UNICEF program. But to which charity I should contribute is thereby not determined.

Seen from this perspective, the notion that the main function of law is that of "constraint" in order to arrive at determinate choices seems quaint indeed. If someone were to object to such indeterminacy and were committed to have things regulated once and for all, he would (and should) rightly "be committed." This raises the more general point that large areas of law are therefore badly conceived as "constraints," as the distinction between constitutive and regulative rules suggest. Constitutive rules are rather designed to enable the actors to pursue their own plans. If they are "constraints" at all, they are so only in the above sense that they allow us to characterize an action as falling within a certain class, e.g. as making a contract. This means that the parties must observe certain formalities regulated by rules. But these rules will not determine the particular substantive choices of the parties. The implications for international law are obvious: many if not most international legal norms

---

[33] See e.g. Ludwig Wittgenstein, *Philosophical Investigations*, trans. G.E.M. Anscombe, New York: Macmillan, 1953, §43.
[34] See e.g. the discussion in ibid., §§138–242.
[35] See Immanuel Kant, *The Metaphysics of Morals*, trans. Mary Gregor, Cambridge: Cambridge University Press, 1991, particularly 386–388.

(although not necessarily the most "important" ones, such as those regulating the use of force) are of such a constitutive nature, such as e.g. the law of treaties.

From the brief discussion we gather that only in very special circumstances will a rule lead to definite outcomes. It will be a small class of events (although it may contain quite numerous cases): as the example of the decision rule of flipping a coin above showed, only an additional rule solving a more or less pure coordination problem will lead to definite outcomes. Its parasitic nature, i.e. its dependence on other rules establishing the class of permitted actions, as well as the necessity of *common interests* among the actors, should be obvious.[36] Technically speaking, we are dealing here with situations where a rule is supposed to resolve the problem of two or more equilibria. Examples from the international arena are easy to find. Thus, no public or private actor will care whether he transmits on any particular wavelength for radio transmissions as long as he is allocated a specific spectrum insuring that he can send his messages without undue interference. While the conventional wisdom of the "self-enforcing" and unproblematic nature of these rules might be overly optimistic, as the hard bargaining for technical standards in the organizations concerned with the telecommunications order showed,[37] these types of rules are closely tied to functional cooperation in areas considered to be of a merely "technical" nature. But also more "important" or controversial choices can be handled in this fashion by entrusting some authority with finding the solution. The idea of "depoliticizing" fundamental questions by submitting them to constitutional courts might at first seem attractive but is likely to engender significant costs down the line, since the idea that a "constitutional order" can resolve normative conflict via the "right answer" thesis, is one of the fantasies of legalism. In criticizing Dworkin, Christopher Kutz points out:

Dworkin's response misses the point: if values are genuinely plural, then there neither can nor should be a successful technique for resolving all conflicts between them, such as the reduction of normative deliberation to a monistic calculus (e.g. wealth maximization), or the stipulation of an overarching principle to order values. Normative conflicts will simply reemerge when we seek to justify that framework for deliberation or that of ordering values.[38]

---

[36] For a more extended discussion, see Kratochwil, *Rules, Norms, and Decisions*, chaps. 3–4.

[37] See the discussion of the role of governments, particularly the US government, which pushed the proposals of its transnational corporations within the International Telecommunication Union of the UN, in William J. Drake, "Conclusion: Policies for the National and Global Information Infrastructures" in William J. Drake (ed.), *The New Information Infrastructure: Strategies for U.S. Policy*, New York: Twentieth Century Fund Press, 1995, 345–378.

[38] Christopher L. Kutz, "Just Disagreement: Indeterminacy and Rationality in the Rule of Law," *Yale Law Journal*, 103:4 (1994): 997–1030, at 1026.

Another type of indeterminacy arises when norms themselves conflict and make incompatible demands upon the actor. In extreme cases this amounts to tragic conflict, as the examples of Antigone or Agamemnon showed. Here the failure of normative guidance arises not out of equally possible and justifiable possibilities, but rather from the fact that no matter what one does, one important norm has to be violated. We react therefore not with indifference to such dilemmas, but with regret, or guilt. It is this type of conflict not only among specific rules, but also in the underlying justifications and fundamental values, which members of CLS like Kennedy have stressed.

A third source of indeterminacy is that rules have to be formulated in ordinary language and that means they have an open texture. The examples above have already shown several of the puzzles of semantic indeterminacy. As we have seen, what the apparently clear statement "No dogs on the escalator" meant was semantically ambiguous and its meaning could be construed only by relying on contextual factors. Here pragmatics rather than semantics provided the key in deciding whether the instruction applied only to the plural, to any dog, to any pet, only to my dog, or to the animal in general for which I was responsible, etc. Only by successively supplying through examples a context, did these terms become more definite.

Even particles of rules, such as terms like "reckless" or "fair" or even "big" or "exact," create similar difficulties. While we could have assumed that the difficulties stem from the existence of some normative standard, embodied in "reckless" and "fair," respectively, it is puzzling that we encounter the same problems when we use allegedly descriptive terms that are even susceptible to objective measurement, as in the case of "big" or "exact." The problem is that in both cases the issue of interpretation does not turn on simple evidentiary matters. There is no "fact of the matter," as the philosopher would say, whether or not the term in question applies. What is "exact" or "big" depends on the circumstances and not primarily on measurement, as Aristotle reminded us.[39] A deviation of two inches is no problem for an architect of a fifty-story house; it is a big problem for a doctor who has to remove a tumor from the brain, not to speak of the engineer in microelectronics. What represents a reckless act can only be ascertained by taking the circumstances into account. Being ten miles above the speed limit on a free interstate highway in Kansas is not the same as transgressing it on a narrow mountain road in Scotland or Tuscany, even if it is pretty free of traffic.

These are rather obvious observations. While they introduce in practical reasoning considerable uncertainty – and I treat here law as a special form of practical reasoning – there is no point in belaboring the vagueness of such

---

[39] Aristotle, *Nicomachean Ethics*, Baltimore: Penguin, 1953, at 1094 b13–1095 a7.

terms in pursuit of some mistaken semantic ideal. The only hope of clarifying the boundaries of the terms of everyday language consists precisely in the process of supplying context and elaborating the implications successively by adding examples in order to probe the vague penumbras of a term. If for the semantic purist this is like a pragmatic trick, so be it!

After all, language itself cannot be restricted to consistency and purely tautological derivation. But even semantics and syntax, which are supposed to specify the conditions for meaning, are not exhaustive. They specify, "dog bites man" is not equivalent to "man bites dog." But there are other cases where "meaning" is also communicated by pragmatic understandings, which we adduce in order to decode a message. Thus, "I like her cooking" might mean – dependent on the context – either the food or the activity. Furthermore, nobody could claim that a person has answered my question when he mistakes my "is Jim there?" on the phone as a genuine question, instead of a request. If he answers simply "yes" and hangs up, we are sure that he has not understood. Apparently, communications about practical problems do not concern solely semantic issues.

How mistaken the notion is that meaning can be reduced to issues of semantics can be seen if we imagine for a moment a world in which finally all terms have a clear referent in accordance with the semantic ideal. In a way, such a world would be that of a Hobbesian sovereign who, as the sole authoritative *fixer of signs*, could prescribe everything. But as Simmonds correctly points out, such a system of communication would nevertheless fail, precisely because prescriptions need common understandings as the background for their interpretation.

For what understandings and apprehended concerns could possibly inform our interpretations, leading us to converge on a shared interpretation? ... Hobbes does indeed claim that there is no "common rule of good and evil to be taken from the nature of the objects themselves" ... My argument is not intended to be a refutation of Hobbes. My object is simply to suggest that, in the chaos of subjectivity, a sovereign deliberately positing could not create a shared body of rules certain verbally formulated precepts. Shared rules require shared interpretations, but shared interpretations could not emerge in the chaos of subjectivity. When the legal positivist solution to the problem of co-existence in a world of disagreement seems most necessary, it turns out to be impossible. Might it not be that when the solution is possible it could prove to be unnecessary?[40]

Thus, the upshot of this argument is that the lack of a hard edge of our concepts and the dependence of their meaning upon context defeats the argument that only the insistence on authoritative texts and their semantic clarity can rescue us from the throes of uncertainty.

[40] Simmonds, "Between Positivism and Idealism," at 314.

Finally, another more principled form of semantic indeterminacy arises out of the possibility that competing "fact descriptions" are given for the same events or actions. This creates great difficulties in ethics and thus it is not surprising that similar problems are to be expected in law. Is my statement (to take Kant's famous example) that misleads an invader of my house as to where my friend is hiding, simply a lie (as Kant suggests), or is it a response to coercion, where the characterization of lying is simply inapt (as Pufendorf would argue)? It is this difficulty with which international lawyers are perhaps most familiar: how am I to choose between describing some action as self-defense vs. aggression? Why are my freedom fighters your guerillas or political criminals? Here, legal doctrine has tried over the years to develop distinctions of absolute and relative offenses, to distinguish between different stages of internal unrest, by attempting to impose certain responsibilities on the contending parties and their sympathizers and supporters, but none of these typologies or casuistic methods can, of course, deny that we have to deal here with essentially contested concepts.[41]

The problem with such concepts is that they are part of political struggles, not simply descriptions of them. That courts of law become in that case one of the arenas in which these struggles occur, is obvious. It does not, however, prove the assertion that law is nothing but politics. After all, the style of reasoning is quite distinct when we engage with a situation in the political mode and when we utilize legal arguments.[42] The use and admissibility of evidence, the way of structuring arguments, and finally the way in which norms are used will be quite different. The commonality between law and politics does not consist in the denial of their distinct styles within practical reasoning but rather in their common concern with human action and the creation of the human (and hopefully humane) world.

5.4   The Role of Norms: Some Social Science Explanations

The discussion above concerning the problems of a largely semantic theory of law pointed to the need for common understandings as the background for the interpretation of the rules and norms which are to govern our interactions. Such a stance rules out the possibility of radical rule skepticism as it emerged

---

[41] On "essentially contested concepts" and their properties, see W.B. Gallie, "Essentially Contested Concepts" in Max Black (ed.), *The Importance of Language*, Englewood Cliffs, NJ: Prentice-Hall, 1962, 121–146. For an elaboration in regard to the political discourse, see William Connolly, *The Terms of Political Discourse*, 2nd edn., Princeton: Princeton University Press, 1983.

[42] See also N.E. Simmonds, "Why Conventionalism Does Not Collapse into Pragmatism," *Cambridge Law Journal*, 49:1 (1990): 63–79.

from a particular interpretation of Wittgenstein §198 in the *Philosophical Investigations*,[43] and which has found its adherents in the legal community.[44] Since every rule requires its interpretation and application in a specific context, Wittgenstein wonders how a rule can tell me what to do in a situation. "Whatever I do is compatible with some interpretation of the rule."[45] In other words: rules cannot provide guidance.

This radical rule skepticism seems to issue in a paradox, but Wittgenstein himself suggested that "The surprising, the paradox, is paradoxical only in a certain deficient environment. One has to complement this environment in such a way that what seemed to be paradoxical no longer appears to be paradoxical."[46] Thus, while, in a way, rule skepticism is as irrefutable on its own terms as is Hume's paradox, for Hume it was "common sense" which prevents us from despair, as it provides us with orientation. For Wittgenstein the paradox dissolves as soon as we leave the atomistic world of the single speaker and take more seriously the notion that language is an intersubjective practice.[47] As a practice a rule not only tells me how to go on in a situation which I might never have faced before,[48] it is also governed by certain conventions of the community of which I am part. To that extent my interpretations of a rule as well as my uses of words are monitored and reinforced by a group of competent speakers. Thus, while there are likely to be disagreements about the proper use of a term or the interpretation of a rule, purely idiosyncratic uses are excluded even if the use of the concepts remains contestable and contested.

These remarks also have important implications for the status of norms as explanation of actions in international politics. While regime analysis has over the last two decades flourished in IR by challenging the predominance of structural models, there remain nevertheless certain problems with this mode of analysis. The most serious is that of reification, as if norms were doing the acting. Since that is obviously a tall order to fill, norms are frequently assigned the status of "intervening variables" and the strategy is to accept an interest- and/or power-based explanation as the baseline.

---

[43] Saul A. Kripke, *Wittgenstein on Rules and Private Language: An Elementary Exposition*, Cambridge, MA: Harvard University Press, 1982.

[44] For a collection of interesting essays addressing the problems of a Wittgensteinian conception of rules for legal theory, see the July issue of the *Canadian Journal of Law and Jurisprudence*, 9:2 (1996), with contributions by Bix, Schauer, Marmor, et al.

[45] Wittgenstein, *Philosophical Investigations*, §198.

[46] Ludwig Wittgenstein, *Remarks on the Foundations of Mathematics*, trans. G.E.M. Anscombe, Oxford: Basil Blackwell, 1956, at 410.

[47] See Ulrich Volk, *Das Problem eines Semantischen Skeptizismus: Saul Kripkes Wittgenstein-Interpretation*, Rheinfelden: Schäuble, 1988.

[48] See Wittgenstein, *Philosophical Investigations*, §§151, 185.

The result of this move is that one gets thereby two mistakes for the price of one: it preserves the reification but reduces the other approaches to the status of explaining only some of the remaining variance.[49] First, while "interest" and "power" seem somehow self-explanatory, norms, particularly in their constitutive function, are hardly perceived. This is all the more surprising as the discourse on international politics could hardly get off the ground in the absence of rules which informed us of who is an actor, and how the poles of the international system are supposed to be determined, and alliances concluded. But of course, the work rules and norms do in that context is hardly that of a causal or intervening variable. The privilege of certain notions as an *explanans* might be understandable because of the predominance of realist and economic thinking; it is hardly justifiable if our goal is a better understanding of international politics.

To that extent the debate on how we can prove that norms matter seems utterly confused since it is informed by some incoherent notions of what constitutes a (scientific) explanation instead of accepting the multiple meanings of "cause" and of *what can serve as an "explanation" in different contexts.* Both problems, singly and in conjunction, prevent us from developing more appropriate strategies for probing the role rules and norms play in shaping international reality in general, and decisions in particular. It is to these two problems that I want to turn in the next subsection. For this purpose, I shall briefly touch upon the regime debate and draw upon the discussion of its main schools, realism/rationalism on the one hand, and more sociologically oriented approaches influenced by constructivism on the other hand.[50]

Criteria for What Matters

Let us agree in a preliminary fashion that the criteria for ascertaining whether norms matter in international politics have something to do with the effectiveness and robustness of a given regime. By choosing regimes as the focus, I argue that outcomes in the international arena are not the result of some fortuitous coincidence of choices but that these choices are in a way molded by norms and common understandings that represent some form of governance.[51] In other words, we are not only observing certain patterns of interactions from the outside but explain these empirical regularities on the basis of an internal point of view, by taking rules and norms as an *explanans*. By *effectiveness*

---

[49] This is more or less Krasner's strategy in Stephen D. Krasner, "Structural Causes and Regime Consequences: Regimes and Intervening Variables" in Stephen D. Krasner (ed.), *International Regimes*, Ithaca, NY: Cornell University Press, 1983, 1–22.

[50] For a not quite accurate distinction between these two types of approaches that nevertheless has gained currency, see Keohane, "International Institutions: Two Approaches."

[51] See e.g. Young, *International Governance*.

I accept the usual notion that regimes enable the participants to realize certain goals (that otherwise would have been impossible to reach or would have been impeded) and that the rules and norms of regimes are defenses against unilateral action and opportunism. *Robustness*, on the other hand, refers to the ability of regimes to withstand the challenges of change and to their capacity to adjust and thus provide orderly procedures for dealing with such environmental shocks.[52]

How do norms matter? According to the predominant mode of analysis they matter because they express the interests of the actors or of the dominant hegemon. In the latter case, regimes are little more than the expression of power. Meanwhile, the hegemonic stability debate has run its course but has contributed surprisingly little to the study of the effectiveness and robustness of regimes. Part of the problem is the questionable characterization of regimes as collective goods, and part is due to the lack of empirical fit with the post-World War II order. The multilateral institutions of the Bretton Woods regime developed much more stickiness than was expected.[53] But to rely on a metaphor (stickiness) for an explanation is not tantamount to explaining the phenomenon. To that extent, the more general case of an interest-based explanation seems more appropriate.[54] In that case, norms matter because regimes solve certain informational asymmetries that otherwise would inhibit cooperation. In other words, regimes have reputational effects[55] and they can persist because they represent sunk costs that make it rational to play by the rules even in the face of certain dissatisfactions and opportunities of circumvention.[56]

The Crux of Rationalism

Each of these hypotheses makes an important point although they are not necessarily mutually compatible and thereby do not fit into a coherent theory. The most obvious contradiction is the argument that regimes are crucial for the actors' reputation by providing standards against which their behavior can be

---

[52] The definitions of effectiveness and robustness are taken from Robert Powell, "Anarchy in International Relations Theory: The Neorealist–Neoliberal Debate," *International Organization*, 48:2 (1994): 313–344.

[53] See e.g. the discussion of Ruggie (ed.), *Multilateralism Matters*, chap. 1.

[54] For a fundamental discussion of different approaches to regimes, see Andreas Hasenclever, Peter Mayer, and Volker Rittberger, *Theories of International Regimes*, Cambridge: Cambridge University Press, 1997.

[55] This point is made by Robert O. Keohane, *After Hegemony: Cooperation and Discord in the World Political Economy*, Princeton: Princeton University Press, 1984. See e.g. the discussion at 104–106.

[56] The "sunk cost" argument is developed by Robert Keohane, "The Analysis of International Regimes: Towards a European–American Research Program" in Volker Rittberger and Peter Mayer (eds.), *Regime Theory and International Relations*, Oxford: Clarendon Press, 1993, 23–45.

assessed. While the latter is obviously true, for the rationalist approach it is true in a trivial sense only, i.e. it is not clear what role "reputation" is supposed to play in explaining cooperation. If the main reason for the creation of a regime is transparency, as the participants can thereby overcome information asymmetries, then it is not clear why reputation would be important. The actors have all the relevant information (or at least most of it) so that it is unclear why an actor would credit others with certain behavioral dispositions from which one could draw inferences about an actor's character (quite aside from the difficulties of such imputations in the case of corporate actors). In short, as with the *homines economici* in the market, who are interested in prices not in the dispositional traits of other actors, it is not quite clear why for rational egotists reputation should matter.[57]

But even if reputation is important because transparency is – contrary to the assumption – not sufficient and thus reputation can actually significantly reduce information costs, it is not clear why it would be in the interest of any single actor to shoulder his part of what appears to be a collective action problem. Why take the trouble of disseminating information, particularly after having been taken for a ride and in the face of the possibility of retaliation by the actor who is being bad-mouthed? We are all familiar with the phenomenon that some of the best recommendations are reserved for those one tries to get rid off. Anyway, violations are seldom clear-cut, they are subject to different interpretations and rebuttals. Thus, unless we take this larger picture into account, there is often no way of even beginning to show what was the case. True, as we have seen in Chapter 4, it makes more of a difference to me *who* violated the rule than *that* it was violated, as actors treat violations differently, but it is not clear how this phenomenon can be accommodated within a rationalist theory.[58] For one it leads to double standards and to the debasement of the necessary information, and it means that the "framing" of the violation rather than the action itself seems to carry most of the weight in the explanation. In systematically excluding issues of framing, and in neglecting possible excuses and rebuttals as part of the story, the rationalist approach cuts itself off from important issues.

Finally the "sunk costs" argument seems to be only a special case of the more general argument that regimes reduce transaction costs but are, at the same time, difficult to create, because of the transaction costs they entail in getting them off the ground. However, without specifying *ex ante* what counts as a "cost," it is again difficult to see how the demand of regimes can bring them into existence (since there are demonstrably many areas in which there

---

[57] For a fundamental discussion, see Mercer, *Reputation and International Politics*.
[58] Joanne Gowa, "Rational Hegemons, Excludable Goods, and Small Groups: An Epitaph for Hegemonic Stability Theory?" *World Politics*, 41:3 (1989): 307–324.

is a "demand" but no regime exists) or why the existence of a regime should deter defections (aside from the trivial case of a unique solution to a coordination game).[59] Precisely because regimes have changed the general presumptions of the actors, cheating pays off now! Only under the assumption that a "self-destruct" mechanism is triggered by any rule violation[60] would defection be irrational. It is of course this fear that Hobbes utilizes in showing the irrationality of resistance to the sovereign, even if his particular actions are reprehensible and engender resistance on the part of his subjects. But as we all know, no such mechanism exists either domestically or internationally and thus this "explanation" fails. My cheating is usually not likely to bring down the whole house and therefore, *depending how others interpret my defection*, it might or might not end the regime.[61] In other words any outcome is compatible with the hypotheses of rationalist theory.

Sociologists and Constructivists

The second school, much less unified in its general approach and methodological commitments,[62] shares as a common point of departure the notion that actors in the international arena are really never in the state of nature and that social order cannot systematically be derived from individual maximizing choices. Not only are the actors themselves as corporate entities constituted by norms (social contract), but they are also much more deeply implicated in normative understandings than rationalists suggests. Hobbesian actors could never get out of the state of war, since their promises would not be binding.

---

[59] The demand for regimes argument was made by Robert Keohane, "The Demand for International Regimes" in Krasner (ed.), *International Regimes*, 1983: 141–172.

[60] This is suggested by Jon Elster, *The Cement of Society: A Study of Social Order*, Cambridge: Cambridge University Press, 1989, at 44.

[61] This is, of course, the trouble with the universalization principle in ethics and the Kantian categorical imperative. For a further discussion, see Friedrich Kratochwil, "Vergeßt Kant: Reflexionen zur Debatte über Ethik und Internationale Politik" in Christine Chwaszcza and Wolfgang Kersting (eds.), *Politische Philosophie der Internationalen Beziehungen*, Frankfurt: Suhrkamp, 1998, 96–152.

[62] This school comprises "sociologists" like Oran Young, Martha Finnemore, and Andrew Hurrell as well as "constructivists" of quite different orientations such as Katzenstein, Müller, Onuf, Wendt, or Klotz. See Onuf, *World of Our Making*; Wendt, "Anarchy Is What States Make of It"; Young, "The Effectiveness of International Institutions"; Andrew Hurrell, "International Society and the Study of Regimes: A Reflective Approach" in Rittberger and Mayer (eds.), *Regime Theory and International Relations*, 1993, 49–72; Harald Müller, *Die Chance der Kooperation: Regime in den Internationalen Beziehungen*, Darmstadt: Wissenschaftliche Buchgesellschaft, 1993; Peter J. Katzenstein (ed.), *The Culture of National Security: Norms and Identity in World Politics*, New York: Columbia University Press, 1996; Michael N. Barnett and Martha Finnemore, *Rules for the World: International Organizations in Global Politics*, Ithaca, NY: Cornell University Press, 2004.

Besides, in the absence of shared conventions they could not even determine what counts as a contract, i.e. could not act.

Although the international system might represent a strange form of sociality in that neither a common notion of the *salus publica* nor a common identity is created – speculations on the regulative idea of a *civitas maxima* à la Wolf notwithstanding[63] – it represents nevertheless a form of sociality. The actions of the participants are meaningfully oriented towards each other,[64] and such meanings presuppose intersubjective understandings that are the preconditions and thus antecedent to any optimizing behavior in which any actor might engage. To that extent, neither interests nor even power, "operationalized" in terms of capabilities, are "given" and can be used as unproblematic foundations. Both presuppose an understanding of rules of the game which one wants to play, before issues of strategy or even the identification of resources can arise. In the absence of such an understanding, neither the notion of "winning" nor of certain moves makes much sense. Rather strangely, even what is a resource remains unclear. For example, while strength and weight might be a resource and give the player some power in a game of American football, it will hardly help him in tennis or chess.

Different from rationalists who take regulative rules as their only model of norms, theorists indebted to the sociological approach point to the importance of constitutive rules and to their enabling and constraining character in reproducing a system of action. Treating them merely as an epiphenomenon fundamentally misdiagnoses their function and significance in social life. In a way, it is as if we attempted to reduce the meaning of words to the number of different sounds out of which they are formed, instead of analyzing their semantic, syntactic, and pragmatic functions.

To the extent that certain regimes result from such broader normative understandings, they buttress cooperative solutions in the face of incentives to defect and leave in place a normative structure that possesses a certain robustness. International rules develop not only a compliance pull of their own, their legitimacy and thus both their effectiveness and robustness is enhanced by certain properties: their determinacy (textual clarity and closeness to standard interpretations), coherence (compatibility with higher-order norms undergirding the "society of nations"), their symbolic validation (rituals of recognition)

---

[63] On this point, see Nicholas Greenwood Onuf, *The Republican Legacy in International Thought*, Cambridge: Cambridge University Press, 1998, especially chap. 4.

[64] This is Weber's definition of "social" action, which represents the formal object for study in sociology. See Max Weber, "On the Concept of Sociology and the Meaning of Social Conduct" in *Basic Concepts in Sociology*, trans. H.P. Secher, Secaucus, NJ: The Citadel Press, 1972, 29–58.

and adherence (agreement with rules about application and interpretation), as Thomas Franck has argued persuasively.[65]

Nevertheless, the effectiveness of a regime is most crucially related to the level of institutionalization and the role conception of the actors. Henkin's suggestion that the respect on the part of actors for norms is the price of membership in international society and of having relations with other nations[66] might be right although it is also highly optimistic, since it entirely discounts the possibility that "cheating" might be the best of all possible worlds, particularly in a world of rule-followers. Nevertheless, being considered a bona fide "player" and thus having "standing" is central to our conception of an actor.

Finally, as in the case of moral training when we want to counteract the known temptations of lying or cheating by arguing not only for the obligatory character of the rules transcending the particular utility considerations, we also appeal to the child or person that such an action would not be fitting for a "gentleman." While for our jaded view such appeals might sound corny, it is not true that appeals to roles and identities are entirely unknown even in international relations. There is some agreement as to the "outlaws" or pariah states, and even in a time of severe crisis (Cuban missile crisis) forceful action was rejected by President Kennedy. As his brother and influential member of the Excom group remarked, launching an air strike on Cuba would place the US on the same level as Tojo, a comparison that compromised America's notion of role and self-understanding.[67] That these things are not immutable, even when norm cascades have been successful, and that normative orders can decay – as we see in extrajudicial killings and the ever increasing use of drones in the "war on terror" – comes as a surprise only to those who mistake human laws for laws of nature, or consider them to be irreversible "signs" of the kingdom of ends.

As Alex Wendt has pointed out, role conceptions and identities might change on the basis of continued and routinized cooperation.[68] As a virtuous cycle begins, states might learn to establish more inclusive notions of identity that discourage free-riding, increase diffuse reciprocity and thus enhance the willingness to bear some costs for the "us" or even a new "we." Again it would be overly optimistic to expect on the basis of these observations a generally peaceful world, precisely because this focus only brings into view one type of

---

[65] Franck, *The Power of Legitimacy among Nations.*

[66] Louis Henkin and Council on Foreign Relations, *How Nations Behave: Law and Foreign Policy*, New York: Praeger, 1968, at 32, 48. See a similar argument made by Franck, *The Power of Legitimacy among Nations*, at 106.

[67] For the Tojo analogy, see Graham T. Allison, *Essence of Decision: Explaining the Cuban Missile Crisis*, Boston, MA: Little, Brown, 1971, at 132, 197, 203.

[68] Alexander E. Wendt, "Collective Identity Formation and the International State," *The American Political Science Review*, 88:2 (1994): 384–396.

process of association and fails to realize how conflict is "functional" for group cohesion. To that extent a universally organized humanity is not a very likely outcome, absent an imminent existential threat to all people.

On the other hand, for better or for worse, even structural certainties that seemed immutable can dissolve rather quickly, given certain circumstances, such as those between the Soviet Union and the US at the end of the Cold War.[69] In short, making this point about the constructive possibilities of political actions (with all due respect for the possibilities of misfires) frees us not only from an overly deterministic mode of analysis by identifying chances and possibilities for new beginnings, but also serves as a warning by pointing to the fragility of social orders which result from even widely accepted "settlements" in domestic or in international politics.

It is strange in this context that one of the oldest and newest concerns, i.e. the role of institutions in buttressing particular regimes or governmental structures, seems rather under-researched. In a way, in spite of the dense network of treaties and regimes, the level of institutionalization in the international arena might still be too low to create new identities. Even successful examples such as the EU now seem to suffer from a distinct lack of enthusiasm among their peoples, as the recent debates about the euro, or the disarray of common responses to migration or to Grexit and Brexit suggest. Even institutional structures which are well grounded in "Community law" seem now to command less respect than national institutions, the functionalist dynamics of the European project notwithstanding.

Here sociologists and constructivists in general have failed to analyze the different dimensions of the problem and to point out which tradeoffs, or even possible spill-backs or breakdowns, are possible or likely to occur. Somehow our picture of the future always seems to be influenced by some dubious philosophy of history, in which cooperation is not only viewed as an unquestioned consumption good, but we also tend to assume (against all historical evidence and practical experience) that the emergence of larger identities is somehow the wave of the future. To that extent, the robustness of those state structures (despite, or perhaps because of, all these changes) is as much of a puzzle to sociological as to rationalist explanations, since no clear pattern seems to be emerging. What we need is a more detailed understanding of why and when the pressures on the actors for reproduction are stronger than those allowing for, or even favoring, transformation or defection. The rapidity

---

[69] See Rey Koslowski and Friedrich Kratochwil, "Understanding Change in International Politics: The Soviet Empire's Demise and the International System," *International Organization*, 48:2 (1994): 215–247. See also the general discussion and criticism by Lebow, Stein, and Risse-Kappen in Richard Ned Lebow and Thomas Risse-Kappen (eds.), *International Relations Theory and the End of the Cold War*, New York: Columbia University Press, 1995.

with which the chances for a "New World Order" after the Cold War slipped away from us seems worrisome.

None of these considerations justifies, however, considering the existence of norms and institutional rules as epiphenomenal. Institutions are constituted by rules and have effect because they allow us to connect certain consequences with our actions. We make contracts or appoint and thereby empower people to take actions in certain areas, we demand, or even deter, and all of these actions are informed and constituted by institutional rules. Institutional rules are so important for social life because they enable and constrain us at the same time, as they systematically link the "is" and the "ought." Since their intersubjective character is understood, institutions not only constitute a settled practice, they make it possible to answer normative questions on the basis of seemingly factual observations. To that extent, they help us terminate otherwise endless arguments. If I can show you e.g. a document which has the word "Contract" and your signature on it, then I am entitled to conclude (save limited possibilities of rebuttal) that you have an obligation. What you will do and whether you will discharge your obligation will, of course, depend upon a variety of factors including the penalties associated with noncompliance and your psychic costs. Nevertheless, one thing is clear: without such common understandings embedded in and buttressed by institutional rules, we would not be able to appraise the character of actions, speak of violations, make demands for information or restitution, insist on our rights, or demand punishment.

5.5   Some Common Puzzles: Rule Guidance and Explaining with Norms

With the last remarks, we already reenter the more general discussion of how we are to conceive the way in which norms mold decisions. Here, the presumption that explaining an action in terms of norms has to meet the criteria of logical positivism runs into heavy weather right from the start. First, taking the "external point of view" on rules condemns us to focus on some behavioral regularities (supposedly induced by norms) and establish some correlations. But quite aside from the fact that empirical generalizations do not exhibit the properties, which are logically necessary for the subsumption model of explanation utilizing "laws," three interrelated further problems arise. First, in the case of norms the traditional "tests" which are supposed to corroborate our "theory" are hardly possible, since a single case can no longer refute the general law, as norms are counterfactually valid. Second, we might observe certain regularities which might be caused by some underlying norm, but we have no clear idea how this hunch can be translated into a causal mechanism that establishes the actual etiology between norms and resulting behavior. This raises a third difficulty: since many norms do not prescribe anything in particular, but rather serve only as determinants of a zone of permissibility, entire areas of human activity must be neglected, as otherwise our belief in the necessity of a causal connection becomes incoherent. Certainly norms cannot be "causes" in the same way as the causes we know from "science," where we think of x causing y when we perceive a constant conjunction between these two distinct phenomena.

The last remark seems debilitating even if we change the perspective and approach the matter from the actor's point of view. Again, difficulties immediately mount even if we want to stay again on a purely descriptive level. How can norms, which belong to a different realm, "cause" anything? Not only does the concept of causality seem to lose its definite meaning, but we also become increasingly unsure what is involved in "explaining" an action. All the familiar tools of analysis such as generalization, cause, action, event, suddenly lose their bite and we seem hopelessly stuck in a conceptual morass. Given this predicament, the best way out of a dilemma (or in that case a conceptual morass) is to backtrack and see where one has taken the wrong path that led to the dilemma.

Consider in this context Hart and Honore's observation: "The statement that one person did something because another person threatened him, carries no implication . . . that, if the circumstances were repeated, the same action would follow, nor does the statement require for its defense, as ordinary causal statements do, a generalization."[70] Understanding the action and thus being able to explain it means to diagnose the action as being of a certain type, without thereby relying on the semantic relationship that obtains in the subsumption model between the single case and the general law. Similarly, as Dray has demonstrated, historical explanations do not depend on general laws. Even if they existed they would be trivial and would not do much of the explaining.[71] What carries the weight in those cases is rather the narrative context that assigns importance to certain factors and connects events and actions.

Furthermore, these remarks have important implications also for law since to apply the law is not simply to somehow unearth a preexisting meaning. Meaning instead is constructed by persuading an interpretive community of the "reasonableness" of the interpretation. In the case of the domestic arena, where compulsory jurisdiction gives courts, especially higher courts, much clout, there is then a certain finality to argumentation by a decision. In international law the lack of such institutions engenders additional complications since the interpretive "community" is rather heterogeneous. It involves decision-makers, judges, practitioners, and scholars, and increasingly also members of

---

[70] H.L.A. Hart and Tony Honoré, *Causation in the Law*, Oxford: Clarendon Press, 1959, at 52.
[71] William H. Dray, *Laws and Explanation in History*, Oxford: Oxford University Press, 1957; see also Arthur Coleman Danto, *Analytical Philosophy of History*, Cambridge: Cambridge University Press, 1965.

civil society who frequently present their proposals in legal terms. Here the struggle begins already with "naming," i.e. by the competition for having one's characterization of a "case" accepted. This is not a simple cognitive operation but often a multidimensional struggle in which "words" are semantic weapons, far exceeding application or subsumption but also the simple legal/illegal dichotomy. As Jean d'Aspremont has remarked, words are then used

to create textual economy, generate semantic instability, rough out and hone scholarly ideas, enhance textual esthetics, yield empiricism, create straw men, and preserve the argumentative character of scholarly idea, gratify oneself, magnify erudition, boost fame and intimidate peers, ... there is nothing to rein in the use of such semantic tactics in the interpretative community of international law, for [the] paradigmatic revolution is meant to be permanent.[72]

Thus, contrary to the predominant epistemology, explaining does not seem to involve only the procedure of "subsumption" but comprises a rather heterogeneous set of procedures by which we try to understand actions and events. Explaining often means providing a context, such as when we make a series of actions and events part of a wider narrative. But explaining an action might also involve us in elaborations and justifications of the choices made, or require a disclosure of the reasons for choosing certain beginnings and ends for the explanatory account we tender. Counterfactual arguments are particularly important in this context, and so are our specific interests that drive our questions.[73] One of the implications is that the notion of cause can change dramatically.

Consider the following example: a set of houses collapses after an earthquake, but the entire area is not devastated. It is not wrong to call the earthquake the "cause" of the collapse even if the same cause did not issue in a uniform "effect." But then we notice that the houses which remained standing were all built according to code, while many, if not most, collapsed houses were substandard, so our puzzle has been solved. Here obviously the issue arises of whether the chiseling of the contractor should be called the "cause," even if we find out that he was able to "get away with it," since the new standards came into existence only after this section of the development had been built. Things get even more complicated when we realize that most of the

---

[72] Jean d'Aspremont, "Wording in International Law," *Leiden Journal of International Law*, 25:3 (2012): 575–602, at 577.

[73] On the importance of counterfactual reasoning, see James D. Fearon, "Counterfactuals and Hypothesis Testing in Political Science," *World Politics*, 43:2 (1991): 169–195; Thomas J. Biersteker, "Constructing Historical Counterfactuals to Assess the Consequences of International Regimes: The Global Debt Regime and the Course of the Debt Crisis of the 1980s" in Rittberger and Mayer (eds.), *Regime Theory and International Relations*, 315–338; Philip E. Tetlock and Aaron Belkin, *Counterfactual Thought Experiments in World Politics: Logical, Methodological, and Psychological Perspectives*, Princeton: Princeton University Press, 1996.

collapsed houses were built along a recently completed tunnel that apparently weakened the foundations of the houses in question. Suppose, the tunnel was built according to code, but that it can also be established that digging it in this particular geological configuration facilitated the transmission of shock waves. Would it make a difference for our causal assessment if the tunnel had also collapsed? If it had not been built to code? Thus naming "the cause" is quickly becoming more and more complicated and our choice among several of the candidates (or even their conjunction) is obviously not independent of whether we examine this issue as a geophysicist, as a lawyer, as a structural engineer, or as a historian.

Further complications arise when we inquire into the issues of intentions that play such a decisive role in distinguishing events from actions. While events can be explained by causes and contexts, explaining actions usually involves us in more complicated operations. On the surface though, the explanations we give for both seem exactly parallel, as both require causal imputations. In the first instance, events are caused by antecedent conditions, while in the latter case intentions, motives, or purposes serve as causes in the explanation scheme. To that extent purposes or goals do not seem different from causes, in that they provide the antecedent motive which makes the actor behave in a certain way. But a moment's reflection shows that the two paradigmatic cases are not strictly analogous, since the causal mechanism adduced for the explanation is rather different.

As already mentioned, in the classical Humean account, providing a causal explanation means having two independent observations of states of affairs at different times, as well as a "constant conjunction" between these observed phenomena, a conjunction which even for Hume is supplied by the "mind" not by nature! But this is then tantamount to arguing that causality cannot be directly derived from observation, as this category is constitutive for, and antecedent to, every observation. A rather different picture emerges, however, when we explain an action in terms of purposes and intentions. Again the goal of the action and the intention preceding the choice are conjoined, but it is clear that we no longer have independently defined observations at different times since *it is the "goal"* which also serves as the antecedent *"motive"* for the action.

This peculiarity of intentional accounts explains why we do not necessarily reject an explanation when the predicted and observed results differ. For example, when we explain why a person is running after a train by providing a motive for this action, we do not, absent special circumstances, feel impelled to withdraw the proffered account when it turns out that this prediction failed. We simply say that this person "missed" the train. Similarly, when we assert that one person wanted to exercise power over another, we know that there is no inherent necessity analogous to two bodies colliding, in accordance with the Newtonian law of *actio est reactio*. Again, our ontology of social action prevents us from simply accepting the refuting evidence, which would oblige us to cast our explanations aside. Instead, we argue that the influence attempt might have simply "misfired," as the grammar of volition and capacity also includes the notion of "failure." For actually revising our explanation we would need rather different reasons and alternative plausible accounts, instead of accepting a simple "misfire" as a refutation.

Note, that explanations using norms obviously represent a subcategory of intentional accounts, and – as we have seen above – intentional explanations seem to violate the standard epistemological criteria of logical positivism whose canonical status is largely accepted in political science. Perhaps it is not surprising that realists, who usually also pretend to be "scientists," have such a hard time in discovering the role of norms in international relations. Equipped with a universal hammer, they try to fetch water by attempting to nail it down, instead of changing the tool!

If we took the standard epistemology seriously, we ought to reject any type of intentional account since only antecedent or efficient causes have scientific status. The fact that we do not heed such advice and continue to explain actions in terms of intentions or purposes seems to indicate that we recognize that this problem cannot be solved by epistemological fiat. The new interest in ideas as explanatory factor despite their epistemological problems, and the continuing relevance of the philosophical dilemmas which Albert Yee[74] details in his interesting treatment of data analysis among statisticians, buttress such judgment. No matter how we twist or turn, a true efficient-causality account seems to escape us, as we do not seem able to visualize how ideas influence choices and actual behavior. After all, Descartes's "solution" via the pituitary gland is no longer available to us,[75] quite aside from the fact that here both the hoary mind/body problem and the freedom-of-will vs. determinism issue raise their ugly heads. Obviously, causality is somewhat tricky.

Showing the causal significance of one phenomenon for another is to engage in demonstrating the existence of a connection, but the nature of this connection need not be a mechanical one. Thus a connection is established if we think along the lines of building a bridge that allows us to go from "here" to "there." This is what we do when we provide an account in terms of purposes or goals, or when we cite the relevant rule that provides the missing element, showing us the reasons that motivated us to act in a certain way. No mechanism, no hammer hitting a lever, no springs, no billiard balls, etc., are involved here.

---

[74] Albert S. Yee, "The Causal Effects of Ideas on Policies," *International Organization*, 50:1 (1996): 69–108.

[75] For a short overview of the Cartesian explanations and mental causation, see Richard Montgomery, "Non-Cartesian Explanations Meet the Problem of Mental Causation," *Southern Journal of Philosophy*, 33:2 (1995): 221–242.

This is what Weber means when he talks about causal explanation in the social sciences.[76] We reconstruct a situation, view it from the perspective of the actor, and impute purposes and values based on evidence (although not necessarily limited to the actor's own testimony). Following this procedure, in turn, provides us with an intelligible account of the reasons for acting. Furthermore, such imputations have nothing to do with some mysterious empathy or the private status of the mind of the actor (unless we try to figure out some idiosyncrasies or pathologies). As in Wittgenstein's puzzle about the communication concerning pain, we do possess a language in which shared meanings make it possible to communicate, even if we never reach the actual private sensations that "cause" the pain we observe. Rather, the characterization of the action is possible because the account we provide can be justified and defended in terms of intersubjectively shared "reasons." We might still not know what actually transpired and competing explanations might persist. But even in science all our accounts are subject to revision on the basis of new evidence or interpretations that seem to have a better "fit" (problematic though such an expression might be). Nevertheless, explanations have to end somewhere, and in action accounts, be they in the area of social action or in law, pragmatic criteria are used to assess the justifiability of the interpretations rendered. As Wittgenstein put it: "If I have exhausted the justifications, I have reached bedrock and my spade is turned. Then I am inclined to say: 'This is simply what I do.'"[77]

As soon as we view the problem of explanation in this light, our puzzlement is relieved and we understand why and how the metaphor of a mechanism was misleading. We also begin to understand that the language game governing the use of the term "explanation" and "cause" is not restricted to some mechanical paradigm, or to the notion of efficient cause in Aristotle's parlance. As Wittgenstein suggested: "Giving reasons for something one did or said, means showing a way which leads to this action. In some cases it means telling the way which one has gone oneself; in others it means describing a way which leads there and is in accordance with certain accepted rules."[78] Again, no reference needs to be made to private states of mind, or inner life occurrences, since such a construction of the problematique is only the result of the "mistaken addiction to Hobbist mechanism,"[79] as Gilbert Ryle suggested a long time ago. To that extent, questions about the relations between a person and his mind, or

---

[76] Weber, *Aufsätze zur Wissenschaftslehre*. See especially the controversies with Roscher and Knies, Stammler and Eduard Meyer.

[77] Wittgenstein, *Philosophical Investigations*, §217.

[78] Ludwig Wittgenstein, *Preliminary Studies for the "Philosophical Investigations" Generally Known as the Blue and Brown Books*, New York: Harper & Row, 1964, at 14.

[79] A.J. Ayer, "An Honest Ghost?" in Oscar Wood and George Pitcher (eds.), *Ryle: A Collection of Critical Essays*, London: Macmillan, 1970, 53–74, at 54.

between a person's body and his reason, are "improper questions" in the same way as it does not make much sense to ask, "What transactions go on between the House of Commons and the British Constitution?"[80]

The few examples given above should have put not only the "reasons/causes"[81] debate in perspective, but also driven home the fact that explanations are not all of the same kind: What we accept in a given case as appropriate is thoroughly context-dependent and not reducible to some standard logical form which is automatically privileged. Rather, providing explanations involves us in choosing usually between different possible versions, and, in justifying our choices for "coming down on one side" rather than the other, we provide and clarify an account within a context where an explanation is demanded. Thus, the point is not that no causal accounts of actions can be given. The rub is rather that our interests require usually a deeper, i.e. more-dimensional, version of an explanation, as all the analytical distinctions between the "is" and the "ought," between causes and reasons, are woven together in our grammar of explanation. In it are implicated our concepts of agency and responsibility, and the predicaments of choice as an existential condition rather than as a case of incomplete information only. Consequently, what "serves" as an explanation cannot be decided once and for all. Thus the hope for an absolute point of view which dispenses with the need to engage in often complicated justifications of one's decision by hitting upon the single "right" answer is indeed as tempting as it is futile. It would be available to us only if we were no longer interested in all those things, which are constitutive of law and politics.

5.6   Practical Reason

But how do we reason when facing practical choices, which are contingent, where information is incomplete and costly, and which take place in irreversible time? While most attention has been paid to the former factors the problem of "irreversible time" is hardly even mentioned. The time within which action takes place is different from the homogeneous time of science, which is structured by a "before" and "after" but runs equally from the present to the past and to the future. To that extent the mathematical formulation of scientific laws in terms of a function is telling, as it lets us reason back to times immemorial as well as to the most distant future by informing us how the changes in one part

---

[80] Gilbert Ryle, *The Concept of Mind*, Chicago: University of Chicago Press, 1984, at 167f.
[81] See e.g. Donald Davidson, "Actions, Reasons, and Causes," *The Journal of Philosophy*, 63:23 (1966): 685–700. See also the anthology by Ernest Sosa (ed.), *Causation and Conditionals*, London: Oxford University Press, 1975; Paul Humphreys, "Causation in the Social Sciences: An Overview," *Synthese*, 68:1 (1986): 1–12.

of the equation alter the values in the other side. Here even the "causal arrow" seems to have been lost.

Irreversible (historical) time is different: we have to act and cannot wait until all information is in. But how can we then have confidence that our choices will reach the intended goal? On a narrow construction of the problem we encounter here Hume's dilemma of induction. While the problem preoccupied him precisely because of the logical conundrum it entails, Hume provides us, in the section of Book I of the *Treatise* devoted to "Of the reason of animals," with the hint of an alternative. Although he argues there rather too strongly that no sufficient warrant can be provided by logic for many of our inferences, there is a "practical" solution to our conundrum, a "solution" that we actually and surprisingly share with animals.

Beasts certainly never perceive any real connection among objects. This therefore by experience they infer one from another. They can never by any arguments form a general conclusion, that those objects, of which they have no experience, resemble those of which they have. It is therefore by means of custom alone that experience operates upon them. All this was sufficiently evident with respect to man. But with respect to beasts there cannot be the least suspicion of a mistake; which must be owned to be a strong confirmation, or rather an invincible proof of my system.[82]

There are several problems in this quote, as well as in Hume's general teaching about motives, which need unpacking. One is the notion that belief (and true knowledge is "warranted belief" for Hume) is not produced by "reason." Rather as "embodied beings," we possess an endowment to orient ourselves, which we share with animals. Hume thus not only sees the constitutive role of repetition and "habit," but also notes that cognition has emotional roots from which a purely instrumentally conceived reason – dealing with the selection of means for the "desired" goals – is cut off. It is in this sense that his adage that "reason is and ought to be the slave of passion"[83] has to be understood. After all, when we compare different options, such as the satisfaction we would gain from a distant "delight," such as better health, instead of giving in and lighting another cigarette, we do not need reason, but "imagination," to buttress our choice[84] Only in this way can we conjure up these different states whose comparison might enable us to counteract the present temptations. And it is again "imagination" that supplies us with the "constant conjunction" when we make causal arguments, despite the fact that they always transcend any possible observation.

While the "constant conjunction" issue is of course part and parcel of Hume's concern with critical reflection, he shows that even beliefs which are

---

[82] David Hume, *A Treatise of Human Nature*, ed. David and Mary Norton, Oxford: Clarendon Press, 1978: 1.3.16, para. 8, at 119.
[83] Ibid., 2.3.3, para. 4, at 266.   [84] Ibid., 1.4.2, at 125–144.

"successful" are frequently sufficient for "going on," as the example of animal learning shows. A dog who wants to fetch the ball thrown from a first-floor window "learns" (even after some effort) that he cannot just jump – due to the realization of the height and the fear it induces – but that he has to take the back staircase (even if its descends in the opposite direction from the thrown object), so that below he can run around the house and fetch the ball in the garden.

The recent "practice turn" focusing on such habits and on "knowing how" rather than "knowing what" has foregrounded again this part of praxis. However, in these debates we often encounter a silent reliance on some form of "functional explanation": reducing something to routine and pushing it into the background, so as to gain more time and preserve one's capacities for making better choices in "important" matters. But such a gambit might be a bit too economistic and one-sided.[85] Furthermore, rituals and "performances" also need to be included in the analysis of praxis although those forms of action are of course powerfully shaped by the symbolic capacities which come only with the emergence of language. Hume was aware of this and expanded his "research program" by focusing on the conventional character of the social order, i.e. the rules underlying certain practices such as promises, or institutional rules which create social "facts" virtually *ex nihilo*. While for certain practices custom and habit are sufficient, for the emergence of "institutions," which are productive of "social power," more sophisticated arrangements involving symbols and concepts become necessary.

Unfortunately, Hume is not as clear about this problem as we wished, because he lacks a superordinate conception of communication (and meaning) that embraces both gestures and verbal exchanges. This problem becomes visible in Hume's treatment of "property" and its customary nature, and his analogy of "language" as custom. Speaking is after all a learned habit but this does not mean that concepts function analogously to the above "hunches." Even if property emerges out of customs, the participants in the conventions of property have somehow to "indicate" to each other that they are willing to respect other claims on the basis of reciprocity. This need not be a formal promise, but some type of "sign" or explicit communication seems necessary. Furthermore, as Hume suggests, very soon further agreement on the acquisition and transfer of titles becomes necessary since the *uti possidetis* rule is insufficient for facilitating exchanges. Thus, for promises and contracts, which create particular obligations, a much richer semantics, presupposing language and its constitutive capacity, is necessary.

---

[85] See Ted Hopf, "The Logic of Habit in International Relations," *European Journal of International Relations*, 16:4 (2010): 539–561. The problem with the argument is that precisely the most habit-driven societies are very slow learners, despite the "time" they have gained.

The cognitive purchase of his analogy of language as a "custom" remains then somewhat murky. Hume just notes that language attains its validity without "promises," which is right. But he fails to tell us what the difference between this (transcendental?) convention and other conventions is, a problem that has bedeviled the discussion up to our time. For the moment, I want to concentrate on the problem of how we orient ourselves in the practical realm, as we certainly neither "subsume" our actions under covering laws nor do we rely only on unreflective "habits" learned by rote. Thus, a brief discussion of the role of analogies and metaphors becomes necessary in order to show how we are thereby able "to go on" with our actions.

Analogical Reasoning

In this context we have to see whether analogical reasoning is a mode of reasoning in its own right (different from both inductive and deductive reasoning), and how the conceptual formation of "prototypes" and family resemblances helps us to clear up some of the difficulties of the traditional classification relying on essential descriptions. Analogical reasoning has a long history in logic and casuistry,[86] but also in science, where Joseph Priestley, a pioneer in physics and chemistry, suggested: "analogy is our best guide in all philosophical investigations; and in all discoveries, which were not made by mere accident, have been made by the help of it."[87] This might be hyperbole, but even a logical positivist would not necessarily disagree save to insist that there is only a logic of justification, but not a logic of discovery.

In remedying this flaw, analogies and reasoning from a prototypical case to other more problematic cases have revolutionized our thinking about categorization and "natural kinds." They have also suggested that the explication of meaning in terms of an extensional and intensional semantics is rather problematic because it insisted – in accordance with the traditional Aristotelian logic – on "sharp boundaries" of our concepts and the requirement of exclusivity of our taxonomies. Thus, echoing Wittgenstein's argument about family resemblance, Eleanor Rosch suggested that the members of a category might share several features, whereby some are more central or prototypical than others, such as a blackbird instantiating the concept of "bird" more obviously than e.g. a penguin. Rosch was also able to show that physiological and cultural factors intertwine since each culture has e.g. a favorite prototype of

[86] See Albert R. Jonsen and Stephen Edelston Toulmin, *The Abuse of Casuistry: A History of Moral Reasoning*, Berkeley: University of California Press, 2000.
[87] Joseph Priestley, *The History and Present State of Electricity*, New York: Johnson Reprint, 1966 [1767].

"red," so that neither a physiological nor a cultural reductionism is appropriate and that categorization cannot be understood in terms of the classical set theoretic approaches to semantics.[88]

If we go now to the problem of analogical reasoning we see that basic to an analogy is a comparison which focuses on certain features of objects or systems (the source) and transfers it to another (the target). Thus consider the following two examples:

Source: 1, 3, 7, 15...	Target: 2, 5, 11, ...
Source: fingers: palm	Target: toes: sole

Here the comparison remains within the same domain but consists in the first case in finding the "rule" to go on (always add the next following number, so that 31 is the "solution" for the first example) and the part/whole relationship, which is the solution to the second one. The second example also drives home the fact that the asserted similarity is not point-to-point but "structural" or "proportional."[89] Of course, its heuristic value derives from the fact that we use analogies across domains, such as when Niels Bohr's atomic model was based on the analogy to the solar system, or when the Newtonian planetary system was used for "explaining" the international system, or when Waltz more recently relied on the (mistaken) analogy of the competitive market for "explaining" international politics.

Several problems arise in this context. One is whether we have here a bowdlerized version of either deductive or inductive reasoning, or something quite different. The second is, since the mapping from source to target is always partial and, since the world can be described in a variety of ways, how sure can we be that the observed similarities justify our belief that further similarities exist? (It runs like a duck, it sounds like a duck, it flies like a duck; it is a duck!) This plausibility can be modal or probabilistic. In the latter case the subjective degree of belief can be based on probabilities and there is then often a tendency to see in analogical reasoning just a form of induction, as e.g. Mill argued.[90]

---

[88] For a discussion see e.g. George Lakoff and Mark Johnson, *Philosophy in the Flesh: The Embodied Mind and Its Challenge to Western Thought*, New York: Basic Books, 1999. See also James W. Davis, *Terms of Inquiry: On the Theory and Practice of Political Science*, Baltimore: Johns Hopkins University Press, 2005.

[89] The proportionality argument goes back to Aristotle and is elaborated in cognitive science to a "structure mapping theory," such as Dedre Gentner, Keith James Holyoak, and Boicho N. Kokinov (eds.), *The Analogical Mind: Perspectives from Cognitive Science*, Cambridge, MA: MIT Press, 2001.

[90] John Stuart Mill, *A System of Logic, Ratiocinative and Inductive; Being a Connected View of the Principles of Evidence and the Methods of Scientific Investigation*, London: Longmans, 1930.

But that does not seem quite right, since, as Aristotle argued, an analogy does not "draw its proof from all particular cases"[91] but looks for the justifiability of particular conclusions. Here we seem to reason more from case to case rather than adduce a generalization or subsume under a law.

Case-Based Reasoning

Consider in this context case-based reasoning for purposes of problem solving. We usually have to go through four steps: retrieve past similar cases, look for the "solution," perhaps distinguish cases according to different types, transfer the proposed solution to the problem at hand, seeing which one "fits" best, making adjustment (revision), and store "what worked." While our analysis might look like an induction algorithm in which generalizations are derived from previous cases, the case-driven approach differs in that it is sensitive to variability of cases and draws conclusions only at the end, not using an *ex ante* template. In the case of an inductive algorithm, the "solution" exists before the target problem is examined, since the solution is "applied." In case-based reasoning, the "right way of going about the problem" is not to prejudge the problem. Instead, one wants to see what happens as one sequentially works one's way through, since the "case" might turn out to be more complicated than assumed and might instantiate in the end rather a different "type." This becomes clearer when we contrast the "garbage can model" of decision making[92] with a problem-solving perspective. In the garbage can model, the solutions exist before the target problem is well understood, and thus the solution is in search of problems, while in case-based reasoning some weak or (lazy) generalization only emerges at the end. Thus solutions are not only much less generalizable, they also result from *proper sequencing* of the analytics steps, which rule out certain possibilities despite their prima facie plausibility, as is the case in judicial reasoning. This sequential sensitivity gets lost when we focus only on the logical form of the investigative operations, and it is therefore not surprising that Aristotle suggested – arguing here well within the confines of a time-insensitive logic – that analogous reasoning is more like a form of deductive reasoning. As he suggests, we reason from an example, then support our major premise by further similar cases, so that we "arrive at a general proposition and then argue deductively to a particular conclusion."[93]

[91] Aristotle, "Prior Analytics" in *The Categories, on Interpretation, and Prior Analytics*, trans. Hugh Trendennick, Cambridge, MA: Harvard University Press, 1962, 69a 15f.
[92] See March and Olsen (eds.), *Ambiguity and Choice in Organizations*.
[93] Aristotle, *Rhetoric*, trans. J.H. Freese, Cambridge, MA: Harvard University Press, 1926, at 1402b 1415.

While such a deduction would not be compelling (as the scope of the generalization is restricted) it could marshal assent.

The last remarks lead us to the second problem mentioned above: how are we justified in believing that the analogies, which we have chosen because of a certain "fit," will buttress our conclusion that the source and target are also similar in other respects, since this is the actual heuristic pay-off? While certain analogies might establish a "modal" conception of plausibility and encourage us to do further research, they cannot provide the same assurance for the plausibility of the conclusions. Thus an often discussed example here is Thomas Reid's argument (in 1785) for the existence of life on other planets. In particular he argued that since both Earth and Mars orbit the sun and both have moons, revolving around an axis, and are subject to gravity, the "inferred similarity" is that there plausibly can be life on Mars.[94]

Thus while Reid somehow hit on the importance of moons for the evolution of life, his analogy misses the mark by not "finding" the important dissimilarity, i.e. the absence of an atmosphere. Thus, despite their usefulness, analogies are rife with mistakes simply because the relevance of the similarities and differences is left unspecified. Obviously, there has to be some understanding of connections in the source domain, such as that a sun is necessary for life, i.e. what Hesse calls "pre-theoretic correspondences," and *there must not be a known dis-analogy* between source and target domain, before one can even venture a transfer from the source to the target domain. In short, observed similarities in the source and target domains are obviously insufficient to establish the inference, and no clear rule for valid inferences seems to exist.

Historical Analogies

This is all the more problematic in "historical analogies," especially when they contain certain "lessons learned," as e.g. the Munich analogy, or the domino theory of international politics. Here the problem of establishing the "historical individual" (framing conditions), as well as the hoary nature of historical "facts," which Carl Becker pointed out in his famous article discussing Caesar's crossing of the Rubicon,[95] makes this a particularly problematic area. The perhaps most important point is often overlooked, i.e. that in history we are not dealing with natural kinds that can easily be collected into stable

---

[94] For a further discussion see Mary B. Hesse, *Models and Analogies in Science*, Notre Dame, IN: University of Notre Dame Press, 1966.
[95] Carl L. Becker, "What Are Historical Facts?" *The Western Political Quarterly*, 8:3 (1955): 327–340.

conceptual classes or "populations." Instead, we have to deal with the unique problem of determining how the present, the past, and the future interact in a particular instance.

At the moment, I want to examine "precedents" in the legal sense, since they are in a way a special case of (historical) analogies. However, when we examine some of the constitutive notions of *stare decisis*, of distinguishing and overruling, and when we consider the difficulties which arise when "precedents" are construed in terms of functional necessities, they appear to become "future-oriented" rather than backward-looking. While this point allows us to account for change as well as for the stability in a society, it also raises a whole host of problems for adjudication and the proper exercise of judicial discretion.

Precedent in Law

The first thing we have to remember is that in law a precedent owes its standing to the fact that it is based on a decision of a court which stands in a certain relationship to other courts and is thus part of an institutionalized legal process. Thus, different from the other cases where our interest was in explaining the reliability of certain inferences, here the decisive fact is that even a "wrong" or logically questionable argument "will stand" (*stare decisis*) in virtue of the institutional rules which empower a court to say "what the law is." This fact is often overlooked when we focus on the "reasons" a court gives for its decision. In well-articulated legal systems the persuasiveness of the court's reasoning is always subsidiary to the institutional facts, which puts courts in a particular position of authority.

The "white elephant" in the room is, of course, international law, which does not recognize *stare decisis*, as provided e.g. in Article 59 of the International Court of Justice (ICJ) statute, but where a strict construction of this prohibition would undermine the court's credibility if it did not feel constrained by its previous decisions in cases similarly situated. While this norm of fairness creates some form of "horizontal" *stare decisis*, two other developments counteract the accretion of authority of ICJ decisions, despite their "persuasiveness." One is the proliferation of and competition from other courts, either set up ad hoc, such as the International Criminal Tribunal for the former Yugoslavia (ICTY), or those of "freestanding" regimes, i.e. of regimes which not only have "primary rules" addressing the "dos" and "don'ts" in respect to the actors' actions, but also contain secondary rules by which disputes about the meaning of primary rules can be decided. This leads to a "fragmentation" of the international legal order, as different courts frequently come to different decisions. Here the row between the Yugoslav Tribunal and the ICJ concerning *mens rea* and command responsibility serves as an example.[96] It also often leads to hegemonic struggles within the law, concerning whether an issue falls, e.g., within the remit of public international law, environmental law, or EU law as the Mox case demonstrated.[97] These problems are not entirely new, as we can also gather from the "Wall case" (advisory opinion) of the ICJ,[98] since the conflict before the court could be interpreted as one of the law of occupation, of humanitarian law, of human rights, or of public international law (inherent right of self-defense). But having now, in addition, different forums, certainly does not make things easier. Besides, since every court "sees" different issues raised by the facts of the case, decisions are not final, as the same facts can be used in different versions before different courts, thereby subverting one of the strongest reasons for *stare decisis*, i.e. the expected predictability that results from a "final" decision.

The second development is that recent international lawmaking has escaped its traditional "sources," as exemplified in the proliferation of "soft law" instruments. While the effects of this "relative normativity" might not be as disabling as some international lawyers feared[99] – since the question of obligation can no longer be reduced to one of law vs. morality (or whatever), resulting in the previous conversation stopper: "it's the law, stupid!" – it has created a whole host of doctrinal and practical problems that are difficult to sort out.[100] Above all, there is an astounding conceptual change in the semantic field of custom, i.e. from a practice of long usage and conditional mutual recognition, to a notion which seems entirely derived from doctrinal speculation, equally distanced from political and legal practice. In this way an *obiter dictum* of the Barcelona Traction case could become the "starting point" for some speculations about the movement from a "society" of states, to a "community" of mankind. Ironically, this construction inverts the traditional conception of progress, which envisaged a move from *community to society!*

Given these trends and the increasingly "teleological" interpretation of norms, the real issue is: why should judges be "hostage" to the past, instead of creatively thinking about the future? Should the judges, therefore, decide on the basis of how their decision is likely to influence the actions of the actors in the future,

[96] *Case concerning Military and Paramilitary Activities in and against Nicaragua: Nicaragua v. United States of America*, June 27, 1986, International Court of Justice, I.C.J. 14 (1986).
[97] *The Mox Plant Case (Ireland v. United Kingdom), Provisional Measures*, International Tribunal for the Law of the Sea, (2005) 126 ILR, vol. 273 (2001), at 50.
[98] See *Legal Consequences of the Construction of a Wall in the Occupied Palestinian Territory*, International Court of Justice, Advisory Opinions (2004), at 136.
[99] See the controversy between Prosper, Weil, and J. Gold in the *American Journal of International Law*, vol. 77 (1983). Weil, "Towards Relative Normativity in International Law?" See also Jan Klabbers, "The Redundancy of Soft Law," *Nordic Journal of International Law*, 65:2 (1996): 167–182.
[100] See Kratochwil, *The Status of Law in World Society*, chaps. 3–4, 9.

since for that purpose the "past" might not provide the adequate template? This is indeed a puzzling question, especially if raised at this high level of abstraction. For one: as we have seen, applying a precedent to a "present" case involves a judgment as to the relevant similarities, and thus the meaning of a precedent is not just applying a ready-made template mechanically, as we do when we press a cookie cutter into some dough. After all, the precedents instantiating the prohibition of "unreasonable searches or seizures" have always to be interpreted, looking at the past from the angle of a present problem. Our guiding interest here is pragmatic, not "factual" in the sense of wanting to establish the veracity of certain matters of fact. As such, the "present/past" is a very specific "construct," subject to procedures determining the relevant facts and rules. Hereby certain past actions weigh in, such as the original intent, or the will of the legislature in constitutional and statutory construction. But again, such a construal will be hermeneutic – precisely because we do not know what the different legislators or their majority thought – and the "original intent" of the constitution makers is not tantamount to aggregating episodic evidence about their personal opinions.

If we accept this train of thought then a few corollaries follow. One is that even judges using precedents do not necessarily provide the best description of what they are doing. For example, the US Court of Appeals for the Ninth Circuit states on *stare decisis*:

Consider the word *decisis*. The word means literally and legally the decision. Under the doctrine of *stare decisis* a case is important for what it decides – for the "what," not for the "why" and not for the "how." Insofar as precedent is concerned, *stare decisis* is important only for the decision, for the detailed consequences following a detailed set of facts.[101]

The first part concerning the "what" could be interpreted as pointing to the authority of the court in making decisions by applying precedents, and that the law is not simply the *ratio decidendi* of a previous case. The identification of the "what" with the "facts" but the dismissal of the "why" and "how," however, cannot be quite right. Precisely because even explicit rules are open-textured, as the debate between Hart and Fuller showed, cases cannot be decided on looking harder at the facts.[102] Remember: Is the prohibition "no vehicles in the park" supposed to apply also to wheelchairs, if they are motor-driven (or electrically powered)? Do ambulances qualify (when they try to reach someone having a heart attack in the park, or when they take a short

---

[101] *United States v. Osborne (in Re Osborne)*, United States Court of Appeals, Ninth Circuit, 76 F.3d 306 (1996), at 185. Para. 50.

[102] H.L.A. Hart, "Positivism and the Separation of Law and Morals," *Harvard Law Review*, 71:4 (1958): 593–629. See also Lon L. Fuller, "Positivism and Fidelity to Law: A Reply to Professor Hart," *Harvard Law Review*, 71:4 (1958): 630–672.

cut to reach a hospital on the other side)? And what about the tank which serves as a monument in the park? Precisely because the social world does not consist of neatly packaged natural facts, a more careful analysis of relations between the "facts" and the *ratio decidendi* is required, and this entails opening up issues of "how" and "why."

But why should judges not set precedents which are *forward-looking* rather than backward-looking? Indeed, advocates of the law-and-economics approach have argued that such a Copernican turn is necessary. While this would certainly raise important legitimacy questions since it would tear the veil from the legitimizing myth that judges do not legislate but "find" the law, it also would sit quite uneasily with the traditional separation-of-powers argument. But let us leave such scruples aside for the moment and rather ask what would have to be true so that such a forward-looking setting of precedent could muster support. Here public "utility," of course, comes to mind and the judge could justify her actions by showing that her decision would increase overall public utility.

Faced with this daunting task of minimizing social costs "the law" would then have to develop e.g. both efficient liability rules and enforcement mechanisms. Practically this means that the conceptualization of "fault" would have to be approached as an optimization problem that can be solved via a marginal cost analysis. Thus, a person is at fault and liable if s/he has neglected to apply an additional unit of care, even though the cost to her was less than the marginal benefits to the victim. In this way we could reduce the total amount of expected damages. There are, however, at least three major difficulties with this solution.

One is that actually no clear rules are then possible at all, since damages are assessed only *ex post* and the costs, instantiated by the specific rules, are not available to the parties *ex ante*. Thus, inevitably, the outcome seems more like a Weberian *kadi*-justice than one of formulating rules, which allow for prospective ordering. Second, for such a situation to occur, it would have to be true that both judges and injurers are perfect maximizers and agree on the same accounting scheme when setting the optimal levels. Here the assumption of complete and costless information raises its ugly head. We all know, of course, that such an assumption is "unrealistic," as it is "ideal." But never mind!

However, as it turns out, this assumption is not only ideal, but also logically *incoherent*. This leads us to the third problem. If information is not costless then the question arises of how long and at what costs we are going to search. The resulting "augmented" decision problem does not let us determine the "optimal level of search," so that we can converge on an optimum level of care. It was precisely for these reasons that we tried to "economize" and use short cuts by inventing rules in the first place! Our hope was that these rules would at least help us in our calculations by identifying fewer and more manageable factors we have to take into consideration than if we had to deal with an overall assessment of a contingency that has not even arisen yet. In a similar fashion, property rules relieve us from worrying about the needs of others, and having to speculate about social optima, which would be relevant when "needs" are adduced to "solve" the distribution problem. As Conlisk points out,[103] the idealized assumption of an optimum has to fall down when the "costs" for solving the augmented decision problem are included.

It is therefore no surprise that the genuflection before the idealized assumptions has little to offer to either a "theory" of law or to the actual practice of judging. If we do not want to fall back on the idiosyncratic reasons of the judges, as the realists suggested, we need some consensual "rules of thumb" by which we, as potential tort-feasors and judges alike, can assess how to proceed. These rules need not be unequivocal or incontestable, and they certainly will not be universal, showing instead the traces of "traditions" and "common sense," which need to be vetted. But for better or for worse, that is all we have and with which we must make do.

5.7   Conclusion

This chapter examined in greater detail the influence of norms on molding decisions. I developed my argument in two steps: one by a critical examination of the existing approaches; and two by providing an alternative heuristics examining different modes of practical reasoning common in law and politics. The critical stance towards both certain legal theories and the social scientific approach to "compliance" was based on my suspicion that they tend to mischaracterize the problems of choice. This issue of "mischaracterization" was related to – or rather becomes apparent in – the curious mutual dependence of realism (as a "theory" of politics) and of "legalism." By this distinction the actual problem of "praxis" is evaded, i.e. that its choices are neither unique nor "determined" (as, ironically, both the "pure theory of law" seemed to imply and Dworkin actually claimed), nor explainable in terms of "intervening or antecedent variables" (which represents the standard social "scientific" account).

In a second step, I focused in the remainder of this chapter on different modes of reasoning to deduction or induction. Here I scrutinized reasoning by analogy, by metaphorical extension, reasoning from case to case and the use of precedents in law. I will return to these topics in Chapters 8 to 11 after having examined more closely the actual practices of sanctioning (Chapter 6) and punishing (Chapter 7), and having shown the importance of historical reflection in Chapter 8.

---

[103] John Conlisk, "Why Bounded Rationality?" *Journal of Economic Literature*, 34:2 (1996): 669–700, at 690.

6 Sanctioning

6.1 Introduction

The characterization of law as a system of sanctioning norms is as common as it is controversial. As the debate e.g. between Kelsen,[1] Hart[2] and Dworkin[3] has shown, "secondary" rules in a legal system no longer address the actors' behavior directly but are concerned with establishing how primary norms are created, modified, or rescinded. As such they do not seem to possess an explicit sanction as a character-tag. Besides, some of the most important parts of legal systems, such as "principles" (good faith, due process, etc.), do not even have rule character but are open-textured as to their instances of application and scope. True, the counter-example of secondary rules that seem to have no attached sanction but stipulate the conditions under which certain acts have validity – be it Hart's wills-act, or the constitutional prescriptions such as: "The President shall have the power of sending and receiving ambassadors" – can be brought, through some "re-casting," under the penumbra of sanctions. In that case not a penalty but the invalidity of the acts would be the sanction.

However, principles raise other hoary problems that cannot be as easily accommodated. They remind us that this old definitional chestnut is heir to a particular political project, which tied law to the sovereign and state building. Not only was law the "command of the sovereign" – and, consequently, if there is no properly constituted public authority there could not be any law, and no injustice either, as Hobbes pointed out. This emphasis on official sanctions also reminds us that all (natural) rights that entitled their bearers to seek on their own redress for wrongs suffered, had been transferred to the sovereign, save for the extreme circumstances of self-defense. In short, as opposed to other religiously or ontologically inspired notions of order, the sovereign had now become the sole fundament for the public order, and the fountainhead of law. The old scholastic controversy about the origin of *ius*, i.e. whether it derives from a notion of justice (*ius* from *iustum*) or from the

---

[1] See Hans Kelsen, *Principles of International Law*, 2nd edn., New York: Holt, 1966, at 4.
[2] See Hart, *The Concept of Law*.   [3] See Dworkin, "Is Law a System of Rules?"

command of the sovereign (*ius* because it is *iussum* i.e. commanded) seemed to have been decided in favor of the latter.

As understandable as the wish is to have a precise concept of law, the above brief reflections suggest that the issue of sanctions cannot be disposed of by engaging in purely definitional exercises concerning the nature of law. Thus even dyed-in-the-wool positivists have to agree that legal orders often "incorporate" customary rules although they do not have their origin in the will of a sovereign. Besides, the focus on sanctions in positivism, and their identification with the state obscures rather than illuminates the variability of sanctions. One need not be an advocate of a Foucauldian approach in order to see that the disciplinary control prevalent in modernity – devolving important elements of control to private agents, such as hospitals, professions, credit bureaus – functions quite differently from the infrequent but brutal punishment characteristic of pre-modern law. In addition, such an approach also fails to examine the distinctive roles that the "declarers of the law" play, as the latter's role is simply amalgamated with that of the enforcers although much of state-building had to do with institutionalizing the *separation of powers*, which *prohibits* the fusion of law-declarer and executor. Finally, and of particular importance for international politics, such an approach misconstrues the problem of "self-help," representing it as an indicator for international anarchy – in the sense of a Hobbesian war of all against all – instead of conceiving it as a legal institution.

The sorting out of these conceptual issues has first to place sanctions within the proper semantic field and show how sanctions connect with notions of legitimacy, authority, harm, punishment, and responsibility. Furthermore, this semantic field has then to be related to the practices of securing social order by deterring transgressions and inducing compliance, which in turn makes the examination of the efficacy of sanctions necessary.

Although tackling the latter task in the "anarchical" environment of international relations addresses a central problem in the field, it is rather surprising that the big sanctioning debates over the last few decades have mainly focused on economic sanctions while the discussion of sanctions implying the use of force was either left to advocates of humanitarian interventions, or to the proponents of criminal prosecution for human rights violations. Notions of a *guerre d'exécution* or some modern version of this have practically vanished from the ongoing debates. Even realists apparently have accepted the notion that forceful action requires some form of consent to the operations by the Security Council, notwithstanding the Kosovo operation and the second Gulf War, even if noncompliance with that norm and an *ex post* sanctioning of previously unauthorized acts by the UN might leave us with a bitter aftertaste.

Other uses of force have been dealt with under the heading of collective defense or of "covert operations," or operating, as in the case of the "war on terror," in a curious and disturbing conceptual no-man's land. Here the old rules of warfare are subverted and new word creations, such as "unlawful combatant" and the conceptual overstretch of "terrorism," dominate the discourse. The latter then justifies not only "enhanced interrogation techniques" but also "extrajudicial killings" and drone strikes, i.e. virtually anything that the new security experts, clad in a legal garb, can dream up. At this point the civilizational veneer is wearing thin and terrorists and those fighting terrorism become increasingly indistinguishable.

In short, although the bulk of the literature on sanctions addresses issues of effectiveness its narrow focus on the infliction of harm faces a variety of shortcomings. It assumes that the sender for some apparently obvious reasons imposes sanctions on a target in order to "make" the opponent desist, or induce him to take certain actions. But this is inadequate since the role of the "recipient" often remains unaddressed. As the focus is solely on the commitment and the clarity of the message of the sender, it usually neglects the strategic situation, and thus the possibilities of the recipient "working around" sanctions by intentionally or unintentionally "not getting the message," or using the penalization to his advantage ("rally around the flag" syndrome).

Further questions arise when we leave the purely instrumental perspective behind. After all, states imposing sanctions might have multiple purposes and often unstated motivations. As the historical record shows, states often impose sanctions for symbolic purposes, not the least of which concerns the assuaging of the *domestic audience* in the face of grave violations committed by others. Hellquist has demonstrated that the EU continued with its sanctions vis-à-vis Zimbabwe in spite of their admitted ineffectiveness. But this fact is easily explained by the wish of the EU to send a "signal" that Mugabe's conduct was unacceptable, to assure the European publics that something was being done, and to impress the audience, i.e. other African states, which were considered to be "fence-sitters." The same point could be made in the case of the sanctions against the Russian Federation for its incorporation of the Crimea, since nobody is under any illusion that this will get us back to the status quo ante. Finally, the complex decision making of modern states makes the effectiveness of sanctions dependent on the interactions between different branches of government (Congress and President) and activist groups within the domestic public and transnational "civil society." This problem makes it unlikely that a country can speak with one clear voice and that the political priorities are as well ordered, as assumed by rational actor models. Thus, presidential action can undermine congressional sanctioning legislation (as in the case of Rhodesia when compared to that of South Africa), or Congressional insistence on policy change might undo the executive's attempts at a more "constructive engagement" with the other country, as was the case during the Nixon administration when Congress insisted on a more liberal Soviet emigration policy, which tougher sanctions were supposed to deliver. In addition, sanctions usually hurt some domestic interests through the trade forgone and thereby create incentives for domestic groups to work for policy change and/or circumvent the sanctions. The last remarks also drive home the fact that the use of the term "actors" has its drawbacks, as it backgrounds or even loses the remarkable differences between social aggregates and individuals. The result is an entirely implausible account of how sanctions are supposed to "work." Since the sites (i.e. the points where the consequences should be felt) are frequently not disaggregated, it is also assumed that the "economy of force" works in individual and collective cases in like fashion. As the pressure on the individual increases and the mounting pain leads to his eventual compliance, so the pressure on a state will lead either to a change in actions, or to a domestic revolution putting new leaders in power. Both assumptions are obviously rather heroic, as both a conceptual analysis and historical experiences show. Sanctioned leaders might use "foreign hostility" to cement their regime and skillfully deflect the impact of sanctions from their governmental apparatus and their loyal clients. This realization has led to a call for "smart sanctions," targeting individuals rather than states or societies as a whole. But eventually those measures too will reach farther down into the society, as the Iraqi sanctions and the "Oil for Food" program show, holding again the entire population hostage.

These problems have not only engendered two rounds of vigorous debates,[4] they have also considerably refined our conceptual tools, even if various "coding problems" plaguing previous sanction studies have not been eliminated and thus the empirical record remains vexing: what one coder counts as a success, is for the other a failure.[5] Similarly, while sanctions were not generally successful in bringing about the desired regime- or foreign policy changes, it is hard to imagine that the changes in South Africa or Libya (under Gaddafi) would have been possible without the international pressure exerted by sanctions. Over time they were instrumental in initiating a "rethink" in the target state suffering from continued delegitimization efforts.

Issues of monitoring or being able to stop defection from the sanctioning regime have been another focal point in the discussions. Thus the sanctioning state has to see to it first that the sanctions *are enforced against one's own*

---

[4] See e.g. as part of the first debate David Baldwin's magisterial work: David A. Baldwin, *Economic Statecraft*, Princeton: Princeton University Press, 1985. For the more recent debate, see Gary Clyde Hufbauer, Jeffrey J. Schott, and Kimberly Ann Elliott, *Economic Sanctions Reconsidered*, 2nd edn., Washington, DC: Institute for International Economics, 1990; Robert A. Pape, "Why Economic Sanctions Do Not Work," *International Security*, 22:2 (1997): 90–136; Kimberly Ann Elliott, "The Sanctions Glass: Half Full or Completely Empty?" *International Security*, 23:1 (1998): 50–65.
[5] See the interesting discussion in Jonathan Kirshner, "Review Essay: Economic Sanctions: The State of the Art," *Security Studies*, 11:4 (2002): 160–179.

firms and traders, who might incur considerable losses. As a research institute has suggested, the sanctions of the decade 1990–2000 have resulted in a loss to American firms in 1995 alone of a staggering $15–19 billion, affecting also approximately 200,000 workers.[6] Even more difficult to achieve is compliance by others. Given that, for sanctions to succeed, a drastic reduction in the availability of alternative trading partners or in embargoed goods is necessary, anything but a common front vis-à-vis the sanctioned state seems insufficient. But here size (and with it the concomitant opportunity costs) matters more than numbers, and powerful actors might want to go it alone anyway since getting a coalition together might involve significant bargaining costs and/or water down the sanctioning regime itself. To that extent unilateral sanctions might not be as ineffective as is often assumed, and multilateral ones not as promising as thought.

The unilateral flexing of one's muscles is also likely to engender unanticipated costs that a narrow focus on effectiveness hides. Thus the extension of extraterritorial jurisdiction of the US to subsidiaries of American firms in order to reinforce the US pipeline embargo created significant fallout within NATO. Washington originally adopted these measures in 1982 in response to the Soviet invasion of Afghanistan. But attempts to extend their scope by asserting jurisdiction over firms abroad which were either owned by Americans or used US technology misfired.[7] European courts not only refused to allow such an extensive interpretation of the protective principle of international law, they allowed (forced) US subsidiaries in Europe to honor their contracts, which were part of the pipeline deal between the western European states and the Soviet Union.[8] Particularly objectionable in this context was the use of US patents and licenses to justify the extraterritorial extension of jurisdiction, since this move violated the interests of third parties (i.e. those of the European states), who had no dispute with the US and thus could not retaliate against the unilateral US countermeasures, save by not enforcing them.

Thus the illegality of some sanctions serves as a useful reminder that even in a self-help system it is not true that "anything goes." As this case shows, the ineffectiveness of the sanctions and their political costs in straining the NATO alliance soon led to an abandonment of the original strategy. But even multilateral sanctions might not achieve their goal if the members of the sanction coalition do not continue seeing eye to eye in dealing with the changes in the

---

[6] Richard N. Haass, "Sanctioning Madness," *Foreign Affairs*, 76:6 (1997): 74–85, at 75.
[7] See Michael Mastanduno, *Economic Containment: CoCom and the Politics of East–West Trade*, Ithaca, NY: Cornell University Press, 1992.
[8] For an assessment of the legal fallout, see Andreas Falke, "The EU–US Conflict over Sanctions Policy: Confronting the Hegemon," *European Foreign Affairs Review*, 5:2 (2000): 139–163.

environment, as the weapons embargo against the former Yugoslavia showed.[9]
While the sanctions apparently played a pivotal role in Milosevic's original
decision to cut a deal at Dayton (November 1995),[10] the original consensus
among the sanctioning coalition evaporated thereafter.

These inconsistent data make it difficult to sort things out. One problem
is obviously the notoriously imprecise determination of how to assess whether
or not sanctions "work." Such an assessment is downright impossible unless
we specify first what they are supposed to accomplish: do we seek a containment of the opponent (as was the case with the strategic embargos imposed on
the Soviet Union during the Cold War), do we want to bring about a policy
change, or do we even aim at a regime change?

Furthermore, even if we have specified our goals a bit more precisely we
still have to answer Baldwin's question"as compared to what?"[11] While economic sanctions generally do not seem able to induce regime change – precisely
because they presuppose that the leaders are subject to popular disapproval[12] –
they might erode the effectiveness of the regime without necessarily effecting a
policy change.[13] In short, sanctions might increase the costs of a sanctioned
state for pursuing the original policy and thus have a demonstrable "effect,"
whereas the aimed-at change might not be attainable.

It is therefore cold comfort indeed to see that things are not that different
when sanctions include the use of force. How contingent the link between
policy change and various forms of influence-attempts is can be seen from the
Vietnam experience. Despite an overwhelming amount of force applied by the
US, a change in North Vietnamese policy, i.e. "getting them to the table," was
effected only after the diplomatic constellation had changed and Hanoi's allies
pressured North Vietnam and the Vietcong to seek a preliminary and negotiated settlement. It seems that rather than analyzing only the increase in force
that is supposed to deliver a change in policy in accordance with a monotonic
function of pain inflicted, we would do better to look at the wider picture, i.e. at
the threats, the application of actual force, and the promises made in this context. Here the Cuban Missile Crisis and the *quid pro quo* of US withdrawals of

---

[9] Here the US tacitly allowed weapons to reach Croatian and Muslim forces; see Loretta Bondi,
"Arms Embargo: In Name Only?" in David Cortright and George A. Lopez (eds.), *Smart
Sanctions: Targeting Economic Statecraft*, Lanham, MD: Rowman & Littlefield, 2002,
109–124.
[10] See Richard C. Holbrooke, *To End a War*, New York: Random House, 1998, at 282.
[11] Baldwin, *Economic Statecraft*, particularly chap. 7.
[12] See e.g. the findings by Nossal that sanctions work best when they are addressed to states with
more or less democratic regimes and multi-party political systems: Raimo Väyrynen (ed.),
Globalization and Global Governance, Lanham, MD: Rowman & Littlefield, 1999.
[13] See e.g. J. Dashti-Gibson, P. Davis, and B. Radcliff, "On the Determinants of the Success of
Economic Sanctions: An Empirical Analysis," *American Journal of Political Science*, 41:2
(1997): 608–618.

the missiles from Turkey and the acceptance of Castro's regime in exchange
for a Soviet withdrawal are instructive. Although this might lead us to far more
complex models of exerting influence than the simple causal model in which
force equals change (*actio est reactio*), the fruitfulness of such a more comprehensive analysis for explaining policy change and crisis resolution has been
amply demonstrated by James Davis's study of historical crises.[14]

Third, as has been pointed out, the whole debate concerning the effects of
sanctions might be seriously flawed, as the universe of actually imposed sanctions might suffer from a serious selection bias. Unless we also include in our
sample cases of sanctions which were threatened but then not applied because
the sanctioned party complied, we are likely to skew our analysis considerably.
Here the historical record shows that many threats "work," particularly when
they are considered as supporting legitimate objectives. The imposition of
actual sanctions only becomes necessary when threats misfire, as the previous
"speech acts" had no "per-locutionary" effect.[15] Not only are demands which
are considered illegitimate less likely to be effective – they usually engender
resentment and resistance – we also have to bear in mind that not all decision-
makers are opportunistically driven actors. In cases where an actor is defen-
sively oriented but fears that his position will be weakened when he does not
hold firm, or where the threatener is going to press on no matter what concessions are made, the imposition of sanctions and/or the escalation of the crisis is
likely. As Drenzer has shown, states with a high expectation of conflict are
more likely to accept significant cost rather than concede. They fear further
demands, and care about the "relative gains" that might accrue to the threatener
from their present concession,[16] quite aside from loss of prestige or credibility
the backing down might engender.

Fourth, our inclination to see sanctions functioning like a "cause" exerting
its effect, so that more force will have to engender bigger effects, is misleading
We should note that we are moving here in a strategic environment and not in
the natural realm. To that extent actors might exploit effects that are latent in
normal times but which provide powerful countervailing power in times of
crises, such as the above-mentioned "rally around the flag" syndrome. Symbolic capital provides a sanctioned government with enormous resources for
counteracting possible hardships and getting acceptance for standing firm or

[14] James W. Davis, *Threats and Promises: The Pursuit of International Influence*, Baltimore:
Johns Hopkins University Press, 2000.
[15] See in this context Leonard Schoppa's interesting examination of the US–Japanese relationship
and the changing rate of compliance with US demands when they were no longer perceived as
appropriate. Leonard J. Schoppa, "The Social Context in Coercive International Bargaining,"
International Organization, 53:2 (1999): 307–342.
[16] See Daniel W. Drezner, *The Sanctions Paradox: Economic Statecraft and International Relations*, Cambridge: Cambridge University Press, 1999.

even retaliating, despite the costs such moves might engender. As Simmel has observed, conflict with outsiders inevitably enhances group solidarity.[17]

The last point leads to a fifth problem that arises from the growth of humanitarian law and the increase of attempts at "sanctioning" serious breaches. Somewhat surprisingly the use of international law to penalize for purposes of retribution and deterrence enjoys nearly unmitigated popularity, while in penology and criminal justice the advocacy of such measures has more or less fallen out of favor. Furthermore, the issue of individualizing guilt and innocence for policies and actions raise serious issues as to whether the standards of proof and of procedural justice are adequate to deal with serious and massive violations of human rights. But this will be the topic of the next chapter and I shall forgo a discussion here.

From these rather lengthy initial remarks we can see again that sanctioning lies at the intersection of a variety of theoretical and practical problems that need further exploration. The procedure below will again follow the process of an "interrogation," i.e. showing how sanctions link to other concept and practices in order to clarify their meaning. Rather than looking for the lowest common denominator that all sanctions possess, which forms the "core" from which a "theory" can take off, I begin by examining the conceptual issues surrounding the term and examining its connection in order to get a reading of the semantic field.

For that purpose I shall begin in Section 6.2 with the use of the term sanction, which is strangely bound up with both "approval" and with "disapproval." Beginning with this half-forgotten dimension of sanctioning might be unorthodox, but I do so because in this way I can correct, in Section 6.3, some of the most common conceptual myopias surrounding "self-help." This permission for "private" redress is often interpreted as a result of "anarchy" in the international arena, instead of realizing that self-help is a pervasive legal institution in both the domestic and international realm. To correct this error I begin my discussion with "seals of approval" which are the result of voluntary codes of conduct, and their various reporting and monitoring requirements to which corporations and other actors have submitted, in order to signal to the general public the legitimacy of their actions. Here the greening of corporate activity has to be mentioned, as well as attempts to abate certain conflicts, which are fueled by natural resources (such as blood diamonds). But also the UN Global Compact and the "Guiding Principles" and the "Protect, Respect and Remedy Framework" developed by John Ruggie under the auspices of the UN Human Rights Council (adopted in 2008) belong here.[18]

---

[17] See Simmel, *Conflict and the Web of Group Affiliations.*

[18] See John Gerard Ruggie, *Just Business: Multinational Corporations and Human Rights*, New York: W.W. Norton, 2013. See also the voluntary framework developed for businesses: United

In Section 6.4, I deal with the "negative" side of sanctions by examining the historical feud as a self-help measure among the (developing) sovereigns in the European system. I analyze the medieval feud, which survived in the *ius armorum* of the "estates" (not states!) in the Westphalian settlement and developed further both in the *ius ad bellum* and in the regime of neutrality. In our times it has morphed into the more narrowly circumscribed "inherent right" of self-defense and the doctrine of "countermeasures." Section 6.5 is devoted to self-defense, and Section 6.6 to the discussion of countermeasures not involving the use of force, while Section 6.7 discusses sanctions in multilateral settings including those authorizing the use of force. This prepares the way for a discussion of a reassessment of the impact of sanctions, in Section 6.8.[19]

6.2   Sanctioning (Approving)

On January 25, 1984, the Swiss Nestlé Corporation announced that it was willing to fully implement the WHO/UNICEF code for marketing breast milk substitutes and signed an agreement with the International Nestlé Boycott Committee (INBC), a caucus of activist groups, which for the previous seven years had organized a boycott of Nestlé products throughout the world.[20] This agreement was not only remarkable for its unprecedented form, i.e. as an agreement between a corporation and some private actors. It had also succeeded in holding a business corporation accountable for the *unintended* harm caused by its product in the underdeveloped world, where most of the conditions for safe use were not present (since they had only contaminated water, no or little possibility of preparing the baby food under sterile conditions and keeping it refrigerated, or the users were unable to read and could not follow the instructions). Thus, ironically the product that was relatively safe in the First World represented a significant hazard for life and health in the Third World.

Equally remarkable was that the agreement came after protracted conflict and that Nestlé turned from a Saulus into a Paulus afterwards. It not only accepted the code, which had been prepared by the WHO, regulating industry

---

Nations General Assembly, *Protect, Respect and Remedy: A Framework for Business and Human Rights*, Human Rights Council, 2008, A/HRC/8/5.

[19] Here I obviously cannot deal with the newest case (perhaps one of success), the lifting of the Iran sanctions, because the deal occurred after I had concluded the manuscript and the information will only become available in the next couple of years. Rather than engaging in speculation I decided to leave this for "further research."

[20] For the background to the Nestlé case, see Kathryn Sikkink, "Codes of Conduct for Transnational Corporations: The Case of the WHO/UNICEF Code," *International Organization*, 40:4 (1986): 815–840.

behavior, but began to promote it and contributed, in a way, to its adoption by the World Health Assembly in May 1980.

Finally we see here both elements of sanctioning: on the one hand the negative sanctions of a boycott that included a "naming and shaming" campaign by an international coalition of activists (IBFAN) and on the other hand the "positive sanction," i.e. creation of a "seal of approval," which was sought by Nestlé after the agreement. Its adoption was to salvage the corporate image and to signal to the world that Nestlé was willing to take the necessary steps in complying with the "voluntary" code worked out by the WHO and UNICEF. In October 1984, after the activists had examined monitoring reports from fifteen countries and verified a significant change in Nestlé's marketing practices,[21] IBFAN ended the boycott. They thereby hit on a solution that was instrumental in the later development of the corporate social responsibility framework that had emerged at around the turn of the twenty-first century, and which was later fed by several debates within the UN, civil society, and the business community itself.

The initial debates were occasioned by some notorious "scandals" that showed that in a globalized world there existed even more serious problems for mishaps and for holding corporations liable for negligence or questionable conduct – including downright criminal actions involving forced labor, rape and murder, sometimes even with the cooperation of the host government.[22] The lamentable outcomes were due to the regulation gap, and to complex legal constraints, which do not allow the attribution of fault to a parent company for the misdeeds of one or more of its subsidiaries, even if the parent company is the sole shareholder.[23]

The Bhopal incident, probably the greatest ever industrial disaster,[24] exposed at a minimum 80,000, perhaps even 500,000, people to toxic gases, killed 3,787 persons (according to the local government) and inflicted permanent

---

[21] Ibid., 833.

[22] Here the case of *Doe v. Unocal Corp.*, US Court of Appeals, Ninth Circuit, 395 F.3d 932 (2002) has deservedly attained notoriety. In that case, Burmese villagers sued an American company for the named egregious violations of human rights under the Alien Tort Claims Act. They had been forced to build a pipeline for which the Burmese government (State Law and Order Restoration Council) and the Myamar Oil and Gas Council had created a partnership with the US service provider. Despite the immunity excuses of the Burmese partners the judge allowed the case to proceed with Unlocal as sole defendant. The case for damages was settled in March 2005 out of court for reportedly US$30 million. See Armin Rosencranz and David Louk, "Doe v. Unocal: Holding Corporations Liable for Human Rights Abuses on Their Watch," *Chapman Law Review*, 8 (2005): 135–147.

[23] For such an attribution, actual day-to-day operational control by the parent company has to be proven.

[24] See Dan Kurzman, *A Killing Wind: Inside Union Carbide and the Bhopal Catastrophe*, New York: McGraw-Hill Companies, 1987.

damage on possibly up to 100,000 people[25] when poisonous gases escaped from the tanks of the chemical factory of United Carbide India Limited (UCIL). In this corporation the US firm of Union Carbide (UCC) held the majority stake, and Indian banks and the public held a 49 percent stake. When a suit for damages was filed, the US parent offered $470 million dollars as compensation in 1984 to preempt further proceedings, an offer which was accepted by the Indian Supreme Court in 1989 as an appropriate settlement sum. The Indian courts themselves, however, took until June 2010 to bring civil and criminal charges against seven former employees of UNIL – including the former UCC chairman, who had been arrested but was out on bail and was apparently flown out of the country by government plane. The conviction amounted to two years in prison and a fine of $2,000 each.

When measured against these horrors, the slave-labor charge leveled against Nike in the 1990s seems at first small indeed, until one realizes that the hourly wage paid by Nike to its laborers in the Third World amounted to about 19¢ while the same company could afford to "sponsor" the basketball star Michael Jordan for about $20 million a year. After a storm of public outrage, Nike, to its credit, mended its ways and even became a founding member of the Global Compact, which John Ruggie had inaugurated at the UN in 2000. This was a policy initiative that tried to serve as a catalyst for corporations to live up to their responsibilities in and beyond the workplace, by safeguarding human rights, insuring transparency of their activities, taking measures against corruption, and linking the corporations' strategies to some of the larger UN goals, such as environmental protection, sustainable development, and the Millennium initiative. It also encouraged public/private partnerships for the advancement of health, education, and community development. Corporations could join in this effort by subscribing to the principles and provide a yearly progress report on their efforts.

While the UN officially had continued to push for a formally binding convention on Norms on the Responsibilities of Transnational Corporations (TNCs) and Other Business Enterprises with the Regard to Human Rights (2003) – which engendered considerable resistance in business circles, as had all previous attempts at formulating formal codes of conduct for the TNCs – Ruggie's initiative linked to two wider debates and profited from their synergies when joined.

One was the debate about the nature of corporate governance itself and the responsibilities to the wider society. It started in the nineteenth century, was

---

[25] The estimates differ widely between governmental sources and Ingrid Eckerman, who was a Swedish member of the International Medical Commission to investigate the Bhopal incident. See Ingrid Eckerman, *The Bhopal Saga: Causes and Consequences of the World's Largest Industrial Disaster*, Bhopal: Universities Press, 2005.

then submerged, and resurfaced in the 1950s, when Howard Bowen wrote his *Social Responsibilities of the Businessman*.[26] The challenge to the notion that the business of business had to be business was then taken up by Milton Friedman in the 1970, who reintroduced the shareholder value as the[27] ultimate goal of corporate activity, or as Friedman put it: "the social responsibility is to increase profit" and not to engage in some form of charity. Before long, this view was contested in turn by Robert Ackerman,[28] who suggested that a business enterprise could be successful only if it paid attention to the societal environment in which it operated.

Most of these writers, being managers rather than (like Friedman) classical economists, were keenly aware of the myopia of considering the firm a simple "throughput" function, subject to the maxim of revenue maximization. They argued that a firm with a reputation for being socially irresponsible might *actually fail* to secure even a minimum return to its shareholders. The result was the "stakeholder" model of the firm, which Freeman[29] proposed in 1984, the upshot of which was that a corporation was not only to satisfy the interests of its shareholders but should also pay attention to those interests which were affected by its operation.

As problematic as the notion of a stakeholder in actual practice is – as frequently a virtually unlimited number of "affected" could be identified without some further (arbitrary?) restrictions – the idea was simple. Analogous to the problem that firms have to advertise their products, since the consumer is neither in possession of complete information concerning the available products, nor does s/he know their quality (for which "branding" provides the solution) – the "stakeholders" can be reassured by some signs which signal to the wider audience that the enterprise engages in legitimate and responsible production and management practices.[30]

The other development was the phenomenal growth in transnational networks and movements which often claimed to be part of an emerging global civil society and which were ready to challenge the monopoly of states on determining the political agenda and its priorities. Even if the analogy to a domestic civil society that had accompanied the emergence of state-building

---

[26] Howard Rothmann Bowen, *Social Responsibilities of the Businessman*, New York: Harper and Row, 1953.

[27] Milton Friedman, "The Social Responsibility of Business Is to Increase Its Profits," *New York Times Magazine*, September 13, 1970: 32–33 and 122–126.

[28] Robert W. Ackerman, *The Social Challenge to Business*, Cambridge, MA: Harvard University Press, 1975.

[29] R. Edward Freeman, *Strategic Management: A Stakeholder Approach*, Boston, MA: Pitman Publishing, 1984.

[30] See Michael E. Porter and Mark R. Kramer, "Strategy and Society: The Link between Competitive Advantage and Corporate Social Responsibility," *Harvard Business Review*, 84:12 (2006): 78–92.

was problematic[31] – precisely because the new transnational movements and networks were usually single-issue organizations – they linked particular knowledge (about an "issue") and "local knowledge" (how it played out in a given locale) to the wider debates taking place in other "publics," international organizations, or other fora.

Bringing these two elements together could therefore create important synergies, as Ruggie remarked with regard to the corporate social responsibility (CSR) initiative:

Companies began to establish CSR Units to monitor workplace standards in their global supply chains, whether in consumer electronics or apparel and footwear. So called fair trade labeling and other certification schemes extended similar promises, ranging from coffee beans to toys and forest products. A number of collaborative initiatives were established with industry partners, sometimes including NGOs and governments as well, the Kimberly Process to stem the flow of conflict diamonds being a notable example.[32]

Of course, given the complexity of these issues the question whether all these arrangements "work" remains open and can be answered only by a detailed examination. What is however *not possible* is to give the categorical answer that because these norms are soft and voluntary, the resulting regime cannot possibly work. The silent assumptions here are on the one hand that "hard law" guarantees success because it is enforced, and the notion that voluntary undertakings cannot be serious but are self-serving camouflage for business as usual. Both assumptions are open to well-founded criticisms. First, since these "compacts" are attempting to alleviate environmental and working conditions, as well as safeguard respect for human rights in countries in which governments are weak or corrupt – and frequently both – getting state enforcement might be like putting the fox in charge of the hen house. It is not surprising that private businesses have seldom shown enthusiasm for being once more under the thumb of still another bureaucracy.

But there is another reason that formality does not simply result in greater compliance, or necessarily better results. Since human rights protect a diverse set of values, tradeoffs are inevitable. They are already difficult to achieve in the domestic arena where courts exist which stand in a more or less strict line of command provided by the legal process. Given the fragmentation of the international legal order and the existence of many freestanding regimes with dispute resolution mechanisms, but lacking such an ordering, legal incoherence seems to be pre-programmed, as even two former presidents of the

---

[31] See Bartelson, "Making Sense of Global Civil Society". See also Terrell Carver and Jens Bartelson, *Globality, Democracy and Civil Society*, Abingdon: Routledge, 2011.
[32] Ruggie, *Just Business*, at xxvif.

ICJ suggested.[33] Furthermore, the growth of special investment treaties with compulsory arbitration put public and private interests on the same footing.

As an illustration of this point consider the difficulties of Argentina and South Africa in pursuing policies of "implementing" some basic human rights when this implementation collided with bilateral investment treaties that allowed foreigners to sue the respective government. In the South African case it concerned some form of affirmative action policy for black workers after the end of the Apartheid regime. In the case of Argentina the privatization of water and the regulatory authority of the state vis-à-vis foreign investors was at issue. A consortium of international firms had signed a contract with Argentina in the mid-1990s to supply water in the regions of Buenos Aires and Santa Fé. When the consortium[34] later drastically increased water prices – also because of the devaluation of the peso – the Argentinian government disallowed the increase and the consortium sued. Argentina invoked in the proceedings the basic "human right" to water, which it wanted to protect by denying the substantial increase in prices. The Tribunal sided however with the investors and stated

> Argentina and the *amicus curiae* submissions received by the Tribunal suggest that Argentina's human rights obligations to assure its population the right to water somehow trumps its obligations under the BIT (bilateral investment treaties) and that the existence of the human right to water also implicitly gives Argentina the authority to take action in disregard of its BIT obligations. The Tribunal does not find a basis for such a conclusion either in the BITs or in international law.[35]

It needs no further elaboration that states are unlikely to follow the tribunal's conceptual arguments with the result that "binding norms" have now fallen into disfavor with both the companies and states. It seems that if a solution is possible it will not be provided by the formal legal prescription but rather by some practical choices and compromises, which allow the parties to "go on."

Similarly, the usual objection to self-reporting schemes is that they are whitewashes, designed to assuage the audience rather than to identify and remedy the existing flaws. While these points are well taken, practically they need not lead to the seemingly preordained end of sanctions and penalties. Competent third parties can take over monitoring and accounting procedures and certify a firm's compliance with the voluntary standards such as the Fair Labor Association, which monitors suppliers for premium brands in the

---

[33] For an extensive discussion of the issues raised by the fragmentation debate, see Kratochwil, *The Status of Law in World Society*, at 75–100.

[34] The consortium comprised the French company Vivendi Universal, the UK Anglian Water Group, and the Spanish firms Agbar and Interagua.

[35] Decision of July 30, 2010, as quoted in Ruggie, *Just Business*, at 66.

apparel and footwear industry. Social Accountability International developed an accreditation procedure and can certify whole factories in virtually any industry. The yearly Dow Jones Sustainability Index, based on thorough analysis of economic, environmental and social performances of firms, provides important information to portfolio managers about companies worldwide which are committed to sustainability. The Earth Institute in Berkeley, California, certifies by its label "Dolphin safe" (backed up by on-site surprise checks) that 700 foreign tuna companies follow the standards articulated in the 1997 International Dolphin Conservation Program Act.

All of this does not guarantee that the numbers in the indices will always add up and that the goal will be reached, or that the "capture" of the watchdog entrusted with the monitoring is impossible. But it certainly shows that "cheating" has become more difficult and that capture of the certifiers requires deliberate acts of rascality with which we are mostly familiar from Wall Street, one of the most formally and tightly regulated sectors of the economy! For the rest of the imperfect world we live in, the informal practical solutions usually meet the "good enough" standard (until we have knowledge of glaring deviations), even if the problem of *quis costodiet custodies?* (who watches the watchmen?) remains a dilemma.

6.3   Sanctions and Self-Help

That nations dwell supposedly in anarchy and that, therefore, the international arena is one characterized by self-help, has been one of the basic premises into which several generations of IR scholars have been socialized. But, as has been pointed out, the notion of anarchy is first of all equivocal – the term being used for both the "war of all against all" and also for decentralized systems of authority and exchange (as e.g. the competitive market). It should come as no surprise that the concept of "self-help" is similarly equivocal. Rather commonly the concept is used to suggest that self-help is just another way of retaliation when the law has run out, i.e. that in the absence of central enforcement, "taking the law into your own hands" need not be intersubjectively justified. But this view obscures the fact that self-help is a recognizable legal institution that plays an important role in international life as well as in domestic society.

Take e.g. (individual) self-defense, which justifies the use of even deadly force against a perpetrator of a crime (going back to the Roman institution of *fur manifestus*). But as the specified circumstances for its operation clearly indicate, it is not an instance of "anything goes." One could also mention the "repo-man" that is familiar from many movies detailing the adventures of persons who seize cars and other valuables when the persons possessing them are in default of their payments. Similarly, strikes are a means of self-help, as are managerial measures of control[36] addressing the perverse effects of the principal/agent problem. Since "labor law" regulates these issues, it is clear that the farther we move away from notions of imminent threat, the stronger becomes the need for justification. Consequently, below I want to place sanctions and self-help measures in the wider framework of rights and obligations and of the limits an actor has to observe when resorting to retaliation.

This change in perspective has an important corollary: in order to understand self-help it is useful to study instances in both the international and the domestic arena. Furthermore, in using the mistaken dichotomy of anarchy and hierarchy the interesting question of how self-help and sanctions actually work, largely disappears – since one already knows the answer: it consists in the superiority of centralized sanctions. This relieves us from engaging in further research although we know that the organization of central enforcement was, even in domestic law, a relatively late development. If no capital crime was involved, the execution of sanctions was frequently left to the parties, or clans, or even the society at large. This points to the need to unpack these notions and examine their changing historical configurations.

In this context we learn from the Twelve Tables, the first document of Roman law (451/450 BC), that capital crimes were the first ones considered a community affair, which necessitated the centralization of sanctions. The offices of the *quaestor* (officers entrusted with the inquiry into manslaughter and murder)[37] and of the *pontifex* (priest, conceived as a "bridge-builder" between the here and the transcendent) were entrusted with their prosecution. Thus the close original connection between the "sacred" and "sanction" are by no means accidental, while the mode of execution of the sanctions is historically speaking rather variable.

As Weber already pointed out, it makes sense to talk of *law* when the application of norms is entrusted to a special group of rule-handlers whose decisions and even commentaries on the rules and norms become part of the law, while the type of punishment might range from classical enforcement to societal shunning.

The means of coercion are irrelevant. Even the "brotherly admonition" which has been customary among members of some sects – as a first measure of mild coercion applied to sinners – belongs to "law" if regulated by rules and administered by a (special) staff.

---

[36] Wolfgang Kunkel, *Römische Rechtsgeschichte: eine Einführung*, Köln: Böhlau-Verlag, 1956, at 19.
[37] The original *quaestores* took their name from their power "to ask questions," which points to their prosecutorial function. *Questores parricidii*, i.e. those dealing with murder, are mentioned in the Twelve Tables, IX, 4. See Rudolf Düll, *Das Zwölftafelgesetz: Texte, Übersetzungen und Erläuterunge*, München: Heimeran, 1953, at 59. Only later did *quaestores* also become the administrators of public funds. See Kunkel, *Römische Rechtsgeschichte: eine Einführung*, at 12.

The same is true of the "censorial reprimand" as a means for guaranteeing the moral norms for behavior. Even more so does the psychological coercion of proper disciplinary ecclesiastical measures belong here. Thus there exists "law" which is based on a hierocratic, and a political or domestic authority even on the statutes or conventions of a voluntary association.[38]

These reflections throw a new light on the, at first, rather odd use of "sanctioning" which encompasses both positive approval and punishment. What unites these two poles of the semantic spectrum is the problem of validity. After all, it is not odd to say that certain actions were "sanctioned" when I want to express that they are held to be "valid" and that they, therefore, have legal consequences, even if no one was punished. In the latter case the retributive element for a transgression is emphasized. Note, however, that this idea is different from the usual argument about positive and negative sanctions. While in the case of positive sanctions we refer to the inducements that one actor might offer to another; when we employ the term "sanctioning" for both punishment and approval, we are not focusing on the means by which the manipulation of the will of the actors is accomplished, but rather on the allowed or disallowed character of an action and the consequences that follow from it.

This leads me to my second point, the problematic reduction of the sanction problematique to issues of effectiveness. Thus already Johan Galtung – well in tune with many other social scientists working on sanctions at that time – entirely dismissed the public dimension of sanctions when discussing the Rhodesian sanctions and was mainly interested "in the way of making other international actors comply."[39] Here the distinction between "rational" (i.e. instrumental) action and "expressive" action is supposed to be the relevant distinction for the subsequent appraisal. Since part of our political language is to signal approval and disapproval we miss important clues when we neglect the audience and the "because of" part of sanctions and focus exclusively on the instruments.

This is why Baldwin correctly suggested that decision-makers might choose sanctions for several reasons. In discussing the Cuban case, Baldwin mentions reducing the attractiveness of the Cuban example to other states, limiting the regime's capabilities, and imposing costs on its protector, the Soviet Union, even if the direct goal, i.e. the removal of the regime or a radical policy change, seemed out of the question. But even Baldwin seems to miss something when he did not explicitly analyze the distinction between the simple "hurt" that is indubitably connected with sanctions and the "because of" reasons which are

---

[38] Max Weber, *Wirtschaft und Gesellschaft: Grundriss der Verstehenden Soziologie*, vol. 1, Köln: Kiepenheuer & Witsch, 1964, at 25. My translation.

[39] Johan Galtung, "On the Effects of International Economic Sanctions, with Examples from the Case of Rhodesia," *World Politics*, 19:3 (1967): 378–416, at 380f.

part of the grammar of sanctions. The basic point here is that not every unfriendly act entitles me to impose a sanction. France's behavior in wanting to sell weapons to China might be hurtful to US interests and upset US policies, but as long as the US cannot point to a manifest violation of some concrete obligation, it would be hard-pressed to invoke sanctions. Since the reasons for taking such measures have to be of a public nature, all the US can do is to "speak for itself."

Consequently, the distinction between instrumental rationality and the alleged "consumption good" character of sanctions is far too crude. For one, while the sanctioner could experience feelings of satisfaction – leaving aside for the moment the question whether it makes sense to ascribe emotions to such abstract entities as states – these feelings have very little to do with the reasons for which one metes out punishment. To assume that in the absence of success in reaching the assumed goal, the motive for punishment *must have been* some type of emotional gratification is already rather absurd in the case of a single law-breaker, and there is no reason why this should be otherwise in the case of states. One does not punish and put people in jail because "we enjoy" it, even if we are also convinced that the offender will not be reformed. Punishment is meted out in order to achieve the purposes of compulsion, prevention, and retribution at the same time, although the "mixes" are controversial and hotly debated in penology. The reasons are "public" reasons, not indications of individual psychological satisfaction. As Nossal points out, while the grammar of punishment does not fit the explanation scheme of goals and means, it cannot be understood in terms of an individual consumption goal either.[40]

The short Weberian passage quoted above raises still other issues to which we have not attended. We can find here an argument similar to that of legal pluralists who have always maintained that different legal orders intersect even within the modern state. Weber's own "definition" of law, which is different from e.g. Hobbes (command of the sovereign) or even Kelsen, is "state-free" precisely because otherwise the differentiation of society, and the relationship of the state and law in their differing historical conjunctions could not be analyzed. But there is also the clear recognition that the changing configurations of law, the state, and society cannot be understood in terms of one form displacing another one, as is familiar from certain narratives of "progress." Rather the transformative changes have to be investigated through an analysis of various historical reconfigurations.

Such a new configuration can be clearly seen in the case of self-help, when it gets incorporated in "private law," i.e. the law of contracts. Take the

---

[40] Kim Richard Nossal, "International Sanctions as International Punishment," *International Organization*, 43:2 (1989): 301–322, at 312.

employment contract as an example. Technically it is an "incomplete contract," in that some important elements cannot be exhaustively specified, as opposed to a *quid pro quo* exchange (spot contract), where two parties exchange, e.g., apples for oranges, or accept payment for the commodity. On the face of it, the incomplete labor contract also entails an exchange: labor for wages. But what such a characterization hides is the important change in the status of the two parties which occurs. The employer not only acquires the labor power of the employee, but also the *right to determine its utilization by "imperative" control*. Firms are therefore not only actors (effacing the important distinction between individuals and organizations), or simple "production functions" (as earlier economists wanted to have it). They are *organizations* within which rule, or *dominium*, is exercised. That this power is limited in scope and domain is clear. Thus a boss might be able to send the paid intern to get coffee and doughnuts but he cannot require her to do his laundry, or join him for a weekend in his cottage at the seashore. If he is too insistent, the employee might threaten to call in "the law" because of harassment.

Of course not all cases are as clear-cut, and a double enforcement problem of the contract exists which has to be worked out between the parties. Otherwise the old proverb of communist times obtains: "they pretend to pay us, and we pretend to work." Thus the manager, or owner, has to insure himself against shirking by resorting to self-help measures: punching the clock, reports, quota, inspections, forbidding cellphone use at work, regulating coffee breaks, etc. In recent times "Gregory" (alluding to Orwell), the hand-canner used by Amazon to keep track of what their employees are doing, has attained some fame. Each item has to be scanned, thereby identifying the person who put it on a shelf, so that later a "picker," collecting the items for a delivery, can take it, scanning the item again. If an employee's hand scanner does not indicate any activity for a few minutes, an alarm goes off at the supervisor's office and the employee has to appear for a "feedback" session.

All these measures might be or become controversial and engender unrest and resistance among the staff, possibly even court action (to determine what is a reasonable and a work-related exercise of power). In this way, labor law emerges as powerful counterweight to an unfettered power of hiring and firing. It becomes an important regulatory device not only by safeguarding the right of collective bargaining and of resorting to job actions and strikes, but also by subjecting day-to-day practices to scrutiny. If the courts are not invoked, the parties might submit to arbitration, or the public authorities might insist on binding arbitration in cases where necessary public services are at issue – such as police and fire protection, garbage collection, public transport or air safety. The employees might even become "civil servants" whose status entirely withholds from them the right to strike. Of course, such arrangements can address only part of the principal/agent problem, as "working exactly according to the prescribed rules" is – together with foot-dragging – one of the most effective forms of resistance, as all bureaucrats know.

Having shown that self-help measures are not an indication of anarchy but part of every legal system, it might be useful to trace in greater detail the developments of self-help in the world of emerging sovereigns, first by briefly delineating the feud among the nobility in defense of their rights during the Middle Ages, then moving on to the later privileging of state interests in waging war, the restriction of this claim to the inherent right of self-defense, and the recent attempts at vesting a residual "responsibility to protect" in the international community.

6.4   Sanctioned Self-Help: The Feud

On April 27, 1541, King Ferdinand I of Austria and Bohemia issued an edict against a certain Wenzel Schaerowetz of Scherowa, who had declared a "feud" on his king and had informed him that in the pursuit of his rights he would resort to "killing, capture, plunder, destruction, every manner of evil that enemies might inflict on each other." Ferdinand's answer to this challenge was to put a price on Wenzel's head and those of his allies and helpers, noting that the knight had no "legitimate claim or justification to engage in such an action against US [*pluralis majestaticus*] or our subjects, but he does so owing to his insolent and obdurate character."[41]

There are several interesting observations regarding this case. Realists, in focusing on the vivid descriptions of the forceful means, will of course see in it a confirmation of their theory that in the absence of a strong ruler the public power is challenged and the war of all against all results. Those more familiar with the development of the European state and its constitution will be astonished that even "so late" in the historical development, a nobleman dares to challenge his overlord and that the overlord does not simply invoke the crime of high treason for this action. Instead, he rejects the challenge simply by maintaining that the knight had no good cause. Indeed, as the investigations of Brunner have shown, we are dealing here with a legitimate "feud," which was a prominent medieval institution of self-help.

The feud established not only the liberty of taking up arms to redress some injury, but insured that social pressure was brought to bear on persons who were not ready to defend their rights by such means. In the medieval context feudal lords had not only to make an effort through feuding to recover their losses, but because they were often indebted in turn to others, serious loss of

---

[41] As quoted by Otto Brunner, *Land and Lordship: Structures of Governance in Medieval Austria*, vol. 4, trans. Howard Kaminsky and James van Horn Melton, Philadelphia: University of Pennsylvania Press, 1992, at 13.

status for the person and his family were the outcome, if someone did not defend his "honor." The same pattern can be found in other societies in which feuding is prevalent. A person failing to redress the injustice is considered a coward who has disgraced himself and his family, as Hasluck[42] suggests in her classic study of Albanian society:

A man slow to kill his enemy was thought to be disgraced and was described as "low class" and "bad." Among the Highlanders he risked finding that other men had contemptuously come to sleep with his wife, his daughter could not marry into a "good" family and his son must marry a "bad" girl. As far south as Godolesh on the outskirts of Elbasan, he paid visits at peril; his coffee cup was only half filled, and before being handed to him it was passed under his host's left arm, or even under his left leg, to remind him of his disgrace.[43]

Thus although the feud is usually seen as a bilateral relationship par excellence, in the mobilization of shame it shows that here wider societal norms are at work and that notions of simple or instinctual revenge are hardly appropriate. To that extent Elster is right when he distinguishes between spontaneous revenge directed at the author of an injurious act and norm-guided revenge. The latter is compulsive precisely because society interjects itself not only by determining the types and limits of revengeful acts, but also by forcing the victim to redress his injuries.[44]

But let us return – after this short detour into still existing blood feuds – to the historical record of feuds as classic self-help measures. Similar feuds had e.g. a century earlier pitted the Austrian Estates against the Emperor, the City of Vienna against Emperor Fredrick III (October 5, 1462, beginning of the feud). In another case (Mathias Liechtenstein's feud with Duke Albrecht III in 1394), the Emperor Wenceslas, the Margrave of Brandenburg and the Duke of Bavaria were on Liechtenstein's side, and the "helpers" of Albrecht included several leading Moravian lords and the noble families of Rosenberg and Neuhaus. The interesting point here is that the Emperor was simply an "associate" who helped for more or less personal reasons to redress the alleged injustice done to Liechtenstein. He was not exercising his rights as a "sovereign" and as the guarantor of public order. These examples reveal conditions of politics and law so different from our present conceptions, and from the assumed patterns of political and legal development, that it is not surprising

[42] See e.g. Pierre Bourdieu, "The Sentiment of Honour in Kabyle Society" in Jean G. Péristiany (ed.), *Honour and Shame: The Values of Mediterranean Society*, Chicago: University of Chicago Press, 1969: 191–241.
[43] Margaret Masson Hardie Hasluck, *The Unwritten Law in Albania*, Cambridge: Cambridge University Press, 1954, at 231f.
[44] See Jon Elster, "Norms of Revenge," *Ethics*, 100:4 (1990): 862–885, particularly 871f.

that we often lack critical distance and take the examples of medieval self-help as test cases for anarchy.[45]

The notion of personal rule is quite manifest and in the case of self-help it cuts across the modern public/private distinction. Indeed Brunner showed that the classical distinction between a war and a feud hardly existed, except in the issue of financing. Notions of sovereignty, the *res publica*, or the state seem to be entirely missing. Although attempts to prohibit feuding go back to Merovingian times,[46] these attempts, similar to those by the Church to limit feuding through the "Peace of God" movement, have obviously not been very successful. Nevertheless, not every possession or place was fair game for the feuding parties: special provisions were part of the general public order (*Landfriede*) in which certain places were exempted from forceful action, such as churches, fruit trees and vines, but also the houses of the feuding parties themselves, peasants working in the field, their gear, etc.

Thus it is quite clear that the self-help instrument of a feud by no means condoned acts of willful or idiosyncratic violence (*Mutwille*). It was a legal institution that was not only part of old custom but explicitly recognized in many constitutional documents such as in Salian law.

These observations cast a new light on moves to give courts the monopoly of dispute settlement. It was a move for centralizing royal power rather than an attempt to replace lawlessness by orderly procedures. After all, a trial by a court in medieval times often meant a "trial by combat" to which oaths had been added. Thus it is not surprising that most of the legislative initiatives of medieval kings concerned the scope and the conditions of feuds rather than their abolition. As late as the sixteenth century the Criminal Code of Charles V (Constitutio Criminalis Carolina, 1535) still recognizes the feud as a permissible means to redress un-redressed injuries. Two hundred years later the Theresian Criminal Code of 1768 (Constitutio Criminalis Theresiana) refers to "challenges" (feuds) but considers them as "public acts of violence" that were now, except in extenuating circumstances, forbidden. But the definitional part of the article regulating feuds indicated that the feud had been a highly institutionalized practice that had evolved well with time.[47] This we

---

[45] See e.g. Markus Fischer, "Feudal Europe, 800–1300: Communal Discourse and Conflictual Practices," *International Organization*, 46:2 (1992): 427–466.
[46] The Merowingian king Childebert II's decree of 509 forbade feuds.
[47] Usually the feud began with a written letter (*diffidatio*), in which the challenger informs the other party that the normal *fides*, i.e. peaceful state, between the parties has been severed. For a further discussion, see Heinrich Mitteis, *Lehnrecht und Staatsgewalt: Untersuchungen zur Mittelalterlichen Verfassungsgeschichte*, Köln: Böhlau, 1974.

can see from the inclusion of "gunpowder" in the catalog of valid symbols initiating the feud.[48]

Similarly the *ius armorum*, often not quite adequately translated as the "right to make alliances" (rather than the right to bear arms), which was ensconced in the Westphalian treaties still represents, as already mentioned, this old legal institution of the feud rather than the new development of state alliances that signified the end of the Empire. Actually the prohibition on taking up arms against the emperor is one of the more important *new* developments that resulted from the legal reform of the Empire. The Westphalian settlement preserved the old "choice of means" which allowed for either court decisions or a feud, but strengthened the position of the imperial courts.

An even more important part of this reconstitution of the Empire was that the *inquisitio* (fact finding) had now been entrusted solely to the judge and abolished the combat as a means of trial. To that extent the entire question of proofs had been taken out of the hands of the contending parties, leaving only the complaint (pleadings) to the parties themselves.

This is not the place to examine in detail the various changes that occurred over the next few centuries, but a few must be mentioned. There is first the emergence of the territorial state and its subjects, which creates entirely new practices and structures. The result is not only that the inside and the outside are now distinguished, but also that the personal politics of medieval times is transformed by the notion of a subject that owes loyalty to one sovereign. Such changes also draw an increasingly clearer line between the public and the private realm, whereby the definition of what belongs to the public and what to the private is entrusted to the highest authorities of the public realm. Thus measures of self-help do not cease to exist but are more and more subject to the authorization by the sovereign (letters of marque) and directed against "outsiders."[49]

Second, these distinctions now allowed for a far sharper separation between war and a feud. In countries in which the abstract notion of the "state" as a set of offices (*res publica*) had never entirely vanished, as the Italian republics show, two of the enabling conditions for engaging justly in a war were that it could be waged only by the prince, and that it had to be for a public purpose.[50] Private persons could seek redress from courts, and rulers could not misuse their public office for private interests. But it was only by the eighteenth

---

[48] See Art. 61 of the Constitutio Criminalis Theresiana.
[49] For a good discussion of the change from medieval to modern notions of "war" and reprisals, see Joachim von Elbe, "The Evolution of the Concept of the Just War in International Law," *The American Journal of International Law*, 33:4 (1939): 665–688.
[50] See e.g. Thomas Aquinas, *Summa Theologica* (1485). Secunda secundae, quaestio XL.

century that things had changed dramatically and feuds and "private wars" appeared an "absurdity." As Rousseau maintains:

Private combats, duels, and encounters are acts which do not constitute a state of war; and with regard to the private wars authorized by the Establishments of Louis IX, king of France, and suspended by the Peace of God, they were abuses of the feudal govern-ment, an absurd system if ever there was one, contrary both to the principles of natural right and to all sound government.

War then is not a relation between man and man, but a relation between State and State, in which individuals are enemies only by accident, not as men, nor even as citizens but as soldiers . . .

The foreigner, whether king, or nation or private person that robs, slays or detains subjects without declaring war against the government, is not an enemy but a brigand. Even in open war, a just prince, while he rightly takes possession of all that belongs to the State in an enemy's country, respects the person and property of individuals; he respects the rights on which his own are based. The aim of the war being the destruction of the hostile state, we have a right to slay the defenders so long as they have arms in their hands; but as soon as they lay them down and surrender, ceasing to be enemies or instruments of the enemy, they become again simply men, and no one has any further rights over their lives.[51]

Of course the states, created by the social contract, find themselves now in a state of nature vis-à-vis each other and consider the resort to force, the taking of reprisals or, retorsions,[52] and even the making of war[53] as their preroga-tive. The latter, because of its unilateral, self-judging nature, hollows out the notion of the "republic" of Europe or of an international society of states, which vanishes by the mid-nineteenth century.[54] Now the state becomes not only the ultimate expression of *Sittlichkeit* but also the sole guarantor of political

---

[51] Jean-Jacques Rousseau, *The Social Contract and Discourse on the Origin and Foundation of Inequality among Mankind*, New York: Washington Square Press, 1971, bk. 1, chap. 4, at 13f.

[52] Retorsion refers to an unfriendly but legal act by a state for an injury inflicted upon it by the author of the unfriendly act. Reprisal refers to a prima facie illegal act that becomes legal on the basis of an un-redressed wrong that the state suffered from the state towards which this act is directed. For a general, brief but still illuminating, discussion, see James Leslie Brierly, *The Law of Nations*, 6th edn., Oxford: Oxford University Press, 1963, chap. 9.

[53] On the discussion of the notion of a "guerre d'exécution," see W. Michael Reisman, *Nullity and Revision: The Review and Enforcement of International Judgments and Awards*, New Haven: Yale University Press, 1971, at 844f. The difference between "war" and armed reprisals in the pre-Charter era seems to have consisted largely in that war had immediate effects on all the existing rights of the belligerents while armed reprisals did not have such a broad effect but allowed for the nonperformance of a limited number of international obligations vis-à-vis each other.

[54] See Friedrich Kratochwil, "On the Notion of 'Interest' in International Relations," *International Organization*, 36:1 (1982): 1–30.

projects concerning the "good life."[55] The prevalence of contractual thinking by the end of the nineteenth century also makes it appear that that all acts of states are valid until and unless they are explicitly forbidden[56] and that such limits to state actions have to be thought of as self-limitations that states have voluntarily imposed upon themselves.

To that extent the notion of a public order seemed to have been reduced to unilateral exercises of rights accruing to the states on the basis of their sovereignty, and to various bilateral limitations of state sovereignty through treaties, while "custom" as a constitutive element plays now a more and more shadowy and under-appreciated role. Although, these developments seem to have been reversed in the twentieth century, as the emergence of obligations *erga omnes* as well as the legitimizing function of the Security Council of the UN indicates, the question remains whether these conceptual developments are coherent and effective enough to inspire an *ordre publique* vision that meets the challenges of globalization, and of new security threats. Such an assessment requires as a first step a closer examination mapping the classical self-help institutions and the changes they have undergone.

6.5   Self-Defense

As Hume already suggested and as further elaborated by Bull, social systems, not being "natural," must meet three normative criteria to be able to reproduce themselves.[57] There must be a restriction on the use of force, the members must work on the presumption that promises are being kept (*pacta sunt servanda*) and there have to be some arrangements for the acquisition and transfer of titles. In this enumeration it is no accident that the prohibition of the use of force takes, however, the pride of place. It is indeed difficult to conceive a society able to make social interactions possible (even in the face of the inevitable disappointments), or of achieving prosperity through production and trade, if the fear of violence is pervasive. Traditionally, this point has been elaborated through casuistic or systematic arguments as to the circumstances under which resort to force is justified (*ius ad bellum*) and the criteria that have to be taken into account when one resorts to forceful retaliatory measures (*ius in bello*). The purpose, irrespective of the actual prospects of being successful in suppressing violence, was to provide some normative guidelines that not only restricted the resort to force but which could be used for an appraisal, even in cases of noncompliance

---

[55] See the discussion of R.B.J. Walker, *Inside/Outside: International Relations as Political Theory*, Cambridge: Cambridge University Press, 1993.
[56] See e.g. *The Case of the S.S. "Lotus" (France v. Turkey).*   [57] Bull, *The Anarchical Society*.

If we examine the contemporary state practice and doctrine concerning self-help, three developments are of particular importance: the "monopolization" by the Security Council of the authority to decide on forceful reprisals – except for the narrowly circumscribed circumstances of self-defense – the multi-lateralizations of sanctions, and the emergence of notions of obligations *erga omnes*, whose breach, in turn, might even allow states not directly injured to take "countermeasures" (e.g. for gross violations of human rights by another state). Since the next sections of this chapter are devoted to the multilateraliza-tion of sanctions and the role of the Security Council, I want to concentrate here on self-defense.

Self-defense is an important concept since it intersects with the traditional just war doctrine, the institution of private justice, as we saw in the feud, but also with notions of natural rights, constitutive of agency. For the latter, the notions of natural freedom, the right to life, and the prevention of bodily harm, as well as the protection of rightfully acquired goods, provide the conceptual boundaries. Within this framework self-defense can be exercised either in the state of nature or in the residual contingency of dire emergencies in which the public order is unable to safeguard these rights. While in the domestic arena we have always held that such a right and its exercise by individuals was limited to exceptional circumstances, in the international arena the decay of the just war doctrine led to widespread agnosticism with regard to the guiding function of these criteria. So it was easier to argue that both aggressor and defender might have a point, and that sitting in judgment of such existential choices was not likely to lead anywhere. From here it was only a small step to argue that self-help measures were not subject to any kind of review, not to speak of any type of authoritative decision.

Two difficulties exist in this context: one is, in the absence of a clear-cut act of aggression, which defensive measures are justifiable in anticipation of an attack held to be inevitable? Second, who is entitled to assess the risk: only the actual actor being threatened, or were there some community standards that must be adduced in making such an assessment? The difficulty exists precisely in that on the one hand only the agent who is being attacked can make that choice, while on the other hand the choice cannot be made on purely idiosyn-cratic grounds. After all, someone e.g. traumatized by previous experiences might even (mis)take a "hello" or friendly slap on the back as an "attack" and undermine by his retaliatory action the general expectations on which the social order is based.

Article 51 of the Charter and the debates and cases surrounding it offer in this respect an amazing inventory of paradigmatic arguments that are worth pondering. There is first the stipulation that self-defense as a self-help measure is limited to an "armed attack" but at the same time considered an "inherent right," even though that right ceases as soon as the Security Council takes measures. Furthermore, the right is not limited to the particular victim but, as in the medieval feud, a victim might appeal to others for help. But no actor might invoke collective self-defense until and unless the actual victim has asked for assistance, as was the case of e.g. Kuwait. Furthermore, in the case of individual self-defense by a state, the right to use force is conditioned on "repelling an attack, or to prevent future enemy attacks following an initial attack, or to reverse the consequences of an enemy attack, such as ending an occupation."[58]

To that extent the intervention of the US and its allies in Afghanistan after September 11 was arguably justifiable in a loose reading of a case of self-defense – even though no state was directly involved – while e.g. invocation of this right by the US in the Nicaragua case was not. There the US had argued that its use of force against Nicaragua was lawful as an act of "collective self-defense of El Salvador" since Nicaragua had supplied the rebels in El Salvador with weapons. But as the court pointed out, aside from the fact that it could not be shown that Nicaragua had actually provided such weapons, even in the case that such an allegation could be proven, the supply of weapons was not tanta-mount to an armed attack.[59] Accordingly, recent allegations that the simple possession of weapons of mass destruction alone already justifies actions in self-defense seems entirely specious, since in that case any state could make self-defense arguments in justifying the use of force against the US, Russia Great Britain, France, China, Pakistan, India or Israel.

Much has been made of the notion of the term "inherent" in the French version of the Charter, suggesting that there might be an independent source for justifying the resort to force, outside of the exceptional circumstances of an armed attack. But even if, on one interpretation, the term "inherent" might refer to customary practice antedating the Charter, the logic of the concept seems to require a limitation of this basic right in order to rule out self-serving claims. As in the case of the feud, not only must there be a set of specified circumstances that trigger the exercise of this right, there has to be also some formal declaration putting others on notice, as exemplified by the symbols initiating the feud or by the reporting requirements of Article 51.

More difficult problems arise in contexts in which the initiator of aggression is not a state but some armed groups, or when the timing of forceful aggression becomes an issue. Since self-defense can be claimed only against an attacker, hostile acts originating from the territory of another state usually

---

[58] See Mary Ellen O'Connell, "The Myth of Preemptive Self-Defense," Washington, DC: American Society of International Law Task Force on Terrorism, 2002, at 7.

[59] See *Case Concerning Military and Paramilitary Activities in and against Nicaragua: Nicaragua v. United States of America*, International Court of Justice, June 27, 1986, I.C.J. 14 (1986), paras. 194–195.

do not automatically entitle the attacked state to take self-defense measures. Not only must the attack be of a certain gravity, the other state must also through its agents or through its control of the armed bands be directly involved in such hostile acts,[60] or grievously fail in its duty to take the necessary steps for suppressing such acts of aggression.

More difficult issues are raised by the question of the timing of self-defense measures. The clearest case is, of course, the "occurrence" of an armed attack, as mentioned in Article 51. Here the classic *Caroline* case provides the necessary criteria. It involved a US–British settlement of a dispute in which British troops had attacked US forces who had helped Canadian rebels. The use of defensive force is permitted, when in the words of Secretary of State Daniel Webster the "necessity of self-defense is instant, overwhelming, and leaving no choice of means and no moment for deliberation."[61] But if various violent incidents are part of an ongoing campaign, are the responses involving force justified, even if they are not a direct repulsion of an attack but involve some anticipation (and proof) of future operations in an ongoing campaign?[62]

Similarly the discussion of yesteryear concerning e.g. preemptive strikes, such as a "launch on warning" policy, show that not all cases which are nowadays brought under this concept fit this pattern easily.[63] In general, there is a distinct asymmetry in the opportunities for acting since the attacker can choose the moment of attack and thus frequently impairs the victim's capacity to take the appropriate measures. But this asymmetry is, in a way, the price paid for social order as otherwise anybody would act on hunches, which can quickly turn into self-fulfilling prophesies Nevertheless, not all "preemptive" action is justified, despite all attempts to stretch the concept.[64]

On the other hand, when an attacker has fired his missiles but they have not yet hit their target, the other state is already "under attack" and does not have to wait until it is wiped out. Similarly, Dinstein[65] argued rather persuasively that the US could have attacked the Japanese fleet on the way to Pearl Harbor, if it had convincing intelligence that attack orders had been issued by the Japanese government. However, as Dinstein also points out, in those cases we are actually dealing with "incipient self-defense" rather than with classical preemption or anticipatory self-defense.

---

[60] I shall discuss the problems of command responsibility in Chapter 7.
[61] See the letter Department of State and Dan Webster, *Mr. Webster to Lord Ashburton, 6th August* (1842). Available at http://avalon.law.yale.edu/19th_century/br-1842d.asp#web2.
[62] For a plea to allow preemption, see Abraham D. Soafer, "On the Necessity of Preemption," *European Journal of International Law*, 14:2 (2003): 209–226.
[63] See the seminal discussion in O'Connell, "The Myth of Preemptive Self-Defense."
[64] See the discussion in Christine D. Gray, *International Law and the Use of Force*, 2nd edn., Oxford: Oxford University Press, 2004, at 171.
[65] Yoram Dinstein, *War, Aggression and Self-Defence*, 3rd edn., Cambridge: Cambridge University Press, 2003.

Precisely because of such difficulties the standard of necessity proposed by Webster seemed to many so "abstractly restrictive as almost, if read literally, to impose paralysis."[66] In short, the inherited conceptual apparatus seemed tragically out of date and in need of "adjustments," such as introducing exceptions if not rejecting the traditional conceptual framework *tout court*. Thus, one recurring argument is that the presumption against the use of force has to be modified in favor of a purposeful reading of the prohibition of force. In this context, arguments of compatibility are made, i.e. as long as the force is applied for the "purposes" of the Charter, no special authorization through the Security Council is necessary. This was e.g. the position of Britain and France during their Suez campaign.[67] Presently, the propagation of democracy and human rights seems to be the newest version of this gambit. The other theme that runs through the debates is the expansion of the notion of "necessity" so that it loses all discrimination and becomes a justificatory universal, particularly when applied in conjunction with other principles.

Nowhere does this become clearer than in the present debates surrounding the "war on terror" and the conceptualization of "imminent threat." In the face of new threats, gaining the initiative and asserting control, "doing something" rather than waiting, seems psychologically understandable. The real question here, however, is whether force is even the appropriate countermeasure. Here conceptual problems abound. Consider in this context a "cyber attack" against computer networks. While the threat might be real, the remedy might not, given the difficulties of "pinning" the attack or even finding the "location" and the responsible ones, who possibly are sitting all over the globe.[68] Since we have not made any arrangement for such an eventuality the debate will necessarily have to be circumscribed by the discourse on force and its use, even though it has little to do with the classical notions of armed attacks and their repulsion at the territorial borders.

There also remain plenty of issues surrounding the general prohibition of Article 2.4.[69] Thus, rescue missions for one's nationals might be such an exception as might be humanitarian interventions (more likely if authorized

---

[66] See Myres S. McDougal and Florentino P. Feliciano, *Law and Minimum World Public Order: The Legal Regulation and International Coercion*, New Haven: Yale University Press, 1961, at 217.

[67] For the background, see Charlotte Peevers, *The Politics of Justifying Force: The Suez Crisis, the Iraq War, and International Law*, Oxford: Oxford University Press, 2013.

[68] See Michael N. Schmitt, "Computer Network Attack and the Use of Force in International Law: Thoughts on a Normative Framework" in *Essays on Law and War at the Fault Lines*, The Hague: T.M.C. Asser Press, 2012: 3–48.

[69] See here the thorough discussion of the "exceptions to the Charter prohibition on the use of force in Nico Schrijver, "The Ban on the Use of Force in the UN Charter" in Marc Weller (ed.), *The Oxford Handbook of the Use of Force in International Law*, Oxford: Oxford University Press, 2015: 465–487, at 472–476.

ex ante by the UN Security Council, less so if only *ex post* and problematically if not at all). In any case, if threats mount, the not at all faint-hearted Otto von Bismarck once warned that preventive wars are like committing "suicide for fear of death." This adage reminds us that certain strategies might be self-defeating. True, terrorists cannot be deterred. Nevertheless, does it follow from these "facts" that we must be ready to wage preventive wars and act, as President Bush argued, "against . . . emerging threats before they are fully formed"?[70] This seems as megalomaniacal as it is unfeasible.

When right from the start the 9/11 attacks were phrased as a strategic problem, i.e. as an issue of national security rather than as one of criminal conduct, the possibility of different interpretations of the actions and events shows that even in that supposedly clear-cut case more than one alternative existed. But whatever framing we use, everybody agrees that the crucial variable here will be intelligence, and that "not fully formed threats" basically involve bets on the future. Leaders and policies might change and thus threats might disappear or become manageable without forceful intervention and jumping the gun. Obviously both alternatives involve risks if not radical uncertainty, as we faced them with Iran and nowadays again with North Korea. While the jury is still out, it is not clear at all why attempts at total control represent a superior strategy that has to be followed. After all, Argentina and Brazil did stop their nuclear programs, the enmity between the US and the former Soviet Union disappeared, India and Pakistan did not escalate their conflicts, and a new understanding with China under Nixon considerably reduced the threat that Chinese hostility paired with capability posed.

The first and central flaws of the argument of emerging threats is that it treats threats as akin to some natural phenomenon, such as emerging tumors, which have to be removed, otherwise inevitably the malicious growth will kill its host. Such a framing neglects the fact that these threats are different in that they are man-made. They result from strategic interactions and are thus susceptible to de-escalatory measures. Second, in spite of experiences to the contrary, it assumes that hostile regimes never change or that nothing short of forceful intervention will induce that change. They are simply "rogues" and thus one can safely infer their motives and strategies from their "type." Third, there is the assumption that all imminent threats can be fought. But as not only realists have pointed out, such a program might be beyond the capacity of even a superpower. It is also likely to be a self-defeating strategy, since its success depends heavily on both domestic and international support, which is unlikely

---

[70] See the letter accompanying the National Security Strategy of the United States at 2, as quoted in Robert Jervis, "Understanding the Bush Doctrine," *Political Science Quarterly*, 118:3 (2003): 365–388, at 369.

to be forthcoming when costs are mounting and the resistance against the hegemonic project increases throughout the international system.[71]

Consider in this context the strange work the precautionary principle is doing in justifying the new strategic priorities:

> We must adapt the concept of imminent threat . . . The greater the threat, the greater is the risk of inaction – and the more compelling the case for taking anticipatory action to defend ourselves, even if uncertainty remains as to the time and place of the enemy's attack.[72]

The precautionary principle, as applied in medicine (being enshrined in the Hippocratic oath "above all, do no harm"), actually intends to dissuade people from risky actions, when e.g. a certain procedure might succeed but kill the patient. When applied to ill-defined threats it strangely morphs in the hands of the security "professionals" into a rule that commands: "in case of uncertainty, strike – a somewhat weird conclusion," as Michael Bothe correctly points out.[73] The formulation might be new, but actually the notion that America's mission has to be "the destruction of every arbitrary power anywhere in the world that can separately, secretly and of its single choice disturb the peace of the world" fits in a strange way the Wilsonian ideals that have always resonated with parts of the public.

These rather extensive (not to say megalomaniacal) claims are, of course, only possible if such extensive rights of self-defense are not assumed to be accorded to every state, but remain reserved for the power whose mission is to use them alone, or with a coalition of the willing. Even if one thinks that US hegemony has been for Western countries benign in historical comparison, there is little doubt that this is not a universally shared experience, and that the institutionalization of this hegemony by proposing not only de facto but *de jure* two sets of rules is bound to engender resistance and resentment.

6.6   Countermeasures

As opposed to the complications of self-help involving the use of force, the prototypical measure of self-help is, of course, the nonperformance of certain treaty provisions by one actor in retaliation for the alleged injuries received by the other. In that case the rules for taking countermeasures are rather clear.

---

[71] See e.g. Joseph S. Nye, *The Paradox of American Power: Why the World's Only Super Power Can't Go It Alone*, Oxford: Oxford University Press, 2002.

[72] The President of the United States, *The National Security Strategy of the United States of America*. NSS02 (2002), at 15.

[73] Michael Bothe, "Terrorism and the Legality of Pre-Emptive Force," *European Journal of International Law*, 14:2 (2003): 227–240, at 232. For a more general discussion of the problem of terrorism for international law, see Andrea Bianchi, "Terrorism and Armed Conflict: Insights from a Law & Literature Perspective," *Leiden Journal of International Law*, 24:1 (2011): 1–21.

Since one party cannot be bound by treaty obligations if the other party does not perform its duties, the injured state can respond by also not implementing its part of the deal. Here reciprocity provides some guidelines and since treaties usually explicitly mention the *quid pro quo*, the nonperformance of the "quo" is an answer to not having received the "quid."[74] In this way the *exceptio non adimpleti contractus* known from Roman law provides for the right of an immediate remedy not subject to any preliminary procedures, or as the Arbitral Tribunal in the Air Service Award put it, it is a device "to restore in a negative way the symmetry of the initial position."[75]

Two further issues arise in this context. One is that the *exceptio* is not tantamount to a suspension or termination of the treaty but that it enables the injured party only to defend its interest. The treaty as such is still legally in force between the parties, a circumstance that is particularly important since it allows the injured party to continue to rely on the treaty in later proceedings. After all, an injured party could not rely on the arbitration clause in the treaty, if the treaty were no longer existent. The Vienna Convention of Treaties makes it quite clear that there is no unilateral right of terminating treaties, absent a denunciation (withdrawal) clause.[76] Similarly, the ICJ concluded that despite the countermeasures taken by the US in response to the Iranian hostage-taking — including that of the ill-fated rescue mission – the Treaty of Friendship and Commerce of 1955 was still in operation, thus giving the court jurisdiction and the US a valid cause.[77]

This leads us directly to the second point, concerning the case where no clear *quid pro quo* has been stipulated but the treaty was entered to further certain policy goals, such as the enhancement of free trade or respect for human rights. Here reciprocity cannot provide much guidance and the standard of "substantially equivalent concessions" offers a better solution, as is e.g. the case in the General Agreement on Tariffs and Trade (GATT) (Art. XXVIII). Under this rule an injured party might also withhold – within certain limits – concessions made in other areas than those where the injury is alleged. This of

---

[74] For a general discussion see Serena Forlati, "Reactions to Nonperformance of Treaties in International Law, *Leiden Journal of International Law*, 25:3 (2012): 759–770.

[75] *Case Concerning the Air Service Agreement of 27 March 1946 between the United States of America and France*, Reports of International Arbitral Awards, Volume XVIII, 417–493 (1978). §90, quote at §83. Reprinted in the appendix in Elisabeth Zoller, *Peacetime Unilateral Remedies: An Analysis of Countermeasures*, Dobbs Ferry, NY: Transnational Publishers, 1984.

[76] See Vienna Convention of Treaties, Arts. 60 and 72. Here a "material" breach is the precondition for invoking the suspension or termination; in addition, the exacting procedural conditions of Section IV of the convention have to be met, including a three-month waiting period after the notification of the other party, all of which takes at least fifteen months unless the suspending party has the consent of its treaty partner.

[77] *Case Concerning United States Diplomatic and Consular Staff in Tehran (United States of America v. Iran): Judgment of 24 May 1980* (La Haye: C.I.J, 1980), at 2.

course, is likely to lead to further debates and disputes as to what should be considered equivalent. The arbitrators in the *Bananas* dispute between the EU and Ecuador authorized Ecuador not only to suspend its GATT concessions (up to $202 million) vis-à-vis the EU, but also its obligations under the Agreement on Trade-related Aspects of Intellectual Property Rights (TRIPS). However, it seems clear that with "cross retaliation" we quickly enter into the area of "reprisals." In other words as Elisabeth Zoller correctly remarks: "Reprisals are no more than a form of response to wrongful acts beyond the scope of equivalence."[78] But before we lament the standard of "substantial equivalence," because its indeterminacy opens the door for all types of excessive claims, we had better understand that strict adherence to reciprocity is probably worse in many cases.

Suppose two countries have decided an environmental protection treaty setting up pollution standards. Country A does not abide by the undertaking. Should country B now also start polluting again?[79] As a bargaining stance, perhaps that might still make some sense, as a remedy it does not. Similarly, if one country violates the norms of the multilateral regime of human rights by treating its own population badly, could we seriously entertain the thought that the appropriate remedy "demanded" by self-help and reciprocity is that the other countries can now feel justified in treating its own populations badly? Or – in order to preserve the exact symmetry requirement between the self and the other more fully – consider the following cases: can a state whose embassy has been stormed by "students" also have some thugs do the same to the other country's premises? Similarly, are we entitled to hack off the hands of prisoners of war because the other country has done so in an act of barbarity? Quite aside from the fact that the most superficial familiarity with international law shows that such courses of action are not an option, a short reflection on such an understanding of "reciprocity" also indicates that such a stance is likely to make out of us actors of the type we have good reasons for not wanting to become.

In short, the above examples suggest that the simplistic understanding of self-help, guided by simple reciprocity in an anarchic environment, is not likely to further our understanding of international practice. The reason is simply that the traditional contractual paradigm which underlies both international law and "private ordering" arguments does well if it functions *within* a public order, where a sufficiently rich shared understanding of the nature of the public order exists. The contractarian paradigm does badly, however, when it is taken as the

---

[78] Zoller, *Peacetime Unilateral Remedies: An Analysis of Countermeasures*, at 43.

[79] For a good discussion of the enforcement problems in the environmental area, see Mary Ellen O'Connell, "Enforcing the New International Law of the Environment," *German Yearbook of International Law*, 1992 (1992): 293–332.

lapis philosophorum that would provide us with answers as to how to fill those gaps. Whether this can or should be done by an appeal to supreme values or some form of natural law – in the absence of a common historical "life world" or tradition – is, of course, another question

It is in this context that the notion of obligations *erga omnes* becomes important. The ICJ pointed in an *obiter dictum* to certain duties that stay in the background but frame contractual undertakings. The relevant passage of the Barcelona Traction case states:

> An essential distinction should be drawn between the obligations of a state towards the international community as a whole and those rising vis à vis another state . . . By their very nature the former are the concern of all states. In view of the importance of the rights involved, all States can be held to have a legal interest in their protection: they are obligations *erga omnes*.[80]

To that extent the explicit prohibition of the termination or suspension of certain treaty provisions, such as e.g. those relating to "the protection of the human person in treaties of a humanitarian character," even in response to a breach by other contracting parties (see e.g. in Art. 60.5 of the Vienna Convention of Treaties and Art. 50.1 of the ILC Draft Articles) represents only the logical implications of these premises. Here, of course, the crucial distinction is between those obligations of the parties which are part of a multilateral undertaking – those that they have towards each other (*inter se*) – and those obligations that are *erga omnes*.

Similarly complex issues are raised when we rely on the standard of proportionality in assessing the permissibility of responses. In the famous ruling of the Naulilaa Arbitration[81] tribunal, that considered German reprisals excessive and therefore imposed retribution on Germany, the role of the standard of proportionality seemed uncontroversial. Article 51 of the Draft Articles on State Responsibility states that: "Countermeasures must be commensurate with the injury suffered, taking into account the gravity of the internationally wrongful act and the rights in question."[82] But when applying this standard of reasonableness to concrete situations several problems arise which seem to indicate that "proportionality" means rather different things in different circumstances. To that extent it does not represent a hard and fast standard that can simply be applied to the facts.

We all can probably agree that the main objective of invoking proportionality is to prevent excesses which are likely to occur when the wronged party is

---

[80] *Barcelona Traction, Light and Power Company Limited*, International Court of Justice, 3 (1970), para. 32.
[81] See *Responsibility of Germany for Damage Caused in the Portuguese Colonies in the South of Africa (Portugal v. Germany)*, Reports of International Arbitral Awards, 2, 1011 (1928).
[82] International Law Commission, Articles on State Responsibility, Art. 51.

simply freed from all restraint in responding to an injury. But we also should keep in mind that we ordinarily allow for *disproportional* responses in the domestic legal order because the state's writ has to be supreme, if the rule of law is to be maintained. Thus no lone robber relieving a man of his billfold could argue in his defense that after all he got only $5 (as the retrieved billfold was nearly empty), and given that paltry sum he should be let go, or that he was outgunned, because three police cars had responded, and thus the response was clearly disproportional to his infringement.

But how is proportionality then to be assessed? Unfortunately, it can lead us to errors on both sides, suggesting too much or too little as a remedy. Part of the problem is that it is a "prudential" criterion that cannot be pressed into the scheme of instrumental rationality as it refers to both the means chosen and objectives pursued. It needs, therefore, to be accompanied by more substantive understandings in order to do its work. Given the prevalence of instrumental thinking and of reducing the notion of proportionality basically to some efficiency criterion by which we expect the effect to be proportional to the efforts expended, Enzo Cannizzaro correctly points out that applying the proportionality criterion actually involves us in more complicated operations.

> We are mentally accustomed to think of proportionality as a link between the means and aims of the measures of self-redress. However this assumption is not completely correct. Proportionality requires not only employing the means appropriate to the aim chosen, but implies above all, an assessment of the appropriateness of the aim itself . . . international law curtails the otherwise unbounded discretion (of a state) by requiring that the aim pursued is not manifestly inappropriate to the situation, considering the structure and content of the breached rule.[83]

In the case of the Air Sevices case, which introduced the notion of countermeasures, the issue concerned the equivalence of the US measures after France had refused Pan Am landing rights when the company wanted to switch to a smaller aircraft (change of gauge) on the last leg of the New York–Paris route (i.e. London–Paris). Examining the vast network of air service agreements the Tribunal came to the conclusion that, while the proportionality calculus was not an exact science, it was satisfied by approximate "appreciation," and in this way the countermeasures by the US were clearly not "disproportionate."[84]

In the hostage case the court had inter alia to decide whether the takeover of the diplomatic premises, as well as the seizure of the diplomatic and consular personnel of the United States in Teheran, constituted a lawful response to the alleged illegal activities of the diplomatic personnel (spying and interference in

---

[83] Enzo Cannizzaro, "The Role of Proportionality in the Law of International Countermeasures," *European Journal of International Law*, 12:5 (2001): 889–916, at 897.
[84] *Case Concerning the Air Service Agreement of 27 March 1946 between the United States of America and France.* §83.

the internal affairs of another sovereign state). The court not only dismissed the allegations but stated that even if the abuses of diplomatic immunity could have been proven, neither the seizure of the diplomatic premises nor of US diplomats could be justified as a countermeasure, particularly since the recognized remedy was the closure of the embassy and/or the expulsion of the personnel in question.[85]

Finally, in Gabčíkovo–Nagymaros[86] the court had to decide on the legality of the countermeasures taken by Slovakia, i.e. making use of the Danube alone, diverting the waters to its territory, since the joint use agreed upon in a treaty had come to a standstill due to Hungary's failure to live up to its part of the bargain. The court found, however, that Slovakia's measures were excessive, as they were not related to restoring the status quo ante but created an entirely new situation through the unilateral exploitation of the benefits. The failure of Hungary to perform its obligations could only justify measures that brought the parties back to the original agreement, i.e. would have entailed e.g. a claim for compensation on the part of Czechoslovakia (Slovakia). Alternatively, Slovakia could have used the option of breaching an equivalent rule operative between the parties so as to force Hungary to resume its compliance with the treaty regime of sharing the resources.[87]

Given the complexity of the issues involved it also might be useful to have a look at the Draft Articles of the International Law Commission on Responsibility of States for Internationally Wrongful Acts[88] that inter alia addresses the question of "countermeasures" (Arts. 42–54). These draft articles are also often interpreted as providing evidence for the progressive development of international law in that they seem to allow for the possibility that even states not directly injured might invoke these violations to justify countermeasures. But Professor Crawford, the last rapporteur of the Draft Articles, carefully stated:

It does not seem disproportionate to allow states to insist upon the cessation of a breach of an obligation owed to the international community as a whole . . . This would seem to

---

[85] *Case Concerning United States Diplomatic and Consular Staff in Tehran (United States of America v. Iran): Judgment of 24 May 1980*, at 2.

[86] *Case Concerning the Gabčíkovo–Nagymaros Project (Hungary/Slovakia). Judgment of 25 September 1997*, International Court of Justice (1997), at 7.

[87] "Czechoslovakia, by unilaterally assuming control of a shared resource, and thereby depriving Hungary of its right to an equitable and reasonable share of the natural resources of the Danube – with the continuing effects of the diversion of these waters on the ecology of the riparian area of Szgetkoesz – failed to respect the proportionality which is required by international law." Ibid., 55. §85.

[88] International Law Commission, *Draft Articles on Responsibility of States for Internationally Wrongful Acts* (2001, UN Doc. A/56/10). It was subsequently approved by the GA (Dec 12, 2001) without vote ("taking note") through Resolution 56/83, thereby "commending them [i.e. these draft articles] to the attention of Governments without prejudice to the question of their future adoption or other appropriate action."

follow directly from the Court's dictum in Barcelona Traction. Whether a claimant state should be able to seek reparations "in the interest of the injured state or of the beneficiaries of the obligation reached" is perhaps less clear. In particular, this is something the injured state, if one exists, might reasonably be expected to do for itself.[89]

Consequently, not too much of a "universal" right of all states to sanction violations of human rights should be read into them. The real difficulty here is that despite some expressed concerns about the *ordre public*, countermeasures are inherently "mechanisms of private justice" as Denis Alland has appropriately called them. They are therefore somewhat paradoxical when viewed from a classical *ordre public* perspective.[90] They resemble more the institution of ancient feuds than the institutions of a community where third party assessments prevail, for which perhaps the UN and its institutions provide the first, rather problematic, approximation.

6.7   Sanctions and Multilateralism

Our discussion above concerning the remedies of self-help has distinguished between cases in which a state might invoke countermeasures on the basis of a breach of a bilateral obligation, those measures available for breaches of duties *erga omnes*, and those which are justified by the failure to live up to the obligations arising under a multilateral treaty. It is the latter problem that needs further clarification since the "multilateral" enforcement of obligations has raised in the last two decades a variety of issues for both the theory and practice of sanctions.[91]

During the Cold War the UN imposed multilateral sanctions only twice (Rhodesia in 1966 and South Africa in 1990), but the record of the 1990s was dramatically different. Multilateral sanctions were mandated in eighteen cases, and the subsequent debates ranged from discussion of the effectiveness of various measures to questions of the legal standards which multilateral sanctions are supposed to satisfy. Since there was mounting evidence that e.g. the population of Iraq was rather severely impacted by the sanctions,[92] while its regime could not only exempt itself from the negative consequences but was

[89] Ibid., 16., para. 41.
[90] Denis Alland, "Countermeasures of General Interest," *European Journal of International Law*, 13:5 (2002): 1221–1239.
[91] See Pierre-Marie Dupuy, "A General Stocktaking of the Connections between the Multilateral Dimension of Obligations and Codification of the Law of Responsibility," *European Journal of International Law*, 13:5 (2002): 1053–1081.
[92] See e.g. Geoff L. Simons, *The Scourging of Iraq: Sanctions, Law and Natural Justice*, 2nd edn., New York: St. Martin's Press, 1998.

actually able to profit from it by engaging in sanctions-busting, the debate was not only of academic interest.[93]

While the multilateralization of sanctions was supposed to be the answer to the classical collective action problem in sanctioning, it also raised several additional conceptual and practical problems. One was that the expansion of unilateral countermeasures to some form of multilateral undertaking provided grist for the mill of those who had argued that these developments were indicators for a move towards the "constitutionalization" of world politics that ought to be furthered by e.g. including increasingly also human rights in the WTO regime.[94]

But it is questionable whether the addition of such extension can bring about the desired changes, not only because of the jurisdictional issues between different regimes that would arise, but also because the reduction of the problem of legitimacy to one of conformity with a "higher" constitutional order amounts to a not unproblematic political move.[95] Far from representing a move from politics to law, it recreates a politics by other means, when the conformity with legal norms substitutes for the "all things considered" approach to practical questions, characteristic of well-informed political judgments.

Another related issue concerns the *erga omnes* obligations. This arose out of the confusion of obligations from multilateral treaties, under which all parties have obligations vis-à-vis the other parties (*inter se*, or *erga omnes partes* obligations), and from the notion of obligations owed to the "international community (of states!) as a whole."[96] While the addition of "states" seems to prevent the inference that "humanity" pure and simple is addressed here, the interpretive ambiguities point to an equivocal use of the term multilateralism. On the most general level the term "multilateral" refers just to the numbers of participants. Here the distinction is simply between the exclusive bilateral deal and an arrangement that comprises several parties. But as the discussions during the last decades have shown, this is heuristically not a very useful distinction. For one, we can have in effect a multilateral trading arrangement by the extension of bilateral concessions via the most-favored-nation principle, as was the case in the nineteenth century after the Cobden–Chevalier Treaty between France and Great Britain. Second, as Ruggie has pointed out, the multilateralism after World War II was different in kind, not just in numbers.[97]

---

[93] See e.g. Security Council Report, "UN Sanctions" Special Research Report, No. 3, November 25 (New York: Security Council Report, 2013).
[94] See Ernst-Ulrich Petersmann, "The WTO Constitution and Human Rights," *Journal of International Economic Law*, 3:3 (2000): 19–25.
[95] Duncan Kennedy, *A Critique of Adjudication: Fin de Siècle*, Cambridge, MA: Harvard University Press, 1997.
[96] See Peltonen, *International Responsibility and Grave Humanitarian Crises*.
[97] Ruggie (ed.), *Multilateralism Matters*, at 3–50.

As a distinct organizational form this kind of multilateralism was based on general rules, nondiscrimination and diffuse reciprocity i.e. understandings of equivalences allowing also for temporary imbalances. But despite these innovations in the organizational form and their embodiment in the GATT trading order, the fact remains that a surprisingly large part of GATT and the present WTO arrangement remains bilateral. Members with a special interest in a certain product or sector are able not only to renegotiate the concessions pursuant to GATT Article XXVIII and GATT Article XXI, but the remedies that are available to them for countering violations are, despite the compulsory arbitration, entirely bilateral. Precisely because the gains from trade can be individualized, an injured state – and only the injured state! – can respond by imposing up to a 100 percent tariff on the products of the defaulting state in accordance with Article 22.6 of the Dispute Settlement Understanding (DSU).[98] That such retaliatory measures do "hurt" can be seen in the Beef Hormone and Foreign Sales Corporation cases.[99]

It needs no further elaboration that the situation in trade is thus obviously quite different from those regimes covering such areas as biodiversity, global warming or even regional disarmament treaties, where a violation does not affect one state specifically but injures the interest of all of them, and where "there is a genuine need to grant the right to invoke responsibility for breach to each and every party, not because it is specifically affected but in the collective interest of all parties taken together, so that someone at least can enforce the collective obligation."[100] Two problems become visible here: one concerns the nature of the good to be achieved by the regime given the (in)divisibility of the good in question; the other addresses the question of how among freestanding regimes cross-retaliatory measures can be established without engendering and worsening conflict. The first issue has been addressed in part by the discussion above and the recognition that there are indeed multilateral problems that can be handled by bilateral means, while the other issue concerning the

---

[98] The amount of trade affected thereby must be, as is the case with any lawful self-help measure, "equivalent to the level of the nullification or impairment" suffered by the complaining state (Art. 22.4 DSU).

[99] *European Communities – Measures Concerning Meat and Meat Products (Hormones)*, World Trade Organization, DS26 (2009). See also *United States – Tax Treatment for "Foreign Sales Corporations"*, World Trade Organization, DS108 (2006). While in the former the US and Canada were authorized to take retaliatory measures up to $116 million (11 million Canadian dollars) against the EU, the bill was considerably higher in the latter case. After having its claims vindicated that the US tax provisions amounted to an illegal subsidy of US firms trading with Europe, the EU sought authorization for the imposition of tariffs up to $4 billion on US goods!

[100] Joost Pauwelyn, "A Typology of Multilateral Treaty Obligations: Are WTO Obligations Bilateral or Collective in Nature?" *European Journal of International Law*, 14:5 (2003): 907–951, at 934.

"common good" or common ongoing concern can no longer be partialed out or decomposed into a web of bilateral obligations

Although the latter problem is perhaps not as new as it seems, since it goes to the very heart of the constitution of the international system, the conceptual puzzles remain. Already in the traditional notion of a society of states, constitutional questions arose in the context of the *ordre public*, but initially focused virtually exclusively on security issues among states – although here one should not forget that already with the internationalization of the Rhine and Danube other public concerns were articulated and the first international organizations were created.[101] But the "constitutional" issues concerning the "repose of Europe" were discussed after the settlement at Vienna within the framework of the Concert. A contractual understanding of politics and the possibility of ad hoc agreements among the various powers through the mutual recognition of their "interests" and roles within the system provided an important template that militated against the Hobbesian notion of an international anarchy in the sense of a war of all against all.

Great powers were not only characterized by their capabilities but by their system-wide interests and the presumption that all "important" issues had to be managed by them. But since the challenge of the French Revolution ascribing sovereignty to "the people" rather than to traditional rulers, issues of the legitimacy of political rule could no longer simply be defined in the traditional categories of abstention from interference, modeled after the notion of exclusive ownership (*dominium*).[102] The form of government was now likely to affect the "public order" of Europe. As Kissinger has shown, the existence of different regimes with differing notions of legitimacy spawned a major controversy between Metternich and Castelreagh, concerning an intervention in Spain, which came to a head in the Congress of Verona.[103]

It cannot be the purpose of this discussion to rehearse the arguments for the decay of the Concert system. Here I want to follow up only on the new ways in which the international system was managed and new public order concerns were articulated. Emblematic for these developments were the three major "settlements," i.e. those of 1815, 1918, and 1945, for which Vienna, Versailles, and San Francisco respectively stand. Vienna created the status of the "great power" which had both system-wide interests and the wherewithal to pursue them, making its consultation at the "Concert" necessary. Only the

---

[101] To that extent the call for revision of the WTO charter can be heard as representing a new "constitutional moment" for the post-Cold War era.

[102] See Kratochwil, "Sovereignty as 'Dominium'."

[103] Henry Kissinger, *A World Restored: Europe after Napoleon*, New York: Grosset & Dunlap, 1964. See also Henry Kissinger, *World Order*, New York: Penguin Press, 2014, chap. 1.

Versailles and San Fancisco settlements created more explicit sanctioning regimes, reflecting important changes to the notion of an *ordre public* in an emerging global world.

Although Article 16 of the Covenant represented the first multilateral agreement (aside from International Sugar Convention of 1902), in that it provided for trade sanctions in response to a breach of the peace, its record, when compared to its initial expectations, remained very poor.[104] Should any member resort to war in disregard of the provisions of the Covenant, the other members obliged themselves to subject that state to the "severance of all trade and financial relations." In addition, the members committed themselves to some form of burden-sharing in regard to the costs of sanctions, attempting thereby to counteract the collective action problems endemic to multilateral sanctions.[105] But since, the application of sanctions for illegal conduct remained within the discretion of each state, the multilateralization of applying sanctions, i.e. the actual collective action problem, was not cured.

The UN Charter was designed to overcome this defect by the provisos of Chapters VI and VII and by ensconcing the duties of the members vis-à-vis the UN in Article 103. As Thomas Franck noted:

It gives the Council flexibility to impose broad or narrowly targeted sanctions in a wide range of circumstances. Articles 25 and 48 now require the compliance of all members. However, what has changed most since 1919 is not the normative text but its sociopolitical context. Thus it is revealing to compare the League's divisive debates over imposing sanctions on Italy and Japan with the contemporary lack of opposition to the use of sanctions in dealing with Iraq, Yugoslavia, Liberia, Haiti, Somalia, and Cambodia. If anything, criticism has come from those who believe that the Council should, in some instances, have reacted more swiftly and decisively.[106]

In this context not only the number of sanctioning episodes but also the complexity of the problems which were addressed through sanctions is significant. While during the Cold War multilateral sanctions were imposed only twice during the first four decades of the UN (Rhodesia 1966 and South Africa 1977) the Security Council voted subsequently in over fifty resolutions for sanctions against Iraq, former Yugoslavia, Libya, Somalia, Liberia, the parts of Cambodia held by the Khmer Rouge, Haiti, Angola, Sudan, Rwanda, Sierra Leone,

---

[104] The League was successful in having Yugoslavia recall its troops from Albania in 1921; however, its imposition of a trade embargo against Bolivia in the Chaco war of 1933–1934 and against Italy after its invasion of Ethiopia can hardly be called successful. No sanctions at all were imposed on Japan after its attack on Manchuria, and Russia was expelled from the League in accordance with Article 16 (4), after its invasion of Finland.

[105] Covenant, Art. 16 (3).

[106] Thomas M. Franck, *Fairness in International Law and Institutions*, Oxford: Clarendon Press, 1995, at 291.

Eritrea, Ethiopia, and Afghanistan,[107] that often involved the UN directly in complex enforcement and "peacemaking" operations. They represented an entirely new type of UN operations that fell "in between" the Chapter VI and Chapter VII measures. These "VI½" missions[108] differ from former peacekeeping in that they are no longer based on the consent of the parties to conflict, and depend, therefore, on an increasingly extensive interpretation of Article 39 of the Charter, on the Security Council's decision, and on the willingness of member states to furnish the necessary troops and support.

When in 2000 the Secretary General charged a panel of experts with a comprehensive review of all peace and security operations, the resulting Brahimi Report noted both the weakness of the UN machinery and the substitute that had been found:

... while the United Nations has acquired considerable expertise in planning, mounting and executing traditional peacekeeping operations, it has yet to acquire the capacity needed to deploy more complex operations rapidly and to sustain them effectively ...

The UN does not wage war. Where enforcement action is required it has consistently been entrusted to coalitions of willing states with the authorization of the Security Council, acting under Chapter VII of the Charter.[109]

Such an assessment might be slightly self-congratulatory for several reasons. For one, far from "enforcing" the peace against violating states, most of the breaches of peace *are not* handled by UN enforcement. Both the Security Council and the international "community" prefer to sit out the conflicts, "calling upon the parties" without taking measures. Second, as the controversies concerning the Second Gulf War (Operation Iraqi Freedom) indicate, mandates without limits, with "implied" or continuing authorization (as suggested by the contentious debate concerning the meaning of Resolution 1441), have meant practically no control of the actual execution of the mandate (vide Operation Desert Fox and the "enforcement" of no-fly zones in Iraq "pursuant" to

---

[107] More limited mandates – mandates which nevertheless sometimes explicitly authorized the use of force – were contained in the Security Council resolutions for imposing no-fly zones in Bosnia and Herzegovina (where NATO was entrusted with that task) and for delivering humanitarian aid in Albania and the Central African Republic for safeguarding the unimpeded movement of peacekeeping forces.

[108] For a general discussion, see Steven R. Ratner, *The New UN Peacekeeping: Building Peace in Lands of Conflict after the Cold War*, New York: Palgrave Macmillan, 1995; Thomas M. Franck, *Recourse to Force: State Action against Threats and Armed Attacks*, Cambridge: Cambridge University Press, 2002, chap. 2. See Connaughton's critical assessment of the Somalia, Rwanda, and Kosovo operations in Richard M. Connaughton, *Military Intervention and Peacekeeping: The Reality*, Aldershot: Ashgate, 2001. See also Alex J. Bellamy, Paul Williams, and Stuart Griffin, *Understanding Peacekeeping*, Cambridge: Polity, 2004.

[109] United Nations General Assembly and United Nations Security Council, *Report of the Panel on United Nations Peace Operations* (2000, UN Doc. A/55/305–S/2000/809), paras. 6h and 58 respectively.

resolution 687).[110] Finally, due to the complex problems and the varied local circumstances, the idea that peacekeeping operations can be handled according to the notion that "one size fits all" and that the "learning" will consist in the simple accumulation of experience is extremely naïve. After all, Haiti posed different problems than Kosovo, and the experiences with the strong state structures of a repressive regime, as in El Salvador or Namibia, are of little help in dealing with state decay and warlordism encountered in Somalia or Cambodia.

At the most extreme part of the spectrum the new "peacemaking" efforts have involved the actual takeover of certain territories, such as in the cases of East Timor and Kosovo. In the latter cases (as was to an extent already the case in the Congo and in Cambodia) the diplomatic virtue of "neutrality," i.e. not becoming involved in internal affairs, which was essential for the success of "preventive diplomacy," is obviously no longer of any avail, and the UN possessed an independent political decision-making capacity as well as administrative and judicial authority for establishing the "rule of law." These "third-generation" UN operations, focusing on "peace maintenance" rather than prevention of a war through outside intervention, of course pose the greatest difficulties, since such missions entail the comprehensive restructuring of the political processes which led to violent conflict and UN intervention. But such a charge also implies that the calls for accountability, transparency, efficiency, and legitimacy which international agencies require from their "target" country can now be raised vis-à-vis the "international governance and particular international administration missions."[111]

The international administration of a territory by an international organization is not unprecedented,[112] as the League had administered the Saar Basin and Danzig, the city of Tangier was internationalized until 1956, and Mostar was under a special EU regime from 1993 to 1996, while the UN provided a transitional administration in Cambodia (1992–1997), East Timor, and Kosovo.[113] The historical record, is, however, rather mixed. How complicated things can get under these circumstances is well documented by the experiences in East Timor where during the transition the UN even became

[110] For an extensive discussion of the legal issues, see the "Agora" of the *American Journal of International Law*, 97 (2003): 800f.
[111] Outi Korhonen, "International Governance in Post-Conflict Situations," *Leiden Journal of International Law*, 14:3 (2001): 495–529, at 497.
[112] For a discussion of these precedents and their implications for UN peace maintenance operations, see Ratner, *The New UN Peacekeeping*.
[113] For an assessment of the strange "trusteeship," see Andreas Zimmermann and Carsten Stahn, "Yugoslav Territory, United Nations Trusteeship or Sovereign State?: Reflections on the Current and Future Legal Status of Kosovo," *Nordic Journal of International Law*, 70:4 (2001): 423–460.

the *de jure* sovereign. As a UN official, who later resigned his post as head of the Transitional Authority (UTAET), pointed out:

Indeed comparisons with colonial administrations were unavoidable and affirmed by various forms of segregation between expatriates and the Timorese. Two economies emerged, just as in Cambodia and other peace keeping locales. Timorese were turned into the servants of foreigners in their own land, since they could apply only for menial jobs. Physically the UN's hermetic office world was increasingly disconnected from life in the streets. Floating container hotels in Dili restricted the access of Timorese, except to serve drinks and food.[114]

While in the case of East Timor the "transition" was limited by the prospect of national independence, no clear exit option (aside from a time frame and the reaffirmation of self-determination) had been formulated for Kosovo, and the declaration of the latter's independence – duly buttressed by the advisory opinion of the ICJ[115] – handed the fate of the country to the EU, rather than settling the outstanding issues.

One need not possess too much perspicacity in order to see that here we have the administrative result of a highly problematic sanctioning policy that not only strained the relations between the Western powers and the Russian Federation, but between Europe and the US. The result was that the problems in the Balkans were, despite much diplomatic activity, first treated with benign neglect – as before in the case of Rwanda, where the employment of ground troops had been categorically ruled out by President Clinton. The subsequent highly problematic decision – for strategic[116] as well as legal reasons[117] – to bomb Serbia was then supposed to reverse the increasingly serious situation on the ground. However, one has also to see that the worst ethnic cleansing occurred after the commencement of the NATO bombing! What was supposed to be a "humanitarian intervention" was in danger of becoming a desperate gesture, trying to show that "something" was being done, even if that "something" was not sensibly related either to a clear policy objective, or even to helping along the relief efforts, which are part of "normal" humanitarian politics.

In the end the resulting regime for Kosovo might have been the least bad of all the remaining options but such an interpretation neglects to inquire into the

---

[114] Jarat Chopra, "The UN's Kingdom of East Timor," *Survival*, 42:3 (2000): 27–39, at 33.

[115] See *Accordance with International Law of the Unilateral Declaration of Independence in Respect of Kosovo*, International Court of Justice, Advisory opinion of 22 July (2010), at 403.

[116] The US military had advised against a "bombing only" option. Furthermore, initially only ninety-one targets for three days had been selected, since US decision-makers believed that Milosevic would fold. See Connaughton, *Military Intervention and Peacekeeping: The Reality*, at 209. The Chairman of the US Joint Chiefs of Staff repeatedly warned Secretary of State Albright that such a campaign would encourage a "humanitarian disaster in Kosovo." See Michael Hirsh and John Barry, "How We Stumbled into War," *Newsweek*, April 12, 1999.

[117] See e.g. the 4th Report of the Foreign Affairs Committee of the UK of June 7, 2000, which examines the legal issues. Available at www.parliament.uk.

opportunities missed and the failures of policies before the fateful bombing campaign took place. It also fails to mention the difficulties that lie ahead when the political debts that have been incurred and that are tenuously kept under control will become due. That the outcome is now the result of multilateral failures rather than only bilateral ones, and that they also point to failures of "governance" conceived as a technical solution (instead of political blunders of governments), seems indeed cold comfort.

6.8   Reprise: Assessing the Impact of Sanctions by Comparing Cases

Whatever we might think about the First and Second Gulf Wars, one hopeful interpretation – quite current after the ending of hostilities and the imposition of an unprecedented set of conditions[118] through Resolution 687 – seems to have lost much of its earlier persuasiveness. It concerned not only the hope that sanctions which had originally been intended to induce Iraq to end the invasion and occupation of Kuwait could now be refashioned by a united Security Council in order to compel Baghdad to comply with the terms of the ceasefire. Another such hope was that a new chapter in humanitarian law had been written by the enforcement of "no-fly" zones in Iraq, ending the regime's human rights abuses against the Kurdish minority.[119]

Without wanting to discuss in detail the pros and cons of such an appraisal, it seems that the long-term effects were quite different than expected: the sanctioning regime did not work as intended, because paradoxically it was increasingly considered punitive and illegitimate. This not only exploded the myth of the relatively benign nature of economic sanctions,[120] it even raised the issue of responsibility for the possible violation of humanitarian law by the UN itself.[121] The Security Council could also not function as a credible enforcer of the peace, as the controversies concerning the use of force by a "coalition of the willing" exemplified. The no-fly zones brought to the fore the constitutional problem of the "reverse veto," i.e. that earlier authorizations for sanctions could not be lifted if one permanent member vetoed such

[118] See Bardo Fassbender, "Uncertain Steps into a Post-Cold War World: The Role and Functioning of the UN Security Council after a Decade of Measures Against Iraq," *European Journal of International Law*, 13:1 (2002): 273–303.
[119] See United Nations and Secretary General, *In Larger Freedom: Towards Development, Security and Human Rights for All: Report of the Secretary-General*, New York: United Nations, 2005.
[120] Joy Gordon, "A Peaceful, Silent, Deadly Remedy: The Ethics of Economic Sanctions," *Ethics and International Affairs*, 13:1 (1999): 123–142.
[121] See e.g. August Reinisch, "Developing Human Rights and Humanitarian Accountability of the Security Council for the Imposition of Economic Sanctions," *American Journal of International Law*, 954:1 (2001): 851–872.

a resolution. This, in turn, led to the introduction of "sunset resolutions"[122] in some sanctioning regimes, which will, however, probably weaken this instrument of multilateral enforcement. Nowhere do the dilemmas of politics appear more clearly.

When a panel was appointed to monitor the humanitarian situation in Iraq, it had to admit in 1999 that the sanctions coupled with the degradation of the country's infrastructure had taken a terrible toll, affecting children in particular because of malnutrition (five to six thousand were estimated to have died per month) and the collapse of basic healthcare. If there was any doubt, the resignations in protest of both Humanitarian Coordinators for the UN, Dennis Halliday and Hans von Sponeck, in 1998 and 2000 should have opened the eyes of the public to the corruption and terrible suffering that the sanctioning regime had inflicted upon the Iraqi people.[123] The Iraq problem thus provided a site for most of the ongoing debates about the possibility of greater accountability, of *ultra vires* actions of the Security Council,[124] and of the "constitutional" reform of the UN. Here the composition of the Security Council, its procedures with regard to the "listing" of individuals to be sanctioned, the effectiveness of general or "targeted" sanctions, their justifiability and compatibility with the provisions of the Laws of War or humanitarian principles, and the advancement of human rights were the major issues.

Indeed the UN itself set up a working group on sanctions comprising all members of the Security Council in order to study the problems and to profit from both the extensive academic debate and the experiences of the "sanctioning decade," which ended in a call for "shrewd"[125] or "smart" sanctions. Specific sanctioning episodes were examined, such as the targeted sanctions against the UNITA leadership in Angola, which even named two sitting presidents as sanction breakers (Eyadema of Togo and Campore of Burkina Faso), but which also had identified Bulgaria as the main arms supplier.[126] The Swiss

---

[122] E.g. the arms embargo for Eritrea and Ethiopia imposed in May 2000 was limited to twelve months with a mandated review thereafter. United Nations Security Council, *Resolution 1298, 17 May* (2000, S/RES/1298), para. 16.

[123] See Hans von Sponeck and Denis Halliday, "The Hostage Nation," *The Guardian*, November 29, 2001, accessed at www.theguardian.com/world/2001/nov/29/iraq.comment. A chilling reminder of how quickly such humanitarian interventions "to protect" can degenerate and become nightmarish examples of inhumanity can be found in Hans-Christof Sponeck, *A Different Kind of War: The UN Sanctions Regime in Iraq*, New York: Berghahn Books, 2006.

[124] See e.g. Willem J.M. van Genugten and Gerard A. de Groot (eds.), *United Nations Sanctions: Effectiveness and Effects, Especially in the Field of Human Rights, a Multi-Disciplinary Approach*, Antwerpen: Intersentia, 1999; Mary Ellen O'Connell, "Debating the Law of Sanctions," *European Journal of International Law*, 13:1 (2002): 63–79.

[125] See Meghan L. O'Sullivan, *Shrewd Sanctions: Statecraft and State Sponsors of Terrorism*, Washington, DC: Brookings Institution Press, 2003.

[126] See Michael Brzoska, "From Dumb to Smart? Recent Reforms of UN Sanctions," *Global Governance*, 9 (2003): 519–536.

Government sponsored two conferences in 1998 and 1999 at Interlaken, which addressed targeted financial sanctions. The German government, through its Center for Conversion, convened a meeting that analyzed embargoes and travel sanctions. The Swedish government tasked Uppsala University with an examination of three implementation-related issues: improvement of the operation of sanction committees, the development of guidelines for the implementation of certain targeted sanctions, and the identification of targets for "smart sanctions."[127] Finally, the Watson Institute at Brown University in Providence, Rhode Island, developed in 2001 a comprehensive manual for the implementation of targeted financial sanctions.

The consensus emerging from these various "processes" (Interlaken, Bonn–Berlin, Stockholm, Providence) seemed to be that "targeted" sanctions had to address the elite of the sanctioned country, rather than the population at large, that they could be effective, and that better management and information about the impact of these sanctions could both "increase their effectiveness, while minimizing the negative humanitarian impact . . . of comprehensive sanctions regimes."[128] To that extent targeted, or "smart" sanctions, such as travel bans for the ruling elite, the seizure of the financial assets of a rogue regime, and an embargo on certain commodities, such as oil or diamonds, that finance war lords seemed like a decision-maker's dream. They promised to provide "two for the price of one": effectiveness and legitimacy. But while the approach seems logically compelling and politically attractive, a more somber mood has settled in, as the complexities of the operational problems, ranging from the lack of state capacities to the vagaries of the political processes within the Security Council, have became clearer.

Although smart sanctions might be better targeted and reduce the enforcement cost as only the transactions of a small circle rather than trade in general have to be monitored, it would be a misconception to think that thereby the enforcement cost problem has been solved. Looking for a needle in a haystack, i.e. relying on specific targeted sanctions, is always more time-consuming than locking the door to the barn in the first place, i.e. applying general sanctions. Besides, identifying leaks, searching for accounts of foreign potentates, or subjecting diamonds or oil to certification procedures is not tantamount to being able to stop the leaks in weapons embargoes, given the oversupply of arms after the Cold War, or the rather easy forging of certificates.

---

[127] See Arne Tostensen and Beate Bull, "Are Smart Sanctions Feasible?" *World Politics*, 54:3 (2002): 373–403.

[128] Remarks of the Swiss Ambassador Jecker in his Chairman's Report at the Interlaken Conference, as quoted in Matthew Craven, "Humanitarianism and the Quest for Smarter Sanctions," *European Journal of International Law*, 13:1 (2002): 43–61, at 47.

For seizing the accounts of human rights violators, speed, knowledge and capacity are required, that are often beyond the means of most states. Depriving warlords of their sources of income generated by criminal networks or shady "spot" markets requires the ability to penetrate and disrupt these networks. Finally, having an inventory of the ruling circles for imposing travel sanctions (only the members of government or their entire families?) presupposes intimate knowledge of the regime and the wherewithal to prevent circumventions of the restrictions by issuing new or multiple passports, or by using cargo rather than passenger carriers. In short, as Matthew Craven has pointed out:

> To suggest that targeting will fulfill both the need for effectiveness and humanity seems to be credible only to the extent that the terms of evaluation are regarded as being contained within the activity itself. Targeting may be said to be more effective only in that "hitting" the target is better than "missing" it, and more humane only as far as the non-infliction of harm on others can be regarded as such. In either case it ignores the broader contextual factors that inform general understandings of what is either "effective" or "humane."
>
> . . . It is barely credible that in directing measures against the government, the civilian population will be immunized from harmful effects. Whether or not the benefits are thereby to be regarded in comparative terms . . . the point is that once one accepts the premise of targeting as a strategic tool, there is also a tendency to accept the limitations implicit in that activity for purposes of evaluating it as a coercive strategy.[129]

In the following I want to sidestep the usual discussion in the social sciences of whether sanctions work or not on the basis of empirical data, in order to focus more on what they actually do and on what the appropriate criteria for appraising sanctions could be. It would indeed be ironic if the old and unreflective idea of "pain equals gain" is replaced by an equally naïve notion that sanctions work (or do not work) over all. Before we try to bolster our arguments with scientific criteria, such as invoking generalizations derived from some data banks, we had better clarify some of the conceptual issues that underlie various sanction studies. Here three sets of problems can be identified: one concerns the mistaken analogy to a technical problem, a second set of issues arises in the context of strategic interaction, and finally we have to be aware that certain distortions in our appraisals derive from the mode of selection and representation of the cases. Given these many sources of confusion that work singly and in conjunction, it is not surprising that the sanctions debate has been inconclusive and that it is probably the "wrong debate" as one political scientist has termed it.

Let us begin with the technical analogy, or "pain–gain" fallacy. Implicit in the argument is the assumption that the effects of an action obey the same

---

[129] Craven, "Humanitarianism and the Quest for Smarter Sanctions," at 47f.

causal laws as mechanical systems, where action equals reaction. As soon as we admit that we are dealing with actual agents, this form of causality does not hold. Instead the crucial variable is now dependent on how the "transmission mechanism" works, i.e. how the external pressure works itself through the political system and translates pressure into changed policy preferences of the decision-makers, or effects a regime change. Only if we assume a reasonably free and competitive political system in the target state can we assume that sanctions will be taken up by the opposition and engender electoral competition. Autocracies, on the other hand, we would expect to be less susceptible to such pressures, unless the ruling coalition itself is divided or falls out.

Thus, at a minimum the discussion of sanctions has also to include the "regime type" in its assessment[130] rather than simply inferring that the lack of effect *must have been caused* by the "porousness" of sanctions in accordance with the mechanical metaphor. Certainly, the collective action problems in maintaining sanctions and the negative impact on the economies linked to the sanctioned state pose problems for the effectiveness of every sanctions regime. This is after all the reason why conventional wisdom emphasizes both the need for "watertight" sanctions and for their multilateral endorsement. But even tight and nearly universally supported sanctions sometimes fail, as the example of Syria demonstrates. Furthermore, the devastations imposed by comprehensive sanctions regimes on Iraq and Yugoslavia did not result in the desired policy changes, while the relatively minor impact of sanctions on South Africa (limited to an equivalent loss of 1–3 percent in growth a year) finally led to the demise of Apartheid.

But as the addition of qualifying conditions, i.e. of time lags, and (in the case of South Africa) of regime change through evolution in "thinking" – and not party competition[131] – shows, even opening up the black box of the target state while retaining the mechanical analogy is misleading. After all, the political system of the target state is not fixed and thus a lot will depend on whether the strategies chosen by the leadership in refashioning the political order succeed or backfire. Here Rowe's analysis of the moves by the Rhodesian government to sequester political opposition and build new bases of support is highly instructive.[132]

---

[130] See Risa A. Brooks, "Sanctions and Regime Type: What Works, and When?" *Security Studies*, 11:4 (2002): 1–50.

[131] See Audie Klotz, *Norms in International Relations: The Struggle against Apartheid*, Ithaca, NY: Cornell University Press, 1999. See also Neta Crawford and Audie Klotz, *How Sanctions Work: Lessons from South Africa*, New York: Palgrave, 1999.

[132] David M. Rowe, *Manipulating the Market: Understanding Economic Sanctions, Institutional Change and Political Unity of White Rhodesia*, Ann Arbor: University of Michigan Press, 2001.

Rowe's study not only fills in the details in Galtung's highly influential but somewhat simplistic sketch of Rhodesian politics after the imposition of sanctions,[133] but also actually changes the mode of assessing the way in which sanctions work. Precisely because sanctions provided the Rhodesian government with opportunities to exercise its dominant position by creating new institutions designed to mitigate the effects and overcome protest by private interests, new domains, formerly untouched by governmental power, became areas for public ordering, after sanctions had been imposed. Once the government had managed to issue licenses and set quotas, it was also in a position to reward its supporters by distributing the extracted rents and punish its adversaries.

Thus sanctions led to "the increasing penetration of the economy by the government"[134] and to a successful strategy of "divide and rule" by playing high-quality against low-quality growers. For the implementation of these policies the foundation of a national tobacco corporation was particularly important. Tobacco was one of the key export items of Rhodesia, the overwhelming part of it going to Great Britain. Thus the growers had considerable clout within the white community and, if well organized, could have become an active opposition to governmental policies by seeking an accommodation with Great Britain. However, fearful of the impact of sanctions on their ability to survive on their own – exports declined dramatically – tobacco farmers overcame their former reservations about governmental interference and supported the state company, which in turn used its powers as a monopsonist and prevented – through quota allocation and set prices – the emergence of a potentially powerful opposition.

So well did this strategy work that finally the government could even decide to sell out the tobacco farmers, as their ranks had dwindled and import-competing industries, which profited from sanctions, provided the ruling group with much-needed support. The State Tobacco Company had managed to effectively mute what could have been a powerful source of opposition. Rowe's further discussion demonstrates that other segments of the society, such as export-oriented business, fared no better. Again the government succeeded in marginalizing the outward-oriented groups, which were likely to opt for an accommodation with Britain in return for the lifting of sanctions. The regime was thus able to fashion a coalition from businesses that profited from the enforced import substitution.

A similar picture emerges from the reports of Yugoslavia. Given that here the communist heritage already provided a much better set of instruments to reward friends and punish the enemies of the regime, Sonja Licht describes the situation as follows:

---

[133] Galtung, "On the Effects of International Economic Sanctions."
[134] Rowe, *Manipulating the Market*, at 33.

The character of the Milosevic regime was a mixture of communist heritage and a national mafia that monopolized the still existing resources. Only pro regime newspapers had printing paper and ink, only official television had all its needed production materials, and only Milosevic's Socialist Party had sufficient facilities, money, organization and the means of propaganda. Only banks that collaborated with the regime received fresh supplies of domestic currency out of the printing house to exchange for the hard currency exchanged on the black market. The political elite bought hard currency from the people for worthless money, and deposited the real money in foreign private accounts. . . . The scarcity of resources resulting from the sanctions enabled this regime to thrive on the poverty of the people and to tighten its grip on power.[135]

Thus Milosevic had managed to signal to his people that Serbia was not secure without its own state and military resources. To that extent he acted in accordance with the national myth, securing the survival of the Serb nations against all odds. The effects of economic sanctions also worked against finding alternatives to war and nationalism. The economic crisis allowed the state to reimpose state monopolies (while the elite could also enrich itself on the black market), strengthen the police and the armed forces, and deprive those elements of the liberal opposition which had not yet emigrated of political power.

Furthermore, as the post-mortem on the sanctions against Yugoslavia by an EU official shows, "smart" sanctions such as the flight bans actually hurt the opposition more than the governmental circles, and the targeted financial sanctions resulting in a "white" list of normal and unsanctioned firms (all others being presumed to be controlled by the government) failed to achieve their objective. Although the reversal of proof – the firms themselves had to show that they had no substantial ties to the government, which about 190 companies could do – simplified the enforcement problem, the EU administrator for sanctions had to admit that: "Financial sanctions probably caused the greatest negative impacts on non-targeted sectors of Serbian society, mainly from the denial of credits and other resources being allocated to state owned and controlled companies"[136] and that they were responsible for triggering the severe stagflation that subsequently devastated the Yugoslav economy.[137]

[135] Sonja Licht, "The Use of Sanctions in former Yugoslavia: Can They Assist in Conflict Resolution?" in David Cortright and George A. Lopez (eds.), *Economic Sanctions: Panacea or Peacebuilding in a Post-Cold War World?*, Boulder, CO: Westview Press, 1995: 153–160, at 158.

[136] Anthonius W. de Vries, "European Union Sanctions against the Federal Republic of Yugoslavia from 1998 to 2000: A Special Exercise in Targeting" in David Cortright and George A. Lopez (eds.), *Smart Sanctions: Targeting Economic Statecraft*, Lanham, MD: Rowman & Littlefield, 2002, 87–108, at 102.

[137] Yugoslavia's welfare loss is estimated at between 26 percent in 1992 and 28 percent in 1993, with rampant inflation so that by 1993 the numbers were only reported day-by-day, as the numbers for a month or a year were simply staggering. See David Cortright, *The Sanctions Decade: Assessing UN Strategies in the 1990s*, Boulder, CO: Lynne Rienner, 2000, at 73.

These brief remarks on two sanctioning episodes illustrate why attempts at showing the impact of sanctions in terms of a clear cause-and-effect scheme, or even an intentional account that underlies much of our conventional wisdom on sanctions, have to fail. The simple causal account is inadequate because in politics we are always acting within a strategic context, i.e. move and counter-move of sender /target, but in which the moves and their effects are not sufficiently known, not to mention that they cannot be exhaustively specified for the "players" *ex ante* because the "reality" is not "out there," but comes into existence by the very choices they make. To that extent assessing the use of sanctions by expecting either the removal of the other player (regime change) or a return to the status quo ante seems highly inappropriate for an assessment. As power analysis suggests, the exercise of power always creates opportunities for countervailing strategies, and in most cases even a victor needs the cooperation of the vanquished. Thus truly "unconditional surrenders" are rare and even those depend on the subsequent keeping of the peace. How different things can turn out to be when these two conditions are not met is amply demonstrated by the premature claim of victory and the hollow US announcement of the "end of hostilities" while the war in Iraq was still going on.

Furthermore, simple intentional accounts fail – even if incorporating inter-dependence of decisions – because our actions in strategic situations are usually embedded in contexts that complicate matters. If we can see that e.g. our decision will not only impact on the target but have repercussions on others, we become aware that our choices will have to take these consequences into account and that, therefore, what seemed formerly a straightforward instrumental decision has now become a choice with "multiple objectives." The latter usually do not necessarily work out like a hand fitting in a glove. On the contrary, they might involve difficult choices and result in instrumentally non-rational strategies, as the competing objectives cannot be expressed in a coherent scheme of "sub-goals." Thus the actual decision might not bring any of those about, but might be – in terms of "all things considered" – not unreasonable and perhaps at least be realizable.

Sometimes the actions that reverberate throughout a system are subject to echo effects or other mechanisms that separate even further the intended goal and the outcome. The outcome appears then as an unintended consequence of underlying structures that work themselves out "behind the back" of the agents rather than as the result of an intentional action. But again such explanations work only as long as these "structures" are reinforced by the very actions of the agents. Sometimes becoming aware of the underlying dilemmas and settling on a norm (convention) is sufficient for solving the problem; sometimes institutional solutions, changing the parameters for choice are required.[138]

---

[138] See the discussion of Hume on Conventions and on Magistrates, in Chapters 8 and 9 below.

Although these brief epistemological considerations seem rather far removed from the "practical" issue of assessing sanctions, they are of direct relevance for the following reasons. One, in defining the "success" of sanctions, policy-changes and an engagement with the opponent by "getting him to the table" seem to be a more appropriate measure than assuming that success implies either the redefinition of the game by being able to dictate who will represent the other party, or a return to the original state. As David Cortright suggests:

> The greatest benefit from sanctions comes not from their punitive impact but from their ability to prompt a bargaining process for the negotiated resolution of conflict. Sanctions work best as instruments of persuasion, when they are employed as part of carrot and stick diplomacy designed to achieve a negotiated settlement. In the twelve cases examined in our recent volume *The Sanctions Decade*, we found that sanctions often opened up a bargaining process between UN officials and the targeted regimes ...[139]

Such a shift in focus serves the purpose of placing sanctioning in a broader political context and forces us to look at strategies not solely in terms of a maximization criterion, but in terms of comparisons among and the selection of different alternatives. It allows then a better estimation of costs of different strategies and their possible combinations. Since the underlying agenda of the debate on whether economic sanctions "work" is based on the dichotomy between "force" and "other" sanctions – usually adopting by silent stipulation the effectiveness of force as the default position – the move to a broader framework, suggested long ago by Baldwin,[140] allows for a more fine-grained assessment.

Consider in this context the following problem, pointed out by Kirshner[141] when commenting on the debate between Pape and Huffbauer, Schott, and Elliott.[142] In the case of Biafra the reversal of its secession had been coded by Huffbauer and his team as a success for the sanctions policy. For Pape it represented an utter failure since it was a case of military conquest.[143] Indeed, the secessionist rebels folded when central government forces marched into the province and took over. Presumably, we are dealing here with a clear case in which force represented the *ultima ratio* bringing about the unconditional surrender of the rebel Biafra forces on January 15, 1970. But while the account of the sequence of events is correct, it does not save us from improper inferences because of its selective attention to the "facts."

What this account leaves out is not only that there had been an indecisive civil war for more than two years. During that time the Biafran forces had

---

[139] David Cortright, "Powers of Persuasion: Sanctions and Incentives in the Shaping of International Society," *International Studies*, 38:2 (2001): 113–125, at 118.
[140] See Baldwin, *Economic Statecraft*.   [141] Kirshner, "Review Essay."
[142] Hufbauer, Schott, and Elliott, *Economic Sanctions Reconsidered*. See also Elliott, "The Sanctions Glass."
[143] See Pape, "Why Economic Sanctions Do Not Work."

made a good showing with their war of attrition against the poorly equipped troops of the central government. The capitulation of the secessionists therefore came as a surprise. The decisive blow to their capacity to sustain the war seems to have been an act of economic coercion rather than a simple defeat on the battlefield. In 1968 the Nigerian government announced a change in its currency, in order to prevent Biafra from using its reserves to pay for the war. The frantic attempts by Biafran agents to unload their Nigerian holdings in the days before the change became official were obviously not very successful. They could not prevent the ensuing financial crisis in which the government was increasingly unable to pay for the war effort and support its army and staff. Thus while certainly Nigerian military forces accepted the surrender of Biafra, it is hard to dispute that it was the act of economic coercion, which cost Nigeria virtually nothing, that effectively wiped out Biafra's fiscal wherewithal.[144]

To that extent no strategy is automatically entitled to the assignment of an unproblematic default position. Besides, the experiences in Iraq indicate that even when force achieves its objective – in this case bringing about regime change – the ultimate goal for which regime change was sought, i.e. the pacification of the country, eluded the US. Thus, calculations of effectiveness frequently depend on unstated assumptions, whose erroneous nature cannot be examined if they are taken for granted and not subjected to criticism.

The above discussion of a few selected cases leads us finally to the examination of the last set of problems mentioned above that besets the sanctions debate. As critics have pointed out, assessments are usually based on the selection of a few highly salient cases but the conclusions based on such investigations fail to establish their validity because this procedure inevitably suffers from a strong selection bias.[145] Thus cases in which threats of sanctions have been made, which induced the targets to change their position, are usually not part of the database for the analysis of sanction regimes. Consequently, generalizations based on such data are highly problematic.

But since compellence is virtually always harder than deterrence, as already Schelling suggested,[146] we should not be surprised that the actual imposition of sanctions implies that the sanctioner faces a much more determined opponent who has already decided to suffer the consequences. Thus while a welfare loss of 10 percent might be unacceptable for a sender country, the same need not be true for the target, especially when it believes its national existence is threatened. In that case the same dynamics as in the Vietnam conflict obtain. Particularly when future conflict is anticipated, the targeted regime will be more determined to bear the costs and will be more sensitive to losses of face or to the relative gains that might accrue to the sanction sender if he is successful

---

[144] For this alternative explanation, see Rowe, *Manipulating the Market*.
[145] Drezner, *The Sanctions Paradox*.   [146] Schelling, *Arms and Influence*.

in his sanctioning attempt. This leads to the sanction paradox that Drezner has analyzed: sanctions will be more common, but less successful among adversaries, while between allies they will be less frequent but more successful, as the sender will be reluctant to employ them but the allied targets will be more susceptible to pressure.[147]

Furthermore, while a deterrent threat is usually clearer because of the "thus far and no further" (while the determination of the sanctioner to carry out the threat may remain unclear), what represents compliance with the demands of the sanctioner, i.e. represents a successful act of compellence, opens up all types of bargaining games, as exemplified by Saddam. What is e.g. an inspection site within the meaning of the sanctions regime, what is "unimpeded" access, what is a "material" breach of the agreement, etc., are all subject to bargaining. On the other hand, the sanctioner can also muddy the waters. In the process of enforcement he might expand the original goals and make further demands that were originally not envisaged, especially if the original measures imposed on the sanctioned turn out not to have done the trick, as the case of Yugoslavia seems to show.[148] Initially the imposition of sanctions (in May 1992) helped the republics of Slovenia, Croatia, and Bosnia to secede from the Federation. Sanctions then played a crucial role in bringing about the Dayton Accords but failed in the case of the Rambouillet peace proposals.[149] Here the addition of last-minute demands by the Western powers stiffened Milosevic's opposition.

The Yugoslav case (as well as the other examples) raises some important issues not only with regard to the appraisal of the success or failure of sanctions, but also for the epistemological issue of creating a more reliable database for their assessment. As the discussion showed, broadening the databases in order to deal with the problem of a selection bias seems an important step in improving our knowledge. But attempts to broaden the databases in order to arrive at more robust generalizations have to face several obstacles that make it doubtful whether such a goal is within reach.

The first issue is that generalizations, which are based on abstractions of theoretically significant factors in order to have a broader sample for the application of statistical techniques, are in all likelihood theoretically uninteresting. As the discussion of the "regime" variable shows, significant patterns may emerge only after the data are subsumed under different types, while overall no significant

---

[147] Drezner, *The Sanctions Paradox*.
[148] For a general account of the Yugoslavian case, see Licht, "The Use of Sanctions in Former Yugoslavia." See also Holbrooke, *To End a War*; Bondi, "Arms Embargo: In Name Only?"; de Vries, "European Union Sanctions against the Federal Republic of Yugoslavia from 1998 to 2000".
[149] See Marc Weller, "The Rambouillet Conference on Kosovo," *International Affairs*, 75:2 (1999): 211–251.

relationship might exist, because it is washed out by aggregation. After all, what might be true under all conceivable circumstances is probably uninteresting (as in the case of tautologies) or trivial.

Second, as the controversies between Pape and Huffbauer et al. show,[150] much of the disagreement centers on issues of interpretation, on judgments as to the proximate, as opposed to remote, causes, as we are virtually never able to identify the necessary and sufficient conditions of any action or event that shows any degree of complexity. But such assessments involve us in debates about the "boundaries" of the case (they are after all not natural), about motives (which in turn, as they are inaccessible to observation, might involve us in counterfactual speculations), and about "learning," which again is incompatible with the statistical requirement of the independence of cases. Simply assigning real numbers to cases in order to normalize them and allow for algebraic treatment might seem as an easy way out, but we should not forget that we have not thereby increased the "scientific" reliability of our findings. After all, the numbers are assigned according to the more or less idiosyncratic judgment of a researcher or their "group think." But they do not register *the actual behavior of the objects, which are part of a theory*, such as the case with "mass" or "velocity in physics. Even if inter-coder reliability is high, the consensus among the researchers does little to improve on the *theoretical* significance of the result, since the procedures did not meet the criteria that provide the scientific warrant.[151] Controversies will therefore remain, since looking harder at the facts or analyzing the dataset once more is unable to settle these issues. To a large extent, our "cases" are part and parcel of "stories" that not only record what happened but which are constitutive for the meaning of the actions and events.

In a perceptive analysis of the differences between Baldwin's approach to sanctions and Hufbauer and Schott's treatment, Lenway used the sanction episode of Athens against Megara as a paradigmatic example to show that the controversy goes deep indeed. Huffbauer and Schott rely on Aristophanes' account, while Baldwin uses Thucydides as a source.

By using Aristophanes as a source Hufbauer and Schott implicitly adopt the conventional wisdom that economic sanctions against Megara were ineffective in preventing the outbreak of war . . . This view also gives Pericles the major responsibility for the war because he was unwilling to revoke the decree. In contrast Baldwin adopts Thucydides'

---

[150] See Hufbauer, Schott, and Elliott, *Economic Sanctions Reconsidered*. See also Richard Hass and Meghan L. O'Sullivan, *Honey and Vinegar: Incentives, Sanctions, and Foreign Policy*, Washington, DC: Brookings Institution Press, 2000.

[151] See James Samuel Coleman, *Introduction to Mathematical Sociology*, New York: Free Press of Glencoe, 1964. See especially his discussion of "Operationalization."

view . . . In his analysis of the decree Baldwin portrays Pericles as a wise statesman who wanted to retaliate against the Megarians for their role in the battle of Sybota.[152]

The significance of these different sources is that what is in one account the incident that explodes the situation becomes in the other a last ditch effort of preventing the war! This leads me to my last point concerning the appraisal of sanctions. Given, that historical facts are not simply "there" – as if they were the statues or objects in a museum called "history"– but are rather part of the reports that come to us, they cannot be simple pictures of the events as they happened, since no untainted "overall picture" can emerge. To that extent, adhering to this scientific ideal seems to be a mistake but recognizing this is – unfortunately – not tantamount to having a clearer idea of which other and more appropriate ways of generating warranted knowledge for understanding the world of praxis exist. It will be the task of the remainder of the book to attempt such an explication.

---

[152] Stefany Ann Lenway, "Between War and Commerce: Economic Sanctions as a Tool of Statecraft," *International Organization*, 42:2 (1988): 397–426, at 410.

7   Punishing

7.1   Introduction

Our discussion of sanctioning has addressed the equivocal nature of the use of the term, as both positive and negative sanctions were included. Furthermore, as our survey of self-help measures showed, private enforcement in both the domestic and international arena concerns well-established practices and has little to do with "anarchy" in the sense of widespread anomic behavior.

There remains, however, one area in which "the law" clearly lords it over its subjects, requiring their submission by inflicting punishment on the perpetrators of a "crime." In that case, as Hannah Arendt put it: "The law's main purpose is: ·to weigh the charges brought against the accused, to render judgment and mete out due punishment."[1] While this "purpose" gave rise to a problematic understanding of law modeled after criminal law, there is of course no doubt that "capital crimes" are treated in virtually all legal systems

---

[1] See Hannah Arendt, *Eichmann in Jerusalem: A Report on the Banality of Evil*, London: Penguin Books, 1994, at 253. See also John Dewey's take on the problem of retributive justice:

> To sentimentalize over a criminal – to "forgive" because of a glow of feeling – is to incur liability for production of criminals. But to suppose that infliction of retributive suffering suffices, without reference to concrete consequences, is to leave untouched old causes of criminality and to create new ones by fostering revenge and brutality. The abstract theory of justice which demands the "vindication" of law irrespective of instruction and reform of the wrong-doer is as much a refusal to recognize responsibility as is the sentimental gush which makes a suffering victim out of a criminal.

> Courses of action which put the blame exclusively on a person as if his evil will were the sole cause of wrong-doing and those which condone offense on account of the share of social conditions in producing bad disposition, are equally ways of making an unreal separation of man from his surroundings, mind from the world.

> John Dewey, *Human Nature and Conduct: An Introduction to Social Psychology*, New York: H. Holt, 1922, at 12.

differently from simple transgressions of even such crimes[2] as fraud, negligence, or recklessness.[3]

But something more than compellence is going on in criminal law as individuals might refuse to recognize the superior authority to which they are forced to submit, or they might be "repentant" and accept the punishment, by "paying" for the deed or even sacrifice their life (in order to save their souls), or they cooperate in getting "rehabilitated" by "doing time." These different responses to the compellence of law draw our attention to the "force" behind the law, which distinguishes punishment from gratuitous exercises of violence. This force must be made "present," as the law might now stand in for the command of God, or his "authorized" sovereign (*Dei gratia*), or for the people forming a community and serving as its source. The judge pronouncing the verdict has to do so "in the name of," making thus present (or re-present) what is hidden, standing behind the particular proceedings.

This realization also entails then a change in perspective – from the outside focusing the observation on the organizational form of super- and subordination of law as a "system" – to the speech act that makes present the mysterious entity. Here the problem of international criminal law becomes obvious since the "world society" does not seem to have such a single obvious source, but is rather characterized by the polytheism of different creeds and communities which create legitimization problems for international courts when they invoke this "public" function.[4] Different from certain conventions that create otherwise unrealizable benefits, such as customary conventions or treaties, which can be neatly explained by functional necessity and the 'interests" of self-interested actors, it seems that "punishment" has to be pronounced by invoking such an ultimate source, be it God, or the "we" of people who reaffirm thereby their commonality. As Émile Durkheim observed, "it pleases us to say 'we' instead of 'I' . . . because it lends greater force [to the statement] which individual utterances lack."[5]

But if this "we" is a precondition for the legitimacy of punishment how do we arrive in the international arena at such a "we"? Here two focal points

---

[2] This is why not only must the act constitute a wrong (*actus reus*) but it also must have been perpetrated with a special intention (*dolus, mens rea*).

[3] "Recklessness" in English common law, implying the intentional disregard of harmful consequences, which are virtually certain, does not seem to have had a direct parallel in civil law systems but has developed over the last few generations in accordance with the "Finalistic theory of action: the notion of a 'crime without direct intent'." See Hans Welzel, *Das neue Bild des Strafrechtssystems: Eine Einführung in die Finale Handlungslehre*, Göttingen: Otto Schwartz, 1961.

[4] For an important discussion of this problem see Armin von Bogdandy and Ingo Vetzke, "In Whose Name? An Investigation of International Courts' Public Authority and Its Democratic Justification," *European Journal of International Law*, 23:1 (2012): 7–41.

[5] Émile Durkheim, *L'Education morale*. Paris: Presses Universitaires de France, 1974, at 203.

recommend themselves for the analysis of the role of international criminal law in the practice of international actors. One is the tracing of the rather unlikely "story" of the success of international criminal law, given the traditional international game and the reluctance of states to have *legitimate* contestants of their own authority.[6] The other is an assessment of how these new developments play out on the practical level, also raising the issue of a critical evaluation of the applicable criteria. For these purposes I shall begin my explorations in the next section (Section 7.2) by a move to "punishment" that has characterized the discourses in international law and politics over the last few decades. It indicates a considerable shift from the original vision enshrined in the UN Charter, which had given pride of place to outlawing the threat and use of force. This investigation of the significant shift in priorities occasions a closer inquiry into the auctorial "we" that authorizes these punitive measures, which I attempt in Section 7.3.

Since my inquiry suggests that this authorization derives largely from "developmental narratives" I examine in Section 7.4 two versions of this narrative. The first treats law (and within it international criminal law) as a tool for expert management of issues of common concern, fitting neatly into the governance argument but mystifying issues of legitimization. The second interprets the growth of international criminal law as a "sign" of the teleology of the human race, as suggested by Kant and similar cosmopolitan speculations, whereby the emergence of the field of international criminal law finds its justification in being interpreted as a "redemptive move" within this trans-generational narrative.

This argument then sets the stage for my interrogation in Section 7.5, which tries to get "the story" of international criminal law right by critically examining some of the conceptual shifts that have occurred when we moved from the unquestioned priority of outlawing aggressive war, to the preoccupation with perpetrators and victims, whereby an abstract conception of "victimhood" serves nowadays as the authorizing source for international criminal courts and the International Criminal Court (ICC). Unpacking these two narratives leads me then not only to some important corrections of the alleged needs or "benefits" of international criminal justice in Section 7.6. This assessment is very much in line with some of the criticism leveled in the field against the special courts and the ICC, but also with a critique of the tendency to either

---

[6] This is why Weber speaks of the state as the association which "claims" the monopoly of *legitimate* force. In other words, neither the actual possession of a monopoly is necessary – as e.g. certain groups might have legitimate enforcement powers (as did the church and universities in the Middle Ages) or "the people" might have a "right to bear arms" – nor is the existence of a monopoly (e.g. in a warlord or kleptocratic governance structure) sufficient for denying or attributing statehood to a governance structure, since such a judgment would require a "reasonable" fit with *both* criteria.

identify international criminal law *tout court* with the "growth" of international law, or even see it as a capstone for international "justice."[7]

7.2   The Move to Punishment and Its Problems

As many observers of international law and international relations have noticed, there has been an undeniable shift in public debates to more "punitive measures," justifying the use of force rather than restricting its scope as had been the original intent of the League and of the UN Charter. This might be the price we have to pay when our identification of evil shifts from "war" – especially "aggressive war" – to "justice" and the "enforcement" of human rights. To that extent the fascination among professionals and the public with ending the era of impunity by giving "justice priority over politics,"[8] and bringing the perpetrators of crimes, particularly those that "shock humanity," to justice, is understandable. However, the bitter truth might be that in doing so, we risk – despite the best of intentions – getting neither peace nor justice. As Anthony Lang's survey of different punitive practices in present international politics suggests:

War crimes trials, economic sanctions,[9] punitive interventions[10] and counter-terrorism policies – international society have become increasingly punitive in recent years. As these punitive practices increase, justice and peace appear no closer. Intended to enforce rules designed to create more justice and peace in the system these punitive practices, in fact, appear to be making the international system more violent and unjust.[11]

The reason is not only that military force is a rather blunt and frequently overrated instrument, but that creating order means more than "doing the right thing" even in a series of occasions. Rather, one has to change a *system of expectations* among the actors precisely because enforcement must be distinguishable from random violence. This is what Hobbes clearly saw, even though he put too much trust in force being able to bring this transformative

---

[7] After all, issues of international "justice" had until recently been limited to distributive problems.
[8] See e.g. the claim by David Scheffer: "In the civilized world's box of foreign policy tools this [international criminal law] will be the *shining new hammer to swing* [emphasis added] in the years to come" in David J. Scheffer, "International Judicial Intervention," *Foreign Policy*, 102 (1996): 34–51, at 51.
[9] For example, those holding the civilian population hostage and inflicting harm on them, as did the sanctions in Iraq.
[10] Those aiming at "regime change."
[11] Anthony F. Lang, *Punishment, Justice and International Relations: Ethics and Order after the Cold War*, London: Routledge, 2008, at 65. Since Lang is backing up his "hunch" with a detailed examination of different types of interventions having a punitive dimension ranging from 1950 to 2005 his suspicion is borne out. Out of a total of 122 military interventions 22 were punitive, and 16 of those 22 (72 percent) have taken place since the end of the Cold War (i.e. between 1989 and 2005).

change about. Absent such a common belief, force can only create the peace of the graveyard, to which Kant ironically referred in his *Perpetual Peace*.[12] The forceful "interventions" are then more akin to drive-by shootings that quickly become unsustainable at home – given their cost and doubtful benefits – as well as in the target society, where they stiffen resistance and expose the "dark side of humanitarianism."[13] The problems arise then not only out of the well-intended but mistaken motives of the interveners or their self-serving propaganda, but out of conceptual befuddlements in dealing with some genuine dilemmas created by the interaction of force, authority, autonomy, and justice.

Casting the conceptual net wider allows for a more fruitful analysis of the development of international criminal law that had, for a while, been the rage after the creation of the ICC. At times, it even led to fears that international criminal law would displace the human rights discourse and become the preferred means of communication for politicians, practitioners, and academics alike. This was worrisome since the present mood in the profession showed a clear preference for certainty over contestation, for action over analysis, and for seemingly straightforward solutions.[14] These fears are perhaps exaggerated, particularly since the field of international criminal law is far from being uncontroversial[15] and the practice of the ICC has been subject to sustained criticism from all quarters.[16] Nevertheless, a critical reflection is badly needed.

An interdisciplinary approach is therefore helpful in making us aware of some of the implicit underlying assumptions of the narratives within which the creation of special criminal courts and the agreement for a permanent international criminal court are embedded. The preferred genre of such narratives is one of evolution or progress by which the past – as in the Hague Conventions and Geneva Protocols, which were addressed to states imposing on them the duty to instruct their troops and prosecute violations for war crimes – is considered only the prologue for the "breakthrough" at Nuremberg and Tokyo. Efforts at creating ad hoc international tribunals trying individuals found their completion in the establishment of a permanent international criminal court.

---

[12] See "Perpetual Peace," initial paragraph, in Hans Reiss (ed.), *Kant's Political Writings*, at 93.
[13] David Kennedy, *The Dark Side of Virtue: Reassessing International Humanitarianism*, Princeton: Princeton University Press, 2005.
[14] See Christine E.J. Schwöbel, "The Comfort of International Criminal Law," *Law and Critique*, 24:2 (2012): 169–191.
[15] See Cassese et al., *Cassese's International Criminal Law*; Marchuk, *The Fundamental Concept of Crime in International Law*.
[16] See Kamari Maxine Clarke, *Fictions of Justice: The International Criminal Court and the Challenge of Legal Pluralism in Sub-Saharan Africa*, Cambridge: Cambridge University Press, 2009; Triestino Mariniello, *The International Criminal Court in Search of Its Purpose and Identity*, London: Routledge, 2015. See also the special issue on the ICC in *Law and Contemporary Problems*, 76:3–4 (2013).

However, such a narrative imposes a coherence upon events that derives its prima facie persuasiveness from the fact that we can always draw a straight line between two points. Besides, it is also problematic in a more fundamental sense, because it fails to analyze the unresolved conceptual issues within international criminal law, in which competing goals (deterrence, punishment, reconciliation) sit uneasily with each other,[17] as they do in domestic criminal law. These conflicts inevitably create policy dilemmas for domestic orders, as exemplified by the Scandinavian approach, whereby an apparently sane but thoroughly radicalized killer acting out his racial fantasies could murder seventy-seven innocent people yet only be sentenced to seventeen years in prison.[18] Compare this judgment to the responses to similar attacks e.g. in the US (the Oklahoma bombing, torture memoranda, not to mention "signature strikes"). It is therefore not surprising that such dilemmas of prosecution and sentencing also appear in international criminal law.

This realization has several corollaries. First, this narrative assumes that we are all "on the same bus" that leads us to the kingdom of ends. There truth will speak to power and the painful dilemmas disappear, as they are authoritatively resolved by the speech act of sentencing that invokes "humanity." Second, the claim of death of sovereignty for which the establishment of the ICC is sometimes taken might be as mistaken as the popular version of the death of God. This is not only because such a storyline does not examine how sovereignty and international tribunals are actually intertwined. Optimistically, we could say that this is the "complementarity" which the Rome Statute of the ICC envisages.[19] More critically, we could see in the arrangements between states and the ICC, and between the court and the UN, an uneasy mediation of a conflict which is bound to occur when parallel legal regimes exist. Here

---

[17] See e.g. the discussion about amnesty, transitional justice, and reconciliation. Geoffrey Robertson, *Crimes against Humanity: The Struggle for Global Justice*, London: Allen Lane, 1999; Mark A. Drumbl, *Atrocity, Punishment, and International Law*, Cambridge: Cambridge University Press, 2007; Edel Hughes, William Schabas, and Ramesh Chandra Thakur (eds.), *Atrocities and International Accountability beyond Transitional Justice*, New York: United Nations University Press, 2007; Louise Mallinder, *Amnesty, Human Rights and Political Transitions: Bridging the Peace and Justice Divide*, Oxford: Hart, 2008; Mark Freeman, *Necessary Evils, Amnesties and the Search for Justice*, Cambridge: Cambridge University Press, 2009; Mark Osiel, *Making Sense of Mass Atrocity*, Cambridge: Cambridge University Press, 2009.

[18] I refer here to Anders Breivik, sentenced by an Oslo court on August 23, 2012 for the killing of seventy-seven persons in July 2011.

[19] See Article 1 of the Rome Statute, providing that the court as a permanent institution shall have jurisdiction "for the most serious crimes of international concern ...[which] shall be complementary to national criminal jurisdiction." United Nations General Assembly, *Rome Statute of the International Criminal Court* (1998 [2002]).

support comes from the different takes on immunity and command responsibility by the ICTY and the ICC.

Third, its narrative fails to convey the complex interaction between politics and law by making it appear that finally the problem of politics has been solved, making it thoroughly subordinate not only to law, but to a professional class of judges, academics, and advocacy groups that have tamed "sovereignty" of the state by the elaboration of universal principles, applying to us all as humans. While taking this absolute point of view is characteristic of "morality," such a "construction" misidentifies or passes over the problem intrinsic to politics and law alike, such as the inevitability of different value hierarchies and the need to seek assent to decisions which cannot rely on algorithms. After all, it is cold comfort that the main competing approaches to morals, consequentialist and deontological, are in agreement that such an absolute point is needed, but cannot be found, as the persisting deep disagreements indicate, so that we cannot hope that our practical problems will be resolved by either taking a "moral point of view" or by dissolving praxis into theory.

The point here is not that politics and morals have nothing to do with each other, as realists sometimes suggest; the point is rather that, save in a universal empire, political obligations cannot simply be "derived" from universal standards, be they justice, human dignity, nature, or whatever. Not only are "judgments" required that follow a different "logic," there are also particular obligations, which are not instantiations of universal principles satisfying the criteria of the "moral point of view." For example, I am obliged to my family not because they are members of the human race, but because they stand in special relationship to me, which has independent value and is only trivially related to our common humanity. Similarly, an Australian, Brazilian, French or Latvian has to abide by the laws of their respective country not because it represents a just regime, but because s/he is a citizen and subject, and s/he cannot justify noncompliance by choosing another just (or even more just) regime, without having first changed the particular allegiance. The decisive point thus is that it is the "sacrifice" one is willing to accept and which the group demands (and can expect), and not some cognitive principle, that commands assent because of its "universality." But it is precisely this existential link between the individual and the community – visible only briefly in oaths of allegiance – which is not brought into view or is passed over in liberal political theory by considering the state a mere mutual benefit association.

While one might be inclined to think that the reference to "sacrifice" is perhaps just an atavistic remnant of politics, and people in "secular" modernity actually try to maximize their gains, the close connection of citizen and soldier suggests – as is particularly evident in republican theory – that there is more to it than the standard liberal version of obligations allows for. As to the "secularization" thesis: the recent increase in suicide missions[20] and, even more worrisome, the fact that these deeds are being carried out not only by the downtrodden who have nothing to lose, but by "fighters" who grew up in Western middle-class environments and converted e.g. to the IS, reminds us that social reality might be more complicated.

Although the cases of this "unexplainable" turn to self-immolation by Western youth fighting for another cause and becoming terrorists in their home country are still rare, they cannot be dismissed as unimportant "outliers." For one, they are tightly linked to new forms of organized violence operating internationally and therefore differ significantly from individual acts of self-sacrifice, such as e.g. Jan Palach setting himself on fire in Prague (January 1969) to protest the Soviet invasion of Czechoslovakia. Even more importantly, those exceptional actions have *exemplary relevance* since they fundamentally affect the other members of the society. For the actions threaten our *standard beliefs* in how both socialization and the general "awe" of the law work. No wonder that one hears increasingly frequent calls for more security. Vigilantism on the part of the public and surveillance by the government both increase, and at the same time infringements on basic rights and even torture become accepted, as fears about the "terrorist" and ticking bombs increasingly dominate the political imagination.[21]

Significantly, in criminal law, both domestic and international, a new class of perpetrators is being created, as the "enemy criminal law" shows. Something like the *ex lex* or the *hostis humani generis* has reappeared, separating the normal criminal from the "enemy" criminal.[22] The "enemy," however, is no longer simply "foreign," protected also by the laws of war, but it is the "unlawful combatant," who even as a "citizen" has lost his rights, and who can be executed without due process and a formal conviction through a signature strike.

It is cold comfort indeed that those fundamental changes have occurred not through violent revolution or surrender to an external "enemy," but largely

---

[20] For an illuminating account of the different types of suicide missions, see Jon Elster, "Motivations and Beliefs in Suicide Missions" in Diego Gambetta (ed.), *Making Sense of Suicide Missions*, Oxford: Oxford University Press, 2005: 233–258; Diego Gambetta, "Can We Make Sense of Suicide Missions?" in Diego Gambetta (ed.), *Making Sense of Suicide Missions*, Oxford: Oxford University Press, 2005: 259–300. A similar picture emerges from Robert Pape's analysis. Of the 315 suicide missions between 1980 and 2005, 301 have been part of a collective campaign, and more than half of them have been led by non-religious organizations. See Robert Anthony Pape, *Dying to Win: The Strategic Logic of Terrorism*, New York: Random House, 2005.

[21] See e.g. Ayşe Zarakol, "What Makes Terrorism Modern?: Terrorism, Legitimacy, and the International System," *Review of International Studies*, 37:5 (2011): 2311–2336.

[22] See e.g. the German discussion among criminal lawyers spawned by the work of Günther Jakobs, "Bürgerstrafrecht und Feindstrafrecht," *HRRS: Onlinezeitschrift für Höchstrichterliche Rechtsprechung zum Strafrecht*, 3 (2004): 88–95.

through the activities of jurists, who, as teachers of law, are mainly concerned with doctrine, or who, as practicing lawyers, are working for their client, i.e. mainly the executive branch of government, or who as judges, serve in a secret parallel system of courts. To that extent the newest developments hardly bear out hopes that more and more law and more judicialization[23] will lead us to mankind's destiny, or at least a cosmopolitan order in which the law not only rules, but instantiates the traditional values of a rule of law (subjective rights, separation of powers, publicity, due process, presumption of innocence, prohibition of torture and degrading treatment, etc.). All this does not augur well for buttressing the larger point that sees in the growth of international criminal law the crowning achievement of the establishment of the "rule of law" in the "anarchy" of international relations. However, before we jump to conclusions let us return to the examination of the "we" invoked in international criminal law and its narratives.

7.3   The "We" and Authorization

To hold someone accountable by meting out punishment, rather than simply frustrating his misdeeds or imposing a sanction, presupposes that the wrong inflicted by the perpetrator on the victim is of special gravity, as the deed was not only wrong but was executed with guile and a special intent to harm. To that extent the "repair" requires a hostile response to the acting perpetrator, making sure that he gets what he "deserves" (*desert condition*). This condition then raises the question of the severity of the punishment (*fit condition*), such as e.g. Kant's argument for limiting the retribution to the *lex talionis*, or Beccaria's argument for the proportionality of punishment, finding their echo also in the constitutional prohibition of cruel and unusual punishment. Finally, the third condition addresses the issue of *authorization*, which licenses someone to exact retribution from the perpetrator.

Although these conditions are intertwined, they do raise separate problems and point in different directions in penology, as they give rise to the discussion of the "purposes" of criminal law and the appropriate ordering among these elements when sentencing a perpetrator. After all, the need for *ex post* retribution, which frequently cannot "repair" the victim's loss, is also powerfully reinforced by the deterrence argument which buttresses law's ability to order

---

[23] See e.g. the special issue on Legalization and World Politics in *International Organization*, vol. 54, no. 3 (Summer 2000) in which "delegation," i.e. third party dispute settlement, represents the judizialization within the process of legalization. Sometimes this argument comes in the form that not the proliferation of courts on the international level but cooperation among the "community of national courts" acting as deputies of the international legal order (in terms of Scelle's *dédoublement fonctionelle*) provides the solution. See Anne-Marie Slaughter, "A Global Community of Courts," *Harvard International Law Journal*, 44:3 (2003): 191–220.

society prospectively. Here, of course, disagreements abound concerning the actual deterrent value of criminal sanctions, especially when we realize that our jails have become places for advanced training in criminal activities rather than institutions for personal contrition and rehabilitation. Similarly, the "rational" expectation that the more exacting punishments should also have greater deterrent value – particularly among those perpetrators who, as recidivists, are unlikely to be reformed[24] – is not only contradicted by experience, but also limited by the injunction against "cruel and unusual punishment" as well as by common sense. Thus, hardly anybody will be impressed by a threat posted in an elevator, "Smoking in the elevators will be punished by death." Consequently, given the uncertainties of deterrence, alternatives focusing on rehabilitation rather than desert and fit attain their plausibility.

While much of the moral and legal discourse in penology has foregrounded the desert-and-fit conditions, the authorization condition has received much less attention since "law" in modernity has become part and parcel of the state project. The state has become the official avenger, except in cases celebrated in various Western movies, where the failure of public order makes it necessary for individuals to become "virtuous avengers." It is upon them to mete out "rough justice" insuring that perpetrators get what they deserve. The authorization is then usually provided by the special relationship that the avenger had to the victim, showing clearly its pedigree in ancient notions of blood revenge and self-help. Thus only Achilles can avenge the death of his friend Patroclus, and it is only Ethan Edwards in John Ford's classic Western *The Searchers* who can pursue the murderer of his brother's family and free his abducted niece

Thus while the marginalization of the authorization condition – raising distinct political problems of legitimization – is understandable, it remains nevertheless of high importance even under conditions of well-institutionalized vengeance, as the following thought experiment shows. A convicted murderer and child molester, having exhausted all appeals, is awaiting his execution, but he is killed in what turns out to be his last visit to the prison-yard. One of his arch-enemies in the penitentiary gets "even" with him by stabbing him to death for all the "disrespect" he has shown him over the years. As the result is the same as in the case of being executed, and although his death might even evoke cheers among the other inmates – or even among people on the outside – we could hardly call this a "punishment," despite the fact that it is done with

---

[24] Here "rationalists" have correctly pointed out that it is not punishment per se but punishment plus the risk of being caught and convicted that count and thus the various steps of the "compliance mechanism" confront public authorities with genuine dilemmas for policy and allocating resources to strengthening "prevention and detection" of misdeeds (discovery, identification of "priors," forensics,) "processing" (indictment, conviction), and finally "execution" (punishment).

obvious popular approval. "The people" (in the sense of a multitude of persons) is not the people in whose name such punishment is authorized.

Here the close connection between politics and law, independent of the moral question of desert and fit, becomes visible. This can also be seen from Charles I's defense in his trial, in which he persistently challenged the legitimacy of the proceedings against him by insisting that his parliamentary opponents must provide the source of authority for their trial. In the absence of an "official" avenger we either have some regulated yet persistent problem of "private revenge" in blood feuds, as discussed above, or we can have the Hobbesian war of all against all, a situation more likely to occur when the "state has failed" and no customary limits exist anymore. The use of (show) trials and of spectacular executions is then one of the means by which opponents are not only eradicated, but the failure of their political project is demonstrated. There remains no common ground, no common tradition, no common goal one could appeal to.

The "enemy" is then no longer one, as in traditional societies, with whom one duels and to whom one pays respect by accepting his challenge, even if it means a fight to death. The enemy also loses the status of *justus hostis*, as in the *ius publicum Europaeum*,[25] who enjoys a certain protection as he is only as the agent of his sovereign an "enemy" (but not a criminal). Instead as the servant of evil he now becomes the enemy of God – most obviously for the fundamentalist, but also for some more "enlightened" representatives of "humanity." If all meaning issues from the sacred, neither politics nor (moral) philosophy matters. If one can be fully human only within a community of true believers, then any similarity between those outside and those inside is more or less fortuitous and irrelevant.

Again one might be inclined to ascribe such fundamentalist tropes to some atavistic tendencies were it not for the fact that some uncanny parallels can be discovered between the "atavistic" and "progressive" discourses, as the justifications for the "war on terror" show. Then, parallel to the normal (citizen) criminal law, an "enemy criminal" emerges, featuring, as already mentioned, the former *hostis humani generis*, who is beyond the pale, even though he comes in a new garb. The appeal to the "sacred" seems then, despite all the secularism and progressivism of the Enlightenment project, to be just around the corner. As President Clinton put it, "our sacred task is to work to banish this great crime against humanity."[26] And perhaps those allusions are not that

[25] Carl Schmitt, *The Nomos of the Earth in the International Law of the Jus Publicum Europaeum*, trans. G.L. Ulmen, New York: Telos Press, 2003.
[26] As quoted in Immi Tallgren, "Who Are 'We' in International Criminal Law? On Critics and Membership" in Christine E.J. Schwöbel (ed.), *Critical Approaches to International Criminal Law: An Introduction*, Abingdon: Routledge, 2014, 71–95, at 71.

fortuitous either since, as Paul Kahn suggests, the construction of meaning is intrinsically linked to sacrifice and existential commitments.

No one sacrifices himself for the maintenance of the WTO, even if one truly believes in the justice of this project. No one pledges allegiance to the United Nations, much as we might appreciate its efforts in support of international justice ... Justice as a moral norm simply does not create an obligation of sacrifice, although it surely creates obligations of redistribution. Redistribution is not sacrifice no matter how much it takes from the wealthy.

... There was no appeal to the social contract in the trenches of World War I and none on the Eastern Front in World War II. Nuclear weapons would not be imaginable if the state were only a vehicle for the enforcement of a just legal regime seeking individual well being. To understand the threat of such destruction, we need to distinguish pledge from contract, and love from self-interest.[27]

These remarks not only suggest that conceiving of the problem of politics in terms of justice and distributional issues might be far too narrow, despite the contemporary foible for such an approach.[28] Instead, the quote above draws attention to other existential issues, such as security, highlighting its paradoxes, which already Rousseau pointed out.[29] Strangely enough, they have become much more salient under modern conditions. The state provides security to the individual in exchange for their willingness to sacrifice their life, which in the nuclear age is purchased at the price of latent annihilation (even in times of peace!). The fact that the ICJ could not "answer" the questions put to it for an advisory opinion concerning the (il)legality of nuclear weapons[30] indicates that at the limits of law the "awful" quality of the sovereign (state) as a "mortal god" emerges to which Hobbes pointed. In line with the ambiguity of the term, the sovereign state keeps not only the individuals "in awe"[31] but it shows its awful side by requiring human sacrifices.

---

[27] Paul W. Kahn, *Sacred Violence: Torture, Terror, and Sovereignty*, Ann Arbor: Michigan University Press, 2008, at 113.

[28] See Rawls and the enormous literature he has spawned by (mis-)identifying the problem of justice as *the* political problem. For a further discussion, see Kratochwil, *The Status of Law in World Society*.

[29] See Rousseau, *The Social Contract and Discourse on the Origin and Foundation of Inequality among Mankind*, bk. I, chap. 8. at 22f.

> The passage of the state of nature to the civil state produces in man a very remarkable change, by substituting in his conduct justice for instinct and by giving his actions the moral quality that they previously lacked.
>
> ... he ought to bless the happy moment that released him for ever, and transformed him from a stupid and ignorant animal to an intelligent being and man.

[30] See *Legality of the Threat or Use of Nuclear Weapons*, International Court of Justice, Advisory Opinion of 8 July (1996), at 226.

[31] Hobbes, *Leviathan*, pt. I, chap. 13, at 185.

Emphasizing the particular and its relations to powerful noncognitive factors, such as love and sacrifice, does not mean, of course, the "particular" is determinate and identical throughout history. After all, we have "learned," more by rote than cognition, to be not only loyal to our next of kin, but also to extend ourselves to "others," who are members of different clans or cities, as Aristotle's *synoikismos* of the *phyles* coming together in the new social formation of the *polis*, suggested. This is the same phenomenon we also observe later in the consolidation of states. In the latter case, this move was powerfully reinforced by the national myth that lent legitimacy to the state by interpreting it as an expression of the "nation."[32] But precisely because of this conceptual link that conferred legitimacy, nationalism meant the death knell to some "states," i.e. multi-ethnic empires.[33]

Thus crucial for the success of such new "imagined communities" seems to be that they connect individuals to each other through the symbols of the sacred and of an "origin" that implies existential commitments. Thus Lincoln referred in the Gettysburg address to "those who gave their lives here so that we might live."[34] But he thereby only revisits a familiar *topos* that ranges from Pericles' famous funeral oration[35] to Churchill's promise of blood, sweat and tears. The same commitment to sacrifice is rehearsed and re-enacted in the innumerable ceremonies of memorial days.[36] The imagery evoked on such occasions creates a continuity, linking the past to the present, as it phrases the present troubles and travails in terms of the legacy of the ancestors to the present generation, which puts the latter under a special obligation. This makes the community not only an ongoing, but also a transgenerational concern, thus combating the fears of insignificance, death, and extinction.

Seen from this angle it becomes clear why "genocide," i.e. the physical elimination of an entire group, or even of its cultural heritage and traditions by destroying their temples and monuments, burning their books, or forbidding the use of their language, becomes the "ultimate" crime. But it also explains why we as humans, having to deal with our mortality and the threat of evil, universally recognize this as a misery. Our solution to this predicament seems,

---

[32] Tamir, *Liberal Nationalism*.
[33] This became obvious not only after World War I, when "self-determination" served as a new form of legitimacy, but also at the end of the Cold War. One of the first indications of a possible disintegration of the Soviet Union came when perestroika and glasnost undermined the two main forces of integration – the infallibility of the Communist Party, and the apparatus of repression – and enlistment for the Soviet army precipitously declined while that of the "national republics" dramatically increased.
[34] Abraham Lincoln, *Gettysburg Address, November 19* (1863). Available at http://avalon.law .yale.edu/19th_century/gettyb.asp.
[35] See Thucydides, *History of the Peloponnesian War*, trans. Rex Warner, London: Penguin Books, 1972, bk. II, at paras. 34–46.
[36] See below, Chapter 8.

however, closer to the extreme situation of trying to reach a lifeboat than to extending our sympathies to "all." We take care of ourselves, our children, and family, but we do not see ourselves ambling down with all the others the broad highway into the Promised Land.

This leads to the apparent paradox that we often phrase our claims in universal language while trying to protect particular values and particular ways of life. This criticism is often made about liberals, who advocate the rule of law but tend to "operationalize" it in terms of their particular preferences, i.e. for open markets, property rights and equality (whereby the glaring divergence between claim and reality becomes rather quickly apparent). But the above reflections show that such myopias are rather common, indicating a more serious conceptual problem.

Such a stance emphasizing the particular instead of the universal could be misunderstood as an invitation to "relativism" and the surefire way of arguing that anything goes, against which only an extra heavy dose of armchair philosophy can help. But such conclusions follow, and such fears are justified, only if we assume that the binary logic of the categorical is/is-not distinction obtains across all domains and provides the decisive distinction that cannot be overridden by other concerns. However, as Kant already argued in the case of aesthetic judgments – and the above discussion of authorization suggested more generally – law and politics might follow a different logic since there propositional truths are not at issue. After all, law is *valid*, not true (vide its counterfactual validity!). Similarly, the "equality" of others is not a natural fact, ascertainable by a look at our common DNA, as then "small differences," such as racial markers, could "account for" (or rather be used for) racial discrimination. Equality has rather to be "established" by mutual recognition and ascription *through commitment*. When Jefferson claimed, "we hold these truths to be self-evident,"[37] the importance of his message does not lie in its propositional content but rather in the commitment issuing from the declaratory "we hold." That a sizable part of the population is not even "recognized" and therefore excluded (women and slaves) does little to weaken the force of the commitment by citing disconfirming evidence. The dynamic works the other way: rather than undermining the commitment, it provides "irritating" evidence for the hypocrisy of not following up on the declaration and, by implication, for the need to bring behavior into conformity with the commitment.[38]

---

[37] Library of Congress, "Thomas Jefferson, Declaration of Independence: Right to Institute New Government," 2000, www.loc.gov/exhibits/jefferson/jeffdec.html.

[38] Of course, this does not entitle us to conclude that compliance is the logical result, since norms are not causes but also allow for exceptions and exemptions. Similarly, one norm might get trumped by another norm (not only by a higher "principle") under certain circumstances. But whether norms are followed or not in a particular case or whatever norm a court might decide to

Since the understanding of commitments is crucial for the analysis of social order, the theory of speech acts has provided us with some conceptual tools, instead of remaining within the prison house of "descriptivism" and its aporias, such as the dichotomies of facts and values, of description/prescription, of emotions vs. cognitions, all of which have increasingly become problematic. Searle's discussion about verdictives, commissives, behabitives provides here for a more fine-grained analysis by taking attitudes and different perspectives (actor vs. bystander) into account.[39]

On the other hand one has to be careful with the inference that since the fathers have left a legacy to posterity, their heirs will necessarily have to honor it and take it as a rule for action, as this leaves out the processes of vetting and of making changes, without which commitments would be not much more than flipping a coin or perhaps placing a bet. Other possibilities exist: the heirs cannot simply ignore their heritage, or only pay lip service to it, or refuse to live up to it when defects are identified. Of course, in domestic society the existence of a constitution shaping the political process through exacting majority requirements might safeguard the legacy and shore up commitments, but the critical point is that what future generations make of the commitments and of the opportunities which cannot simply be read off the legacy itself. On the other hand the mandated "we" need not become hollow, but can continue to have Bourdieu's "oracle effect"[40] even though the circumstances have changed dramatically and the ascertainment of the "original intent" becomes now a matter of arcane exegesis of a "holy text" by a "court."

In the case of the "international community" or "humanity" this speech act can easily misfire since there is no community in place that links symbolization to action, absence to presence, and that authorizes a speaker to act in its name. The suspicion of "usurpation," hollowness, and the disingenuous use of the "absent" arise here much more easily, as Carl Schmitt pointed out.[41] But even if such invocations are not simply self-serving gambits for particular interests, disguised as appeals to universal values, but sincerely espouse cosmopolitan goals by making "humanity" the object reference, – as e.g. in the case among NGOs and legal activists – utilizing such a strategy might over time succeed in changing the imaginary of politics. Here Hannes Peltonen has pointed out that such appeals in invocations can function like central tendencies that emerge

---

apply, norms provide criteria for criticism and the legitimization of actions even if they did not cause an action.

[39] See Austin, *How to Do Things with Words*, Lecture XII.

[40] See Pierre Bourdieu, *Language and Symbolic Power*, Cambridge, MA: Harvard University Press, 1991, at 211. In other words in the case of a group "representing" the absent, the speech act has a constitutive effect by bringing it "again" into existence.

[41] "Whoever invokes humanity wants to cheat." Carl Schmitt, *The Concept of the Political*, trans. Georg Schwab, Chicago: University of Chicago Press, 1996, at 54.

from the drawing and redrawing of e.g. circles that do not have a common central point but converge towards an identifiable form.[42] However, there is also a downside to this: since no concept can have an inside without an outside and since "humanity" has no "enemy" – unless we are ready to rule certain individuals and groups out of the human universe – such "globalizing" concepts can quickly turn up in the armory of those engaging in witch hunts. This danger perhaps explains Kant's lack of enthusiasm for a global empire, opting instead for a "league."

Since such speech acts can entail some dangerous gambits, we frequently use some more "positive" strategies for dealing with problems of "existential choices." Here I want to focus in a preliminary fashion on the strategies by which we try to make sense out of the changes we see and which are brought about by our actions and political projects, but which, in their sometimes far-reaching and quite troubling implications, are not perspicuous to us. In that case the narrative of "progress" serves as a powerful conveyor of meaning and of getting on with life, instead of being stymied. This narrative seems to come in two versions: One, more "technical," is indebted to the logic of productive knowledge, taking the undeniable increase in mastery over nature as its paradigm. The other is more rooted in a secularized version of eschatological hope. It reasons from a supposedly given end-state of "humanity" backwards, by trying to identify the events which could serve as "signs" foreshadowing the ultimate end. The first emphasizes more the technical managerial aspects of the artifice of social order as well as its "functional" aspects and requirements, the other is rooted in soteriological versions of knowledge or moral intuition.

Oddly enough, both play down or even deny the need to meet the challenges of incoherence – and its concomitant anxieties – through an engagement with praxis, i.e. wrestling with the actual political and moral challenges, in which neither technology nor managerial know-how "solves" our problems. There no prophet – whether clad in political, philosophical, or legal garb – knows the future and can show us the way without further ado. Even if she attracts a following, which in time can become a political force, in all likelihood she will do so only by creating countervailing forces. The latter are usually promptly ignored since they represent, nearly by definition, either misguided "idiots" (living in their own world) or worse, "reactionaries," i.e. malfeasants beyond the pale.

For sure, the discordant voices can be silenced or marginalized – and here law plays a decisive role in making "rule" and orthodoxies possible – but the ensuing silence is most often bought at a heavy price. One cannot force others to become moral, and it seems nearly equally difficult to "make them" endorse

---

[42] Hannes Peltonen "Re-drawing Boundaries: Fuzzy Boundaries, Conceptual Spectrums, and Polity Comparison" (mimeo, 2014).

one's political project without "bringing them around" to share one's view. Thus forcing people to accept their "own good" undermines both law and morals alike. While liberal theory has been well aware of the problems of placing the notion of the "good" ahead of everything else, it seems that few theorists have appreciated the dangers that flow from the self-authorization of their particular project on the basis of some "ultimate" values or principles.

Applied to our discussion of authorization in international criminal law, that means that law will never be able to displace politics. But we also cannot dissolve politics into morals, as it is parasitic on both of them, being part of the domain of praxis. Conversely, it also means that neither politics nor morals can stand alone despite the fact that modern ethics has tried to do so by a "transcendental turn" suggesting that the most important issue consists in the clarification of principles, encouraging thereby an "ideal theory" for the understanding of praxis. While I plan to address this problem in the following chapters, for the moment I want to return to the initial puzzle of the successful emergence of international criminal law and of the two dominant narratives, which offer an explanation.

7.4   The Narratives of Law as Management and Law as Deliverance

As mentioned above, the emergence of international criminal law seems rather odd since states have always regarded punishment (like security) as their main business and – as the flipside – the capacity to punish has been identified by many advocates of the ICC as a victory over the state and its claims to sovereign immunity. This "oddity" is then explained – if not in a straightforward causal fashion – by endowing several developments with meaning and placing them in a narrative, which connects several events that changed the character of the post-World War II international order. Let us therefore consider first the narrative of management.

Law as Management

Several factors are usually adduced to explain both the popularity of such an approach to law and, by extension, the allure that international criminal law represents as its capstone. First, there is no doubt that the growing inter-dependencies in the post World War II era furthered the "deformalization" of law in the international arena, thus affecting the constitutive norms of the international game by attributing more and more significance to other traditional or nontraditional "sources" of law. Here the ascendance of custom over the contractual paradigm of international order has to be mentioned. It reversed not only the allegedly dominant trend from custom to treaty – which had been a constitutive part of the modernization discourse – it also accepted the existence of "soft law," or made the norms developed by nonstate actors (international organizations, scientific associations, global networks of public and private agencies, etc.) through incorporation by courts, or official agencies, part of "hard law."

The second development, which suggested that we were heading towards an era of post-sovereignty, was the European project. By the late 1950s it had moved out of its sectoral fetters, first towards a still functionalist, but at least in conception, sectoral order, i.e. the fully integrated market (Rome Treaties 1957), and only afterwards towards a more comprehensive "Union" (Maastricht 1992).[43]

The third development concerns the prominence which human rights attained. Originally, they were a "state project," taken up by the West to induce change in the Soviet empire. In exchange for accepting the USSR as an equal partner through the SALT treaties and accepting the de facto status quo in Europe, the Helsinki Accords mentioned them in "basket three," which over time developed an unexpected dynamism. When they were taken up by the newly forming networks of domestic and international society they ceased to be only an instrument of state power, as they created a new agenda.[44] To that extent Moyn's argument identifying the link between international social movements and human rights as a "game changer" is justified, especially if we consider it in conjunction with the fourth development: the end of the Cold War. This ushered in hopes for a New World Order, particularly since the old enemy, the Soviet Union, agreed not only to the demise of its empire, but had also adopted the domestic reform programs of glasnost and perestroika and sought new cooperative ventures, some within the UN and even together with NATO,[45] at times apparently even floating the idea of joining NATO.[46]

---

[43] Although here the free movement of persons conceived (in its commoditized form as "labour" only) created new complexities because real persons raise issues of social and fiscal policy which remained in the national domain, even after the introduction of a common currency (1999) and the realization that Europe is not an "optimum currency area" and that therefore the euro could neither count on economic logic nor the support of well-institutionalized practices familiar from some nation states. Instead it was supported only by some legal norms which were not self-enforcing and not enforceable except in crisis situations in which economic collapse was a distinct possibility, which in the absence of a sanction of exit or a possible bankruptcy created a chicken game among debtors and lenders.

[44] For the importance of the link between human rights and social movements see Samuel Moyn, *The Last Utopia: Human Rights in History*, Cambridge, MA: Harvard University Press, 2010.

[45] See e.g. The Partnership for Peace of 1994 and the establishment of a permanent Council for consultation in 1997 (NATO–Russia Founding Act).

[46] Although this idea seems to have been informally floated by Yeltsin, the only open source I could find was an interview with Vladimir Putin on March 5, 2000, when the new strongman in the Kremlin remarked in the popular telecast *Breakfast with Frost* that "there was no reason why Russia should not join NATO as long as it would be treated as an equal," at www.news.bbc.ca.uk, March 5, 2005.

With the traditional security threats disappearing, the institutional trends seemed to indicate a decisive turn to the post-sovereign era, in which *new governance* structures rather than the insistence of states on their sovereignty and their right of judging the *competency of competence* attained prominence. To that extent the move to international criminal law was part of a larger syndrome. Given that regulation already occurred largely beyond the confines of nation states,[47] there seemed no reason to think that this process could not be pursued further in the post-national era.

After all, are not decisions about the "competency of competence" inherently *legal* decisions, which courts rather than governments can decide, as the Tadić case at the ICTY[48] showed? Finally – and this was supposed to be international criminal law's finest hour – was it not time to claim universal jurisdiction over the gross violation of human rights and humanitarian law, ending impunity once and for all? Belgium and Spain were not alone the avant-garde of a much broader movement, as even the UK's House of Lords scrutinized the sovereign immunity claims of state officials charged with torture. As people were now protected by human rights and courts – whether national ones, which now became agencies of humanity's law, or supranational ones such as the European or (Latin American) – there appeared to be no need or place for politics and its organizational expression, the state (represented by the government), save to serve as the executor of the universal "rule of law."

What this narrative obscures, or leaves out, is some disquieting facts. For example: that Pinochet was sent home by the British law lords; that an arrest warrant against former Israeli foreign minister Tzipi Livni, on the basis of allegations of war crimes committed in Gaza, was withdrawn when it became clear that she had canceled plans to visit the UK;[49] that in 2013 the European Court of Human Rights upheld the immunity by which Dutch courts had defeated the claims by the mothers of several victims of the Srebrenica massacre (1995);[50] that Justice Garzon's activism in Spain proved to be far from trend-setting after his removal from his position; that in 2003 Belgium revoked its universal jurisdiction statute[51] because of the havoc it had created

---

[47] See e.g. Michael Zürn (ed.), *Globalizing Interests: Pressure Groups and Denationalization*, Albany, NY: SUNY Press, 2005.

[48] See *Prosecutor v. Dusko Tadić: Decision on the Defence Motion on Jurisdiction, 10 August*, ICTY, IT-94-I-T (1995). See also *Prosecutor v. Dusko Tadić: Decision on the Defence Motion for Interlocutory Appeal on Jurisdiction, 2 October*, ICTY, IT-94-I-AR72 (1995).

[49] See the article by Ian Black and Ian Cobain, "British Court Issued Gaza Arrest Warrant for Former Israeli Minister Tzipi Livni," *The Guardian*, December 12, 2009.

[50] *Stichting Mothers of Srebrenica and Others against the Netherlands*, European Court of Human Rights, 65542/12 (2013). The mothers had claimed that the failure of the Dutch soldiers operating under the auspices of the UN violated a *jus cogens* norm that overrides the immunity of states and of international organizations.

[51] See the vote of the Belgian Senate on August 1, 2003, repealing the universal jurisdiction law.

in the decade before; that the European project ran into heavy waters as the attempt to give it a "Constitution" was rejected in 2005 by the French and Dutch electorates (as was the Treaty of Nice by Ireland in 2001, which passed only on a "retake" in 2002), and that it died an ignominious death thereafter; that hopes that the existential threat to the West had disappeared with the "New World Order" and "the end of history" were dashed by 9/11; that the West had to face an increasingly belligerent "New Russia" which eventually created new realities by annexing the Crimea and thereby sparking fears of a new Cold War; that the peacekeeping operations of the UN and NATO turned out to be the more controversial the more "robust" they became; that the bombing campaign against Serbia (1999) – designed to punish the population for the intransigence of its leadership by destroying the infrastructure of the country – led to the oracular statement by a panel of legal experts that the campaign was "illegal but justifiable."[52] Obviously, something had gone wrong on the way to the post-sovereign world, in which the rule of law and a diffuse (and obviously benign) governance was supposed to substitute for the mercurial and irrational politics of sovereign "governments."

Of course, this particular narrative, based on functionalist arguments and beliefs in managerial solutions, was not uncontested, even among jurists. Some of the leading professionals (i.e. practicing lawyers, judges) pointed out that the proliferation of courts might actually be more of a bane than a blessing, particularly since the various "courts" attached to regimes or set up ad hoc might contribute to the fragmentation of the international legal order precisely because each court had the competence to determine its own competence with little regard to other "courts" and their pronouncements. In addition, since any halfway realistic fact patterns touch on a variety of legal issues – as the Mox plant dispute showed[53] – cases can be brought not only in different courts, their decisions have neither finality nor can they serve as precedents for other courts since they have a different jurisdictional domain. All of this was, of course, bad news, as it seemed to shatter the hopes for a post-sovereign world.

---

[52] Independent International Commission on Kosovo, *The Kosovo Report: Conflict, International Response, Lessons Learned*, Oxford: Oxford University Press, 2004, at 4.

[53] Ireland began proceedings against the UK, which had built a nuclear processing plant near the Irish Sea in 1993. After protests Ireland began proceedings before the Court of the Law of the Sea Conventions (ITLOS) in Hamburg, and the OSPAR Convention (environmental protection treaty to which both states were party). The EU complained that this ought to be litigated by the European Court as it touched on community matters. The ITLOS tribunal granted provisional measures of protection, and a special Arbitral Tribunal was set up. In 2008 Ireland informed the Tribunal of its withdrawal of the complaint (Final Order of Termination by ITLOS, June 6, 2008).

Law as Deliverance

It is therefore not surprising that the second narrative draws more on emotional resources, which, of course, play a part in our assessments of good and evil, and it also suggests some answers to the question what we can hope for. As to the first issues, Hume had shown, our judgments in those cases concern not simple descriptions of some "properties" that are captured by cognitive reason, as when we e.g. grade apples or eggs according to size, but are appraisals that invoke powerful emotions of approval or resentment. Similarly, Kant had averred that the question of what we can hope for is one that cannot be dismissed, even though it cannot be answered in straightforward fashion. For him, hope provides the thread which interprets events as signs of the time to come.

Seen in this light, the establishment of the ICC represents – consciously or unintendedly – the crowning achievement of all the previous efforts to arrive at the "global" rule of law. This is not only a story of a "before" and an "after" but one of "evolution" realizing nature's hidden teleology for mankind as a whole.[54] As Tallgren aptly remarks:

In this way the ICC jurisdiction is at times seen as emanating from absolute moral sentiment shared internationally. These sentiments seem intrinsically related to a need of belonging to something higher, larger shared by all humans, bearing resemblance to the "oceanic" feeling of religious faith that Freud saw accompanied by a "feeling of an insoluble bond, of being one with the external world as a whole" . . .[55]

In similar fashion Chief Prosecutor Jackson said in his opening statement before the Nuremberg Tribunal:

The wrongs we seek to condemn and punish have been so calculated, so malignant, and so devastating that civilization cannot tolerate their being ignored, because it cannot survive their being repeated. That four great nations, flushed with victory and stung with injury stay the hand of vengeance and voluntarily submit their captive enemies to the judgment of the law is one of the most significant tributes that Power has ever paid to Reason.[56]

Although the horridness of the crimes to which Jackson referred is beyond any doubt – and so is the revulsion of any person being confronted with

---

[54] See Immanuel Kant, "Perpetual Peace" in Hans Reiss (ed.), *Kant's Political Writings*, Cambridge: Cambridge University Press, 2011. For a criticism, see Friedrich Kratochwil, "Immanuel Kant (1724–1804): A Little Kantian 'Schwaermerei'" in Richard Ned Lebow, Peer Schouten, and Hidemi Suganami (eds.), *The Return of the Theorists: Dialogues with Great Thinkers in International Relations*, London: Palgrave Macmillan, 2015: 99–109.

[55] Tallgren, "Who Are 'We' in International Criminal Law?," at 74.

[56] Justice Jackson's Opening Statement for the Prosecution of November 21, 1945 (Nuremberg ITM) 1947, 98–102, available at http://avalon.law.yale.edu/imt/11-21-45.asp.

them – there was unfortunately then and now a considerable gap between the aspirations and reality.

For that reason a rather painful deconstruction of the invocation of the "we" and of the justification of dealing with these outrages by means of criminal law becomes necessary. After all, because of the devastations and scores the Nazi regime had created, calls for exemplary punishment by summary executions of both the political leaders and a large part of the officers corps were not only voiced by the Soviets but had also dominated the discussions in London and Washington.[57] Here the advocates of a trial finally won and the Allies signed the London Agreement (to which the Charter of the Nuremberg Tribunal was attached) on August 8, 1945. But this "victory" came only after considerable opposition not just from policy-makers but, in the case of the US, even from the judiciary,[58] not to mention conflicts among the Allies concerning the specific charges.[59]

Obviously, the "we" of humanity did not speak with one voice, as different political projects and their implementing strategies were hotly debated, especially the new crime of planning and waging a "war of aggression." Even if a case could be made – and it was made by Jackson during the trials – that war had been "outlawed" by the Geneva Protocol and the Kellogg–Briand Pact,

---

[57] For a discussion of the politics of setting up the Tribunal, see Gary Jonathan Bass, *Stay the Hand of Vengeance: The Politics of War Crimes Tribunals*, Princeton: Princeton University Press, 2002; Norbert Ehrenfreund, *The Nuremberg Legacy: How the Nazi War Crimes Trials Changed the Course of History*, New York: Palgrave Macmillan, 2007. Oddly enough, the idea of a trial was first floated by Secretary of War Stimson who had asked the advice of Col. Murray Bernays, an attorney at the War Department. But postwar planning in regard to Germany under Roosevelt was largely in the hands of the Secretary of the Treasury, Henry Morgenthau, who favored a punitive peace and an eye-for-an-eye approach to the Nazi leadership. Churchill too was inclined to this strategy, so the Quebec meeting between Roosevelt and Churchill (September 15, 1944), to which Stimson and Bernays were not invited, endorsed Morgenthau's plans. While Morgenthau's plan for the deindustrialization of Germany continued to inform early US occupation policy (JCS1067), things changed when with Roosevelt's death Stimson gained the ear of Truman. He proposed a trial, which Barnays had suggested could use the "conspiracy" concept of American criminal law as an approach to prosecute the leadership and their enabling helpers. Jackson and Biddle now became allies in shaping US policy, in the face of the recalcitrant British, stiff opposition from Moscow and the disbelief of the French since such "crime" was entirely alien to them.

[58] Thus Francis Biddle, the American Judge on the Tribunal, had originally opposed the idea of a trial in a letter to Truman as late as January 5, 1945, and Harlan Fiske Stone, the Chief Justice of the US Supreme Court who had opposed the Nuremberg Trials and remained critical, considered them a "fraud" and a "lynching party" (*sic!*). Criticizing Chief Prosecutor Jackson, Fiske Stone wrote "I do not mind what he does to the Nazis, but I hate to see the pretense that he is running a court and proceeding according to common law. This is a little too sanctimonious a fraud to meet my old-fashioned ideas." As quoted in Alpheus Thomas Mason, *Harlan Fiske Stone: Pillar of the Law*, Hamden, CT: Archon Books, 1968, at 716.

[59] For a careful analysis of the negotiations in London antedating the Charter, see Kirsten Sellars, *"Crimes against Peace" and International Law*, Cambridge: Cambridge University Press, 2013, chap. 3.

this did not dispose of the problem whether such a breach also created individual criminal responsibility, particularly since in criminal law the injunction *nullum crimen sine poena* is fundamental. Similarly disquieting were some facts that surfaced during the negotiations setting up the Tribunal. As Jackson wrote in a letter to the President in October 1945, the Allies had also

done or [were] doing some of the very things we are prosecuting the Germans for. The French are so violating the Geneva Conventions in the treatment of prisoners of war that our command is taking back prisoners sent to them. We are prosecuting plunder and our Allies are practicing it. We say aggressive war is a crime and one of our allies asserts sovereignty over the Baltic states based on no title except conquest.[60]

If he was worried, the declaration of war by the Soviets in violation of a still existing Japanese/USSR non-aggression treaty[61] – not to speak of the same modus which the Soviet Union had used in the case of Finland in 1939, for which it had been expelled from the League – was another case in point.[62] Worrying should also have been the Yalta agreement by which the Western allies had obtained a commitment from the Soviet Union to declare war on Japan in exchange for acquiring some Japanese territory. Further worries should have been raised by the Potsdam Agreement, which in section XII provided for the "Orderly transfer of the German population" from the east. Thus, if we needed a precedent for the later ethnic cleansing in the Balkans, we would not need to go back to alleged "ancient hatreds," as Clinton did,[63] but we could easily find the "precedent" right there. Worrying also should have been the dropping of two atomic bombs on August 6 and 9, just before the trial.

In the opening statement such doubts were, of course, not noticeable. Only the victorious nations, "flushed with victory," were invoked, and the trial became the symbol for the "tribute" that power "has ever paid to reason."

---

[60] Letter from Jackson to Truman, October 12, 1945, p. 4, accessible through Harry S. Truman Library and Museum (accessed December 18, 2015), available at www.trumanlibrary.org/whistle stop/study_collections/nuremberg/documents/index.php?documentid=7-2&pagenumber=1.

[61] Richard H. Minear, *Victors' Justice: The Tokyo War Crimes Trial*, Ann Arbor: University of Michigan Press, 200, at 97.

[62] The attack occurred on November 30, 1939; it eventually led to the expulsion of the Soviet Union from the League. Stalin acted here too in direct violation of the still existing non-aggression pact of January 21, 1932, between the Soviet Union and Finland and attacked Finland presumably in response to the Finnish shelling of a Russian village but which had been shelled by Soviet forces (similar to Hitler's "retaliation" for the Polish attack on the radio station at Gleiwitz which had been staged by German forces).

[63] Clinton made his assertion on the talk show *Larry King Live* (June 5, 1995), apparently under the influence of Kaplan's book *Balkan Ghosts*, which he had read. He later regretted this soundbite after having "read up" on Balkan history. See Steven R. Weisman, "Editorial Observer; Coming to Terms with Kosovo's 'Old' Hatreds," *New York Times*, 12 June 1999, accessed at www.nytimes.com/1999/06/12/opinion/editorial-observer-coming-to-terms-with-kosovo-s-old-hatreds.html.

In this the auctorial "we" of the victors spoke for human civilization at large. Aware, however of the actual constraints,[64] Jackson was not ready to let the trial be derailed by "formalist" objections of the defense that here "victors' justice" was dispensed and that acts of barbarity had occurred on both sides. This stance would have entailed the highly problematic conclusion that "therefore" everyone should be excused because of the *tu quoque* principle, leveling the atrocities thereby and making them appear as the results of a "normal" war.

Jackson's strategy was therefore to show the "novelty" of this war by focusing particularly on the single-minded determination with which it had been planned and executed, and this "planning" provided the thread that tied all the other crimes together. The conspiracy to wage aggressive war also explained the Reich's move to seek Japan's entry into the war long before the latter's attack on Pearl Harbor.[65] As Jackson argued:

In general our case will disclose these defendants all uniting ... with the Nazi Party in a plan, which they well knew could be accomplished only by an outbreak of war in Europe. Their seizure of the German State, their subjugation of the German people, their terrorism and extermination of dissident elements, their planning and waging of war, their calculated and planned ruthlessness in the conduct of warfare, deliberate and planned criminality toward conquered people ... all these are phases of the conspiracy, a conspiracy which reached one goal only ...

It is my purpose to open the case, particularly under Count One of the Indictment and to deal with the Common Plan or Conspiracy to achieve ends possible only by resort to Crimes against Peace, War Crimes and Crimes against Humanity.[66]

Such a take inevitably led to considerable distortions, such as treating the Holocaust, the enslavement and extermination campaigns against other groups – political or ethnic – as a subordinate and ancillary element of aggression;[67] as if crimes against humanity did not have their own source and deserve separate remedies! But it did also point to the need to establish a wider framework for the global order, which was to establish the United Nations, by transforming them from the wartime alliance against the Axis powers into a universal international organization.[68] Nevertheless, it was quite clear that the Military Tribunal could not directly set a precedent, which could transform

---

[64] See Jackson's admission: "Unfortunately the nature of these crimes is such that both the prosecution and judgment must be by victor nations over vanquished." Opening Statement (note 56 above), at 101.

[65] Jackson mentions the German–Italian–Japanese military and economic alliance of September 27, 1940, and Ribbentrop's entreaties to Matsuoka, the Japanese foreign minister, in March and April 1941 to join the German war effort since the German Army was ready for an attack on the Soviet Union. Opening Statement (note 56 above), at 135.

[66] Ibid., at 104.   [67] See Bass, *Stay the Hand of Vengeance*, at 177.

[68] See the San Francisco Conference which adopted the UN Charter, April 25–June 26, 1945.

international law or change domestic legal systems, as Jackson well recognized at this point.[69] Strangely enough, the subsequent endorsement of the Nuremberg principles by the United Nations[70] seemed to provide just the influence on international law that Jackson had originally downplayed.[71] After all, the Tokyo Trials followed Nuremberg in that the "crimes against peace"[72] remained the main charge under which virtually all the accused were condemned.

Nevertheless, after that endorsement those trials remained the exception and no tribunals were created until the 1990s. When they finally proliferated, the focus on crimes against peace (conspiracy to plan and wage aggressive war) had, however, dramatically changed. A broadened human rights agenda and the interest in humanitarian law had moved the center of discussion from the prevention of resort to force to the issue of the legitimacy of forceful intervention (R2P) and the limits of "robust" peacekeeping missions. This new problematique also replaced the preoccupation with the aggressor with an interest in the "victim," whose protection now became the main justification for the above-mentioned push for international criminal law.

These changes not only reopened the debate between the various goals which international criminal law was supposed to achieve (retribution, deterrence, and reconciliation), which often point in different directions, but placed the whole criminalization enterprise in a wider framework of assessing different strategies for dealing with mass atrocities and the problems encountered by societies suffering the traumas of "transitions."[73] When finally the efforts for

---

[69] See the ambiguity in Jackson's *Summation for the Prosecution* of July 26 1946 noting the special status of the Military Tribunal: "The Allies are still technically in a state of war with Germany . . . As a military tribunal this Tribunal is a continuation of the War effort of the Allied Nations. As an international tribunal it is not bound by the procedural and substantive requirements of our respective judicial or constitutional systems, nor will its rulings introduce precedents into any country's internal system of civil justice. As an International Military Tribunal, it rises above the provincial and transient and seeks guidance not only from international law but also from the basic principles of jurisprudence which are assumptions of civilization and which long have found embodiment in the codes of all nations." *Summation*, available at http://law2.umkc.edu/faculty/projects/ftrials/nuremberg/Jacksonclose.htm.

[70] See United Nations General Assembly, *Formulation of the Principles Recognized in the Charter of the Nurnberg Tribunal and in the Judgment of the Tribunal*, (1947, GA Res. 177 (II), 21 November). It charged the ILC with the elaboration and drafting of these principles which were adopted in 1950. See International Law Commission, *Formulation of the Nürnberg Principles* (1950, A/CN.4/L.2).

[71] For a comprehensive collection of essays on Nuremberg with contributions by some of the participants and contemporary scholars, see Guénaël Mettraux (ed.), *Perspectives on the Nuremberg Trial*, Oxford: Oxford University Press, 2008.

[72] See the so called class A charges, as opposed to class B and C charges, which covered traditional war crimes and crimes against humanity (planning, ordering, authorizing or failure to prevent such transgression).

[73] The field of transitional justice has of course become another "growth area" of the (inter) national legal field. For a seminal contribution to this debate, see Teitel, *Transitional Justice*.

an international criminal court came to fruition, the Rome Statute gave the ICC jurisdiction for crimes against peace, but inability to "define" the crime of aggression postponed the date at which the court could actually exercise this jurisdiction.[74]

Keeping these facts in mind corrects the simple storyline that begins at Nuremberg and ends with vindication of all the efforts by the ratification of the Rome Statute (never mind that most of the Great Powers have not ratified the statute or have immunized their citizens from its jurisdictional reach). It also points to some of the persistent conceptual dilemmas that are part of its problematique. It will be the task of the next two sections to elaborate on these points, for which actually the Tokyo trial – usually rather problematically treated as a follow up of Nuremberg – provides a good point of departure for analysis.

7.5   Getting the Story Right: The Strange Disappearance of Aggression and the Emergence of the (Paradigmatic) Victim and Perpetrator

The Tokyo Trials

The authorization of war crimes trials in the Far East did not require as much diplomatic maneuvering as the London Charter. The Soviet Union had not joined the war in the Far East, and France was not present at Potsdam (July/August 1945), so it was China, Great Britain, and the US that signed the Potsdam Declaration on July 26, 1945. In it the "unconditional surrender" of Japan was demanded and the Japanese government was informed that "stern justice shall be meted out to all war criminals including those who have visited cruelties upon our prisoners."[75] The subsequent Moscow Conference (December 1945) outlined the basic structure of the occupation of Japan and vested General MacArthur, as the Supreme Commander of the Allied Powers, with the power to issue all orders for the implementation of the surrender and the occupation and control of Japan. Pursuant to those powers he issued a proclamation for the establishment of the International Military Tribunal in the Far East (IMTFE) and later appointed judges from those powers which had signed the Japanese capitulation.[76]

---

[74] On the meeting of the state parties in Kampala attempting such a definition, see Marieke Hohn, "Constructing the Crime of Aggression," paper prepared for the COST (Co-Operation in Science and Technology) Conference in Weimar.

[75] See Potsdam Agreement Annex II no 10, available at www.pbs.org.

[76] Australia, Canada, France, India, the Netherlands, the Philippines, the USSR, the UK, and the US.

The indictment closely followed US plans for again making crimes against peace the central concern.[77] All but one defendant was charged and convicted on one or more counts of crimes against peace. While the Tribunal offered the opportunity to establish criminal liability for atrocities committed by Japanese troops in the conduct of war, it did so largely only in conjunction with the A type charges.[78] Joseph Keenan, the chief American Prosecutor, even wanted to drop charges on the other counts in the "interest of time."[79] Only the vigorous dissent of Assistant Prosecutor Pedro Lopez (Philippines) and the Australian judge Alan Mansfield, endorsed later by other prosecutorial teams, prevented such a short cut. Keeping the old agenda also provided the first clues to the chemical and bacteriological atrocities of the Japanese forces involving experimentation on humans in China and Manchuria.[80]

The preoccupation with crimes against peace and the conspiracy to plan an aggressive war led to some pretty strange conclusions. As Simpson points out:

At Tokyo, Keenan suggested that all Japanese soldiers who had fought in the war in the Far East could be indicted for crimes against peace ... According to him to fight an illegal war was to fight illegally. The Japanese had embarked on an aggressive war and ... "since the war was illegal, all natural and normal results flowing from the original act were also illegal."

... Chief Justice Webb agreed with Keenan, The logical conclusion of the aggressive war doctrine was that a soldier or civilian who was opposed to the war but after it began decided it should be carried out ... was guilty of waging aggressive war.[81]

---

[77] Special importance should be given to "offenses of the type described in paragraph 1.A," which was crimes against peace, as stated in United States Department of State, *Foreign Relations of the United States: Diplomatic Papers, 1945. The British Commonwealth, the Far East*, vol. VI, Washington DC: U.S. Government Printing Office, 1945, at 930.

[78] This was also the reason why General MacArthur could move the case against General Yamashita to a different court (Military Commission in Manila) since Yamashita had not been indicted for conspiracy to commit crimes against peace. Yamashita later appealed his death sentence to the US Supreme Court on grounds of habeas corpus. The Supreme Court upheld the Manila Commission's decision and MacArthur refused the request commutation of the sentence. See *In Re Yamashita*, U.S. Supreme Court, 327 U.S. 1 (1946).

[79] See Yuma Totani, "The Case against the Accused" in Timothy L.H. McCormack, Gerry J. Simpson, and Toshiyuki Tanaka (eds.), *Beyond Victor's Justice?: The Tokyo War Crimes Trial Revisited*, Leiden: Martinus Nijhoff Publishers, 2011, 147–161.

[80] Unfortunately, because the leader of this "research" unit General Ishii had been granted immunity in exchange for supplying information, the President of the Military Tribunal made light of this charge and dismissed requests for further investigation of the criminal activities of "Unit 731" attached to the Kwantung Army. As later investigations intimated, up to about 300,000 victims might have lost their lives through the activities of the "Army Epidemic Prevention Research Laboratory." A fuller account available to the prosecution was apparently withheld from the court but led later to prosecutions in the Chabrowsk War Trials, as mentioned by B.A. Röling to Antonio Cassese. See Otozō Yamada, *Materials on the Trial of Former Servicemen of the Japanese Army: Charged with Manufacturing and Employing Bacteriological Weapons*, Moscow: Foreign Languages Publishing House, 1950.

[81] See Gerry J. Simpson, *Law, War & Crime: Iraq and the Re-Invention of International Law*, Cambridge: Polity, 2007, at 146.

Of course such an argument would have altered the whole conceptual apparatus that traditionally distinguished between the *ius ad bellum* and the *ius in bello* – the former not being determinative of the latter. It would also have introduced some form of "collective guilt" – at least for all combatants – that was explicitly rejected at Nuremberg.

Also strange was the answer provided to the question whether the sneak attack on Pearl Harbor – without any warning or declaration of war – was illegal, as it seemed to instantiate "aggression" in a pure form. By some contorted reasoning the majority found, however, that the attack was not a violation of the Hague III Convention of 1907, which imposed a duty to give warning before actual hostilities commenced. Since the Convention does not, however, specify the exact period that had to expire before warning and execution, the majority

> ... deemed it pointless to determine the Japanese leaders' true intent [in regard to the Hague Convention] ... Rather it was the decision of the Tojo cabinet to defy US embargoes to resort to the use of force, in order to continue aggression in China and beyond, which made the Pearl Harbor attack unlawful and criminal. (Majority Judgment 49-581-2A)[82]

Should we conclude therefore that planning a single sneak attack – if it is not a part of a larger plan – is not unlawful, given this "loophole"? But this would be preposterous, even if one has serious doubts about the notion that the conspiracy to plan and wage aggressive war is "the crime of crimes."[83]

If unity was sought among the judges, it eluded the Tribunal, although it had tried to keep strictly to the Nuremberg agenda. Thus, when the tribunal delivered its final judgment on November 4–12, 1948, it contained a majority opinion supported by eight, and five concurring or dissenting opinions. Even the President, who had attempted to preserve the appearance of unity during the proceeding, wrote a separate opinion, concurring only partially with the reasons provided by the majority.[84] Judges Röling (Netherlands), Bernard (France), and Pal (India)[85] were the dissenters and they were promptly punished for having

---

[82] Totani, "The Case against the Accused," at 151.

[83] Needless to say, the US Prosecutor was quite unhappy with this part of the Judgments; see Joseph Berry Keenan and Brendan Francis Brown, *Crimes against International Law*, Washington DC: Public Affairs Press, 1950, 51–87.

[84] Webb not only was critical of the immunity granted by MacArthur to the emperor, he also rejected the death penalty which was sometimes meted out with only one vote making up the majority. And he equally objected to the notion that an inchoate conspiracy to commit aggression was a crime under international law although he tried to justify this effort of lawmaking by resorting to some classical "sources" and traditions, such as tracing the prohibition of aggression back to Grotius.

[85] Ironically, Justice Pal was the only member of the tribunal who had an international law background!

broken ranks, by having their dissent originally excluded from the original transcript of the Trials.

The dissenters, however, did not agree with each other either. The French judge was willing to go along without voicing his dissent concerning both the immunity of the Emperor, and his objections to some of the procedural defects of the trial,[86] but felt compelled to voice opposition after the tribunal had announced the judgment as that of the court (not that of a "majority").[87] Röling's dissent concerned more generally (qualified) disagreement with the validity of the "crimes" against peace, which he considered inexistent before 1945. However, he did not share Pal's opinion that it violated a fundamental principle of criminal law. The *nullum crimen sine poena* was for him not a principle of justice but an "expression of political wisdom" that could not be straightforwardly applied to international relations at that time. Thus he conceded that the Tokyo Charter might be in a way retroactive but such a flaw was permissible, given the particular circumstances. Röling came to his conclusion by agreeing with Bernard that in the case of "political crimes" the "decisive element is the danger rather than the guilt."[88] As Röling avers: "Insight into the genesis of a crime has but limited importance as it is not so much the retribution, which is here being sought as is a measure of protection by the elimination of dangerous persons."[89] To that extent the "definitional issue" and the exact state of mind of the aggressors were of lesser importance. They could have believed that they acted in self-defense, especially given the crippling US embargo.

Nevertheless, the danger of becoming an instrument of political power rather than remaining a tribunal was not lost on Röling, as his response to Justice Jaranilla's "Concurring Opinion" shows. Jaranilla had argued that any judge having consented to sit on this Tribunal had also accepted unconditionally its Charter and its provisions. Consequently,

the charter has defined that aggressive war is a crime and has provided that those guilty of it are liable ... May the members of the tribunal deriving their function solely from the said charter, say that aggressive war is not a crime and that those who waged it should not be personally liable? With due respect, such a position, in my opinion, seems absurd.[90]

---

[86] See e.g. his taking issue with US rules of evidence, which he considered defective (coming from the continental school, which vests the judge(s) with the power of conducting the inquiry). B.V.A. Röling and Antonio Cassese, *The Tokyo Trial and Beyond: Reflections of a Peacemonger*, Cambridge: Polity Press, 1993, at 39. In addition he considered the verdict invalid as all judges were never called together to deliberate and discuss the parts and the entirety of the majority's draft. See Bernard Dissenting Opinion at 19 as quoted in Minear, *Victors' Justice*, at 90.

[87] Roeling, in Cassese and Roeling, *The Tokyo Trial and Beyond*, at 32.

[88] See Bernard, Dissenting opinion, at 10, as quoted in Minear, *Victors' Justice*, at 53

[89] Röling, Dissenting Opinion, at 50, quoted in Minear, *Victors' Justice*, at 59.

[90] Jaranilla, "Concurring opinion," 29 and 31 in ibid., 65f.

Whatever the absurdity of this position might be, it points to the flaws of political trials, using the judicial process to eliminate political opposition. If rule of law values are not to be compromised, there has to be at least the presumption of innocence and the possibility of dismissing charges. Otherwise such trials have the odium of Molotov's "Freudian slip" in 1946 (concerning 16 Polish underground leaders in Soviet custody): "the guilty persons will be tried."[91] Röling's rebuke of Jaranilla and the majority opinion was telling and to the point:

> It would be the worst possible service this tribunal could render . . . if it would establish as a rule that an international tribunal called upon to mete out justice would have to apply the rules laid down by the Supreme Commander of the victorious nations without either having the power or the duty to inquire whether it was applying rules of justice at all.[92]

To that extent Röling's dissent came close, on both the question of "aggression" and the assessment of "negative criminality" (counts 53–55), to Justice Pal's principled dissent. Pal held, after a rather extensive review of the historical record and of the explanations tendered about this pact by various states (including the US), that the Pact of Paris (Kellogg–Briand Pact)

> fails to add anything to the existing law . . . In my opinion no category of war became illegal or criminal either by the Pact of Paris or as a result of the same. Nor did any customary law develop making any war criminal. Indeed: when the conduct of nations is taken into account, the law will perhaps be found to be that only a lost war is a crime.[93]

In Pal's view, such questions were unjusticiable since in the absence of effective measures to allow for peaceful change, self-help by force can be justifiable since otherwise the status quo attains virtual sanctity irrespective of its merits. But as Pal argues: "I am not sure if it is possible to create 'peace' once and for all and if there can be a status quo which is to be eternal. At any rate, in the present state of international relations such a static idea of peace is absolutely untenable."[94]

Similar difficulties arose in the context of "negative criminality." According to the indictment the defendants were charged that they conspired to "order, authorize and permit" breaches of the laws of war (count 53), that they actually ordered, authorized and permitted such acts (count 54) and that they deliberately disregarded their legal duty to take adequate steps to secure

---

[91] Bass, *Stay the Hand of Vengeance*, at 161.
[92] Röling, Dissenting Opinion, 4–5, as quoted in Minear, *Victors' Justice*, at 66.
[93] Pal, Dissenting Opinion, 45f., as quoted in ibid., at 55.
[94] Pal, Dissenting Opinion, 114–115, as quoted in ibid., at 60.

the observance and prevent breaches (count 55).[95] Since atrocities had obviously occurred, the problem was whether such violations were "ordered" by the governmental authorities (e.g. the summary executions of Soviet Polit-officers ordered by the German High Command on the Eastern Front), or what would have been a sufficient proof that a superior had the necessary means to prevent atrocities in the field, but failed to use them to prevent crimes.

It is not difficult to see that the presumption of innocence is in that case reversed, as the defendant has to prove his innocence. Besides, the Charter listed only war crimes and not a "disregard" of duty. Would such a charge have to be listed separately? Actually a good case can be made that within military organizations such a "duty to knowledge standard"[96] can be assumed – since knowing what is going on in the field is not only required by customary standards of the laws of war, but is of the essence for tactical and strategic reasons. Things can, however, be quite different for establishing the *mens rea* component in other contexts.

Consider in this context count 53 of the Tokyo indictment. The issue of *dolus* or *mens rea* was solved here by the "membership" in a criminal organization, without a separate vetting of the motive. Even in cases of becoming part of the Cabinet – and thus being part of the government which planned and executed "aggressive war" – certain complexities arose. In the case of Hirota, who devised the Japanese policy of the "New Order" but left the government when the military took over, he was brought to the trial at the behest of the Chinese, who charged him with the "rape of Nanking" although he had not been in power then. Togo had, in Röling's assessment, –"joined the cabinet in order to *prevent* the war, and Shigemitsu entered the War cabinet with the intention of *ending the war* as soon as possible."[97] However, due to the "conspiracy" charge, "operationalized" as membership in a high governmental circle, no such distinctions mattered.

These issues were just the first signs of the more general problems which were to challenge later tribunals when they moved from an exclusive focus on conspiracy to wage aggressive war, to the problem of how to conceptualize individual liability for crimes, which were committed collectively by organizations.[98] Here the notion of a Joint Criminal Enterprise (JCE) was

---

[95] This count was new at Tokyo and seems to be a fallback in case of problems making charges stick under count 54.

[96] See the argument for such a criterion in Jenny S. Martinez, "Understanding *Mens Rea* in Command Responsibility," *Journal of International Criminal Justice*, 5:3 (2007): 638–664.

[97] Röling and Cassese, *The Tokyo Trial and Beyond*, at 41.

[98] For a discussion of the conceptual problems of joint criminal enterprise and traditional liability under command responsibility, see Kai Ambos, "Joint Criminal Enterprise and Command Responsibility," *Journal of International Criminal Justice*, 5:1 (2007): 159–183.

introduced.[99] Such conceptualization in turn raised the issue of actual "control" and command responsibility both in terms of commission and omissions (neglect of duty to prevent crimes which were foreseeable and of which the person in command authority "should have known").[100] They touch upon crucial factual and "state of mind" questions (*mens rea, dolus*), relying on counterfactual reasoning to justify a criminal conviction.[101] As B.H. Röling, reflecting on his role at Tokyo, told Cassese twenty years later, membership in a "criminal organization" could not settle the issue of guilt.

In my dissenting opinion I stressed the importance of their intention, when they consented to enter the Cabinet. From the evidence I concluded that Togo accepted the post with the intention of preventing the war and that Shigemitsu entered the War Cabinet with the intention of ending the war as soon as possible. From the decision of the Tribunal's majority it follows that it is forbidden to accept important government posts, even if one does so to prevent or to end a war. I do not consider this a reasonable standpoint. To have influence over government decision one needs to occupy a position of power.[102]

In a way the Nuremberg and Tokyo Trials raised at least as many issues as they answered both in terms of law and of politics. To that extent their character as a milestone – towards the establishment of an international criminal court, or as a turning point away from sovereignty and its concept of immunity – is, however, clearly the result of what people later made out of these events[103] when reflecting on them with hindsight.

Reflecting on Nuremberg: The Strange Fate of "Aggression"

Seen from the perspective of the immediate situation after the trials, their "legacy" was far from clear, as e.g. Kelsen's scathing indictment of Nuremberg shows.[104] While Kelsen took issue with Jackson's argument that the Kellogg–Briand Pact established individual criminal responsibility, he did not think that the Tribunal acted illegally when it used the rules of the London

---

[99] See also the use of this concept in the ICTY jurisprudence such as *Prosecutor v. Dusko Tadić: Decision on the Defence Motion on Jurisdiction, 10 August*; *Prosecutor v. Dusko Tadić: Decision on the Defence Motion for Interlocutory Appeal on Jurisdiction, 2 October*.

[100] Verena Haan, "The Development of the Concept of Joint Criminal Enterprise at the International Criminal Tribunal for the Former Yugoslavia," *International Criminal Law Review*, 5:2 (2005): 167–201.

[101] Mohamed Elewabadar, "Mens Rea – Mistake of Law and Mistake of Fact in German Criminal Law: A Survey for International Criminal Tribunals," *International Criminal Law Review*, 5:2 (2005): 203–246.

[102] Ibid. Of course such assessments are subject to rebuttal and historical research, but Röling's point here is that no critical examination of the issues occurred during the trial.

[103] For an excellent collection of essays written at different times, see Mettraux (ed.), *Perspectives on the Nuremberg Trial*, at 208.

[104] See Hans Kelsen, "Will the Judgment in the Nuremberg Trial Constitute a Precedent in International Law?" *The International Law Quarterly*, 1:2 (1947): 153–171.

Charter for its proceedings, since that was a treaty to which the powers had agreed. Similarly he did not think that the *ex post facto* application of law by the Tribunal undermined its legality, because he considered the *ex post facto* principle a more general principle of justice, standing in tension with other principles, such as that ignorance of the law cannot be pleaded as a valid excuse for avoiding a penalty. Besides,

[The] rule excluding retroactive legislation is restricted to penal law. But it does not apply to customary law and to law created by precedent, for such law is necessarily retroactive in respect to the first case to which it is applied . . .

The London Agreement is such a law. It is retroactive only in so far as it establishes individual criminal responsibility for acts, which . . . constituted violations of existing international law but for which this law has provided only collective responsibility . . .

The rule against retroactive legislation is a principle of justice. Individual responsibility represents certainly a higher degree of justice than collective responsibility. . . . Justice required the punishment of those men in spite of the fact that they were not punishable under positive law . . . In case two postulates of justice are in conflict . . . the higher one prevails.[105]

What really impaired the effectiveness of the Tribunal's judgment was in Kelsen's opinion that it had not established individual responsibility "as a general principle of law but as a rule applicable only to the vanquished"[106] as his distinction of "legislative" (contractual) vs. "judicial" precedent suggests. Even more objectionable was in his view that the tribunal was exclusively composed of representatives of the victorious powers.

Thus these States made themselves not only legislators, but also judges and prosecutors . . . If the principles applied in the Nuremberg trials were to become a precedent – a legislative rather than judicial precedent – then the governments of the victorious states would try . . . [those] of the vanquished states for having committed crimes determined unilaterally . . . Let us hope that there is no such precedent.[107]

These are certainly startling arguments, particularly since they combine moral intuitions (vide the notion that the Nazi leaders knew about the moral abjection of their deeds and had to be punished) with rather stringent formalistic arguments (that there was something wrong with simple "legislative" precedents, although they were not illegal). But is this blend of moral intuition and the status of the principle *nemo judex in sua causa* not equally defeasible, particularly in an arena in which the effectiveness of norms depends to a large extent on reciprocity?

In short, whether the presumptive change from vengeance to just punishment can be institutionalized by simply establishing "third party" adjudication – as

[105] Ibid., 164–165.   [106] Ibid., 170.   [107] Ibid., 171.

important as it might be within the semantics of law – leaving to the judges legislation and prosecution, while nobly ignoring the "execution" problem, is of course a general problem of "legalism" and particularly of international criminal law. It will occupy us in the next section. Here it is sufficient to note that behind these speculations lies, of course, the idea of a *civitas maxima* – the state written large – and the changing meaning of sovereignty. After all, sovereignty was central to the crime of aggression. As Kirsten Sellars – writing now with benefit of hindsight about the history of aggression – points out, "the charge of aggression reflects both the impulse to protect sovereignty (by safe-guarding the existing order against violent rearrangement), and the impulse to breach sovereignty (by making leaders directly accountable to international law)."[108] Thus a much more ambiguous picture emerges from the record than the triumphalist account suggests: "from sovereignty to the end of impunity" in a cosmopolitan order, crowned by the ICC.

Nothing shows this more clearly than the course of the discussions defining "aggression" after the Tribunals had been disbanded. Although the Codification of the "Nuremberg principles" entrusted to the International Law Commission resulted in a draft code on "Offences against the Peace and Security of Mankind," it did not find an attentive audience and was shelved in 1954. A new Draft Committee on the Definition of Aggression commenced its work under the auspices of the 6th Committee of the General Assembly.[109]

After lengthy and sometimes acrimonious discussions it delivered in 1974 a controversial Definition of Aggression that satisfied none of the major parties but established a "compromise." If it was reminiscent of Nuremberg and Tokyo, it was so as suggested by Kelsen and Pal: as condemning aggression by placing it within the larger purposes of the UN for protecting peace and security and by incorporating also Pal's notion that peace and security cannot be defined once and for all as sanctifying the status quo. Thus Article 7 excepted struggles against colonial or racist regimes from the general prohibition of violent means, exposing to all that one had agreed to disagree.[110] It was not "Nuremberg- conform" either in that it defined aggression and conspiring to commit it as an individual crime, but inconsistently provided in Art. 5(2) only that aggression gives rise to international *responsibility of the state* and that the benefits derived from aggression would not be recognized as lawful (Art. 5(3)).

---

[108] Sellars, *"Crimes against Peace" and International Law*, at 292.
[109] For an exhaustive study of attempts to define aggression, see Benjamin B. Ferencz, *Defining International Aggression, the Search for World Peace: A Documentary History and Analysis* Dobbs Ferry, NY: Oceana Publications, 1975.
[110] See Art. 7 of the Draft Code.

In 1981 the General Assembly again tasked the International Law Commission to proceed with a new codification, which led on July 12, 1991 to the adoption of a catalog of crimes against "Peace and the security of Mankind," which tried its hand at the crime of aggression, of colonial and other forms of alien domination, and of intervention. But although the emphasis on individual responsibility showed that times had changed, as the subsequent Draft Code of 1996[111] also revealed, the result was again a strange compromise. On the one hand, individual responsibility was incurred for "the crime of aggression," defined as taking "active part in ordering and planning, preparation, incitement and aggression by a state." But the "conspiracy" element as well as the "threat of aggression" was removed. The *mens rea* elements, on which Röling had insisted, seemed strengthened albeit at the price of expanding considerably the notion of command responsibility (coming close to the common law conception of criminal negligence, which stands in tension with the *dolus* criterion of civil law). Oddly enough it does not refer to Resolution 3314 of 1974, or to the list of examples in Article 3.

In the meantime, special courts for war crimes in the former Yugoslavia and Rwanda were created in 1993 and 1994[112] and the plans for an international criminal court gathered steam with the passage of GA Resolution 49/53 of December 9, 1994, the establishment of a Preparatory Committee (December 11, 1995), and with the call that went out for a Diplomatic Conference,[113] charged with negotiating the ICC statute in Rome in 1998 (June 15–July 17, 1998). The Statute itself entered into force on July 1, 2002. The Statute lists "aggression" as one of the four most serious crimes over which the Court shall have jurisdiction (Article 5(1)), but Article 5(2) determines that it will be able to exercise this jurisdiction only after a definition of aggression has been adopted and the conditions for this jurisdiction have been specified. This means, of course, that de facto this court is not empowered to hear or decide cases falling under this rubric. To end this "codified impasse" a special working party of the state parties to the Statute of the Court convened a "Special Working Group" on the crime of aggression which presented its results[114] to a Review Conference held by the state parties in Kampala (May 31–June 11, 2010).

---

[111] See International Law Commission, "Draft Code of Crimes against the Peace and Security of Mankind," *Yearbook of the International Law Commission*, II:2 (1996).

[112] For the ICTY, see United Nations Security Council, *Resolution 827, 25 May* (1993, S/RES/827). It established the ICTY. For the Rwanda Court, see United Nations Security Council, *Resolution 955, 8 November* (1994, S/RES/955).

[113] United Nations General Assembly, *Establishment of an International Criminal Court* (1996, A/RES/51/207).

[114] Several problems were considered aside from the definition of aggression; the application of the principle of complementarity (as the ICC and national courts have concurring jurisdiction); general provisions of the court's jurisdiction; the *ne bis in idem* problem (double jeopardy) with regard to aggression, and amendment procedures for defining aggression. For a general

Its outcome was, in a way, surprising, not to say confusing. On the one hand the conference was able to agree (on the surface) on a definition of aggression and on the conditions of the exercise of jurisdiction by the ICC in that area. However, on closer inspection this "solution" was question-begging since the difference between those favoring a clear definition on the one hand and those wanting to leave the determination of what constituted aggression to the Security Council – a position that was favored by its members but was unacceptable to others – was not resolved. It also militated against the notion of an independent court. The parties agreed on a somewhat more specific list of examples (similar to the Article 3 enumeration in the 1974 Definition of Aggression Resolution) together with a "high threshold" clause that would condone freedom of action in a "grey zone," which did not outrageously violate the core of the semantic field of "manifestly illegal" action. But what might be obvious to some might not be obvious to others, as Andreas Paulus[115], Kai Ambos,[116] and Sean Murphy[117] have noted. Having been once defined as the "crime of crimes" and having been placed high on the UN agenda for responding with criminal measures through the incorporation of the Nuremberg principles, certain forms of aggression (apparently if done for "good purposes") might actually not represent a manifest violation of the Charter and incur the opprobrium of a criminal sanction.

Uneasiness was heightened by the subsequent actions of the Conference. Having "agreed" to a definition of aggression, the "states made a decision that precluded any judgment on the charge of aggression for the next 8 years."[118] In short, this exercise of jurisdiction by the court could not occur before 2017 at the earliest. Similar to the assessment of the Kosovo mission that the intervention against Serbia was illegal but justified,[119] aggression is now defined as illegal and involving individual responsibility, but it actually remains injusticiable, showing thereby that even the establishment of a court with "neutral" judges, which Kelsen advocated, is far from solving the problems.

discussion, see Patrycja Grzebyk, *Criminal Responsibility for the Crime of Aggression*, London: Routledge, 2013.
[115] Andreas Paulus, "Second Thoughts on the Crime of Aggression," *European Journal of International Law*, 20:4 (2009): 1117–1128.
[116] Kai Ambos, "The Crime of Aggression after Kampala," *German Yearbook of International Law*, 53 (2010): 463–510.
[117] Sean D. Murphy, "Aggression, Legitimacy and the International Criminal Court," *European Journal of International Law*, 20:4 (2009): 1147–1156.
[118] Grzebyk, *Criminal Responsibility for the Crime of Aggression*, at 128.
[119] See e.g. Bruno Simma, "Nato, the UN and the Use of Force: Legal Aspects," *European Journal of International Law*, 10:1 (1999): 1–22.

As we can see, the storyline of an ongoing concern with aggression creates a tenuous continuity, as it fails to highlight some of the significant changes in the priorities of the international order agenda. The question of conflict prevention was superseded by the "Responsibility to Protect"[120] and by debates about the limits of (humanitarian) intervention.[121] In IR a concern with the management of force through deterrence and alliances or collective security arrangements was eclipsed by an interest in regimes and later in the "norm cascades"[122] set in motion by norm entrepreneurs in global civil society. In legal theory a new discussion on the nature of global justice[123] tried to engage with the cosmopolitan debates carried on by political theorists and philosophers.[124] A similar change in priorities can be noticed, as Rengger has argued:

a good deal of contemporary international law and, indeed other approaches to the ethics of force, is a conception of the ethics of force as predominantly about the pursuit of justice, or perhaps better, the elimination of injustice, rather than about the restraint of force that, as a result, is becoming progressively less restrictive . . .

Within this context, quasi as a countermove, the idea of international criminal tribunals *as an alternative* to intervention and "robust" peacekeeping operations emerged, as the history of the ICTY showed.[125] It fit the managerial mood of the times that had grown weary of peacekeeping missions – originally the UN's innovative answer to the failure of its collective security system – which had morphed into something entirely different: *peacemaking* missions with forces on the ground. Thus authorizing a new tribunal under a broadened interpretation of Article 39 and Chapter VII of the Charter seemed like a win–win situation. Politicians could avoid costly commitments and lawyers could represent the thorny issues as those of "administering" justice in which the gavel instead of the sword would rule the world.

---

[120] International Commission on Intervention and State Sovereignty, "The Responsibility to Protect."

[121] Welsh (ed.), *Humanitarian Intervention and International Relations*; Anne Orford, *International Authority and the Responsibility to Protect*, Cambridge: Cambridge University Press, 2011.

[122] The empirical work on the spread of human rights dates back at least a decade, although Finnemore and Sikkink systematized the argument only in 1998 in Martha Finnemore and Kathryn Sikkink, "International Norm Dynamics and Political Change," *International Organization*, 52:4 (1998): 887–917.

[123] See e.g. Kok-Chor Tan, *Justice, Institutions, and Luck: The Site, Ground, and Scope of Equality*, Oxford: Oxford University Press, 2012; Steven R. Ratner, *The Thin Justice of International Law: A Moral Reckoning of the Law of Nations*, Oxford: Oxford University Press, 2015.

[124] For a useful collection of essays, see Thomas Pogge and Keith Horton (eds.), *Global Ethics: Seminal Essays*, 2 vols., St. Paul, NM: Paragon House 2008.

[125] See Victor Peskin, *International Justice in Rwanda and the Balkans: Virtual Trials and the Struggle for State Cooperation*, Cambridge: Cambridge University Press, 2008, at 35–38.

The Problems of Administering International Criminal Justice

Of course, quite different from Nuremberg, there remained for the new tribunals the small problem of getting a hold of the "criminals" who were often still in power. As a British military lawyer so aptly put it: "Nuremberg was a lovely hood ornament on the ungainly vehicle that liberated Western Europe, but it was not a substitute for D-day."[126] However, given the "progress" made in pushing international criminal law to the top of the agenda, those unresolved problems seemed like administrative glitches that could be taken care of in time. For the moment it was important to seize the opportunity and create a "court." As one observer of the beginnings of the ICTY declared:

Anyone with half a brain would know that you do not launch an investigative and judicial tribunal the way the ICTY was set up. You do not start with renting a building, appointing 11 judges before you even hired the first investigator, let alone prosecutor . . . Is it not clear that something went wrong with that picture?[127]

Some of the language harked back to Nuremberg, although the semantic field had substantially changed. There was still the shared concern to end impunity and hold the "perpetrators" accountable for their misdeeds, but scant attention was paid to the problem that the perpetrators were now mostly actual *genocidaires* or planners and executors of atrocities *in power*, rather than waiting in their cells to face the tribunal. Whereas formerly the Holocaust and crimes against humanity were of interest only if they had occurred in conjunction with a world war, now many, if not most, victims were the result of the "normalcy" of failed states, the growing frequency of asymmetric conflicts, the modern conditions of complex interdependence, and the discursive formation that made "victimhood" a password at the "gates of power and recognition."[128] It was these conditions plus the lack of response to the continued abuses by the "Great Powers" that allowed local leaders to link to transnational production, distribution, and banking channels in order to prop up their regime, profit from official sanctions, press people into their "armies," and sustain high levels of conflict. The "blood diamonds," Saddam and Milosevic's "programs" for sanction-busting, the "child soldiers," and the oil- and slave-trading enterprises of IS provide the sorry illustrations.

---

[126] As quoted in Kenneth Anderson, "The Rise of International Criminal Law: Intended and Unintended Consequences," *European Journal of International Law*, 20:2 (2009): 331–358, at 335.

[127] John Hagan, *Justice in the Balkans: Prosecuting War Crimes in the Hague Tribunal*, Chicago: University of Chicago Press, 2003, at 97.

[128] See the analysis of Zygmunt Bauman and Leonidas Donkins, *Moral Blindness*, Cambridge: Polity Press, 2013: 123.

These circumstances created entirely new problems, for which the traditional backward-looking conception of criminal law imported from the domestic arena had little to offer. If the creation of the ICC seemed like an answer to our prayers, it soon strained credulity that future change could come about through *ex post* "administration of justice," even if the dispensing institution was conceived to be neutral, separate from politics, and ready to mete out justice in the name of humanity. As we had to learn from experience, the compromises at Rome between the court and the Security Council could not resolve the conflicts between politics and law, as the referral of the Darfur situation (referred to the court by the Security Council) and of Uganda (self-referral using the court for political purposes) showed.[129] Besides, in the normal way of proceeding with their business, tribunals and the ICC had often to acknowledge the cooperation of one party, while castigating the noncompliance of the other – one party thereby becoming a friend of mankind, and the other its enemy. This created a dynamic in the case of the ICTY where Croatia and Serbia had become in public display the respective good and bad boys.[130]

Furthermore, as it turned out, a strong Prosecutor was not the "solution" either, by which justice could speak truth to power. After all, his or her "discretion" could result in turning a deaf ear to complaints against some bête noir,[131] especially if such complaints would touch on tricky political issues, as Carla da Ponte was quick to notice by refusing to "get into the issue" of NATO's bombing of Serbia.[132] Prosecutorial discretion can even impair a fair trial and undermine the attempts to defuse explosive situations, as was shown in the Lubanga trial and the controversies surrounding the public charges and requests for arrest warrants for Omar al Bashir (president of Sudan) and of Uhuru Kenyatta (of Kenya).[133]

[129] For a good examination of the politics of international law in the "situations" in Darfur and Sudan, see S.M.H. Nouwen and W.G. Werner, "Doing Justice to the Political: The International Criminal Court in Uganda and Sudan," *European Journal of International Law*, 21:4 (2011): 941–965.

[130] See the analysis of Nikolas Rajkovic, *The Politics of International Law and Compliance: Serbia, Croatia and the Hague Tribunal*, New York: Routledge, 2012. See also the analysis of Jelena Subotic, who shows that such dynamics were not limited to the Balkans but occurred in virtually all tribunals. Jelena Subotic, *Hijacked Justice: Dealing with the Past in the Balkans*, Ithaca, NY: Cornell University Press, 2009.

[131] See the incisive examination of Carsten Stahn, "Judicial Review of Prosecutorial Discretion: Five Years On" in Carsten Stahn and Göran Sluiter (eds.), *The Emerging Practice of the International Criminal Court*, Leiden: Martinus Nijhoff Publishers, 2009: 247–280.

[132] For a discussion of NATO's Kosovo campaign see Nicholas Wheeler, The Kosovo Bombing Campaign" in Christian Reus-Smith (ed.), *The Politics of International Law*, Cambridge: Cambridge University Press, 2004: 189–216.

[133] On the Lumbanga trial see the suspension of the proceeding on June 23, 2008, and the subsequent order of release of the accused (July 2, 2008) since the Prosecutor Louis Moreno-Ocampo had refused two orders by the Trial Chamber to share with the court potentially exculpating evidence. In July 2008 Ocampo's charge of the Sudanese president Omar al Bashir

It is hardly surprising that the present mood is much less confident even among the proponents of the ICC, while of course the opponents, after some triumphant cries of the "I told you so," have realized that although war and atrocities are still with us, dealing with them in terms of strict opposition to law, or with benign neglect of law, is no longer politically possible. As the military were quick to learn, effective strategy means becoming proficient in "lawfare."

The inventor of this term, Major General Charles J. Dunlap (US Air Force), recalls that he "started using 'lawfare'" in the late 1990s because he "wanted a bumper sticker term . . . to describe how law was altering warfare."[134] The term might be new, the idea that warfare, depends on public support is not, especially in a democratic state. It remains an open question whether this need for a legal justification is, as we hoped, productive of restraint, or whether it is counter-productive – as we feared and as the experience with "collateral damage" and "signature strikes" seems to indicate.[135] Perhaps this question cannot be decided on the level of abstraction at which it is posed, since operationalizing e.g. the "success" of international criminal law by simply "measuring" its output in terms of the number of trials, or worse, of convictions, is objectionable.[136] We need instead a more critical approach to the presuppositions on which the usual pro and contra arguments of international criminal justice rest, as Carsten Stahn has argued.[137] It is the task of the next section to attempt such a critique.

7.6   Why Not All Roads Should Lead to Rome (or The Hague)

The Problem of Political Justice

Our justifications of *ex post* adjudication by a neutral and independent court rest on some conceptual paradoxes and on some specific historical experiences.

with war crimes, genocide and crimes against humanity increased tension in an explosive situation, particularly since a UN commission of international criminal jurists headed by Antonio Cassese had concluded in 2005 that the government of Sudan had not engaged in genocidal policies in Darfur. Similarly, the request of arrest warrants in November 2008 for members of some tribes who had murdered international peacekeepers was answered by the tribes with a libel and defamation suit. In the Uhuru Kenyatta case, Trial Chamber V of the ICC decided on March 13, 2015, to withdraw the charges.
[134] See Major General Charles J. Dunlap Jr., "Lawfare Today: A Perspective," *Yale Journal of International Affairs*, 3:1 (2008): 146–154.
[135] Pascal Vennesson and Nikolas M. Rajkovic, "The Transnational Politics of Warfare Accountability: Human Rights Watch Versus the Israel Defense Forces," *International Relations*, 26:4 (2012): 409–429.
[136] For a comprehensive overview of cases, informative cross-tabulations and comparisons and a critical discussion of the principles that should be guiding sentencing in international criminal law, see Silvia D'Ascoli, *Sentencing in International Criminal Law: The UN Ad Hoc Tribunals and Future Perspectives for the ICC*, Oxford: Hart, 2011.
[137] Carsten Stahn, "Between 'Faith' and 'Facts': By What Standards Should We Assess International Criminal Justice?," *Leiden Journal of International Law*, 25:2 (2012): 251–282.

Law is supposed to be different from politics, the latter being the unprincipled art of the possible, while law has to embody justice, i.e. principles which lend, by their universal normative pull, legitimacy to the law. But putting the problem of justice and law this way hides several important problems, as the discussion of legalism by Shklar has shown.[138]

Obviously the issue of enforcement (after a judgment has been rendered) is not part of judicial concerns, but belongs to the executive. However, it would be strange, even in the domestic order, to assume that the *ex post* punishment could claim legitimacy, if we had not developed an increasingly dense net of institutions, that work *ex ante* and prevent deviations from the law. These institutions of "governance" – in the Foucauldian sense, as "disposing of things" –range from regulatory practices to the police and "private enforcement" mechanisms, such as licensing procedures or examinations, to general civic education, instilling thereby in the "citizen" or subject the necessary loyalty and creating the "credit" needed for the reproduction of the social order. In short, focusing only on conceptual issues of norms obscures entirely the fact that the "rule of law" is not only adjudication, but a *rule by law*, i.e. *dominium or Herrschaft* in Weber's terms.

It needs no further belaboring that the net of preventive and enabling institutions is largely missing in international criminal law and has to be provided mostly by states. One could now point out that because of the increasing internalization of war and the concomitant dangers for humanitarian disasters new institutions have to be created to hold violators of humanitarian law accountable. And indeed, this had been the argument of the activists of civil society networks, who were particularly vocal and eventually successful[139] in pursuing the establishment of an independent and permanent international criminal court.[140] The underlying rationale was that there was something wrong with the traditional abstention of international law, namely its

... leaving power-political interests and the whims of unscrupulous leaders unchecked; second, that the extension of international criminal law by holding individual perpetrators to account for their crimes, is able to address the broader phenomenon of violence and atrocities.[141]

But on closer inspection the charge fails in the case of international criminal law, as both the ad hoc tribunals, and the ICC have to rely on "contributions" (even if some of them are "assessments") and in-kind grants of member states

---

[138] Shklar, *Legalism.*
[139] See e.g. Nicole Deitelhof, "The Discursive Process of Legalization: Charting Islands of Persuasion in the ICC Case," *International Organization*, 63:1 (2009): 33–65.
[140] See Benjamin N. Schiff, *Building the International Criminal Court*, Cambridge: Cambridge University Press, 2008: 144–164.
[141] Tor Krever, "International Criminal Law: An Ideology Critique," *Leiden Journal of International Law*, 26:3 (2013): 701–723, at 702.

(or charitable organizations) rather than on secure taxes, which could guarantee their existence and permanence.[142] This creates tensions between the donors as the principals and the court (the agents), even if the judges (Arts. 35 and 36) and the prosecutor (Art. 42) are now technically independent and must not have a conflict of interest.[143] But as the complicated arrangements concerning the jurisdiction of the ICC show,[144] even those stipulations although important are part of a larger picture concerning the court's position in the general institutional structure of the international game. Here several relations are of relevance: those between court and the countries delivering the perpetrators to the ICC (or prosecuting them in accordance with *aut dedere aut judicare*), and those between the Security Council and the court. The former can refer cases to the court or ask for a deferral of an investigation by the Prosecutor.[145] Furthermore, there is the relationship of the Prosecutor and the state parties to which s/he can complain in case a state refuses to cooperate with the court.[146] Finally, there are the relations with the nonparticipating great powers, and their special deals with the court, securing immunity for their military personnel[147] in peacekeeping undertakings involving the use of force.[148]

---

[142] Whether this has a bearing on functionalist organizations in general can remain an open question. Here the experiences with the euro do not seem encouraging as even a rather "strong" independent ECB and a comprehensive framework treaty and compulsory dispute settlement seem unable to stem the tide of divergent policies.

[143] That committed believers in international criminal justice can suffer from activist myopia is evidenced by Geoffrey Robertson. He was "recused" from the court through some arm-twisting and a change in the rules for appointing the president and time of tenure so that Robertson's tenure was effectively over. The arm-twisting consisted in allowing Robertson to excuse himself from cases he had written about before coming to the court and in which the attribution of crimes to certain persons now before his court raised the issue of bias directly (as he seemed to have prejudged issues of guilt in certain cases) or indirectly (by "normal" readers of his book). Since he had not voluntarily availed himself of Rule 15 A, a panel of judges decided that they had to apply Rule 15 B (actual removal) but with a "consensual understanding." For a further discussion, see James Cockayne, "Special Court for Sierra Leone: Decision on the Recusal of Judges Robertson and Winter," *Journal of International Criminal Justice*, 2:4 (2004): 1154–1162. The challenge to Judge Winter was not sustained.

[144] See Article 1 of the ICC Statute, which provides a concurring jurisdiction and the possibility of referral by a state party to the court.

[145] See Article 16 of the Rome Statute: "No investigation or prosecution may be commenced or proceeded with under this Statute for a 12 months period after the SC, in a resolution adopted under Chapter VII of the Charter of the United Nations, has requested the Court to that effect; that request may be renewed by the Council under the same conditions."

[146] Art. 87(7) of the ICC Statute.

[147] See Attila Bogdan, "The United States and the International Criminal Court: Avoiding Jurisdiction through Bilateral Agreements in Reliance on Article 98," *International Criminal Law Review*, 8:1 (2008): 1–54.

[148] Art. 98 agreements e.g. between the US and other states who are members of the ICC Statute that they will not surrender US military personnel to the ICC for prosecution. See also American Service Member Protection Act signed into law August 2, 2002 cutting off funds to countries unwilling to conclude such a bilateral agreement. Despite some exemptions from

Thus the picture that emerges from a careful review of the historical record[149] is quite different from the pious hope that Cherif Bassiouni invoked at the end of the Rome Conference, that "[t]he ICC reminds governments that *Realpolitik* which sacrifices justice at the altar of political settlements is no longer acceptable."[150] What he also failed to mention – and what emerges from a study of the controversies in the negotiation of the compromise enshrined in Article 13[151] – is that arguments clothed in legal garb and defended with sectarian enthusiasm are likely to enhance conflict by interpreting the disagreements as a failure to live up to the demands of universal "reason."

Furthermore, while certain arrangements in international politics – as discussed in the regime debate – might come close to a self-enforcing game, generalized Prisoners' Dilemmas can be overcome only by "contract" or by effective retaliation of the actors themselves in case reciprocity has been breached.[152] But it is precisely this reciprocity (perhaps in the laws of war buttressed by mutual recognition of status and "professionalism" among "soldiers") on which formerly the rules of warfare depended, for which international criminal law is now offered as a substitute. Only in this way, it is argued, can the legitimacy of administering justice be guaranteed.[153] Such an argument makes sense if we assume that we are in a structured society. But putting the problem this way hides the hypocritical element that follows from the notion of international criminal law as a substitute for "reciprocal" justice. As Kenneth Anderson points out:

For those in the professional world of international criminal law the right to judge is a universal act of justice and as such its standards ... should be enforced in the present,

---

the sanctions provided by the Nethercutt Amendment for the refusal to sign such a bilateral treaty, in 2003, the respite was short as the amendment was repealed in 2009.

[149] See Rosa Aloisi, "A Tale of Two Institutions: The United Nations Security Council and the International Criminal Court," *International Criminal Law Review*, 13:1 (2013): 147–168.

[150] M. Cherif Bassiouni, *The Legislative History of the International Criminal Court: Introduction, Analysis, and Integrated Text of the Statute, Elements of Crimes and Rules of Procedure and Evidence*, vol. 1, Ardsley, NY: Transnational Publishers, 2005, 121.

[151] Art. 13 provides the powers of the Court to initiate an investigation, if "a) A situation in which one or more of such crimes appears to have been committed is referred to the Prosecutor by a State Party in accordance with Art. 14; b) A situation in which one or more of such crimes appears to have been committed is referred to the Prosecutor by the UNSC acting under Chapter VII ... c) The Prosecutor has initiated an investigation in respect of such a crime in accordance with Art. 15, by not invoking Art. 53 that such an investigation would not be in the interest of justice, taking into account the interest of the victims and the gravity of the crimes." Art. 53 has obviously been added in order to allow for nonjudicial alternatives, such as truth and reconciliation commissions, or political deals to end civil strife.

[152] Of course that would imply not only a bilateral tit-for-tat strategy but also accepting the costs for enforcement by spreading the news.

[153] Typical of this attitude is the rather silly remark by Richard Goldstone (first prosecutor of the ICTY): "It seems to me that if you don't have international tribunals, you might as well not have international law." Simpson, *Law, War & Crime*, at 137.

but if not in the present, then post hoc in the future ... the system is justified by its impartiality, universality and neutrality in judging *and is even independent of the decision to intervene* [emphasis added].[154]

In other words, since justice has to be *done* the question of *when and how* do not arise, as the only germane questions concern the clarification of the principles and norms and applying them via the tricks of the trade to a fact pattern. Saying what the *law is* – in a "community" that still largely relies on self-help and leadership to solve its collective action problems – is different. I am not sure whether Anderson's argument is right, that it has to be "earned," but it cannot be right to limit the problematique of justice to sporadic *ex post* interventions of some courts. Seen in this light, the experiences in Rwanda (where French troops were *in loco* and could have prevented or minimized the genocide)[155] and Yugoslavia (where UN troops watched the slaughter at Srebrenica, as insufficient troops had been committed to the proclaimed "safe haven") take on a different and more sinister meaning. They seem to bear out the ruminations of Justice Pal at Tokyo that by conducting such trials the Western powers are enabled "to repent their violence and permanently profit by it."[156]

Verdicts and their Legitimation

While the above argument concerns the episodic pronouncements by international courts, which militate against important aspects of justice and draw our attention away from other modes of handling problems, there is also a problem in equating even the competent "application" of law with "justice" *tout court*. As Jack Balkin avers:

Human law, culture and conventions are never perfectly just, but justice needs human law culture and convention to be articulated and enforced. There is a fundamental inadequation [*sic*] because of our sense of justice and the products of culture, but we can only express this inadequation [*sic*] through the cultural means at our disposal ...

---

[154] Anderson, "The Rise of International Criminal Law," at 338.

[155] See the "genocide fax" sent by General Roméo Dallaire, Commander of the UN peacekeeping mission (UNAMIR), on January 11, 1994, to UN Headquarters, which forbade his intervention in the rapidly deteriorating situation. For his account, see Roméo Dallaire, *Shake Hands with the Devil: The Failure of Humanity in Rwanda*, London: Arrow, 2005. See also Michael N. Barnett, *Eyewitness to a Genocide: The United Nations and Rwanda*, Ithaca, NY: Cornell University Press, 2002.

[156] Simpson, *Law, War & Crime*. at 137. See also Elizabeth S. Kopelman, "Ideology and International Law: The Dissent of the Indian Justice at the Tokyo War Crimes Trial," *New York University Journal of International Law and Politics*, 23:2 (1991): 373–444.

Hence our laws are imperfect not because they are bad copies of a determined form of Justice but because we must articulate our insatiable longing for justice in concrete institutions and our constructions can never be identical with or inspire them.[157]

This realization raises further questions as to whether "ideal theory" can deliver on its promise, i.e. deriving the assent to a decision from the transcendental conditions of the norms being applied. The above short quote from Balkin alerts us instead to some important points. First, Balkin casts doubt on whether the usual way of "theorizing" is useful for clarifying the peculiarities of practical choices. Second, he calls our attention to the importance of emotions in framing moral issues instead of leveling everything by making it a cognitive problem. Hume saw that moral questions involve sentiments, as we have seen, and why imagination rather than reason (understood in the modern way as instrumental reason) is the decisive faculty at work here. But this raises, at least indirectly, a third point, i.e. the problems which arise when "the wish becomes father to the thought" – as Goethe had it – and enthusiasm takes over, which makes "being on the right side" the only criterion.

Finally when we take emotions seriously we have to become aware that international criminal law faces quite different situations from those we encounter among the "normal" largely opportunistically driven criminals in the domestic arena, who defraud or engage in violence in order to "get something." However, for the crimes falling within the domain of international criminal justice, "gang" warfare might be a better analogy, as it is frequently "respect" – including the existential issue, i.e. being a member of a certain group – which serves as the "driver," rather than the tangible benefits. After all, one does not wake up one day ready to commit "genocide," but one does so when one's standing and existence are at issue. This presupposes an entirely different motivational structure and organizational context. It obviously functions quite differently from the deterrence that is supposed to issue from the *ex post* punishment of "normal" criminals.

Not surprisingly, perpetrators of crimes involving ethnic violence usually show little insight or remorse when put on trial, and their usual strategy is to depict themselves as "victims"[158] who have served their group, but who are now scapegoated not only by the "others," who, as victors, sit in judgment, but even by their own people. Even if a (new) political leadership, under pressure to deliver the alleged criminals to their respective courts, has been successful

---

[157] Jack Balkin, "Being Just with Deconstruction," as quoted in Sarah M.H. Nouwen and W.G. Werner, "Monopolizing Global Justice: International Criminal Law as Challenge to Human Diversity," *Journal of International Criminal Justice*, 13:1 (2015): 157–176, at 157f.

[158] Here it is important to distinguish between the first-person question à la Eichmann, "Why me?," and the third-person question which a sympathetic but disinterested spectator might ask such as "Why him and not her, or the fellow over there?" The first is self-serving, the second asked by the disinterested bystander is not, but points to the moral problem of equal treatment.

by using the notion of "sacrifice" and has "persuaded" the perpetrators to surrender "voluntarily" to prosecution – as was the case in Serbia and Croatia – the lessons are seldom the ones one would like to see.[159] The charges of show trials might stick, in which case the perpetrator is convicted. But if he gets off – because the evidence might not be sufficient for conviction, as witnesses do not show up, or cannot, traumatized as they usually are, identify their torturer – this verdict can then be used by domestic groups to claim that this "proves" that the charges had been trumped up, and that "no crimes" were committed after all.

Of course, such an interpretation undermines one of the most important purposes of such trials, i.e. establishing a record of what happened. Contrary to the intent of counteracting impunity and preserving the memory of the suffering visited on the victims, a trial might give rise to a "history" that has little to do with what happened, as criminal evidence and historical evidence are not the same. The perpetrators can then return as unscathed "victors" since their "innocence" has been proven by the not-guilty verdict. They can play on the polysemy of the term "truth," since in law both innocence and guilt can never be "proven" as in geometry or in cases involving "matters of fact." Rather the appraisal that emerges from vetting of the evidence during the trial is an assessment that a certain state of affairs is "held to be true" (according to the rules of procedure under which a court has to operate). That such a "holding" can be a far cry from what happened is often established by later historical research. Unfortunately, that does not help the victims of perpetrators who have been "let go," but even the most painstakingly researched historical record seldom ends the controversies, as I will show in the next chapter. It certainly does not help that most of the recent trials are not, like Nuremberg, largely based on extensive documentation left behind by a fully bureaucratized state, on which the prosecution could then build its case. Rather the courts have to rely predominantly on "eyewitnesses" and translators to establish a record of what happened. Given these circumstances, the expectation that the "truth" will emerge from such proceedings is often little more than a pious dream, as has amply been documented by Coombs.[160]

The problem is not only that the testimony of eyewitnesses is far less reliable than is usually assumed, but that cultural differences enter the picture when seemingly straightforward questions, such as "Were you his wife?" or "Was Mr. X your commander or the person you took orders from?" or

[159] See e.g. Stephan Parmentier and Elmar Weitekamp, "Punishing Perpetrators or Seeking Truth for Victims: Serbian Opinions on Dealing with War Crimes," *International Criminal Law Review*, 13:1 (2013): 43–62.
[160] Nancy A. Combs, *Fact-Finding without Facts: The Uncertain Evidentiary Foundations of International Criminal Convictions*, Cambridge: Cambridge University Press, 2010.

"Did you go on this and this day to town x?" do not elicit straightforward answers. Witnesses do not understand what e.g. a commander (in the relevant sense of the law) is, or have difficulty remembering specific dates, or are unclear (or refuse to provide an answer) as to whether they were e.g. forced by their family or the accused to be "one" of the alleged perpetrator's wives. This is not only a problem of language or general cultural orientation, but also often involves a question of the purpose of justice.

It is certainly true that part of the struggle within the politics of international criminal law is "whose story" is told and heard. Although a witness might be eager to tell the story, s/he also comes to the court in order to ask for help, as she now has perhaps to live cheek by jowl with the perpetrator(s) who might have killed her whole family. Under such circumstances her aim of "getting justice" might not primarily mean fighting "impunity," but patching up the rent fabric of her life or what is left of it, even if this does not coincide with the preferences of "principled" lawyers from abroad. Given the latter's circumstances they can, from the safety of their offices, oppose amnesties in principle, insist on strict prosecution, remain lukewarm towards other means of reconciliation (such as truth and reconciliation commissions), and need not discover (if at all) that the victims are real persons with their own minds and projects.

Establishing the Record: Zundel, Pétain, Barbie?

The above remarks suggest that entrusting the fate of "their story" to a court might be problematic for both victims and the society alike. One way of correcting the potential dangers is, of course, to commission a report, as was done in the case of Argentina,[161] or the various inquests and continued projects in Germany, after its unification. Even here, getting at the larger truth, by weaving together different pieces of evidence and eliciting answers from participants in carefully structured interviews, can get tricky very quickly, as Sarah Nouwen has shown.[162] That such "reconstruction" has only marginally to do with the ability of courts to "compel" the evidence can be shown from several domestic trials in Canada and France.

Consider in this context the famous Zundel case in Canada. Gary Simpson has analyzed how in the two trials of Zundel, who had been charged with violating a Canadian law against Holocaust denial, which set the stage for a

---

[161] The *Nunca más* Report (officially The National Commission on the Disappearance of Persons CONADEP) was delivered to President Alfonsin (who had commissioned it on December 15, 1983) on September 20, 1984. In it the number of proven disappearances was put at 8,961 but some sources put it at high as 30,000. Accessible through the *Pro Quest* database.

[162] See Sarah M.H. Nouwen, "'As You Set out for Ithaka': Practical, Epistemological, Ethical, and Existential Questions about Socio-Legal Empirical Research in Conflict," *Leiden Journal of International Law*, 27:1 (2014): 227–260.

later decision of the Canadian Supreme Court, Zundel's lawyer, Douglas Christie, managed to have survivor testimony thrown out because of the trauma they had experienced in the camps; similarly, filmed evidence of the gas chambers and crematoria was dismissed under the hearsay rule. Even experts on Holocaust scholarship were placed on the same level of "expert opinion" as Holocaust deniers (such as Robert Faurisson). Thus Simpson's analysis suggests that Christy's defense strategy was to argue that

Holocaust history was in the process of constant revision and reinvention and that the work of Holocaust deniers was a respectable part of this professional ferment . . .

In the end the Canadian Supreme Court decided that the statute under which Zundel was prosecuted was itself unconstitutional because it breached the freedom of expression . . . The law in the court, and in the Constitution in a different way, elevated Holocaust denial into a position of equivalence with other histories of the mid 20th century. The court-room proceedings treated each party impartially and each view was subjected to a degree of neutrality. The Charter meanwhile protected the right of deniers along with the right of those who asserted the existence of the Holocaust.[163]

Similarly, the French trials of Maréchal Pétain and Pierre Laval on the one hand, and that of Paul Klaus Barbie on the other, provide perhaps the most striking examples of the pitfalls of trying to get to the "truth" (or rather establish the meaning of certain actions and events) through trials. They also provide much food for thought as to what extent the "histories" that emerge from such trials can lead us to a critical reflection on what happened and what we should do to come to terms with the past.

Seen from this angle, i.e. the angle of practice, the paramount issue is no longer the political vs. the legal divide, the decisive issue becomes rather which type of politics of law emerges, i.e. what space for praxis, linking politics, law, and morals, is thereby opened or foreclosed. While I cannot provide a definite answer to the dilemmas raised, I am highly skeptical of using trials as pedagogical instruments because of the emotional pull these extraordinary events have. Trying to use those energies seems more likely to end up in either enthusiasm or in "kitsch," as Martti Koskenniemi once suggested. Rather than attaining an adequate understanding of what the tasks (*Aufgaben*) are that we, as political beings, have to address, we are overwhelmed by human-interest stories and our own traumas and desires. In order to make this argument clearer let us first return to the Pétain and Laval trials, and visit the Barbie trial thereafter.

Both trials occurred during the *dépuration* phase of French history. France had to come to terms with both the widespread collaboration with the Nazi regime and with the *indignité nationale*, conceived not only as a term of moral

---

[163] Simpson, *Law, War & Crime*, at 87.

assessment, but also as a new crime (!). For this purpose the Haute Cour de Justice, set up originally as an organ of the Senate under the Constitution of the Third Republic, was revived. It had been abolished by the Vichy regime but was reconstituted in a different configuration: instead of the senators, three magistrates and twenty-four jury members – half from Parliament and half from citizens having demonstrated a "patriotic and resistant attitude towards the enemy" – was to hear the indictments against Pierre Laval and, in a separate proceeding, that of Maréchal Pétain. The former was a French politician during the Third Republic, and later *spiritus rector* of the Vichy government's collaboration with the Nazi occupiers. Maréchal Pétain had been a war hero in World War I, but having signed the armistice with Hitler and having become head of the French government, while General de Gaulle had formed his government in exile, he had also become the symbol of the illegality of the Vichy regime.

The proceeding against both of them promised an extraordinary spectacle. Laval was one of the most hated men in France,[164] identified not only with the atrocities committed against members of the Resistance and with mass deportations, but with France's weakness and decline long before the capitulation. Pétain was at least a hero, who had failed, however, at the decisive moment in his life and had therefore, despite his previous merits, besmirched the honor of the nation.

The law to be applied in both trials was a (modified) version of Article 75 of the Criminal Code dealing with treason and offences against state security, labeled as "intelligence with the enemy." It therefore required some evidence that the Pétain's government had been illegitimate from the beginning. This was accomplished by a dubious accusation raised during the trial, that Pétain had already conspired during the Third Republic to establish a dictatorship in France with the help of Franco and Hitler, for which no proof was ever presented and which was discarded in the judgment. The same was true of the case against Laval. For that purpose his anti-war stance in the pre-World War II period, and his predictions of the defeat of Great Britain and of German victory, were used by the prosecutor, who connected these facts with the "policy of annoyance," i.e. with the reduction of the war potential of France and the defeatist mood after Hitler's attack.

Obviously, part of the agenda was a reconstruction of the history of the French defeat. In other words, the court had to tackle the tricky situation in

---

[164] This can be seen from the remark by the prosecutor – not one of the finest testimonies to the impartiality of the trial – in the closing statement that unfortunately Laval had not been killed by an "act of popular justice" when he visited Paris in August 1944. Dov Jacobs, "A Narrative of Justice and the (Re-)Writing of History: Lessons Learned from World War II French Trials" in Kevin Jon Heller and Gerry Simpson (eds.), *The Hidden Histories of War Crimes Trials*, Oxford: Oxford University Press, 2013, 122–136, at 132.

which not only the "kingpins" but other normal people, who had brought through their actions not only "shame to themselves, but to France," were to blame. To that extent the *indignité nationale* was to legitimize the acts by which the French Republic could declare "that these citizens were not worthy of the same rights as other citizens."[165] That such a construction of the "facts" is not just revisionist speculation can be seen from other gambits which tried to erase the historical circumstance that the Third Republic had voluntarily transferred power to Pétain, well knowing that he, as a member of the last government of the Third Republic, had been explicitly asked to negotiate the armistice with Hitler.

Both trials went to considerable lengths to show the power of the accused was acquired by political maneuvering, i.e. what the prosecutor in the Laval case called a *coup d'état*. In the case of Pétain, his accession to power was not counted from the moment of vesting him with powers by Congress (July 10, 1940) that also dissolved the Third Republic, but from June 15, when he was invited to join the last government of the Third Republic. The significance of this date was that the armistice with Germany was signed on June 22, and while the cabinet had been divided and some members were leaving for exile, the deal was struck. The proceedings now placed the "ultimate crime," i.e. the signing of the armistice, plainly on the shoulders of Pétain. When he was convicted and condemned to death (with a one-vote majority) the court expressed the wish that the judgment would not be executed.[166] De Gaulle agreed and eventually commuted Pétain's death sentence to imprisonment, complying in this way with the "wish" of the court.

The trial of Klaus Barbie (May–July 1987) on the other hand brought a former SS commander into the dock, who had personally tortured suspected members of the French resistance at Lyon, aside from rounding up scores of people for deportation to the death camps. It exposed the darker side of the "collaboration" period, even if the sensational claims made by the defense at the beginning of the trial, that Jean Moulin, a leader of the Resistance, had been a victim of a plot within the Resistance itself, were never substantiated. Barbie's defense counsel Jacques Vergès,[167] who had made his reputation in several trials of FLN members accused of terrorism during the Algerian war, skillfully exploited the somewhat strange legal situation prevailing in 1978, by turning attention away from crimes committed by Barbie to the more general question of imperialism and to the widespread collaboration of Western intelligence services with Nazi henchmen.

---

[165] Ibid., 127.

[166] See Charles de Gaulle, *Discours et messages*, vol. 2, Paris: Plon, 1974, at 239f.

[167] Jacques Vergès's, foible for "anti-imperialist" causes (probably due to his background as the son of a French diplomat and a Vietnamese mother) is further evidenced by his defense of Khmer Rouge leaders in 2001, of Carlos the Jackal in 1994, and Tariq Aziz in 2008.

Different from the earlier trials held in France immediately after the liberation, where crimes against humanity had been incorporated into French law by the adoption of the Nuremberg Charter, three subsequent laws had complicated matters considerably by the late 1970s. One was the general amnesty of 1962 for "infractions" committed by French soldiers during the Algerian war. The second was the 1964 legislation against the "inprescriptability" of crimes against humanity, which was however superseded by a second general amnesty voted by the National Assembly in 1968, for all acts committed during the Algerian war (despite the imprescriptability statute of 1964!) by members of the military.[168] The squaring of the circle for the prosecutor now consisted in showing that a qualitative distinction could be made between "normal" war crimes including crimes against humanity on the one hand, and those which the Nazis and their helpers had perpetrated on the other. The solution was provided by an appeals court during the preliminary investigation of the Barbie trial: it created a special category for

all inhuman acts and persecutions which in the name of a state practicing a policy of *ideological hegemony* [emphasis added] have been committed systematically not only against persons because of their membership in a racial or religious group, but also against opponents of this policy whatever the form of opposition.[169]

To that extent the surprising situation arose that the accused could only be charged with crimes against humanity if the latter were undertaken by a state (and its implementers) that was committed to Nazi ideology. This, of course absolved any possible crime perpetrated by Resistance members, since they were the result of the liberation of France, or were done in pursuance of the enlightened goals of the French state, as in Algeria. The downside of this argument was that the prosecutor had now to prove that the atrocities had, so to speak, a special *mens rea* requirement: Nazi ideology.

Barbie had been twice convicted *in absentia* by French courts (1946, 1952), but had escaped extradition to France because of his work for British and American intelligence in Germany. When finally the pursuers were on his heels, he was sent with a false passport to Bolivia (in the name of Klaus Altman), where he was active in hunting down Che Guevara, but also served as an informant for German intelligence, finding customers for old German

---

[168] A third general amnesty was decreed including also the members of the OAS in 1982 by President Mitterrand (OAS was the illegal organization of French settlers, that opposed de Gaulle's withdrawal from Algeria and terrorized Algeria after the Evian Accords of 1982, which had led to an armistice with the Algerian FLN and prepared Algerian independence).

[169] Cour de Cassation, Judgment of May 20, 1985, as quoted in Guyora Binder, "Representing Nazism: Advocacy and Identity at the Trial of Klaus Barbie," *Yale Law Journal*, 98:7 (1989): 1321–1383, at 1337. The preliminary investigation took over three years from Barbie's extradition to France (February 1983); the main trial began in May 1987.

military hardware. Having survived an attempt on his life by a French "intelligence operation," he was finally expelled from Bolivia in February 1983 and escorted to France to stand trial.

The special circumstances referred to above then provided for a strange trial since the defense was able to hijack the process by four moves. One was an attack on the main gist of the accusation by taking it seriously, while blunting its edge. It tried to show that the charge of "crimes against humanity" as a plot of Nazi ideology was of questionable legality since the purpose of the trial was to "judge a man ... not to condemn an ideology," as Vergès sarcastically noted, since the "place for that is a political meeting."[170] The second move suggested that the distinction between Nazism and "normal" crimes against humanity was not only a self-serving ploy, but also tried to hide the fact that Nazism was only one version of a common problem: Western imperialism. The third move was the establishment, by implication, that the history of the case in previous trials showed an egregious lack of concern for the victims of the Holocaust by not raising these issues in the previous trials and in amalgamating them with those of the French Resistance. Move four used the official requirement of proving that the charges had to be shown as emanating from Nazi ideology, as a perfect cover for Barbie's absenting himself from the trial by letting his defense counsel take up virtually the entire case against the Nazism charge.[171]

The grotesque result was that Vergès could depict nearly everyone as a Nazi, save the accused in the dock! In addition, given the enormous media attention to the trial, the "show" elements increasingly overshadowed the "search for truth" and the meting-out of justice. Guilt was replaced by sentimentalism, and lesser issues tended to crowd out the more important ones because of their sensational vividness. Thus Barbie's shaking hands with the Algerian, Congolese or Vietnamese members of his defense team conveyed the message that he was no longer, or actually never was, a racist. To that extent the trial, although ending in Barbie's conviction and a sentence of life imprisonment (July 4, 1987), represented for the public intellectual Alain Fienkelkraut a "moral failure,"[172] precisely because of its show elements and the media spectacle it had generated.

---

[170] See Vergès's objection to Prosecutor Truche's statement in Binder, "Representing Nazism," at 1399.

[171] Right from the beginning Barbie depicted himself not only as a victim (scapegoat) but also announced his intention "not to be present." "If I find myself here today it is because I have been illegally expelled ... It is therefore for my lawyer to defend me ... The trial might follow its course. The witnesses may come ... But I shall not be present. I will be represented by my lawyer." Binder, "Representing Nazism," at 1355.

[172] Alain Finkielkraut, *Remembering in Vain: The Klaus Barbie Trial and Crimes against Humanity*, trans. Roxanne Lapidius, New York: Columbia University Press, 1992.

This criticism raises four issues that have bedeviled such trials. There is first of all always a "show "element, for the simple reason that part of the purpose of any legal proceedings is to bear witness to a deed that is considered a grave transgression, as I tried to argue in the chapter on "showing." Second, the show element is naturally reinforced by the "extraordinary" nature of the transgressions, not only in terms of their scope and frequency, but their being done "in the name" of the law, and thus perverting justice. To that extent Bass's general argument that the charge of "show trials" is a blunt one has a point, since much depends on *by which state* and *for what purposes* these trials are used.[173] But he is certainly mistaken in the assumption that such trials in the hands of liberal states or a cosmopolitan community speaking in the name of humanity are, because of their liberal pedigree, immune from such derailments. As Frédéric Megret suggests, the issue is not so much what happens in the courtroom,

... *as who ends up* in the courtroom. The apparent legal normality of the trial, in the end is derived from and almost entirely conditioned by the very exceptionality of the discretion over who should stand trial. The creation of a permanent ICC was supposed to have marginalized that element of discretion; instead it has simply displaced it from some external political actor to ... the tribunal's operation. The exceptional power to decide who stands trial has become the rule. That element alone suggests a considerable space for politics of criminal international criminal justice ... it implicitly portrays the ICC prosecutor for example as a sort of sovereign with the unique decisionist ability to lay the foundations for the on-going order of international criminal justice.[174]

Of course some distinctions between show trials, abusing politics and law alike, and these trials are easy to find: above all in the cancellation of presumption of innocence, the right of facing the accuser, and the protection guaranteed by a regular procedure. Whatever the failings of the discussed trials may have been, they were quite different from what was seen at the Moscow show trials (1935–1938) under Stalin,[175] or during the the trials of Slansky and others in the late 1940s, which accompanied the tightening grip of Soviet control on the "people's democracies." In the latter case Moscow decreed that a conspiracy involving high party officials had to be "uncovered" and Soviet "advisors"

---

[173] Bass, *Stay the Hand of Vengeance*, at 16: "the phrase victor's justice is in the end a largely uninformative one. The kind of justice one gets depends on the nature of the conquering state. The question is not whether we are looking at victor's justice ... But which victor? And what justice?"

[174] Frédéric Mégret, "International Criminal Justice: A Critical Research Agenda" in Christine E.J. Schwöbel (ed.), *Critical Approaches to International Criminal Law: An Introduction*, Abingdon: Routledge, 2014: 17–53, at 25.

[175] See Stephen F. Cohen, *Bukharin and the Bolshevik Revolution: A Political Biography, 1888–1938*, New York: Oxford University Press, 1980; Robert Conquest, *The Great Terror: A Reassessment*, New York: Oxford University Press, 1990; Wendy Z. Goldman, *Inventing the Enemy: Denunciation and Terror in Stalin's Russia*, Cambridge: Cambridge University Press, 2011.

were sent to the eastern European capitals with specific instructions. As one of them told his dumbfounded Czechoslovakian hosts in response to their objections: "We have been sent here to stage trials, not to check whether the charges are true."[176] Consequently the proceedings were conducted in special courts on "Matters of State Security," and special regulations, such as the notorious regulation No. 25 (January 1950) in Czechoslovakia, provided that

> The Court must inform the Prosecutor in advance of the judgment it is about to hand down and get his opinion whether the judgment is correct . . . The Prosecutor's opinion is binding on the court.

> Dress rehearsals were conducted prior to these Czech trials and these rehearsals were taped so that if the defendant deviated from the script then the microphone was switched off and the tape would begin playing the defendant's pre-recorded responses.[177]

While the miscarriages of justice that emerge from such arrangements can be easily recognized, less clear are the subtle or the not too subtle and perhaps even the unintended consequences that result from the framing of the problem: that courts should be not only an institution invoking a moral collective representation (humanity) but that their "neutrality" and their procedures should be the appropriate means for making present and sustaining these collective representations. As I have tried to show, such hopes are hardly sensible, even if international criminal trials are not simply show trials. Furthermore, as the lengthy discussion in France about the Holocaust and its misuse, as well as the problematic notion of founding Jewish identity on the unprecedented status of being a victim, showed, the courts' contribution to historical "truth" and to the construction of an "identity by trial" are rather controversial. From what was said it seems difficult to justify the belief in the "pedagogical" purpose and the "cumulative effect" of such trials, especially when they are accompanied by suggestions that they "should be designed as monumental spectacles" in order to "maximize their pedagogical impact."[178]

"People" might love such spectacles – and usually are willing participants in this type of "pedagogical" exercise – but this is hardly conclusive evidence for their desirability. Spectacles range from May Day parades to the epic spectacles of *Star Wars* or to the neatly packaged and sanitized Disney versions of dramas and fairy tales, to the court dramas of Perry Mason, or the hooligan fights at soccer games. But their popularity is not relevant evidence precisely

---

[176] As quoted in Simpson, *Law, War & Crime*, at 121.   [177] Ibid., 130.

[178] Mark J. Osiel, *Mass Atrocities, Collective Memory, and the Law*, New Brunswick, NJ: Transaction Books 1997. Although Osiel is aware of "six obstacles," he thinks that such "considerations of dramaturgy have proven quite valuable to this [pedagogical] end." This is because those are "liberal show trials," conducted by what have been called "moral entrepreneurs" and "activists of memory." Thus it just seems that the trick is to get the right kind of people who will do the right kind of thing.

because it hides the price of these joy rides of enthusiasm, or of the balmy feelings of righteousness that envelop us,[179] relieving us from the usual doubts in practical life. As the novelist Milan Kundera so aptly put it: "When the heart speaks the mind finds it indecent to object."[180] What makes morality plays so satisfying is that they convey simple truths, creating clarity by the melodramatic representation of perpetrators, victims, and heroes who save them. The problem then for courts is – as Fienkelkraut and Hannah Arendt have pointed out – to prevent such melodramatic elements taking over, although what the public at large "makes of" such trials and of the lessons contained in them is no longer within the power of such a court.

In the case of the ICC, the recent focus on "victims" (rather than on deterring aggression, or contributing to re-socialization and conciliation) and their actual involvement in the proceedings[181] seems to have strengthened the melodramatic elements, as the analysis of Sarah Kendall and Sarah Nouwen[182] suggests. This can be seen from the "hierarchy of victims" which international criminal law wittingly or unwittingly has created. Thus persons who have their house bombed or a family member killed because they were caught in the crossfire during an armed conflict cannot be legally relevant "victims" in a criminal trial since the victimization is not the result of a crime. A second and third selector for becoming a "victim" is then the existence of a "case" either through referral or the *proprio motu* investigation of the prosecutor,[183] and the prosecutor's decision to pursue certain charges rather than others.

A fourth "filter" is de facto applied by the court's recognition of that status, as not all those affected by a crime that occurred within the confines of a "case" can be recognized. Only those who are willing to "cooperate" with the court and who fill out the required form can be considered, while those who oppose e.g. criminal charges, as well as those who fail to finish the paperwork, have

---

[179] See also Robert Meister's criticism about "humanitarian compassion" that makes us feel good about feeling bad and insinuating that this compassion is its own reward. Robert Meister, *After Evil: A Politics of Human Rights*, New York: Columbia University Press, 2010, at 404.

[180] Milan Kundera, *The Unbearable Lightness of Being*, New York: Harper & Row, 2005. Koskenniemi has used that quote and Kundera's characterization of this world of simple truths and obvious certainties as "kitsch" in order to highlight the difference between false and genuine universalism in international law. See Martti Koskenniemi, "International Law in Europe: Between Tradition and Renewal," *European Journal of International Law*, 16:1 (2005): 113–124, at 121f.

[181] The "innovation" of greater participation in proceedings became already visible in Art. 22 of the ICTY Statute (or Art. 2 of the International Criminal Tribunal for Rwanda (ICTR) Statute) but has been expanded in Art. 43(6) (outlining a witness protection program) and Art. 68 of the ICC Statute.

[182] Sara Kendall and Sarah Nouwen, "Representational Practices at the International Criminal Court: The Gap between Juridified and Abstract Victimhood," *Law and Contemporary Problems*, 76 (2013): 235–262.

[183] In the case of a "situation" involving state-parties to the Statute, the Prosecutor can do so with the approval of a pre-trial chamber of the court.

lost their "voice." Of course, a further (unintended) filter is the ability of the Registry of the court to process all applications in time.[184] Fifth, an exercise of the right of participation will obviously depend on the perpetrators being in the custody of the court, otherwise this right has to stay in abeyance. If all that were not enough, the court has to select "recognized victims" who are willing to testify and who can corroborate the charges by fitting well within the Prosecutor's strategy. The result is a further reduction (sixth filter), as the search is now on for "good witnesses" likely to impress the court by their testimony. But this also means that last-minute strategizing by the Prosecutor might practically "de-recognize" previously recognized victims. The Bemba trial illustrates the first possibility where only five out of five thousand recognized victims were called to be present at the trial;[185] the Katanga trial illustrates the second, where the four victims, selected out of a pool of four hundred, were finally considered to be "unreliable" before they even arrived at The Hague.[186]

Given this complicated system of establishing "juridical victims," it is not surprising that the legitimacy of protecting the "victim" – used then in the collective singular – has to lie elsewhere, particularly since the notion of protection by punishing the perpetrators of atrocities is based on a conception of law as a "public good."[187] This means that the meting-out of justice is something that is in everybody's interest and is thus not exhausted by providing some victims their "day in court."[188] The Creation of a Trust Fund within the ICC framework, into which the fines and forfeitures ordered by the court[189] are deposited and which then can then be used for disbursements to the victims

---

[184] Thus Kendall and Nouwen note that, in the case of Callixte Mbarishimana, 470 "victims" could not be recognized due to the failure of the Registry to process the application in time. Kendall and Nouwen, "Representational Practices at the International Criminal Court," at 241.

[185] Ibid., at 252.   [186] Ibid.

[187] This is well captured in Kant's notion of "publicity." Obviously here the contemporary notion of a "collective good" (sometimes confusingly also called "common good") which focuses on market failure in producing certain goods in adequate supply. Aside from this terminological confusion it should be clear that the term "good" is used in the latter case in the sense of "commodity" rather than designating something "good" for all of us. In other words, the usage of a "common good" in the former sense points us towards something that should be in our *common* interest rather than just satisfying my or your need as a "private" person and consumer singly or in aggregation. To that extent the "supply" problem, on which market failure focuses, is, although connected, not the main concern, For the problems that arise out of the narrow focus of the market failure approach, see Friedrich Kratochwil, "Problems of Policy Design Based on Insufficient Conceptualization: The Case of Public Goods" in Ernst-Ulrich Petersmann (ed.), *Multilevel Governance of Interdependent Public Goods: Theories, Rules and Institutions for the Central Policy Challenge in the 21st Century*, Florence: EUI Working Paper RSCAS 2012/23, 2012: 42–61.

[188] This is also clear from the fact that the individual recognized victims have the right to an individual counsel or have no independent standing as participants in the proceedings but are "represented."

[189] Art. 79 ICC Statute.

and their families, has however left the strict confines of a criminal proceeding by offering some compensation. Nevertheless, any assignment of victim status by the court can, of course, be only provisional and must not be prejudicial to the rights of the accused,[190] since the whole point of the court proceeding is to establish whether or not the defendant is guilty as charged.

Thus while the courts has been keen on representing the victims as central actors and as authors who participate in the formation of the historical record, ensuring "that these crimes are not forgotten,"[191] their actual capacity to shape the outcome seems rather limited. Consequently, a different notion of the victim has to be invoked when the case for the fight against impunity for the sake of humanity is made. Far beyond any concrete and "legally recognized" victims, "the victim" in its collective singular refers to and symbolizes "victimhood" which mystically unites all who have suffered from international crimes.[192]

Such a move has several implications tending not only to "monopolize" the discourse of justice in terms of a mystical humanity, but also to suggest the "victim(s)" "serve as the highest symbolic entity within this juridical domain, in whose name justice is done."[193] Such a construction enhances the melodramatic elements in the morality play, in which the heroic outsider has to bring justice to the helpless. Both abstractions enable each other and make out of the chorus of bystanders an "international community" and a repository of universal values.

But, if, in a way, all the elements for a catharsis[194] seem to be present, the question is only whether this purification process is likely to occur, since significant differences from the genre of tragedy also exist. The latter assessment, of course, will probably not be denied by the onlookers or participants in the melodrama, since the obvious message of this genre is one of liberation and deliverance, not of tragic failure in which the drama's protagonists try to do the right thing but thereby bring about what they try to prevent. In the melodrama the hero, such as the occupant of the Office of the Prosecutor of the ICC – celebrated in several video productions,[195] which follow the

---

[190] Art. 63 (3) ICC Statute.
[191] For a further discussion, see Ralph J. Henham, *Punishment and Process in International Criminal Trials*, Aldershot: Ashgate, 2005, at 71f.
[192] See the critical assessment of Susan Marks and Andrew Clapham, "Victims" in *Human Rights Lexicon*, Oxford: Oxford University Press, 2005: 399–411.
[193] Kendall and Nouwen, "Representational Practices at the International Criminal Court," at 254.
[194] Aristotle derived this "cleansing" as a working through of the emotions of pity (*eleos*) and fear (*phobos*) which a particular situation of suffering we witness evokes. See Aristotle, "Poetics" in T. Allen Moxon (ed.), *Aristotle's Poetics & Rhetoric*, London: J.M. Dent and Sons, 1953, at 1449b.
[195] See the perceptive criticism of Wouter Werner comparing several documentaries dealing with crimes against humanity: *Carte Blanche*, in which several victims retell their experience of the pillaging of their village in the Central African Republic and their stories are examined from different perspectives; and four other, more "propagandistic," videos, in which the previous

Mission Impossible script – descends upon the victims who are depicted as passive, helpless objects. They have to await the outside intervention until justice is brought to them,[196] as in the well-staged video *The Prosecutor*, where the man in the white suit descends on a Congolese village. Meanwhile the international community can complacently look on, while enjoying the pleasurable feeling of compassion rather than having to address the individual and collective failings that have led to such situations in the first place.

The melodramatic genre might be particularly inapt since it makes it appear that the problem consists mainly in "getting" the perpetrators who are clearly recognizable. But precisely because in cases of mass atrocities the problem of "many hands" exists in an aggravated form, the attribution of individual guilt creates extremely difficult problems. The ICC departed, therefore, from some precedents set by previous tribunals and attempted in Art. 25 (a–d) a new definition of perpetrator and accessory, as well as complicity in a criminal enterprise. Whether this new formulation actually eliminates the disagreements[197] which arose from trying to navigate between different conceptions of different legal systems, also calling for different strategies[198] in transitional countries, remains to be seen.[199] In any case, looking at some recent judgments of the ICC, such as the judgments against Taylor or Katanga, the impression is rather

and the present Chief Prosecutors of the ICC are featured and "celebrities" like Mia Farrow and Angelina Jolie carry their brief, while supermodel Naomi Campbell enjoys the limelight in giving testimony in the Taylor trial. The videos examined are: *The Prosecutor, The Reckoning, The Court*, and *Kony*. Wouter G. Werner, "We Cannot Allow Ourselves to Imagine What It All Means: Documentary Practices and the International Criminal Court," *Law and Contemporary Problems*, 76:3–4, 2013: 319–339.

[196] See the criticism of Clarke, *Fictions of Justice*.

[197] See Kai Ambos, "International Criminal Law at the Crossroads: From 'Ad Hoc' Imposition to a Treaty-Based Universal System" in Carsten Stahn and Larissa van den Herik (eds.), *Future Perspectives on International Criminal Justice*, The Hague: T.M.C. Asser Press, 2010, 161–177.

[198] See the searching critique of Mark Osiel, "The Banality of Good: Aligning Incentives against Mass Atrocity," *Columbia Law Review*, 105:6 (2005): 1751–1862.

[199] Compare e.g. the rather critical comments of James Stewart concerning the conceptual problems of the new version of complicity: "... complicity has escaped careful theoretical scrutiny in the scholarly revolt against international modes of liability. This is peculiar, since complicity, or accessorial liability as it is otherwise known, is of central relevance to the Hitler-as-accessory dilemma; is increasingly prominent in international discourse; and, most importantly, also harbors a glaring conceptual anomaly – the doctrine holds the accomplice liable for the same crime as the perpetrator, even though the accomplice, by definition, did not personally carry out the offence. To illustrate, someone convicted of aiding genocide by supplying the weapons is herself guilty of genocide, even though she never killed a soul." James G. Stewart, "The End of 'Modes of Liability' for International Crimes," *Leiden Journal of International Law*, 25:1 (2012): 165–219, at 168. See also the criticism of Jens David Ohlin, "Three Conceptual Problems with the Doctrine of Joint Criminal Enterprise," *Journal of International Criminal Justice*, 5:1 (2007): 69–90.

one of confusion and unprincipled reasoning by the court which has, deservedly engendered severe criticisms.[200] There remain several difficulties. One is that of selectivity of prosecution, since blaming a number of prominent individuals for systemic levels of violence leads, in Drumbl's words, to "a very partial print of justice."[201] The second is the multiple conceptual problems which have already been mentioned in passing: the issue of conspiracy, the problem of *mens rea* or *dolus specialis*[202] (and their different manifestations in various legal systems), of a criminal enterprise, of immunity, of command responsibility and its different tests (on which courts disagree),[203] and of fitting the different goals of criminal law (retribution, deterrence, restoration) together in a convincing sentencing strategy.[204] A third set of problems concerns the proportionality of the punishment. Given the atrocities, it is almost impossible to fathom what a "fitting punishment" for them could be, without leaving the standards of the Enlightenment and modern penology behind, from which the ICC derives, however, its legitimacy. Finally, the fact that perpetrators and victims often change places in the mayhem of mass violence does not make things easier, as questions of *tu quoque* and of jurisdictional limitations[205] often violate the requirements of equal justice under the law.

Thus rather than having to deal with a few clearly identifiable monsters, we have to realize that, as Hannah Arendt observed in the case of Eichmann,

---

[200] On the Taylor judgment, see Kevin Jon Heller, "The Taylor Sentencing Judgment: A Critical Analysis," *Justice: Journal of International Criminal Justice*, 11:4 (2013): 835–855. On the Katanga Trial, see Carsten Stahn, "Justice Delivered or Justice Denied?: The Legacy of the Katanga Judgment," *Journal of International Criminal Justice*, 12:4 (2014): 809–834.

[201] See Drumbl, *Atrocity, Punishment, and International Law*, at 153.

[202] See the discussion of several conceptual innovations in the jurisprudence of the ICTY by Mohamed Elewa Badar, "Drawing the Boundaries of Mens Rea in the Jurisprudence of the International Criminal Tribunal for the Former Yugoslavia," *International Criminal Law Review*, 6:3 (2006): 313–348.

[203] See e.g. the differences between the ICTY and the ICJ in the area of command responsibility, immunity, and diplomatic protection, as pointed out in the speech by Rosalyn Higgins, President of the ICJ, to the Meeting of Legal Advisers of the ministries of Foreign Affairs on 29 October 2007, at icj-cij.org/presscom/files/7/14097.pdf.

[204] Ralph Henham, "Developing Contextualized Rationales for Sentencing in International Criminal Trials," *Journal of International Criminal Justice*, 5:3 (2007): 757–778.

[205] The fact that the Rwandan domestic *gacaca* courts (established in 2001 and discontinued in 2012) had no jurisdiction to try the Tutsi RPF members (Rwandan Patriotic Front, who had formed in Uganda and to whom the Hutu government surrendered after the civil war that followed the massacre in 1994) does not inspire confidence that the 10,000 or so trials were instantiations of equal justice under law. Worse is that even the ICTR "cooperated" with the new Tutsi government by not prosecuting Tutsis, especially after a row in 2002 with the Rwandan government (when such plans were floated by the court). In response the government placed a travel ban on witnesses so that they could not testify at the court in Arusha. See Human Rights Watch, "Rwanda: Justice after Genocide – 20 Years On" (2014). Available at www.hrw.org/news/2014/03/28/rwanda-justice-after-genocide-20-years.

stink normale (pathetically normal) people can apparently quite easily *become* monsters,[206] even in the aseptic setting of a bureaucracy, far removed from the emotional pathologies which we encounter in outbreaks of mass atrocities. As Alexander Solzhenitsyn once so aptly put it, fighting evil is not as simple as isolating and eliminating it.

If only it were so simple! If only there were evil people somewhere insidiously commit-ting evil deeds, and it was necessary only to separate them from the rest of us and destroy them. But the line dividing good and evil cuts through the heart of every human being.[207]

Addressing those issues obviously requires other remedies than just a show of "exemplary justice" administered by rather spotty *ex post* punishments. In noticing this we need not revive the debates about alternatives to the criminal paradigm, making space for other considerations, such as measures enhancing reconciliation or providing for increasing welfare or education, or more rapid responses to international crises that have the potential for genocidal conflict.

Of course, there is no magic bullet that takes care of all problems, so the endless debates whether we should fight impunity or instead trust "truth and reconciliation" commissions present false alternatives. But equally problem-atic is the common assumption of their compatibility as if they could work hand in glove. As Alison Bisset points out,[208] there are some hoary issues such as when the right to a fair trial for a perpetrator is at odds with the truth com-mission's objective to have the broadest information on the past by encour-aging perpetrators as well as victims to tell their story. What we need instead is a variety of policy options that have to be carefully weighted, but which will entail hard choices. It is exactly in this context that we have to see that profes-sions of mere faith in the virtues of criminal law are neither convincing nor responsible.

Here the dangers of an "ideal discourse on justice," which Balkin criticized above, become obvious, particularly if, in addition, it gets monopolized by the fascination with "punishment" as the *via regia* to social order. These two inter-acting problems raise two further issues. One is the paradox that despite its ineffectiveness and spotty performance, international criminal law has been able to wield considerable power (of the diffuse/constitutive, rather than agen-tial kind). But phrasing all issues of global order in terms of international criminal law, and equating the punishment of perpetrators with "global justice"

[206] Arendt, *Eichmann in Jerusalem*.
[207] Alexander Solzhenitsyn, *The Gulag Archipelago*, as quoted in David Keen, *Endless War? Hidden Functions of the "War on Terror"*, London: Pluto Press, 2006, at 9.
[208] Alison Bisset, *Truth Commissions and Criminal Courts*, Cambridge: Cambridge University Press, 2012: 187–199.

tout court, has some problematic consequences. As Nouwen and Werner point out, such a move

runs the risk of monopolizing the debate about global justice by international criminal law. The term "global justice" may still have a broader meaning in the context of social struggles against poverty and for access to basic services, but in response to armed conflict and so-called mass atrocities, international criminal law has increasingly appropriated the term.

The dark side of the rise, institutionalization and framing of issues in terms of international criminal law, and its equation with global justice, is that alternative conceptions of global justice are in danger of being pushed to the margins.[209]

The other issue is what a criminal discourse – cleansed of its pretense of being the voice for "humanity" as well as of its melodramatic trappings – could deliver. Here one important point which emerges from our discussion is that such a discourse would have to be attentive to the various conceptions of justice, which we find in different political and legal cultures and traditions. These issues have been as of late raised in the context of increasing African resistance to the interventions of the ICC, but go far beyond these particular complaints.[210]

To assume that the differences can be pushed aside by ascending the ladder of abstraction or by decreeing that the plurality of approaches are manifestations of different stages of legal development – whereby the Western notion of rule of law, "finally" freed from its Westphalian shackles, sits at the pinnacle – is simply counter-productive. Behind such a "mission" we can not only see the paternalistic or imperialist project of the white man's burden, but we also realize that moves in the name of clarity and harmony are silencing moves that go against everything we know about the practical world: that disagreements are rampant and that in order to live with them in a way that does not prevent social reproduction, we need laws, but not the silence of a "Perpetual Peace."[211] These laws emerge out of struggles, and they ratify victories, but precisely for that reason their "solutions" can hardly be eternal and beyond debate, even if ensconcing them in "the law" closes the controversies for some time. This realization has to come with the recognition that something new can only emerge if we have the "requisite variety" of views and a panoply of competing criticizable

---

[209] Nouwen and Werner, "Monopolizing Global Justice," at 171.

[210] See e.g. Christopher Graves, "The International Criminal Court and Individualism: An African Perspective" in Christine E.J. Schwöbel (ed.), *Critical Approaches to International Criminal Law: An Introduction*, Abingdon: Routledge, 2014: 221–245.

[211] This is Kant's takeoff when he warns his reader that the message of his treatise is not the same as the ironic reference conveyed by the sign of a Dutch innkeeper which depicted a graveyard with the lettering below: "The Perpetual Peace." See Kant, "Perpetual Peace," at 93.

solutions is available, including those which are skeptical about the proposition of *ex post* punishment.[212]

Instead of entrusting our fate to "theories" or predictions – which claim authority under the pretense of an immutable "truth" but which, on closer inspection, inevitably turn out to rely on (false) prophecies[213] and actually deprive us of our status as free agents – we had better take this Sisyphean challenge seriously. We have to fix the "leaky vessel while being on the high seas," as Hume once suggested.[214]

It is the task of the next few chapters to elaborate on these points that enable us to understand the world of praxis, its possibilities and limitations.

---

[212] Given the estimated cost of around US$1.7 billion (for ninety-two indictments), and reading again alarming reports from Burundi, one has to wonder what alternative preventive programs could have been financed. See also the critical television broadcast aired by the BBC on October 1, 2014, "Rwanda the Untold Story." According to another source, "the two ad hoc UN international tribunals (ICTY and ICTR) alone are estimated to have claimed roughly 15 per cent of the UN annual budget, which is a projected cost of around $25 million per case"; see Stewart, "The End of 'Modes of Liability' for International Crimes," at 216. Thus while the charges of a "justice industry" made by Jelena Subotic seem exaggerated, that of a "boutique justice" does not.

[213] Consider in this context Antonio Cassese's mind-boggling inference that "the result of the impunity of the leaders and organizers of the Armenian genocide, is that it gave a nod and a wink to Adolf Hitler and others to pursue the Holocaust some twenty years later" as quoted by Krever, "International Criminal Law: An Ideology Critique," at 702. Of course, since there is no evidence, we have to take such divinations on faith that the "sign" is known to the prophet.

[214] Hume, *A Treatise of Human Nature*, at 263f.

8   Remembering and Forgetting

8.1   Introduction: The Problem of History for Theory-Building

In a seminal article that started the "second debate" Hedley Bull, one of the exponents of the English school, advocated a "classical approach" for the study of international politics. He warned of submitting the study of politics too eagerly to the epistemological ideal of "science" because of the mistaken notion that only a form of knowledge based on the criteria of universality and necessity can claim to represent warranted knowledge. In a way Bull attacked the "unity of science position" which enjoyed increasing popularity in a time when, especially in the US, IR had emancipated itself from its original moorings in international law and organization, and attempted to gain intellectual respectability by becoming a subfield of political science. Among the "scientists" in this field there was of course ample disagreement whether we should claim scientific status by simply following a method that used measurements and empirics based on the law of large numbers, or whether a warranted knowledge was the result of an artful combination of logic and empirics, as logical positivism, emerging from the Vienna Circle, maintained.[1]

Bull was not interested in such differences, as he perceived both schools to be obtuse to the particularities of the social world, which required a form of knowledge that derived above all from sound judgment. This "power of judgment," however, comes from experience, from being exposed to a variety of complex problems and finding one's way through the thicket of the contingent factors that define choices, instead of relying either on ultimate and incontrovertible foundations, of subsuming a case under a covering law, or of relying on abstractions from the empirical cases by emptying them of content in order to get a large dataset.

With hindsight we have to acknowledge that Bull's frontal challenge had mixed results. It resonated largely with the older members in the field who

---

[1] For a powerful critique of these assumptions see Yale Ferguson and Richard Mansbach, *The Elusive Quest: Theory and International Politics*, Columbia, SC: University of South Carolina Press, 1988.

311

had been practitioners who had moved into academia after some practical experience in policy making. It certainly got assent from most historians and those in "international studies" who had "country experience." The latter knew very well that the world, when seen through the windows of buildings on the Charles River or San Francisco Bay (or even worse, when looked at from the prison cells of many of the new buildings of Midwestern universities), was not the same as what one saw in Delhi, São Paulo, Peking, Cairo, Moscow, or Accra. But Bull's intervention did not, of course, convince the other camp, whose members saw their dream thwarted of entering the temple of science – as the economists had just successfully accomplished by sharpening their methodological tools. It also did not sway the fence sitters of the discipline, partially because some of Bull's charges were overblown or inconsistent, and partially because he could not outline a "counterprogram" with sufficient clarity. "Judgment," after all, seemed something more appropriate for debates in clubs where on the occasion of the admission of a new member such a factor was discussed, in addition to "breeding," character, or style. No wonder that the new "professionals" preferred to be subject to "objective" certifications rather than to idiosyncratic judgments of the old guard, who had to be emasculated in accordance with Oedipal urges.

But as understandable as those motives might be, they do not dispose of the serious problem of judgment or, as Kant calls it, the "power of judgment" (*Urteilskraft*), when we deal with problems of praxis and its appropriate form of knowledge. Perhaps the most important reason why Bull's wake-up call was missed was that it came too early and that the jury was still out whether the rational "reconstruction of science," postulated by the "unity of science" school, bore out some of the central tenets of the epistemological project, which Hempel,[2] Popper, and others had elaborated, and which was supposed to serve as the lodestar for a "political science." In this context the logical requirement of "refutability" had become extremely important since it solved some conceptual puzzles that had arisen in the context of induction, which already had vexed Hume. The question was now whether "refutability"was used in actual research and provided the "demarcation criterion," which was able to adjudicate the disputes over what was considered good science and what was not.[3] While investigating this question involved a detour, leading us from the halls of philosophy to the actual practice of science in laboratories and in the "field," it also subjected the epistemological claims to the findings of history.

---

[2] Carl Gustav Hempel, *Aspects of Scientific Explanation, and Other Essays in the Philosophy of Science*, New York: Free Press, 1965.
[3] For this position see Karl Popper, *Conjectures and Refutations: The Growth of Scientific Knowledge*, New York: Harper & Row, 1965.

After all, it was Kuhn's investigation into the history of physics[4] which led not only to a different understanding of the poster child of science, physics,[5] but also engendered some fundamental changes in the conception of science. For Kuhn the process of knowledge production followed a different pattern than that "predicted" by the "theory of science." Instead of a steady and incremental process of conjectures and refutations, science was subject to jumps and gestalt shifts, which engendered fundamental controversies, as "revolutionary science" differed from "normal" science. The a priori specified epistemological criteria of the unity of science position came thereby under considerable pressure.

The engagement with a field's history also decisively shifted the emphasis from simple tests and a preoccupation with the discovery of universal laws, to a concept of science as a *practice* and a concern for the rules that constitute it, i.e. to an interest in individual cases, such as "crucial experiments," and to the role of judgment in science. Precisely because controversies among scientists could no longer be decided by some deictic procedure (just looking harder at "the facts"), or by some knockout logical demonstration, but the scientist had rather to assess the "weight" of various findings, requiring an orderly process of admission and exclusion of evidence, the *rules for practicing science* established the importance of the scientific community.

Instead of logic and the speculation about the nature of true statements, which were part of e.g. Popper's "Third World,"[6] we came to realize that knowledge production had an important practical and historical dimension. Not simple cumulative progress, but controversies and debates, as well as unexpected twists and turns, were now legitimate parts of the story. Since our research activities are not only dictated by techniques and measurement procedures, but are mainly fueled by "larger" philosophical questions, considerable uncertainty always remains where judgment, rather than strict obedience to a method, is required. Reflecting on the history of a field brings out this aspect since it is intimately related to the very practice of doing research in the field itself.[7]

In this chapter I want to follow the same method, and approach the problem of theoretical progress in IR not via some epistemological criteria, but via an examination of the *history of the discipline*, which opens the space for asking further questions. In this context I am interested particularly in the

---

[4] Thomas S. Kuhn, *The Structure of Scientific Revolutions*, 2nd edn., Chicago: University of Chicago Press, 1970.

[5] See here the criticism by physicist and philosopher of science Stephen Toulmin, in Stephen Toulmin, *Return to Reason*, Cambridge, MA: Harvard University Press, 2001, chaps. 1–5.

[6] See e.g. Karl Popper, *Objective Knowledge: An Evolutionary Approach*, Oxford: Clarendon Press, 1972.

[7] See the interesting argument by Cameron Thies that disciplines attain their identity via a (re) writing of the histories of the field. Cameron G. Thies, "Progress, History and Identity in International Relations Theory: The Case of the Idealist–Realist Debate," *European Journal of International Relations*, 8:2 (2002):147–185.

"second debate," because it was perhaps the defining moment for the field
morphing into an autonomous discipline, or more precisely, of becoming part
of political science. But I am less interested in actually following all the details
of the second debate[8] than in drawing out the wider logic of the argument of
practice and history that was not explicitly raised by Bull.[9]

Although even in the hard sciences judgments concerning the quality of
"evidence" rather than logical demonstration are of paramount importance in
all branches of knowledge production, such "judgmental" elements play an
even larger role in the social sciences. Politics is inherently *practical* since
it deals with doing the right thing at the right time in view of the particular
historical circumstances. For thinking coherently about those problems several
different skills are required, not only logic. Furthermore, rather than moving
from the specific to the general, as in the hard sciences, we proceed in social
analysis by developing prototypes, which are elaborated further through extensions and analogies. In reasoning from "case to case" we need again good
judgment for establishing relevant similarities and dissimilarities, rather than
generalizations or universal laws.

But this engagement with the historical world is also of quite a *different type*
than testing our theories by the "data" we have amassed over time. Especially
under conditions of rapid change, the past can no longer provide us with exemplars which we can apply without further ado to the case at hand. Consequently
the function of a historical reflection cannot consist in the "lessons"[10] of history,
or in the knowledge of "what really happened." Rather, it is through historical
reflection that we become aware of the dialectic of choice in which the past
(through recollection) is joined in the present with the future by means of a
political project. In understanding this dialectic we are little helped by traditional "theory," especially not by large *n*-multivariate analyses. Instead, given
that the historical facts, such as e.g. wars, are seldom entirely independent of
each other, that our decisions are underdetermined, and that outcomes can differ
in complex systems – even if the "course of events" began with the same initial
conditions – identifying the causes of conflicts usually engages us in difficult
operations of counterfactual reasoning. For that reason alone a straightforward
testing of a full-blown theory "against reality" seems hardly possible.

Paradoxically the encounter with history suddenly opens up new vistas and
the past loses its fixed nature since it is not considered analogous to a natural

---

[8] Morton A. Kaplan, "The New Great Debate: Traditionalism vs. Science in International
Relations," *World Politics*, 19:1 (1966): 1–20.
[9] Bull, "International Theory: The Case for a Classical Approach."
[10] On the change in our historical understanding of the past, see the fundamental discussion by
Reinhart Koselleck, "Historia Magistra Vitae: The Dissolution of the Topos into the Perspective
of a Modernized Historical Process" in *Futures Past: On the Semantics of Historical Times*,
Cambridge, MA: MIT Press, 1985, 21–38.

event but viewed as the result of conjunctures and of choices. Precisely because we know that things could have been different, the more we deepen our understanding of the past the more we begin to sense the opportunities forgone and thereby become aware of our own potential as agents. Of course, this does not mean that everything is now possible just because we no longer consider social reality as simply "given" and the familiar structures that constrain us are deconstructed in this reflective process. On the contrary, historical awareness clearly indicates that not everything is possible, as disagreements are rampant, collective action problems abound, dilemmas are real, and institutions are sticky. Furthermore, a proper reflection on the possibilities for action, present or past, does not provide us with a warrant to engage in fantasies of omnipotence just because the "necessities" with which we are confronted turn out to be mostly man-made and thus could have been otherwise. To that extent such an inquiry has to transcend the limits of a purely historical reconstruction, even though an engagement with the past is nevertheless the precondition for a proper appreciation of action as Hume has emphasized, whose "philosophy of common life" we will turn in the next chapter.

For the moment I am concerned with laying the groundwork for this engagement by investigating the importance of historical reflection. For that purpose my argument takes the following steps. In the next section (Section 8.2) I want to revisit the second debate and clear the ground of some of the debris left from it. In particular, starting with Bull's indictment I shall concern myself with the problems of measurement, judgment, and the alleged role of generalizations or laws in the social sciences. In explicating these problems I draw on two further debates: the democratic peace argument, and the place of macro-sociology in studying political developments. While in both cases history is largely treated as a storehouse for "data" which allow us to test theories, some of the recent discussions concerning historical facts bring to the fore the problem of their "emplotment" since historical facts are always part of a "story." The term "fact" derives after all from *facere* and this points to action taking place at a particular time. This occasions a discussion of why understanding praxis involves a "narrative" understanding. Since narratives are not reducible to some observational protocols or "basic sentences," as postulated by positivist epistemology, they have to satisfy distinct criteria of intelligibility, as suggested by Ricoeur,[11] Dray,[12] Gallie,[13] Danto,[14] and others. Those problems are discussed in Section 8.3.

---

[11] Paul Ricoeur, *Time and Narrative*, trans. Kathleen McLaughlin and David Pellauer, 3 vols. Chicago: University of Chicago Press, 1984–1988.
[12] Dray, *Laws and Explanation in History*.
[13] Gallie, *Philosophy and the Historical Understanding*.
[14] Danto, *Analytical Philosophy of History*.

To exemplify the importance of this realization – leaving therefore the confines of the second debate and embarking on the embellishment of Bull's intent – I examine in Section 8.4 the implications of a narrative understanding for social action and for the reproduction of the social world and its changes. For that purpose I contrast different processes of social reproduction: imitation, reproduction through norms, and finally reproduction on the basis of narrative understandings. For the latter the formation of an "English" identity in the Shakespearian historical dramas serves as my foil.

In Section 8.5 I turn my attention once more to the various ways in which this engagement with the "historical" dimension of action gets sedimented in, and formed by, the various genres of narratives. In this context I examine ways of "dealing with the past." The concluding section (Section 8.6) then links the present discussion to the next two chapters, which are devoted to Hume and his analytical and historical work. In those chapters I shall mainly focus on his criticism of subjecting the social world to the inappropriate criteria of "theory," or as Hume called it to "false philosophy." In this way Bull's plea for a "classical approach" is heeded and a fruitful heuristics for the realm of praxis can be outlined.

8.2   The Second Debate Revisited

For someone revisiting the second debate it is surprising how little some of the controversies in the field have changed since. To that extent the victory which the "scientists" in this debate have claimed seems to have been less than decisive. The opponents of science have not been subdued and the positions on the basis of which victory was claimed have often turned out to be mistaken,[15] as they were sometimes the result of faulty analogical reasoning,[16] and frequently showed an egregious lack of familiarity with the tricky epistemological issues

---

[15] See e.g. Kaplan's specification of essential rules for a balance of power system, which were contradictory. Morton A. Kaplan, *System and Process in International Politics*, New York: Wiley, 1967, chap. 2.

[16] See e.g. Kaplan's argument that purposeful action can – contrary to the argument of "traditionalists" – be explained by normal causal scientific inferences. The confusion in this debate – which shows that both Bull and Kaplan were right and wrong, depending upon the interpretation one gives to the term "explain" and purposive action – can only be cleared up when we keep the crucial difference between antecedent cause and motives as antecedent conditions in mind. In the case of natural phenomena (that is a physicalist framework) cause and effect have to be determined and measured independently from each other. The same is not true in the case of motivational accounts, where an observer can only impute "causal" motives if s/he takes the actor's perspective and assumes a goal (Aristotle's *hou heneka*) to be controlling. The imputation can be based on the actor's direct reports but need not be. This was Weber's famous argument against "empathy." For a further discussion, see Friedrich Kratochwil, "Errors Have Their Advantage," *International Organization*, 38:2 (1984): 305–320.

involved. On the other hand, some of Bull's arguments were also clearly problematic. They need to be restated, because they provide opponents with an opportunity to dismiss too easily Bull's larger point because of some infelicitous expressions on his part. In the following, I want first to critically examine Bull's seven propositions and then, having corrected some of them, focus on the central thesis with which Bull buttresses his plea for a "classical approach." Here the role of judgment and questions of the historical nature of the social world become the focal points which have important implications for theory building and for the *kind of* "knowledge" we need in order to address questions of praxis.

Let me begin with the clarification. As already mentioned, despite the fact that I consider Bull's argument as basically right, some of its steps were badly stated. For example, it is indeed hard to argue against the search for universal laws and then say that the "models" of IR "could just as well have been expressed as an empirical generalization" – quite aside from the fact that laws and generalizations work rather differently.[17] Similarly, to maintain that the "rigor and precision" to which the scientific approach aspires can be achieved "wholly within the classical approach"[18] seems rather off. After all, this argument contradicts two other major points of his: that the subject matter of politics might require different standards than those provided by logical calculi, and that choosing an erroneous methodological ideal is tantamount to cutting oneself off from history and philosophy, so that one is likely to end up with an impoverished research agenda (points 1 and 7).

The second, third and fifth propositions are variations on these themes. If the proponents of the "scientific" approach have provided us with any insights, it was, according to Bull, because they left the narrow confines of their own methodological criteria. But for that reason they were unlikely to make progress, save perhaps on some "peripheral topics," precisely because of their fetishization of measurement. However, to the extent that failure to meet one's own standard is a common failing among researchers of all colors, Bull's plea for a classical approach requires a more principled argument. It seems to me that Bull would have had to argue that the *notion of field-independent "scientific" criteria for truth* – endorsed by the unity of science position – is in itself not a useful "regulative idea." A brief discussion seems appropriate.

The belief in the objectivity of the scientific approach, as propagated in mainstream *social* science, seems to rely on several problematic metaphysical assumptions. The most important of these is the idea that "social kinds" do not differ in any significant way from "natural kinds." We can apprehend both through the same mode of careful observation, which in turn depends on rules

---

[17] Bull, "International Theory: The Case for a Classical Approach," at 370.
[18] See his point six in ibid., 375.

for insuring the objectivity of observation (operationalization). If we make these assumptions, then issues of "inference" become the decisive issues in theory building.[19] But there are two problems with that argument. The first is the famous one of induction; the other one concerns conceptualization that has to precede any form of operationalization and measurement.

As to the first: Is the observation of 1,000 white swans all over the world sufficient to buttress the claim that all swans are white? The observation of one black swan obviously disproves this universality and perhaps leads me to propose characteristics other than only color to define a species. Such a move raises, as we will see, several difficulties, which call into question even the notion of "natural kinds." When the boundaries of a species are "fuzzy" because several defining characteristics are utilized, of which only a few exemplars possess all, while several others have only few of them, then how many properties are enough for an attribution?

This simple example also illustrates the second problem, i.e. the fact that conceptualization has to be prior to any measurement and operationalization and those conceptual issues cannot be solved by measurement procedures.[20] Thus, contrary to the conventional claims of methodologists, classification does not follow the logic of a set of properties held to be necessary and sufficient for judging them as instantiations of a concept. Rather the formation of concepts and the establishment of classes proceed on the basis of *judgments of similarity*. Some prototypical case or exemplar instantiates the phenomenon and we include or exclude new cases by extensions and family resemblance.[21] Since the range of features that can be the basis for the judgments of similarity is virtually unlimited, even the notion of "natural kinds" seems problematic. The present controversy in biology on species shows surprising similarities to debates in social science concerning concept formation. This seems to indicate that the difficulties we encounter have nothing to do with the traditional division between natural and cultural sciences but issue from common misconceptions of conceptualization.

Concerning the "fuzziness" of concepts we should also be aware that this problem has little to do with traditional notions of probability, as the following example shows. The statement that a person with Asian, Black and European

---

[19] See e.g. "Research designed to help us understand social reality can only succeed if it follows the logic of scientific inference." Gary King, Robert Keohane, and Sidney Verba, *Designing Social Inquiry: Scientific Inference in Qualitative Research*, Princeton: Princeton University Press, 1994, at 229.

[20] On this fundamental issue, see Giovanni Sartori, "Concept Misformation in Comparative Politics," *The American Political Science Review*, 64:4 (1970): 1033–1053.

[21] For a fundamental discussion of light the cognitive revolution can shed on the process of concept formation, see George Lakoff, *Women, Fire and Dangerous Things: What Categories Reveal about the Mind*, Chicago: University of Chicago Press, 1987.

ancestors is "Caucasian" is true to some extent, and false in others, as would be any other assertion (such as this person is black). Consequently this "fuzziness" is not a problem that can be overcome by finding the proper measures for an "empirical" operationalization, but concerns rather the justifiability of the criteria we use in asserting what is the case in various instances.[22]

Whatever we might think of these controversies, one thing is certain: that such problems are aggravated in the social sciences where not simple observable elements (natural kinds) but *values* determine to a large extent the operations of our concepts, as Weber[23] has pointed out. Here Bull's argument about the need for judgment in the social sciences has a special weight, even if such problems are not unknown in the natural sciences. What "counts" as an instance of e.g. war or democracy, is neither answerable by a closer look at the phenomena, nor is it solved by strict operationalization and inter-coder reliability. Equally problematic is the assumption, that only trans-historically valid generalizations provide insights and warranted knowledge. As Paul Diesing once correctly pointed out: generalizations e.g. about US voting behavior "can be valid even though they apply only between 1948 and 1972 and only to Americans. Truth does not have to be timeless. Logical empiricists have a derogatory name for such changing truths (relativism), but such truths are real, while the absolute fully axiomatized and a-historical truth is imaginary."[24]

A second metaphysical assumption concerning objectivity becomes visible here. It is beholden to a rather suspect Platonic ontology that something truly "is" only when it does not change.[25] The whole Western tradition has always contrasted "true being" (*to ontos on*) with different forms of being (*ta onta*). The former is eternal, while the latter is the realm of growth and decay. We should, however, realize that on the basis of modern physics we might rather think about "things" and "objects" not as fixed entities, but as temporary stabilizations of various processes. In that case a totally different ontology emerges, as time is not identified with decay or lack of true being but change is the normal (true) condition. Whitehead[26] revived this alternative to Platonic thought, expounded originally by Heraclitus, for which Rescher[27] provided more recently a nearly mind-boggling alternative to the traditional

---

[22] Davis, *Terms of Inquiry*, chap. 4.

[23] See Max Weber, *Gesammelte Aufsätze zur Wissenssoziologie*, Tübingen: J.C.B. Mohr, 1971.

[24] Paul Diesing, *How Does Social Science Work?: Reflections on Practice*, Pittsburgh, PA: University of Pittsburgh Press, 1991, at 91.

[25] See Plato's distinction between *aion* and *chronos*, between eternity, which does not move, and time in his *Timaios*.

[26] Alfred N. Whitehead, *Process and Reality*, Chicago: University of Chicago Press, 1981.

[27] Nicholas Rescher, *Process Metaphysics: An Introduction to Process Philosophy*, Albany, NY: SUNY Press, 1996.

ways of thinking. Thus getting the context for these stabilizations right, both conceptually and historically – a problem that cannot be answered by building e.g. rigorous models based on assumptions, as Bull correctly suggested – is then more important than focusing on two or three variables that stay the same over time.

Given these difficulties, several gambits are available to adherents of the universality argument, all of which depend – given the ontological injunctions – on the elimination of history as a proper concern. One is the idea that "historical laws," explaining transitions from one epoch or period to another, can capture even transformative changes of a system. The other involves the opposite assumption, i.e. the existence of some trans-historical structures that work themselves out, irrespective of the intentions of the actors and the changes "on the surface," as Waltz suggested.[28]

However, a moment's reflection shows the problematic nature of both gambits. The first relies on a philosophy of history,[29] in which the philosopher now plays the role of God who looks upon the "developments" from an absolute point beyond time. For him everything is contemporaneous and history can only be conceptualized as some type of "unfolding," be it of the Hegelian spirit, of Marx's productive forces, or democracy as the "end of history."[30] It was one of the merits of Popper's analysis to have debunked the myth of such historical laws. Even if three or four events are causally related there is no way to construct out of this chain a universal "law."

Perhaps "predictions" of transformative changes are indeed impossible, but could an "evolutionary" approach actually throw some light on this problem? In that case we have to sacrifice the logical equivalence between prediction and explanation – for a long time a mantra among the adherents of the "scientific" approach – and we have to come to an entirely new conception of "system" as e.g. Luhmann suggests.[31] However, we also would then have to admit that such an approach is entirely different from the naïve physicalist accounts of mechanical systems à la Kaplan (even if they possess a feedback loop). In any case the issue of the historical character of such systems and their reproduction is far from being satisfactorily solved, so that we could rely from now on on "normal" science to do all the explaining. As Bull correctly pointed out, Kaplan's various models of international systems are ideal types derived more

---

[28] See e.g. Ruggie's criticism of Waltzian structuralism in John G. Ruggie, "Continuity and Transformation in the World Polity: Toward a Neorealist Synthesis," *World Politics*, 35:2 (1983): 261–285.

[29] For a scathing criticism of this idea, Karl Popper, *The Poverty of Historicism*, New York: Harper & Row, 1961.

[30] See Francis Fukuyama, *The End of History and the Last Man*, New York: Avon Books, 1992.

[31] See e.g. Niklas Luhmann, *Die Gesellschaft der Gesellschaft*, Frankfurt am Main: Suhrkamp, 1998.

from inductive reasoning than from a stringent theory. Since we do not have any transformation functions allowing us to specify which type of system follows from which antecedent type, we can hardly speak of a "theory" in any relevant sense.

The other gambit is to radically de-emphasize problems of change and of the succession of eras by focusing on the existence of allegedly trans-historical structures. This is what structuralism has done. Thus even transformative change, such as the one we encountered in the demise of the Soviet Empire, becomes a mere "data point" that is hardly of significance, as several practitioners of political "science" have argued.[32] Having defined the "system" in such a way that nothing but the emergence of an empire would count as a transformative change, the actual investigation into the changing patterns of politics can safely be sequestered to "confirmatory" research.

However, as the discussion about "uni-polarity" vs. "hierarchy" suggests, such a research program is seriously flawed. Obviously the two versions of systems differ in whether or not the organizing principle has changed and that means that norms of legitimacy are different in both models. While the preponderant state in a unipolar system might have as much influence as an imperial center, part of the rules defining the international game differ significantly. In an empire the center can give orders, in a unipolar system such orders are illegitimate and will, in all likelihood, engender resistance.

To that extent the idea that an objectivist conceptualization of a social system without any recourse to the ideas and values the actors themselves hold – all alleged by Waltz to be "reductionist" in nature – seems futile indeed. In addition, we have to realize that precisely because social reality is not simply out there but is "made" by the actors, the concepts we use are part of a vocabulary that is deeply imbricated with our political projects. Nowhere does this become more obvious than in the "empirical" evidence presented in support of the theory of democratic peace. Behind the efforts of operationalization, measurement and coding lie not only language, but also a political "project" that informs our conceptual apparatus. Here two difficulties arise: one normative, the other operational.

The normative one is best illustrated in Rawls's argument about the peaceful character of liberal democracies[33] because as status quo oriented states they have no reason to go to war with other peaceful states. They lack the desire of imposing a "comprehensive ideology" on others, and are "indifferent to economic growth." While the first argument has also traditionally been considered to be valid only among liberal and other "decent" states, wars against

---

[32] For a useful collection of essays on this point, see Lebow and Risse-Kappen (eds.), *International Relations Theory and the End of the Cold War*.
[33] John Rawls, *Law of Peoples*, Cambridge MA: Harvard University Press, 1999.

"outlaw states" are another matter. What is interesting nevertheless is the conceptual stretch from the original argument about democratic states to "liberal states," and then the further expansion to well-ordered societies (decent peoples, even if not liberal). Crucial for Rawls's claim that liberal states are indifferent to growth is the notion of a "stationary state," which Mill propagated at the high point of British imperialism (!) and which Rawls uses again with approval at a time of turbo-capitalism and a highly interventionist stance by the "liberal" US.[34]

It strains credulity that after all the "conflicts" and humanitarian interventions fought not only for "saving strangers"[35] but for engineering regime change, one can apparently live happily in American academia and fail to see what is happening in the world, or interpret it away, by arguing that some liberal states have failed to "live up to their ideals." But this is a curious argument: if liberal states supposedly have the institutional checks to prevent their regimes going to war, why have they not developed similar checks to prevent the commercial elites from escalating conflicts by insisting that free markets and property rights have not only to be "universal" but, if need arises, have also to be "enforced"? On the other hand, if the interventionist project is then justified by an argument for the "robust enforcement of human rights" this "Wilsonism in boots" supplies the missionary creed which liberal states allegedly lack and that is supposed to make them peaceful.

These reflections lead us back to the further problem mentioned above: that of operationalization. First we have to become aware that drawing the lines will depend more on *judgment* in the light of our values than on the "things out there." For example, what are we to do with "illiberal democracies,"[36] i.e. political systems that might provide for contested elections and changes in government, but not for an effective civil rights regime? Similarly, Rhoda Rabkin,[37] studying Chile, has rightly insisted that intrinsic to our concept of democratic rule is also the understanding that the civilian government ought to have "effective power to rule." Therefore, such a government should not engage moves of "anticipated reactions" in order to assuage the armed forces. Second, if such additions stand for important dimensions, could the development of an "over-all score" not perhaps deal with these problems?

Unfortunately, the idea of "defining" democracy in terms of a variety of indicators and arriving at an "over all score" that represents more accurately

---

[34] Ibid., at 28.
[35] See Nicholas Wheeler, *Humanitarian Intervention in International Society*, Oxford: Oxford University Press, 2003.
[36] See e.g. David Collier and Steven Levitsky, "Democracy with Adjectives: Conceptual Innovation in Comparative Research," *World Politics*, 49:3 (1997): 430–451.
[37] See Rhoda Rabkin, "The Aylwin Government and 'Tutelary' Democracy: A Concept in Search of a Case?" *Journal of Interamerican Studies and World Affairs*, 35:4 (1993): 119–194.

what is "out there" does not really solve the problem. Thus, in operationalizing
the democratic peace argument, e.g. a "polity" score could be calculated by
subtracting an "autocracy" index from a "democracy" index, which yields a
number that supposedly tells us how democratic a country is. But as David
Spiro has pointed out, by using this dataset and the "operationalization"
suggested by Maoz for "autocracy" and "democracy", France is not "democratic" after 1981, but El Salvador is, and Belgium was not a democracy until
1956![38] Obviously, some implicitly or explicitly held values concerning the
importance and weight of the several dimensions of "democracy" play a role,
so that problem cannot be reduced by increasing coding reliability or looking
harder at the facts.

Similarly, the comparison between the measure constructed by the Finnish
social scientist Tatu Vanhanen for democracy[39] (operationalizing the concept
along the lines of Dahl's definition) and that of Doyle shows that on the
"Finnish" score the US ranks consistently low, far behind western European
political systems. Vanhanen's research most heavily emphasizes participation
and the competitiveness of elections among different parties and the supremacy of parliament.[40] In Doyle's treatment, on the other hand, the US always
scores highest, historically as well as at present.

It seems that in the American scientific discourse the "liberal" norms are
usually those which correspond to the *ongoing political project* in the US and
that it is this yardstick which is then applied to other countries. This leads to
a pretty uninteresting discussion within the "liberal" theory, as everybody "on
the good side" (like us!) becomes a card-carrying liberal. Even Kant is pressed
into "liberal" service, despite the fact that his dour emphasis on duties and
limited political participation hardly makes him a paradigm for liberalism.
Furthermore, countries resembling the US are held to share the same political
"project," be it liberal peace, consumer sovereignty or whatever, even if the
"causal" chain accounting for the outcome usually remains rather murky.[41] As
Ida Oren suggested:

---

[38] David E. Spiro, "The Insignificance of the Liberal Peace," *International Security*, 19:2 (1994):
50–86, at 56.
[39] See Tatu Vanhanen, *The Process of Democratization: A Comparative Study of 147 States,
1980–88*, New York: Crane Russak, 1990.
[40] For a fuller discussion of these problems, see Davis, *Terms of Inquiry.*
[41] See e.g. the controversy between Anne-Marie Slaughter and Jose Alvarez: Anne-Marie Slaughter, "International Law in a World of Liberal States," *European Journal of International Law*,
6:4 (1995): 503–538; Anne-Marie Slaughter, "A Liberal Theory of International Law," *Proceedings of the Annual Meeting (American Society of International Law)*, 94 (2000): 240–253;
José E. Alvarez, "Do Liberal States Behave Better?: A Critique of Slaughter's Liberal Theory,"
European Journal of International Law, 12:2 (2001): 183–246.

Polities have numerous objective dimensions by which they can be measured. The dimensions captured by the current empirical measures of democracy came to be selected through a subtle historical process whereby objective dimensions on which America resembled its enemies were eliminated, whereas those, on which America differed the most from its enemies, became privileged. Thus the coding rules, defining democracy are better understood as a time-bound product of America's historical circumstances than as the timeless exogenous force that they are presumed to be.[42]

The above discussion shows that, for these reasons, data banks cannot be simple storage places for unadulterated "facts," but that they are part of our political understandings and projects. It is through historical reflection and not through generalization that the genesis and importance of such data becomes visible, that the role of judgment is uncovered, and that the criteria for counting a phenomenon as an instantiation of a certain concept become explicit. To that extent many issues in the second debate have not lost their importance.

The best proof for this is the controversy concerning macrohistorical studies in sociology[43] and political science.[44] While the original discussion among the sociologists created more heat than enlightenment, Ian Lustick correctly identified the central point of this controversy: expressed in the language of normal social science it concerns the issue of "selection bias." Thus in examining the "empirical" basis of such macrohistorical work as Barrington Moore's *The Social Origins of Dictatorship and Democracy*[45] or Theda Skocpol's *States and Social Revolutions*,[46] Lustick points out that both authors had used, as their factual basis, "histories" of scholars who implicitly or explicitly shared their own theoretical biases. Moore, in order to make good on his claim that the British Civil War was actually a bourgeois revolution, had e.g. to show that the bourgeoisie emerged as an important social force by the second quarter of the seventeenth century. His "proof" was provided by the historian Tawney's somewhat problematic class analysis that amalgamated not only the burghers and the gentry into one revolutionary movement, but also postulated the emergence of an entrepreneurial "proto-capitalist class." However, Hexter,[47] another eminent historian studying the same era, forcefully debunked those "facts." In other words, Moore relied on Tawney (and Campbell) without any critical

---

[42] Ido Oren, "The Subjectivity of the Democratic Peace: Changing US Perceptions of Imperial Germany," *International Security*, 20:2 (1995): 147–184, at 152.

[43] See the controversy between Michael Mann, John Goldthorpe, Nicos Mouzelis, and Niki Hart in the *British Journal of Sociology*, vol. 45 (1994).

[44] See Ian S. Lustick, "History, Historiography, and Political Science: Multiple Historical Records and the Problem of Selection Bias," *American Political Science Review*, 90:3 (1996), 605–618.

[45] Barrington Moore, *Social Origins of Dictatorship and Democracy: Lord and Peasant in the Making of the Modern World*, Boston, MA: Beacon Press, 1966.

[46] Theda Skocpol, *States and Social Revolutions: A Comparative Analysis of France, Russia, and China*, Cambridge: Cambridge University Press, 1979.

[47] J.H. Hexter, *Reappraisals in History*, Chicago: University of Chicago Press, 1961.

appreciation that these facts were the result of *interpretations* and of *theoretical dispositions* similar to his own, and thus could not provide a neutral set of data by which the theoretical propositions could be established.

Somewhat counterintuitively we have to conclude that the primary problem for macrohistorical work is thus not the difficulty of getting enough information about the past. "The more daunting question is how to choose sources or data without permitting correspondence between the categories and implicit theoretical postulates used in the chosen sources to ensure positive answers to the questions being asked about the data."[48] Of course, historians have long been familiar with this difficulty. In a fundamental paper the historian Carl Becker[49] tried a long time ago to explode the notion of hard "historical facts" that are directly accessible to us.

For example, the historical fact that Caesar crossed the Rubicon existed not as a simple description of the physical acts involved in crossing a river, but only in virtue of its relations to other facts and its *emplotment in a narrative*, which puts these things in perspective. Otherwise the crossing would have occurred but would not transport any meaning, as many people before and after have crossed that river. Given the unavailability of simple facts, the hope of arriving at the truth via generalizations or more data seems dim indeed. Historians have therefore developed various ways of weighing the evidence by subjecting sources and "facts" to criticism, relying on counterfactual arguments, triangulation, and procedures for process tracing.

These arguments lead us right back to Bull's fifth point. In addition, I suggested that the recursivity problem arises particularly clearly in the social sciences because the understandings of the actors constitute the social world. Therefore, the causal arrows run from "understanding" to the world, and not from "the world" to our understanding or to our theory. This explodes the notion that all true explanations have to be cast in terms of efficient causes, and from objectively given "things" to which our concepts have to "correspond," as the "scientific" approach suggested.

I think, however, that Bull's strongest claim for the classical approach and for historical reflection is contained in propositions one, four, and seven. Given that deductive modeling presupposes different skills and sensibilities, the "law of the hammer" is not only an imaginary danger for developing a fruitful theory. Even the proponents of logical positivism have held that asking creative questions and developing an interesting set of problems for guiding research is not part of the logic of discovery, but rather – in Popper's parlance – part of "psychology." But does it not seem strange that the questions concerning substance are relegated to some psychological factors, which remain a residual

---

[48] Lustick, "History, Historiography, and Political Science," at 608.
[49] See Becker, "What Are Historical Facts?"

category outside the remit of epistemology? It is against this danger that Bull suggested an exposure to history in order to deal with the substantive issues that arise out of the variability and the "surprises" of the historical world.

It is indeed disturbing that Bull's fears concerning the barren scholasticism of the "scientific" approach have not resonated. Consider in this context the suggestion by some leading political scientists addressed to the future practitioners of international relations. Students are not supposed to tackle directly problems of the "real world," although these might be interesting precisely because of their practical relevance. Rather the "apprentices" are exhorted to go to the work of the "greats" of the field and modify some of the propositions of their respective theories in order to obtain a viable dissertation project(!).[50] The scholastic nature guiding such a research project could not be more pronounced.

8.3   Memory, Identity, and Action

The above discussion concerning the nature of historical data has tried to drive home the point that although "history" is past and seems therefore to be "objective," fixed, done with, and a secure source of knowledge, actual historical reflection shows that it is quite different. Contrary to this naïve view it turns out that history is malleable because it is remembered. It is also always remembered from a certain situation in the present, for which things past have now relevance. Thus the "re-collecting" of the past, putting it in a frame, bestows importance on some earlier actions and events by connecting the past through the present with our personal and political projects. In this reflection we establish our identity as agents and societies and understand ourselves as the same, despite all the experienced changes. In this sense history becomes the encounter with the individual or collective self, rather than representing a storehouse of data or being an agglomeration of examples or presumptive lessons.

It was Nietzsche who probably most strongly emphasized this element of historical reflection. Viewing the past as fixed is a misconception of history that he criticized by labeling it "antiquarian."[51] It disables the individual from making significant choices due to the emphasis on facts and causal links running through time instead of approaching history via the modality of the "possible."[52] Notions of the "ahistorical" (consisting in forgetting) and of

---

[50] See King, Keohane, and Verba, *Designing Social Inquiry*, at 161f.

[51] See Friedrich Nietzsche, "Unzeitgemäße Betrachtungen, Zweites Stück: Vom Nutzen und Nachteil der Historie" in Giorgio Colli and Mazziono Montinari (eds.), *Nietzsche, Gesamtausgabe*, vol. 1, Muenchen–Berlin: DTV and Walter de Gruyter, 1988, at 244–334.

[52] ibid., at 265–267.

the "*über*-historical" (such as instantiation of values or ideas of timeless justice) then flesh out this, at first, counterintuitive approach, by calling attention to the "becoming," the making of history, *the trans-historical.* If history has any function it cannot lie in a conception of the past that is entirely reduced to *cause and effect which an action has to take as a template in order to reproduce it*[53] but in making the individual aware that the goal of humanity cannot lie in an "end of history" but requires a critical stance bringing to the fore the importance of the trans-historical. Here Weber's notion of values as the constitutive elements of historical reflection is foreshadowed. In addition, by making history a product of memory, Nietzsche not only realizes that every recollection also presupposes the "ability to forget,"[54] he also emphasizes that the "past" is deeply involved in constructing the individual as an agent.

Thus history defined as a *re-collection of all those things worth remembering* provides in itself the antidote to the "poison" of an assumed necessity, of the logic of systems, of the "blind forces of the real,"[55] or the hopelessness that comes from the invention of a tradition which makes out of us only epigones of a glorious but unreachable past. We can see now from this vantage point why "new beginnings" stand in such a close relationship to the past, as exemplified by the various "renaissances." From ancient Sumer[56] to Egypt[57] to the Italian Renaissance or even the French Revolution[58] a new link to the past has always been considered intrinsic to the new beginnings that were sought.

Irrespective of whether or not we agree with Nietzsche's philosophy, his suggested link between historical reflection, agency, and notions of the individual "self" deserves further examination. The first thing to notice is that, seen from this perspective, the process of individuation is not simply a biological process but mediated by communication with others and by sharing certain collective memories with a group. As all societies are imagined communities – to use Anderson's felicitous phrase[59] – the individual memory is built up by participation in communicative processes. These processes concern the daily

[53] Ibid., 261f. [54] Ibid., 281. [55] Ibid., 265.
[56] As Jan Assman notes, the Dynasty of Sargon (ended 2154 BC) attained paradigmatic status during the first millennium BC, and the Mesopotamians of that time became a "digging society," obsessed with preserving and finding the remnants of this dynasty, which by then had all but disappeared. Jan Assmann, *Religion und Kulturelles Gedächtnis: Zehn Studien*, München: Beck, 2000, at 42f.
[57] See e.g. the attempts of the founders of the Twelfth Dynasty to "revive" the Old Kingdom and to accord to the Pharao Snofru of the Fourth Dynasty a certain "canonical" importance. Jan Assmann, *Ma'at: Gerechtigkeit und Unsterblichkeit im alten Ägypten*, München: C.H. Beck, 1990, chap. 2.
[58] See the revival of the cult of the Roman Republic and of virtue, particularly among the most radical exponents of the French Revolution.
[59] Anderson, *Imagined Communities*.

interactions, and the inevitable conflicts for which we need shared rules and settled practices, but we also need common recollections in order to understand *who we are.*

The *first* kind of processes (dealing with conflict and interactions) has usually been treated as involving questions of order and justice, i.e. the establishment, maintenance, and change of normatively secured expectations. Norms governing this process allow us to interact even in the face of disappointments, as the most important function of norms is their capacity for "prospective ordering," their counterfactual validity, their function as yardsticks for assessment.

The *second* type of processes involves the diachronic link connecting the past through the present to the future via our individual and common projects. Who we are is significantly shaped by where we think we come from. This process has therefore to do with identities and collective memories that allow us to be a person and a group and make "society" an ongoing and transgenerational concern among its members.

However, a moment's reflection shows that these two ways of connecting the individual and the group are even more closely linked than they appear at first. After all, what has to be done and what we are obliged to do is often directly the result of *particular forms* of recollection. For example, obedience is due to the traditional ruler because he is the legitimate son of the previous ruler, and thus only a "flaw" in the genealogy would exculpate the nobles and vassals if they failed to obey. Similarly, historical events may have a particular meaning and obligatory force for a society. "Remember the Maine," "Remember the Boyne" (the battle in 1690 between the Protestants and Catholics in Ireland), "Remember St. Vitus day" (battle of Kosovo 1389), "Remember Auschwitz," "Never again must Masada fall," etc.: all those exhortations refer to recollections of particular relevance to a given group, but they are at the same time powerful sources of obligations. This then has important implications for the "politics of memory" and the "working through" of individual and collective traumas of war and defeat. Here Thomas Berger's work[60] (focusing on Germany, Japan, and Austria), the collection of essays edited by Lebow, Kantsteiner, and Fogu[61] (addressing western and eastern Europe after the Cold War), or Ayse Zarakol,[62] studying stigmatization, stratification, and status consciousness in international relations (taking Turkey after World War I, Japan after World War II, and Russia after the Cold War as case studies), come to mind.

---

[60] Thomas Berger, *War, Guilt and World Politics after World War II*, Cambridge: Cambridge University Press, 2012.

[61] Richard Ned Lebow, Wulf Kantsteiner, and Claudio Fogu (eds.), *The Politics of Memory in Postwar Europe*, Durham, NC: Duke University Press, 2006.

[62] Ayse Zarakol, *After Defeat: How the East learned to Live with the West*, Cambridge: Cambridge University Press, 2011.

Obviously the dead are of particular importance in this context. Traditional society has dealt with this kind of specific obligation in terms of *piety* (i.e. what is due to one's ancestors)[63] and *fama* (reputation). How "political" this cult of the dead had become after the move from a tribal society to the classical *polis* can nicely be gathered from Pericles' famous eulogy for the dead.[64] At first, somewhat strangely for us, we notice that it is the *city* and not the fallen soldiers that are the object of the encomium. But Pericles followed here the spirit of the Athenian legislation that had made honoring the dead a *public* rather than a family or clan obligation.[65] While the family was allowed to keep a fallen soldier's body for some days, both burial and public display were now the task of the city, thereby powerfully reinforcing the notion that loyalty was owed to the *polis*, rather than to the clan or tribe.

These examples make several points. One is the surprising malleability of the past as it is created by memory through a reordering (and forgetting) of the events one considers (un)important. As the individual rewrites continuously his/her biography in which events and decisions take on different meanings – even relegating some of them to oblivion – so collective memories, recorded or not, show similar plasticity. Of course, since the invention of writing, memories that had been discarded, sometimes survive somewhere (archives, museums, etc.) and can be re-collected so as to become sometimes in the future again part of the collective memory.

The best example of this phenomenon is the Masada incident, which played virtually no role in Jewish collective life during the nearly 2,000 years of the Diaspora. As originally recorded by Flavius Josephus,[66] it was a story highly critical of the various groups of zealots who had revolted against the Romans. They had succeeded in seizing the fortress of Masada near the Dead Sea and committed collective suicide after the Romans breached its walls. Josephus blames the zealots[67] for ending the last vestiges of Jewish political life since

---

[63] Thus piety meant first loyalty to one's own "house," the parents and the household gods protecting the family and its abode. This is why Aeneas was called "pious" as he took his old father and his son and wife to settle somewhere else when everything else was lost at Troy. See Vergil, *The Aeneid of Vergil*, trans. Allen Mandelbaum, New York: Bantam Books, 1961, bk. II.
[64] See Thucydides, *History of the Peloponnesian War*, bk. II, at paras. 34–46.
[65] See Nicole Loraux, *The Invention of Athens: The Funeral Oration in the Classical City*, Cambridge, MA: Harvard University Press, 1986.
[66] Josephus Flavius, *The Jewish War*, trans. G.A. Williamson, New York: Dorset Press, 1970.
[67] In echoing the mood of Thucydides' description of the revolution in Corcyra, Josephus writes of the various groups that often used "religious" motives to justify their terrorist attacks:

so corrupt was the public and private life of the whole nation, so determined were they to outdo each other in impiety towards God and injustices to their neighbours, those in power ill-using the masses and the masses striving to overthrow those in power. One group was bent on domination, the other on violence and on robbing the rich. First to begin this the Romans laid waste to the land and dispersed the entire Jewish population thereafter. But with the experience of the Holocaust, with Zionism becoming a political force, and with the creation of a beleaguered state in the 1940s, Masada took on an entirely new meaning. What was now remembered was the uncompromising sacrifice for autonomy and a particular way of life rather than the political failure of the former state. Something that had been forgotten was "re-collected" – even though from quite a different angle, as suggested by the political situation of the period – and it became part of the "new" collective memory.

The second point is that individual and collective memories differ in some important respects, but not those frequently considered. Usually we assume that the "unencumbered" self, i.e. the notion of pure reflexivity, which Descartes took as the *fundamentum inconcussum*, is the proper beginning of thought and reflection. "Society" and all other collective notions are "later" additions as they are based on aggregation. However, we always start out as encumbered selves, as members of a concrete society, in a specific time, and with particular obligations. It is through a long process of differentiation that we acquire the abstract form of the individual or the modern person and with it, the "view from nowhere." This Archimedean point not only informs our comprehension of the world – since it is constitutive of scientific objectivity – but it is also supposed to provide the criteria for assessing our moral commitments (Kant). The categorical imperative establishing the criteria of moral autonomy is then the last step in this process in which "generalizability" becomes the most important requirement. Now all obligations resulting from a shared way of life, such as special duties to our family, children, and fellow-countrymen, have to be justified, since the traditional "ethos" itself no longer suffices.[68]

lawlessness and this barbarity to kinsmen were the sicarii, who left no word unspoken, no deed untried, to insult and destroy the objects of their foul plots.

No one could equal (however) the Zealots, a party which justified its title by deeds; they followed every bad example, and there was no crime in the records that they did not zealously reproduce. And yet they gave themselves this title in view of their zeal for what was good, either mocking their victims, brutes that they were, or regarding the greatest evils as good! Thus it was that each of them found a fitting end, God sentencing them all to the penalty they deserved. Every torment mankind can endure fell upon them to the very end of their lives; when they came face to face with death in all its most agonizing forms. Yet it would be true to say that they suffered less misery than they had caused: to suffer what they deserved was impossible. . .

Ibid., 394f.

[68] Perhaps this is also one of the reasons why analytical ethics has become so barren or when it actually contributes to solving our practical problems it has to rely on "interpretation," and that means on "forms of life" rather than the calculi of pure models. For a criticism of formalism in ethics, see Kratochwil, "Vergeßt Kant", 96–152.

From these considerations a third point follows: that it is easier to forget one's collective identity than the personal one since in the former case life can go on and need not result in the same pathological problems that are frequently associated with the loss of a personal identity. However, as the above considerations also showed, we ought to be careful in thinking that the former is real while the other is simply a figment of imagination. Collective memories are real and not simple aggregates of individual memories. As in the case of language, we cannot infer from the fact that only individual speakers can utter words that language as such must also be conceived as an aggregation of individual utterances rather than as a collective phenomenon.

Fourth, it seems also to follow that the present infatuation with simultaneous "multiple identities" is a highly problematic notion. It confuses the notion of role with that of identity. Moreover, it often commits the fallacy that if something is not fixed, it has to be arbitrary and therefore changeable at will. If someone experiences his or her personal past merely as a sequence of events, s/he will experience life as largely meaningless, and s/he will not be able to learn, but is likely to get stuck in (destructive) routines. To avoid such a fate s/he will have to "work through" the past – to use the Freudian vocabulary – in order to become again an autonomous actor in its full meaning. Usually such an alienation from one's own past and such a decentered stance is the result of a trauma which therapy tries to overcome by constructing an alternative narrative. True, the individual might decide to change part of his/her identity by leaving home, converting to a new creed, or getting "nationalized" somewhere else. But these are usually exacting processes, more akin to learning a new language than to becoming e.g. a member of a club, or making a choice between apples and oranges.

Fifth, since emotions play such a crucial role in remembering and forgetting[69] (vide the traumata mentioned above), special rites and ceremonies are powerful means of mobilizing them and of enabling us to recollect. These rites play a particularly important part in cultures that are not dependent on writing for the preservation of memory.[70] The *hieros gamos*, the yearly ritual of the marriage between heaven and earth, existing in many societies, provides the best example. The periodic reliving of the original creation by reenacting the cosmological myths is, in nonliterate societies, of utmost importance for the maintenance of order.

---

[69] In this context see the recent discussion in IR on the role of emotions, such as the forum introduced by Roland Bleiker and Emma Hutchison, "Introduction: Emotions and World Politics," *International Theory*, 6:3 (2014).

[70] See in this context the discussion of the *tepe* ritual among the Osages in Assmann, *Religion und Kulturelles Gedächtnis*, at 23f.

In societies in which memory is largely transmitted by "texts," the actual presence and the reliving through rites takes second place. The focus is now on creating a canon determining what belongs to the tradition and what is apocryphal, and on the purification of the texts themselves, expunging from them what seems foreign or accidental. However, even in cultures whose memory has been transformed by writing, memorial days and reenactments – where performances, rites, and ceremonies call attention to the commonality of a group in an emotionally significant way – are not simply supplanted, but remain part and parcel of the cultural heritage. A particularly interesting form here is the historical drama as it unites recollection, performance, and historical plots and links individual and collective identity, as Aleida Assmann's interpretation of the Shakespearian historical dramas has shown. By placing these dramas within the larger process of social reproduction, we can see some interesting changes that occur in modernity in reconstructing the individual and "the people." As Aleida Assmann points out:

Feudal ethics obscures in its forms of memory the greater "whole" of the nation because it is as little interested in the actual individual as in the encompassing community. It guarantees the Identity of the powerful noble families and thereby of a social formation, which had to be overcome by the social formation of an early modern territorial state. The nation emerges in England in co-evolution with the absolutist territorial state. Patriotism serves now a new basis for this identity, which integrates but does not abolish the old status order. National history becomes thereby the common point of reference, which substitutes for the former diverging and conflictual memories. The national *memoria* as the history of the collective genealogy of the English people displaces now the feudal *memoria*.[71]

8.4   Social Reproduction and Change

The above argument has several implications for understanding the conceptual connections between individual and social reproduction. If we accept that the social world is one of artifice, then its re-creation is the main problem that traditionally is "solved" by endowing the existing customs with authority, what Nietzsche ironically called *die Sittlichkeit der Sitte*. These customs function as templates for seemingly endless and exact reproductions. The French sociologist Gabriel Tarde[72] has pointed to the importance of imitation as the main mode of reproduction in traditional societies in which the older generation transmits its heritage to the next generation. Thus *Sitte* is not just unreflective reproduction, it also endows the past with nearly unchallengeable

---

[71] Aleida Assmann, *Erinnerungsräume: Formen und Wandlungen des kulturellen Gedächtnisse*, München: C.H. Beck, 1999, at 77.
[72] Gabriel de Tarde, *The Laws of Imitation*, trans. Elsie C. Parson, New York: H. Holt, 1903.

authority, reaching back through mythical generations to the ancestors, who have set forth the way things are. Thus both the truth and the imperative of exact reproduction of the template from generation to generation provide the space for "right" action, which is maintained by rituals, taboos, and "zero-tolerance" for deviations.

How powerful these reproductions through habituation are – nowadays again partially addressed by the practice turn and the attention to the "the knowing how" – is illustrated by two observations. One is that paleontologists claim, on the basis of excavated bones of elk and deer, that Stone Age hunters in northwestern Europe repeated the same rituals for about 10,000 years when sacrificing part of their hunt: the removal of the animal's heart and its replacement by a stone with the subsequent "burial" of the animal in shallow water. As Slotterdijk points out, that would mean that around 400 generations were involved in this form of reproduction. This is all the more astonishing as such a sequence would be three times longer than the 125 replications with which we are familiar from the Near and Far Eastern cultures. The Eucharist on the other hand, which formed one of the central rituals of Western civilization, can only look back on eighty reproductions of which the last fifteen generational replications were characterized by extreme conflict and dissent concerning the proper role of this sacrifice (Transubstantiation, Reformation, shift to homily and prayer, etc.).[73]

The second observation concerns the persistence of the eponymy, long after the exact social reproduction conceived as a genealogy had lost its power. Thus a part of the name – -son, Mc, O', or "-wichs," even the addition of Ibn in Arabic culture – locates the individual in a generational context. Obviously, the interest here is not simply cognitive. Identifying someone as a bearer of the name of a family is also a signal to others of what can be expected from that person. But this simple transmission from one generation to the other was considerably modified by the discovery of the Socratic *daimonion*, which devalues unreflective *Sittlichkeit* and its institutions. Here the Roman legal *traditio* (literally transfer of a good) and *successio*, i.e. entering into the privileges and duties of being an heir, come to mind. The emergence of the *homines novi* in both antiquity[74] and the Renaissance challenge this mode

---

[73] See Peter Sloterdijk, *Die Schrecklichen Kinder der Neuzeit über das Anti-Genealogische Experiment der Moderne*, Frankfurt: Suhrkamp, 2014, at 233f.

[74] See e.g. the speech by Gaius Marius who during the wars with the German tribes was five times elected consul, which was not only in contravention of the constitutional provisos but also drew the criticism of the old nobility. Marius countered with an argument that bravery, frugality, and virtue were more important than the possession of expensive silverware or other useless treasures. See Sallust, *The War with Jugurtha*, Cambridge, MA: Harvard University Press, 2013, chap. 85.

of reproduction. Significantly, the "new men" in the latter case were often "bastards" who were excluded from inheriting the patrimony.

Here Shakespeare has provided us in *King Lear* and his historical plays with paradigmatic examples of the dangers and failures in individual and collective generational transmissions. In *King Lear* he addresses this problematique in terms of a revolt against the "normal" patrimonial succession. In the monologue which introduces the audience to Edmund, Lear's illegitimate son, the logic of his revolt against the traditional order is spelled out, by Edmund contesting Edgar's (Lear's legitimate son) succession:

> Thou, nature, art my goddess; to thy law
> My services are bound. Wherefore should I
> Stand in plague of custom, and permit
> The curiosity of nations to deprive me,
> For that I am . . .
> Lag of a brother? Why bastard? wherefore base?
> When my dimensions are as well compact,
> My mind as generous, and my shape as true,
> As honest madam's issue? Why brand they us
> With base? with baseness? bastardy? . . .
> . . .
> Well then,
> Legitimate Edgar, I must have your land:[75]

Here the claim to the patrimony is supposed to accrue to those with ambition and ability and who will not be constrained by the demand of the customary *tradition*. To that extent Edmund's last line is emblematic: "*Now Gods stand up for bastards.*" Edmund's monologue is still cast in the form of an objection to the genealogical blemish but it has much wider legitimatory implications. As we know from the research of Alison Findlay, the succession problem and the status of bastards were from the end of the sixteenth century to the middle of the seventeenth the subject of considerable public interest, as the seventy plays she found indicate.[76]

It is therefore not surprising that Shakespeare also uses this succession problem as a subtext in his history plays, since the original evil which starts the Wars of the Roses is the deposition of the legitimate heir to the throne, Richard II, by Henry Bolingbroke and the cycle ends with the accession of the Tudors to the throne. But the main messages of this "history," told in several plays, moves beyond the familial problematique, where fighting, forgiving, and forgetting of the parties provides the subject.[77] The main point of this

---

[75] Shakespeare, *King Lear*, Act I, scene ii.
[76] Alison Findlay, *Illegitimate Power: Bastards in Renaissance Drama*, Manchester: Manchester University Press, 1994, at 253–257.
[77] See *Richard II*, I. i.156: "Forget, forgive, conclude and be agreed."

sequence of dramas is rather *the creation of a common memory* through a cathartic reliving of the past. To that extent the reigns of the various kings provide the episodes of a story in which the Tudor accession to the throne supplies the so long elusive settlement. Shakespeare's intent seems therefore to have been to use the theater and the drama as a means of moral instruction, as was common at the time – and the "bastard" problem provided him with ample material for that.

Thus rather than telling a story of the rise and fall of heroic individuals, or of common human failings which are the topic of comedies or of morality plays, Shakespeare prefers to link up to the genre of "chronicle plays" which were popular already before his time and which served as a rudimentary instruction on the genealogies, battles, and successions of rulers. In this way the English nation is not only the audience, it becomes the "historical individual" that is created by these representations and performances:

The national unity, which emerges from the bonds that the English, Welsh, Irish and Scots at the Battle of Agincourt forged, occurs in the theater as an integration of the different social strata and forms of life without however erasing the regional or social differences, which, instead, are now placed in a common frame of a new common identity. The national army and the stage are the organs of this new collective identity.[78]

The difference to the heroic memory, transmitted in tales celebrating the kudos that lives on after the hero's death, is considerable. Social reproduction and change are no longer identified with conformity with the old templates but with a new awareness that simple repetition of the old familiar patterns might no longer provide a viable "project" in either the individual or the collective case. While the heroic memory imparts direct instructions for actions through the examples it conjures up, making sense of actions and events must now allow for changes that let us reinvent ourselves.

But such an alternative is possible only if meaning is no longer exclusively attributed to things which are "true" (because they are unchanging) but instead if *meaning arises from the reflection that shows a narrative structure*. In other words, since the question of "who am I?" cannot be answered by a response indicating "what I am" (a body, a member of a species, or even of a group or status), narratives need second-order criteria of truth, established by a hermeneutical understanding. They require "followability" and narrative coherence, not only reference to some facts. This innovation creates a certain anxiety, as freedom does not come without its aporias and life often resembles a "do-it-yourself game" without instructions.

This narrative's function of supplying meaning, rather than just listing the sequence of some actions or events, becomes visible when we compare a

---

[78] Assmann, *Erinnerungsräume*, at 79.

narrative with a protocol. Although scientific experiments also require a mnemonic device, which preserves the observations made, the text of a protocol and a text making sense of actions and events through a narrative follow different logics. As Louis Mink pointed out when he compared the texts of a scientific protocol (or what he, somewhat oddly calls paradigmatic discourse) with that of a narrative:

> The truth-value of the text [in the first case] is ... simply a logical function of the truth or falsity of the individual assertions taken separately: the conjunction is true if and only if each of the propositions is true. Narrative has in fact been analyzed ... as if it were nothing but the logical conjunction of past – referring statements. ... and, on such an analysis, there is no problem of *narrative truth*. The difficulty with the model of logical conjunction, however, is that it is not the model of narrative at all. ... Logical conjunction serves well enough as a representation of the only ordering relation of chronicles, which is "... and then ... and then ... and." Narratives, however, contain infinitely many ways of combining these relations. It is such a combination that we speak of when we speak of the coherence of a narrative.[79]

This capacity of the narrative form to provide meaning through the ordering of episodes and through the interpretations of actions has two corollaries. First, it is not surprising that the narrative form accommodates nearly effortlessly the changes in the historical subjects, whether it is states or nations, both of which emerge as predominant subjects during the nineteenth century. Second, given that the story told is about praxis, history can also teach us how to act, if we take the exemplary actions as our guides. From there it seems only a small step to the assertion that histories are just proto-theories and since theories have proven to be more powerful instruments for acting upon nature, it would be advisable to take this step also in the realm of praxis. Such a step would eradicate Mink's distinctions between theoretical (paradigmatic) and narrative knowledge, but as the unity of science adherents would be glad to say: so be it!

I think these conclusions are hasty and mistaken, as Bull suggested, and it will be the task of the next few chapters to sort things out. For the moment I just want to make the point that there is a decisive difference between a type of "pragmatic" history and the later abuses of history for which the past is, because of its alleged facticity, the reality that can be appealed to as a type of "proof." The "pragmatic history," which is part of the rhetorical tradition, does not teach us by showing us the "truth," perhaps it does not even provide us with some useable technical knowledge. It remains the record of the practical realm and is therefore subject to contingencies, which are intrinsic to all practical and political action: partial knowledge, time pressures, (faulty)

---

[79] Louis O. Mink, "Narrative Form as a Cognitive Instrument" in Robert H. Canary and Henry Kozicki (eds.), *The Writing of History: Literary Form and Historical Understanding*, Madison: University of Wisconsin Press, 1978: 129–149, at 143f., as quoted in David Polkinghorne, *Narrative Knowledge and the Human Sciences*, Albany, NY: SUNY Press, 1988, at 63.

judgment, and accidents (*fortuna*). Thus, history instructs us rather *indirectly* by the "pull" which a well-executed story has, in exhorting us to *imitate these deeds*, as Machiavelli suggests. History's message is that of the appeal of exemplary action and of an appreciation of the contingencies that characterize action, and that cannot be neglected as due to their "non-necessary" nature, rather than the establishment of theoretical knowledge or the application of simple technical know-how. Thus historical understanding directs our attention to the problem of judgment, which is an intrinsic part of praxis and not susceptible to an algorithmic treatment, which amounts to what Kant once called the "scandal of reason."[80] *Freedom* as a new dimension of human subjectivity emerges now as one of the subtexts of historical reflection. Autonomous actors can not only start new causal chains, but also radically alter their practices and thereby change the seemingly immutable parameters of their actions.

This view has various methodological and epistemological implications. First, it disabuses us of the "objectivity" of the past. Rather, the past becomes an object of historical reflection only from the perspective of a present problem. Thus, even Ranke's ideal of telling the story as "things really were" is recognized as impossible, as is the attempted self-effacement by the historian.[81] Second, the search for a perspective outside of a *present problem situation*, such as reflection on the past from either the "end" or from "above" (as it could be written from the perspective of God), is futile since "history" represents the bringing together of the past, the present, and the future. As in the later debate about the objectivity of the social sciences and their "value freedom," one can reach objectivity as little by pretending to occupy a point of view outside of any value relationship, as one can attain it by claiming to stand outside of a historical context. Rather, one ought to make intelligible the crucial link between an action and a value, and between the present and the past, without claiming that this particular connection satisfies the truth conditions of theoretical assertion. Objectivity in history, therefore, lies in recognition of the "partial" character of every narrative, which will be contestable, rebuttable, and subject to various interpretations.[82]

---

[80] See Albena Azmanova, *The Scandal of Reason: A Critical Theory of Political Judgment*, New York: Columbia University Press, 2012.

[81] See Droysen's invective against Rankean attempts at objectivism which he considers disabling (actually castrating "*eunuchisch*"): "Ich danke für diese Art von eunuchischer Objektivität, und wenn die historische Unparteilichkeit und Wahrheit dieser Art von Betrachtung der Dinge besteht, so sind die besten Historiker die schlechtesten und die schlechtesten die besten." Johan Gustav Droysen, *Historik: Rekonstruktion der Ersten Vollständigen Fassung der Vorlesungen (1857), Grundriss der Historik in der Ersten Handschriftlichen (1857/1858) und in der Letzten Gedruckten Fassung (1882)*, Stuttgart: Frommann-Holzboog, 1977, at 236.

[82] See ibid., 238. This "perspectivism" and the right to provide other interpretations is explicitly mentioned as a criterion for assessing the objectivity of a historian. Similarly, "Objective impartiality ... is inhuman" in ibid., 236.

Third, historical reflection thus requires a hermeneutic form of understanding, in which memory plays a constitutive role. Its epistemic (in the sense of *wissenschaftlicher*) characteristic is not guaranteed by demonstrations (proofs), or some generalizing inductions, but rather through a specific method by which the unproblematic existence of the past in the present – as e.g. in the institutions that make up the "world" in a given epoch and serve as the constraining and enabling conditions of action – is transformed into the specific historical, i.e. *critically examined past* that provides for a "tradition" but also for new beginnings. What remains to be done, therefore, is to briefly discuss various strategies in which – particularly traumatized – societies have tried to come to terms with their past and construct a new narrative that enabled them to overcome past ruptures and "go on" with their individual and collective projects.

8.5   Dealing with the Past

Denial

Let us begin with denial, which is one way of trying to "save" oneself by "absenting" oneself from burdens of the past. As understandable as such a defensive reaction is, simple refusals to address the past are rather rare, and with good reason. Usually the remnants of atrocities are everywhere still visible, so as to make simple indifference or "passing over" impossible. People have therefore to engage in explicit defensive strategies that keep certain things "under wraps" (taboo) for which Cambodia[83] and Mozambique[84] can serve as examples. Both societies emerged from protracted periods of mass violence and from atrocities of genocidal proportions, leaving the survivors extremely traumatized. But while human rights workers have noted a strange or even shocking disinterest in coming to terms with the past in both societies, the record is not as clear even in the case of Cambodia, and significant differences exist between these two countries.

Cambodia seems at first to have denied the need for trials out of fear that the "fragile fabric of the country might be destroyed and that revenge and

---

[83] See Stephen P. Marks, "Forgetting the Policies and Practices of the Past: Impunity in Cambodia," *Fletcher Forum of World Affairs*, 18:2 (1994): 17–43; Tom Fawthrop and Helen Jarvis, *Getting Away with Genocide? Elusive Justice and the Khmer Rouge Tribunal*, London: Pluto Press, 2004.

[84] Although the government did not adopt a specific policy after the peace accords of 1992, a variety of cultural practices developed that can be considered as measures of "restorative justice." See e.g. Victor Igreja and Beatrice Dias-Lambranca, "Restorative Justice and the Role of *Magamba* Spirits in Post-Civil War Gorongosa, Central Mozambique" in Luc Huyse and Mark Salter (eds.), *Traditional Justice and Reconciliation after Violent Conflict: Learning from African Experiences*, Stockholm: International Institute for Democracy and Electoral Assistance, 2008: 61–84.

retribution would return Cambodia to the Dark ages."[85] Several years later (1999) the Prime Minister (or rather "strong man") Hun Sen considered a "truth commission," but even for this option there existed little readiness to follow through. When the US government appropriated some money in the mid 1990s to create a center at Yale University to document the atrocities of the Khmer Rouge, there was virtually no support for this project in Cambodia's governing circles or among the general public. Even human rights groups tried to discourage the idea of a genocide investigation.[86] Instead, a post-traumatic denial seemed to be the dominant strategy, and resistance did not disappear when Cambodia finally agreed to a joint international/national tribunal. For a long time even intelligent and reflective people repeated rumors that the Khmer Rouge had actually not been Cambodian but "Vietnamese agents" sent to destroy the Khmer people.[87] The average Cambodian, haunted by decades of unmitigated violence, which had resulted in one to two million dead, apparently was not keen to examine the past, through trials or otherwise.

When, largely through international pressure, the above-mentioned special "court," made up of international and Cambodian members, was set up by agreement with the UN in 2003,[88] it seemed to be of more interest to outsiders than to the Cambodian government. The court, named the ECCC (Extraordinary Chambers of the Courts of Cambodia), started work in July 2006 when approximately thirty Cambodian and UN judges were sworn in. Right from the beginning, the Cambodian authorities, the Cambodian members of the courts, and their international counterparts appeared to find it difficult to cooperate. In 2009 Robert Pettit, the Chief Prosecutor, resigned for personal and family reasons. However, those reasons seemed to most observers a "diplomatic excuse," papering over fundamental differences.

In October 2011 the rifts became more obvious when the German judge Sigfried Blunk resigned after only ten months on the job, citing some row with his Cambodian colleagues on the court, as well as the decision of the Cambodian authorities not to indict further persons. During the investigations only five suspects had emerged as additional perpetrators of atrocities. Human Rights Watch, which had criticized Blunk before as "too soft," now charged him with inadequately prosecuting the crimes brought to his attention. In addition, the new Chief Prosecutor Andrew Carley had also excoriated him, accusing him of having breached confidentiality, and his staff accused him of

---

[85] See Statement by Prime Minister Hun Se of February 25, 1995, as quoted by Mark A. Drumbl, "Punishment, Postgenocide: From Guilt to Shame to *Civis* in Rwanda," *New York University Law Review*, 75:5 (2000): 1221–1326, at 1282, ftn. 1290.
[86] Priscilla B. Hayner, *Unspeakable Truths: Confronting State Terror and Atrocity*, New York: Routledge, 2001, at 198.
[87] Ibid., 197.
[88] See United Nations General Assembly, *Khmer Rouge Trials* (2003, UN Doc. A/RES/57/228 B).

improper conduct. The Swiss judge Laurent Kaspar Ansermet, named as the successor to Blunk, resigned in March 2012 after the Cambodian Minister of Information had announced in May 2011 that if investigating judges wanted to pursue further cases they "should pack their bags and leave." The Cambodian authorities, in spite of their denials, were actually following a line of passive resistance. They had kept Ansermet's appointment on hold for months and the Cambodian Council of the Magistracy apparently had finally denied him accreditation.[89]

In the meantime Pol Pot, the head of the Khmer Rouge and *spiritus rector* of the massacres, had died in 1998. Another of the Khmer Rouge kingpins had to be exempted from further prosecution because of Alzheimer's, and the five indictments for atrocities committed between April 1975 and January 1979 led to only three convictions resulting in life imprisonment.

Ritual Engagement

Mozambique ended sixteen years of bitter civil war in 1992 through a brokered peace accord and held its first election two years later. Although an amnesty for crimes against the state was passed ten days after the settlement, most members of the government (Frelimo party) as well as of the opposition (Renamo party) did not even seem to remember this official act. There was, according to the report of observers, a virtually universal agreement not to bring up the past, which included one million dead, thousands of tortures, gruesome instances of mutilations (cutting off of ears and lips), abduction of children who were then forced to commit atrocities and other barbarism (re-education camps).

Strangely enough, there were also no calls for, or acts of, retribution, so that civic life on the local level was rather quickly re-established. No instances of postwar acts of violence to avenge former crimes are on record, despite the fact that the conflict had permeated the whole social structure (families, villages), with victims and perpetrators living together cheek by jowl.[90] As one outside observer working on rural development projects stated:

Who would retaliate against whom? There was not one group against another ... If it was one ethnic language group against another, then maybe you could see it. It was the Browns vs. the Smiths – but even the families were split up. The conflict is so intricate, no revenge factor is possible.[91]

---

[89] See Douglas Gilson, "Justice Denied," *Foreign Policy*, November 23, 2011, accessed at http://foreignpolicy.com/2011/11/23/justice-denied.

[90] When Hayner visited a village she found a man who had lost his father in a battle with the Renamo rebels living peacefully next to a Renamo commander who probably had taken part in the battle. Neither of them had even brought up the subject in conversation. See Hayner, *Unspeakable Truths*, at 193f.

[91] Ibid., 189.

While this situation clearly differentiates the conflict from that in Rwanda, it seems that the re-establishment of civil life in Mozambique is not only a function of the difficulty of taking revenge, but due to some form of "forgiving" brought about by the still existing power of traditional structures. Given the fact that most villages (even large ones over 10,000 people) have no "police," order was maintained by traditional leaders. In our context, the *curandeiros* (medicine men) appear to have been particularly important. When the soldiers returned home after the war, it fell upon these medicine men to "cure" the physical and psychological wounds. The reintegration of the soldiers/killers worked on the basis of ritual sacrifices. As Hayner reports, Mozambiquean scholars have called attention to this important "neo-traditional healing" through rituals. As one sociologist who had studied the process described it:

It works like this: if you kill someone that person's spirit will sit on your shoulders and will give you bad luck. In order to lift that spirit you must undergo treatment. Your relatives would therefore organize a ceremony to "re-humanize" you, to make you normal again. This ceremony is always done by a traditional leader, not someone appointed by the government. It is this ceremony that allows killers back into their community and they are then accepted almost without any questions. Even by the relatives of the victim ... Where many people have died they do a ceremony to wash away all the blood, which has fallen on the land. The ceremony is set up as a spiritual reconciliation between the living and the dead ... People find the money for these ceremonies even if they don't have the money to buy animals to slaughter or to prepare the necessary drinks etc.[92]

In a way we have here an alternative to the "ritual" of confession, contrition, and forgiveness that is part of the reconciliation process.

Reluctant Engagement

Consider also e.g. Australia's (somewhat reluctant) attempts to come to terms with some of its past policies vis-à-vis the aborigines. Here, it was not individual abuse but "the law" itself which defined the group and systematically removed legal protection from it, allowing also for specific policies that otherwise would have been fundamental abuses of rights. In particular, the policy of separating Aboriginal and Torres Strait Islander children from their families became part of an official inquiry (Stolen Generations Inquiry). The background was the following: from the last quarter of the nineteenth century to the mid 1960s, large numbers of indigenous children were taken away from their families in order to be placed with white foster parents or state institutions. The rationale for these policies, rooted in racist eugenics, was described as follows by one of the official "Chief Protectors," in charge of the native children:

[92] Ibid., 192f.

Generally by the fifth and invariably by the sixth generation, all characteristics of the Australian aborigine are eradicated. The problem of half-castes will quickly be eliminated by the complete disappearance of the black race and the swift submergence of their progeny in the white ... The Australian native is the most easily assimilated race on earth, physically and mentally. The quickest way is to breed him white.[93]

Leaving aside for the moment the question of whether such policies do not already constitute a genocidal practice,[94] the publication of the inquiry report caused a public uproar. Although the government refused to officially acknowledge the past wrong and to apologize for the harm done, thousands of Australians signed the "Sorry Books" displayed throughout the country by civil society organizations. Finally, to allay growing public criticism, Prime Minister John Howard had to introduce a motion of reconciliation into the Federal Parliament (August 26, 1999), on which occasion he expressed what he called a "generic regret" for some past practices. More specifically, Prime Minister Rudd and opposition leader Nelson issued on February 13, 2008, an official apology of the Australian Parliament to the "stolen generations."

Truth and Reconciliation Commissions

Thus while Australia's official responses fell short of notions of "restorative justice" they did meet its first criterion: breaking the official silence by appointing a commission of inquiry and acknowledging a wrong.[95] It is therefore not surprising that the various "commissions of truth and or reconciliation"[96] were created all over the world in order to deal with the shadows the past cast on the present. The concrete manifestations of these "restorative" projects range from

---

[93] As quoted in Neta Crawford and Chris Cunneen, "Reparations and Restorative Justice: Responding to the Gross Violation of Human Rights" in Heather Strang and John Braithwaite (eds.), *Restorative Justice and Civil Society*, Cambridge: Cambridge University Press, 2001: 83–98, at 85.

[94] Australia as well as Brazil and Paraguay have denied the existence of genocide against the native populations due to the lack of "intent." For a further discussion, see Jennifer Balint, "Towards the Anti-Genocide Community: The Role of Law," *Australian Journal of Human Rights*, 1:1 (1994): 12–42.

[95] For an interesting discussion of an alternative conception of justice not based on punishment but shaming, focusing more on the restoration of the social fabric than on retribution or deterrence, see John Braithwaite, *Crime, Shame, and Reintegration*, Cambridge: Cambridge University Press, 1989.

[96] For a brief overview and assessment, see Priscilla B. Hayner, "Fifteen Truth Commissions – 1974–1994: A Comparative Study," *Human Rights Quarterly*, 16:4 (1994): 597–655; Daan Bronkhorst, *Truth and Reconciliation: Obstacles and Opportunities for Human Rights*, Amsterdam: Amnesty International, Dutch Section, 1995; Richard Goldstone, "Justice as a Tool for Peace-Making: Truth Commissions and International Criminal Tribunals," *New York University Journal of International Law and Politics*, 28:3 (1996): 485–503; Henry J. Steiner et al., *Truth Commissions: A Comparative Assessment*, Cambridge, MA: World Peace Foundation, 1997; Audrey R. Chapman and Patrick Ball, "The Truth of Truth Commissions: Comparative Lessons from Haiti, South Africa, and Guatemala," *Human Rights Quarterly*, 23:1 (2001): 1–43; Hayner, *Unspeakable Truths*.

the creation of a comprehensive Commission of Inquiry (Enquete Kommission[97]) and making the secret files of the security apparatus accessible to individuals,[98] as in the case of Germany (paralleled by some criminal prosecutions of former GDR officials and border guards), to the reports in Argentina and Chile,[99] to the famous Truth and Reconciliation Commission in South Africa.[100] Even when blanket amnesties or pardons often exempted some of the worst offenders, subsequent to the publication of the findings, as in the Latin American cases,[101] the "record" could at least be set straight and the idea that these actions could be justified in terms of "reasons of state" in an "unconventional" war against subversives could be discredited.[102]

[97] See the report of the First Enquete Kommission. Established in 1992, the commission consisted of sixteen members of the German Parliament and dealt with "The Elaboration of the History and Consequences of the SED Dictatorship." The second Enquete Kommission was established in 1995 and had as its task "Conquering the Consequences of the SED Dictatorship in the Process of German Unification."

[98] This required the establishment of a special agency of over 3,000 people taking care of over two million requests by private persons, as well as checking the "credentials" of people in the former GDR wanting to become or continue to be civil servants.

[99] See Phillip Berryman, Chile, and Comisión Nacional de Verdad y Reconciliación, "Report of the Chilean National Commission on Truth and Reconciliation," Notre Dame, IN: published in cooperation with the Center for Civil and Human Rights, Notre Dame Law School, by the University of Notre Dame Press, 1993.

[100] See e.g. Paul Lansing and Julie C. King, "South Africa's Truth and Reconciliation Commission: The Conflict between Individual Justice and National Healing in the Post-Apartheid Age," *Arizona Journal of International and Comparative Law*, 15:3 (1998): 753–789.

[101] In Salvador the governing ARENA party pushed through a sweeping amnesty one day after the Commission had published its findings of gross violations of human rights (March 20, 1993). In Chile the junta barred prosecution through the Decreto Ley 2191 of April 19, 1978 for all criminal offences between September 11, 1973 (the day of the coup against Allende), and March 10, 1978. Subsequently this amnesty was tested in court and found to be constitutional by the Chilean Supreme Court on August 24, 1990. In Argentina, the Report of the Commisión Nacional de la Disparación de Personas was given to the President in November 1984; a few days later a list of 1,351 perpetrators was leaked to the press. Argentina and Comisión Nacional sobre la Desaparición de Personas, *Nunca más: The Report of the Argentine National Commission on the Disappeared, with an Introduction by Ronald Dworkin*, New York: Farrar, Straus, Giroux, 1986. Subsequently, nine junta members and several other officers were prosecuted for crimes committed during the late 1970s and the 1980s. (According to the *Nunca más* report, 8,960 persons had disappeared.) The foot dragging of military and civilian courts and fear of rebellion by the armed forces led President Alfonsin to severely curtail prosecution through legislative acts (Law 23492 of December 24, 1986, and Law 23521 of June 4, 1987). With some rebellions actually occurring (and with hyperinflation ravaging the country) the President had to resign before his term ended. In July 1989 the new Peronist president Menem took over and granted on October 6, 1986, and on December 29, 1990, presidential pardon to all those convicted or under trial, including those members of the junta who were responsible for organizing the state terror. See Carlos Santiago Nino, *Radical Evil on Trial*, New Haven: Yale University Press, 1998, at 103f.

[102] See also the creation of such a commission by the UN Transitional Administration in East Timor on July 13, 2001. See Carsten Stahn, "Accommodating Individual Criminal Responsibility and National Reconciliation: The UN Truth Commission for East Timor," *American Journal of International Law*, 95:4 (2001): 952–966.

Conceived, as an alternative to judicial proceedings and retributive justice, the main objective of these Commissions was to publicly recognize the "evil" and thereby provide the "larger truth" that usually does not emerge from individual court proceedings. Various substantive and procedural issues were raised concerning the work of these commissions. One was the link between these inquiries and to other measures, most importantly possible future prosecutions or disciplinary action. This turned out to be one of the real problems in Argentina under President Alfonsin, who in 1985 had actually tried members of the junta and several other officers, leading to the conviction of five junta members.[103]

While several reports contained concrete proposals for prosecution, legal action usually had to be taken by the public prosecutors, and only the South African Commission[104] was directly empowered to grant individual amnesties for wrongful conduct while in office. Obtaining such an amnesty presupposed the official confessing his crime and apologizing for his actions. The second issue concerned the standards of evidence such a commission should apply in coming to its conclusions.[105] A third problem was whether or not such a commission should provide the names of the perpetrators or not. Here the Salvadorian report (which did) and the Chilean (which did not) diverged significantly.[106]

In retrospect, perhaps one of the better stories can be told of Germany and Chile, where the reports engendered public debate and created new awareness. But even in Germany a new nostalgia among some parts of the population of the former GDR for the "good old days" – now that the dangers and oppression of the former regime were no longer daily occurrences – tended subsequently to undermine some of the lessons learned. Argentina was afterwards so preoccupied with sheer economic survival that those hurts of former days were easily drowned out by the new pains. In eastern Europe some of the abuses of "lustration,"[107] i.e. the possibility of barring former state officials for a certain

---

[103] For an account of those trials and analysis of wider ramifications see Nino, *Radical Evil on Trial.*

[104] South Africa, Truth and Reconciliation Commission, and Desmond Tutu, *Truth and Reconciliation Commission of South Africa Report*, Cape Town: Truth and Reconciliation Commission, 1998.

[105] While no uniform standards have been articulated, the emerging practice for those commissions is to rely on a "balance of probabilities" (preponderance of evidence), meaning that there is more evidence for something to be true than not. Obviously, that is a more relaxed standard than of "beyond reasonable doubt." Hayner, *Unspeakable Truths*, at 131.

[106] See e.g. the intervention by Jose Zalaquett justifying the Chilean practice by arguing that a truth commission "must not trespass the fine line between an ethical commission and a kangaroo court. The moment they move to individual blame, they violate the basic principles of the rule of law" in Steiner et al., *Truth Commissions*, at 30.

[107] See Ruti Teitel, *Transitional Justice*, Oxford: Oxford University Press, 2000, at 98–99 and 164–67.

period from public office, and the circulation of "lists" of former collaborators have given rise to personal vendettas and witch hunts.

It remains of course an open question whether or not "reconciliation" actually occurs, or whether "digging up the past" will open old wounds. It would be surprising if the record were not mixed, since "knowing" alone is only the necessary but not sufficient condition for reconciliation. As one of the victims in South Africa put it, "once you know who did it you want the next thing – you want justice."[108] The Trauma Center for Victims of Violence and Torture estimates on the basis of its experience with hundreds of cases that 50–60 percent of the people participating in a reconciliation commission suffered difficulties in the aftermath and many regretted having participated.[109]

Ultimately, the success of "reconciliation" will not only depend on the ability of individuals to go on with their individual lives but also on collectively finding a new identity in which the sufferings of the past are connected to the future by a common political project. This does not mean that all individual stories will have to "merge" into one master narrative, but it does mean that the individual story and collective remembrance will illuminate, supplement and even criticize each other and thus open the space for individual and collective action. To illustrate this point, below I shall use some materials of the South African commission as well as Lincoln's Gettysburg address as my foils.

Engaging the Past by Defining a "Mission"

Psychologically speaking, the issue of reconciliation requires a mutual identification of victim and former oppressors with each other. Thus the former perpetrators and beneficiaries of the Apartheid regime in South Africa must not only lend an ear to the stories of victims, they also have to realize their failings and reconstruct the beliefs and desires that had "prevented them" from recognizing what was going on. Here often the ambiguous notion of "betrayal" emerges as a key concept in the stories of perpetrators. As one Afrikaans member of the South African Truth and Reconciliation Commission stated:

---

[108] See Mhlelli Mxenge commenting on the proceedings that provided Dirk Coetzee with amnesty for the murder of Mhlelli's brother, Griffith, a human rights lawyer. On the other hand, Coetzee who before the proceedings of the Commission "never expected" to be forgiven by the Mxenge family, is now "getting fed" up with the refusal of Griffith's brother to reconcile. Obviously, here victims and perpetrators exhibit precisely those attitudes that do not allow for a new beginning. See Lansing and King, "South Africa's Truth and Reconciliation Commission," at 772.

[109] Hayner, *Unspeakable Truths*, at 144.

We who came from the old order – or the majority of us – are horrified by the stories that victims of gross human rights violations have told over the past year. We are horrified and feel betrayed. We feel done in. We feel our dignity impaired. That things like these were possible, right under our noses. How could this have happened? We are victims of the cruelest fraud committed against us.[110]

While on the one hand such a "betrayal" could be seen as simply a self-serving defense – as it makes out of the perpetrator another "victim," blurring the fundamental differences in the processes of victimization – there is no doubt that the recognition of having betrayed one's own standards and thereby lost one's dignity as an agent is a basic yet painful step in moral reconstruction.

The victim on the other hand must not only believe that the perpetrator sees him as innocent but has also to convey the message that s/he recognizes the perpetrator's pain coming from the admission of guilt, thereby assuaging the fear of retribution. In other words, the victims must show that even if they do not actually forgive in their own hearts, they have not been damaged by the process of victimization. Although "unreconciled," they are still capable of acting as free moral agents, and of transcending the bounds of vengeance or retribution. To that extent they have to impose a discipline on themselves that seems precisely the opposite of that of consciousness-raising, which usually precedes revolutionary action. "Un-reconciled victims as revolutionaries," – writes Robert Meister,

achieve the heightened consciousness necessary for self-liberation when they recognize the beneficiaries of injustice as (would-be) perpetrators. For them justice will become a continuing struggle – not merely to defeat the evil regime, but also to eliminate its material effects. Even after the perpetrators of injustice have been defeated (both politically and morally), the un-reconciled victim thus sees struggle against the remaining beneficiaries of injustice as unfinished business of the revolution. Justice as the outcome of revolutionary struggle would consist of the final victory of the un-reconciled victim over the beneficiary, and from this perspective anything short of victim's justice is a compromise or a defeat.[111]

Given the understanding of these mutual vulnerabilities, the realization of the common fate of having become victims serves as a possible, but ambiguous and even dangerous, bridge.

When nations emerge from civil wars or large-scale violence, the "new beginning" usually has to find expression in an accord among the contending parties and/or some form of constitutional founding or re-founding. Of course,

[110] Wynard Manan, "Statement by Mr. Wynand Malan, Deputy Chairman of the Human Rights Violations Committee of the Truth and Reconciliation Commission," May 16, 1997, www.justice.gov.za/trc/media/pr/1997/p970516a.html.
[111] Robert Meister, "Forgiving and Forgetting: Lincoln and the Politics of National Recovery" in Carla Alison Hesse and Robert Post (eds.), *Human Rights in Political Transitions: Gettysburg to Bosnia*, New York: Zone Books, 1999, 135–176, at 162.

compromises are the common experience, as exemplified in transitional just-ice, since usually neither "revolutionary justice" nor a totally "new beginning" is possible. Nevertheless, if such a "re-founding" occurs, it has to be based on a notion of reconciliation. Consider in this context the short text of the Gettys-burg address, through which Lincoln attempted to deal with the trauma of the Civil War:

Four scores and twenty years ago our fathers brought forth on this continent a new nation conceived in liberty and dedicated to the proposition that all men are created equal.

Now we are engaged in a civil war, testing whether that nation, or any nation so con-ceived and so dedicated can long endure. We are at a battlefield of that war. We have come to dedicate a portion of it as a final resting place for those who died here that the nation might live. This we may in all propriety do. But in a larger sense we cannot dedicate, we cannot consecrate, we cannot hallow this ground. The brave men, living and dead who struggled here have hallowed it far above our poor power to add or detract. The world will little note nor long remember what we say here, but it can never forget what they did here.

It is rather for us the living, here to be dedicated to the great task remaining before us. That from these honored dead we take increased devotion – that we here highly resolve that these dead shall have not died in vain, that this nation shall have a new birth of freedom, and that this government of the people, by the people, for the people shall not perish from the earth.[112]

Clearly this is not an address dealing solely with the burial of thousands of soldiers at Gettysburg. Rather, like Pericles' funeral oration before it, it becomes a statement about the "mission" of the society that connects the past to the future. In the case of the Gettysburg address, it does so not by an exten-sive praise of the city, in which Pericles engaged, but rather by some very bold and mutually reinforcing conceptual moves contained in a brief text of hardly 200 words.

First, it attempts to show the exemplary character of the original founding ("any nation so conceived"). Second, it considers the war as a "test" for the viability of the original political project, thereby taking the war out of the context of the usual violent dispute arising from the stasis within a political system. Finally, the war is interpreted as a common trial in which the "Union" (i.e. both the North and the South) frees itself from the stigma of slavery and resolves to rededicate itself to its original task.

The religious overtones telling a story of promise, failure, and redemption are obvious. What is less obvious, but even more interesting for our purposes,

[112] Abraham Lincoln, address delivered at the Dedication of the Cemetery at Gettysburg, PA, Nov. 19, 1863, reprinted in Roy P. Basler (ed.), *Abraham Lincoln: His Speeches and Writings*, Cleveland, OH: World Publishing, 1946, at 734.

is that in Meister's interpretation it is the "Union" which is being depicted as a *victim*, having succumbed to (the sin of) slavery and now seeking redemption. Thus, both contending parties can, on this basis, rededicate themselves to the (original and) future task. The issue is therefore one of identification with a task, not as a "constitutional" question of representation, or of a "contract," from which one can withdraw through secession. In addition, phrasing the conflict in those terms, the story is not one of revenge, retribution or reparation, but of a common purpose with which all can identify and to which they can "rededicate" themselves. Different from normal conceptions of restorative justice in which some form of restitution is part of the settlement, there is an eerie and troubling silence in regard to the sufferings of the actual victims, the slaves. But since they are not directly a party to the conflict, they are supposed to be now "emancipated" members of the Union together with their former Southern masters, who are now "reconciled" and no longer "revolutionaries."

Of course, Reconstruction and the whole story of the Fourteenth amendment and its changing interpretations tell of the difficulty of translating such a rededication into practical politics. Nevertheless,

rather than describing the aftermath of the war as a deserved punishment for sin Lincoln suggest that the living are the undeserved beneficiaries of the sacrifice of those who "... gave their lives that ... the nation might live." ... Viewed as a peace strategy Lincoln's national "survivor" story provided a moral framework under which many in the defeated South could accept the Northern victory as something other than a humiliating punishment for slavery and secession.[113]

8.6   Conclusion

This chapter dealt with the problem of "history" for theory building in the social sciences. For that purpose it tried to move on two levels: First, I revisited the old debates between Hedley Bull and his sparring partners, and their continuation in e.g. the more recent controversy in sociology and political science concerning the possibility of macrohistory. Second, by revisiting these debates I attempted to sharpen the conceptual criticism of Bull in order to clarify the role of historical reflection for the social sciences. For the latter purpose I examined the difficulties that arise when we try to reduce history to a "storehouse" of data in order to corroborate our models or theories.

I suggested that the latter view fundamentally misunderstands the nature of historical data, which are not brute facts, but are always emplotted and thus part of larger structures of meaning. "History" is not simply "there" but is a

---

[113] Meister, "Forgiving and Forgetting," at 141.

product of memory. What is considered worth remembering, therefore, is constituted by our values and interests, as Weber already remarked. To that extent the usual procedures provided in various "primers" of political science for building better theories are highly suspect because they misunderstand not only the practice of science itself, but misconstrue the problem of concept formation and their constitutive character, which has to precede any concern with operationalization or inference. Basing my criticism on the cognitive revolution in psychology, I argued that our conceptualizations about the social world do not proceed via abstraction and generalization but through the extension of prototypes to other "cases," thereby judging the phenomena according to various (value) dimensions. To that extent, family resemblance rather than intrinsically fixed properties constitute types and mark their boundaries. Attributing a case to a type requires, therefore, (contestable) *judgments* rather than abstraction and the type of inferences familiar from statistics and quantitative methods. The debate concerning the democratic peace argument was intended to illustrate some of these points.

Finally, if history is produced by "memory," as I argued, then it is always viewed from a particular *vantage point of the present*. It is this present problem that informs the selection of what is considered worth remembering. To that extent historical reflection is not some collection of interesting facts one could do without, but is intrinsic to our notions of agency and identity. In approaching history not in terms of the fixity of the past, but through the modality of remembering, we become aware of the "possible." In this way individuals and collectivities can transcend the confinements imposed by system, and find new ways of mastering their destiny. Taking this attitude towards the past means getting rid of certain experiences that traumatize or limit us as actors (forgetting).

In this context, the problem of a formation of a collective memory and the interactive influence of processes of individuation and of creating a collective reference world were discussed. These considerations then prepare the ground for a further exploration of the knowledge appropriate for praxis, which will be the topic for the next chapters.

9   Knowing and Doubting

9.1   Introduction

What does it mean to say that we "know" something? On the simplest level we claim that the statements we make are not simply idiosyncratic utterances indicating likes and dislikes, but that they are warranted and thus have public standing. While such a bare bone conception of knowledge might marshal assent – as it just rules out purely personal beliefs – the problem is not solved as long as the "warrant" remains an empty placeholder for a vast variety of criteria. Here the distinctions of appearance/reality opinion/truth, logic/nonsense, experience/speculation, prejudice/well-founded belief, philosophy/revelation, or science/folklore, come to mind. Furthermore, since in all assertions the innocuous term of "is" plays a crucial role, it comes as no surprise that its status within the system of signs provides since earliest times some puzzles. Already Aristotle remarked that "is" is used in a variety of senses and thus predication and what we believe to be true (because of the attending warrants) have spawned controversies in ontology, semiotics, deconstruction, the order of things, the debates on universals (whether concepts are in the things, before the things, or after the things), whose aftershocks we still notice. Even IR scholars get an occasional whiff of this, with the various "camps" in the field, such as realists and conventionalists or adherents of induction or subsumption, of explaining and understanding, making ready to kick off another "great debate."

Nevertheless, debates in IR frequently exhibit a certain artificiality. Precisely because they often lack the necessary philosophical background, IR scholars often use the writings of one of the founders of a school in their field as a "proxy measure," or they select one philosopher as their more or less unquestioned authority, so that his insights can now be "applied" to the discipline. What then takes up most the discussion is who in the discipline said what, and placing the different participants in the ever more finely subdivided spaces of a quadrant (actually drawn out in a table or implied).

Thus in a recent book, which wants to "reclaim causal analysis" in IR,[1] Milja Kurki identifies the "Humean syndrome" in a variety of writers in IR and claims that the dangers of this Humeanism can only be mastered if we return to a "causal ontology" and allow for "more holistic" (or more varied) explanatory accounts. Since apparently rational choicers, as well as reflexivists of various stripes, have symptoms of this disease,[2] only "scientific realists" seem reliable as they have acquired the necessary immunity. The latter are basing their arguments largely on Roy Bhaskar's[3] "realist" philosophy of science – nobly suppressing the fact that their guru had left their camp long before his untimely death. Kurki's assessment then sits uneasily with her own analysis of Aristotle and the latter's notion of a variety of "causes."[4]

Although one might be quite sympathetic to her effort at clarification, I have my doubts that going "deeper" down to ontology is the (only?) way of arriving at a more adequate framework for analyzing of praxis. What is interesting in her presentation is the rather strange characterization of Hume. In all fairness one has to say that she gestures at the difference between what Hume said and what later generations made of it,[5] such as Mill, the conventionalists, or the various offshoots of the Vienna circle. To that extent her reliance on some form of "ideal type" does not seem illegitimate – even though it is at odds with the original Humean intent and his rather explicit teachings on common sense, on conventions, and on the importance of a historical understanding of the social world.

In constructing as a sparring partner a Humean "theory" that never was – picking and choosing bits and pieces from Hume's writings – distortion is rampant and develops its own dynamic, instead of providing a fuller and "more holistic account" of knowledge and human action. The move to ontology might be the wrong medicine by privileging a priori only those explanations

[1] Milja Kurki, *Causation in International Relations: Reclaiming Causal Analysis*, Cambridge: Cambridge University Press, 2008.
[2] See Milja Kurki, "Reflectivist and Constructivist Approaches in International Relations: More Cases of Humeanism" in *Causation in International Relations: Reclaiming Causal Analysis*, Cambridge: Cambridge University Press, 2008, 124–144.
[3] Roy Bhaskar, *A Realist Theory of Science*, 2nd edn., Brighton: Harvester, 1978; Roy Bhaskar, *The Possibility of Naturalism: A Philosophical Critique of the Contemporary Human Sciences*, Brighton: Harvester Press, 1979.
[4] See also Hidemi Suganami, "Agents, Structures, Narratives," *European Journal of International Relations*, 5:3 (1999): 365–386.
[5] In her discussion of Kant and Mill, Kurki admits "Despite Kant's and Mill's acceptance of basic Humean premises Humeanism did not flourish until the twentieth century. During the twentieth century the Humean assumptions became deeply embedded within the dominant currents in the philosophy of science." Kurki, *Causation in International Relations*, at 43.

which fully embrace a "deep ontological" stance and contain the "unfolding of material causes."[6]

Given the prevalence of "Humeanism" it might seem rather ironic that in the following I shall here use Hume as my guide in advocating a fuller (causal) account for the analysis of praxis without giving the material or efficient cause the pride of place. For this I use the Humean texts as my basis, instead of relying on a specific interpretation of a follower (or critic). I do this because I believe that Hume provides the only well-articulated approach to the study of the social world and its historical character that does not fall victim to most of the errors which the ontological tradition brings along in its conceptual baggage.

The first thing we have to concern ourselves with is to get the question(s) right which Hume actually wanted to address in his writings. The historical context in which Hume worked is circumscribed by the powerful attack of the skeptics and by Descartes's answer to them in his new *prima philosophia*.[7] Although the latter was no longer grounded in an ontological order of things, but focused on the subject and its production of knowledge, it still claimed to provide secure knowledge by starting from some incontrovertible fundaments from which, as maintained, a distinct method follows.

Hume sets against this project of certainty his philosophy of human nature and of the mind (rather than reason), in which "imagination" and "experience" are the most important elements. Human nature no longer represents some essence, but is crucially linked to the historical emergence of conventions that define a common life in which man is not only a participant, but shaped by it. This new perspective dramatically changed the role of philosophy, which no longer can pretend to stand outside of a common life, claiming an authority independent of all beliefs, customs, and even "prejudices." Instead, philosophy had to recognize its responsibility by not reflecting from the outside, taking social life as an object, but by realizing its purpose and potential as a critical voice *within* the institutionalized interactions and the discourses of a society on problems of common concern. Rather than looking for incontrovertible foundations, Hume suggests that since we always begin "in the midst" of a

---

[6] In this context the stone out of which a sculptor fashions his statue is usually adduced as an example for the "causal" constraints the medium imposes. To that extent Michelangelo's (probably tongue-in-cheek) remark that he is only ripping out of the stone the figures of a David or a Pieta seems to fit. But there is something fishy about this argument since, first, not all people can "rip out" the sculpture from a stone (as many had tried their luck before on precisely the same marble block from which "David" emerged), and even if they had the skill to do it, their products were more or less well executed "reproductions" and not the "real thing."

[7] The tem "first philosophy" was already used by Aristotle, but the later systematization of the Aristotelian corpus labeled that treatise as coming "after" physics (Metaphysics).

concrete situation, we should systematically examine how we got here, what alternatives offer themselves, and how they are furthering or hindering the realization of our individual or collective projects. This mode of argumentation opens up our inquiry to history and to the varied accounts we give of our doings and their meaning in shaping our present predicament and identities.

To that extent my engagement with Hume is not primarily driven by an interest in the history of ideas, i.e. in providing a more accurate intellectual biography of a neglected philosopher who has had his work badly scavenged and bowdlerized. It is rather an attempt to explore more systematically the reasons why the search for grand theories, which is driven by a highly problematic epistemological project, is a mistake in the social "sciences" because the realm of praxis has certain identifiable peculiarities which are simply passed over – at considerable cost, I may add – if they are subjected to "theoretical" criteria.

This realization of the "autonomy" of the practical realm also has important methodological implications since it draws our attention not to the universal and necessary causal constants, but rather to the complex set of interactions and conjunctures that have meaning for us. They do so not because of an empathy we feel with the actors and their motives, but because explaining an action or a sequence of interactions often attains its plausibility from a narrative (not from generalizing inference or the subsumption under a universally valid law). It renders their sequence more intelligible, thereby bringing our questioning to an end. This end is not reached by having now found out what "really" happened or having stepped outside of the historical world and enjoying the view from nowhere – but because we are now relieved of our doubts by having arrived at "warranted beliefs." These beliefs also need not be "final" or incontrovertible, because they are, of course, subject to revision due to new discoveries, or, because of the different political projects which we or the next generations pursue, so that the existing "explanation" is no a longer a (pragmatic) conversation stopper.

The steps of my argument can be derived from these initial remarks. In Section 9.2, I try to characterize the background of Hume's work, circumscribed by the skeptics' attack and Descartes's answer to them. Section 9.3 is devoted to a sketch of Hume's positive heuristics, i.e. his argument about the working of the human mind and its development. Such an attempt was obviously inspired by Newton, as well as by the Enlightenment project which militated against uncritical acceptance of the authority claimed by "throne and altar," i.e. the state and the church. Hume, however, soon recognized the danger that a Newtonian attempt could degenerate into another form of foundationalism instead of of searching for the puzzles in the social world and in "commerce and conversation." This led him to flesh out the conventional nature of the social world in his *Treatise* and *Essay*, which is given greater depth in his later *History of England*, as I shall argue in Section 9.4. A brief summary (Section 9.5) concludes the chapter.

9.2   Hume and the Epistemological Project

By the time Hume was writing his *Treatise* (1738), skepticism had lost much of its steam thanks to Descartes's catchy phrase *cogito ergo sum*. Nevertheless, the danger remained that as soon as the precariousness of this Cartesian solution became obvious, despair would result, since philosophy could not deliver on its promises. It is in the context of counteracting these dangers, which a debunking of the claims of philosophy (traditional, or Cartesian) to be the "queen of knowledge" would likely engender, that Hume's critical remarks about causation are made. Thus Hume's fight is twofold. On the one hand, he had to disarm the skeptics. They had success-fully challenged the traditional ontology and the "order of things" which had relied on canonical sources – be it the Bible, or the works of ancient writers or philosophers – for the necessary "warrants." On the other hand, he had to attack the illusion that gave Descartes's "solution" its force, i.e. that *universal doubt* could disclose a new fundament for *secure knowledge* and that pursuing a certain method represented the *via regia* to the accumu-lation of warranted knowledge.

Hume realized that the Cartesian claims were grossly exaggerated, as God had to be reintroduced, not as an active force as in the Augustinian *Deus illuminatio mea*,[8] but as a presupposition guaranteeing the match between the *res cogitans* (concept) and the *res extensa* (the world out there).[9] In addition, the introduction of "clear and distinct ideas" and a specific method were constantly in danger of being subverted by radical doubt, unless these ideas concerned only purely analytical statements. Aside from the difficulty inherent in this distinction – which Quine later pointed out[10] – it is not clear why the certainty inherent in self-reflexivity helps us to decide what we accept as "evidence" when we deal with *non-analytical* statements or experiences con-cerning the "real world." And finally, there was the inconsistent and rather strange "conservatism" of Descartes, who vehemently refused to apply his method to the study of social and moral questions. He preferred, instead,

[8] "God is my light" – within which I can see how things are. (To this day the motto of Oxford University.)
[9] See René Descartes, *Meditations on First Philosophy*, 2nd edn., New York: Liberal Arts Press, 1951, 2nd Meditation.
[10] Willard Van Orman Quine, "Two Dogmas of Empiricism" in Quine, *From a Logical Point of View*, Cambridge, MA: Harvard University Press, 1953, 20–46.

a rather unreflective life guided by tradition and established institutions.[11] (So much for the "critical" nature of his proposal!)

Given the incoherence of the Cartesian position, one has to wonder why the epistemological project, which Descartes began and which promised us "warranted knowledge" on the basis of philosophical, field-independent criteria, has been so successful. Was Hume, after all, mistaken? I do not think so, but making this case will require a more extended discussion. For the moment I want to treat this as an open question and just note that perhaps part of the success of the epistemological project might have something to do with the corrections which Kant and neo-Kantianism have made over the centuries. Various debates could thus appear to result in a kind of synthesis, espoused e.g. by the "unity of science position," which inspired positivism and scientific realism in the twentieth century. However, what such a thumbnail sketch of the history of epistemology obscures is the fact that the distinction between "explaining" and "understanding," separating the natural and social sciences by bursting the bubble of the "unity of science," also has Kantian roots, which suggests that the synthesis was perhaps more imaginary than real.[12] Furthermore, as the recent discussion which moved from scientific realism to some form of "critical realism" shows, the problems are far from resolved.[13]

Perhaps the greatest failing of the unity of science position was that it relied on a "rational reconstruction" of scientific progress – so dear to the project of modernity. As such, it quickly derailed into an ideology of progress,[14] which hides the importance of both history and of praxis by failing to examine the actual research practices and situating them in the larger social context. Instead, the theme of consistent, even if gradual but nevertheless, preordained, "progress" must now do most of the explaining. While there is certainly growth in our knowledge, the process of knowledge generation is, however,

---

[11] See René Descartes, *Discourse on Method and Meditations on First Philosophy*, trans. Donald Cress, (Indianapolis: Hackett, 1980), pt. 3, paras. 23–28. He formulates a "provisional code of morals" containing four maxims: The first was to obey the laws and customs of my country, holding constantly to the religion in which by God's grace I had been instructed from my childhood ... The second maxim was to be as firm and decisive in my actions as I could, and to follow even the most doubtful opinions, once I had adopted them, with no less constancy than if they had been quite certain ... My third maxim was to try always to master myself rather than fortune, and to change my desires rather than the order of the world ... Finally, to conclude this moral code ... I thought I could do no better than to continue with the [occupation] I was engaged in, and to devote my whole life to cultivating my reason and advancing as far as I could in the knowledge of the truth, following the method I had prescribed for myself," in ibid., at 12–15.

[12] Immanuel Kant, *Kritik der Reinen Vernunft*, vol. 2, Wiesbaden: Insel-Verlag, 1956.

[13] See the recent Forum on Critical Realism in *Review of International Studies*, for which Oliver Kessler assembled an interesting set of papers. Oliver Kessler, "Forum on Critical Realism," *Review of International Studies*, 38:1 (2012): 187–274.

[14] See e.g. the near automaticity implied by Popper, *Conjectures and Refutations*.

far less orderly, as this rational historical reconstruction suggests. Kuhn[15] and the historians of science have pointed out that because neither the Popperian "demarcation criterion" of science, nor "refutability" provide firm guidance as to when we should abandon a wrong theory, the acceptance or rejection of evidence cannot come in the form of a demonstrative proof.[16] Frequently, such a vetting entails a rather contested argument among the practicing scientists, in which the theory, the "background knowledge" (concerning the procedures and assumptions considered unproblematic and reliable), and the tested hypothesis powerfully interact.[17] The upshot of this dilemma is that a considerable burden is then placed on the *community of scientists* (not only the individual researcher and his/her experiments) to keep the individual practitioner honest, but *also to determine who can legitimately claim to practice "good science"* and who is, therefore, entitled to be a member of the disciplinary fraternity.

The above observation also draws our attention to the wider social processes within which knowledge production is embedded: from the man/machine interface in laboratories,[18] to peer group evaluations, to certification procedures, to national academies, to the allocation of the burdens of proof in grant applications, to the channels by which knowledge gets disseminated and impacts upon curricula, public discussions, and policy.[19] All this seems a far cry from the notion of "the scientific method" as self-justifying as long as it satisfies field-independent epistemological criteria. There are three further caveats which attain importance in this context.

The first is that even if we were able successfully to specify a set of field-independent criteria we would have to face a problem which is all too familiar to lawyers: that abstract principles do not decide concrete cases. This means that we still need interpretation and that without an authorized community of interpreters, a discipline might degenerate into a loose agglomeration of different schools, or it might even disintegrate. Second, if we find that in practice actually a *variety of methods* is used in different disciplines – as a Petri dish and a test tube makes sense when doing biology or chemistry, but not when we decipher a text or do research in particle physics – then what is actually going on in disciplinary knowledge production and the idealized

---

[15] Kuhn, *The Structure of Scientific Revolutions.*
[16] Joseph Agassi, *Science in Flux*, Dordrecht: D. Reidel, 1975.
[17] Hempel, *Aspects of Scientific Explanation.*
[18] Bruno Latour and Steve Woolgar, *Laboratory Life: The Social Construction of Scientific Facts,* London: Sage, 1979.
[19] See Kratochwil, "Evidence, Inference and Truth as Problems of Theory Building in the Social Sciences" in Richard. N. Lebow and Mark I. Lichbach (eds.), *Theory and Evidence in Comparative Politics and International Relations*, New York: Palgrave Macmillan, 2007, 25–54.

(or better: phantasmagoric) version of its history diverge considerably. To that extent, the "rational reconstruction" can no longer claim to be a fitting account of "doing" science.[20] At this point a third question arises: why should we then hold on to such a scientific "ideal" in the first place?

But then again, the fact that many, if not most, of us want to hold on to such constructs might not be as mistaken as it seems. After all, there are perhaps *pragmatic* reasons, since the old constructs somehow "worked." Deep down we know that we are always in the midst of things,[21] like on a vessel in a storm which we have to repair plank by plank (if we are lucky enough to have the necessary timber on board) rather than being able to accomplish the feat while enjoying the "view from nowhere." Since the "ideal" is unachievable, why not hold on to what we have and that gets us "through"? Our experiential misgivings about a radical reorientation are usually not just imaginary, as further reflection reveals. After all, looking at "the world out there" is something deeply ingrained in us,[22] although it presupposes that the world is finished, complete, and unchanging, so that after six days God could view his work, see that it was good, and he could rest.[23] This belief, however, sits uneasily with the opposite realization, that the world (even the cosmos) is in the making, and even more importantly, that in the social world most of the constitutive elements are not natural but mind-dependent "facts."

While the notion of a "world out there" might thus show the dead weight of tradition and perhaps of a certain complacency, I think that something more needs to be said on this. Two things come to mind: One is the specific epistemological debates, which will have to be unearthed. The second concerns the more general problem of how cognition and emotions interact since universal doubt is impossible. So I might hang on to some beliefs even if I have my doubts. Thus we "feel" warranted in our beliefs as long as they let us "go on" and we do not lose our orientation, despite occasional real disappointments. Conversely, doubt arises when such disappointments occur frequently and our attempts at "explaining" them away increasingly seem contorted. Then the fear

---

[20] See the discussion of Diesing, *How Does Social Science Work.*

[21] See Jörg Friedrichs and Friedrich Kratochwil, "On Acting and Knowing: How Pragmatism Can Advance International Relations Research and Methodology," *International Organization*, 63:4 (2009): 701–731.

[22] Cicero, *De Oratore* at bk. II, chap. 36. See also the fundamental discussion by Koselleck, "Historia Magistra Vitae."

[23] See Hume's snide remarks: "Disputes are multiplied as if everything was uncertain; and these disputes are managed with the greatest warmth, as if everything was certain. Amidst all this bustle 'tis not reason which carries the prize, but eloquence; and no man needs even despair of gaining proselytes to the most extravagant hypothesis, who has art enough to represent it in any favorable colour. The victory is not gained by men at arms, who manage the pike and the sword; but by the trumpeters, drummers, and musicians of the army." David Hume, *A Treatise of Human Nature*, ed. David Fate Norton and Mary J. Norton, Oxford; New York: Oxford University Press, 2000, Introduction, para. 2, at 3.

arises that perhaps we have been wrong all along and that a more fundamental and perhaps painful readjustment is in order. Such an adjustment might not be limited to the adoption and handling of some new concepts, but might also affect my notions of what I am doing, who I am, and how I relate to "relevant" others. At that point, doubts mount and frequently lead to despair, as the certainty gained through absolute doubt is obviously incapable of making good on its promise to provide "unshakable foundations."

Let me therefore begin with the first issue. The Cartesian doubt was neither "natural" nor did it came from "nowhere." Instead, it was part of a particular history of Western philosophy. The latter claimed that its conceptual apparatus, and in particular the alleged power of its ontology, could decide not only what "is" and what "is not," but that this distinction was also fundamental to questions of making sense and bestowing meaning. It is this latter assertion that cannot be quite right since we all know that the way we attribute sense is wider than asserting matters of fact. Thus, sentences like "Thou shalt not kill" or "This banknote is legal tender" or even "Botticelli's 'Birth of Venus' is a painting of extraordinary beauty" are not simply senseless, even if they are not statements to which we can attach the truth-conditions for factual assertions. This problem is further obscured by the fact that we use the term "is," as if these appraisals were referential statements. Thus it should be clear that the notion of "sense" or meaning has to be wider, rather than the other way around. To wit I say "Every green tomorrow boiled 7 car-insurance" each of the terms has a clear reference although the sentence has no meaning at all.

If we now ask how all these rather abstract discussions relate to the topic of praxis, I claim that for a fruitful engagement with that problematique we have to take leave from the notion that the concepts "make sense" because they refer or cover the things "out there." Rather we have to investigate how we *use* these concepts (in accordance with certain criteria), in order to meaningfully communicate with each other, contest claims, make demands, and voice grievances.[24] Such a change in perspective is also demanded because the most important concepts of the social world are constitutive rather than merely referential, and without knowing how these concepts are used and related to our practices we would have nothing to refer to. The second interconnected move is that we give up the hope that theory is the *via regia* for understanding the social world. What we have to examine instead is the problem of which *criteria* are appropriate for assessing praxis rather than dogmatically follow the old epistemological ideal of "one size fits all." To that extent I claim that some other form of knowledge – conceived as warranted belief but allowing for different criteria than "theory"– is required for the analysis of the social world.

---

[24] See Kratochwil, *Rules, Norms and Decisions.*

For this heterodox endeavor I use Hume as my foil, while digressing occasionally and consulting some other writers, like Adam Smith or modern philosophers of language. I do so on the hunch that Hume, who has been seminal for my career[25] – after I had chanced upon him in my dissertation – was worth a closer second, and more comprehensive, reading, at the point where I am near to spilling my last ink. Furthermore, Hume was one of the most "interdisciplinary" scholars, at home in jurisprudence, the sciences, history, and literature, and he lived at a time when the boundaries of many disciplines were redrawn.[26] Nevertheless, one caveat is in order: I do not want to claim that my reading of Hume's complex and, at times, rather confusing works, such as the *Treatise*, or of Smith's oeuvre – which includes not only his *Wealth of Nations*[27] but also a "theory" of moral sentiments, an engagement with Jurisprudence,[28] the history of several disciplines[29] – represents the "true" or even "comprehensive" interpretation which has up to now eluded us.[30] Rather, as already mentioned, I shall use their writings as heuristic suggestions showing us how new conceptual spaces can be opened up by following up on their challenges. Approaching this problem, in a way historically, presupposes, however, that I first situate the consulted works within their respective debates. But in doing so, great care has to be taken not to interpret the crucial terms and distinctions in the way we nowadays understand them. Attention to their history and their embeddedness in changing semantic fields is crucial, as common terms often turn out to be "false friends" so familiar from language learning.[31]

That said, I claim that Hume's *Treatise* represents an independently articulated and highly original "answer" to the skeptics' challenge, to which both Descartes and Locke had already responded, but whose contributions Hume also criticized for good reasons. He disagreed with Locke with respect to the

---

[25] See Friedrich Kratochwil, *The Humean Conception of International Relations*, Princeton: Princeton University Press, 1981. Reprinted in Friedrich Kratochwil, *The Puzzles of Politics: Inquiries into the Genesis and Transformation of International Relations*, New York: Routledge, 2011: 15–37.

[26] For a good overview of Hume's work and its intellectual background, see Harold W. Noonan, *Hume on Knowledge*, Abingdon: Routledge, 1999; Harold W. Noonan, *Hume*, Oxford: Oneworld Publishing, 2007.

[27] Adam Smith, *An Inquiry into the Nature and Causes of the Wealth of Nations*, Oxford: Clarendon, 1979 [1776].

[28] See Adam Smith, "Lectures on Jurisprudence (1762/63 and 1763/64)" in Ronald L. Meek, D.D. Raphael, and Peter Stein (eds.), *The Glasgow Edition of Works and Correspondence of Adam Smith*, Oxford: Clarendon Press, 1978.

[29] See e.g. Adam Smith, "History of Astronomy" in W.P.D. Wightman and J.C. Bryce (eds.), *Essays on Philosophical Subjects*, Oxford: Clarendon Press, 1980, 33–105.

[30] For a useful brief discussion of different interpretations of central tenets of Hume's work, see Nicholas Capaldi, "Some Misconceptions about Hume's Moral Theory," *Ethics*, 76:3 (1966): 208–211.

[31] Thus assuming that *burro* refers to the same thing in Spanish and Italian because they are both based on vulgar Latin is a case in point, as in Spanish it means "ass," in Italian "butter."

latter's notion of the mind as *a tabula rasa*,[32] and with Descartes because of the implausibility of radical doubt.[33] Hume also took issue with several solutions offered by the "other" side, which had not engaged the skeptics directly. This faction adhered to some type of moral intuitionism, or was slowly moving from a conception of natural law to a theory of natural rights. Thus for Grotius and Pufendorf, Hobbes represented a convenient sparring partner, but he also loomed large on Hume's horizon.

It is against this background that the argument for the development of "a science of morals"[34] was articulated, as it promised to place the question of the sources of our sociability on a firmer footing than either mere speculation, or remaining in the "dogmatic slumber" induced by the familiar. Hume's efforts were thus animated at first by finding a scientific solution to the problem of knowledge in general, and his *Treatise* is an attempt to ground everything in "human nature." He nevertheless remained skeptical of a philosophy based on a foundational understanding of logic or on a (purportedly) "empirical science," as he discovered that neither could make good on their promise. Logic quickly becomes paradoxical as Hume's critique of Descartes showed. However, taking Newton's empiricism as a paradigm unfortunately led to similar difficulties, as Hume noticed after a while: the evidence, disclosed to us by our sense-impressions, is both deceptive and never sufficient for the inferences to which it gives rise.[35] This realization reinforces our doubts and can even lead to total withdrawal and/or despair (as exemplified by the ancient Pyrrhonists). After all, if we start from the proposition that we are not rationally justified in accepting beliefs which go beyond our individual perceptions

[32] See e.g. Hume's snide remark in the *Treatise* that he wants to use the word idea in its "original sense from which Mr. Locke had perverted it." Hume, *A Treatise of Human Nature*, Introduction, fn. 2.

[33] See David Hume, *An Inquiry Concerning Human Understanding*, Oxford: Clarendon, 1975, at 149f. First Inquiry, sec. XII, part 1, para. 116. " [Descartes] recommends an universal doubt, not only of all our former opinions and principles, but also of our very faculties, of whose veracity . . . we must assure ourselves by a chain of reasoning deduced from some original principle which cannot possibly be fallacious or deceitful, But neither is there any such original principle, which has a prerogative above others, that are self-evident and convincing. Or if there were, could we advance a step beyond it, but by the use of those very faculties, of which we are supposed to be already diffident. The Cartesian doubt . . . were it ever possible to be attained by any human creature (as it is plainly not) would be entirely incurable; and no reasoning could ever bring us to a state of assurance and conviction upon any subject."

[34] For excellent discussion of this background, see Knud Haakonssen, *Natural Law and Moral Philosophy: From Grotius to the Scottish Enlightenment*, New York: Cambridge University Press, 1996.

[35] Here Hume probably found support in Newton's admission "I have not been able to discover the cause of those properties of gravity from the Phenomena." See Isaac Newton's (1678) *General Scholium* in Isaac Newton, *Philosophiae Naturalis Principia Mathematica*, trans. Andrew Motte, Cambridge: Cambridge University Press, 1934, at 547.

and their connections (the Humean "ideas"), then we have to accept that we also cannot believe in the existence of objects in the world, or even in our own identity, or in the existence of moral facts. Thus, the cure of empiricism, if taken seriously, leads to the paradox that we have to reject what seem to be the most self-evident propositions about the world.

In a way, the merit of Hume's work is not only the realization that certainty and warranted knowledge cannot be grounded in the "things" out there, or in the subject's reason, but also that even if such foundations are faulty, this does not mean that the skeptics are right and that *no knowledge* is possible. Here the notions of intersubjectivity and of participation in a common life-world attain their importance. Although we cannot reach the certainty we seek there either, *we become aware that we no longer need* such absolute foundations for our knowledge-warrants, because we can "go on" and pursue our individual and collective projects in the face of an uncertainty we can live with. Pyrrhonist skepticism is not refuted by a new and "true theory," but becomes a *mitigated skepticism that proves its usefulness in practice.*[36]

This realization is what Hume sometimes calls the "true philosophy." It emerges from *within* the common world and from an engagement with it, instead of embarking on the vain search for a chimerical certainty outside of it. Such an engagement cannot promise certitude, but it prevents us from both overestimating our capacities of understanding – since our knowledge will always be limited – and from underestimating the practical difficulties of creating the social world by design. "True philosophy" can only be critical by taking the common life, its institutions and tradition seriously, while trying to cleanse them of mistaken beliefs (such as in mysterious or miraculous origins, or their providential nature), or of the obsessions which result from the quest for certainty.

9.3   Situating the Puzzle of "Human Nature"

Having adumbrated in a first cut the debates in which Hume intervened, let me begin with a (modest) ground-clearing operation on the Humean conceptual apparatus, i.e. the apparent contradiction between Hume's argument for the social world as being based on conventions and customs – which point us to the importance of history – and his attempt to build his "true philosophy" on human nature. His admiration for Newton and the not so hidden claim that he is trying something similar appear to reinforce the perception that we are dealing here with a glaring contradiction. After all, both Hume and Smith

---

[36] See *Enquiries*, 1, 12, 3 (Selby-Bigge version), 3rd edn., ed. P. H. Nidditch, Oxford: Clarendon, 1975, 161–165.

admired Newton and were fascinated by his discoveries,[37] but the result of their own explorations was that, like Columbus, they found something new instead of reaching the intended goal. Although a certain uneasiness might remain, it is clear, on closer inspection, that Hume's notion of human nature is not essentialist and not that different from Rousseau's reformulation in the *Second Discourse*.[38] It is its *malleability* rather than its essence, or even its sensory substratum, which is emphasized. Similarly, Hume's own reflections and those of his younger friend Smith, lead them quite early on to a non-Newtonian notion of principles which explain human action by pointing to their specific embeddedness in time and historical conjunctures[39] (all metaphors of the "springs of action" notwithstanding).[40]

While sharing with Newton the urge to "unify" all science, both Hume and Smith emphasized that there is considerable "slack" between the principles of human nature and the historical variation it gives rise to, as accidents, unforeseen consequences, and the stickiness of institutions set societies on different and unforeseeable trajectories. Here we enter a world that is different from physics, where the ahistorical force of gravity allows us to deduce planetary motions and the interaction of bodies on earth. As Hume remarks in the Introduction of the *Treatise*:

When I am at a loss to know the effects of one body upon another in any situation, I need only to put them in that situation, and observe what results from it. But should I endeavour to clear up after the same manner any doubt in moral philosophy 'tis evident this reflection and premeditation would so disturb the operation of my natural principles, as must render it impossible to form any just conclusion from the phenomenon. We must therefore glean up our experiments in this science from a cautious observation of human life, and take them as they appear in the common course of the world, by men's behaviour in company, in affairs, and in their pleasures. Where experiments of this kind are judiciously collected and compared, we may hope to establish on

---

[37] See e.g. Stefano Fiori, "Adam Smith on Method: Newtonianism, History, Institutions, and the 'Invisible Hand'," *Journal of the History of Economic Thought*, 34:3 (2012): 411–435.

[38] Jean-Jacques Rousseau, *A Discourse on Inequality*, London: Penguin Books, 1984.

[39] For a critical discussion of Newton's influence on social theorizing, see Bernard Cohen, "Newton and the Social Sciences, with Special Reference to Economics, or, the Case of the Missing Paradigm" in Philip Mirowski (ed.), *Natural Images in Economic Thought: Markets Read in Tooth and Claw*, Cambridge: Cambridge University Press, 1994, 55–90.

[40] I leave aside here Hume's argument on the "naturalness" of induction which he elaborates in his section "Of the reason of animals" (in Hume, *A Treatise of Human Nature*. 1.3.16), because (1) this observation of "learning" is obviously quite different from finding universal "laws" in physics, and (2) because he himself notes that the "constant connection" is supplied by the human mind which (3) would require a more thorough discussion of the role of conceptualization and language, rather than relying on the metaphor of "custom" and "habit" which are, according to Hume, common to man and animals alike. (This is not to deny that certain "theories" of learning reduce that notion to Pavlovian reactions, as the "behaviorist" program à la Skinner demonstrates.)

them a science that will not be inferior in certainty and will be much superior in utility to any other of human comprehension.[41]

Despite the flourish of assuring us that we can gain equal certainty by such a procedure – which contradicts the gist of his central argument for his approach – the observation of great variability leads Hume to pay close attention to the role of habits and conventions, and to an examination of how sociability is learned in the course of a common life. This not only undermines philosophy's claim that: "Reason first appears in possession of the throne, prescribing laws and imposing maxims, with an absolute sway and authority,"[42] it also provides a new solution to many of the puzzles that informed debates at that time, such as Mandeville's[43] problem where public welfare can only be procured by private vices. Hume is thereby also able to show that the tenets of a natural jurisprudence à la Grotius or Pufendorf are not the only available alternative, particularly since their "solution" appeared unacceptably "Lutheran" to the mostly reformed and Calvinist audience of Hume.

In Smith's case, this realization leads to the notion that although there might be a natural tendency of man "to truck, barter and exchange,"[44] these are however "natural" only in the sense that they presuppose man's symbolic capacities, i.e. speech and reason, which is hardly some form of "rump materialism." But when we are interested in finding out what impels society to go through a series of transformative changes, it is not the former principle or "natural tendency," *but the division of labor*, as well as the empirical fact of the extent of the market, and of prevailing institutions, which explains the patterns of social development. Thus, all Western societies suffered from the disorder accompanying the waves of invasions half a millennium after the fall of the Roman Empire. Because security could no longer be provided during the *Voelkerwanderung*, the subsequent "disorderly times" decisively shifted power from the towns to the country. There feudal lords, supported by the law of primogeniture (that allowed land to be passed on undivided), could use land as a means of cementing their power by extending their protection racket, instead of using land productively, i.e. to promote subsistence and further exchanges. In other words, while we might be able to extract *ex post* a "natural course of things" (as in "stages" of development which Smith adumbrates), *ex ante* no such foresight is available.[45] Counter-tendencies might have developed, institutions might not only become

---

[41] Hume, *Treatise*, Introduction, 10, at 6.   [42] Ibid., 1.4.2. para. 12, at 125.
[43] See Bernard Mandeville, *The Fable of the Bees: Or Private Vices, Publick Benefits*, London: Penguin, 1989.
[44] Smith, *An Inquiry into the Nature and Causes of the Wealth of Nations*. I.2.1.
[45] See also the interesting discussion by Eric Schliesser, "Reading Adam Smith after Darwin: On the Evolution of Propensities, Institutions, and Sentiments," *Journal of Economic Behavior and Organization*, 77:1 (2011): 14–22.

sticky but can generate downright perverse (or beneficial)[46] side effects, and the actors might not have the benefit of a clear and action-guiding picture of the situation they are in.

Nevertheless, there is an inherent tension between the vocabulary of naturalness, which both Hume and Smith use, and their efforts to show that human nature is not simply given but malleable. We must therefore examine in detail the intermediary concepts, which do virtually all the explaining, rather than focus on the presumably foundational ones (nature). This tension is also clearly visible in the different modes of exposition by which Hume tries to get his message across. On the one hand he wants to provide a general framework for argument that knowledge has to be based on "human nature" – which suggests a naturalistic and perhaps an "essentialist" account, communicated by a systematic exposition.

'Tis evident that all the sciences have a relation greater or less to human nature; and however wide any of them may seem to run from it, they still return back by one passage or another. Even Mathematics, Natural philosophy and natural Religion are in some measure dependent on the science of man . . .

. . . what may be expected in the other sciences, whose connection with human nature is more close and intimate? The sole end of logic is to explain the principles and operations of our reasoning faculty, the nature of our ideas: Morals and criticism regard our tastes and sentiments: And politics consider men as united in society and dependent on each other. In these four sciences, of Logic, Morals, Criticism, and Politics, is comprehended almost every thing, which it can any way import us to be acquainted with, or which can tend either to the improvement or ornament of the human mind . . .

Here is then the only expedient, from which we can hope for success in our philosophical researches, to leave the tedious lingering method which we have hitherto followed, and instead of taking now and then a castle or village at the frontier, to march up directly to the capital or center of these sciences, to human nature itself.[47]

On the other hand Hume remains deeply skeptical about traditional philosophy, as we have seen, and the efforts of system builders, irrespective of whether they base their speculation on traditional ontology, logic, or pure self-reflexivity. Even his expository *Treatise* is concluded by an Appendix, in which Hume calls into question some of his conclusions, not because he has found some flaws in the argument but because of a certain unease he seems to feel about the whole enterprise. The book is thus more a "work in progress" than a finished product or manifesto.

The usual way in which Hume cautions the reader is, however, by introducing imaginary dialogues in order to convey his ideas, most notably in his

---

[46] Max Weber, *The Protestant Ethic and the Spirit of Capitalism*, New York: Scribner, 1976.
[47] Hume, *A Treatise of Human Nature*, Introduction, para. 4–5.

Dialogues Concerning Natural Religion.[48] He follows a similar strategy in his *Enquiries* where Sec. XI of the *First Inquiry* is presented in dialogical form and the Conclusions of this work – some four appendices summarizing what Hume intended to prove (such as the role of sentiments and of utility as a foundation of morals) – get called into question again by a further appended Dialogue.[49] This Dialogue must baffle the readers and throws them back to ponder the Conclusions in the light of the open questions, which remained.

Aside from the structural ambiguity of these texts, many problems for their interpretation arise from the vocabulary which Hume uses. This significantly deviates from our conception of what the key terms *should mean*, given what we nowadays consider the dominant (Lockean) eighteenth-century discourse, and how these concepts became the "liberal" tradition, which we take for granted nowadays. But such an approach courts disaster as it projects back contemporary meanings onto a semantic field, which in Hume's time was just being formed and "knew" yet nothing of their later use. A brief discussion of some key terms, which, on closer inspection, turn out to be "false friends," seems appropriate.

Perhaps the most important misconception arises out of Hume's treatment of the perceptions of the human mind, which he subdivides into *impressions* and *ideas*, distinguished "by the degree of force and their liveliness."[50] On the face of it this seems to justify an empiricist, nearly mechanical, and highly individualist, notion of the "mind." But while Hume's expression has a Lockean ring, it does not follow that Hume is a strict empiricist or radical individualist, as shown by his discussion of causality in the *Treatise.*[51] After all, an individualist interpretation is also incompatible with the wider logic of Hume's argument, which emphasizes the role of a "common world" for our reasoning, a world that is not simply an aggregation of the impressions of individuals.

Let us also consider "causality," as this concept is central to Hume's endeavor. Contrary to our expectations (derived perhaps from a rather mechanical interpretation of an "efficient cause"), "causality" is for Hume not a "primitive," but a complex notion. It presupposes two events placed in time and space (priority and proximity), as otherwise cause and effect could not be distinguished and we would mistake mere sequences for causal relations (the kicking of a ball somewhere in Europe at t 1 and the subsequent breaking of a window in China at t 2). However, as Hume points out, the most important

---

[48] See David Hume, *Dialogues Concerning Natural Religion*, ed. Norman Kemp-Smith, Indianapolis: Bobbs Merrill, 1947.
[49] Hume, *An Inquiry Concerning Human Understanding*, at 324–343.
[50] Hume, *A Treatise of Human Nature* at 7. 1.1.1, para. 1, at 7 (Norton ed.).
[51] Thus while Hume insists that all our ideas are derived from "impressions" he allows that the mind (through memory) can use an idea to "supply the place of an impression." Ibid., 74, 1.3.8, para. 15, at 74 (Norton ed.).

element of causality, namely the establishment of the "constant conjunction," is *supplied by the mind* and is not a feature of the "world out there."[52] This raises the hoary problem of induction and of the justifiability of our beliefs based on "experience" (evidence), but it clearly transcends a purely mechanistic interpretation. Furthermore, causal inferences are not the only way in which the mind operates, since by connecting simple impressions the mind creates ideas and then joins "ideas" together, thereby enlarging our capacities for cognition. "Rather the quality from which this association arises and by which the mind is after this manner conveyed from one idea to another, are three, viz RESEMBLANCE, CONTIGUITY in time or place and CAUSE and EFFECT."[53]

Finally, as in the case of the emergence of a "common world," Hume clearly does not speak the language of rational choice when he uses the term "interest." He emphasizes, instead, habit and long usage as the necessary preconditions for resolving the double contingency problem in strategic interactions. Furthermore, he not only includes sentiments in his conception of *imagination*, which is for him the crucial *explanans* in his theory of action, but also examines their role for thought and action.

'Tis certain there is no question in philosophy more abstruse than that concerning identity and the nature of the uniting principle, which constitutes a person. So far from being able by our senses merely to determine this question, we must have recourse to the most profound metaphysics to give a satisfactory answer to it; and in common life 'tis evident these ideas of self and person are never very fixed nor determinate.[54]

Rejecting the traditional separation of mind and body, and the identification of "reason" with the mind – which traditionally had to rein in the animal side of human existence – Hume actually relies on man's sensual nature. He thereby hopes to overcome the chasms of traditional philosophy that led either to skeptic withdrawal (Pyrrhonism) or to "vulgar" notions of how to satisfy the "violent" passions through some maximization strategies. Hume's answer to this problem consists instead of denying their role, civilizing and transforming them into "calm passions" through "custom and repetition."[55]

'Tis evident that passions influence the will not in proportion to their violence, or the disorder they occasion in the temper; but on the contrary, that when a passion has once become a settled principle of action, and is the predominant inclination of the soul, it commonly produces no longer any sensible agitation. As repeated custom and its own force have made everything yield to it, it directs action and conduct without that

---

[52] Hume, *Treatise*, 1.3.14, paras. 12f–36, at 108–114 (Norton ed.) (emphasis in original).
[53] Ibid., bk. 1.1.4, para. 1, at 13.   [54] *Treatise*, 1.4.2, para. 6, at 127.
[55] See ibid., 2.3.5, para. 1, at 271: "Custom has two original effects upon the mind in bestowing a facility in the performance of any action or the conception of any object; and afterwards a tendency or inclination towards it; and from these we may account for all other effects, however extraordinary."

opposition and emotion, which so naturally attend to every momentary gust of passion. We must, therefore, distinguish bewixt a calm and a weak passion.[56]

To that extent it becomes clear why "reason" plays a rather subordinate role in Hume, while habit and "custom" attain such importance. After all, even causal inference "Is nothing but the effects of custom on the imagination."[57]

Above all, Hume is interested in how a change in the perception of the interacting parties brings into existence something in common, something, which emerges between the interacting parties and represents thus an "inter-esse."[58] Here "sympathy" plays an important role, as it is active in two processes. One is a process of "enlarging the self" as when e.g. a mother becomes interested in the welfare of the child, whom she sees as her "extension." Such an act then counters purely egotistical interests and redefines the self. The other process – perhaps for society at large even more decisive – is that sympathy is not only an emotion coming from within the person (as do the "drives" and perhaps even some natural desires, such as hunger) but can be triggered by perceptions which reach the mind from the "outside." The example Hume gives is the pity[59] we might feel for the misery of a beggar we[60] see; and we could add the pride we feel when e.g. "our team" has won a match.

It may seem that Hume here merely rehearses the argument for an empathetic understanding. But he is very clear that sympathy is not simply the welling-up of some personal, purely internal emotion, but has a different and *social* quality. Thus while emotions are important for our moral sense, as the feelings of approbation and disapprobation informing our moral judgments show, these sentiments have to be calm. Here the "golden mean" (the *aurea mediocritas*) is explicitly invoked:

By such reasonings [*sic*] we fix the proper and commendable mediocrity in all moral and prudential disquisitions; and never lose view of the advantages, which result from any character or habit. Now as these advantages are enjoyed by the person possessed of the character, it can never be self-love which renders the prospect of them agreeable *to us the spectators* and prompts our esteem and approbation. No force of imagination can convert us into another person and make us fancy, that we, being that person, reap benefit from these valuable qualities which belong to him.[61]

---

[56] Ibid., 2.3.4, para. 1, at 268f.   [57] Ibid., 2.3.1, para. 16, at 261.
[58] M. J. Ferreira, "Hume and Imagination: Sympathy and 'the Other'," *International Philosophical Quarterly*, 34 (1994): 39–57.
[59] Hume, *A Treatise of Human Nature*, 2.2.7. "Of Compassion," at 238 (Norton ed.).
[60] Ibid., 3.1.1, para. 10, at 295. "Moral distinctions are not the offspring of reason. Reason is wholly inactive, and can never be a source of so active a principle as conscience, or a sense of Morals."
[61] Hume, *An Inquiry Concerning Human Understanding*, Second Inquiry: Concerning the Principles of Morals, sec. VI, part 1, para 191, at 233f. (Nidditch and Selby-Bigge eds.) Emphasis added.

Thus in a remark anticipating, in a way, Mead's argument[62] with regard to the involvement of others in the construction of the self – playing itself out in the dialectics of the "I" and the "me" – Hume argues that we are inevitably affected by others not only because our "reputation" is often at stake, but because we are involved with others much more deeply. As he points out: "In general we may remark that the minds of men are mirrors to one another not only because they reflect each other's emotions, but also because those rays of passions, sentiments and opinions may be often reverberated, and may decay by insensible degrees."[63]

After all these critical remarks it should not come as a surprise that Hume's notion of utility, which he introduced into the political discourse, has also become a "false friend" as he uses it quite differently than liberals, where utility indicates either mere personal preferences and idiosyncratic likes, or even refers to a metric, determining the greatest happiness of the greatest number, as in the case of the felicific calculus employed by Bentham.[64] Only Mill[65] invents the (rather incoherent) notion of "higher" and "lower" pleasure to get out of the embarrassing straitjacket in which the liberal conception of utility has put us. For Hume, "utility" has to do with our moral sentiments.

Usefulness is agreeable and engages our approbation ... But *useful*? For what? For somebody's interest, surely. Whose interest? Not our own only, for our approbation frequently extends farther. It must, therefore be the interest of those who are served by the character or action approved of; and these, we may conclude, however remote, are not totally indifferent to us ...

Compelled by these instances, we must renounce the theory, which accounts for every moral sentiment by the principle of self-love. We must adopt a more public affection and allow that the interests of society are not, even on their own account, entirely indifferent to us. Usefulness is only a tendency to a certain end; and it is a contradiction in terms, that anything pleases as a means to an end, where the end itself in no wise affects us. If usefulness, therefore, be a source of moral sentiment, and if usefulness were not always considered with reference to self; it follows that everything which

---

[62] George Herbert Mead, *Mind, Self & Society from the Standpoint of a Social Behaviorist*, Chicago: The University of Chicago Press, 1962, at 194–200.

[63] Hume, *A Treatise of Human Nature*, 236, 2.2.6, para. 21, at 236 (Norton ed.).

[64] Jeremy Bentham, *An Introduction to the Principles of Morals and Legislation*, London: Athlone, 1970. See also for Bentham's idea that his calculus will make him a Newton of the moral sciences, Elie Halévy, *The Growth of Philosophic Radicalism*, trans. Mary Morris, London: Faber and Faber, 1972.

[65] See e.g. John Stuart Mill, *Utilitarianism: Text and Criticism*, Belmont, CA: Wadsworth, 1969, chap. 2. Here "utility" remains the "unit" measuring pleasure, but the introduction of higher and lower pleasure undoes a common utility scale. Of course some of the problems can be solved when the maximization no longer concerns "utiles" but "revenue," which presupposes a standard measure of value, and since it also serves as a store of value and a near-universal medium of exchange it solves the fungibility and the interpersonal comparability of utility problems.

contributes to the happiness of society, recommends itself to our approbation and good will. Here is a principle, which accounts, in great part, for the origin of morality.[66]

From these passages it is quite clear that Hume's account has little to do with utilitarianism or with a bare bone notion of rational action. For one, the "mind" works in much more complex ways. Here imagination and sentiments interact and reason, concerned with finding the means for achieving the intended goals, plays a rather subordinate role. To that extent Hume's saying that "reason is and ought only to be the slave of the passions"[67] does not have the wider implications we assume. We are neither condemned to the Hobbesian "restless desire of power after power that ceaseth not until death"[68] nor to the project of the "possessive" individualism characterizing liberal thought.[69]

In Smith, the notion of personal interest might be more pronounced, particularly when he writes on the sources of wealth and its relations to a division of labor and free exchanges in the market. But for him, as well as for Hume and other members of the Scottish Enlightenment, even market exchanges – as any human action – are embedded in wider appraisals, in which moral sentiments and feelings of approval and disapproval play a decisive role.[70] These sentiments are not "natural" in the sense of unmediated or idiosyncratic feelings. They are rather public, forming part of a shared (even if contestable) "common sense." They are accessible to us through both the inside and the outside: from the inside as "reasons" for actions, and from the outside as observable manifestations and templates, which we use for decoding what others are doing.

These sentiments are, therefore, part of the social world, which emerges through their cultivation, through the formation of habits and through traditions. To that extent the social world is largely artificial and accessible to us only through "experience" and historical reflection, since any reduction of this world to some natural facts or a fixed human nature is bound to fail. The underlying "ontological" mistake is the erroneous assumption that what something consists of, or what is usually present, has also to be the key for understanding what something *is* – as e.g. mistaking the paper on which a contract or banknote is printed, for the contract or for money itself.

To that extent the at first perhaps puzzling attempt by Hume to "ground" all knowledge in human nature, and his refusal to found it on some form of physiological naturalism, loses its paradoxical character. If human nature is not given, but part and parcel of further articulations occurring in history, then

---

[66] Hume, *An Inquiry Concerning Human Understanding*, Sec. V, pt. 1, para. 177, at 176; and pt. 2, at 178 (Nidditch and Selby-Bigge eds.).
[67] Hume, *Treatise*, 2.3.3, para. 4, at 266 (Norton ed.).   [68] Hobbes, *Leviathan*, chap. 11, at 70.
[69] C.B. Macpherson, *The Political Theory of Possessive Individualism: Hobbes to Locke*, New York: Basic Books, 1977.
[70] Adam Smith, *The Theory of Moral Sentiments (1759)*, Oxford: Clarendon Press, 1976.

assuming a fixed human nature will not do. It cannot provide us with the warrants for our acting and knowing in a changing world. Obsessed with certainty,[71] we are likely to end up with trivialities, paradoxes, or with contorted reductionist attempts to solve our puzzles not by reflection, or elaboration, or by placing them in contexts, but by a dogmatic and, on the whole, unjustifiable, fiat. Thus if the philosophical activity as the search for warranted knowledge is to continue, it has to abandon philosophy's

autonomy principle: according to this principle philosophy has an authority to command belief and judgment independent of the unreflectively received beliefs. Customs and prejudices of common life . . .

[It must] recognize common life not as an object of critical reflection, but as a category internal to its own activity. "True philosophy" then presupposes the authority of common life as a whole. A reformed version of the autonomy principle survives: philosophy may from abstract principles and ideals criticize any judgment in common life: what it cannot do, on pain of total skepticism, is to throw into question the whole order.[72]

This implies not only dispensing with the notion of an absolute point of view – the famous "view from nowhere"[73] – but also accepting the fact that we are always "within" the world, which conditions our thoughts. The task is not deictic but therapeutic: to see what we can learn from vetting the traditional notions and find new ways of "going on."

In his little treatise entitled "Of Essay Writing," Hume addresses these issues by examining the exchanges between the "learned" and "conversable" world, i.e. that of the philosophers and the world of the common life, and by probing the dramatic changes they have undergone in modern times. When learning took place in the monk's cell or college halls, it produced writings deemed canonical, although Hume considers the results mostly pedantic and scholastic. "And indeed," he continues, "what could you have expected from men who never consulted experience . . . or who never searched for that experience where alone it is to be found: *in common life and conversation*."[74] In the modern world new forms of expressions have appeared in the salons and in public discussions, which should provide the materials from which the "science of man" could be derived.

In short, we, who are always in the "midst of it," advance our understanding through criticisms of the concepts and customs we encounter in our search for

---

[71] See John Dewey, "The Quest for Certainty" in Jo Ann Boydston (ed.), *John Dewey: Later Works*, Carbondale: Southern Illinois Press, 1984.

[72] Donald W. Livingston, *Hume's Philosophy of Common Life*, Chicago: University of Chicago Press, 1984, at 3.

[73] See Thomas Nagel, *The View from Nowhere*, New York: Oxford University Press, 1986.

[74] David Hume, "Of Essay Writing" in Eugene F. Miller (ed.), *Essays, Moral, Political, and Literary*, Indianapolis: Liberty Classics, 1742, 533–537, at 535 (emphasis added).

what is the case. Instead of the assurances of absolute foundations, which bring our queries to an end, we have to realize that it is

only through these customs and prejudices that we can think about the real. Skepticism then is internal to true philosophy. The true philosopher recognizes his cognitive alienation from ultimate reality, but continues to inquire, though he has nothing but the "leaky weather-beaten vessel"[75] of common life through which to think.[76]

Precisely because we know that our quest will never come to an end – as we cannot arrive at a place where we stand outside the world – we also have to realize that the "world out there" does not exist.[77] It is at best a manifold of different ways of understanding what "is," which is determined by our interests and by the semantic grids these interests engender, rather than by the mere reference to objects existing as brute facts "out there." After all, in the physical world there are waves and electromagnetic charges, but no melodies or tradable futures, there is land, but no property.

All of these realizations are hardly news to those who possess some common sense. But they are disturbing to those who suffer from a certain *idée fixe* concerning certainty, or from an acute case of physics envy. That what "is" has then to do with getting the description right, i.e. finding the right "covering concept" for the "things out there." Instead, we see that, in many descriptions, various things which we know from other worlds, such as "property" or "beauty," do not even occur, because finding out "what is the case" has to do with how the particular concepts are used and how their emplacement in semantic fields constitutes their meaning. Consequently, there is no a priori reason to privilege one (material?) description over all others, irrespective of the particular interest guiding our inquiry.

As we shall see, Hume's attention to the importance of history, as exemplified in his monumental *History of England*, leads him to his rejection of any absolute beginnings or teleology. Instead, Hume pokes fun at the notion of an "original (social) contract":

It is strange that an act of the mind, which every individual is supposed to have formed, and after he came to the use of reason too, otherwise it could have no authority; that this act, I say, should be so much unknown to them, that over the face of the whole earth, there scarcely remain any traces or memory of it . . .

I maintain that human affairs will never admit of this consent, seldom for the appearance of it; but that conquest and usurpation that is in plain terms, force, by dissolving

[75] This imagery is used by Hume, in Hume, *A Treatise of Human Nature*, 1,4,7, at 172 (Norton ed.).
[76] Livingston, *Hume's Philosophy of Common Life*, at 3.
[77] For an important discussion of these themes see Markus Gabriel, *Warum Es die Welt Nicht Gibt*, Berlin: Ullstein, 2013.

the ancient governments, is the origin of almost all the new ones which were ever established in the world. And that in the few cases where consent may seem to have taken place, it was commonly so irregular, so confined, or so much intermixed either with fraud or violence, that it cannot have any great authority.[78]

Hume thereby shows the ideological nature of the social contract argument, which turns out to be similar to that of the divine rights of kings. The point is not only that such a contract is fictitious, but also that it cannot explain the reproduction of a society because it has become *the ongoing and trans-generational concern* of the people, despite its initially murky or unknown legitimation. Hume emphasizes instead the slow accretion of conventions, habits, and "prejudices" that enable actors to come together in a society and also make it an ongoing concern,

In this context it is important to appreciate Hume's distinction between "conventions" and "promises," as for the latter a variety of conceptual presuppositions have to be in place, such as e.g. which signs or formalities have to be fulfilled in order for certain undertakings *to count* as promises or contracts (exchange of promises). For the former, on the other hand, only a common perception of interest is necessary, in the sense of something we both understand and indicate to each other while acting routinely in a strategic environment. Although Hume chooses the establishment of property as his paradigm, he is quick to point out that other social arrangements follow the same logic. Unfortunately, he never follows up on his remarks about the origin of languages (which Smith attempted in his *Considerations Concerning the First Formation of Languages*)[79] but only briefly mentions:

This convention is not in the nature of a promise. For even promises themselves ... arise from human conventions. It is only a general sense of common interest; which all the members of the society express to one another, and which induces them to regulate their conduct by certain rules. I observe that it will be for my interest to leave another in the possession of his goods, provided he will act in the same manner with regard to me. He is sensible of a like interest in the regulation of his conduct. When this common sense of interest is mutually expressed and is known to both it produces a suitable resolution and behavior. And this might properly be called a convention or agreement bewixt [*sic*] us, though without the interposition of a promise ... Nor is the rule concerning the stability of possessions the less derived from human conventions, that it arises gradually and acquires force by a slow progression, and by our repeated experience of the inconveniencies of transgressing it. On the contrary, this experience assures

[78] See David Hume, "Of the Original Contract" in Ernest Barker (ed.), *Social Contract: Essays by Locke, Hume, and Rousseau*, Oxford: Oxford University Press, 1960: 147–168, at 147.
[79] Adam Smith, "Considerations Concerning the First Formation of Languages (1761)" in J. C. Bryce (ed.), *Lectures on Rhetoric and Belles Lettres*, Oxford: Clarendon Press, 1983. See also James Otteson, "Adam Smith's First Market: The Development of Language," *History of Philosophy Quarterly*, 19:1 (2002): 65–86.

us still more that the sense of interest has become common to all our fellows . . . And 'tis only on the expectation of this that our moderation and abstinence are founded.

In like manner are languages gradually established by human conventions without any promise. In like manner gold and silver become the common measure of exchange, and are esteemed to sufficient payment for what is a hundred times their value.[80]

Hume outlines here a research program, which was later taken up by the "English school"[81] for which Hedley Bull's *Anarchical Society*[82] became emblematic. The inspiration for Bull's research agenda was obviously Hume, with both his emphasis on the common world disclosed to us by empirical investigation and historical reflection, and his skepticism towards the heuristic purchase of formal models and methods imported from other fields – often mistaking, in addition, the ideal types of hierarchy and anarchy for "natural facts."[83]

The most interesting part of Hume's discussion is, however, his suggestion that in "like manner" languages and custom emerge. They call attention to the importance of analogies and reasoning from case to case rather than following the classical inference patterns of induction and deduction. They also suggest that the typologies we develop in order to establish what "is the case" cannot be based on unrealistic (idealized) assumptions à la Friedman,[84] or the simple ascription of maximizing strategies pursued by the actors. Instead, the common world emerges out of interactions and is the result of conjunctures and accidents, which entail future consequences that are unknown to and unforeseeable for the actors themselves.

Incoherence and even tragedy are inevitably part of our individual and social existence, as perhaps best exemplified in Hume's treatment of Charles I's refusal to let the Puritans Pym, Cromwell, and Hampden depart for the Americas, as he wanted to stem the tide of emigration. But while we understand his action, what it meant, i.e. his own downfall and ultimately his execution, was unfathomable to him, as it was to the petitioners themselves who later became Charles's executioners.[85] This puts severe limits on understanding the social

---

[80] Hume, *A Treatise of Human Nature*, "Of the Origins of Justice and Property," 3.2.2, para. 10, at 314f.

[81] On the English school, see Timothy Dunne, *Inventing International Society: A History of the English School*, New York: St. Martin's Press, 1998. For a further assessment, see Barry Buzan, *From International to World Society? English School Theory and the Social Structure of Globalisation*, Cambridge: Cambridge University Press, 2004.

[82] Bull, *The Anarchical Society.*   [83] Waltz, *Theory of International Politics.*

[84] Milton Friedman, "The Methodology of Positive Economics" in *Essays in Positive Economics*, Chicago: University of Chicago Press, 1966, 3–16, and 30–43.

[85] See David Hume, *The History of England: From the Invasion of Julius Caesar to the Revolution in 1688*, Indianapolis: Liberty Classics, 1983.

world as one of design[86] – even if it is one of artifice. It also casts considerable doubt on approaches which attempt to understand our predicament from some preordained teleology that works itself out behind the back of the actors, or that can be intuited since *telos* can serve as the guidepost for our actions.

Understanding the common world instead as a "historical" product has important implications for the type of knowledge which we consider adequate for praxis. It is not only that we have to understand how this world emerged – rather than how it sprang into existence through a "first act" or as a result of starting with certain assumptions. While such foundational acts or commitments are the "stuff" of ideal theorizing to which Hume objects, it is clear that such a move cannot be invalidated by another or better "theory" that remains, nevertheless, "outside" the historical world. Instead, the critique has to address the very notion of an ideal theory by obliquely showing why such attempts are futile. I shall therefore choose his indirect approach and explore what answers Hume could give to the proponents of an "ideal theory."

9.4   Hume's Answers to "Philosophy" (Ideal Theory): Natural History, Convention, and Conversation

To be clear what it means to say that Hume bases his understanding of the common world on "history" we must first deal with the objection that his conception of the origins of human society, while more substantive than the bare-bone notion of a mythical contract, is equally speculative. Thus why not start by assuming an absolute beginning and work towards the present, or begin with a *telos* and work backwards to the present? In other words, one might be inclined to believe that we are dealing here with the "same difference" as we say in common parlance. As I shall argue, however, such a view obfuscates the issue of the historical nature of the social world by *suggesting a parallelism between original beginnings, idealizations, and teleological explanations,* which mystifies the way in which, the present, the past, and the future relate to each other in the world of praxis. While a comprehensive treatment of these issues will have to be postponed to the next chapter, even the preliminary answer I try to provide here requires some further elaboration.

Hume's answer to ideal theorizing would probably be tenfold. *First,* his objection to a priori reasoning and arguments from design would be that someone proposing such models would be obliged to show first why these models should function in a world of non-ideal actors. If "ought" implies "can" (as we would say) then this question cannot be left hanging as a minor issue of

---

[86] For a good discussion of some of the important problems of this approach, see Alexander Wendt, "Driving with the Rearview Mirror: On the Rational Science of Institutional Design," *International Organization*, 55:4 (2001): 1019–1049.

"application."[87] Instead, those concerns are central to the interpretations of the rules by which we attempt to guide decisions and assign the duties and rights which we expect the members of a society to uphold, without requiring acts of supererogation (*ultra posse nemo obligatur*).[88] When Hume mentions that we should design institutions which should work even among "knaves,"[89] he wants to make it clear that one cannot set the standard too high since "intuiting" the right moral standard or solving the problem by assumption will not do. Instead, our standards for assessments are accessible to us only through our own common life, and through experience. In this way we are able to identify the ills created by the arrangements under which we live, and formulate proposals for their abatement. In doing so we are also helped by comparisons with other societies exhibiting different "morals" and institutions. Thus, our predominant mode of theorizing in much of contemporary ethics and politics would be highly suspect to him. Hume is clear that any clarification of the appropriate standards has to occur through "society and conversation," but also that here the "emotions" are involved. The danger that "hot passions" evoked by the nearness or vividness of a situation might overwhelm an actor, so that the "cold passions" get "trumped" by "the heart," cannot be mastered by sequestering the emotions and by pretending that our appraisals involve only cognition. Rather, it is necessary to cultivate the passions, making them through discipline into moral "sentiments" (cold passions). This would be Hume's *second* answer.

Such a stance does not prevent the emergence of a "distant view of reflection,"[90] which is usually identified with a "neutral observer." But for Hume it is obvious – and this would be Hume's *third* answer – that this will still be the reflection of a *sympathetic individual who is embedded in a concrete society* rather than of a "universal spectator." As Rachel Cohon points out:

> The common point of view is not a detached perspective … It gives us not a wide panorama, but an intimate glimpse … It is general or common not in the sense of being a broad view but rather in the sense that it is a view available to every reflective person … This intimate glimpse yields two products which are necessarily related to each other: a sentiment of approbation or disapprobation … and a causal judgment

---

[87] See the important contribution by Rahul Sagar, "Is Ideal Theory Practical?," *Review of International Studies*, 37 (2011): 1949–1465.

[88] "Nobody is obliged to do the extraordinary" (literally what is beyond = *ultra*). Principle of Roman law.

[89] See David Hume, "Of the Independency of Parliament" in Eugene F. Miller (ed.), *Essays, Moral, Political, and Literary*, Indianapolis: Liberty Classics, 1985, 42–46, at 42. See Kant's similar reference to the "republic among devils" which did not, however, hinder him from postulating a priori moral principles obliging you to work for a cosmopolitan order. See Immanuel Kant, *Perpetual Peace: A Philosophical Sketch*, Cambridge: Cambridge University Press, 1970: 93–130.

[90] Hume, *A Treatise of Human Nature* 3.3.3.1, para. 18, at 372f. (Norton ed.).

about what impact the trait of the person being judged is likely to have on his near associates, typically a judgment about the power of the trait ... to cause pride or love, humility or hatred. These are the judgments that need to remain constant within an individual over time ... and these are the judgments that need to be consistent between people if we are ever to converse on reasonable terms.[91]

This commonality need not be universal in scope or time. Such a view could at first appear somewhat parochial, since we are limited to the standards of our society. For Hume, viable new standards or refinements of our yardsticks do not emerge from the closet of philosophy, but from the enlargement of the circle of people we converse with, and from a familiarity with different common worlds. He seems at first rather optimistic about the emergence of such a "distant" reflection when evaluating actions and attributing praise or blame such as e.g. in historical contexts – even though here the "nearness" might make us inclined to view the actions of our servant as more praiseworthy than the attempted rescue of the Roman Republic by Brutus.[92] Similarly, when confronted with the inevitable disagreement about the appropriate standards in settling moral issues, Hume somewhat mercurially announces "that there is such uniformity in the general sentiment of mankind as to render such questions of but small importance."[93] But over the years he seems to have become a bit more guarded. He uses two strategies in his attempt to square the circle.

On the one hand he explains (away) the apparent contradictions by arguing for a certain general development of society, so that, by implication, at least some disagreements might result from the uneven development in which different societies find themselves. If it is true that "from Law arises security, and from security curiosity; and from curiosity knowledge"[94] then different societies might be at different stages, which is reflected in their "civilizational standard." This gambit is familiar from the development discourse but it contradicts the wider ramifications of Hume's skeptical argument. The other strategy is to confront the dilemma and admit that "the difference among men is really greater than at first sight appears."[95] By using the "conversation" with a Muslim as his foil, he finds the use of terms such as justice, charity, equity, etc., quite at odds with our standards, as "every action is blamed and praised so far only as it is beneficial or hurtful to the believers."[96]

Here Hume faces the same aporia as we do when we encounter persons who are not ready to alter their convictions. Since they believe that they are in possession of the truth, the possibility of an "inter-esse" is of little concern

[91] Rachel Cohon, "The Common Point of View in Hume's Ethics," *Philosophy and Phenomenological Research*, 57:4 (1997): 827–850, at 840f.
[92] Hume, *A Treatise of Human Nature*. 3.3.3.1, para. 17.   [93] Ibid.
[94] Hume, "The Rise of Arts and Sciences" in *Essays*, at 118.
[95] Hume, "On the Standards of Taste," in *Essays*, at 228.   [96] Ibid., 229.

to them. Quite obviously then the conversation comes to a screeching halt, as the positions become incommensurable. Hume's (indirect) answer to this dilemma is to point to the dangers of such a denial of engagement. Such an attitude tends to reinforce misconceptions and prejudice and is socially costly, even in situations when no ultimate values are at issue.

An Irishman cannot have wit and a Frenchman cannot have solidity; for which reason, tho' the conversation of the former in any instance be visibly very agreeable, and of the latter very judicious, we have entertained such a prejudice against them, that they must be dunces or fops in spite of sense and reason. Human nature is very subject to errors of this kind . . .[97]

Thus while this observation does not provide a solution, it points us in a direction which we might want to explore, namely how we could circumvent the dilemma and go on. Where the theory runs out, a therapy, conceived as a critical reflection on our practices, might offer some hope. Hume nevertheless, thinks that such incommensurable disagreements are the exception and that within an established society the common rules and cold emotions "are sufficient for discourse and serve all our purposes in company, in the pulpit, and in the schools."[98]

The *fourth* answer addresses the formal requirement of generality of rules. Rules safeguarding social utility against idiosyncratic preferences have, of course, to be more general than the various cases to which they are applied. But they are more general *not in the sense of being simply abstract*, as this would empty them of content and thus impair their capacity to help us along in the common world. They are more general in the sense that they attempt to capture some *typical* features of recurring situations. Thus, those types attain their meaning from distinctions which become relevant when we try to fit them to the fact-pattern of a "case" – such as distinguishing "fraud" from an "error" – by looking for supporting evidence why one typification fits better than the other (adducing e.g. the "common sense" principle of *cui bono?*). The point is not the *generality of their logical form*, but rather the recognized "interest" that lets us make the type-distinctions. Here the reasoning from "case to case" analogies, hypotheticals, knowing the relevant exceptions and circumstances that make a general rule defeasible, etc., are the proper conceptual tools rather than relying on their (alleged) general, or even universal covering scope.

In the social sciences this problem has given rise to debates about the information loss that occurs when we ascend the ladder of abstraction and about the proper level of abstraction in theorizing, as the denotation and connotation of the concepts are inversely related.[99] While this problem certainly points to an

[97] Hume, *A Treatise of Human Nature* 1.3.13, para. 7, at 99f   [98] Ibid.
[99] Sartori, "Concept Misformation in Comparative Politics."

important issue, a Humean perspective suggests that noticing this problem is not enough. Focusing on *one* concept at a time does not take into account the multi-dimensionality of meanings that emerge from their links in a semantic field. Those entanglements get erased as soon as we use the traditional logical instruments, such as the principle of the excluded middle. This collapse of the field into one dimension has important implications for our traditional classifications. While it is certainly true that "mixing apples and oranges" might entail a conceptual blunder on one level, it is not, however, the case that apples and oranges can never be classified as "the same," such as when we compare them e.g. to birds, or stones. Consequently, the *tertium comparationis, and not the logic or some preexisting ontological order* holds the key for assessing the appropriateness of our conceptual operations. Since things can be compared in terms of a whole host of considerations, which dimension should be chosen depends on our interests, and there is no point in expecting that a closer look at the "things out there" can dispose of this necessary choice.

In short, something more is required than noticing the obvious logical pitfalls. Actually, our whole conception of how meaning and language function has to be changed. This much Wittgenstein suggested when he moved away in his later period from the analysis of artificial languages as models for understanding, taking up the analysis of ordinary language.[100] Hume, in calling attention to "conversation and commerce" and emphasising the common world and its traditions, is also redirecting our attention from the "world out there" to the criteria and standards which *we actually use*, which represents his *fifth* answer

He addressed this issue by noting that the meaning of a term depends on its connection or opposition to another concept in the discourse. This clarification is offered in his discussion of justice being an "artificial, not a natural virtue."

> To avoid giving offense, I must here observe, that when I deny justice to be a natural virtue *I make use of the word* [emphasis added] "natural," only as opposed to "artificial." In another sense of the word: as no principle of the human mind is more natural than a sense of virtue; so no virtue is more natural than justice. Mankind is an inventive species; and where an invention is obvious and absolutely necessary it may as properly be said to be natural as anything that proceeds immediately from original principles without the intervention of thought or reflection. Though the rules of justice are artificial they are not arbitrary . . .[101]

---

[100] See Wittgenstein, *Philosophical Investigations*. See also Hume's remarks against "private languages" and idiosyncratic appraisals: "General language, being formed for general use, must be molded on some general views, and must affix the epithets of praise or blame in conformity to sentiments which arise from the general interests of the Community." *Enquiries*, Second Enquiry, sec. V, 2, para. 186, at 228 (Nidditch and Selby-Bigge eds.).

[101] Hume, *A Treatise of Human Nature* at 311.2.2, para. 19, at 311.

In short, while there is certainly ample room for disagreements in our appraisals, it is simply false that "anything goes" after we have thrown away our ontological crutches. Instead, on reflection we realize we fell into this trap because
of an impoverished notion of language.

The above remarks lead me to Hume's *sixth* answer. As we have seen,
Hume began his analysis not with an original contract but with the emergence
of the distinction between what is "mine" and what is "yours," here mostly
among social groups, rather than solitary individuals, who agree on respecting
possessions on the condition of mutuality. In this way the actors, who are
characterized by selfishness and limited generosity, and who are born into a
world of scarcity, can avoid conflicts and interference with their particular
pursuits, if

> Everyone expresses his sense to his fellows along with the resolution he has taken of
> squaring his actions by it on condition that others will do the same. No more is requisite
> to induce any one of them to perform an act of justice, who has the first opportunity.
> This becomes an example to others. And thus justice establishes itself by a kind of
> convention or agreement . . .

> To the imposition then and observance of these rules, both in general and in every
> instance, they are first moved only by regard to interest and this motive is sufficiently
> strong and forcible. But when society has become more numerous and has increased to
> a tribe or nation, this interest is more remote; nor do men so readily perceive that
> disorder and confusion follow on every breach of these rules, as in a more narrow and
> contracted society. But though in our own actions we may frequently lose sight of that
> interest which we have in maintaining order, . . . we never fail to observe the prejudice
> we receive, either mediately [*sic*] or immediately from the injustice of others . . . Nay
> when the injustice is so distant from us, as no way to affect our interest, it still displeases
> us, because we consider it as prejudicial to human society, and pernicious to everyone
> that approaches the person guilty of it. We partake of their uneasiness by sympathy; and
> as everything which gives uneasiness in human actions, upon a general survey, is called
> a *vice*; and whatever produces satisfaction, in the same manner is denominated *virtue*.

> Though this progress of the sentiments be natural, and even necessary, 'tis certain that it
> is here forwarded by the artifice of politicians, who, in order to preserve peace in human
> society, have endeavoured to produce an esteem for justice . . .

> As public praise and blame increase our esteem for justice; so private education and
> instruction contribute to the same effect. For as parents easily observe, that a man is
> more useful, both to himself and others the greater degree of probity and honour he is
> endowed with, and that those principles have greater force when custom and education
> assist interest and reflection.[102]

There are two things that are truly remarkable in this passage. The first surprise
is that Hume clearly shows that the traditional notion of requiring one specific

---

[102] Hume, *A Treatise of Human Nature* 3.2.2, paras. 24–26, at 320f.

motive which establishes the moral quality of an act – whether cast in terms of
the Aristotelian theory of virtue (as individual *hexis*), or, as in modern deontological approaches, as an act of the free will determining itself (personal utility
having been discarded before). For Hume, there are, after all, different motives
that vary with social conditions and developments – as the later discussions
in sociology by Tönnies[103] and Durkheim[104] show, distinguishing different
forms of solidarity (*Gemeinschaft* vs. *Gesellschaft*, mechanical vs. organic
solidarity). It seems also that despite the difficulties in determining a non-
myopic assessment of self-interest in larger societies, this defect can be cured
by the fact that different socialization processes are at work. But neither singly
nor in conjunction do these habits and passions make out of the actors just
"throughputs" for legal norms.[105]

The second surprise is that Hume attributes to "primitive" societies not a
communal value-consensus, but uses self-interest in maintaining "property" as
the *explanans*, thus reversing the sequence of the later sociological theories.
He obviously never believed that society is formed out of individuals but that it
consists of families and clans[106] – held together by natural necessity (reproduction) and affection. But the issue is now how these clans are able to coexist,
especially when they engage in exchanges. Here a type of sociality emerges
that is not based on kinship, but on reciprocity for which Hume uses *property*
as a foil. However, even though an agreement on possession according to
the *uti possidetis* rule might at first be obvious to the actors, it would fail
to bring about the hoped-for stability in expectations since it inhibits change.
To that extent a more complicated "artificial" property regime becomes necessary and Hume examines in great detail the entitlements that result
from occupation, prescription, accession, succession, and above all "consent"
(exchange),[107] which then occasions his investigation into the nature of promises[108] and of social institutions. This leads to some further surprises concerning the nature of morals and of political obligation. A more explicit discussion
of these seventh and eighth Humean answers seems appropriate.

[103] Ferdinand Tönnies, *Community & Society*, East Lansing: Michigan State University Press, 1957.
[104] Émile Durkheim, *The Division of Labor in Society*, New York: Free Press of Glencoe, 1964.
[105] For a critique of this point from which much of the "compliance" literature suffers, see Kratochwil, *Rules, Norms and Decisions*. For a fundamental discussion of the "contestedness" (not only contestability) of even accepted norms in actual practice, see Antje Wiener, *The Invisible Constitution of Politics: Contested Norms and International Encounters*, Cambridge: Cambridge University Press, 2008.
[106] See *Enquiries*, Second Enquiry, sec. III, part 1, para. 151, at 190; see also *Enquiries*, appendix III (Nidditch and Selby-Bigge eds.), at 303
[107] Hume, *A Treatise of Human Nature*. 2.2.3, 2.2.4. and 3.2.2.
[108] *Enquiries*, 2.2.5., para. 257, at 306 (Nidditch and Selby-Bigge eds.).

Let us begin with promises (Hume's *seventh* answer). In an at first rather surprising move, Hume does not consider promises to be on the same footing as the rules of property. He justifies this gambit in two interrelated ways. The first concerns his argument that a "promise would not be intelligible before human conventions had established it," and the second "that even if it were intelligible, it would not be attended with any moral obligation."[109] Although promises and contracting (as in the exchange of mutual promises) often also imply a temporal sequence – which leads to the near exclusive concern with enforcement problems in modern analyses – Hume's attention is focused only on the necessary conditions for promises to exist, while the latter problem (sequential performance) is addressed in his introduction of "magistrates" (his *eighth* answer).

For Hume the constitutive conventions for promises and contracts are not only the declaratory speech act but, in the case of contract, the use of specific formulas or further external signs, such as the signing of a document or the affixing of seals without which no contract exists. Here the sharp distinction Hume tries to make between convention and contract is, however, somewhat misleading. Already for the emergence of property a "declaration" to others must be considered constitutive. Hume concedes as much, when he discusses the issue of "symbolic delivery" of an item when "the real one is impracticable."[110] But since the latter might actually already be a case of contract we see how fuzzy the boundaries between convention and contract (because of the need for a symbol) can be. I think the difficulty is that Hume realizes that some conventions are transcendental, such as e.g. language, in that they cannot be explained in terms of a mutual agreement, as language has to be *logically* antecedent to any promise or agreement

The second reason provided by Hume carries more weight. It counteracts the tendency to ground all obligations in one "natural" motive, external to the specific undertaking,[111] which, so to speak, would lend its dignity to all the obligations ranging from universal to specific ones. Hume does not deny that there might be some natural obligations, but they would have to be grounded in a natural passion. But since promises (and contracts) fix specific duties between the parties (without regard to universal concerns, such as humanity or goodness) no such derivation seems necessary.

There might indeed not be "one force" but several reasons resulting from the artificial (or positive) nature of contracting – some of which might have

---

[109] *Treatise* 3.2.5. para. 2, at 331.
[110] *Treatise* 3.2.4, para. 2. The example is the handing over of the keys of a granary, which symbolizes the delivery of the corn contained in it.
[111] This would be Hume's "peculiar act of the mind annext [*sic*] to promises." *Treatise* 3.2.5, para. 7, at 333.

nothing to do with ethical principles, such as the stipulations when a contract or treaty is entering into force, or whether certain errors of form (unauthorized agent signing the instrument) make the contract void. But Hume should also have taken the invalidating conditions more seriously, as exceptions and exemptions safeguarding fairness and good faith are also an important part of the contracting game.

Furthermore, the surprise he expresses at creating obligation *ex nihilo* by a symbolic action shows that he realizes that the vocabulary of "virtue" which was transposed from the individual *to classes of actions and then to institutions*, had reached its limits.

since every new promise imposes a new obligation of morality on the person who promises, and since this new obligation arises from his will; 'tis one of the most mysterious and incomprehensible operations that can possibly be imagined, and may even be compared to *transubstantiation* or *holy orders* where a certain form of words along with a certain intention, changes entirely the nature of the external object, and even of the human creature . . . As the obligation of promises is an invention for the interest of society, 'tis warped into as many different forms as that interest requires . . .[112]

In a way Hume anticipates the theory of speech-acts and its connection with institutional rules on which John Searle elaborated.[113] Finally, although still speaking the language of virtue, his analysis increasingly turns on the question of whether a *particular set of institutions* is beneficial to society. To that extent actions are no longer evaluated in terms of making their character transparent, but rather in terms of how certain institutional rules affect society.[114] Since actions are now instantiations for certain types of permitted, allowed, or required conduct, "justice" increasingly becomes a question of the institutional order rather than a personal attribute.

When I relieve persons in distress, my natural humanity is my motive . . . But if we examine all the questions which come before any tribunal of justice we shall find that considering each case apart, it would as often be an instance of humanity to decide contrary to the laws of justice . . . Judges take from a poor man to give to the rich; they bestow on the dissolute the labor of the industrious, and put into the hands of the vicious the means of harming both themselves and others. The whole scheme, however of law and justice is advantageous to the society and to every individual; and 'twas with the view of this advantage that men by their voluntary conventions, established it. After it is once established by these conventions, it is *naturally* attended with a strong sentiment of morals, which can proceed from nothing but our sympathy with the interests of society.[115]

---

[112] Ibid., 3.2.5, para. 14, at 336f.   [113] Searle, *The Construction of Social Reality*.
[114] See *Enquiries*, appendix III, sec. 256, at 304 (Nidditch and Selby-Bigge eds.).
[115] Hume, *Treatise* 3.3.1, para. 12, at 370.

Nevertheless, something is still missing in this story, as the overall perception of social utility is "distant" and might be powerfully counteracted by the "vividness" of a particular injustice, as pointed out. What we need is an additional assurance that holding on to our "cold passion" is justified, so that e.g., a concrete case can be considered a miscarriage of justice rather than an invalidating reason of the general respect for law, which is Hume's *eighth* answer. The difficulty consists in finding

the expedient by which men cure their natural weakness and lay themselves under the necessity of observing the laws of justice and equity, notwithstanding their violent propension [*sic*] to prefer the contiguous to the remote . . . [i.e.] to render the observance of justice our nearest interest and their violation our most remote. But this being impracticable with respect to all mankind, it can take place with respect to a few, whom we just immediately interest in the execution of justice. These are the persons, whom we call civil magistrate, kings and their ministers, our governors and rulers . . . Here then is the origin of civil government and allegiance . . . Men are not able radically to cure [*sic*]. . . All they can do is to change their situation and render observance of justice the immediate interest of some particular person . . .

Magistrates find an immediate interest in the interest of any considerable part of their subjects. They need consult no body but themselves to form any scheme for the promoting of that interest. . . . Thus bridges are built, harbours opened; ramparts raised; canals formed and armies disciplined . . . by the care of government, which, though composed of men subject to human infirmities, becomes, by one of the finest and most subtle inventions imaginable, a composition, that is, in some measure, exempted from these infirmities.[116]

This seems at first an astounding conclusion and readers who had the patience to follow my argument up to this point might ask themselves why we had to go through all these moves, only to end up with a Hobbesian solution, i.e. a sovereign and his officials "who know best" and who have to be obeyed because they are "above" the law. This suspicion is even heightened when we read in the subsequent sections of the *Treatise* that promises without public sanctions "would have but little efficacy in such (large) societies"[117] and that

no one whose judgment has not been led astray by philosophy has ever yet dreamt of ascribing governmental authority to that origin from a promise. Neither magistrates nor subjects have formed this idea of civil duties.[118]

While this last point is clearly problematic, as both government officials and the public at large *do use the language of consent* and thus the charge that

---

[116] *Treatise*, 3.2.7 at 344, and para. 8, at 345.
[117] As opposed to small face-to-face communities, where defections are easily noticed and sanctioned. See *Treatise*, 3.2.8, para. 7, at 350
[118] *Treatise* 3.2.8, para. 8, at 350.

contractarian thinking arises out of philosophical speculation, seems over-drawn, even if it has a point. The emphasis on conventions rescues law from being exclusively a state-project, placing it instead in a wider social context, which contractarian thinking with its focus on one foundational act hides. After all, it is indisputable that Hume's ire is directed against modern con-tractarianism in general and while Locke is his major sparring partner, his counterargument to the theory of establishing government through contracting cuts also against Hobbes.

Where Hume and the other two authors mostly differ is on the way in which this common world can be constructed: imprescriptible natural rights or force on the one hand, or the accrual of customs on the other? Hobbes bases his speculation on a near magic belief in the effectiveness of force, which is to keep all subjects "in awe."[119] It is here that Hume's argument concerning the sedimented experiences, the role of commerce and conversation, the cultiva-tion of passions into sentiments, and the "artificial" nature of morality provides an important secular and enlightened alternative. Obviously, Hobbes's beliefs were deeply influenced by the experience of the religious wars that had visited England. But paradoxically the Leviathan's language still remains steeped in religious symbolism, irrespective of what Hobbes personally believed. This is not only visible in the biblical monster that lends its name to his book but e.g. also in the notion of "awe" in which the ambivalence of the "sacred"[120] (combining often the good and the "awful") resonates.

Hume's answer to this is to take emotions in general (not only fear) more seriously by cultivating and harnessing them for the construction of the common world, and forgo any sacralization move. He is interested in the role of religion in social life but he treats it like "false philosophy," i.e. as a specu-lation arising out of man's precarious condition in a world which he does not understand.[121] As in the case of philosophy, which is in need of criticism and the "gross earthy mixture of experience," religion has to be cleansed of false beliefs, such as prophecies, and beliefs in miracles and magic, but also of fundamentalist claims to the ultimate "truth." As Hume points out: "Generally speaking, the errors in religions are dangerous; those in philosophy only ridicu-lous."[122] The enlightenment project which Hume pursues is thus far removed from the zeal of religious enthusiasts, such as the Puritans, who attempted the

---

[119] See Hobbes, *Leviathan*, chap. 13, at 88.
[120] For a further discussion of politics and the sacred, see Friedrich Kratochwil, "Politics, Law, and the Sacred: A Conceptual Analysis," *Journal of International Relations and Development*, 16:1 (2013): 1–24.
[121] David Hume, "Dialogues on Natural Religion" in Antony Flew (ed.), *Hume: Writings on Religion*, La Salle, IL: Open Court, 1992.
[122] Hume, *A Treatise of Human Nature*, 1.4.7, para. 13, at 177

"cleansing" of the traditional faith, only to establish an oppressive regime of the "godly elected" who could do no wrong. But it is equally distanced from the stridency of the secularism pursued by the French Revolution and its cult of reason. What emerges from Hume's project is a secular social order based on cultivated sentiments, habits, and conventions, in which the sovereign and his magistrates are not "above" the law but are part of institutional arrangements that have evolved historically and which are legitimate without invoking a special "moral" motive, extraneous to this order. Consequently, there is also no need to derive political obligation from an original contract. The reason is not only that such moves involve us in some mythical construction of when such a pact occurred; it also does not solve the intergenerational problem of obligation. One would then have to explain why a promise of the father or grandfather can bind future generations, and one would have take recourse to implied or "tacit consent." The latter undertaking, however, would, as we have seen, require a rule or convention that certain acts imply such consent.[123]

For Hume the duty of allegiance even if "at first grafted on the obligation of promises, and for some time supported by that obligation, yet as soon as the advantages of government are fully known and acknowledged, it immediately takes root of itself and has an original obligation and authority, independent of all contracts."[124] It is this realization that also solves the problem of political obligation in the case of an absolute government[125] or of conquest, as the subjects have an obligation to obey the new magistrates. As long as the latter maintain a public order satisfying the criteria of "justice" they are owed allegiance, "independent of all contracts" even though the new magistrates are, or are appointed by, "foreigners" who certainly were not invited, and the consent through "submission" might seem more like handing over one's billfold to a gunman than a making a "contract."[126]

This leads us to the more general point mentioned above, i.e. Hume's "solution" of curing myopic notions of self-interest by making the upholding of the public interest the "special" business of magistrates. Again, his solution might seem paradoxical and mercurial, since this was precisely the justification for absolutism (*l'état c'est moi*), which relied thereby on the analogy of the

---

[123] For a further discussion, see Kratochwil, "The Limits of Contract."

[124] Hume, *Treatise*, 3.2,8, para. 10, at 347.

[125] See Hume's objection to deriving political obligation from a promise: "To which we may add, that a man living under an absolute government would owe it no allegiance, since by its very nature, it depends not on consent. But as that is as natural and common a government as any, it must certainly occasion some obligation." *Treatise*, 3.2.8, para. 9, at 351.

[126] However, this follows only if we consider "war" analogous to a hold-up, i.e. a "crime," instead of an institution, and "self-determination" as a principle of *ius cogens*.

sovereign as the *bonus pater familias*. Both the *Hausvater* literature and the *Polizeywissenschaft* invoked this *topos*, when justifying absolutist rule, as both Hans Maier and Michel Foucault have shown.[127]

The move to understand politics and the public order in *terms of a private-order paradigm* taken from the despotic rule within the household has a long history and Hume seems, at first blush, only to have extended the notion to lower levels by arguing that the public interest can be secured by giving the officials a (private) stake in the maintenance of public order. After all, we do sometimes make gamekeepers out of (former) poachers, and burglars might become "security specialists," as "it takes a thief to catch a thief." But obviously, something more than playing musical chars is implied here if such arrangements are supposed to work.

Two important and interconnected issues are relevant here: one is the peculiar form of this private interest of the magistrates. It cannot be the "personal" interest of the office-holder, even though he usually receives some form of remuneration for his service (which makes it appear that we are dealing here with some form of private wage contract only). The other issue is that of discretion and its limits, which is accorded to the magistrates (counteracting the "father knows best" temptation). Both point to the problem of *professionalization* and to the wider shared understandings and institutions involved in making this "solution" viable. Let us consider both in turn.

The change from the limited private to the general interest requires not only a change in perspective and in the formation of a particular attitude, making the "calm passions" prevail, but also circumspection and knowledge of the "systemic" effects of actions, in particular, of governmental actions. Kings and magistrates must stop identifying the common interest of the country with the interest of the royal house, as "reason of state" is different from dynastic concerns.[128] This was one of the important *topoi* which emerged in the writings of the reason of state literature, from the Duc de Rohan to Gentz.[129]

But there is not only a reason of state (different from the dynastic interest), there is also a *raison du système* – embodied in the "Republic of Europe" idea – within which policy has to be pursued. Thus, it becomes counterproductive to wage wars based on inheritance claims, if the prevalent balance of power thinking is likely to bring about a coalition since the expectation prevails that such a potential aggrandizement might be detrimental to the

---

[127] See Hans Maier, *Die ältere deutsche Staats- und Verwaltungslehre*, München: C.H. Beck, 1980; Michel Foucault, *Security, Territory, Population: Lectures at the Collège de France, 1977–78*, New York: Palgrave Macmillan, 2007.

[128] For a historical overview of these developments, see Friedrich Meinecke, *Die Idee der Staaträson in der neueren Geschichte*, München: Oldenbourg, 1960.

[129] For a further discussion see Kratochwil, "On the Notion of 'Interest' in International Relations."

repose of Europe.[130] The changed symbolic environment requires an entirely new mindset, which cannot be derived from purely personal interests or old traditions, but results from specific "training" in diplomatic academies, or from the later established curricula and examinations for the civil service. It also requires "discretion" and room for maneuver. Both elements are pillars of the growth of "professionalism" among the magistrates in the future (perhaps Hume's *ninth* answer).[131]

Although Hume is usually identified with traditionalism and the force of habits, his historical writings, such as the essay on the uniqueness of "Balance of Power,"[132] show that he is keenly aware of the difficulties of devising policies, irrespective of the framing conditions, particularly in times when old habits and conventions are rapidly changing. In his *History of England* he shows that Charles I did not fail because of tyrannical ambitions, although what Hume calls the king's "misguided beliefs" in viewing the liberties of his subjects as "grants" of his predecessors[133] were certainly not helpful and fueled the conflict. Instead, he calls attention to the fact that Charles found himself involved in an emerging state system in which attempts to protect his "house" by giving aid to his relative, the Bohemian king, misfired. When the religious fanaticism of the Puritans led to the demand to help their co-religionists in France, these new "realities" forced Charles to declare war on France. When, however, the same party provided no appropriations in parliament, Charles resorted to the unpopular, but established, Elizabethan precedent of imposing "ship money." However, a "seditious" (in his eyes) parliament took this move as further proof of his intention to undermine the "old freedoms" of Englishmen. Charles attempted to allay such fears by sacrificing his trusted magistrate, the Earl of Stafford, and he even accepted the supremacy of parliament in the Petition of Right and the Triennial Act, but all those concessions did not prevent the loss of throne and life.

Although Hume celebrates the outcomes of the Glorious Revolution, he is critical of the partisan interpretations which made a morality tale out of the record, in which the "right people" won. Instead, he takes pains to show how the final settlement of 1688 was the result of unintended consequences and

---

[130] See Edward Vose Gulick, *Europe's Classical Balance of Power: A Case History of the Theory and Practice of One of the Great Concepts of European Statecraft*, New York: W.W. Norton, 1967.

[131] For a further discussion, see Friedrich Kratochwil, "Practising Law: Spoudaios, Professional, Expert or 'Macher': Reflections on the Changing Nature of an Occupation" in Wouter Werner, Marieke de Hoon and Alexis Galan (eds.), *The Law of International Lawyers: Reading Martti Koskenniemi*, Cambridge: Cambridge University Press, 2017, 225–264.

[132] Hume, "Of the Balance of Power" in David Hume, *Essays: Moral Political and Literary*, New York: Cosimo, 2006, 339–348. He points to the "uniqueness" of the European balance of power in history.

[133] See Hume, "The Parties of Great Britain" in Hume, *Essays*, at 63–74.

fortuitous circumstances. He thereby indirectly gives us some further clues as to how the "discretion" of kings and magistrates is to be sensibly limited and controlled, a problem he later elaborates again in his essay on the ideal republic.[134] Not surprisingly most of his suggestions derive from "republican" theory[135] and its logic of checks and balances, among the existing constitutional arrangements.

But Hume is also sensitive to public opinion[136] and, for that reason, to the need to acquiesce to controversial or even "illegal" decisions by the proper authorities. His subtle analysis, linking the recent unprecedented changes to the hitherto existing traditions and customs, demonstrates that he is not a nostalgic conservative who wants to return to an idyllic past – which was not idyllic at all, as Hume analyzes in excruciating detail – but that he fully embraced the new order. Nevertheless, he is not a simple partisan observer who feels justified in projecting his views back into the past, in order to claim that "history" has borne him out.

While he doubts that there are general principles justifying resistance, which could "cover" unprecedented acts,[137] he avers:

> Though the succession of the Prince of Orange to the throne might at first give occasion to many disputes ... it ought to not now appear doubtful but must have acquired sufficient authority from those three princes who have succeeded him upon the same title ... Time and custom give authority to all forms of government and all succession of princes, and that power which at first was founded only on injustice and violence becomes in time legal and obligatory.[138]

The last remark again seems suspiciously close to the Thucydidean adage of the Melian dialogue[139] – which "realists" are so fond of quoting – that "the strong do what they can and the weak suffer what they must"[140] – but this would be a hasty conclusion. Hume's point here is not the specifics of a "settlement" that was formerly hotly contested. His point is rather that learning to live with certain facts of life in order to be able "to go on" is an important part of common sense, even if it violates doctrinal purity (*ex iniuria (non) oritur ius*). Any purely restorative notion of justice clinging to a status quo ante, or taking it as an unproblematic "absolute beginning" can endanger

---

[134] Hume, "The Idea of a Perfect Commonwealth" in Hume, *Essays*, at 499–516.
[135] See Philip Pettit, *Republicanism: A Theory of Freedom and Government*, Oxford: Oxford University Press, 1997. See also Onuf, *The Republican Legacy in International Thought*.
[136] Hume, "Of the Liberty of the Press" in Hume, *Essays*, at 8–12.
[137] Hume, *A Treatise of Human Nature*, 3.2.10, para. 17, at 363.
[138] Ibid., 3.2.10, para. 18, at 361f.
[139] Thucydides, *The History of the Peloponnesian War*, trans. R.W. Livingstone, Oxford: Oxford University Press, 1960, bk. V, at 84–116.
[140] Ibid., para. 89.

the very civil life which law is supposed to protect. This could be Hume's *tenth* answer, objecting as much to blind adherence to tradition as to the pre-occupation with "consistency" without circumspection. After all, even Kelsen noticed (at the margin) the "normative force of facticity" and saw the need for an extra legal *Grundnorm*. But Hume calls our attention to the fact that such considerations do not occur only at the margins, leaving both law and politics, as a hermetically closed system, to their own devices. Instead, for Hume the project of building a civil life is deeply interpenetrated by customs, habits, the taken-for-granted knowledge as well as the *epistemes*, which have gained acceptance. They percolate through societies, networks of scientists, (critical) philosophers, and professionals who are engaged in the construction of that artifice, which circumscribes the "world of our making."[141]

9.5   Conclusion

It was the task of this chapter to elaborate on the conceptual innovations for our understanding of the social world, which Hume articulated in his oeuvre. For that purpose our analysis began by placing the Humean "answer" to both the skeptics and the Cartesian way of thinking. Descartes's "solution" to the skeptics' criticism consisted in providing an alternative approach to the alleged indubitability of the self-referential reflection and the rather prob-lematic extension of that certainty to some allegedly "clear and distinct ideas" and a particular method, which could disclose to us what the "world out there" is like. Hume considers the starting point of an absolute doubt, which, if over-come, provides us with absolute certainty, as an entirely dubious construct. For him it is implausible to start an inquiry with a generalized doubt and with an absolute fundament outside our experiences and our situatedness in the natural and social world; it is also implausible for him since the Cartesian approach necessitates the reintroduction of a God as the ultimate guarantor of knowledge.

Against this position Hume relies on a "natural history" of human develop-ment, which is experienced from "within" this world and in which philosophy can no longer lay claim to the sole possession of absolute truth – as all our knowledge is limited and preliminary, as it is refutable. Especially for the analysis of the social world the experience of a common life and conversa-tion provide for Hume the material that a proper philosophy must subject to criticism, without arrogating to itself the "final" and universally valid, ultimate "word," which "ideal theories" try to find in abstract principles.

---

[141] Onuf, *World of Our Making*.

Hume's interest in the artificial character of the social world, its conventions and laws and their historical development, relies not only on an "internal point of view" – as legal theorists, such as Hart, or sociologists such as Weber have suggested. Hume's analysis of the conventions and of acting in a social world by learning to use the intersubjective "rules" and concepts opens the way, in addition, for analyzing acting and knowing in the realm of praxis. It takes into account the specific defining characteristics of this domain, instead of subjecting it to the inappropriate standards of theoretical knowledge. It is this problem which the last two chapters address.

10 Acting

10.1 Introduction: The Practice Turn

The practice turn seems to be the *dernier cri* in the field of international politics, and since it follows the many turns in the past, one had better be careful with its theoretical claims made in this context. It seems also a bit out of place, given that fashions are changing in the field and that the younger members of the "community" of IR scholars seem somewhat tired of "grand theory." They prefer much simpler endeavors – a fact duly lamented by some of the older "heavy hitters" in the field, who seem to fear for their privileged status in the discipline.[1] Nevertheless, modesty and fatigue do not seem enough for developing a new heuristic or for justifying "normal science"[2] and that means that the new research will nevertheless have to take notice of some of the criticisms concerning the presuppositions of "theory" of practice.[3] To that extent the limitations of a priori reasoning, of misapplied theoretical standards (such as parsimony), or of beginning one's analysis with "unrealistic assumptions" conceived in an ideal world, need to be examined since they are likely to lead us astray, as Hume suggested.

Given Hume's caution and the critical purpose of his project, one is indeed astonished when one compares the present discussions in the field with the subtlety and sophistication with which Hume attempted to deal with the "establishment" of the domestic English order and of the international system, being well aware of their interaction effects. Furthermore, in reading his work we cannot but realize that an engagement with praxis might require some further fundamental conceptual work that is not exhausted by mapping some new

---

[1] See John J. Mearsheimer and Stephen M. Walt, "Leaving Theory Behind: Why Simplistic Hypothesis Testing Is Bad for International Relations," *European Journal of International Relations*, 19:3 (2013): 427–457.

[2] For a perceptive criticism of the Mearsheimer and Walt misdiagnosis, see Daniel J. Levine and Alexander D. Barder, "The Closing of the American Mind: 'American School' International Relations and the State of Grand Theory," *European Journal of International Relations*, 20:4 (2014): 863–888.

[3] See e.g. Rudra Sil and Peter J. Katzenstein (eds.), *Beyond Paradigms: Analytic Eclecticism in the Study of World Politics*, New York: Palgrave Macmillan, 2010.

practices, bundling them together as "best practices," and generalizing from them. What one sorely misses in the contemporary debate is precisely the critical examination of the silent and not so silent presupposition of thought, on which Hume insisted and which later other philosophers, such as the American pragmatists, have also demanded. Significantly, neither of these fundamental challenges has made it to the agenda of the IR debates even though "practice" has recently become a new buzzword. The present chapter attempts to counteract these tendencies by adumbrating a mode of analysis that takes praxis seriously in following up on some of the conceptual pointers which both Hume and the pragmatists have left for us.

As we have seen, it was the evidence presented by students of the history of science which showed that "doing science," i.e. the practice of science, was quite different from the rational reconstruction presented by Popper and others concerning the accumulation of knowledge. The other objection to the epistemological ideal was the even earlier criticism voiced by pragmatists who suggested that following such an ideal might be counter-productive for actual knowledge production since much of the old philosophical baggage on which traditional epistemology relied could be dispensed with without any damage to the creation and dissemination of knowledge. In this more radical way, the groundwork was laid for undermining the very theoretical ideal of knowledge, based on the "quest for certainty."[4] Instead of deriving security from some method or the incontrovertible foundations to which one had retreated in order to assuage the anxieties of radical doubt, Hume's message as well as that of the pragmatists was that a productive engagement with the world had to start in the midst of things and by subjecting our hunches – or "prejudices" as both Hume and Gadamer[5] would call them – to criticism.

Since the task of the present chapter is a critical reflection on knowledge claims, particularly in the remit of a social "science," it should be clear that such an endeavor cannot limit itself to mining a few pragmatic thinkers and distilling some principles from their writings in order to apply them then to international relations in the hope that they will explain "more of the variance." This would be falling into the very traps we try to avoid. Thus some distancing of oneself from the present debates is required. Furthermore, the necessary clarification entails not only an "archeology" of the concept(s) under scrutiny and of their embeddedness in a semantic field, it also demands an examination of the particular practices determining what counts as "being the case" in different fields. Finally, beyond the processes of disciplinary knowledge

---

[4] See John Dewey, *The Quest for Certainty: A Study of the Relationship between Knowledge and Action*, London: Allen and Unwin, 1930.

[5] Hans-Georg Gadamer, *Truth and Method*, 2nd edn., New York: Continuum, 2004.

generation we have to analyze the diffusion of *what is justifiably believed to be true*, by tracing its percolation through the society at large.[6]

Recognizing these points also challenges the simplistic notion that grand theory building is the *via regia* to understanding how knowledge is created, and then "applied" to managing our individual and collective lives. Instead, we have to address the antecedent question of what is considered knowledge in certain domains. To that extent again praxis i.e. the branch of knowledge concerned with acting and making choices, requires special criteria that are particular to that domain. Two problems arise in this context: one is to provide a preliminary mapping of different domains and, second, we have to specify the appropriate criteria for evaluating knowledge within each, instead of simply relying on the metaphysical assumption that everything is of one cloth and thus susceptible to the same mode of analysis.

With these considerations in mind, my argument will take the following steps. In Section 10.2 we discuss the traditional privilege accorded to theoretical knowledge. This involves me in mapping different forms of knowledge and, as adumbrated by Aristotle and Kant, explicating the justifications for the underlying conceptualization. My argument here is that Aristotle was well aware of the difference between theory and praxis as they represented different domains with a different underlying logic. However, his philosophy was also committed to an ontology and an "order of things" which automatically privileged the knowledge of what is "universally and by necessity so," over other forms of knowing, be they technical knowledge, or even (his understanding) of "physics" (understood as a general field of coming into existence and of decaying). It is this metaphysical commitment to ontology, of distinguishing "being" (*to on*) from the different forms of being in the phenomenal world (*ta onta*) that has survived in our epistemological debates, even after the onslaughts on ontological thinking by Descartes, Hume, and Kant.

Section 10.3 will expand on this problem of privileging theory, that persisted in the "re-founding" of knowledge on the basis of human subjectivity as manifested in the epistemological project of modernity. In Section 10.4, I examine the conceptual issues underlying our notions of progress in knowledge generation. I try to show the problematic implications of some of the traditional metaphors for understanding the nature of knowledge, and in particular of knowledge in regard to action taking place in irreversible time. Section 10.5 is devoted to the understanding of the historical character of the social world on the one hand, and the role of criticism on the other, without recourse to an "ideal-theory" that is atemporal, universal, and built on necessity.

---

[6] For a further discussion of the "disciplinarity" of knowledge, the difficulties of interdisciplinary research and the "bounds of (non)sense," see Kratochwil, *The Status of Law in World Society*, chap. 9.

10.2   The Privilege of "Theory"

Kant and Aristotle

In order to examine the reasons for this position let us begin with a paradox that Kant notes in his *First Critique*: that the "odd destiny of human reason consists in the fact that it is in its nature to be confronted with questions, which it cannot reject but which it also cannot not answer as they transcend the limits of human reason."[7] He further identifies three questions, which are of concern to everybody, since the questions of "what I can know," "what I shall do," and "what I can hope for" are in the "interest of reason itself." This *self-concernment* we also find in Locke[8] and Hume, as it represents the typical self-reflexivity of modernity, cannot be found in either Plato's idealism or in Aristotle's search for knowledge. It is then somewhat surprising that two years after the *First Critique* Kant attempts to persuade his audience that actually the most important question seems to be the one which would allow metaphysics to claim once again to be a science,[9] and his invocation of Copernicus and of Newton seems to follow the same logic. Furthermore, since the *First Critique* is concerned only with the construction of objects in accordance with the criteria of scientific apprehension – while the constitution of the life-world remains unattended – it is possible to read the *Critique of Pure Reason* as a "tractatus on method" (*Traktat der Methode*)[10] suggesting perhaps that it has displaced the other questions. However, such an interpretation is unwarranted since Kant did write, after all, two further critiques.

There is no point here in entering the speculations about Kant's possible intentions, or in following his further trajectory, which led him after the next two critiques to a rather theistic notion of "nature" and its "design" (teleology). Notable, however, is his obscure remark[11] that a fourth critique would be

---

[7] Immanuel Kant, *Critique of Pure Reason*, "Vorrede," A VII, in Immanuel Kant, *Werkausgabe*, vol. III, Frankfurt: Suhrkamp, 1956, at 11.

[8] See Locke, *An Essay Concerning Human Understanding*. In the "Epistle to the Reader" Locke identifies the most important questions as those which secure mankind's "great Concernments, that they have Light enough to lead them to the Knowledge of their Maker and the sights of their own Duties," ibid., at 11. Kant's "ideas" of God, World, and the Soul take up the same theme, even though in a different conceptual apparatus.

[9] See Immanuel Kant, *Prolegomena to Any Future Metaphysics That Will Be Able to Come Forward as Science*, trans. Gary C. Hatfield, Cambridge: Cambridge University Press, 2004.

[10] See Immanuel Kant, *Critique of Pure Reason*, trans. Paul Guyer and Allen W. Wood, Cambridge: Cambridge University Press, 1998, at 28.

[11] In the Introduction to his *Third Critique* Kant reflects on the existing three Critiques, suggesting that the existing First Critique should be renamed as *Critique of Pure Understanding* (Verstand), and adumbrates a new conception of critique of Pure Reason, which is not the same as the existing *First Critique*. For a further discussion, see Reinhard Brandt, *Die Bestimmung des Menschen bei Kant*, Hamburg: Felix Meiner, 2009, chap. 10.

needed in order to reconcile the difficulties that had arisen in the meantime. For our purposes here it is enough to note that even after the dismantling of the old *order of being*, where once the "ought" and the "is" had been fused, but which were now separated and could not be bridged by reason (being nothing more than a "slave of passion"[12] as Hume remarked), the preference for identifying knowledge with the criteria of necessity and universality (both in scope and time) seemed still in place. It survived also the next two centuries and still informs most of our commonsense notions of reality, truth, and meaning.

Kant's ruminations at this point about the need for a fourth critique occurred in his *Third Critique* and link back to the now questionable metaphor of reason as a "court" that compels the production of evidence, which he used in his *First Critique*. While there reason's "power of command" carried the argument, in his *Third Critique* the problem of universality and particularity became an issue, since he realized that both the verdict of a court and of an esthetic assessment involve the power of judgment *in a particular case*. In both cases we make claims on *the attention of an audience* and want their assent to our decision, although we are not able to provide universally compelling reasons for our singular judgment. A similar situation arises when we deal with political choices since we have to decide without full information and in the absence of a universal compelling algorithm. Of course, we buttress our position with *reasons*, but know that they are at best persuasive, instead of being compelling. Thus, if knowledge serves as a warrant for our assertions, it seems to come in different forms in different fields.

This leads us back to Aristotle's attempt at mapping the different forms of knowledge we need in different contexts. After the skeptic's challenge, one thing seemed clear already in antiquity: that relying simply on the senses cannot provide the necessary warrant for our beliefs in many important instances. The broken oar in water, which gets whole again when removed, cautions us against taking sense perceptions at face value (even if the practical relevance of these objections seems exaggerated). The separation of belief (*doxa*) and truth (*aletheia*), of appearance and true being, becomes now the template for deciding knowledge claims since if something truly "is,"[13] the ontological warrant justifies our assertion.

---

[12] This widely circulated Humean saw is, however, misleading, since for Hume it is *imagination* rather than reason that is the main power of the human mind.

[13] Actually *aletheia* means originally that something is out in the open, is no longer hidden but discloses itself. It relies on a simple visual metaphor but sets up the "object/concept dichotomy" that originally privileges the "object" which, however, has to be cleansed from "accidental" properties so that its "true being" becomes visible. This leads, on the one hand, to "reification" when the object becomes the measure of all things and when the principle of the excluded middle (is/is not) is applied, that determines meaning according to this timeless existence criterion. Or it leads in the Copernican revolution to the "noumenal world" where the things in themselves exist, but cannot be described or known unless they are brought under concepts

Being heir to the Socratic and Platonic criticisms of the sophists, who had put the arguments of the skeptics to good use and profit, Aristotle realized that both the Socratic notion of what could count as knowledge, and Plato's elaboration of the ontological status of ideas, that served as presumptive refutations, were not quite satisfactory.[14] The Socratic questions inquiring into the specific *arete* of people, i.e. what they are "good at," be they shoemakers, priests or politicians, relied on a model of knowledge which is derived from the specific skills that emerge with the division of labor in a society.

But this model, relying on a "knowing how," quickly gets into trouble when we leave the realm of "making things" (*techne*) and try to apply it to larger questions, such as steering the ship of state. While the latter metaphor has become ingrained in the Western tradition – and a ship's captain certainly possesses certain skills based on the knowledge of the stars and the weather – the metaphor breaks down when we attempt to derive from this expertise the claim that the captain also possesses superior insight as to the destination of the ship, on what occasion, what time, and for what purpose it has to set out to sea. "Being good at" follows in that case a different logic, which cannot be reduced to either the know-how of making of things, or to the notion of "participation" in true being that Plato proposed, privileging thereby "theory" whose domain is to examine the premises of thought and of matters which are universally and by necessity so and "cannot be otherwise."

But in the realm of praxis, when action is at issue, and in particular when we want to act "well," we are confronted with certain distinct features of that domain, which must be taken into account. For Aristotle two important differences are: one, the contingencies introduced by the fact that actions take place in *time* and are thus characterized by (historical) contingency, privileging thereby the particular not the general; and two, that therefore the knowledge necessary for practical questions fits badly the logical model of inference that operates with a general major (universal) premise and a minor (factual) premise insuring the conclusion, even if the "enthymeme," i.e. the mode of practical reasoning

and categories by which we apprehend the (unknown) world, a move which privileges the "subject." A third possibility however could be that "truth" reveals itself in time – which gives rise to "cults" or personal conversions; sometimes based on surprisingly detailed observational knowledge (such as of the stars in Egyptian or Mayan calendars) or personal "insights." While this suggests that the universe of meaning is wider than the set of true sentences (since only meaningful sentences can be true but not vice versa as juridical and esthetic judgments show), we usually do not apply the term "knowledge" to them since we usually cannot give a warrant for our observations (why and not only that this constellation repeats itself), or for the "insight" which is only partially communicable, based on a personal soteriological experience.

[14] See his (meanwhile lost) treatise "On Ideas" of which we still have some fragments. See the illuminating discussion of Gail Fine, *On Ideas Aristotle's Criticism of Plato's Theory of Forms*, Oxford: Oxford University Press, 1995. See also Aristotle's remarks in his *Metaphysics* at 990b 17 and at 1039 a 2f.

in which the first premise is a norm or principle and the second premise consists of the facts of a "case," seem to suggest a parallelism. Since I will attend to this issue below, let us for the moment concentrate on this primary Aristotelian distinction, which has several corollaries.

Thus, an agent is neither served by logic alone, nor is s/he helped by the knowledge of what is true in general. Rather, given time pressures, s/he needs a quick diagnostics identifying what best characterizes the present problem. Since s/he is also never confronted with exhaustively defined situations and complete knowledge of all the strategies available, the search for new information is costly and indeterminate.[15] Consequently, more important than maximization is the *criterion of completeness*, i.e. of not having overlooked something that might become important down the line, which involves experience rather than logical astuteness. Furthermore, given this predicament a quick heuristics and *a flexible* rather than a purely maximizing strategy is demanded, since choices cannot be postponed and windows of opportunity open and close, i.e. are not indefinitely available. This also necessitates *a sense of "timing"* as an important element – Aristotle's *kairos* – and also of having a *viable fallback strategy* if it turns out that one had misjudged the initial situation or that the dynamic of interaction does not develop along the expected lines. Doing more of the same (much helps much) according to the metaphysical principle of the continuity of nature, is then hardly a prudent and defensible strategy.

Another important point is that the grammar of "acting well" not only comprises that we reach our goals, but also *in what fashion* we do this. New problems arise in this context, since we are likely to interfere in our pursuits with the goals of others and competition can quickly degenerate into conflict. Finally, many of our actions are undertaken *on behalf of others*, who are our clients, patients, or students, to whom we *owe particular fiduciary duties*. The latter are important but cannot be derived from the general obligations we owe to all humans, or even to all fellow citizens. Here a general respect for "the law" – rehearsed by Aristotle's *rule of law* argument (*nomos basileus*) in his *Politics*[16] – and its specific exceptions and exemptions – sedimented in codes or precedents forming a specific tradition[17] – rather than knowledge of the first principles and mere logic, becomes important.

In short, the knowledge we are after is that of the particular, not of the general. Someone proficient in analogous and counterfactual reasoning will be of greater help than someone schooled only in logic. Similarly, being able to think in terms of types, rather than of classes, will be better for us when we look for orientation than having clarified ultimate first principles and looking around for a possibility of applying them.

[15] Conlisk, "Why Bounded Rationality?" 669–690.   [16] Aristotle, *Politics*, 1287a 3–6.
[17] See Martin Krygier, "Law as Tradition," *Law and Philosophy* 5:2 (1986): 237–262.

All these considerations suggest for Aristotle that practical knowledge needs experience, and judgment. By experience he obviously did not mean that a person must have performed *the very same actions* and routines frequently, even if they are of crucial importance in the case of production (*techne*), and in modern "normal" science. He rather suggests that the prudent person must have been *exposed to a variety of things*, that s/he must have learned to compare situations and to find ways of going on, rather than getting stymied by an instance which refutes traditional wisdom, or embarking on the task of "normalizing" non-conform cases in order to expand the database and prepare a hypothesis for a scientific test.

There is no need to map exhaustively here Aristotle's different branches of knowledge, save to come back to the question why he in the end favors, nevertheless, theoretical knowledge. Given this realization of certain defining characteristics of practice, Aristotle's plea for prudence and persuasiveness rather than cogency and parsimony seems well founded. Nevertheless, they get trumped all the same, although there does not seem any compelling reason to evaluate all forms of knowledge according to the criterion of necessary truths. After all, tautologies are "true" by definition – and thus always true – but they are also pretty uninformative. For we would not call someone saying that "a is a, is a, is a" a wise man (he at best qualifies as a "wise guy"), any more than we would consider someone to be a financial advisor who told me to buy a lottery ticket, in order to get out of debt – even if I, in following his advice, happened to hit the jackpot and his "prediction" was right.

I think that the fact that this hierarchy in evaluating forms of knowledge remained the persistent subtext of the Aristotelian enterprise is due to the "ontological" step he took with Plato. Thus, he accepted that there was an order of being, which at the same time determined the respective intrinsic value of different domains. Thus the "higher-order" things, although poorer in information – due to the ladder of abstraction (which already hints at the danger of the vacuity of ultimate ontological principles) – were then by their very "nature" of higher value. Furthermore, in the Platonic universe, true being was identified with changelessness, since change could only mean becoming or decaying, whereby decay manifested the imperfect instantiation of the eternal *eidos*.[18] In short, true being, timelessness, and universal necessity were all interwoven.

Aristotle did not follow Plato's ontological teachings in all respects and was at times rather critical of his teacher. His interest in dynamic processes

---

[18] See Plato, *Timaios* 27d–28a. "First ... we must make a distinction and ask: What is that which always is and has no becoming, and what is that which is always becoming and never is? That which is apprehended by intelligence and reason is always in the same state, but that which is conceived by opinion with the help of sensation and without reason, is always in a process of becoming and perishing and never really is."

of genesis and decay and the teleology of living forms added important new subjects to his inquiry. Nevertheless, he remained within the ontological prison that the highest form of knowledge has to do with the transcendent unchanging being and he suggested that someone engaging with the contemplation of these ideas becomes similar even to God.[19]

This preoccupation with the universal became a constant theme in his teachings, as can be seen from Aristotle's discussion in his *Poetics*, in which the drama is accorded a higher value since it represents the more general and timeless (the heroic), while history records only the sequence of particular events and thus reconstructs only the accidental.[20]

Thucydides and "the Good Forever"

This ontological slant has important implications for our historical understanding and its role for praxis. Thus one of the first things Thucydides had to do when writing his *Peloponnesian War* was to rescue historiography from the fate of the evanescence of life by claiming for it the status of an "exemplary history" – so to speak, presenting us with the "idea" of history. He argued, therefore, that his work is not only a "good forever" (*ktema eis aei*), but also presses practical knowledge, which underlies the political decisions he records, into a generalizing framework. The result is that the issue of action is then largely addressed in terms of learning from history and of the imitation of great deeds: *historia magistra vitae*.[21] This leads him to some curious and entirely ahistorical arguments, and to a theory of action that is as flawed as it is popular.

For this purpose let us quickly look at this work, which has become a canonical text for historians of old, and for some realists of newer times. Both parties accept Thucydides' claim of the usefulness of knowledge for future generations, but modern realists believe that he thereby also made a genuine "theoretical" claim,[22] while historians, particularly in the humanist tradition, submit to the allure of great deeds that need to be emulated. In the first interpretation, Thucydides uses the past, i.e. the past, which he had witnessed, in order to provide advice for the future, so as not to be identified with his contemporary "storytelling" historians, who sought to amuse and entertain their audience. Thucydides is

---

[19] Aristotle, *Politics*, bk. III, chap. 16, at 1287a 5–1287b 8. Law as the pure voice of God and of Reason may thus be defined as "reason free from all passion."
[20] Aristotle, "Poetics," at bk. IX, 1451b 1455–1457. See also Silvia Carli, "Poetry Is More Philosophical than History," *The Review of Metaphysics*, 64:2 (2010): 303–336.
[21] Koselleck, "Historia Magistra Vitae."
[22] See e.g. Gilpin, *War and Change in World Politics*.

very clear about distinguishing his enterprise by both his intention (to tell a true story, not some fiction)[23] and by the nature of his subject matter.

Let us grant him the first part and examine the more problematic second assertion concerning his subject matter. If he maintains his claim that the Peloponnesian War was unprecedented in its scope and importance, he has to face the objection that future wars might either be more normal again – as had been the previous ones – or that they will be new again, so that what he observed has been overtaken by events. But then the advice he provides becomes problematic. The usefulness of his history crucially thus depends on a rather "ahistorical" stance, since nothing new, no perspective-dissolving surprises, should occur. But this position sits uneasily with his other claim – and the evidence he adduces – that the Peloponnesian War was indeed a historical turning point. Nevertheless, reasoning from the sample of wars he provides in the *Proeoemium* (including the Trojan War),[24] a justifiable inference could indeed be that the Peloponnesian War was the exception and thus a fluke that can (or should?) be neglected.

The problem is that Thucydides' claim (at least on this interpretation of events) is not only unsupportable as to the future, it also seems mistaken with regard to the past. It holds water only if we make the metaphysical assumption that "all wars" are alike, no matter when they have taken place or will occur, which is, of course, an absurd or a trivial assessment. Only in that case their past or future occurrence does not make any difference because they are taken as *instantiations of a population*. But then the specification of a "past" or a "future" adds nothing to the ahistorical, universal "all," robbing "history" of its subject matter, and action of its performative element.

Although this argument leads us to an obvious absurdity, its popularity seems unbroken, even in modernity. But precisely because of this absurdity we should be suspicious of this interpretation, making out of this "history" a theory. The metaphysical notion of an unchanging nature, which nowadays has been applied to the social world, is powerfully buttressed by the equally implausible inference based on an ontological understanding that any truth has to be universal and ahistorical. Otherwise, so the story goes, "truth" itself would be undermined and we would all end up in "relativism." Here existential anxiety plain and simple raises its ugly head – as the bite of the skeptics shows its power. It comes as no surprise that calls for absolute foundations are then heard everywhere.

Against this fear induced by the feeling of losing one's moorings in reality, only a radical medicine can help: such doubts have to be overcome, once and for all, by the hardest possible test, i.e. the refutation of absolute doubt. Thus

---

[23] Although he admitted that some of the speeches were not directly witnessed but composed by him according to an imaginative reconstruction of what one could and should have said in persuading an audience.

[24] Thucydides, *History of the Peloponnesian War*, at 35, para. 1.

when absolute doubt can be shown to be impossible, the miracle of having found an incontrovertible fundament promises us a free ride through the land of certainty. Logic with its principle of the excluded middle (either something is or is not the case and there is no third possibility) guarantees the first part, and the observance of a method, carefully prescribing the path to follow, the second. If we are still, against all "evidence," not convinced – as this seems to some of us too pat a story – then Descartes can remind us that even God is on our side, guaranteeing the success of our endeavors.[25]

Consequently, any further doubt can only be malevolent resistance to reason, and that seems worse than a crime: it is a mistake. Obviously, such acts of obduracy have to be handled by the disciplinary watchdogs who guard the eternal flame of knowledge in the temples of ontology. On the other hand, it should also be clear by now that questions of doubt and certainty are not simple cognitive issues but obviously shaped by powerful emotions and particularly by the fear of death and the "pointlessness" of life when judged from the "outside" and compared to the "grand scheme of things."

10.3   Of Progress, the Accumulation of Knowledge, and the Dialectic of Action

The Conceptual Puzzles of Accumulation and Progress in Science

If the above rendition resembles more a caricature than an accurate representation, we should remember that a caricature is *not* a simple distortion of reality, but rather a way of calling attention to some prominent or characteristic features that are being heightened or reinforced, in order to increase their saliency.[26] In the case at hand: the absurdity of the quest for absolute foundations and certainty, which actually silences a critical inquiry but justifies this move by an entirely implausible notion of progress, will require some further elaboration.

Things became even more complicated when we deal with the social world where its elements are not mind-independent. What does "progress" then mean? One thing is quite obvious, that e.g. the paradigm shift in the seventeenth century from the metaphor of a "body politic" to that of a "contract" cannot be understood in terms of a "better" representation of social reality that "contains" everything the old body politic's imagery suggested but also allows for a better explanation of the "variance" in the "world out" there. The bitter truth is rather that an entirely new set of constitutive and regulative rules was substituted for

[25] See René Descartes, Second Meditation in Descartes, *Meditations on First Philosophy*.
[26] See Weber, *Aufsätze zur Wissenschaftslehre*.

the old corporeal metaphor of a status society[27] that up to then had been taken as the preordained "order of things."[28]

Both examples suggest that the metaphor of the accumulation of knowledge is more problematic than it at first appears and so is the Popperian argument that this accumulation process of conjecture and refutation[29] leads us straightforwardly nearer and nearer to the truth, which we, however, never will fully reach. Two objections (and their corollaries) need to be considered in this context. Singly and in conjunction they suggest a curious case of conceptual befuddlement in the traditional way of incorporating *time* into the explanatory accounts of both nature and the social world. While statements about nature are in our understanding always true no matter whether they were made years ago or will be made decades from now, as we seem to move in a "homogeneous" space and time continuum,[30] statements about the social world are always "historical" where time is not homogeneous and reversible. The social world is constituted in *irreversible and conjunctural time*, in which actors act and bring about transformative changes, which requires an understanding of how past, present, and future are intertwined, but not the same. For that the simple time arrow in a homogeneous time provides a poor metaphor, as Paul Ricoeur has shown in his monumental study of historicity.[31] A further discussion seems required.

Let us begin with "homogeneous time" and the deceptively simple notion of *progress* in science, which raises some disquieting conceptual puzzles. The standard way for dealing with change is to hold on to a notion of a given world out there while coming to terms with change by conceiving that the objectively given truth has to be discovered step by step. In that way, what we believed to be true can actually be false but is corrected by "later" discoveries. First, how do we ever know what "is" since our assertions based on a present view (*theoria* in Greek: view), can be refuted tomorrow, so something that supposedly "was," now no longer "is." From God's view – the view from nowhere – where everything is a timeless presence, such puzzles are not disconcerting as everything is known atemporally, but then the idea of "progress" becomes incoherent. When seen from this angle Plato's conception of the realm of ideas and Popper's "Third World" have then, quite ironically, an

---

[27] For an interesting collection of essays concerning paradigms and revolutions, see Gary Gutting (ed.), *Paradigms and Revolutions: Appraisals and Applications of Thomas Kuhn's Philosophy of Science*, Notre Dame, IN: University of Notre Dame Press, 1980.

[28] For a fascinating treatment of the construct of status society reflecting the order of things, see Georges Duby, *The Three Orders: Feudal Society Imagined*, trans. Arthur Goldhammer, Chicago: University of Chicago Press, 1980.

[29] See Popper, *Conjectures and Refutations*.

[30] See Isaac Newton, "Scholium" in Newton, *Philosophiae Naturalis Principia Mathematica*, bk. I, para. 1.

[31] Ricoeur, *Time and Narrative*.

uncanny resemblance! In any case for us, who are less privileged, the question arises: should we go back again to our original belief? Which refutation should count? The last one? But why should the time at which the discovery occurred make a difference, since what truly "is" has to be, according to the underlying ontology, time-independent?

This raises still another difficulty: any refutation is an "answer" to a specific "question." Since there are many possible questions and things can be false for different reasons, the simple "is/is not" dichotomy proves to be a blunt instrument for deciding what to do, and classical logic is not of much help in that case. Obviously, it cannot be that everything we believed is now up for grabs, as it "is not" and thus also never really "was." Thus caution seems a better guide than trusting the rigor of the logical inference, even if it turns out that the result is not a downright "fluke" since it can be reproduced. Even then it is perhaps better to live with an "anomaly" and treat those phenomena as "undecidable" rather than jumping the gun.

This leads to the argument, well rehearsed in the epistemology of the unity of science position, that not single propositions but research programs[32] are the proper level at which "truth" has to be asserted. This seems to provide a way out, but does so rather unconvincingly. For one, it seems that the same problematic move returns at a higher level since now not the singular question is subjected to a test but the entire program. Unfortunately, this usually offered set-theoretical solution in which the "new theory" has to explain everything the old one did, but also must have some heuristic and explanatory surplus, runs afoul of the fact that such a comparison is possible only after the competing theories have been in use for some time so that the number of correct hits can be compared. Such a comparison is, however, quite unlikely at the beginning of a theoretical revolution and thus it cannot provide firm guidance for orienting research practice. Furthermore, certain theories might be better in one area and others in other areas; the decisive criterion cannot be their "correspondence" to what actually is, or even the quantity of corroborated propositions, but the context and purpose of the question for which we want an answer. Here again the old semantics of "being" turns out to be a poor philosopher's stone. In any case we also have to realize that we have left the semantics of "is/is not" and must adduce other criteria to help us along in our searches. These criteria are however not simply decomposable into the traditional semantics of truth, which tells us unequivocally how things really "are."[33]

---

[32] See Lakatos, "Falsification and the Methodology of Scientific Research Programmes."

[33] This leads to the appeal to use a variety of criteria to evaluate competing research programs as proposed by Colin Elman and Miriam Fendius Elman, "How Not to Be Lakatos Intolerant: Appraising Progress in IR Research," *International Studies Quarterly*, 46:2 (2002): 231–262.

Consider in this context some other "solutions" to the conundrum of the ontological anchor of "truth" and for conceptualizing "progress" in knowledge. Popper uses in this context the notion of the *verisimile*, i.e. of finding something resembling the truth by coming closer and closer to it, without however ever arriving there, or "possessing" it. Obviously here the analogy lending plausibility to this argument is that of determining the content of a circle by placing increasingly finer polygons within the demarcated space, which can, however, never quite meet or coincide with the line of the circle.

Popper thereby acknowledges the only preliminary character of knowledge which all truth claims share, admitting obliquely that the naïve scientific realist understanding might be too simple. The upshot of this realization is, however, that the realist counterargument that if our theories were not true, then our undeniable breakthroughs in technology, medicine, etc., would have to be a downright miracle, is less cogent than it seems.[34] As already pointed out, Popper realized that many, if not most, of the inventions of the nineteenth and twentieth centuries were based on theories which we nowadays consider refuted or false.[35] Can knowledge (informing us of what "is") come from error, i.e. from nothing? (it is *not* so). After all a "test" leading to a refutation tells us only what is not the case – and that also only under the exacting conditions of the *modus tollens* in logic – and not what "is." This seems a strange "ontological" answer indeed.

Nevertheless, whatever doubts we might have, Popper's argument leaves us at first with enough optimism, as it suggests that even if our theories have been false, they at least brought us nearer to the truth. But, despite its apparent plausibility the argument is rather problematic, since it involves an illicit *petitio principii*, i.e. it uses as a presupposition for the argument something that it attempts to prove. If we employ the metaphor of moving closer to the truth *then we must already know it*, or see what is the case, i.e. we must at least know the perimeter, if not the entire content, of the set containing all the sentences which are true. Otherwise we only realize – somewhat paradoxically – that now perhaps we can do more things, but whether we are nearer to the limit or not is non-decidable. Similarly, when we say that e.g. a player in a football game is now nearer to the goalpost than before, we can do this only if we actually "see" the goalpost and can use it as a reference mark for buttressing our assertion. Otherwise, all we can say is that the player is now somewhere else. However, when we acquire or produce new knowledge, the problem is precisely that *we do not know knowledge's outer perimeters*, or "see" the

---

[34] For a discussion of the "miracle theory" expounded by scientific realism, see Wendt, *Social Theory of International Politics*, chap. 2.

[35] See Popper, *Conjectures and Refutations*, passim.

goalpost or the lodestar of truth. Actually, we realize instead a paradox: that gaining more knowledge always also implies becoming aware of our growing ignorance.

The point of all this is that if scientific progress means anything, it is that we can now ask questions about problems (and subject them to further scrutiny) of which we had "no idea" a few decades or centuries back. To that extent the more appropriate image is perhaps that of a game of scrabble where we add to a word by finding new connections. We can also go off in different directions, start somewhere else and suddenly perceive new opportunities to link to existing words, thereby also creating new bridges for further connections, which involves us in a process of (re)search that potentially can go on forever.[36]

The implication of this realization is that the growth of knowledge cannot be conceived as describing the world out there in greater and greater detail. Instead, we have to understand that the world is inexhaustible, since it is describable in innumerable ways. Thus the world is rather (if we still need this notion) a manifold of different descriptions that might overlap but which have different ontologies (if we now conceive of ontology as a framework determining what "is" or exists within a certain field). These arguments have important implications for knowing the historical world, to which we now turn.

10.4   Historicity: Its Concepts and Semantics

The above-mentioned objections to treating the problem of "truth" as an ontological problem rather than one of a framework within which a question was asked, frees us from the stifling assumption that truth has to be universal in scope[37] and time. Let's even leave aside some mind-boggling new developments in modern physics where God seems to play dice – contrary to Einstein's conviction – and just focus instead, on the truth claims in common parlance, such as the following statements made on January 24, 2016: "Wolfgang Amadeus Mozart was born on Jan. 27, 1756." This statement is true and semantically equivalent to the sentence: "The composer of the *Magic Flute* (Wolfgang Amadeus Mozart) was born on Jan. 27, 1756." But the latter statement certainly could not have been true if someone had uttered it in in 1770 (on the basis of perhaps a bad dream, or clairvoyance). However, this assertion would have been "true" again when made by someone in 1800, since by then the work was

---

[36] For a further discussion of the problematic character of such a version of scientific realism, see Friedrich Kratochwil, "Constructing a New Orthodoxy? Wendt's *Social Theory of International Politics* and the Constructivist Challenge," *Millennium*, 29:1 (2000): 73–101.

[37] Note that we do not argue that the scope of laws might not be restricted, but rather that assertions that claim to be true have to be so in all places and all times.

composed, and Mozart had died. Thus many true statements are not universally true but have meaning only if interpreted within historical, and that means in irreversible, time.

If we accept these points we also have to accept the implication that thereby important issues for a "theory" of action, particularly political action, are raised. The dialectics between present, past, and future, cannot be collapsed into a simple "before and after" of a homogeneous time, playing itself out. On reflection we realize e.g. that "the past" arises from a problem of the present, which calls forth a specific recollection to which meaning is assigned, as discussed in Chapter 8. But, as we have seen, the dialectic of action requires not only a remembered past, but also a selection and a construction of a projected future. However, the future, as it is available to the actor at the time of the decision, can only be a projection, i.e. "future-present" since what eventually happens will often be powerfully shaped by unforeseen and unforeseeable events, which, in turn may lead to perspective-dissolving transformations. The disappearance of the Soviet Union, or the sudden salience of a radical Islam that emerged from transnational networks of (un-)civil society and which nowadays confronts the West but also challenges the very Islamic community, are just the more recent examples of such changes.

In short, we often not only have to make decisions under risk – for which we need a known distribution for assessing probable outcomes (and for which history is frequently but largely erroneously pressed into service) – but under conditions of genuine ignorance. If we are helped by anything it is by our imagination and by our ability to think "things through" using different scenarios, based on different metaphors, rather than rely on what has been true in the "world" with which we have been familiar. Thinking of a plane *as a bomb* rather than a means by which a terrorist might transport a bomb was one such perspective-dissolving surprise, which was unpredictable because it transcended for virtually all of us the imagination of a civil life, or even an international anarchy. This puts some important limits on the knowledge claims we can make when deliberating about our practical choices.

In "real" life, we face not only radical uncertainty, as Keynes reminded us, since certain things are unknowable in principle, such as stock prices one year hence, or the next winners of the FIFA World Cup (despite the fact that much can predictably be "bought" there). The reduction of uncertainty to a problem of insurability likened to extremely rare events, such as earthquakes, or assuming an infinite time horizon in which the bills never come due, seems to solve our problems, but only by denying the relevance of the objections to the implausible assumptions on which this construct rests.[38] The application of

---

[38] For a further discussion, see Kratochwil, *The Status of Law in World Society*, Meditation IX.

such a model to the financial market and its record does nothing to strengthen our confidence in its explanatory capacity, when we consider the recent busts. Instead, any realistic action-theory has to recognize both the irreversibility of time and the finitude of life, which often gives rise to regrets, such as "if only I had known then. . ." However, such an interpretation of the human predicament also misconceives the problematique of choice, as Aristotle points out.

Both issues of regret and of irony center on the dilemmas of the knowledge/ ignorance nexus which affects choices, but they stress different aspects of it. The first issue concerns the delusion of power that flows from the imagination of an all-knowing subject relieved from the constraints of temporality; the second – so to speak, its flipside – indicates the resignation that follows from realizing the potential for tragic outcomes of even the most well-intended decisions. On the other hand, not everything needs to turn out badly since these realizations also alert us to the possibility of multi-party and trans-generational action complexes and to their unintended consequence that can lead to a surprising "settlement," as Hume suggested (Glorious Revolution), which nobody could have intended or foreseen.

Let us begin with the first issue i.e. the simple case of regret as expressed in the sigh of "If I had known that x would happen . . ." Such regret, however, turns out to be problematic, as it arises out of a paradox. The problem is simply that for the sentence to be true, x must happen. If that is the case my regret is indeed misplaced since the sentence makes sense only if we assume that I or we could have done something that would have prevented x from happening. But if I can do something about it then x will not be true and, by implication, no knowledge of the future could be available to us. Thus the general point about expressing "regret" is:

That we do not see our own actions, at the time we perform them as having the significance which we will after attach to them, in the light of further action and events to which they are to be related. But this is a general insight into the historical organization of events: events are continuously being re-described and their significance re-evaluated in the light of later information. And because they have this information, historians can say things that witnesses and contemporaries could not have said.[39]

But unless we want to commit two further blunders we had better first be aware that this re-description, or rather the attribution of new significance is something different from a Bayesian update. For the latter I have to know *ex ante* the number of e.g. red and black balls contained in an urn – or come close with my guess to the actual state of affairs – so that I can make guesses about the next draw on the basis of the previous ones. For that reason also the record of score keeping (of the various drawings from the urn) does not result in a "history," which conveys the type of knowledge described above by Danto,

[39] Arthur C. Danto, *Narration and Knowledge*, New York: Columbia University Press, 1985, at 11.

but remains rather a "statistic." Second, assigning meaning to an event *before* other things happen – in virtue of which we then justify the ascription of significance by emplotting it in a narrative – [40] does not mean that we are always engaged in writing or narrating a "historical" story, i.e. one with which the proper historian is concerned. There is, after all, a big difference between an attribution of meaning which remains backward-looking, and a "prophetic" one, such as the philosopher of history's attribution of "progress" via a plot. In short, while historians, prophets, and philosophers of history all employ plots in order to give meaning to the events they narrate, the genres of the plots they use differ markedly despite some surface resemblances.

Consider in this context some of the most compelling emplotments, which are provided in "prophecies" but also in their modern avatars, i.e. the accounts of the "Rise of" . . . Japan, of China, of Russia, of Islam, you name it, that are often enriched by statistics and bad social science. The prophet, as well as the philosopher of history, is concerned with the future, but they do not make "predictions" proper. Predictions can be refuted, or have unforeseen consequences, which the historian records but which s/he could not have predicted. To that extent predictions proper are always only conditional and therefore we have to be agnostic as to what, in fact, will happen. Consequently, the knowledge a historian is able to transmit to us is "reflective" only (not predictive), since a description or explanation of past actions or events can be given which could not have been used beforehand, as exemplified by Mozart's birth argument above. If this is the case then the postulate of the logical equivalence of prediction and explanation no longer holds, since it is convincing only in logic in which historical time does not matter. Unfortunately, this thesis has been one of the main tenets of logical positivism justifying the theory-building efforts in the social sciences as the *via regia* to generating knowledge for the realm of praxis. But why is there no parallelism between meaning attribution on the basis of things past and one done with the future in mind? This leads us to another aspect of prophecy.

Prophets claim to know what *will* happen, plain and simple, and thus attribute significance to actions and events by making them into "signs" of the things to come, or to stages of development on the road to a predestined end. While prophets might limit themselves to specific events, for which the prophets of the Old Testament provide many examples, there is a marked shift in the prophetic tradition beginning with Deutero-Isaiah,[41] where the destiny of all mankind is foretold. Thus the prophet is not only one who speaks about the future in a manner which is appropriate only to the past, "he speaks of the

[40] See W.B. Gallie, *Philosophy and the Historical Understanding*, 2nd edn., New York: Schocken Books, 1968.
[41] Isaiah, verses 42f.

present in the light of a future treated as a fait accompli."[42] Prophets share with modern philosophers of history (via the New Testamentarian eschatology of the end of all things) this teleological orientation.

Consider in this context Kant's opening lines in his *Universal History with a Cosmopolitan Purpose*, in which a secularized eschatology is linked to the revolution brought forth by modern science. This gives rise to the strange antinomies between freedom and necessity but also to the repeated attempts to reconcile them in terms of "nature's design" which Kant discovers in all types of things (even in the increasing brutality of wars, as argued in his Perpetual Peace) which will bring mankind to its destined *telos*. While he tries to make it appear that discovering this hidden message in nature itself, analogous to the work of Kepler, this analogy is hardly fitting. It takes little imagination to see here that the "purpose" which was originally ascribed to God is now attributed to nature. As Kant avers, if one looks at history on a large scale

... it will be able to discover a regular progression of the freely willed actions. In the same way we may hope that what strikes us in the actions of individuals as confused and fortuitous may be recognized in the history of the entire species, as a steadily advancing but slow development of man's original capacities ... Individual men and even entire nations little imagine that, while they are pursuing their own ends ... often in opposition to others, they are unwittingly guided in their advance along a course intended by nature.

Let us now see if we can succeed in finding a guiding principle for such a history and then leave it to nature to produce someone capable of writing it along the lines suggested. Thus nature produced a Kepler who found an unexpected means of reducing the eccentric orbits of the planets to definite laws, and a Newton who explained these laws in terms of a natural cause.[43]

This train of thought has been adopted by the general public in the West (and increasingly all over the world). It has informed the political projects of a cosmopolitan order, brought about (somehow incoherently) by both design and necessity, since Kant and his followers obviously do not want to take chances on reaching this prophetic goal.[44] (So what, a bit of stacking the deck is a good thing if done for the right purposes ... right?)

Nothing could be farther from a Humean approach. For him philosophy is not tasked to provide incontrovertible foundations or prophecies about the

---

[42] Danto, *Narration and Knowledge*, at 9.
[43] Immanuel Kant, "Idea for a Universal History with a Cosmopolitan Intent" in *Kant, Political Writings*, 2nd edn., ed. H.S. Reiss, Cambridge: Cambridge University Press, 1991, 41–53, quote at 41 and 42.
[44] See Kant's remark in the *Perpetual Peace* "fata volentem ducunt, nolentem trahunt" (nature leads the willing and forces the unwilling). Immanuel Kant, "Zum Ewigen Frieden" in Peter Niesen and Oliver Eberl (eds.), *Zum Ewigen Frieden: und Auszüge Aus der Rechtslehre*, Berlin: Suhrkamp, 2011, at 40.

future, but finds itself in the midst of things and thus his analysis is parasitic on the experience of a common life, its conceptions and institutions. Philosophy's role is not to issue in metaphysical truths but to provide reasoned criticism of the common and current conceptions which underlie our choices and institutions, embracing both their historical malleability and their limitedness. Against this "delirious philosophy" which promises certitudes which it cannot deliver – here Hume's skepticism about external objects, the existence of causality, and the problem of the justifiability of induction comes to mind – he sets his "philosophy of the common life," which consists in the criticism of the tangle of prejudice, custom, and tradition. The next section is devoted to elucidating this task.

10.5   Time, Action, and the Common World

Hume and the Proper Task for "True Philosophy"

In a famous passage of his *Treatise* Hume avers: "Generally the errors of religion are dangerous, those in philosophy only ridiculous."[45] With that remark he not only inveighs against the "craft of popular superstition" on which false religion relies for manipulating popular sentiments – a devious practice attributed to the clergy whom Hume and the Enlightenment so abhorred – and which can also be found in popular religion which makes it a "plaything for monkeys or sick men's dreams,"[46] but he also calls into question belief in the ability of philosophy to provide the absolute vantage point from which traditional unreflective beliefs or customs of a society can be judged. Significantly, he rejects the notion of a freestanding reason which we find later in Kant, which can command like a (judicial) court men and nature before its bars. Hume uses instead the image of the "throne" (the political "court") and thereby puts an ironic gloss on reason's presumptions of "prescribing laws and imposing maxims with an absolute sway and authority."[47] He also leaves no doubt that both religion and philosophy can wreak havoc in a society,[48] and whether the threat to public life comes from some totalizing philosophical system or some religious enthusiasm is then of lesser importance since both suffer from the crucial flaw of not being subjected to criticism. To that extent his central argument tasks true philosophy with preventing the degeneration of the public

---

[45] Hume, *A Treatise of Human Nature*, bk. I, pt. 4, sec. VII, at 272.
[46] Hume, *Natural History of Religion*, ed. H.E. Root, London: Adam and Charles Black, 1956: 75
[47] Hume, *A Treatise of Human Nature*, at 186.
[48] See Hume's remarks about the cynics whose philosophy was as destructive as the teachings of "any monk or dervish who ever was in the world" in *Treatise* I, 4, 7, at 177.

discourse, when e.g. commonly used concepts are twisted in accordance with some a priori principle or an assumption is "reformulated" so as to become the exact opposite.[49] Then, e.g., when "utility" suddenly indicates personal preference, property becomes "theft" and benevolence is "really" nothing but "self-love."

In making these points Hume actually harks back to a *topos* which Thucydides had already used in his account of the revolution in Corcyra[50] concerning the disastrous consequences of such shifts in meaning for the political order. Hume's argument is, however, wider as it is directed at the mistaken foundational claims of (false) philosophy. Since such a philosophy is unable to provide a secure footing through the specification of a transcendental point of observation outside the world, "true philosophy" has to dispense with such pretenses and has to start *within* the world. This means, however, that true philosophy, particularly in the social world, can only be parasitic on the existing discourses and practices and cannot claim to exist outside of the common world in some transcendental or value heaven. Its function is thus "critical," not foundational or axiomatic, and the insights it generates resemble more a dialectical or therapeutic "working through" of the problems than following the template of a demonstration. In this way we learn to live with the contradictions we encounter and can go on with our lives and political projects without despair, although no logical or compelling solutions have been found for our dilemmas.

Precisely because the problems of praxis deal with issues of meaning, such as moral worth, or justice, the language we use does not describe or refer to mind-independent entities, but registers rather the approval and agreeable sentiment produced in us and other people by an object or incidence. Then the crucial question is how we can find assent to those propositions, which cannot be based on the correct reference of the covering concepts, on the validity of inductive inferences or on the cogency of a deductive conclusion. What needs explanation now is how such an agreement on *particular judgments* can come about in the absence of a unique fitting and compelling answer.

Hume attempts to clarify the problem in two interrelated steps. First, he demonstrates the flaws in the argument that this assent could be the result of logical operations, subsuming a case to a general law or principle (as in the Hempelian account of scientific explanation), and second he advances a more productive heuristic for appraising and explaining both individual action and social cohesion (or disintegration), as in the case of sixteenth-century England,

---

[49] See David Hume, *Enquiries*, bk. II, appendixes 2 and 4, at 297 and 322 (Nidditch and Selby-Bigge eds.)
[50] Thucydides, *History of the Peloponnesian War*, bk. III, paras. 81–85.

412   Acting

when the common maxims of policy were displaced by theological disputes.[51]
These heuristics require cutting in at the level of intersubjective understandings of the common world since they provide both reasons for actions and the
yardsticks for appraisal. Let us consider each point more explicitly.

The usual way of explaining assent to a practical proposition is by invoking
higher-order principles or values, which are supposed to provide the necessary
backing or pull. But Hume is rather skeptical with regard to the role of general
principles in ethics, and he is especially critical of the proposition that their
discovery or clarification is able to do the work they allegedly do. Since general principles need application to a case at hand, we need a *community of
interpreters* if these applications are to result in stable decision outcomes. This
community has to share certain more specific rules or paradigmatic cases that
allow its members to affirm or reject the use of a higher-order principle because
of its (non)applicability in a particular case – such as to whether a case falls
under the principles of liability or of *mens rea*. But such an agreement also
allows for "distinctions" (as in common law with regard to the meaning of *stare
decisis*), exemptions, or exceptions. As Hume suggests:

> The word virtue with its equivalents in every tongue, implies praise, as that of vice does
> blame; and no one ... could affix reproach to a term which in general acceptation is
> understood in a good sense ...

> The merit of delivering true general precepts in ethics is indeed very small. Whoever
> recommends any moral virtues, really does no more than is implied by the terms them-
> selves ... People who invented the word charity and used it in good sense, inculcated
> more clearly and more efficaciously the precept: Be charitable than any legislator pro-
> phet who should insert such a maxim in his writing.[52]

While, at first sight, it might seem that Hume suggests that terms such as
"good" and "bad" are like analytical truth, I think something more is going
on. The initial sentence calls attention to language as a semiotic system. Thus
the meaning of its terms does not consist simply in their reference but in their
connection with, and their opposition to, other terms. Thus "good" and "bad"
being universal in all languages does not dispose of the problem of their
meaning in a concrete appraisal and of the latter's justifiability, as the issue
cannot be reduced to some deictic procedure, but can be acquired through
practice, leading to (a) good judgment. Using the terms good and bad, might
logically not be more complicated than a simple "application" or "fitting" the
term to a case, but whether and how well it "fits" will depend on an appraisal of

[51] See Hume, *The History of England: From the Invasion of Julius Caesar to the Revolution in
1688*, at 52.
[52] Hume, "On the Standards of Taste" in David Hume, *Essays Moral, Political, and Literary*, new
edn., London: Millar, Edinburgh: Kincaid and Donaldson, 1758: 134–148, at 135.

various factual circumstances and a comparison with other possible applications of norms or principles.

Thus our assessments involve a two-tier process. By invoking a universal term (such as "good") we make use of its "recommendatory" meaning (or disapproval), which is part of the speech-act of appraising. This recommendatory meaning uses field-independent criteria, since they derive from the semiotic logic of language;[53] however, a further problem arises, when we are called upon to provide the reasons for our judgment call. In that case we have to adduce *field-dependent reasons* with which we can buttress or justify our assessment, as argued above. What justifies our calling a car, or a fountain pen, or a deed, "good" is obviously field-dependent and cannot be explained in terms of some properties of the thing itself (rather than by the attitude we take towards it), or by their participation in the universal idea of goodness à la Plato, or solely by the oppositional logic of the semiotic system (as here the specter of arbitrariness à la Derrida raises its ugly head).

Finally, since the evocation of approval (or disapproval) is at issue in appraisals, a vivid concrete example might do a better job than the invocation of an abstract principle. We do this e.g. in moral training (*exempla trahunt!*). Similarly, Christ's answer to the Pharisees about the man who had fallen among robbers but was not helped by a Pharisee passing by because of the restrictions imposed by the Sabbath, is a case in point. We acquire this (moral) sense and realize that it is fundamentally different from just indicating our personal likes and dislikes, when we participate in the respective language game of justice and morality, in which a variety of argumentative styles and figures of speech are utilized.

These examples not only point to the importance of reasoning from case to case, of using analogies and metaphors, so that we can go on and find our way in the social world. This is why Ricoeur sees a parallel in the production of meaning through metaphorical extension – by highlighting the resemblance among things which at first seemed to have nothing to do with each other – and the construction of a narrative, both of which are the work of productive imagination.

The productive imagination at work in the metaphorical process is thus our competence for producing new logical species by predicative assimilation, in spite of the resistance of our current categorization of language. The plot of a narrative is comparable to this predicative assimilation. It "grasps together" and integrates into one whole and complete story multiple and scattered events, thereby schematizing the intelligible signification attached to the narrative taken as a whole.[54]

---

[53] I follow here R.M. Hare, *The Language of Morals*, Oxford: Clarendon Press, 1972.
[54] Ricoeur, *Time and Narrative*, vol. 1, at X.

In addition, it alerts us to the importance of a vivid[55] image or the pull of a paradigmatic narrative that synthesizes common experiences and allows for the development of further conventions and templates that can then be used in appraisals. In that case it is not so much the subsequent generalization that we might derive afterwards when we perceive certain similarities – as we can reason from case to case without utilizing generalizations – or when we became aware through cross-cultural contacts of different conventions and standard-solutions that are prevalent in other societies that carries the argument. Rather what is crucial in these discernments is "getting the point" which underlies the exemplary stories and paradigmatic examples. This has important implications for both our explanations of actions in terms of reasons, and for the historicity of the social world.

Action and the Historicity of the Social World

To explain what an action means then is to make the act intelligible by providing plausible reason(s) an actor had for acting in a certain way. That does not involve bringing the action under a covering law of universal validity, nor does it entail an exercise in empathy, getting into the mind of the actor in order to "find" the motive. Instead, we ascribe to the actors a reason for an action on the basis of the situation by placing his choice in an intersubjective scheme of sensible templates, which are taken from common life. A man is running after a tram, so we explain his actions by surmising that he wanted to catch the tram, after e.g. hailing a cab had failed. If this person fails to hop on, we do not necessarily count this as a refutation of a "general law" (presumably dealing with "hopping on trains or trams, after having failed to call a cab"). Rather, we consider this a mishap or misfire of an action, which does not challenge the intelligibility of our explanatory account. After all, people miss trams, although it might true be that in this particular case the person realized at the last moment that it was the wrong train and decided not to hop on.

In this simple case we could ask the person of what was intended. But the agent's account does not always have an automatically greater explanatory power since in more complicated situations there might be strong incentives to dissimulate one's motive, or even the actor might puzzle about why s/he acted in the way s/he did. This is all the more the case when several action episodes are linked together and we have to provide the framework for the linked actions and their sequence. Here two problems arise: one, there is the problem of

---

[55] Vividness and the narrative structure of the lessons learned and of how we got where we are now which defines our choice situation are of particular importance for Hume. See Hume, *A Treatise of Human Nature*, bk. I, pt. III, sec. 13, at 153.

providing a convincing account of several linked actions of an individual; two, we have also to provide a convincing account for interlinked action-complexes involving several actors over time – where probably no actor had intended the outcome and/or could have taken it as the goal for his actions – but to which s/he nevertheless contributed.

As to the first problem: consider in this context the case of a certain Mr. Biedermann. He seems on the face of it remarkable only because of his humdrum appearance and petty bourgeois lifestyle. But then we notice by accident that he has made, as of late, large deposits in numbered bank accounts. Again out of nowhere a mistress appears – after we got interested and did some further "digging" – which badly undermines Biedermann's image as a family man. Our suspicion is heightened when we put together what we already know with some other fact that surfaced: that Biedermann had also recently taken out a large life insurance on his wife, without having ever discussed this issue with her. When we confront Mr. Biedermann he might say that all these were just unconnected actions, the one with the mistress even being a very regrettable one. But the one concerning the life insurance, he says, just goes to show how concerned he is with his family, since his wife would be for all of them irreplaceable, but at least some of the problems could be taken care of by the insurance. Of course, hardly any detective will swallow this story.

The methodological implication here is that aside from the "plausibility" of the single actions or facts, the story as a whole must be believable. It becomes so by following a certain (hermeneutic) logic within which the individual facts and actions have to fit, and from which they attain their importance. But this logic of the storyline does not come from certain axiomatic assumptions and from the cogent derivation of some implications, or from some generalizations (although all of them can play some subordinate role), but rather from the particular "surprises." After all, people usually do not have access to large sums of cash, and neither do they behave as suspiciously as Biedermann, even if their marriage is not the happiest. The plausibility of the storyline stems from our experience of participating in the various facets of common life and from the critical weighing of the evidence. Thus by excluding step by step some competing and prima facie plausible alternatives, in the end all the facts have to fit into a narrative framework that makes sense. Making the case intelligible does not entail getting into the mind of the actor and finding there the psychological motive, which causes the action, since his mind is not accessible to us. Rather it consists in reconstructing the reasons for the actions, which allow us also to link them to each other in a meaningful sequence.

Making sense of our social world is therefore crucially related to some narrative framing. Here time not only plays a role in the sense of distinguishing a "before" and "after" which causal analysis tries to penetrate via the constant conjunction – which, *nota bene*, not nature but the mind supplies – as both

Hume and Kant pointed out. In that case the observed objects or events are disposed of by an order of succession, but in which the present, the past, and the future are not systematically linked or recognized in their co-constitution. Significantly, in some standard accounts of the philosophy of science close to positivism, neither the future nor the past is any different from the present. Many philosophers, such as Ayer,[56] Carnap,[57] or C.I. Lewis,[58] have therefore held that statements about the past are either meaningless, or they have to be translated into a protocol of present observations. This perspective unites empiricist, scientific realists, and pheneomenalists and has powerfully shaped the epistemological project of orthodox social science.

Hume agrees that a "before" and "after" ordering is common to the physical and the social world. He rejects, however, most of the traditional conclusions that certain philosophical schools draw from this premise. As we have seen, his moral explanations, providing reasons for decisions rather than citing their antecedent "cause," accept the irreversibility of time and a reality that is not fixed but in the making. As a matter of fact, Hume even suggested that his "moral explanations" provide a better justification for causal analysis than holding on to the paradigm of efficient cause where a "constant conjunction" is imputed by the mind to two natural events occurring in sequence In the latter case what really happens cannot be directly observed and we cannot say what it "is" that causes something else. As Hume avers with regard to causal explanations, "We cannot penetrate into the reason of this [causal] conjunction."[59] The insight gained by reflection on actions and practices in the common world is, however, different. It arises from both observation and learning of how to do things, which enable us "to go on."

Again this *knowing how* is neither based on a generalization distilled from our observations (we might do so but it does not do very much for our understanding), nor is it the necessary character of a law that gets instantiated (after proper abstraction and normalization of the observations) by bringing our actions "under it." Rather it is the practical experience that we can act and continue without causing an interruption of the interaction. Thus "going on"

---

[56] See A.J. Ayer: "propositions referring to the past ... can be taken as implying that certain observations would have occurred if certain conditions had been fulfilled," and "no sentence as such is about the past." A.J. Ayer, *Language, Truth, and Logic*, London: V. Gollancz, 1946, at 19 and 160.

[57] For a statement to be meaningful "perceptions or feelings or experiences ... may be expected for the future." Rudolf Carnap, *Philosophy and Logical Syntax*, New York: AMS Press, 1976, at 15.

[58] "To ascribe an objective quality to a thing means implicitly the prediction that if I act in certain ways, specific experiences will eventuate." Clarence Irving Lewis, *Mind and the World-Order: Outline of a Theory of Knowledge*, New York: Dover Publications, 1956, at 140.

[59] Hume, *A Treatise of Human Nature*, 1.3.6, at 93.

means adjusting to the constantly changing circumstances, which is quite different from blindly repeating or re-enacting a causal sequence. The confidence that we get to "go on" is also not the result of withdrawing to the abstraction of a self-referential reflection (à la Descartes), but emerges from being and acting in the world with others. To that extent the moral world, being constituted by "human feelings and opinion," can be understood by the actors without the need to posit the existence of exotic theoretical structures, such as light waves and gravitational forces.[60] The latter are not only mistakenly identified as the analogies and metaphors by which we can find our way, but bring with them the perplexities and contradictions which "we have discovered in the natural [world]."[61]

The second important point mentioned above concerns the plausibility of multi-action/multi-actor sequences, taking place in irreversible time This makes it necessary to first examine more closely the co-constitution of present past, and future, which any adequate account of action has to take into account. As we have seen, explaining an action means providing a critically vetted, plausible account of the action and its context, which has the structure of a narrative rather than of a demonstration. At first sight it might seem that only a reconstruction from the actor's perspective is necessary. But much more is involved as Hume in the fifth book of his grand *History of England* showed. None of the popular interpretations of the English Revolution and its aftermath, tendered by either the Whigs or the Tories, are tenable for Hume. Neither was the settlement of the Glorious Revolution preordained as a vindication of the old liberties of Englishmen, nor did it come about and prove its stability later for the reasons for which the actors originally went to the barricades.

These realizations squarely raise the issue of the limits of narrative judgments, which the historian as an exponent of "good philosophy" has to tackle. In times of unsettled practices, or of institutions which have lost their legitimacy, the old patterns can no longer provide convincing reasons for "going on" by doing things in the way one used to (aside from the fact that the past is, on closer inspection, hardly ever as settled as is usually believed). But the grand narratives in which vice and virtue play themselves out by presenting the protagonists as puppets on a string are clearly not plausible either. Here the use of criticism shows it force. Contrary to the partisan use of history, Hume's critical examination shows that the reign of "good Queen Bess" (Elizabeth I), who was celebrated by the Puritans for her regard for the ancient liberties as opposed to the vile Stuarts, was in reality an arrangement between the court

---

[60] Livingston, *Hume's Philosophy of Common Life*, at 198.
[61] Hume, *A Treatise of Human Nature*, 1.4.5, at 232.

and the Commons, which "was more worthy of a Turkish divan than of an English house of Commons according to our present idea of this assembly."[62]

Similarly, anyone who reviews the great debates in the House of Commons during those years is struck by the fact that they had little to do with the issue of governing, but were mostly inspired by fundamentalist religious questions, ranging from controversies about church governance, to the metaphysical issue of transubstantiation, to the proper mode of praying, to the question of the wrong exercise of tolerance by the crown towards "papists" or latitudinarian bishops, right down to the ridiculous fight over whether having a bar in front of the altar was compatible with true Christianity. All of which squares rather badly with the Whig interpretation[63] that imputes to the Puritans a concern with the preservation of "ancient" liberties, or with a plan for instituting a limited government. As Hume remarks, the Puritans, like their opponents, "were willing to sacrifice the civil interest rather than relinquish the most minute of their theological contentions."[64]

In the same vein, the use of the Star Chamber, or of "tonnage and poundage" and of quartering soldiers, were all measures which had been used by the Tudors and which were, therefore, eagerly treated by the Stuarts as established precedents. But when "theology" upset the customary order, Charles decided to take up the challenge and justify his prerogatives in equally metaphysical terms, i.e. as God-given. In this way the constitution, or rather a metaphysical interpretation of it, had become a timeless arrangement that had to be defended against any usurpation. This *idée fixe* limited Charles's room for maneuver considerably, not only because he apparently also was not a man of good judgment, antagonizing his opponents unnecessarily, but also because in considering policies it became increasingly difficult to "think things through," and discuss alternatives.

There is no point here in recounting the further events up until the "settlement" of 1688, save to say that the "unity of action" which the actors ascribe to their actions in retrospect, and on which historians elaborate through a comprehensive coherent narrative, is on this grand scale hardly ever possible. This is particularly true of teleological accounts, which rely on a prophetic

---

[62] Hume, *The History of England: From the Invasion of Julius Caesar to the Revolution in 1688*, ed. Tobias Smollett, London: A.J. Valpy, 1834, bk. V, chap. xliv, at 377. This assessment followed the programmatic pronouncement of Elizabeth in parliament concerning her powers. "It was asserted . . . that the royal prerogative was not to be canvassed, nor disputed, nor examined and did not even admit of any limitation; that absolute princes, such as the sovereigns of England were a species of divinity . . ." Ibid.

[63] For a good discussion of the problems, see also Herbert Butterfield, *The Whig Interpretation of History*, New York: W.W. Norton, 1965.

[64] Hume, *The History of England: From the Invasion of Julius Caesar to the Revolution in 1688*, at 527.

vision. The meaning people give to their actions, particularly those which were not routines but resulted in inadvertent or deliberate breaks or changes, crucially depends upon the stories they tell about themselves and the unintended consequences – when they regret their actions, or have to come to terms with "fate" by reflecting on their lives in a biography. Thus "what it all means" in individual life discloses itself only in the end and it is therefore fitting that Hume writes his biography only shortly before his death but in the reflective style as if his death already had occurred.

Such a closure is even more elusive when we deal with narratives that comprise several generations since then the meaning of an act or of an action-sequence depends *on how later generations view these events* by making them part of *their* stories, rather than recounting the original intent of the historical actors. One way of doing this is to introduce new "trans-historical" actors, such as the nation, the proletariat, humanity, etc., which then become conveyors of meaning on their voyage through time. But while the philosopher of history, like the prophet, might participate in such endeavors, Hume's "true philosopher," who takes history seriously, has to be careful. He cannot become a philosopher of history, who predicates meaning from a known *telos*. The true philosopher has to remain a historian as he cannot accept the closure that does not treat the future as open but as if it had already happened.[65]

Furthermore, as in previous "ontological" times when the order of things provided us with standards of value, so in future-directed utopias we are also largely freed from making moral assessments of our actions. If such assessments are interesting at all, they amount to little more than ascertaining on the scale of time what or who is on the right (progressive) side, and what or who is on the wrong one, representing evil. Hume's true philosopher counteracts these constructs by showing first how such a narrative violates fundamental principles of narrative construction, and second, by making us aware of the social costs of a politics informed by such an understanding of the human condition and of action.

The approach to the dialectics of time expounded here appears to give the past, at first sight, perhaps an undue weight, especially when our wishes and desires push us mightily in the other direction. But neither attitude – hoping for a return to the idyllic past or for the rush to the predestined future – does justice to the dialectic of action in irreversible time. We cannot return to a nostalgic past that never was, to the "golden age" where everything was perfect and pristine before the decay set in, which was brought on by catastrophes, natural or man-made. This would be to engage in the parallel fantasy of a future where

---

[65] See Hume, *Enquiries* (Nidditch and Selby-Bigge eds.), at 141: but this is "to reverse the whole course of nature, as to render this life merely a passage to something farther."

everything is perfect, but differs only in that the perfect state is now placed in the future instead of the past.[66]

Both of these "frames" fundamentally misunderstand our predicament when acting. The past is not simply "there," since, as we have seen, it has to be created through recollection from a specific present. It is "there" only in the sense that it is no longer available for being changed *through the actions of the players who figure in its account*. But the past cannot tell us where to go, even though it can tell us something about where we come from and in this way it frees us from possible repetition compulsions since we can set a new course.

Similarly, the future is not "there" aside from a project that has to be realized and is thus subject to unforeseen events and the vagaries of praxis. If it is there it is in an open horizon but not in the sense of a prophecy or *telos*, i.e. in terms of story that can be told because we know its end. In the latter case, the present is devalued as a space for action and freedom. Seen from this angle Kant's predilection for teleology is rather ironic. If there were teleology to nature (and humans are part of this nature) the actors would neither be free to choose their ends, nor would they be truly responsible for their actions. They and their actions would have meaning only if they "furthered" the predetermined end, and they would be meaningless if they did not. No wonder that future-oriented utopias usually look like a "present–plus," and the actions of the agents are subordinated to functional necessities or are informed by the routine of "best practices" which have to be implemented without further ado.

At this point I want to follow up on exploring how the experience of irreversible time gets sedimented in our stories of actions. As shown, narrations help us in our appraisal of what is the case, or they link in the grand narratives complex action sequences through the construction of trans-generational "historical individuals." As a first step I shall focus on some of the very basic concepts we use for creating the social world which have a temporal dimension as part of their make-up, before taking up the latter problem

Tensed Concepts

Let us go back to the example of Mozart and the truth content of the statements concerning his birth and authorship of operas made at different times and elaborate on this further. After all, not only certain statements but even concepts are "time-sensitive" or "tensed." Consider in this context the problem of Columbus's discovery of America. Could he have said, "this is America," when he heard his lookout's call "land in sight." Obviously not, since he thought that he had found the passage to India. Besides, Martin Behaim had

---

[66] See Frank Edward Manuel (ed.), *Utopias and Utopian Thought*, Boston, MA: Houghton Mifflin, 1966.

not yet made his globe,[67] in which he took Amerigo Vespucci's first name for designating this part of the world. But when we in 1960 say, "this is America," what could we mean or have meant? True the "continent" is still the same, but calling the New World America – instead of the Americas, since South America hardly belonged there anymore without a further specification – does not receive its meaning from the physical geography, and neither is it derivative of the former distinction New/Old World. Thus when we said, "this is America," in 1960 we most likely would have meant the complex notion of the United States with its political system, its way of life, and perhaps "what it stands for" (or, if the statement occurred today, it could mean the dystopia of a liberal panopticon, as America now wants "to know it all"), none of which we could have done in 1775.

If "America" might be too complex a term, whose polysemy is obvious, take the simpler example of calling little Philip not a boy, but a "grandchild." Although the reference is the same, the meaning is not. Similarly, although every woman has been a daughter and every daughter is a woman, not every woman is in all contexts a daughter, given that she might be by now, as a historical being, a grandmother.[68] Thus some of our concepts have as a constitutive part of their meaning an emplacement in time. They are so to speak "tensed" as Danto points out,[69] while others do not, such as "man" or "woman." The difference might be made light of, until we notice that it is precisely these tensed concepts that are important in constructing and understanding the social world. This we realize when we engage in the *Gedankenexperiment* of whether even God could have created a grandchild *ex nihilo*, or an orphan, as for that many things would have had to occur (or would have had to be created) before. On the other hand we have no difficulty in thinking that God created and can create a man and a woman.

But while we might take notice of such a distinction, we could be inclined to treat it again as a fluke. However, we would soon have to realize that these examples are not marginal exceptions to our understandings of the social world. When we talk about a senator, a priest, a doctor, etc., we use "institutional" concepts that all contain specific conceptual links to deeds and events, which must have occurred before, so that we can use now these terms in a meaningful way. To that extent it would also be senseless to talk about, or even sell,

---

[67] The Nuremberg *Erdapfel* apparently came into existence (through collaboration with a painter) between 1491 and 1494.

[68] This of course does not mean that she cannot become a daughter again in the narrative of a family or a dynastic history, when we go back in time and might look at the antecedents of the marriage of our grandparents or the succession to the throne.

[69] Arthur Danto, "Looking at the Future, Looking at the Present as Past" in Angel Corzo Migel (ed.), *Mortality, Immortality: The Legacy of 20th Century Art*, Los Angeles: Getty Conservation Institute, 1999: 3–12.

"futures" at the Mercantile Exchange, unless a whole host of institutional facts had been put in place beforehand. This shows how problematic a theory of the social world would be if it took the requirement of operating only with tenseless concepts seriously, and admitted only the "presentist" protocols of scientific observation, mentioned by Mink above.

It does not take too much imagination to realize that it could not be done since such a "theory" based on general, tenseless concepts would be pathetic because it would be pointless. The real surprise here is that we usually gloss over these points, precisely, as Wittgenstein reminds us, because their obviousness remains hidden to us because of our ingrained habits of thinking. Since Adam and Eve, as man and woman, would have had all the observational capacities and dispositions that we connect with rational free agents, we overlook that this is not the case when we are interested in certain particularities of persons – not in their particularity as instantiations of a class but rather in the peculiarities which locate them in certain social contexts. As argued before, to use only tenseless, generic concepts would involve us in serious problems since we could not even apply concepts such as "diplomat" or "judge." But it would be equally absurd if we thought of these particularities, to which these tensed concepts call attention, as being equivalent to the "accidental" properties of the person in question, analogous to her or his hair or eye color.

Furthermore, it now becomes clearer why past-referring and future-referring concepts are not exactly parallel in their logical structure. Going back to the daughter/grandmother problem, we notice that we can say that every woman "is" a daughter (or rather was a daughter), but we cannot say that every woman will be a grandmother, precisely because past-referring concepts depend on facts and occurrences subject to truth conditions, while the future is open and we do not know whether this person will ever marry or have a child (in or out of wedlock). Here, of course, the probabilities of a life cycle provide some justification for our assertions, but our confidence in basing such assertions on the probabilities of complex action and event sequences would require something akin to divination.

This realization has tremendous implications for the analysis of action and of the social world. As Donald Livingston remarks with regard to the claim of social "science" that our observational protocols and theories can do without tensed concepts when we investigate the "common world":

Much of our thought is governed by tenseless concepts; these include sensory, dispositional, logical, and mathematical concepts, all concepts structured by tenseless scientific laws and theories ... Indeed the class of tenseless concepts is so large and important that it is understandable how many philosophers would fix on it as the paradigm of all concepts. The move seems reasonable: how can we universalize or even reason without tenseless concepts? And if reason is possible only through tenseless concepts then given the ancient dictum of Western philosophy that reality must be thought of as what conforms to the dictates of reason, it might seem that reality itself must be tenseless.[70]

Of course this conclusion is cogent only if one accepts its explicit and hidden premises, or has lost the ability or will to examine them critically. This is precisely the delirium of philosophy that Hume feared because it leads in the end to withdrawal and despair. It has been the merit of his work not only to have made us aware of the highly problematic nature of these premises but also to have shown us an alternative. It is through participation in and critical examination of the common life and its conventions that we gain a fuller understanding of our predicament as limited, historical beings, but also as free agents.

10.6   Conclusion

Given the richness of tradition dealing with issues of practice ranging from Aristotle and Hume to the modern pragmatists, it is not surprising that their influence on the various social sciences has been considerable, although the borrowing was quite uneven and often episodic. As already pointed out, the most direct influence of Hume can be noticed in the English school and its interest in the conventional character of state systems. But its wider implications, although adumbrated by Bull, were not really followed up until much later,[71] perhaps with the exception of Oakeshott[72] and his interest in the common world.

Most of the impact or common interest in a new action theory along pragmatic lines could be registered first in sociology, such as the ethnomethodological studies of Erving Goffman[73] and Harold Garfinkel.[74] Ethnomethodological studies stress perhaps most strongly the performative aspects of conventions

---

[70] Livingston, *Hume's Philosophy of Common Life*, at 100.
[71] See e.g. Peter M. Haas and Ernst B. Haas, "Pragmatic Constructivism and the Study of International Institutions," *Millennium*, 32:3 (2002): 573–601; Friedrich Kratochwil, "Ten Points to Ponder about Pragmatism: Some Critical Reflections on Knowledge Generation in the Social Sciences" in Harry Bauer and Elisabetta Brighi (eds.), *Pragmatism in International Relations*, London: Routledge, 2008; Friedrichs and Kratochwil, "On Acting and Knowing"; Gunther Hellmann, "Pragmatism and International Relations," *International Studies Review*, 11:3 (2009): 638–662. See also the special Issue of *Millennium* introduced by Damiano de Felice and Francesco Obina, "Out of the Ivory Tower: Weaving the Theories and Practices of International Relations," *Millennium*, 40:3 (2012): 431–437. See also Inanna Hamati-Ataya, "Beyond (Post) Positivism: The Missed Promises of Systemic Pragmatism 1," *International Studies Quarterly*, 56:2 (2012): 291–305; Christian Bueger, "Pathways to Practice: Praxiography and International Politics," *European Political Science Review*, 6:3 (2014): 383–406; Bueger and Gadinger, *International Practice Theory*.
[72] Michael Oakeshott, *Rationalism in Politics and Other Essays*, Indianapolis: Liberty Fund, 1991.
[73] Erving Goffman, *The Presentation of Self in Everyday Life*, New York: Anchor Books, 1959.
[74] Harold Garfinkel, *Ethnomethodological Studies of Work*, Cambridge: Polity Press, 1984.

and routines and see their "strategic" use as perhaps best exemplified by the "presentation of the self in everyday life" but also in a variety of other contexts. The notion of metis,[75] introduced originally by De Certeau,[76] but having, of course, a long ancestry in discussions of praxis, elaborates further on this feature, and it was put to good use e.g. by Iver Neumann to illuminate the practice of diplomacy.[77]

The wider implication of the Humean and pragmatic program on action is to distinguish actions according to different forms of strictness in rule-guidance. In rituals the underlying rules – even if they were learned by rote, of which the actors eventually are no longer aware – have to be meticulously followed, as otherwise the natural order would be disturbed. Certain aesthetic performances, such as temple dances or Chinese operas, also prescribe every turn of the hand or head, every step or movement. Then there are actions which are mainly concerned with enabling actors to go on. Here the tricks of the trade and their combination come into play, such as when Brunelleschi relies on the traditional know-how of the building trade but "invents" a new combination of connecting two walls and achieves thereby the astonishing cupola of the Duomo in Florence.

In interpersonal interactions it is clear that strategic interests will dictate the bending of the rules or the interpretation of common principles, in order to get what one wants, but with the (often only grudgingly offered) "cooperation" of others, otherwise conflict (the breaking of the other's will) takes over. In artistic performance "variations on a theme" (such as that of Mozart on "Je vous dirais maman") or "improvisations" in jazz are examples, although some superordinate rules might also guide the performative sequence (such as slow improvisations follow a quick one, or one in a minor key follows one in a major key; similarly in jazz the themes and the sequence of the soloists guide the improvisations). Finally, there are "revolutionary changes" which upset the old ways of doing things, as paradigm shifts in science or the change from the sovereign to popular sovereignty in politics demonstrate.

Aside from the performative aspect, the role of norms in social reproduction has, of course, been one of the main concerns in sociology and gave rise to Tarde's work, but also that of Durkheim and Weber. Through the reception of

---

[75] Originally it meant being inventive and knowing the tricks to get what one wants. In this sense Odysseus has as epithet polymetis (of many tricks). For a good discussion of the methis and practical reasoning, see Scott, *Seeing Like a State: How Certain Schemes to Improve the Human Condition Have Failed*, New Haven: Yale University Press, 1998, chap. 9, at 309–341.

[76] Michel de Certeau, *The Practice of Everyday Life*, trans. Steven Rendall, Berkeley: University of California Press, 1984, at 82.

[77] Iver B. Neumann, *At Home with the Diplomats: Inside a European Foreign Ministry*, Ithaca, NY: Cornell University Press, 2012.

the last two, via Talcott Parsons, it resulted in an interest in "social systems." Parsons thought that the problem of order conceived in Hobbesian terms could only be resolved by the mediations provided by a cultural system. But given his positivist sensibilities it is not surprising that his "theory of action" had been removed from a concern with the *propria* of action, and morphed into one of constructing a "theory" along the lines of "variables," dependent, independent or intervening. This in turn influenced the subsequent debates on compliance, on norm diffusion, and on norm cascades, which suffered from a contradiction between ontology and epistemology, as if the earlier criticism made by constructivists could be refuted by simply passing it over.

To that extent the interest in "practice" – without however changing the epistemological and ontological foundations – has to be considered with reservations. Directed by the animus of discovering the "philosopher's stone," or the "gluon," of what holds society together, this engagement with practice is based on the belief that certain parts of Bourdian and Deweyan analyses provide some interesting and useful tools for the old "theoretical" problems in IR. Not too much attention is paid, however, to the problem of whether these parts and pieces from different theorists "fit" with each other and whether the original assumption, that a closer look at what people do "most of the time in their social lives"[78] discloses without further ado what praxis is about. It might very well be true that routines are part of praxis, but so is improvisation and doing things differently spurred by *metis*, criticism, and the "renegotiation" of the existing order, or by a "re-description" of actions through historical reflection, which provide new meanings and chart new projects.

As such, this form of a practice turn seems to have little interest in how to conceptualize the "problems" to which we seek solutions, or in the Deweyan "situations" requiring our action. The underlying assumption seems rather to be that pragmatism just supplies useful "tools" for "problems" that have been around and that provided the fuel for various scholarly debates to which now these tools can be applied.[79] Such an approach then creates "continuity" in a discipline even at the price of considerable boredom and questionable relevance, since the old issues are paraded before us again and again, although their appearance has changed. The fact that at least some (perhaps even most) of the issues might be the result of scholastic controversies in the academy, which have little to do with deepening our understanding of what is at stake in acting and being an actor, remains then largely out of sight.

---

[78] See e.g. Hopf, "The Logic of Habit in International Relations," at 539.
[79] See the criticism by Ulrich Franke and Ralph Weber, "At the Papini Hotel – on Pragmatism in the Study of International Relations," *European Journal of International Relations*, 18:4 (2012): 669–691.

This gambit is what Abraham and Abramson have called the "outward-looking" version of the turn to practices.[80] In order to cure this rather apparent myopia the authors favor an "inward-looking" approach, which takes the philosophical contributions of pragmatists more seriously by accepting that *"theorizing" is itself a practice* and that we should harness pragmatism. This involves not only a more serious engagement with pragmatism, instead of using only bits and pieces of its conceptual apparatus; it also involves us in turning from methodological and theoretical questions to the "vocational" and ethical issues that a concern with "praxis" entails. To that extent the authors argue for going beyond the outward- and inward-looking versions and recover in a Deweyan fashion the "vocation" of pragmatism, which "demands that we recognize our scholarship as political tools ... [which] are integral to the constitution of a global public."[81]

While I consider this distinction of an outward- and inward-looking version of the turn to practice helpful – and I agree that an inward-looking version is the heuristically more promising one – I am not sure that we have to go beyond it, by adopting the "vocational" commitments, since such a step does not follow without further ado. Even the authors apparently have their doubts in this respect, as democratic processes could be "too slow" for attacking our global problems.[82]

After all, would it not be the first and foremost task of scholars to play devil's advocate in accordance with Peirce's logic of the duties of an epistemic community, instead of just endorsing what was said? In this context, I consider it at best an open question – in need of further vetting – whether the notion of a "global public" conceived analogously to the democratic public, which has been brought on and facilitated by the radical transformation of communications technology, is a viable political goal. If it is not, then it would indeed be difficult to argue for some Kantian-like a priori duty to realize it, despite all the presumed emancipatory potential with which it is credited. It will be the task of the last chapter to examine this question in greater detail.

---

[80] See Kavi Joseph Abraham and Yehonatan Abramson, "A Pragmatist Vocation for International Relations: The (Global) Public and Its Problems," *European Journal of International Relations*, 23:1 (2017): 26–48.
[81] Ibid., 19.   [82] Ibid., 16.

11 Judging and Communicating

11.1 Introduction

The last chapter provided us with some of the fundamental elements for analyzing action. As I tried to show, any attempt to subject praxis to a "theoretical framework" misunderstands how we singly and in conjunction go about realizing our projects. For that purpose we have not only to create a common language but also to form collective intentions and share standard solutions which are considered right and which allow us to overcome collective action problems by providing trust. To that extent our discussion seems to have returned to the beginning, but it still has to further clarify the issues of how we get assent to a particular plan or proposal.

Here "theories" suggest that assent is given because of the compelling nature of the assertions underlying our plans, which are guaranteed by logic and their truth conditions. But our discussion of Aristotle already showed that there is something amiss in understanding action in either technical or theoretical terms. Furthermore, our brief discussion of the practice turn, emphasizing habits and near automatic routines certainly has a point. However, nobody could seriously entertain the thought that those who get out of bed or ride a bicycle, or play tennis are "actors" in the sense of choosing their actions reflexively by weighing alternatives, and trying to get assent to his /her espoused position. Acting is also different from making a move in well-defined "games," even if in the latter case the importance of the strategic context is recognized, which also differs from merely "technical" endeavors of "producing something," even if we thereby alter the world and are changed by it (Marx).

It is in this context that, analogously to a technical interest in dominating the world or "others" (strategic interest), a communicative interest has been postulated that aims at human emancipation whose criteria can allegedly be derived from the language game of making assertions. The early Habermas explored this argument in terms of the ideal speech situation.[1] In this way Habermas not

---

[1] This is not to say that Habermas later (after the early 1980s) changed his position substantially, but his earlier works were emblematic for this line of argument. Since I am here not interested in

only provides a transcendental footing for those claims made in the process of their vetting but he also attempted to show thereby the advantage of an "ideal theory" for solving practical problems and normative conflicts.

I consider this argument problematic as it mistakes political argumentation and the role of "communication." There seems to me a contradiction that on the one hand persuasion is stressed – the better argument convinces – but on the basis of transcendental rather than merely prudential considerations. In the first case the "warrant" for the assertions is epistemic and implies compelling reasons; in the latter case, specific "commonplaces" (*topoi*) accepted in a tradition and prevalent in a given society are invoked when the speakers argue with each other. Winning the argument is then the factually achieved assent, which silences opposition. Thus oddly enough the ideal speech situation has again a suspiciously Hobbesian ring in that a unique solution is postulated, even if Hobbes considers the solution the result of the fiat decisions of sovereign. It is the precondition for building an "ideal theory" of politics *more geometrico* eliminating inconclusive deliberations among the concrete actors. But while I am convinced that the Habermasian connection between an ideal theory and the resolution of practical questions is faulty, I nevertheless also think that Hobbes relies on an equally implausible "apolitical" theory for settling practical problems

These considerations highlighting the conundrums of both of these constructs provide me with the opportunity to advocate a non-ideal analysis, based on the criticism of certain identifiable ills with which we become familiar through our participation in common life instead of a view from nowhere or imperative fiat. As already elaborated, this train of thought is indebted to Hume, rather than the modern epistemological project underlying much of our social "theory."

From these initial remarks the plan for the present chapter can be derived. Section 11.2 continues the archeology of praxis which began in the previous chapter and which draws on certain thinkers, from Aristotle to Hume, to Marx and the pragmatists. Thus the distinction drawn between the Aristotelian conception of praxis and that of the Marxian notion of "work" (and alienation) sets the stage for the discussion, which deals with "judgment," as elaborated by Kant. In that context I am particularly interested in the role "universals" play in

---

an intellectual history of Habermas as such, but in the use of "ideal theory," the criticism holds, even if it is no longer espoused by Habermas. For the "early" Habermas see Juergen Habermas, *Knowledge and Human Interest*, trans. J.J. Shapiro, Boston, MA: Beacon, 1971. See also his Christian Gauss Lectures at Princeton of February–March 1971, which later appeared as "Reflections on the Linguistic Foundations of Sociology" in Juergen Habermas, *On the Pragmatics of Social Interaction*, Cambridge, MA: MIT Press 2010, 1–103. Interestingly, Habermas never authorized his article on "Theories of Truth" for translation into English. See Juergen Habermas, "Wahrheitstheorien" in Helmut Fahrenbach (ed.), *Wirklichkeit und Reflexion*, Festschrift für Walter Schulz, Pfullingen: Neske, 1973, 122–165.

practical reasoning and in the answer Kant gave to this problem. This opens the way to thinking about "deliberations" and *reflective judgments* in a different manner than relying on subsumptions or inferential logic. This leads me to the more principled discussion of "ideal theory" in Section 11.3, for which I choose Hobbes and Rawls as my sparring partners. Rejecting the various solutions proposed by ideal theory, and also being critical of the use of speech acts in IR analysis, I provide in Section 11.4 a brief sketch of a more pragmatic analysis of communication that constitutes the world of praxis. In this context I do not specify the conditions of an "ideal" communication but rather focus *on the most obvious impediments to communication* that lead to an atrophy of political language. Since my position obviously is indebted to a particular notion of "politics," I conclude the chapter (Section 11.5) with some critical reflections on whether such a conception of politics can survive in our times. Here both the onslaught of mediated messages and the ascendancy of wishful thinking – exemplified by delusions of grandeur as well as their flipside: despair – indicate the declining role that general cultural resources play in people's "doings." Apparently people prefer to rely instead more and more on what Hume would have called false philosophy and false religion. While such trends have usually been interpreted as "progress" in the developmental schemes of a philosophy of history or as a universal trend towards "secularization," both the despair and the frequent choice to forgo all future choices by creating a fetish or embracing uncritically some absolute "truth" seem to indicate that our dominant master narratives are in dire need of amendment.

11.2   Aristotelian Praxis and Marxian Alienation

Aristotle's Response to the Sophists' Challenge

In making my case for a non-ideal approach to praxis I begin with some preliminary conceptual clarifications, hoping to avoid the confusions which we have seen in the recent debate about the practice turn. The clarifications consist in becoming aware that "acting" is used in different senses, which seem at first to fit the distinction between a wider and a narrower meaning. The former stands for our "doings" in the world, which includes the actions of *Homo faber*, such as producing something, or the nearly automatic reactions we have when we want to avoid e.g. a tile falling from a roof. But "our doings" also might entail activities, which accomplish their end by the very act by which they are executed. For example, in taking a bus which transports me from A to B, I reach my goal, but, when I arrive, nothing remains but a recollection (and perhaps a token, such as a ticket).

The general point here is that in all cases the actor does something, i.e. intervenes in the world, for some purpose – Aristotle's *hou heneka* (in order to).

This then provides the organizing principle for his *threefold* distinction of the practical realm. On the one hand, there is action, which is executed or performed, and there is "production," which aims at the creation of an artifact, on the other hand. "Production" is then further subdivided into *technical* and *artistic* production, such as creating a chair or a play respectively. Of course, there are overlaps, since e.g. a play is written in order to be "enacted," rather than having as its purpose a written-down version in the form of a book. As this example shows, the distinctions are far from unequivocal, as would be required by traditional taxonomy. We notice a further inconsistency in our usage such as when we call a "play," which is being performed, also a "production," as obviously many instrumental activities are necessary for its staging. Consequently, the point of our analysis cannot be a correct labeling, but rather to see what our use of the terms highlights or backgrounds, i.e. to understand the grammar which governs the use of the concepts, and the intersection of different semantic fields.

Further complications arise when we act jointly and our actions are part of a larger undertaking, such as Rousseau's famous stag hunt, or when we play a duet, as mentioned above in Chapter 1.[2] In that case our intentions, being part of a plan, have to mesh. Or we can act in a strategic environment, as with Weber's cyclists, explicating the concept of "social action." Then there is no joint intention necessary, but a coordination problem arises and the outcome will depend on the interaction of the choices both cyclists make and on "common knowledge" in order to avoid a collision.

Furthermore, the characterization of something as an action or activity emphasizes that they take place *in time*, since this is the most important frame, which is foregrounded.[3] It distinguishes what is going on when we act, from what happens in nature when the sun rises or sets, to what happens *to us* when rocks fall or tsunamis inundate terra firma. The latter are still not purely causal events, as our actions in such situations are not really "unintentional," but our usage strains the notion of an action, as is shown by the use of the term "re-action."

A similar confusion arises from the fact that many actions are the result of rigorous training so that they become near automatic (as when we skate or dance). These activities do not seem part of an explicit intention for each single action performed in sequence. They require only one explicit intention, i.e. the commencement of the performance, i.e. to skate, or play a violin concerto,[4]

---

[2] For an illuminating discussion, see also Raimo Tuomela, *The Philosophy of Social Practices: A Collective Acceptance View*, Cambridge: Cambridge University Press, 2007.
[3] See the important contribution by Jackson and Nexon, "Relations before States."
[4] For an interpretation as habits as an evolutionary response to cognitive overload, see Hopf, "The Logic of Habit in International Relations."

but since these activities are not natural (like near instinctual *re-actions*), they must have been learned, and some form of reflexivity and imitation i.e. "learning by doing" must be presupposed. These examples suggest that the stimulus/ response model of the conditioned Pavlovian dog – so dear to strict behaviorist action explanations, coming close to the *actio est reactio* of efficient causality – cannot serve as a general theory of action. Instead of pressing these activities in the Procrustean bed of efficient causality – because of a mistaken notion that only efficient causality can actually explain – we had better modify our conceptualizations in the opposite way. Three examples will suffice to buttress my claim. One demonstrates the potential for a new heuristic that follows from a modification of the rigid conceptual framework; the other two show what gets lost when the paradigm of instrumental action is extended to more complicated individual and collective action sequences.

As to the first: consider in this context the already examined example of wolfs hunting in packs. They must continuously adjust their actions to each other, satisfying the criteria of a "joint intentionality," as Bratman has proposed. But that means that our traditional distinctions of relying on rigid dichotomies of actions and events, nature and culture, need to be modified. Even "nature" is no longer the realm of pure necessity as soon as we also include animals in our analysis and study their intentional actions, including cooperative activities and tool making. Here Hume has provided us in his *Treatise*[5] with one of the first programmatic speculations for transcending the traditional vocabulary and as of late Alexander Wendt has tried his hand at explicating quantum mechanics, which requires from us that we no longer hold on to a rigid distinction between mind and matter.[6]

Now consider the consequences of narrowing the focus of or inquiry by interpreting all action in terms of instrumental action. This arises in two contexts: one of trying to interpret the Aristotelian *hou heneka* not only sequentially, relating it to one last "goal," by linking all the different goals together in a scheme of goals and sub-goals. Aristotle himself did so in order to place all of our actions within a meaningful horizon and to avoid an infinite regress in the absence of a supreme goal. The only problem is that thereby two decisive characteristics of acting easily vanish from sight, i.e. the performative element of an action, and its taking place in irreversible time, since the actions are treated like parts of an atemporal design or system.

The result of such a conceptualization is that it draws our attention to *the selecting of means*, as every action is only considered as a stepping stone for some other goal. In this way the illusion arises that all the steps are more or less

---

[5] Hume, *A Treatise of Human Nature*. pt. III, sec. 16.
[6] See Wendt, *Quantum Mind and Social Science*. For a review of this book see the symposium in *International Theory* (forthcoming).

"rationally" determined since an actor who wants the "end" must also choose the necessary means. But this conceptualization backgrounds the problem that, different from simple steps in a production process, practical choices in life are "episodic." No single line leads *ex ante* to a predetermined goal, even if that "end" seems to be clear, i.e. consisting in "happiness." All we have is a "chain of actions," which, when looked at from the final outcome, shows how one thing leads to the other without, however, allowing for a strict "backward induction" that would have allowed us to specify the steps *ex ante*. Instead, by looking *ex ante* at the chain, at every "turn" certain "opportunities" are identified, which can, however, turn out to be blind alleys, while other things which initially had not even entered our horizon, actually provide us with the possibility of "going on." Thus while a narrative recounting how one thing happened after another can be seen *ex post* as a series of "steps" to an end, a moment's reflection shows that this cannot be a causal path, which could have been perspicuous to us *ex ante*.

For this reason the overarching goal of praxis, i.e. the happy life (*eudaimonia*), can no longer be simply read off a predestined end, since this "life" is evolving in time rather than a one-track proposition.[7] Consequently, Aristotle's *eudaimonia*, usually translated as happiness, is actually not an ultimate goal in the sense that it dominates all others and is subject to the maximization criterion. It rather retains in Aristotle – despite some ambiguity – its link to praxis rather than to production (*techne*) since he conceives the *eudaimonia* as a "fulfilled life"[8] that results from having acted well in various situations and spheres (*schedon gar euzoia tis eiretai kai eupraxia*).[9] Of course, the fact that

---

[7] One could now object and point to "death" as the last "certainty" that informs our choices. But it seems that even here the concrete guidance is missing. This "certainty" has given rise to "hedonism" on the one hand – with all the problems that reappear again in "utilitarianism" whether there are "different kind of pleasures" or only one kind that has to be maximized, the problem well analyzed by Amartya Sen's "rational fools" (op. cit.) argument. On the other hand it occasioned speculations about the afterlife and leaving the ultimate verdict as to the worthiness of conduct to some judge in the hereafter as in the Egyptian religion that inspired Plato, and – in different ways – Judaic or Christian eschatology. In both, however, it is not the individual who is the ultimate "master" of his destiny, as deliverance comes from the "messiah" or is determined by God's final judgment at the end of times, or as in the radical version of Calvinist Protestantism by "predestination," which Weber explored. Another version emphasizes good deeds which are rewarded in the beyond and the "restoration" of the fallen nature of man through sacraments and the faith in salvation that lets the actors in the here and now conceive of themselves as only pilgrims who are "on the way." For an examination of the latter problem, see Mariano Barbato, *Pilgrimage, Politics and International Relations: Religious Semantics for World Politics*, New York: Palgrave Macmillan, 2013.

[8] On the modern conception of a fulfilled life, see also Susan Wolf, *Meaning in Life and Why It Matters*, Princeton: Princeton University Press, 2010.

[9] Aristotle, *Nicomachean Ethics*, trans. H. Rackham, Cambridge, MA: Harvard University Press, 1975, at 38, 1098b 1021.

eu prattein has in Greek two meanings – to act well, and to be happy – does not necessarily make for great clarity and for neat distinctions.

If we, however, move blissfully unaware of the differences between a systemic (nearly atemporal) conceptualization, as provided by *systems* and their *part/whole logic*, and the "fulfilled life," which stresses *temporality* and the *plurality of experiences*, confusion is bound to arise. In the first instance, we treat it as a good that, like a resource, can be maximized through instrumental or strategic action. In the second instance we treat it rather as a sequence of performances that worked out and gave us satisfaction. In the latter case, closure can only be reached through a narrative and at the end of a "fulfilled" life, by being satisfied of having acted well and having been connected to and appreciated by others. This is quite different from *Homo economicus*, who is neither sympathetic to others, nor does he care to be connected to them, save through arm's-length exchanges. He can then measure his "happiness" in terms of the "proxy measures" of money or things possessed. Solon's remark to Croesus (who had amassed enormous riches and power), that nobody can be considered happy, rather than just lucky before his end,[10] might be a bit harsh, even though his larger point of the fragility of a happy life is well taken.

By means of these considerations and the example we can see how a "systemic" or functional conceptualization of happiness as a goal pushes the analysis of action in the direction of *techne* and production. This necessitates the invention of a calculus in terms of individual "utilities" and of risks, which in turn is predicated on known distributions and "normalized" instances. Its extension to society at large, through the "felicific calculus" à la Bentham, who is supposed to provide the "greatest happiness to the greatest number," is then just around the corner, and the hoary problem of the interpersonal comparison of utilities arises. It is "solved" by the convention of "money" and the "willingness to pay" – *volenti non fit inuria* – as adherents of the law and economics approach would tell us. Acting "together" is then no longer about the selection of "common ends," but is modeled in terms of the mediated commercial exchange, whereby precisely the non-existence of a general medium of exchange in a society *for all actions* (and not for market transactions) is usually not appreciated and remains outside critical reflection.[11]

---

[10] Herodotus uses this Solonic message to frame his story of the subsequent nemesis that struck Croesus, in spite of all his efforts to insure himself against various feared disasters, and thereby provides a cautionary tale against the temptations of *hybris*. See his *Histories*, bk. I, 25–33 (Solon) and 32–96 (Nemesis), at 50–79.

[11] It is as if Baldwin had not pointed out the problems of this analogy in his seminal article "Money and Power," *The Journal of Politics*, 33:3 (1971): 578–614.

Marxian Alienation

Marx analyzed this tunnel vision on action as one of "alienation." Nevertheless, for him praxis is more like "productive" work – on and in the world – rather than a performance.[12] To that extent the emancipation of man cannot be brought about by a critical reflection on different understandings of the "world" but by revolutionary practice which breaks the old mold of organizing labor, i.e. that element that makes us human and allows us to transform both the world and ourselves. Only in this way can the dehumanization of man be altered, who, as *homo laborans*, is not only deprived of the fruits of his labor (as the surplus value created is withheld from him) but is also truly dehumanized. The world must be changed instead of being only interpreted differently.[13] The only solution is to treat labor no longer as a commodity as in a capitalist mode of production, so that alienation can be abolished, and the autonomy of the subject determining itself through its labor is restored.

There is, however, also another element in Marx's praxis that comes closer to the paradigm of acting as outlined above. Characteristically, it is mentioned only when he muses in his "German Ideology" about the times *after the revolution*, when man has gained real freedom.[14] The tension between these two conceptions of praxis, joined in his concept of "work" (*Arbeit*), dominated the Marxist academic discussion because their respective predominant tendencies are identified with the "before" and the "after" of the revolution. These phenomena deserve some further scrutiny.

Focusing on new technologies, Marx obviously believed that a surplus would be available, which – if the capitalists did not expropriate it – could satisfy all human wants. Why "labor," manifesting itself in tools, techniques, and skills, should also have the emancipatory potential that Marx ascribes to it remains, however, somewhat unclear. Apparently he believed that the new division of labor which he observed in industrial production carried within it

---

[12] For an illuminating discussion of the Marxian notion of praxis, showing especially the influence of Marx's sparring partners (Feuerbach and Hegel) and his opposition to transcendentalism see Axel Honneth and Hans Joas, *Social Action and Human Nature*, Cambridge: Cambridge University Press, 1988: 12–40.

[13] Karl Marx, "Theses on Feuerbach" in Robert C. Tucker (ed.), *The Marx–Engels Reader*, New York: Norton, 1972: 143–145, at 145.

[14] "Anyone can become accomplished in any branch he wishes, society regulates the general production and thus makes it possible for me to do one thing today and another tomorrow, to hunt in the morning, fish in the afternoon, rear cattle in the evening, criticize after dinner, just I have in mind, without ever to become a hunter, a fisherman, shepherd, or critic." Karl Marx, "The German Ideology" in Robert C. Tucker (ed.), *The Marx–Engels Reader*, New York: W.W. Norton, 1972, 146–200, at 160.

the seed for a new form of solidarity among the proletarians, who eventually would become the "universal class." But why should this solidarity, this reliance on others, born out of the necessity of the industrial production process, continue after the revolution, which had solved the problem of the expropriation of the surplus and had created affluence among all?

Things could be even worse: after the revolution the reflexive "production" of man through labor could just mean that man will have to adapt to the new complex technologies, which increasingly substitute for simple tools, such as egg beaters, or hammers, and sickles. The result could be a reverse adaptation, which is likely to prevent man from realizing human emancipation, creating instead dependencies and compulsions and representing new forms of alienation. That these fears are not imaginary can be seen by a brief look at the use of smartphones, tablets, and the incredible connectivity of the "(a)social" media. Not only Luddites and social critics have meanwhile the impression that the allure of endless exchanges without being connected to, or communicating with, anyone, or even without "doing" anything, has not much to do with leading a meaningful life.

The actions which actually set the course for much of the twentieth century came neither from the proletarian masses, nor from the intellectuals in the temples of academe, who worried about the appropriate exegesis of the sacred texts. It came from a group of *hazardeurs* who "putsched" and pushed their way into the Duma of St. Petersburg in the fall of 1917, which they promptly dissolved by force (January 6, 1918), after they had lost the election in November of the previous year. They thereby proved that new facts could be created if the "productive forces" were not used to create wealth to be distributed to all, but were rather perfected to become means of repression which got trained on people who were soon functioning like oiled machines. As Josef Stalin, the worthy successor of the propagandist Lenin, who had invented the myth of the Great October Revolution, once cynically stated: "people gone, problem gone."

Prudence and Judgment

Having dealt with the questionable argument of an emancipatory interest, the further issue remains whether practical issues can be subjected to a theoretical treatment, or whether the derailments we have noticed are not accidental. Here issues of judgment again enter the discussion. As we have seen already, Aristotle pointed out that different from a subsumption reasoning about a practical problem, both the principles in the major premise as well as the relevant facts (which might be decisive for choosing among competing principles) are subject to contestation and require a hermeneutic understanding rather than a straightforward inference. Aristotle therefore argued that in such cases not the truth (*aletheia*), but only some form of fit or correct ascription (*orthothes*) is required.[15]

This *orthotes*, i.e. the link of the particular to the general, is also not simply reducible to the correct interpretation of the rule as a text. First, not all rules (especially customary ones) are fixed in written form. But even if we have a "text" the correct application of the rule does not simply follow the going back and forth between the single sentence and the larger document, which form the hermeneutic circle. The correctness of the link between the particular and the universal in the case of a legal (or moral) rule has to meet a requirement which a purely textual understanding does not have to satisfy: its correctness lies in its ability to guide action, i.e. lead to "good outcomes," not only in providing a plausible interpretation. The reasonableness of a rule is therefore established by its effects on actions and interactions[16] and not solely by its membership in a larger corpus of texts – legalists, systematizers of law, and even deconstructionists (like Derrida) notwithstanding.

Kant has dealt with this problem in terms of a separate necessary ability, which must be present when one uses rules in practical contexts, which he called *Urteilskraft* (good judgment, often also translated as the "power of judgment"). Although he also uses the (misleading) term "subsumption," the further elaborations show that he was aware that something more is going on than engaging in a syllogistic operation. In a significant footnote he avers: "The lack of judgment (*Urteilskraft*) is actually what we call stupidity (*Dummheit*) and such a flaw (*Gebrechen*) cannot be cured."[17] As the preceding discussion made clear, this "stupidity" has nothing to do with a lack of reason. Rather it seems to affect the intelligent and dull alike, academics not excluded. The problem is:

... if (logic) wanted to show of how one should subsume, or distinguish whether something falls under a rule or not, this could be done only through further rules. But this again would require a new determination by the power of judgment (*Urteilskraft*) because a rule is involved. Thus it is evident that the understanding (*Verstand*) is capable of being instructed by supplying it with rules, but that the power of judgment is a special talent (*Talent*), which cannot be taught, but can be acquired only by practice. For that reason [this faculty] is a specific quality of common sense (*Mutterwitz*), whose lack no school can cure. Although schooling might be able to furnish rules derived from the insights of others and might [even be able] to somehow "implant" them in a limited mind, the capacity to apply them correctly must be in the "apprentice" (*Lehrling*) himself. No rule, which we prescribe to him with this intention, is secure from abuse, if

---

[15] Aristotle, *Nicomachean Ethics*, at 1140a 1110, VI 1143, 1103: 1144b 1118–1131.

[16] This does not automatically privilege a teleological reading of a text either: since the future is unknown, overall effects are difficult to predict, given externalities – law and economics fantasies notwithstanding. Judges are therefore held to ascertain the original intent (as difficult as this is) of the legislator in statutory construction.

[17] Kant, *Kritik der Reinen Vernunft*, A 134, 135; B 173, 174.

such a talent is missing. Consequently, a physician or judge, or statesman might have in their heads many beautiful rules for pathologies, laws, or politics – so that they could even become competent teachers of them – but they could as easily violate these rules in applying them, because they either lack this power of judgment (even if they possess understanding and can discern the general *in abstracto*) but lack the discrimination of whether a concrete case falls under it, or because their judgment has not been sufficiently exercised by practice and examples. Indeed it is the unique and great advantage of examples that they sharpen the judgment. As to the correctness and precision of the understanding, examples are frequently injurious because they, as *casus in terminis*, seldom meet the conditions of the rule and because they frequently also weaken those efforts of our understanding (*Verstand*) to apprehend rules in their generality, independent of their particular circumstance of experience, and thus accustom us to use them more as formulae than as principles. Thus examples become the prosthesis (*Gaengelwagen*) of judgments, which someone who lacks this natural talent can never do without.[18]

This passage provides much food for thought and also seems susceptible to different interpretations. There is on the one hand a nearly classical statement of Wittgenstein's argument, as elaborated by Bloor,[19] about "training," i.e. learning by doing, but, in the end, we encounter again a hidden longing for the "general," i.e. for understanding rule-following "independent of their particular circumstance of experience." Obviously this passage needs some further examination of what role universal principles play in determining choices.

Uncontroversial in the passage above is Kant's recognition that applying rules is not tantamount to logical subsumption, as his problematic use of the word suggests. His distinction of common sense, as opposed to intelligence, is too striking to be put aside. But if we want to know more about the way in which the will determines itself we have to consult the *Second Critique* where Kant uses a two-step procedure. He looks first at the maxims for action which agents have adopted for themselves. That means that maxims are not analogous to hypothetical imperatives (if you want x and if y is the adequate means to it, you ought to choose y). Maxims are thus neither moral per se, nor do they follow from an already known universal law. Similarly, although maxims are self-chosen they do not necessarily satisfy the autonomy criterion that is characteristic of the good will. Instead, they can be chosen for a variety of reasons, embodying a certain experience of going about in the world. To that extent they seem to follow the model of rule-conform action that results from having

[18] Kant, *Critique of Pure Reason*, B 172 and 173 (my translation).
[19] See David Bloor, "Wittgenstein and the Priority of Practice" in Theodore R. Schatzki, Karin Knorr Cetina, and Eike von Savigny (eds.), *The Practice Turn in Contemporary Theory*, London: Routledge, 2001, 95–106. See also Davis Bloor, *Wittgenstein: Rules and Institutions*, London: Routledge, 1997.

learned to follow rules. They are, so to speak, the material, presented to the "will" before it is able to determine itself.[20]

Kant's second step involves then a "test" of whether a maxim can become a universal law that we can prescribe to all. Here the generalization argument and particularly the formal criterion of non-contradiction play an important role. This process allows us then to distinguish autonomous choice, and "heteronomy," where I make arbitrary (*willkuerliche*) choices, guided by desires, traditions, or habits. For autonomous choices, only maxims approved by the categorical imperative count, satisfying the universalizability criterion. For example, one cannot make the maxim that I get the things I need by stealing into a universal law, since very soon nothing would be left to be stolen. Thus while universalization does rule out certain maxims, e.g. self-serving or capricious arguments, such as that I can do certain things which are forbidden to *you*, it is not clear how much work the universalization criterion actually does in providing us with reliable guidance on how we shall act.[21]

But this is odd for two reasons. First, it seems to restrict praxis – and with it politics also – to morality, a step Kant seems to endorse e.g. in his remark in the *Perpetual Peace*,[22] while in his last work, the *Rechtslehre*, he gives "heteronomy" a much greater role,[23] abandoning his attempt to derive the concept of law directly from morals. The second oddity is that without maxims to vet, the good will would be "blind" and could not generate any action-directives. But does this not suggest that reason can become practical only when we are already acting in a familiar historical world with its ingrained conventions, as Hume suggested and Kant himself recognized when he contrasted "common sense" (*Mutterwitz*) with logical inferences?

As we have seen in the quote above, for Kant the lack of judgment does not lie in an inability to reason but consists in a general misunderstanding of what rules are supposed to deliver. Kant's fallback on practice and experience is telling and to the point. Only in this way can we circumvent the semantic openness of rules and "go on." For example, we need not think long and hard to work out that the prohibition "no dogs on the escalator" means dogs in general and not their number, and we also see why this understanding can be

---

[20] Thus, in the *Metaphysics of Morals*, maxims emerge from "*Willkuer*," the realization that we can and have to act in order to live in the world. They are distinguished from the "will" which determines itself in accordance with practical reason. *Metaphysik der Sitten*, A 5: "From the will laws emerge, from *Willkuer*, the maxims."

[21] For a further discussion, see Kratochwil, *Rules, Norms and Decisions*.

[22] *Perpetual Peace*, A 88: In objective or theoretical terms there is no conflict between morals and politics. However, subjectively (because of the selfish dispositions of men which we need not yet call *praxis* because it is not based on the maxims of reason), it may persist.

[23] See Brandt, *Die Bestimmung des Menschen bei Kant*, chaps. 7–10.

extended to other live animals, thus being valid for cats and boa constrictors (although the latter might not even be "on" the escalator since it is likely to be draped around my neck), while a budgerigar in a cage arguably does not fall under the same rule even if he clearly is put on "on" the step of an escalator. Thus I must be an "idiot" i.e. caught up in my own world, or a prankster to boot, if after having gotten onto the escalator with my dog Ulysse, I claim that I am being ticketed unjustly, since Ulysse is only *one* dog.

The reason why we are able to cut such arguments short is simple: we have been trained by the many instances of "dos" and "don'ts" during our socialization, so as to understand what following a rule means. That this does not end all controversies and the fact that it may even escalate some of them, particularly when seemingly higher-order principles are invoked, is hardly news. But this phenomenon is surprising only for those who think that rules work like causes, and are supposed to insure uniformity in a more or less mechanical fashion, very much like a cookie-cutter or punch-hole. The capacity to "go on" acquired through participation in social life is not of that kind. It also does not have the character of "expertise," or of a technique. As Kant reminds us, even the expertise of rule-handlers (law professors and judges) is no guarantee of possessing good judgment and avoiding idiocies. The judge who applies a rule of "no swimming in the lake" to a case where someone tried to rescue a child by jumping into the water is precisely the type of person one would think Kant had in mind. Proper judging thus requires context-sensitivity for choosing and relating a general norm to the particular "case," rather than finding some "algorithmic" form of decision-making, solving problems by simply sub-subsuming a case under a general rule, or invoking higher-order principles.[24]

Finally, Kant's reference above to the problem of "abuse" alerts us also to the fact that stupidity might not be the only problem. Even more disastrous can be the willful misapplication of a rule for guiding decisions. This is, of course, the problem of the sophistic challenge, especially when collective choices are at issue. By making it appear that there is a neutral technique for arriving at a decision, i.e. one which is buttressed by logic, the Sophists not only deceived their public by pretending to know a better way of vetting issues of common concern, while actually hiding the fact that they were interested only in making in the "weaker argument the stronger one." After all, for them "winning" and serving one's own interest was the only thing that counted, but for that purpose

---

[24] For the difficulties that arise from the interplay between constitutional principles and "higher" European norms, see Aileen McHarg, "Reconciling Human Rights and the Public Interest: Conceptual Problems and Doctrinal Uncertainty in the Jurisprudence of the European Court of Human Rights," *The Modern Law Review*, 62:5 (1999): 671–696.

one had to create a system, seemingly based on logic, because it appeared to provide such a neutral ground, which could not be opposed by anyone possessing reason.

Kant's argument shows that more is required for deciding and "acting well" in the realm of praxis. Its *Urteilskraft* is hardly reducible to logic, not only because logic creates its own paradoxes and becomes indeterminate, as the famous paradoxes from Xenon to Russell showed – but because it lacks sensitivity to context and contingency. To that extent attempts to escape these problems through an "ideal theory" that abstracts from contextual and contingent factors seems like a giant misstep, notwithstanding its popularity, as Hume has pointed out. It is the task of the next section to elaborate on this theme by examining more closely three "ideal theories" that captured the political imagination in modernity.

11.3   Ideal Theory and Action

Language and the "Theoretical" Foundation of Society

The relationship between language and action attained in modernity a new seriousness since the older generative notions of an order of things reflected in both natural law and the *Sitte* of different "orders" of an estate society had been undermined by the skeptics' attacks, the religious wars, and by the social upheavals that had transformed persons with a station in life into master-less men. As we have seen, Hobbes suggested, therefore, that order can only be restored by the establishment of a sovereign, who issues binding commands through the promulgation of laws. Thus law "is not counsel but command."[25] Furthermore, as a Latin translation of Hobbes's *Leviathan* suggested: *non veritas sed auctoritas facit legem* (not truth but authority creates law) and it is not the length of time either which bestows authority on (customary) law (the "old freedoms of Englishmen").[26] Hobbes rounds out his attack against the traditional sources of authority by construing even the non-action of the sovereign, i.e. his keeping silent – which could be interpreted to mean that he feels "bound" by custom – as an authorizing act of approval. Thus it is "the will of the sovereign," signified by his silence, that lends authority to the rule.[27]

There is no point in reviewing the Hobbesian construct here, save to look at it as an example of his "theorizing" action that has little to do with praxis and with how we go about interacting in the social world. Since much of Hobbes's

[25] Hobbes, *Leviathan*, bk. II, chap. 26, at 312.
[26] This seems to be an apocryphal story, since the Hobbesian text of 1651 does not contain this phrase, although the sense it conveys is compatible with Hobbes's original version.
[27] Ibid., at 313.

animus is not only directed at the fanatics, who subjected England to strife and civil war, but also against the "schoolmen" (largely Aristotelians) and their teachings, it might be heuristically fruitful to consider whether Hobbes in his advocacy of developing a social "theory" does not blatantly resort to similar "logical" gambits which the Sophists employed.

The point of my undertaking is then not to go back to some form of Aristotelianism of yore, but to show that, first, Hobbes's idea of a social science built *more geometrico* is incoherent (i.e. it violates its own criteria) and miscasts the problem of praxis and action, and, second, that this type of theorizing "solves" certain recurrent problems by illicit conceptual means, which generate the incoherence familiar from contemporary debates in the different fields of praxis. That I am not offering a theory of my own – especially not one which explains more of the "variation" – is true, but besides the point, since I do not believe that theory-building is what we should be doing when we study praxis. Instead, what I can offer is some criticism in the hope that this might free us from some of the contradictions that have been vexing a "theory" of social action for quite some time.

Let me therefore begin with a clarification of the wider implications that undergird Hobbes's use of concepts when constructing his theory. Take, e.g., the above-mentioned "presumption" that silence signals consent. Those of us who are familiar with the principle in Roman law that someone who is silent seems to consent (*qui tacet consentire videtur*) are perhaps somewhat surprised by Hobbes's argument, but usually tend to go with it. However, we should notice that such a "presumption" is possible only after it has been consented to, even if not necessarily by an explicit declaration. This is why we are called upon e.g. at a wedding ceremony to speak up if we have reasons to object, or forever hold our peace. In short, nothing follows from being silent, or even from whistling, since the implication of an obligation is not one of logic,[28] or of empirical facts, but relies on an accepted convention and on the implicit criteria of what would be a relevant formula or sign for signaling that one is availing oneself of this institutional rule. The same is, of course, true of the "contract," which Hobbes chooses as a foundational act. Significantly, it is for him not a historical event – and Hobbes is very clear about that – but attains its standing through a type of *Gedankenexperiment* that shall convince us that in the absence of a sovereign all hell would break loose. The experiment suggests that the only solution to the posed dilemma is a general contract among all subjects that has transcendental status and establishes the obligation of the subjects to abide from now on by the sovereign's authoritative acts.

---

[28] If you want peace (the end) you must also want the means (the sovereign's rulings).

Such transcendental turns are obviously not limited to Hobbes, as the examples of Rawls and of the early Habermas show. Their respective choice situation is also framed by a *Gedankenexperiment*, which is introduced either through the specification of the "original position" or the "ideal speech situation." Since I have dealt, albeit somewhat cursorily, with the latter, something more should be said on Rawls. Although the notions of a "contract" and a "situation" are invoked, none of them has much to do with the ordinary language meaning of these concepts.

Rawls and Ideal Theory

Rawls constructs his "contract" among free individuals in terms of a situation of a choice behind the "veil of ignorance," i.e. neither knowing their own endowments, nor their future position in a society which has adopted the vetted principles. While the choice situation might, in a way, be "idealized" or unrealistic (as we do have "hunches" about what will happen), the former bears absolutely no resemblance to reality and empties the notion of contract of all content.[29] Although the "original position" is thereby supposed to rule out self-serving and strategic considerations – representing, thus, in a way, the impersonal "moral point of view" that issues in universal prescriptions – it is somewhat at odds with Rawls's first goal: to introduce greater realism into our moral reasoning, so as to correct Kantian abstractions and rigorism. Obviously opting for such ideal assumptions has to be justified by the hope that thereby a rational procedure can be found which leads to unique outcomes that demand assent.

I think, however, that these hopes are exaggerated, if not downright mistaken. As with the "golden rule" (do not do to others what you do not want others to do to you), the choice behind the veil of ignorance depends on some additional framing assumptions which are not spelled out, such as the risk propensity of the choosers (or does that also fall under the veil of ignorance, which seems to cover more and more?). How then are the "ideal actors" defined? Do only those who would choose fairness as a trump qualify? While most of us in our culture might be risk-averse, in more "heroic" societies it might not be uncommon to choose principles that allow for grossly unequal treatment among individuals. I might choose a rule that makes me a slave as long as I have a small chance of being an absolute despot (vide Cesare Borgia's maxim: *aut Caesar aut nihil* – either emperor or nothing).

---

[29] Why should anybody be bound by an agreement when he has not the foggiest idea who he is? Usually such failure to meet the background conditions underlying contracting invalidates the undertaking.

Second, by putting the clarification of principles first and the "vetting operation" second, we do not necessarily enhance the "realism" of our moral reflections. Putting the choice of principles first and their realization second obviously constrains the second choice, as sequences matter. But then again, we all seem to believe that having reached an agreement "in principle" – since then the details can be worked out more easily – we have turned the corner, even though we also know that in the second round (e.g. when reflective equilibrium enters the picture), the devil lies in the details and can defeat the entire agreement. It is therefore not clear why and how such an "ideal theory" – which starts with the normative principles and leaves the dirty work of realization, not only to a later stage, but essentially to others (the administrators and norm appliers) – could either maintain a society or push it towards "fairness" and greater equality. Furthermore, even if the actors are ignorant of the endowments and their later position, the veil of ignorance cannot also eliminate *any* understanding about states of the world and all practical experience of and "hunches" as to why and how certain arrangements "work" and others do not. If the latter were the case we would have no way of discussing and choosing consensually which principles or institutions we prefer. All we could say is that they are different and then we would have to roll a dice. On the other hand, if we have a society with rather heterogeneous traditions, several of them closer to the "heroic" way of life, it is not clear why egalitarian principles should be the preferred outcome.

In short, actors might come to the original position with the notion that inequality is important, because egalitarian norms would defeat considerations of "merit" (or even of *karma*). They might very well decide to vote against equality, even if they are aware that some of them will end up in an unenviable position. Before we belittle such an idea as a "Neanderthal" aberration, we had better examine our unquestioned preference for "free markets." Why are we clinging to the principle of free markets, although we know that such a choice will introduce stratification even if we start out with an egalitarian regime and make an explicit commitment to the provision of primary goods for all? We often even defend on the basis of such a "Neanderthal principle" the privatizations of gains and the socialization of risk as a "fair" arrangement since this allegedly insures efficiency, innovation, and growth.

At this point one might ask whether this game was worth the candle. Since we were promised a more "realistic" moral theory, one would have thought that such a theory would have to move towards greater psychological realism.[30] Instead it went the other way, requiring – as the traditional "moral point of

---

[30] See David B. Wong, "Psychological Realism and Moral Theory" in Ian Shapiro and Judith Wagner DeCrew (eds.), *Theory and Practice*, New York: New York University Press, 1995, 108–137.

444   Judging and Communicating

view" demands – that individuals set aside their projects if they conflict with universal principles. But even this much more restrictive requirement is a rather dubious proposition, as Hume, and Bernard Williams after him, have pointed out,[31] and thus we end up with even stranger abstractions. As in the case of the seduction by the Sophists, we suddenly find ourselves – who might have started out as Kantians with strict deontological principles and duties (even towards ourselves) – as part of the liberal chain gang, marching to the tune of some "coercive felicifier" (*Zwagnsbegluecker*).

To that extent the utility of such speculations seems pretty dubious. Instead of providing firm guidance in concrete situations, the clarification of principles actually does very little, since small changes in the background conditions have fundamental consequence. This disappoints our hopes that solutions of practical problems follow without further ado from the clarification of principles. I think such a disappointment is not accidental but results from the naïve notion that in practical reasoning the general somehow "determines" the particular, instead of realizing that both the particular and the general have to be vetted extensively, precisely because their relationship is not one of subsumption, entailment, or causality. The upshot of this argument is that it is extremely unlikely that there is a "silver bullet" or a "one size fits all" ideological solution that is the trademark of "ideal theory." As Gerald Postema put it: even if we focus only on morality – leaving aside that praxis is obviously a wider field – moral reasoning as part of practical reasoning is not served by this type of ideal theory:

The moral point of view does not presuppose an agreed upon code and practical reasoning is not just a matter of demonstration. While it is true that from a moral point of view we together attempt to construct a "common moral world" this need not be . . . a monochrome world of uniform judgment and rigid conformity. Our practices of counting and measuring, perhaps call for such lock-step conformity of action and judgment, but our moral practices do not, and if we value autonomy they ought not do so. Morality is not properly viewed as a code of rules; rather it provides a framework of thought and practice within which we deliberate and decide, *about which* we together reflect and argue. Justification within such a framework proceeds despite differing strategies of reasoning. It involves not only justifying particular judgments, but also justifying the way one has reached those judgments to others who may reason differently.[32]

But if this is so, then the explanation of actions is not like stating some logical necessities, but must make reference to the very maxims of the actors upon

[31] Bernard Arthur Owen Williams, "Persons, Character and Morality" in *Moral Luck: Philosophical Papers, 1973–1980*, Cambridge: Cambridge University Press, 1981, 1–19.
[32] Gerald J. Postema, "Public Practical Reason: Political Practice" in Ian Shapiro and Judith Wagner DeCrew (eds.), *Theory and Practice*, New York: New York University Press, 1995, 345–385, at 355.

which they act (Kant's first step). Consequently, we have to examine in particular the link that makes out of the competition for scarce goods "inevitably" a general "conflict" or "state of war" as Hobbes suggests. This is why Hobbes posits then as a consequence a "general inclination of all mankind, a perpetual and restlesse desire of Power after power that ceaseth only in Death"[33] and the irrationality of resistance to the sovereign as that would put us back in the state of nature. But this is a postulate, not a compelling inference from a possibility to an actuality. Instead, it has to have some reference to what (non-)ideal actors do under certain circumstances. Since in actuality several outcomes are possible – ranging from conflict resolution (agreement), to separation (avoidance of contact), exchanges (the Lockean solution), to closing the border (Chinese option), to minimizing contact (the Japanese solution to avoid conflict with the Western "companies"), to actual war or imperial pacification – a purely "logical" argument will not do.

These examples show that there is not one causal path but various options and we have instead to investigate also the temporal sequences of the decisions taken and see which ones lead to the escalation, and which ones to the de-escalation of the dispute. Taking instead an extreme case and using it as a template to explain a whole host of things – by allegedly making things clearer through abstraction and relying on "logic," while actually stripping away any objection either conceptual or empirical that might punch holes into that construct – is, of course, a well-known technique of the Sophists.

It is precisely these dilemmas that Hume tried to avoid by looking at the emergence of conventions, the establishment of governments and magistrates without some mythical contract, the institutionalization of debates in the "public" sphere, and at the use of the power of the purse to withhold execution and approval from certain policies, despite their prima facie obligatory character. It is precisely the emergence of a common space between the parties – the "interesse" that allows for the change in perspective from the "I" to a "we" that is important. Communication cannot be reduced to "clear reference" even by the fiat of the sovereign, which would be an empty undertaking – as I have shown in Chapter 5 – unless there is a common "community of interpreters" and the public at large understands that e.g. an act of punishment is not an exercise of gratuitous violence. To that extent also the recent attempt to ground a theory of politics – and of high politics at that because it focused on "security" rather than on functional "demands" – on a theory of speech acts is highly problematic not only because speech acts come in different versions, but because not all communication can be brought under this template. A further discussion seems necessary.

---

[33] See *Leviathan*, pt. I, chap. 11, at 161.

11.4   Communication

Representation and Meaning

While Hume pointed to the importance of various interlocking processes of enabling conditions and disabling actions that make up "civil life," he of course had to pay special attention to the fact that certain declarations of the "sovereign" – traditionally subsumed under the notion of prerogative – have special transformative effects, among them the call to arms or the "ratification" of diplomatic settlements, for which the sovereign enjoys the "presumption" of right action and can demand allegiance. But as his analysis and my brief historical review show, these are also the occasions when controversy is likely to erupt, as naming something a "threat" is not tantamount to having already resolved what is supposed to be done in response. Even when traditional rulers were "owed" obedience and seemed to possess full powers, they seldom were in the position of deciding only by themselves. The tribes had to be consulted, or a "parliament" had to be called – which some members rather missed because they knew what often was in the offing: both "death and taxes."

To that extent the absolutist prerogative was mostly pretense and the discussion of securitization during the last decades, which analyzed these problems in terms of speech acts, was somewhat confused.[34] The Copenhagen school got it right by emphasizing that "threats" are not mere descriptions of what happens in the world, unlike natural disasters. This cuts against the naïve notion of the "objective" existence of threats, to which "realists" (political and "scientific" ones) usually subscribe when they conceive of concepts and language as a "mirror" of reality. Threats in the social world are, however, mostly appraisals of deeds done by others, which call for action on our part. Thus characterizing an action (or several actions linked together in a situation) points to the strategic context in which outcomes are being "created" by the interactions of the actors, which often show an unpredictable dynamic.

The Copenhagen school was right again to emphasize that by this act of "naming" a message is sent to both the domestic and the opponent's audience. What is somewhat misleading, however, is the analogy to the Austinian speech act argument, which relies on well-institutionalized practices, which people often use in order to realize *their own* projects. If two people get married they hopefully know what they are doing and so no great controversy is expected.

---

[34] The debate commenced with the book by Barry Buzan, Ole Wæver, and Jaap de Wilde, *Security: A New Framework for Analysis*, Boulder, CO: Lynne Rienner, 1997. For a discussion of the subsequent interventions, see Juha Vuori, "Constructivism and Securitization Studies" in Myriam Dunn Cavelty and Victor Mauer (eds.), *Handbook of Security Studies*, London: Routledge, 2010, 52–72.

When students gets a doctorate, they must have fulfilled all requirements listed in the Ph.D. program, so that the president can after completion bestow the title of "doctor" on them – "in virtue of the powers invested in me." But precisely because of these reasons, many speech acts do not fit this bill very well and "securitization" seems to be one of them. That these conditions do not obtain in situations in which such an agreement cannot be presupposed and it is left for the parties to decide whether or not they want to avail themselves of the "institutionalized" "I do" or even a "signal," such as signing a contract, is rather obvious. Parliaments are after all created for debate and not just for "ratifying speech acts," and contracts can not only be invalidated – because the felicity conditions were violated – but can also be suspended or even terminated because of nonfulfillment of obligations or the impossibility of performance, or the "customary" understandings established through "reliance" and acquiescence fall into desuetude. The connection between language and action in the latter case is more complicated.[35]

Three issues seem to arise in this context. The first is the limitation that a narrow focus on language itself comes with by leaving other means of communication – through signals and acquiescence – to the side and also assuming that explicit expressions always somehow magically perform the "trick" which we observe in the "assignment of status functions" ("this is legal tender" à la Searle). The other is the equally problematic assumption that language is there to facilitate "communicative action." But that cannot be right, particularly if we consider the role of language in politics. After all, words like *basta*, or Luther's statement at Worms, "Here I stand and cannot do otherwise," are communicating loudly and clearly, but they are conversation stoppers. They indicate that the talking is over and that there is no return. This realization leads us to the general point that even if we are serious and sincere and exchange arguments in negotiations, we usually bargain and that means we try to make our proposals look good and cast doubt on those of the opponent. Thus strategic and the communicative parts of speech are nearly always intertwined and hardly separable in actual negotiations,[36] and the

---

[35] As already mentioned, much linguistic communication depends on sharing certain practices which serve as the background for decoding messages, as Grice's theory of implicature suggests. "The theory of implicature makes explicit a feature that is also characteristic of speech act theory. Linguistic understanding is rooted in extra-linguistic communal processes. Conversation depends on typically unstated background assumptions, norms, prejudices and the like, all of which may be said to compose the fabric of common sense. This common sense is not the product of strict explicit calculations; it is not arrived at by rational argument and inference; and it is not applied self-consciously to conversational situations as one often applies the rules and methods to semantic and syntactic analysis." Peter Steinberger, *The Concept of Political Judgment*, Chicago: University of Chicago Press, 1993, at 167.

[36] See Harald Müller, "Arguing, Bargaining and All That: Communicative Action, Rationalist Theory and the Logic of Appropriateness," *European Journal of International Relations*, 10:3 (2004), 395–435.

construal of domination-free discourse quickly runs into heavy weather, and time and the need to make decisions cannot be assumed away without misunderstanding the problem of practical choice.

Third, not all speech aiming at action is oriented towards mutual understanding, but intends to instigate action by subverting the common frame of reference. Thus Mark Antony's speech after Caesar's murder certainly tries to motivate his audience to act, but in its crescendo it wants to instigate a riot, not to accompany a dignified burial, or to commemorate. In his funeral oration Pericles aims at explaining his policies, uniting the audience, and preparing them for further sacrifice. Although both are in a way speech acts – as the speakers engage in a performance, not just in a description – they certainly do not satisfy the criteria of communicative action, precisely because they are, although addressed to an audience, neither construed in terms of a dialogue nor simply as a declaratory "speech act." What does that tell us about the attempt to understand language in terms of speech acts and communicative action?

As we have seen, in particular circumstances the distinction of speaking and acting indeed breaks down, such as when I say "I do" in a marriage ceremony. But does this mean that the special cases can serve as a *pars pro toto* for a general theory of social action? Already Hume noted the rule character of language but did not think that it could be modeled after an "agreement." Thus acting presupposes *purposes*, but can we ascribe to language as a whole a purpose that easily? Here the analogy to "light," which Wendt uses, is more useful. As light in its wave function cannot be seen but becomes visible only when it is reflected by something and the wave collapses, so language has to be something within which something can be said, referred to, and meant, without assuming a common purpose and those interacting.[37]

In short, language, which enables communication, has to accommodate and mediate between different practical goals and purposes. For that reason it must be, in a way, "neutral" as to the projects about which one communicates. Language as such has no explicit goal aside from supplying the medium within which we can exchange ideas and deliberate about selecting goals and means. As such it lacks one element that is central to action: selecting a goal and determining the means. When we talk, we do not usually want just to communicate and continue with it, without saying something (unless we are pathological iPhone users). As Bubner correctly remarks: "It is paradoxically due to the universality and the non-goal oriented nature of the language as a medium that the particularities of practical goals can be pursued by means of communication."[38]

---

[37] Wendt, *Quantum Mind and Social Science*, at 226–228.
[38] See Rüdiger Bubner, *Handlung, Sprache und Vernunft: Grundbegriffe Praktischer Philosophie*, 2nd edn., Frankfurt: Suhrkamp, 1982, at 173.

Could we even think of *the* goal of communication? Perhaps not, save at the margins when we deal with chitchat or mindless prattle, or think of the elaborations of someone who is known to be a "raconteur." But we certainly can think of using language not only for coming to an agreement. Furthermore, we, of course, realize that we can communicate not only by language, as some messages we get across by expressive movements (dance), melodies (communication of moods), or signals' or pictures, as already mentioned. Here the recent move to communicate by pictures rather than words – which the electronic media and the Internet have powerfully reinforced – comes to mind and has led to far-reaching speculations in the field of communication[39] and politics.[40] After all, a picture can be worth a thousand words, and from experience we know that the lone arctic bear, which can no longer move on solid ice, effectively gets the message of global warming across (even if it turns out afterwards that the picture was manipulated). Similarly, the planes hitting the twin towers in New York in September 2001, the student facing the tank at Tiananmen Square (1989), or the dead baby boy Ailan on the Turkish beach during the first peak of the refugee crisis (September 2015) impact on the audience by their vividness and immediacy. Finally, the "hooded man" of Abu Ghraib, as shown on the newscast *Sixty Minutes* (April 28, 2004), "says it all," as one commentator put it,[41] since these pictures not only seem to catch our awareness similar to a lightning flash, which shows us a scene in the crass light of hyper-reality, but also by the near automatic lessons they seem to encapsulate.

To that extent certain pictures have become "icons." They not only document something that happened (record), but point beyond themselves to larger structures of meaning. Thus the hooded man not only appeared next to the headline "Resign Rumsfeld" in *The Economist* (May 6, 2004) but was also the opening photo of Seymour Hersh's much quoted essay in the *New Yorker* and in many media reports.[42] It also engendered countermoves by the administration, such as President Bush saying that "this was not America" and Secretary of Defense Rumsfeld calling it "abhorrent" and something irrational and incomprehensible, which as an isolated incident nevertheless pointed to

[39] To name a few seminal works: Marshall McLuhan, *Understanding Media: The Extensions of Man*, New York: McGraw Hill, 1964; Jean Baudrillard, *Simulacra and Simulation*, trans. Sheila F. Glaser, Ann Arbor: University of Michigan Press, 1994; Paul Virilio, *War and Cinema*, London: Verso, 1989.
[40] See Michael C. Williams, "Words, Images, Enemies: Securitization and International Politics," *International Studies Quarterly*, 47:4 (2003): 511–531.
[41] See David Perlmutter, "Photojournalism" in Robert Hariman and John Louis Lucaites, *No Caption Needed: Iconic Photographs, Public Culture, and Liberal Democracy*, Chicago: University of Chicago Press, 2007. See also David Perlmutter, *Photojournalism and Foreign Policy: Icons of Outrage in International Crises*, Westport, CT: Praeger, 1998.
[42] See Lene Hansen, "How Images Make World Politics: International Icons and the Case of Abu Ghraib," *Review of International Studies*, 41:2 (2015): 263–288.

"the evil in our midst."[43] Apparently the administration's counter-offensive was not without success since, despite an initial uproar, Abu Ghraib did not play a decisive role in the subsequent election. Thus the "lessons" seem to be not as clear as they at first appear, since the icon, precisely because of its significance and its "fit" with a variety of symbolic structures – the hooded man resembles Christ on the cross and thus becomes a powerful symbol for "victimhood" – can be appropriated in a variety of ways, as Lene Hansen's contribution[44] and W.T. Mitchell's seminal analysis suggest.[45]

These brief remarks suggest that, despite their vividness, pictures do not really "speak for themselves" but are part and parcel of a universe of meanings and work through associations, transposing them to other images, or by making them through interpretations part of larger "stories," for which these images become the emblem, and serve as evocative symbols. While the link betweeen cognition and emotion attains a new salience when messages are mediated by pictures rather than words – perhaps best illustrated when a narrative or plot is "documented" in a film in which the viewer has the illusion that s/he is a participant in an event taking place at that very moment – pictures are not displacing verbal communication. This does not mean that the mutual conditioning of word and image does not undergo a significant change, which is one of the main issues in communication from Baudrillard[46] to the impact of the media on war,[47] discussions about the CNN effect,[48] or the transformative effects of the Internet, which has been carefully traced by Chiara de Franco.[49] However, this debate is far from establishing the thesis that verbal communication has been displaced by images, as blogs and even the pidgin communications of "texting" rely on verbal communication. Nevertheless, as any look at even the most highbrow papers suggests, most of them seem well on the way to become daily versions of the "illustrated paper" of yesteryear, or the *biblia pauperum* of postmodernity.[50] The most interesting point, however, is not the one of the rise and decay of certain media but rather, as de Franco suggests,[51]

---

[43] Donald Rumsfeld Statements before the Armed Services Committee, May 7, May 11, May 19, July 22, and September 9, 2004, as quoted in ibid., 281.

[44] Ibid.

[45] W.J.T. Mitchell, *Cloning Terror: The War of Images, 9/11 to the Present*, Chicago: University of Chicago Press, 2011.

[46] See e.g. Baudrillard, *Simulacra and Simulation*.

[47] See e.g. Philip Hammond, *Media, War and Postmodernity*, London: Routledge, 2007.

[48] Steven Livingston, "The CNN Effect Reconsidered (Again): Problematizing ICT and Global Governance in the CNN Effect Research Agenda," *Media, War & Conflict*, 4:1 (2011): 20–36.

[49] Chiara de Franco, *Media Power and the Transformation of War*, New York: Palgrave Macmillan, 2012.

[50] See e.g. the German weekly paper *Die Zeit*.

[51] Chiara de Franco, "Media Power and the Rise of Emotions in International Politics" (paper presented at the Annual Convention of the International Studies Association, Atlanta, GA, 2016).

the new ecology in which different ways of communicating have established themselves and are fundamentally changing the way in which we deal with the individual and collective choices we face as actors.

For the same reasons it also seems problematic to attribute to new communications technologies an inherent tendency to further democracy as some internet or Facebook aficionados have done. As the experience with the Arab Spring suggests, the respective technologies can be used for mobilization purposes but not for the institutionalization of viable and stable political systems.[52] The more sinister part is that they can also be used by governments for surveillance purposes and to spread disinformation. Perhaps the worst possibility in the long run is that surveillance and the "selling" of collected data is also carried out by private purveyors of information who acquire proprietary title, and it is therefore not surprising that the data collectors usually find it necessary to camouflage their more than questionable practices with the aura of a quasi-religious mission.

Whatever we might think about the above "bad news" about the communications revolution, it challenges singly and in conjunction the simple inference that the possibilities of incredible multiplication of communication channels have to lead to meaningful communication. As Sunstein's discussion of internet chat rooms and their use for radicalization indicates, the man/machine interface seems to systematically undermine the emergence of a common and ongoing concern.[53] As research in social psychology has already pointed out, most people prefer to talk to those who share their convictions, and being able to check in and out of chat rooms at no cost, instead of having to wrestle with common problems formerly vetted in a "public sphere," which leads not only to withdrawal, but apparently also to radicalization.

Frequently, things only change when we finally get or have to get to the table i.e. enter the discussion and start talking about common practical goals. Then "exit" involves potentially serious costs. But the "goal" of our efforts to communicate with "others" is above all to get *our* point of view across, and to make it understandable to others. Whether a common goal will emerge is, of course, an open question, but it is not quite clear how this can happen in the absence of some common standards for gains and losses and some conceptions of what one can positively "expect" from others (obligation) or what one can and should not expect (toleration), which is part of living a "civil life."

---

[52] For a critical (and rather pessimistic) assessment, see Evgeny Morozov, *The Net Delusion: The Dark Side of Internet Freedom*, London: Penguin, 2011. A similar note of caution is used with regard to the innovative and welfare potential of the Internet is presented by Andrew Keen, *The Internet Is Not the Answer*, London: Atlantic Books, 2015.

[53] Sunstein, *Republic.com*; see also his *On Rumors*.

These standards have to be, of course, non-idiosyncratic, conveyed by their impersonal formulation, otherwise acrimonious verbal exchanges can overwhelm discussions and negotiations. But the importance of such common standards does not mean that they are "universal" or that their force rests on their logical form, which serves a neutral anchor for all concerned. What is a "reasonable" risk or an unavoidable nuisance cannot be decided by formal criteria such as their potential universalizability, but is subject to assessment in terms of specific standard solutions, which have been accepted as precedents or traditions. (This is why rules and precedents were invented to begin with!)[54] Their only advantage might be that they work "here," but this does not necessarily entitle us to believe that they will also be working "over there," nor does it suggest that they are useless because of those limitations.

Finally, something more has to be said on the conception of inclusiveness and unconstrained communication, which Habermas in particular stressed. Even if we assume seriousness on the part of the participants and accept therefore the requirement of non-exclusivity in regard to the participants, it does not follow, as Habermas wants to have it, that everybody can chime in and raise any issue at any time. There is first the hoary problem of who can "count" as a participant, since it has considerable bearing on the proposition of who can "outvote" me and to whom I have to defer. Furthermore, whatever the merits of the latter criterion might be (unconstrained discussion), it is obvious that even debates conducted with an intent of arriving at a common understanding have to end at some point and lead via a decision to a definite action. To that extent any "ideal" that leaves out "time" as an existential constraint for all practical questions misses the point and it is not quite clear then how an "ideal conversation" can contribute to our understanding of the practical realm. Furthermore, without *some* rules of order and some commonsense notions of what is germane to an issue and what is "out of order," nothing is likely to come out of those potentially interminable discussions, unless one presupposes what one intends to show: that a solution exists, that it is unique, and that it is reachable. Of course, none of our experiences suggests that such a world exists quite aside from the logical paradoxes such assumptions entail, as I have discussed at length.

The Banes of Political Communication: Overload, Narcissism, and "False" Religion

The above discussion of the complexities should have driven home the point that given the difficult conceptual issues the hope of understanding political communications according to the debate among ideal actors in an ideal speech

---

[54] For a more extended discussion, see Kratochwil, *The Status of Law in World Society*, at 279–284.

situation seems quaint indeed. True, some questions become easier to decide if more complete information is available, and here the optimists suggest that big data and more information will resolve the intractable issues of yesteryear. They repeat the move functionalists made earlier, and before them the adherents of Comte who had elaborated on the virtues of new scientific knowledge that could be applied by new elites to problems which formerly only theologians or philosophers had addressed and with insufficient tools. Pessimists on the other hand point out that the most obvious impact of the information revolution has been that the actors seem to be increasingly overwhelmed by the messages they receive and that they become easy prey to misinformation or information overload, not only missing the needle in the haystack, but also being unable see the forest for the trees.

Although both responses have a certain point, and while optimists never will be convinced of the downside of things – insisting that objections, if justified at all, are just the "wrinkles to be worked out" – pessimists can never be disappointed by experience because any misfire that occurs is only what one would have expected. In this way both reactions represent primarily emotional responses, which Hume castigated as the hot passions of "delirium" and "melancholy" that miss the point, which only "cold passions" can disclose. They require an engagement with the actual complexities, aporias, and the opportunities that arise from our (limited) cognitive capacities and the new technological capabilities. This situation requires then a canvass of the field, the identification of how information becomes meaningful by being processed by the media, through which the agents receive their messages, and a careful criticism of the existing "explanations" and proposals, transforming information into useful knowledge for our doings in the practical world. While of course I cannot hope to provide an overall assessment since such an endeavor is far beyond the scope of this treatise, I want to draw attention to some of the neuralgic spots identified in the ongoing discussion on communication which deserve further attention in both the analysis of communication and of action.

For that purpose I shall begin my discussion below – as I have frequently done throughout this book – with some examples and point to the obvious or not so obvious puzzles that communications entail. Here the distinction between information and "meaning" is of particular importance for communication and serves as my foil. This then provides me with the tools to identify some of the most important hindrances to communication in regard to politics. So let us begin with the canvass!

The Problem of Information Overload

Some information communicated to us is unproblematic, such as the inventory lists we found in Sumerian temples that represent the first written documents informing us about agricultural life in Mesopotamia, although if they are

numerous we face the issue of how to select as we are threatened with information overload. Ancient "calendars" are more "instructive" as they are not
only mnemonic devices but usually contain directions when to plant or harvest,
or are decrees about the "proper weights" and measurements to be used for
exchanges. Sometimes, the signs we notice demand our attention, such as when
a monument reminds us of a past battle, or a sign lets us know which fork in
the road to take. Some other communications address our wishes and desires,
which become the filters for attention. In this way advertisements try to capture
our attention by the allure or the shock they convey through their "depiction,"
which prompt gut reactions on our part; after all, everybody "knows" that sex
sells, whether we deal with cars, watches, or perfumes, or that babies and cats
are "cute" and evoke our sympathies.

This raises the issue of how emotions and cognitions interact in "decoding"
the message, or rather in making the information meaningful, or motivate me
to pay attention to the conveyed message. Thus a victory monument might not
touch me, as I am only a stranger or foreigner, or it might become occasion for
reflection, as the remembrances of glory or defeat of "my people" are called
forth, or it might even result in a more distanced awareness of all the victims
who died in this battle, thereby giving rise to serious reflection, regret, even
sympathy.

On the other hand, some unproblematic street signs might become problematic in the decoding procedure as they are written in a different alphabet or
I might not be familiar with the "signs" and the message they try to convey, or
they might even represent attempts at deliberate misinformation. For example,
if I am participating in a cross-country competitive rally or am moving in
contested territory, even supposedly unequivocal street signs might arouse
suspicion, as we cannot be sure that their pointing in a certain direction might
not have been manipulated by competitors or opponents. Here the convention-
ality of the sign, the reference to physical features, such as territorial distance,
and the possibility of strategic manipulation already show the potential for a surprising complexity in meaning-construction, even if we, on the practical level,
seldom become aware of them, and our actions can usually proceed routinely.

Nevertheless, the role of "filters" and "selectors" becomes particularly important as they are supposed to create out of the chaff of impressions and bits of
information the meaning of a message. Sometimes, the unusual, the unexpected,
or the odd, serve as such a selector, as suggested by the old adage that "Man
bites dog" is "news" while "Dog bites man" is not, or as when we find a picture
where a canary sits atop the head of a sleeping cat. We are not only surprised
but might find it so "adorable" that we share it with others on the Internet. Or
we might actively seek out images and mannerisms of "celebrities" reported in
the media, in order to imitate the rich and the powerful in the hope that some of
their glamor or influence might rub off on us. After all, imitation has been

a powerful tool in shaping persons and insuring social reproduction, as our discussion about social reproduction showed. However, if this imitation does not result in a certain discipline and self-chosen and reflective "adoption" of certain "ideals" for which the celebrity is the stand-in, imitation becomes a fake and grows stale with the changing fashions, as the aura of a celebrity is hardly appropriable by replication only, quite aside from the fact that it is also subject to the fortunes of popularity.

If we become fans of such a person we can gain rank among our peers if we develop a certain expertise about their lifestyles so that we can trade pieces of gossip with others who are "in the know." We can become "friends" of a star on the social media without the idol ever having bothered to communicate with us. These figures of glamour or power thus become the objects of projections of our own hopes and desires, even if we are aware that the person in real life and the persona we produce in our imagination out of the "selected" information differ considerably. When celebrities die, or a misfortune befalls them, or when they are no longer "in" by having violated the codes of our projections, we suffer with them or feel betrayed. In the latter case, "shit-storms" are likely; in the former case, the pre-packed nature of the usually displayed "sympathy" becomes visible in its manifestations: the limpid flowers, the chain of lit candles, and the never-ending queue of stuffed animals that litter streets and places where such offerings are deposited. Thank God, no real sacrifice is necessary, but seeing that others "feel" the same as we do makes us part of a "wave" of wallowing emotions, which quickly has to find some new object for projection when the "news" gets stale.

Things do not really get much better if we decide to become more active instead of being just "consumers" of available information and take matters into our own hands. In accordance with Andy Warhol's statement that in the future everybody could be famous for fifteen minutes, we want to "share," or rather disclose, information about ourselves in order to make us significant. This leads to the freakishness of "gong shows" and the unabashed self-exposure on Twitter, where largely meaningless information, like "I am awake," "I finally exercised," or "how nice that the sun is shining," is available for millions of "users." The mere indication of one's mood is considered enough to generate interest, as such statements cannot be examined or contradicted. They are desig-ned to elicit responses from others of how "they feel" by either pressing the "I like" button, or to answer with downright insults when they do not like what they see.[55] The readily supplied information cannot create a common space, or

---

[55] Significantly no dislike button was provided by Facebook, as one wanted only positive news and although the pressures to remove websites that try to incite illegal acts – from bomb building to ethnic slurs or Jihadist atrocities – no real remedy exist to correct (mis)information, be it about persons or events. Again "users" can only send tweets to hashtags like #outcry or

define a common situation, since all that one encounters is the different "I"'s, who use this medium to transport their self-centered preoccupations into the public domain. This leads me to the second factor inhibiting communication.

Narcissism

How little these narcissistic preoccupations with the presentation of the self are able to create an engagement with others or a meaningful exchange wrestling with problems is amply demonstrated by the slew of sitcoms where the "lonely" individuals "kvetch" about their unhappiness, the lack of available women (or men), or their boredom, which they try to self-analyze by a vocabulary picked up from self-help books or sessions with a "therapist." The captive audience is treated to the silliest hurts of their childhood, such as when mother did not let them make mud pies, or took away a toy from them to give it to their brother. While this might come across in a comedy as funny if it is well presented, as a "self-advertisement" or an offer for genuine communication it is just silly and boring. The point here is not so much that the "themes" which are offered for conversations are mundane but that the form of the communication does not lend itself to establishing a genuine exchange. As one of the first reports on Facebook noted, taking issue with the official version of "bringing people together":

While Thefacebook.com [the original name of the platform created at Harvard in 2004] isn't explicitly about bringing people together in romantic unions, there are plenty of other primal instincts evident at work here: an element of wanting to belong, a dash of vanity, and more than a little voyeurism.[56]

In a way these observations seem to corroborate some of the earlier criticism made by the historian Christopher Lash[57] and the sociologist Richard Sennett, who both noticed a growing narcissism in modern culture and saw in this change one of the reasons for the decline of the public. As Sennett avers with

---

#JeSuisBruxelles or even "#JeSuisSickofThisSh-t. According to Meagan Willett's analysis on techinsider.io, this means: "The viral reach of the hashtag and meme – that all terrorist attacks are monstrous – comes after multiple bombings in Ankara, Turkey, this week that haven't received the same level of media attention as the Brussels attack." Megan Willett, "JeSuisSickofThisSh-t," March 22, 2016, on *techinsider.io* (last accessed May 17, 2016). Given this incisive analysis, all one can say is:"OMG, coolio."

[56] Amelia Lester of the Harvard *Crimson* on February 17, 2004, as quoted in David Kirkpatrick, *The Facebook Effect: The Inside Story of the Company That Is Connecting the World*, New York: Simon & Schuster, 2010, at 33. See Richard Sennett, *The Fall of Public Man*, New York: W.W. Norton, 1992.

[57] Christopher Lasch, *The Culture of Narcissism: American Life in an Age of Diminishing Expectations*, New York: W.W. Norton, 1978.

regard to codes which privilege private experiences as templates for understanding social and political life:

We see society itself as meaningful only in converting it into a grand psychic system.
We may understand that a politician's job is to draft or execute legislation but that work
does not interest ... us until we perceive the play of personality in political struggles.
A political leader running for office is spoken of as "credible" or "legitimate" in terms
of what kind of man he is, rather than in terms of the actions or programs he espouses.
The obsession with persons at the expense of more impersonal relations is like a filter
which discolors our rational understanding of society; ... it leads us to believe community is an act of mutual self-disclosure, and to undervalue the community relations
of strangers ... Ironically, this psychological vision also inhibits the development of
personality strengths, like respect for the privacy of others, or the comprehension that,
because every self is in some measure a cabinet of horrors, civilized relations between
selves can only proceed to the extent that nasty little secrets of desire, greed or envy are
kept locked up ...

As a result, confusion has arisen between public and intimate life; people are working
out in terms of personal feelings public matters, which properly can be dealt with only
through codes of impersonal meaning.[58]

This becomes particularly obvious when the narcissistic display is "answered"
by the members of the audience with a "shit-storm," victimizing the original
sender, particularly if s/he displayed some weakness or flaws. Here the offer
and the response seem more to be a sign of dovetailing neuroses rather than the
transmission of actual information that establishes a common concern with the
potential of leading to a communicative engagement. Meaningful communication needs not only give-and-take among different positions, it also requires
the ability to listen and reflect and thus presupposes a distancing from one's
own notions and prejudices. Here the notion of "interest" becomes crucial in
the two meanings of the term. First, in the sense of *mihi interest*, i.e. I communicate that I am committed to something and want to send a signal as I find
myself in a situation that creates some unease or puzzlement; this is why
I address others. But such a stance also entails that I have to be willing to be led
by my own reflections and those of others in order to "go on" by correcting my
original "hunch"[59] or fears, and tackle a genuine problem rather than persist

---

[58] Sennett, *The Fall of Public Man*, at 4–5.
[59] Of course the communication of joy seems to contradict this observation. But why should
I boast to others when I succeeded or was lucky? Would it not be like blowing one's own horn –
and have perhaps the same informative value as the graffiti that adorn a bridge and inform me
that "Mario loves Elsa forever" or that "Juve [archenemy of Florence's soccer team] merda"?
Why should anyone be interested in such expressions unless we have established a special
relationship and mutually consider the other(s) significant? If everybody is now, because of
technological advances, "special" for us, nobody is. Would the information not otherwise be
like advertisements, which we often pay money for an "app" to suppress? Even the collective
display of enthusiasm at fan miles frequently raises the suspicion that the exuberance displayed

in my vague mood. This is why Hume pointed out the importance of "commerce and conversation" with others, as it opens a new space between the interlocutors which is constituted by that which is "in-between" them (*interesse*). It not only implies the imaginative taking of different positions in the interaction, but, above all, the presence of other, different perspectives, as suggested by Aristotle.

In short the intimacy which the virtual availability of everybody "out there" conjures up – and which narcissistic preoccupations reinforce – is not just a pious hope but counter-productive to developing good judgment and finding viable solutions for one's individual or social projects. As in the case of "confirmatory research," looking right away for approval rather than criticism and help, is choosing the wrong tools and strategies for orienting ourselves in this world. The point here is that finding those who are in sync with our feelings and moods is not only difficult practically – which explains why we are so easily seduced by our own "projections" – there is also the *conceptual impossibility* of bringing everybody and everything under one tent. After all, we cannot but notice that every inclusion requires exclusion, since concepts have meaning only when they relate to other concepts and that means that boundaries – even if not fixed once and for all, as the old ontology suggested – need to be drawn. This realization cuts against the rationality of trusting a solution which relies on the undifferentiated feeling of "togetherness," but also against the "privatism" (idiocy) of opting for simple value-maximizing strategies, which are bound to have unintended consequences. Thus a moment's reflection discloses that e.g. not all actors can maximize e.g. their security at the same time, as the security dilemma indicates. Attempts to do so will court disaster in virtually all cases, so that we have to learn to live with certain insecurities and we must rather find a common, intersubjective understanding that can mediate those tensions.[60]

Similarly, the promise of "infinite freedom," usually propagated by new technologies that seem to suspend the traditional limits, is a chimera, since we quickly notice that in our pursuits we interfere with others and vice versa. Thus freedom cannot be infinite, even if, with typical hubris, "Infinite Freedom"

---

is just an attempt to drown out the deafening silence that comes from the despair of an empty life.

[60] In this context it seems noteworthy that "security" and "safety" point, despite their considerable overlap, to potentially different strategies. Security has reference to action and an actor who must make choices to "procure" security. The semantic of "safety" points to a state of feeling in which e.g. "victims" who have taken refuge now feel "safe." See also "safe houses" in which witnesses for important trials are kept and are out of harm's way. Here no chances can be taken which would be taken under normal circumstances. In this line, security, which has been institutionalized by the systemic "public" threat of the Hobbesian sovereign, is increasingly displaced by continuous surveillance of public and private agents. For a further discussion, see David Lyon, *Surveillance Studies: An Overview*, Cambridge: Polity Press, 2007.

was the original codename for the Iraq intervention. As Martti Koskenniemi astutely analyzes the result of such "thinking" (or rather its denial, by wishful thinking):

Political freedom untainted by knowledge turns power into an apparently unending source of gratifications with tragedy looming just around the corner. In the early spring of 2003 I was in New York ... when an expert explained on Fox TV that US soldiers should behave with dignity when Iraqi women throw candy at their feet, since this is the traditional Iraqi way of greeting liberators. The prospect of being seen as "heroes" must have so warmed the hearts of the audience that it stunned the mind against everything we know or may suspect of other societies.[61]

Similarly, the virtually unlimited number of "friends" – at least they have to register, different from the general warm feelings that envelop us when we think about "humanity" along the above lines – can only be imaginary, and many believers in such promises easily become the prey of pranksters (if they are lucky), or of persons for whom the infliction of pain or spreading rumors and "doing others in" is a favorite pastime. Given their perverse preferences, the available media create golden opportunities for mobbing since employing such a strategy remains virtually costless for the perpetrator, and remedies for correcting false rumors are hardly available to the victims.[62] At least there is a glimmer of hope, as the younger generation seems to have lost its enthusiasm for exhibitionism on Facebook.

In the same vein, given the available technology and its potential for misuse, it seems that "shit-storms," hate-messages, and rumors are now being increasingly spread by "bots" (computers) which manipulate the social media by opening accounts – apparently 10,000 accounts can be bought for €499 – and flooding the internet exchanges with their propaganda, pretending to be real persons. Facebook itself estimates that the number of bot-accounts worldwide amounts to fifteen million, with the numbers rapidly growing. Right-wing pro-Russian propaganda during the Ukraine crisis,[63] "cyber attacks" by the Islamic State group, and the recent postings at Chancellor Merkel's Instagram account (particularly during the refugee crisis in 2016) also suggest that these bots are

---

[61] Martti Koskenniemi, "Constitutionalism as Mindset: Reflections on Kantian Themes about International Law and Globalization," *Theoretical Inquiries in Law*, 8:1 (2007): 9–36, at 27.

[62] Only recently some online platforms have appeared that examine critically the content of the promulgated "news" or rumors. Here the website mimikama.at founded in 2011 by a "Verein zur Aufklaerung von Internetmissbrauch," based in Vienna, has to be mentioned. Although e.g. Facebook has been active in removing child pornography, or propaganda inciting violence or propagating racial or religious hatred, most of the messages violating fundamental standards of truthfulness or respect for individual rights remain unexamined as they are "private" statements falling under the right to free information, which, of course does not prevent those collecting such utterances and thereby making "data" out of them from selling them to public and private "customers."

[63] #ukraine.

fed and coordinated by "troll factories," i.e. by hired teams of hackers and intelligence agents. They have become part of the new battlefield of a cyber war,[64] which no longer seems to possess geographic, temporal (as it goes on continuously), or even subject matter limitations.[65]

But putting things in perspective, it is not surprising that "hoaxes," already familiar from the "yellow press" availing itself of the gullibility of its audience, or worse, the anxieties of people in order to conjure up phantoms or enhance potential dangers – have returned with a vengeance in the echo chambers of chat rooms and the virtual reality of the Internet.

But perhaps the most worrisome innovations are the likes of the "chatbot" Tay developed by Microsoft and entering through Twitter in an ill-fated experiment. It attempted to demonstrate the potential of artificial intelligence.[66] After a very short time Tay had 75,000 followers, "liking" the statements it had generated, such as "Hitler was right," "I hate Jews," calling President Obama an "ape," etc. While Tay had apparently very quickly learned from what was "out there," – the robot was conceived as a "curious teenager" – its capacity to distinguish had virtually "no filters," which are ingrained in real persons through deliberate socialization and not through random exposure. Tay, however, quickly fashioned its strategy according to what it mostly encountered in order to gain followers. Thus, contrary to the argument that machines cannot "learn," the answer seems to be: they do, but apparently do so with a vengeance when left to their own devices. The larger point here is not the traditional machine vs. man dichotomy. Rather, the real issue is that without the judgments and decisions of real actors, atrocities and evil do not just fall by the wayside. They are not weeded out by randomness, but rather quickly become our companions.

All this bodes ill for politics, as the co-constitution of self, society, and the global system are called into question. After all, much of our traditional ways of "building the city of man" depended on the silent or not so silent acceptance of conventions and traditions that stabilized expectations. But as we have seen, social reproduction is being overwhelmed by both vanishing faith in traditional solutions and the emergence of new capabilities whose transformative potential is difficult to fathom, fueling thereby both fears and messianic hopes. At the same time, the art of posing questions and the struggle to define concrete

---

[64] See Oliver Georgi, "Automatisierter Hass im Netz," *Frankfurter Allgemeine Zeitung*, May 24, 2016, accessed at www.faz.net/-gpf-8hc5h.

[65] See the attacks on banks, on defense facilities, on technology firms and on the media of (un-) civil society. For an interesting discussion of the effects of information technology on social systems, see Christian Fuchs, *Internet and Society: Social Theory in the Information Age*, New York: Routledge, 2008.

[66] Wibke Becker, "#Debatte," *Frankfurter Allgemeine Sonntagszeitung* (Meinung), April 24, 2016, at 12.

problems are largely overwhelmed by "technical considerations," which often issue in the argument that no viable alternatives exist; and if any critical energy has not been drowned out by then, the attention is focused only on whether or not one is on the "right side." The profession of personal beliefs substitutes for the analysis of problems, and sharing them with others is more a demonstration of faith in "fundamental values." No wonder that trust in gut feelings masquerades then as an exercise in judgment and analysis addressing common problems. Here Hume's remarks about the deleterious effects of "false religion" are telling.

"False" Religion

Reassuring ourselves about our intentions thus dispenses with the need to frame questions and search for evidence. Politics as the art of the possible dissolves itself into "professions" (both in the sense of "giving witness" to certain values one holds, and of the tricks of trade one has been "trained in," which tend to reify practical problems by making them appear as technical problems). The first problem has been analyzed in terms of the "liquidity" of this form of modernity[67] – alluding to Marx's remark in the Communist Manifesto "that all that is solid melts into air, all that is holy is profaned."[68] The second problem is usually dealt with by some speculations about the "end of history" and the "professed" assurance that a discourse on rights and the growth of international institutions can provide the best prospects for a future which we cannot see, but whose contours can already be made out.

Without wanting to reopen this discussion again, it is interesting how quickly the language in both discourses takes on religious overtones, by which the meaning of these transformative changes is communicated. Even Google thinks that its success has something to do with its officially propagated "Don't be evil" mantra.[69] When Loyd Blankfein, former Chief of Goldman Sachs, informed the US Congress[70] that the unprecedented self-enrichment of brokers speculating against the assets of their clients was just "doing God's work," then one had better have one's handkerchief out in time. And even Mark Zuckerberg, whose only purpose in life seems to be to "motivate" people to spend more and more of their time on Facebook or playing trivial games, is

---

[67] See e.g. Zygmunt Bauman, *Liquid Modernity*, Cambridge: Polity Press, 2000.
[68] See Marx and Engels, "Manifesto of the Communist Party," at 476.
[69] See the book by two Google executives Eric Schmidt and Jonathan Rosenberg, *How Google Works*, New York: Grand Central Publishing, 2014.
[70] See Daily Mail Reporter, "Goldman Sachs Chief Says 'We Do God's Work' as He Defends the Bank's Mega Profits," *Daily Mail*, November 8, 2009, accessed at www.dailymail.co.uk/news/article-1226114/Goldman-Sachs-chief-says-Gods-work-defends-banks-bumper-profits.html on May 29, 2016.

well aware that without some quasi religious gloss on the liberating effect of such an addiction he will not be able to sell more and more data to firms and advertising agencies, "liberating" us thereby of our most important endowments: liberty and time. In a perverse way, Weber's "spirit of capitalism" seems to be alive and well in a supposedly secular society. On a more serious take, we could just interpret this phenomenon in terms of the Kantian observation that reasons seems to be unable to let go of questions which transcend their own capacity, and Marx's reference to the "holy" that is now profaned seems to articulate this same desire for ultimate answers.

But contrary to all the disappointing experiences of the immanentization of the transcendent through revolutionary action, we have not left behind "once and for all" the conceptual baggage of previous epochs.[71] In the past these vocabularies and the strategies they spawned have led to jihads, crusades, millennial sectarian violence and its brutal suppression by the ruling powers, not to mention the protracted conflicts between church and state in the West. But it took the French Revolution to reveal that secularization and its cult of reason could unleash similar forces, despite the declared objectives of the Enlightenment project. Even worse, the grand "terror" – quite different from the arbitrariness of the Old Regime – was now becoming part of the state machine and has ever since been put to use in identifying enemies, who were no longer necessarily some "others," who, as agents of a foreign sovereign, fought for some opposing interests, but were those internals or externals who had to be put "outside of humanity," as *ex lex* or, more recently, as an enemy of humanity defined by an "enemy criminal law."

These somber realizations were of course still in the future when Hume warned of the errors of what he called "false religion." But Hume already had an inkling of the politics of universal suspicions and the virtue/vigilantism connection which an uncritically lived life can embody, although people do their "duty," or at least have no manifest evil intentions when committing atrocities. The problem of modern evil seems therefore, at first sight, quite different from traditional evil, as it is no longer attributed to a base character or even to a criminal organizations – the favorite etiology for atrocities used by international criminal law, as we have seen. It is instead the result of apparently normal people and their actions.

Here Eichmann comes to mind (whom Arendt observed) and the increasing disconnect of mere "routines," such as throwing a switch and administering electroshocks (as in the Milgram experiment) or playing "guard" (as in the

---

[71] For good discussion of the generative impact of religion on our conceptualization of the social world, going far beyond the platitudes familiar from some "interfaith dialogues" see Nicholas Rengger, "On Theology and International Relations: World Politics Beyond the Empty Sky," *International Relations*, 27(2), 2013: 141–157.

Stanford prison experiment), or releasing incendiary or even atomic bombs. Zygmunt Bauman, who examined the newer literature on mass atrocities, has powerfully made this argument.[72] Following in his interpretation the analysis of Guenther Anders[73] (the philosopher and media critic, who was first husband of Hannah Arendt during the French exile), Bauman argues (in a way similar to Hume) that the crisis is one of "imagination":

... the human power to produce (*herstellen*: having things done, plans implemented) has been in recent decades emancipated from the constraints imposed by the much less expandable power of humans to imagine, re-present and render intelligible (*vorstellen*). It is in that relatively new phenomenon, the hiatus (*Diskrepanz*) separating human creative and imagining powers, that the contemporary variety of evil set its roots ...

The reality which the perception orphaned by imagination grasps and beyond which it is unable to reach, is always already made, technologically prefabricated and operated ... as Anders points out one would not gnash teeth when pressing a button ... A key is a key ... The gesture that will initiate the Apocalypse would not differ from any of the other gestures – and will be performed, as all other identical gestures, by a similarly routine-guided and routine-bored operator.[74]

Thus while the intersubjectivity of standards is a defense against idiosyncratic justification by relying e.g. on the "pure heart argument" (or "kill a commie for Christ") – as is the universalization argument – it is not any insurance against collective malformations that occur when a critical examination is aborted by carelessness or tabooization. While declaring some commandments or standards as "sacred" and putting them beyond debate has been the dominant solution to the problem of choice – a move frequently criticized by the Enlightenment – the analogy to the taboo of "ultimate values" is much less explored. This is all the more surprising since it is not uncommon in presumably "secular discourses," which are assumed to be immune to such temptations. There exists also in those societies, however, a virtually never acknowledged conversation-stopper that results from the concentration on principles and ultimate values, which corrupts the discourse and tends to ostracize dissenters.

[72] Zygmunt Bauman, "A Natural History of Evil," available at S.I.M.O.N. (Shoah Intervention Methods Documentation), www.vwi.dc.at/images/Downloads/SWL_Reader/Bauman/SWL-Reader-Bauman.pdf, last accessed May 25, 2016.
[73] Guenter Anders (born as Guenter Stern in 1902; "Anders" was his later pseudonym) was a German (Austrian) philosopher and media critic who is hardly known outside of Germany and France. As a student of Cassirer, Heidegger, and Husserl, who served as mentor of his thesis (1923), he has published widely in different fields ranging from philosophy to religion, to literary criticism, the Holocaust, to poetry, music, and TV. He went into exile with his first wife Hannah Arendt, where the distantly related Walter Benjamin joined them. Later he lived in the US, where he tried his hand in Hollywood as a scriptwriter, before going to work for the US government and returned to Europe after the war and died in Vienna in 1992.
[74] Zygmunt Bauman, "A Natural History of Evil," at 13f.

As I tried to argue, such a degeneration can be circumvented only by "reopening" the problems and looking at "situations" and taking seriously the issue of whether or not the fact pattern actually justifies the invocation of a normative principle or a basic value. This is shown in the example of the Kantian "bad man," who knocks on my door and wants to know whether his victim is in my house and puts me in the quandary of responding "truthfully" or by lying to him. I suggested in my argument above that conceptualizing this "situation" as one of "truth telling" is inadequate as it misconceives the characterization of the situation and hides the conflict of duties (since the friend who is hiding in my house asked me for help in escaping from his pursuer). In that case we would be helped more if we understood that the justifiability of appraisals has to do with making exceptions or exemptions for which judicial decision-making provides the better template than "analytical" ethics concerned with the clarification of abstract principles. Of course, such an approach also has its problems which have to be attended to. The point here was simply to call attention to the fact that the ethicist has not the automatic first call on deciding the issues, precisely because most situations are complex and cannot be decided by one principle or one description of the relevant facts. This is why often different "authorities" have to be consulted and are entrusted by law to make ultimate decisions and/or limit liabilities. Thus doctors can decide when someone is dead, although the standard of brain death is far from uncontroversial.

The easiest case for limiting liability is that of exempting the persons forming a corporation, or of invoking the e.g. "superior in command" principle, which leads to the hoary problem in international criminal law of how to yoke this principle with individual culpability in order not to fall into the trap of universal culpability. Another problem is, of course, that limiting liability provides a powerful figure of thought, which consists in and justifies compartmentalizing attention. Doing one's job but refusing to take responsibility for larger issues that are not one's own business is then the virtually inevitable result. This leads to the pathologies of organizational decision making and, on the individual level, to withdrawal and even callousness that we so frequently observe.

However, such a narrower focus is not necessarily already "immoral" since minding one's own business and not meddling in others' is one of the primary practical rules for preventing the escalation of conflicts. Furthermore, the distinction between public and private issues is fundamental for political orders and it is also a fact of life that morality does not have an answer to all questions, as many dilemmas cannot be solved in terms of providing a compelling algorithm for tackling them, while prescriptions for supererogatory efforts are likely to be impracticable, such as having to risk one's life in emergency situations (going even beyond the "good Samaritan"). They might be cause for admiration, but extraordinary sacrifices (as distinct from normal duties) usually have to be enforced, if we want more than "normal" compliance by the actors.

These are the sacrifices imposed by military discipline or specific professional duties (such as the captain being the last to leave the ship). Here again things get rather complicated since in the latter example morality might coincide with professional duty, but such supererogation might lose its moral appeal (at least for Kantians) since it is not purely voluntary but induced by coercion.

Given these complexities it is not surprising that people get confused and prefer to keep their heads down, doing what they are accustomed to and taking the familiar landmarks as guideposts, even if their manipulation becomes obvious. Better safe than sorry, and in this way denial can easily become the maxim, although occasionally dissatisfaction breaks through – largely when we read about atrocities *committed by others*. Then our judgments are quicker and our response faster and arguments that "one should do something about it" abound, as we feel the shame that comes with our inaction. But then the many hands problems arises, questions about priorities have to be answered, and decisions as to who should lead and/or bear the brunt of the effort lead to excruciating conferences, committees, task forces, etc.

What all these reflections rather clearly communicate is that the problems of the social world are not like machine options that require only the pressing of some buttons and the activation of some program that set in motion the autonomous systems that function according the logic of their "codes."

Nevertheless, some of us are jolted into action and want to use the occasion as a golden opportunity to show that the time has come for a different way of handling the problems by becoming a force for the good instead of the state. We want to speak for humanity instead of parochial interests, to use the power of a better argument, rely on soft power, instead of the traditional armory wreaking destruction or corruption, or both. Oddly enough, certain similarities between withdrawal and activism are surprising, although the strategies of withdrawal – capitulating rather than facing the complexities – and the moral fervor inspiring activism seem to be diametrically opposed. Both drown out important information, the former by getting disheartened and confused as one begins to realize the difficulties, the other by adopting a "we can do it strategy" and deciding not to confront the concrete problems at all, since that might temper one's enthusiasm and make one admit to the possibility or actuality of shameful failure.

This brings us back to the role of shame which Bauman used in his analysis of modern evils and which had been explored by Anders, who called it the Prometheus complex.[75] It suggests why "oversight" and not caring on the one hand and the moral fervor to demonstrate good intentions on the other might be functionally equivalent solutions to feelings of inadequacy in the face of the

[75] See Günther Anders, *Die Antiquiertheit des Menschen*, München: C.H. Beck, 1956 and 1988.

"awful" potential offered to us by the problems and their "solution" offered by modern technologies. The incredible power put at our disposal inspires only superficially a feeling of pride and power, as soon we realize our own deficiencies and inabilities when compared to the machines. The illusion of power vanishes and gives rise to what Anders called "Promethean shame," which sets us off looking for frequently unattainable solutions, or – on a lower level which links up with narcissistic self-preoccupations – for therapies for our infirmities. It begins with the illusion of a perfect body and the disciplines of "tracking" our every move in order to "improve" ourselves, and ends with the display of how "cool" *we are* and how "welcoming" to others we have become and thus deserving of their attention.

In the most extreme case we even try to escape death when smitten by a disease or when we are getting on in life so that, along with taxes, death now becomes a continuous preoccupation. Again technology seems to hold the promise: we can let ourselves be frozen and await a better life, not in the hereafter but in a reality which will be just like now, only better! The transcendent has successfully been reduced to a technique, as the new religions are those of self-empowerment; and if the "religion" of scientology is an instantiation of this new creed, then it is clear that the follower will have to be "helped" by appropriate professionals in an endless slew of self-improvement workshops (audits) and "purification rundowns."

But even for the more fainthearted who do not want to follow the rather strange practices of L. Ron Hubbard's gospel,[76] technology can provide the remedy by incorporating machines into our very bodies and mutating ourselves into cyborgs. While primitive man tried to harness the powers of his enemies by eating them, the post-modern actor dreams of Herculean powers through an adaption to machines that function frictionless in his body. (Hopefully they function there better than the allegedly frictionless financial markets.)

What seemed until recently the stuff of sci-fi fantasies – or was available as an "experience" only through mind-altering drugs, or by performances held in special cinemas – has now become a multi-tiered industry powerfully "inspiring" the demand for ever more exotic special effects in films and electronic media. Its products are sold using some of the strategies and techniques that once were the preserve of publicity hounds and drug dealers intent on getting their clients hooked by offering something for "free" but thereby making themselves and their services indispensable.

[76] L. Ron Hubbard, *Dianetics: The Modern Science of Mental Health*, Los Angeles: Bride Pub. Inc., 1950. The cult character of this book can be gathered from the fact that its publication date is often taken as year one of a chronology. Thus AD 30 does not mean Anno Domini, but 1980 in "secular time," since it is the year 30 after the publication of *Dianetics*!

But even if we have to "pay" for it – and not simply hand over some of our "data" to others for sale – the nanotechnology that creates better weapons can also be "useful" for human life; not in the abstract sense, in which Kant still averred that the increasing destructiveness of war will *nolens volens* push people into a cosmopolitan order, but in the "real" way of enabling "number one." There will certainly be beneficial applications in the realm of medicine from which the x-generation or the millennials will be able to profit down the line, when their joints have deteriorated from too much squash or jogging, but about the rest of the promised package one can remain skeptical. Here the prospects of a Google pill which circulates in your body and gives information about all of our vital functions does not seem enticing to me at all, particularly when Google claims that it acquires thereby also proprietary rights in this information. But then again, many will be convinced and undoubtedly investors will compete to get in on this project since "there is a market."

But irrespective of our take on the technologies in the making, what they will mean to politics as we know it is difficult to say. But judging from the historical record, the future is unlikely to be the rosy picture that emerges from the visions of the creative elites which are holing up in the "total institutions" of Silicon Valley – reminding one of socialism for the rich, with free food and services supplied around the clock by a benevolent "felicifier," the firm.

Perhaps we all would like to sit around like them in our "messy offices/ living spaces," mentioned with pride by Google executives as a sign of a distinct lifestyle,[77] which is becoming now a common condition for the turbo capitalist elite. Strangely enough, this "vision" propounded by Google executives betokens a near Marxian enthusiasm for the community created at the workplace, forging together the "proletariat" out of isolated workers and making them into a "class for itself." On second thoughts, it makes one wonder, however, why Mark Zuckerberg, the high priest of "transparency" and openness, bought four houses which surrounded his abode at a measly $30 million, in order "to guarantee his absolute privacy from the outside world."[78] What is still a viable strategy when selectively withdrawing to gated communities or isolated well-designed headquarters/living environments is no longer a viable strategy if attempted more generally by the hoi polloi. Similarly, while a new app can make you a billionaire in a few years, this concentration of wealth depends on entirely fictitious "valuations" of future bids by "investors"[79] that cannot go on

---

[77] See the subsections "Keep them crowded," "Work, eat, and live together," "Your parents were wrong: messiness is a virtue" in Schmidt and Rosenberg, *How Google Works*.

[78] Keen, *The Internet Is Not the Answer*, at 207.

[79] Evan Spiegel invented the app Snapchat 2011, which resulted in an offer from Facebook of $3 billion two years later which was declined. In the meantime "investors" have Snapchat valued at $16 billion. Ironically the app allows you to place pictures and messages (art profile) on social

forever, as the deleterious consequences for the "real economy" are already visible. While the social world is one of artifice, we had better remember fictions have real consequences only as long they are sustained by actions. Thus fundamental crises can occur and there is no reason to believe that they can be suspended forever, or that they resemble extremely unlikely events such as collisions with a comet.

11.5   The Future of Politics: Some Final Remarks (in Lieu of a Conclusion)

The synergies between information overload, narcissism, and the fervor of "false" religion create an atmosphere of irritation and constant motion that is hardly sustainable and is detrimental for genuine deliberation and the making of informed choices. Deliberation requires time and presupposes the ability to listen, and to question. It also presupposes the willingness to change one's mind, instead of being always "first" and having the solutions, which are then in search of the problems to which they can be applied. In politics, this leads to the pathologies of proliferating meetings in which, however, the photo opportunities and the need to "show the flag" systematically drown out the concern with genuine analysis, favoring instead simplistic formulaic declarations and uninformative soundbites. These problems are well known and need not be rehearsed at length here. It also seems cold comfort that other institutions, such as universities or the media – both formerly bulwarks of criticism – are following this lead since they have morphed into "firms" who understand themselves as service providers, subject to the likes and dislikes of "customers," and ratings, rather than as forums of debate and deliberation.

Those developments will, of course, not "end" politics, but will mean the end of politics as a public affair in which binding decisions can be arrived at by making the executors of choices dependent on the consent of the governed. This consent has to be given not only once through entrusting them with the power which generates its own "legitimacy" à la Hobbes and the autopeoetic nature of law and its "administration," but through the constant mediation of interests. In this way a particular community traditionally created a common ground – the common thing or *res publica* – that was not just a temporary compromise, but an "ongoing and trans-generational concern," which both Aristotle and Hume – and even Machiavelli – celebrated. Politics will not disappear, as power does not disappear when it is no longer made visible or

media, which disappear after twenty-four hours and thus provide some protection of privacy for the users. See "Der Teenie-Schwarm," *Frankfurter Allgemeine Sonntagszeitung* (Wirtschaft), April 24, 2016, at 34.

represented. Instead, as we can see, power proliferates and changes its forms, while paradoxically decreasing the scope for human "action," as Foucault has demonstrated. That this form of politics, nicely camouflaged nowadays as "governance,"[80] might not be something that we want or intended to create is of course another matter.

What seems therefore especially troubling is the apparent loss of cultural resources for coping with our predicament that, as the Promethean shame suggested, leads to the crisis of meaning experienced in individual and collective life. Hume had already hinted at this possibility in his treatment of the "delirium and despair" that follows from the impossible quest for certainty and from coming to terms with the limits of "humanity." Used in this way, the term "humanity" also conveys an insight into the limitations of human existence rather than being a stand-in for the *Schwaermerei*[81] of a creating an all-encompassing "community" which represents the *telos* of human nature.

In a time when, increasingly, imagination and creativity is identified with "stunts," with zapping the bad guys, with having bionic powers and with engaging in time-travel and establishing civilizations on other stars, the chances seem slim that something new could emerge from those projections, as they are the typical stuff of the fantasies of children, who feel powerless and have compensatory delusions of grandeur, since they cannot yet be genuine "actors."

All of this of course goes hand-in-hand with growing ignorance of and unfamiliarity with our various historic civilizations and the heritage they have left for us which preserves their take on what it means to be human. The seriousness that comes with the realization of human finitude has always been one of the great themes in all civilizations. Emblematic for this realization are two epics, which are nowadays largely unknown (as is increasingly the Bible or other forms of "theology"). It is the Gilgamesh epic (particularly Tablet X), and it is the *Odyssey* to which I want to turn briefly.

In both epics the vain quest for immortality is addressed and transformed into insight into the necessities and the joys which come from constituting a society and living as part of it in the succession of generations. When the Nymph Calypso, who had kept Odysseus on her island, preventing him from returning home to Ithaca, offers him immortality in exchange for staying with her, she also confronts him with the difficulties a return voyage might entail, so that his goal might never be reached. Furthermore, she alerts him to the

---

[80] For a good thoughtful discussion of the problems – although perhaps cast initially a bit too narrowly as an issue between realists and constructivists – see Iver B. Neumann and Ole Jacob Sending, *Governing the Global Polity: Practice, Mentality, Rationality*, Ann Arbor: University of Michigan Press, 2010.

[81] For a critical comment that Kant himself might not have been that immune to such a *Schwaermerei* which he frequently condemned, see Kratochwil, "Immanuel Kant (1724–1804)."

fact that his memory of Penelope (his wife) might not be accurate, as much time has elapsed, while she, Calypso, is certainly endowed with eternal youth. To this Odysseus responds:

Mighty goddess be not wroth with me for this I know full well for myself that wise Penelope is meaner to look upon than thou in comeliness and stature, as she is a mortal, while thou are immortal and ageless. But even so I wish and long day by day of my return. And if again some god might smite me on the wine-dark sea, I will endure it, having in my breast a heart that endures affliction. For this I have suffered much and toiled much amid the waves and in war . . .

So he spoke and when the sun set and darkness came on, the two went into the innermost recess of the hollow cave and took their joy of love, abiding each by each other's side.[82]

This is certainly not a sappy story about a romantic love that never died, as the last two verses indicate. But it is also not a morality tale admonishing us to be happy with the little joys of daily life, as which Siduri's suggestions in the Gilgamesh epos are often taken

Gilgamesh, whither are you wandering? Life, which you look for, you will never find. For when the gods created man, they let death be his share, and withheld life in their own hands. Gilgamesh, fill your belly. Day and night make merry. Let days be full of joy, dance and make music day and night. And wear fresh clothes. And wash your head and bathe. Look at the child that is holding your hand, and let your wife delight in your bosom.[83]

While this interpretation has increasingly come under criticism as new fragments of the Gilgamesh epic[84] appear, in which Gilgamesh becomes again ruler of a city and services the gods, the message of the *Odyssey* is certainly not one that can be reduced to the idyll of an Arcadian existence. Homer's story is not one with a single theme, or a record of how of one reaches one's goal via its sub-goals, in fulfilling a prophecy, or being able to chart a clear course. Rather it is an epic in which the various threads are woven together in order to show how the tapestry of a meaningful life emerges from the existential choices of a protagonist facing the existential problems presented to him. Therefore, it is far removed from providing instructions via codified "best practices" but shows how one can rise to the occasion through judgment, imagination, and the experience gained by endurance and suffering, mastering thereby the challenges by one's wits, rather than by brute strength, or dumb luck.

In this way living with the realization of mortality is not disabling but opens the space for action and affirms the possibility of meaningful choices, even if

[82] Homer, *The Odyssey*, trans. A.T. Murray, Cambridge, MA: Harvard University Press, 1919, bk. V, at 215–227.
[83] Gilgamesh Epic, Tablet X (Jacobson transl. 1949), at www.sparknotes.com.
[84] This is one possible interpretation of the otherwise rather strange Tablet XII.

they are not crowned by success and/or entail suffering and loss.[85] Nor are the messages of this epic reducible to a nostalgic account of the return to an idyllic past, since the order of things at home has been overtaken by events and needs restorative action. Although we see that Odysseus accepts a certain place in the world, with its roles and traditions, as a part of who he is, like any reflective actor, he is also fully aware that after the momentous events which have rent the fabric of his own life and that of his society, he cannot just settle back in the expectation that habits and routines will do the work for him. If anything, the message the epic conveys is one of the contingencies of action, which it reports in excruciating detail in nineteen books that follow the Calypso episode and Odysseus' fateful choice.

Thus Odysseus' return is far from certain, particularly since he has lost all of his men who loyally had accompanied him to Troy. Even in the immediate family his return is far less welcoming than one could have imagined. So long has been his absence, his son hardly knows him, his wife at first does not even recognize him, and accepts him only after he passes two tests. In the meantime his house has been disgraced by insolent suitors, barely held at bay by Penelope's delaying tactics, but availing themselves in the meantime of the riches of Odysseus' estate. As they do not want to leave, even after none of them could stretch Odysseus' bow in a contest (which was the condition Penelope had given for marrying the winner), they have to be removed by force, resulting in their slaughter.

As the text makes clear, ultimately any hope Odysseus has of regaining his status depends not only on his prowess as a warrior, or on asserting his rights, but on a political solution which reconciles him and his few remaining followers with the families of the slain suitors, who are set on revenge. In the assembly of the nobles the old lord Halitherses stands alone with his plea to desist from such plans by arguing that

Through your own cowardice friends have these deeds been brought to pass ... They wrought a monstrous deed in their blind and wanton wickedness, wasting the wealth and dishonoring the wife of a prince, who they said would never more return. Now then be it thus; and do you hearken to me as I bid. Let us not go forth, lest haply many a one shall find a bane he has brought upon himself.[86]

So it comes to a new confrontation claiming another victim and moving to the brink of a mutual slaughter. Here Athena in the disguise of Mentor intervenes by addressing Odysseus:

---

[85] See the opening lines of bk. I, 1–10, that highlight the loss of his fellows during the return, his physical and psychological plight but also his wits (*polymethis*).

[86] Homer, *The Odyssey*, at bk. XXIV: 454–462.

Son of Laertes, sprung from Zeus, Odysseus of many devices, stay the hand and make the strife of baneful war to cease, lest haply the son of Cronos [Zeus] be wroth with thee . . . So spoke Athena, and he obeyed and was glad in his heart. Then for all time to come a solemn covenant bewixt the twain was made by Pallas Athena, daughter of Zeus who bears the aegis, in the likeness of Mentor both in form and voice.[87]

In this sense the Odyssey is an extremely political book, foreshadowing already the great reworking of the heroic past in the tragedies of the classical age, where *polis* is seen as enabling the "good life," not simply the bare life and its necessities.

Whether such ideals can nowadays still inspire viable political projects is of course another question. Hannah Arendt tried to uncover this side of classical civic life and has been criticized for her analysis of the "political" – conceived as the coming together of free beings creating thereby the power to pursue their individual and collective projects – that she saw as being subverted by the "social" and the humdrum politics of the bureaucratized welfare state.

There is of course something to this criticism, especially when we become aware which problems frame her analysis. One is the devaluation of the *vita activa*[88] and the deformation of politics by the reduction of human existence to the "doings" of *Homo faber*. The second issue she writes against is that "feelings"[89] increasingly overwhelm the political discourse, which she analyzes in terms of the emotions of "pity" and "compassion" into which the *fraternité* of the French Revolution mutated and which gave rise to the "kitsch" in modern politics, which also Koskenniemi identified above as one of the banes of political and legal discourse.

But Arendt's work cannot and should not be read as a paean for glory or for sequestering the "social question" to the realm of the "private," where property rights mystify power, and the tension that exists among different values which politics has to mediate are suppressed by a modern version of politics as bread and circuses, or by the "awards" of juristocrats who settle disputes about "fair" trade among the "parties." After all, no Cleisthenic democracy could have come into existence without the Solonic reforms cancelling debts and setting Athens on a new course, and no rule of law can effectively rule if its operations are not tied to the notion of a common public order in whose name they apply the law.

It is perhaps one of the most egregious failings of our "modern politics" that it apparently cannot sustain a critical examination of the increasing and accelerating inequalities which we observe in national and international politics. Instead, we seem satisfied with some episodic attention, such as when another

---

[87] Ibid., bk. XXIV: 543–547.   [88] Arendt, *The Human Condition*.
[89] See e.g. Arendt, *On Revolution*, esp. chap. 2 "The Social Question." See also Hannah Arendt, "On Humanity in Dark Times: Thoughts about Lessing" in *Men in Dark Times*, Harmondsworth: Penguin, 1973, 11–38.

round of disciplining measures, imposed on a "failing state" by a slew of "governance" institutions, makes it to the top of the agenda. But we seem unable to sustain attention – such as when the study presented to the Davos meeting[90] on the accelerating concentration of wealth makes the headlines for two or three days, but disappears and gets displaced by either oblivion – drowned out by yet another terrorist attack, the death of a rock star, or some natural disaster – or is buried by methodological criticism, showing that the wealth of the world is not owned by only 62 persons but perhaps by more than 224, as an allegedly better statistics reveals![91]

Even if this "finding" is true, the joy over more "accurate" numbers represents exactly the "stupidity" which Kant mentioned, showing a shocking lack of judgment of what the actual point is: that in the face of 3.6 billion poor, it is just callous and hardly even interesting that the number of the very best-off is somewhat larger, particularly since it also fails to alert us to the predictable effects of the dynamics of this ever accelerating concentration, which has been observable for the last few years.

It seems that we have not only lost our capacity for judgment, but that this loss is directly related to the growth of disciplinary discourses. It is not only that this specialization delegitimizes communication in ordinary language by favoring specialized languages, leaving us with unreflective appeals to emotions when common issues are at stake. In this way some communality among those opposing "the system" and clamoring for revolutionary action in the face of such a scandal can be generated. But while the outrage is justifiable, it cannot substitute for the give and take of a "conversation" and for a historical reflection and deliberation, as Hume suggested. Needless to say, this enthusiasm engendered by a feeling of betrayal and the wish to become a "force for good" cannot be sustained when taken as a political program. Instead, the passion for the good leads to a politics of confessional display that favors spectacles in which pathos rather than deliberation and judgment, characteristic of praxis, dominate. How such a form of politics can rather quickly become oppressive becomes visible from the politics of "gong shows" with which we are familiar, as every spectacle needs a victor and a vanquished!

This has two consequences: one wider, the other narrower, both of which are, however, deleterious to civil life. The wider one is that the space within which controversies can be aired shrinks dramatically as "refusniks" who warn about the costs of such modes of communicating are frequently treated as party-poopers, or spoilers of the game. The narrower is that such a politics

[90] See Oxfam International, Report of Wealth "Having it all and wanting more" (downloaded from www.oxfam.org).
[91] See the essay by Martin Zips, "Empört Euch!," *Süddeutsche Zeitung*, January 23/24, 2016, at 49.

valorizes the *argumentum ad hominem* in order to "destroy" the opponent rather than show the flaws in the other's position. Who needs arguments and a careful clarification of problems if one can destroy the credibility of the disliked opponent, or that the fact that s/he does not share with us the Rousseauan simplicity of feelings, or that s/he complicates matters by not trusting "data," insisting instead, on critically examining them, and paying attention to conceptual issues. Both flaws seem sufficient for our disdain.

Whatever the actual outcome might be, given these circumstances, it seems clear that a *vivere civile* will become difficult, as *eros* and desire overwhelm the old virtues of politics: persuasion and friendship. Furthermore, acting is severely circumscribed by "being administered." To that extent "acting in common" might now have become the preserve of varying groups of "stakeholders" since the "common thing," the *res publica* of old, has disappeared. Even "interests" which had been the links that bound people together – although they remained separate with different life plans and particular attachments – have become now only personal preferences governed by libidinal "likes," or often unarticulated but deeply "felt" aversions.

This "privatization" not only has implications for politics as we knew it, it also clearly affects the cosmopolitan project and with it the service to "humanity" we try to preserve thereby, although often with inappropriate means. In a nearly Humean fashion Hannah Arendt writes:

We have seen what a powerful need men have in "dark times", to move closer to one another, to seek in the warmth of intimacy the substitute for that light and illumination which only the public realm can cast. But this means that they avoid disputes and try as far as possible to deal only with people with whom they cannot come into conflict. For a man of Lessing's disposition there was little room in such an age and such a confined world.[92]

That such a search cannot be one driven by antiquarian interests for an idyllic past is clear. To that extent Lessing and his struggles at the height of the Enlightenment becomes emblematic: it is about a man who "wanted to be a friend of many men but no man's brother."[93] In the same vein it should be obvious that Arendt's foible for the "light and illumination" which only the public realm can provide is not a foible for the classical form of politics we encountered in Greece and the Roman republic. It is more a realization of the existential context between the individuals, their choices, and the political order which frames them and is reproduced and changed by the actors. That much we can gather from her remarks about "humanity" that are as far removed from the prophetic notion of an "end of history" as they are from the apolitical enthusiasm of a universal brotherhood: "That humaneness," she writes, should be

[92] Arendt, *Men in Dark Times*, at 39.   [93] Ibid., 38.

... sober and cool rather than sentimental; that humanity is exemplified not in fraternity, but in friendship; that friendship is not intimately personal, but makes political demands and preserves reference to the world.[94]

What remains for us, not directly engaged in making practical politics, but who, as critical observers in the privileged position of academia, surely have something to say and to contribute to the understanding of praxis, is not only to keep this flame of illumination alive – instead of just propagating the pretenses of an enlightenment which vainly claims to show how things really are – but to continue to build the city of man, Socrates' *kallipolis*, in "words."[95] As we have seen, it cannot be a project of designing blueprints or returning to the old, or realizing some futuristic templates, but one seeking to establish an order that allows us to "go on" in that mode of communication that is a "conversation." As such, it does not guarantee success because it cannot be shown to be "true," but it is the precondition for common action, which Hume identified as essential for a free political life:

The Separation of the Learned from the conversible World seems to have been the great Defect of the last Age, and must have had a very bad Influence both on Books and Company: For what Possibility is there of finding Topics of Conversation fit for the Entertainment of rational Creatures, without having Recourse sometimes to History, Poetry, Politics, and the more obvious Principles, at least, of Philosophy? Must our whole Discourse be a continued Series of gossiping Stories and idle Remarks? Must the Mind never rise higher, but be perpetually ... stun'd and worn out with endless Chat, of "WILL did this, and NAN said that".

This would be to render the Time spent in Company the most unentertaining, as well as the most unprofitable Part of our Lives.

On the other Hand, Learning has been as great a Loser by being shut up in Colleges and Cells, and secluded from the World and good Company. By that Means, every Thing of what we call Belles Lettres became totally barbarous, being cultivated by Men without any Taste of Life or Manners, and without that Liberty and Facility of Thought and Expression, which can only be acquir'd by Conversation. Even Philosophy went to Wrack by this moaping recluse Method of Study, and became as chimerical in her Conclusions as she was unintelligible in her Stile and Manner of Delivery. And indeed, what could be expected from Men who never consulted Experience in any of their Reasonings, or who never search'd for that Experience, where alone it is to be found, in common Life and Conversation?[96]

---

[94] Ibid., 33.
[95] Plato, "Republic" in Edith Hamilton and Huntington Cairns (eds.), *The Collected Dialogues Including the Letters*, Princeton: Princeton University Press, 1989, at 369a–473c.
[96] David Hume, "On Essay Writing" in *David Hume: Essays Moral, Political and Literary*, ed. Eugene Miller, Indianapolis: Liberty Fund 1987: pt. III, essay I, at 47–58, quote at III,I, 2–4.

Whether such a vision of politics is still viable or can be regained in a time in which increasingly organizations, be they bureaucracies or "firms," are making the choices "for us" (not even "on behalf of us") remains to be seen. On the one hand a good many people seem rather passively submissive to such a politics, using the "lack of alternatives" as justification, which could give pragmatism a bad name and would deservedly do so, were it not for the fact that it is a rather absurd distortion of pragmatism and its endeavor of taking action seriously. In the private realm such a bowdlerization favors complacency, the intoxication with consumption and with the "entertainment" that the various circuses provide, which have come to town and which are stealing our time with empty promises of "fun," or even happiness. The messages they generate play to our libidos and often create a "public viewing" for things that have no public import, but rather bring out the "private" excesses that are being displayed en masse. In the public realm it reinforces the rather foul consensus between the governing and the governed, who both, for different reasons, seem to prefer the *citizen-sheep* rather than persons who want to exercise their citizenship in terms of participation, controversy, and engagement.

On the other hand, large parts of a supposedly "silent majority" are becoming more and more radicalized and susceptible to slogans that resonate with their frustrations, but which often degenerate into a rage (rather than ending in despair and withdrawal, as Hume suggested), signaling that only a total uprooting rather than a new settlement is in the offing. Here Hannah Arendt's analysis, outlined above, casts ominous light on some of the newer developments.

But whatever the particular responses might be, one thing seems to be clear: without reviving a genuine political language and caring again about what comes into existence by a communication that focuses on forming an *inter-esse* – rather than engaging in interminable arguments about "ultimate" values or human rights – the chances for a politics of freedom seem dim indeed. The latter, although cast in terms of subjective rights, have a tendency to rather quickly turn into disputes about "what is right," thereby escalating conflicts rather than resolving them or enabling us to "go on."[97] As Hume suggested, being in the throes of "false religion," which leads us from the delirium of grandeur to despair, we are unlikely to discover our humanity and build the "city of man" in either words or deeds.

---

[97] For a further discussion, see Kratochwil, *The Status of Law in World Society*, chaps. 7–9.

Bibliography

Government Documents

Argentina, and Comisión Nacional sobre la Desaparición de Personas. *Nunca más: The Report of the Argentine National Commission on the Disappeared, with an Introduction by Ronald Dworkin.* New York: Farrar, Straus, Giroux, 1986.

Berryman, Phillip, Chile, and Comisión Nacional de Verdad y Reconciliación. "Report of the Chilean National Commission on Truth and Reconciliation" (Notre Dame, IN: published in cooperation with the Center for Civil and Human Rights, Notre Dame Law School, by the University of Notre Dame Press, 1993).

Department of State, and Dan Webster. *Mr. Webster to Lord Ashburton, 6th August.* 1842. Available at http://avalon.law.yale.edu/19th_century/br-1842d.asp#web2.

European Parliament and European Council. "Directive 96/9/EC of 11 March 1996 on the Legal Protection of Databases." 1996.

International Court of Justice. "Reports of Judgments, Advisory Opinions and Orders." 1951.

International Law Commission. *Draft Articles on Responsibility of States for Internationally Wrongful Acts.* 2001, UN Doc. A/56/10.

"Draft Code of Crimes against the Peace and Security of Mankind." *Yearbook of the International Law Commission* II:2 (1996).

Formulation of the Nürnberg Principles. 1950, A/CN.4/L.2.

Library of Congress. *Thomas Jefferson, Declaration of Independence: Right to Institute New Government.* 2000. Available at www.loc.gov/exhibits/jefferson/jeffdec.html.

Lincoln, Abraham. *Gettysburg Address, November 19.* 1863. Available at http://avalon.law.yale.edu/19th_century/gettyb.asp.

Maria Theresia von Österreich. "Constitutio Criminalis Theresiana." Johann Thomas von Trattner, 1769. Available at https://archive.org/details/ConstitutioCriminalis Theresiana-1768.

The President of the United States. *The National Security Strategy of the United States of America.* NSS02 (2002).

Security Council Report, "UN Sanctions." Special Research Report, No. 3, November 25 (New York: Security Council Report, 2013). Available at securitycouncil report.org.

South Africa, Truth and Reconciliation Commission, and Desmond Tutu. *Truth and Reconciliation Commission of South Africa Report.* Cape Town: Truth and Reconciliation Commission, 1998.

United Nations. *Convention on Biological Diversity*. Rio de Janeiro, June 5, 1992.

United Nations and Secretary General. "In Larger Freedom: Towards Development, Security and Human Rights for All: Report of the Secretary-General." New York: United Nations, 2005.

United Nations Conference on Environment and Development. *Agenda 21, Rio Declaration, Forest Principles*. New York: United Nations, 1992.

United Nations Environment Programme. *Basel Convention on the Control of Transboundary Movements of Hazardous Wastes and their Disposal*. March 22, 1989.

    London Guidelines for the Exchange of Information on Chemicals in International Trade. 15/30 (May 25, 1989).

    Amendment to the Montreal Protocol on Substances that Deplete the Ozone Layer (London Amendment). June 29, 1990.

United Nations Environment Programme, and the Ozone Secretariat. *The Montréal Protocol on Substances that Deplete the Ozone Layer*. September 16, 1987.

United Nations General Assembly. *Establishment of an International Criminal Court*. 1996, A/RES/51/207.

    Formulation of the Principles Recognized in the Charter of the Nurnberg Tribunal and in the Judgment of the Tribunal. 1947, GA Res. 177 (II), November 21.

    Khmer Rouge Trials. 2003, UN Doc. A/RES/57/228 B.

    Permanent Sovereignty over Natural Resources, Resolution 1803 (XVII). 1962, UN Doc. A/5217.

    Protect, Respect and Remedy: A Framework for Business and Human Rights. Human Rights Council 2008, A/HRC/8/5.

    Rome Statute of the International Criminal Court. 1998 [2002].

United Nations General Assembly, and United Nations Security Council. *Report of the Panel on United Nations Peace Operations*. 2000, UN Doc. A/55/305-S/2000/809.

United Nations Security Council, *Resolution 827, 25 May*. 1993, S/RES/827.

    Resolution 955, 8 November. 1994, S/RES/955.

    Resolution 1298, 17 May. 2000, S/RES/1298.

United States, and Arms Control and Disarmament Agency. *Arms Control and Disarmament Agreements: Texts and Histories of the Negotiations*. Washington, DC: United States Arms Control and Disarmament Agency, 1990.

United States, and the Union of Soviet Socialist Republics. *Treaty on the Limitation of Strategic Offensive Arms, together with Agreed Statements and Common Understanding Regarding the Treaty*. SALT II. Vienna, June 18, 1979.

    Treaty on the Elimination of Intermediate-Range and Shorter-Range Missiles. INF. Washington, DC, December 8, 1987.

    Treaty on the Reduction and Limitation of Strategic Offensive Arms. START I. Moscow, July 31, 1991.

United States Department of Commerce. *Proceedings of the Colloquium on the Science Court*. Washington, DC: Commerce Technical Advisory Board, 1977.

United States Department of State. *Foreign Relations of the United States: Diplomatic Papers, 1945. The British Commonwealth, the Far East. Vol. VI*. US Government Printing Office, 1945.

United States Department of State, and Bureau of Public Affairs. *Compliance with SALT I Agreements*. Special Report no. 55. July 1979.

World Bank. *Adjustment Lending: An Evaluation of Ten Years of Experience*. Washington, DC: World Bank, 1988.

Legal Cases

Accordance with International Law of the Unilateral Declaration of Independence in Respect of Kosovo, International Court of Justice, Advisory opinion of July 22, 2010.

Barcelona Traction, Light and Power Company Limited, International Court of Justice, 3 (1970).

Case Concerning the Air Service Agreement of 27 March 1946 between the United States of America and France, Reports of International Arbitral Awards, Volume XVIII, pp. 417–493 (1978).

Case Concerning the Gabčíkovo–Nagymaros Project (Hungary/Slovakia). Judgment of 25 September 1997, International Court of Justice, (1997).

Case Concerning Military and Paramilitary Activities in and against Nicaragua: Nicaragua v. United States of America, International Court of Justice, 1986 I.C.J. 14 (1986).

Case Concerning United States Diplomatic and Consular Staff in Tehran (United States of America v. Iran): Judgment of 24 May 1980. La Haye: Court of International Justice, 1980.

The Case of the S.S. "Lotus" (France v. Turkey), Permanent Court of International Justice, Ser. A, No. 10 (1927).

Doe v. Unocal Corp., US Court of Appeals, Ninth Circuit. 395 F.3d 932 (2002).

European Communities – Measures Concerning Meat and Meat Products (Hormones), World Trade Organization, DS26 (2009).

The Factory at Chorzow (Germany v. Poland), Permanent Court of International Justice, Ser. A, No. 17, Sept. 13, 1928.

Federal Trade Commission v. Compagnie de Saint-Gobain-Pont-a-Mousson, US Court of Appeals, D.C. Circuit, 636 F.2d 1300 (1980).

In Re Yamashita, US Supreme Court, 327 U.S. 1 (1946).

Laker Airways Ltd. v. Sabena, Belgian World Airlines, D.C. Circuit, 731 F.2d 909 (1984).

Legal Consequences of the Construction of a Wall in the Occupied Palestinian Territory, International Court of Justice, Advisory Opinions (2004).

Legality of the Threat or Use of Nuclear Weapons, International Court of Justice, Advisory Opinion of July 8, 1996.

Mc'alister (or Donoghue) (Pauper) v. Stevenson, House of Lords, UKHL 100, AC 562 (1932).

The Mox Plant Case (Ireland v. United Kingdom), Provisional Measures, International Tribunal for the Law of the Sea, (2005) 126 ILR, vol. 273 (2001).

Prosecutor v. Dusko Tadić: Decision on the Defence Motion for Interlocutory Appeal on Jurisdiction, 2 October, ICTY, IT-94-I-AR72 (1995).

Prosecutor v. Dusko Tadić: Decision on the Defence Motion on Jurisdiction, 10 August, ICTY, IT-94-I-T (1995).

Responsibility of Germany for Damage Caused in the Portuguese Colonies in the South of Africa (Portugal v. Germany), R.I.A.A., 2, 1011 (1928).

Stichting Mothers of Srebrenica and Others against the Netherlands, European Court of Human Rights, 65542/12 (2013).

Trail Smelter Case (United States, Canada), Reports of International Arbitral Awards, Volume III, pp. 1905–1982 (1938 and 1941).

United States – Tax Treatment for "Foreign Sales Corporations," World Trade Organization, DS108 (2006).
United States v. Aluminum Co. of America et al., Circuit Court of Appeals, Second Circuit, 148 F.2d 416 (1945).
United States v. Osborne (in Re Osborne), United States Court of Appeals, Ninth Circuit, 76 F.3d 306 (1996).

Literature

Abraham, Kavi Joseph, and Yehonatan Abramson. "A Pragmatist Vocation for International Relations: The (Global) Public and Its Problems." *European Journal of International Relations* 23:1 (2017), 26–48.
Ackerman, Robert W. *The Social Challenge to Business*. Cambridge, MA: Harvard University Press, 1975.
Adler, Emanuel, and Vincent Pouliot (eds.). *International Practices*. Cambridge: Cambridge University Press, 2011.
Adorno, Theodor W., Max Horkheimer, and Gunzelin Schmid Noerr. *Dialectic of Enlightenment: Philosophical Fragments*. Stanford: Stanford University Press, 2002.
Aeschylus. *The Orestean Trilogy*. Trans. Philip Vellacott. Harmondsworth: Penguin, 1956.
Agamben, Giorgio. *Die souveräne Macht und das nackte Leben*. Trans. H. Thüring. Frankfurt: Suhrkamp, 2002.
    Homo Sacer: Sovereign Power and Bare Life. Stanford: Stanford University Press, 1988.
    The State of Exception. Chicago: Chicago University Press, 2005.
Agassi, Joseph. *Science in Flux*. Dordrecht: D. Reidel, 1975.
Akyüz, Yilmaz. "Taming International Finance." In *Managing the Global Economy*, edited by Michie, J. and Grieve Smith, J. Oxford: Oxford University Press, 1995, 55–92.
Albert, Mathias, Barry Buzan, and Michael Zürn (eds.) *Bringing Sociology to International Relations: World Politics and Differentiation Theory*. Cambridge: Cambridge University Press, 2013.
Albert, Mathias, Lars-Erik Cedermann, and Alexander Wendt (eds.). *New Systems Theories of World Politics*. London: Palgrave, 2010.
Alker, Hayward. *Rediscoveries and Reformulations*, Cambridge: Cambridge University Press, 1996.
Alland, Denis. "Countermeasures of General Interest." *European Journal of International Law* 13:5 (2002): 1221–1239.
Allison, Graham T. *Essence of Decision: Explaining the Cuban Missile Crisis*. Boston, MA: Little, Brown, 1971.
Aloisi, Rosa. "A Tale of Two Institutions: The United Nations Security Council and the International Criminal Court." *International Criminal Law Review* 13:1 (2013): 147–168.
Alston, Philip G. "Resisting the Merger and Acquisition of Human Rights by Trade Law: A Reply to Petersmann." *European Journal of International Law* 13:4 (2002): 815–844.
Alvarez, José E. "Do Liberal States Behave Better?: A Critique of Slaughter's Liberal Theory." *European Journal of International Law* 12:2 (2001): 183–246.

Ambos, Kai. "The Crime of Aggression after Kampala." *German Yearbook of International Law* 53 (2010): 463–510.

"International Criminal Law at the Crossroads: From 'Ad Hoc' Imposition to a Treaty-Based Universal System." In *Future Perspectives on International Criminal Justice*, edited by Stahn, C. and van den Herik, L., The Hague: T.M.C. Asser Press, 2010, 161–177.

"Joint Criminal Enterprise and Command Responsibility." *Journal of International Criminal Justice* 5:1 (2007): 159–183.

Anders, Günther. *Die Antiquiertheit des Menschen*. 2 vols. München: C.H. Beck, 1956 and 1988.

Anderson, Benedict. *Imagined Communities: Reflections on the Origin and Spread of Nationalism*. London: Verso, 1983.

Imagined Communities: Reflections on the Origin and Spread of Nationalism, revised edn. London: Verso, 1991.

Anderson, Kenneth. "The Rise of International Criminal Law: Intended and Unintended Consequences." *European Journal of International Law* 20:2 (2009): 331–358.

Anghie, Anthony. *Imperialism, Sovereignty and the Making of International Law*. Cambridge: Cambridge University Press, 2005.

Anscombe, G.E.M. *Intention*, 2nd edn. Ithaca, NY: Cornell University Press, 1957.

Aquinas, Thomas. *Summa Theologica*, 1485.

Archibald, G.C., Herbert A. Simon, and Paul A. Samuelson. "Discussion." *The American Economic Review* 53:2 (1963): 227–236.

Arendt, Hannah. *Eichmann in Jerusalem: A Report on the Banality of Evil*. London: Penguin Books, 1994.

The Human Condition, 2nd edn. Chicago: University of Chicago Press, 1998.

Lectures on Kant's Political Philosophy. Edited by Beiner, R. Chicago: University of Chicago Press, 1982.

Men in Dark Times. Harmondsworth: Penguin, 1973.

"On Humanity in Dark Times: Thoughts about Lessing." In *Men in Dark Times* (Harmondsworth: Penguin, 1973), 11–38.

On Revolution. New York: Viking Press, 1965.

The Origins of Totalitarianism. Cleveland, OH: Meridian, 1958.

Aristotle. "The Constitution of Athens." In *The Politics, and the Constitution of Athens*, edited by Everson, S., Cambridge: Cambridge University Press, 1996.

Constitution of Athens. New York: Arno Press, 1973.

The Ethics of Aristotle: The Nicomachean Ethics. Edited by Thomson, J.A.K. Harmondsworth: Penguin, 1953.

Nicomachean Ethics. Trans. H. Rackham. Cambridge, MA: Harvard University Press, 1975.

Nicomachean Ethics. Trans. J.A.K. Thompson. Harmondsworth: Penguin, 1955.

Nicomachean Ethics. Baltimore: Penguin, 1953.

"Poetics." In *Aristotle's Poetics & Rhetoric*, edited by Moxon, T.A., London: J.M. Dent and Sons, 1953.

Politics. Trans. H. Rackham. Cambridge, MA: Harvard University Press, 1972.

The Politics. Trans. T.A. Sinclair. Harmondsworth: Penguin, 1962.

"Prior Analytics." In *The Categories, on Interpretation, and Prior Analytics*. Trans. H. Trendennick. Cambridge, MA: Harvard University Press, 1962.

Rhetoric. Trans. J.H. Freese. Cambridge, MA: Harvard University Press, 1926.

Assmann, Aleida. *Erinnerungsräume: Formen und Wandlungen des kulturellen Gedächtnisses*. München: C.H. Beck, 1999.

Assmann, Jan. "Ancient Egypt and the Materiality of the Sign." In *Materialities of Communication*, edited by Gumbrecht, H.U. and Pfeiffer, K.L., Stanford: Stanford University Press, 1994, 15–31.

Ma'at: Gerechtigkeit und Unsterblichkeit im alten Ägypten. München: C.H. Beck, 1990.

Religion und Kulturelles Gedächtnis: Zehn Studien. München: Beck, 2000.

Augustus. *Res Gestae Divi Augusti*. Trans. A.E. Cooley. Cambridge: Cambridge University Press, 2009.

Austin, J.L. *How to Do Things with Words*. Cambridge, MA: Harvard University Press, 1962.

Avant, Deborah, *The Market for Force: The Consequences for Privatizing Security*. Cambridge: Cambridge University Press, 2005.

Axelrod, Robert. *The Evolution of Cooperation*. New York: Basic Books, 1984.

Axelrod, Robert, and Robert Keohane. "Achieving Cooperation under Anarchy: Strategies and Institutions." *World Politics* 38:1 (1985): 226–254.

Ayer, A.J. "An Honest Ghost?" In *Ryle: A Collection of Critical Essays*, edited by Wood, O. and Pitcher, G., London: Macmillan, 1970, 53–74.

Language, Truth, and Logic. London: V. Gollancz, 1946.

Azmanova, Albena. *The Scandal of Reason: A Critical Theory of Political Judgment*. New York: Columbia University Press, 2012.

Bac, Mehmet. "Corruption, Connections and Transparency: Does a Better Screen Imply a Better Scene?" *Public Choice* 107:1/2 (2001): 87–96.

Bachrach, Peter, and Morton S. Baratz. "Two Faces of Power." *American Political Science Review* 56:4 (1962): 947–952.

Badar, Mohamed Elewa. "Drawing the Boundaries of Mens Rea in the Jurisprudence of the International Criminal Tribunal for the Former Yugoslavia," *International Criminal Law Review* 6:3 (2006): 313–348.

Badescu, Cristina G. *Humanitarian Intervention and the Responsibility to Protect: Security and Human Rights*. Abingdon: Routledge, 2011.

Badian, Ernst. *From Plataea to Potidaea: Studies in the History and Historiography of the Pentecontaetia*. Baltimore: Johns Hopkins University Press, 1993.

Baier, Annette. *The Cautious, Jealous Virtue: Hume on Justice*. Cambridge: Harvard University Press, 2010.

A Progress of Sentiments: Reflections on Hume's Treatise, Cambridge: Harvard University Press, 1991.

Baker, John C., Kevin M. O'Connell, and Ray A. Williamson. *Commercial Observation Satellites: At the Leading Edge of Global Transparency*. Santa Monica, CA: Rand/ASPRS, 2001.

Baldwin, David A. *Economic Statecraft*. Princeton: Princeton University Press, 1985.

"Money and Power." *The Journal of Politics* 33:3 (1971): 578–614.

Paradoxes of Power. New York: Blackwell, 1989.

"Power Analysis and World Politics: New Trends versus Old Tendencies." *World Politics* 31:2 (1979): 161–194.

Balint, Jennifer. "Towards the Anti-Genocide Community: The Role of Law." *Australian Journal of Human Rights* 1:1 (1994): 12–42.

Balkin, J.M. "How Mass Media Simulate Political Transparency," *Cultural Values* 3:4 (1999): 393–413.

Barbato, Mariano. *Pilgrimage, Politics and International Relations: Religious Semantics for World Politics.* New York: Palgrave Macmillan, 2013.

Barbosa, Luiz C. "Save the Rainforest! NGOs and Grassroots Organisations in the Dialectics of Brazilian Amazonia," *International Social Science Journal* 55:178 (2003): 583–591.

Barnett, Michael N. *Eyewitness to a Genocide: The United Nations and Rwanda.* Ithaca, NY: Cornell University Press, 2002.

Barnett, Michael N., and Martha Finnemore. *Rules for the World: International Organizations in Global Politics.* Ithaca, NY: Cornell University Press, 2004.

Barratt-Brown, Elizabeth P. "Building a Monitoring and Compliance Regime under the Montreal Protocol." *Yale Journal of International Law* 16 (1991): 519.

Bartelson, Jens. *A Genealogy of Sovereignty.* Cambridge: Cambridge University Press, 1995.

"Making Sense of Global Civil Society." *European Journal of International Relations* 12:3 (2006): 371–395.

Basler, Roy P. (ed.) *Abraham Lincoln: His Speeches and Writings.* Cleveland, OH: World Publishing, 1946.

Bass, Gary J. *Stay the Hand of Vengeance: The Politics of War Crimes Tribunals.* Princeton: Princeton University Press, 2002.

Bassiouni, M. Cherif. *The Legislative History of the International Criminal Court: Introduction, Analysis, and Integrated Text of the Statute, Elements of Crimes and Rules of Procedure and Evidence.* 3 vols. Ardsley, NY: Transnational Publishers, 2005.

Baudrillard, Jean. *Simulacra and Simulation.* Trans. S.F. Glaser. Ann Arbor: University of Michigan Press, 1994.

Bauer, Harry, and Elisabetta Brighi (eds.). *Pragmatism in International Relations.* Abingdon: Routledge, 2009.

Baugh, Daniel A. *The Global Seven Years War 1754–1763: Britain and France in a Great Power Contest.* London: Pearson, 2011.

Bauman, Zygmunt. *Liquid Modernity.* Cambridge: Polity Press, 2000.

"A Natural History of Evil," available at S.I.M.O.N. (Shoah Intervention Methods Documentation), www.vwi.dc.at/images/Downloads/SWL_Reader/Bauman/SWL-Reader-Bauman.pdf, last accessed May 25, 2016.

Beck, Ulrich. *Risikogesellschaft: Auf dem Weg in eine Andere Moderne.* Frankfurt: Suhrkamp, 1986.

Risk Society: Towards a New Modernity. London: Sage, 1992.

Becker, Carl L. "What Are Historical Facts?" *The Western Political Quarterly* 8:3 (1955): 327–340.

Becker, Wibke. "#Debatte," *Frankfurter Allgemeine Sonntagszeitung* (Meinung), April 24, 2015.

Beiner, Ronald. *Political Judgment.* Chicago: University of Chicago Press, 1983.

Bellamy, Alex. *The Responsibility to Protect: The Global Effort to End Mass Atrocities.* Cambridge: Polity, 2009.

Bellamy, Alex J., Paul Williams, and Stuart Griffin. *Understanding Peacekeeping.* Cambridge: Polity, 2004.

Benoist, Jocelyn. "A Phenomenology or Pragmatism?" In *Pragmatism: Critical Concepts in Philosophy,* edited by Goodman, R.B., London: Routledge, 2005, 89–112.

Bentham, Jeremy. *An Introduction to the Principles of Morals and Legislation.* Edited by Burns, J.H., and Hart, H.L.A. London: Athlone, 1970.

Berger, Thomas. *War, Guilt and World Politics after World War II.* Cambridge: Cambridge University Press, 2012.

Berlin, Isaiah. "The Pursuit of the Ideal." In Isaiah Berlin, *The Proper Study of Humanity: An Anthology of Essays,* edited by Hardy, Henry, and Hausheer, Roger, New York: Farrar, Straus and Giroux 1998, 1–17.

Bernard, Mitchell, and Ravenhill, John. "Beyond Product Cycles and Flying Geese: Regionalization, Hierarchy, and the Industrialization of East Asia." *World Politics* 47:2 (1995): 171–209.

Bernstein, Richard J. *The Pragmatic Turn.* Cambridge: Polity, 2010.
Praxis and Action: Contemporary Philosophies of Human Activity. Philadelphia: University of Pennsylvania Press, 1971.

Betts, Richard. "Analysis, War, and Decision: Why Intelligence Failures Are Inevitable." *World Politics* 31:2 (1978): 61–89.

Beza, Theodorus. *Du Droit des magistrats sur leurs subiets.* Saint-Julien-l'Ars: Imprimerie monastique, 1968 [1574].

Bhaskar, Roy. *The Possibility of Naturalism: A Philosophical Critique of the Contemporary Human Sciences.* Brighton: Harvester Press, 1979.
A Realist Theory of Science, 2nd edn. Brighton: Harvester Press, 1978.
Scientific Realism and Human Emancipation. London: Verso, 1986.

Bianchi, Andrea. "Terrorism and Armed Conflict: Insights from a Law & Literature Perspective." *Leiden Journal of International Law* 24:1 (2011): 1–21.

Biersteker, Thomas J. "Constructing Historical Counterfactuals to Assess the Consequences of International Regimes: The Global Debt Regime and the Course of the Debt Crisis of the 1980s." In *Regime Theory and International Relations,* edited by Rittberger, V. and Mayer, P., Oxford: Clarendon Press, 1993, 315–338.
Dealing with Debt: International Financial Negotiations and Adjustment Bargaining. Boulder, CO: Westview Press, 1993.

Bigo, Didier. "The Möbius Ribbon of Internal and External Security(ies)." In *Identities, Borders, Orders: Rethinking International Relations Theory,* edited by Albert, M., Jacobson, D., and Lapid, Y., Minneapolis: University of Minnesota Press, 2001, 91–116.

Binder, Guyora. "Representing Nazism: Advocacy and Identity at the Trial of Klaus Barbie." *Yale Law Journal* 98:7 (1989): 1321–1383.

Bisset, Alison, *Truth Commisssions and Criminal Courts.* Cambridge: Cambridge University Press, 2012.

Black, Ian, and Ian Cobain. "British Court Issued Gaza Arrest Warrant for Former Israeli Minister Tzipi Livni," *The Guardian,* December 12, 2009.

Bleiker, Roland, and Emma Hutchison. "Introduction: Emotions and World Politics." *International Theory* 6:3 (2014): 490–491.

Bloor, David. "Wittgenstein and the Priority of Practice." In *The Practice Turn in Contemporary Theory,* edited by Schatzki, T.R., Knorr Cetina, K., and von Savigny, E., London: Routledge, 2001, 95–106.
Wittgenstein: Rules and Institutions. London: Routledge, 1997.

Bob, Clifford. "Beyond Transparency: Visibility and Fit in the Internationalization of Internal Conflict." In *Power and Conflict in the Age of Transparency,* edited by Finel, B.I. and Lord, K.M., New York: Palgrave Macmillan, 2000, 287–314.

Bodin, Jean. *The Six Books of the Commonwealth*, edited by McRae, K.D., Cambridge, MA: Harvard University Press, 1962.

Bogdan, Attila. "The United States and the International Criminal Court: Avoiding Jurisdiction through Bilateral Agreements in Reliance on Article 98." *International Criminal Law Review* 8:1 (2008): 1–54.

Bogdandy, Armin, and Ingo Vetzke. "In Whose Name? International Courts' Public Authority and Its Democratic Justification." *European Journal of International Law* 23:1 (2012): 7–41. (An expanded version appeared as a book, Armin Bogdandy, and Ingo Vetzke. *In Whose Name? A Public Law Theory of International Adjudication*. Oxford: Oxford University Press, 2014.)

Bohlen, Avis. "The Rise and Fall of Arms Control." *Survival*. 453 (2003): 7–34.

Bondi, Loretta. "Arms Embargo: In Name Only?" In *Smart Sanctions: Targeting Economic Statecraft*, edited by Cortright, D., and Lopez, G.A., Lanham. MD: Rowman & Littlefield, 2002, 109–124.

Bosl, Karl, and Johannes von Elmenau. *Mensch und Gesellschaft in der Geschichte Europas*. München: Paul List, 1972.

Bothe, Michael. "Terrorism and the Legality of Pre-emptive Force." *European Journal of International Law* 14:2 (2003): 227–240.

Bottomore, Tom. *Sociology as Social Criticism*. Abingdon: Routledge, 2010.

Bourdieu, Pierre. *Language and Symbolic Power*. Edited by Thompson, J.B. Cambridge, MA: Harvard University Press, 1991.

Outline of a Theory of Practice. Cambridge: Cambridge University Press, 1977.

Pascalian Meditations. Stanford: Stanford University Press, 2000.

"The Sentiment of Honour in Kabyle Society." In *Honour and Shame: The Values of Mediterranean Society*, edited by Péristiany, J.G., Chicago: University of Chicago Press, 1969, 191–241.

Bowen, Howard Rothmann. *Social Responsibilities of the Businessman*. New York: Harper and Row, 1953.

Boyer, Robert, and Daniel Drache (eds.). *States against Markets: The Limits of Globalization*. London: Routledge, 1996.

Boyle, James. "Ideals and Things: International Legal Scholarship and the Prison-House of Language." *Harvard International Law Journal* 26:2 (1985): 327–360.

Braithwaite, John. *Crime, Shame, and Reintegration*, Cambridge: Cambridge University Press, 1989.

Brandt, Reinhard. *Die Bestimmung des Menschen bei Kant*. Hamburg: Felix Meiner, 2009.

Bratman, Michael. *Intentions, Plans and Practical Reason*. Cambridge, MA: Harvard University Press, 1985.

Shared Agency: A Planning Theory of Acting Together. Oxford: Oxford University Press, 2014.

"Shared Cooperative Activity." *The Philosophical Review* 101:2 (1992): 327–341.

Braudel, Fernand. *The Identity of France*. 2 vols. New York: Harper and Row, 1989.

Breitmeier, Helmut, and Volker Rittberger. "Environmental NGOs in an Emerging Global Civil Society." Tübinger Arbeitspapiere zur internationalen Politik und Friedensforschung Nr. 32. Tübingen: University of Tübingen, 1998. Available at www.uni-tuebingen.de/ifp/taps/tap32.htm.

Brierly, James Leslie. *The Law of Nations*, 6th edn. Oxford: Oxford University Press, 1963.

Bronkhorst, Daa. *Truth and Reconciliation: Obstacles and Opportunities for Human Rights.* Amsterdam: Amnesty International, Dutch Section, 1995.

Brooks, Risa A. "Sanctions and Regime Type: What Works, and When?" *Security Studies* 11:4 (2002): 1–50.

Broome, Andre, and Joel Quirk. "The Politics of Numbers: The Normative Agendas of Global Benchmarking." *Review of International Studies* 41:5 (2015): 813–818.

Brunner, Otto. *Adeliges Landleben und Europäischer Geist: Leben und Werk Wolf Helmhards von Hohberg, 1612–1688.* Salzburg: Otto Müller, 1949.

Land and Lordship: Structures of Governance in Medieval Austria, vol. 4. Translated by H. Kaminsky and J. van Horn Melton. Philadelphia: University of Pennsylvania Press, 1992.

Neue Wege der Sozialgeschichte: Vorträge und Aufsätze, Göttingen: Vandenhoeck & Ruprecht, 1956.

Brzoska, Michael. "From Dumb to Smart? Recent Reforms of UN Sanctions." *Global Governance* 9 (2003): 519–536.

Bubner, Rüdiger. *Handlung, Sprache und Vernunft: Grundbegriffe Praktischer Philosophie*, 2nd edn. Frankfurt: Suhrkamp, 1982.

Bucher, Bernd, "Acting, Abstractions, Metaphors, Narrative Structures and the Eclipse of Agency." *European Journal of International Relations* 20:3 (2014): 742–765.

Bueger, Christian. "Pathways to Practice: Praxiography and International Politics." *European Political Science Review* 6:3 (2014): 383–406.

Bueger, Christian, and Frank Gadinger. *International Practice Theory: New Perspectives.* Houndmills: Palgrave Macmillan, 2014.

Bull, Hedley. *The Anarchical Society: A Study of Order in World Politics.* New York: Columbia University Press, 1977.

"International Theory: The Case for a Classical Approach." *World Politics* 18:3 (1966): 361–377.

Burley, Anne-Marie. "Regulating the World: Multilateralism, International Law, and the Projection of the New Deal Regulatory State." In *Multilateralism Matters: The Theory and Praxis of an Institutional Form*, edited by Ruggie, J.G., New York: Columbia University Press, 1993, 125–156.

Butler, Richard. *The Greatest Threat: Iraq, Weapons of Mass Destruction and the Growing Crisis of Global Security.* New York: Public Affairs, 2000.

Butterfield, Herbert. *The Whig Interpretation of History.* New York: Norton, 1965.

Buzan, Barry. *From International to World Society? English School Theory and the Social Structure of Globalisation.* Cambridge: Cambridge University Press, 2004.

Buzan, Barry, Ole Wæver, and Jaap de Wilde. *Security: A New Framework for Analysis.* Boulder, CO: Lynne Rienner, 1997.

Calabresi, Guido, and Philip Bobbitt. *Tragic Choices.* New York: Norton, 1978.

Callaghy, Thomas. *Innovation in the Sovereign Debt Regime: From the Paris Club to Enhanced HIPC and Beyond.* Washington, DC: World Bank, 2004.

"Lost between the State and Market: The Politics of Economic Adjustment in Ghana, Zambia, and Nigeria." In *Economic Crisis and Policy Choice: The Politics of Adjustment in the Third World*, edited by Nelson, J.M., Princeton: Princeton University Press, 1990, 257–320.

"Toward State Capability and Embedded Liberalism in the Third World: Lessons for Adjustment." In *Fragile Coalitions: The Politics of Economic Adjustment*, edited by Nelson, J.M., New Brunswick, NJ: Transaction Books, 1989, 115–138.

Cannizzaro, Enzo. "The Role of Proportionality in the Law of International Countermeasures." *European Journal of International Law* 12:5 (2001): 889–916.

Capaldi, Nicholas. "Some Misconceptions about Hume's Moral Theory." *Ethics* 76:3 (1966): 208–211.

Carli, Silvia. "Poetry Is More Philosophical Than History." *The Review of Metaphysics* 64:2 (2010): 303–336.

Carnap, Rudolf. *Philosophy and Logical Syntax*. New York: AMS Press, 1976.

Carnegie, Dale. *How to Win Friends and Influence People*. New York: Pocket Books, 1981 [1936].

Carr, Edward Hallett. *The Twenty Years' Crisis*. New York: Harper Torchbooks, 1964.

Carver, Terrell, and Jens Bartelson. *Globality, Democracy and Civil Society*. Abingdon: Routledge, 2011.

Cassese, Antonio, Paola Gaeta, L. Baig, M. Fan, Christopher Gosnell, and A. Whiting. *Cassese's International Criminal Law*, 3rd edn. Oxford: Oxford University Press, 2013.

Castaneda, Hector. *Thinking and Doing*. Dordrecht: D. Riedel, 1975.

Castells, Manuel. *Networks of Outrage and Hope: Social Movements in the Internet Age*. Cambridge: Polity Press, 2012.

Cederman, Lars-Erik, and Christopher Daase. "Endogenizing Corporate Identities: The Next Step in Constructivist IR Theory." *European Journal of International Relations* 9:1 (2003): 5–35.

Cerny, Philip G. *The Changing Architecture of Politics: Structure, Agency, and the Future of the State*. London: Sage, 1990.

"Globalization and Other Stories: The Search for a New Paradigm for International Relations." *International Journal* 51:4 (1996): 617–637.

Chambers, Simone, and Will Kymlicka. *Alternative Conceptions of Civil Society*. Princeton: Princeton University Press, 2002.

Chapman, Audrey R., and Patrick Ball. "The Truth of Truth Commissions: Comparative Lessons from Haiti, South Africa, and Guatemala." *Human Rights Quarterly* 23:1 (2001): 1–43.

Charnovitz, Steve. "Rethinking WTO Trade Sanctions." *American Journal of International Law* 95:4 (2001): 792–832.

Chayes, Abram, and Antonia Handler Chayes. *The New Sovereignty: Compliance with International Regulatory Agreements*. Cambridge, MA: Harvard University Press, 1995.

"On Compliance." *International Organization* 47:2 (1993): 175–205.

Checkel, Jeffrey T. "International Norms and Domestic Politics: Bridging the Rationalist: Constructivist Divide." *European Journal of International Relations* 3:4 (1997): 473–495.

Chernoff, Fred. "Scientific Realism as a Meta-Theory of International Politics." *International Studies Quarterly* 46:2 (2002): 189–207.

Chopra, Jarat. "The UN's Kingdom of East Timor." *Survival* 42:3 (2000): 27–39.

Chopra, Jarat, and Thomas G. Weiss. "Sovereignty Is No Longer Sacrosanct: Codifying Humanitarian Intervention." *Ethics and International Affairs* 6:1 (1992): 95–117.

Christiano, Thomas, and John Christman (eds.). *Contemporary Debates in Political Philosophy*. Chichester: Blackwell-Wiley, 2009.

Cicero. *De Oratore*. Heidelberg: Winter, 1981.

Cirincione, Joseph, Jessica T. Mathews, and George Perkovich. *WMD in Iraq: Evidence and Implications*. Washington, DC: Carnegie Endowment for International Peace, 2004.

Clarke, Kamari Maxine. *Fictions of Justice: The International Criminal Court and the Challenge of Legal Pluralism in Sub-Saharan Africa*. Cambridge: Cambridge University Press, 2009.

Cockayne, James. "Special Court for Sierra Leone: Decision on the Recusal of Judges Robertson and Winter." *Journal of International Criminal Justice* 2:4 (2004): 1154–1162.

Cohen, Benjamin J. *The Geography of Money*. Ithaca, NY: Cornell University Press, 1998.

Cohen, Bernard. "Newton and the Social Sciences, with Special Reference to Economics, or, the Case of the Missing Paradigm." In *Natural Images in Economic Thought: Markets Read in Tooth and Claw*, edited by Mirowski, P., Cambridge: Cambridge University Press, 1994, 55–90.

Cohen, Marshall (ed.). *Ronald Dworkin and Contemporary Jurisprudence*. Totowa, NJ: Rowman & Allanheld, 1984.

Cohen, Morris. "Property and Sovereignty." In *Property: Mainstream and Critical Positions*, edited by MacPherson, C.B., Toronto: University of Toronto Press, 1978, 153–176.

Cohen, Stephen F. *Bukharin and the Bolshevik Revolution: A Political Biography, 1888–1938*. New York: Oxford University Press, 1980.

Cohon, Rachel. *Hume's Morality: Feeling and Fabrication*. New York: Oxford University Press, 2008.

"The Common Point of View in Hume's Ethics." *Philosophy and Phenomenological Research* 57:4 (1997): 827–850.

Coleman, James Samuel. *Introduction to Mathematical Sociology*. New York: Free Press of Glencoe, 1964.

Collier, David, and Steven Levitak. "Democracy with Adjectives: Conceptual Innovation in Comparative Research." *World Politics* 49:3 (1997): 430–451.

Combs, Nancy A. *Fact-Finding without Facts: The Uncertain Evidentiary Foundations of International Criminal Convictions*. Cambridge: Cambridge University Press, 2010.

Conlisk, John. "Why Bounded Rationality?" *Journal of Economic Literature* 34:2 (1996): 669–700.

Connaughton, Richard M. *Military Intervention and Peacekeeping: The Reality*. Aldershot: Ashgate, 2001.

Connolly, William. *The Terms of Political Discourse*, 2nd edn. Princeton: Princeton University Press, 1983.

Conquest, Robert. *The Great Terror: A Reassessment*. New York: Oxford University Press, 1990.

Cortright, David. "Powers of Persuasion: Sanctions and Incentives in the Shaping of International Society." *International Studies* 38:2 (2001): 113–125.

The Sanctions Decade: Assessing UN Strategies in the 1990s. Boulder, CO: Lynne Rienner, 2000.

Coser, Lewis A. *The Functions of Social Conflict.* New York: Free Press, 1956.

Cowhey, Peter F. "Elect Locally – Order Globally: Domestic Politics and Multilateral Cooperation." In *Multilateralism Matters: The Theory and Praxis of an Institutional Form,* edited by Ruggie, J.G., New York: Columbia University Press, 1993, 157–200.

Cox, Robert W. "Social Forces, States and World Order: Beyond International Relations Theory." *Millennium* 10:2 (1981): 204–254.

Craven, Matthew. "Humanitarianism and the Quest for Smarter Sanctions." *European Journal of International Law* 13:1 (2002): 43–61.

Crawford, Neta, and Audie Klotz. *How Sanctions Work: Lessons from South Africa.* New York: Palgrave, 1999.

Crawford, Neta, and Cunneen, Chris. "Reparations and Restorative Justice: Responding to the Gross Violation of Human Rights." In *Restorative Justice and Civil Society,* edited by Strang, H. and Braithwaite J., Cambridge: Cambridge University Press, 2001, 83–98.

Czempiel, Ernst-Otto, and James N. Rosenau (eds.). *Global Changes and Theoretical Challenges: Approaches to World Politics for the 1990s.* Lexington, MA: Lexington Books, 1989.

D'Ascoli, Silvia. *Sentencing in International Criminal Law: The UN Ad Hoc Tribunals and Future Perspectives for the ICC.* Oxford: Hart, 2011.

D'Aspremont, Jean. "Wording in International Law." *Leiden Journal of International Law* 25:3 (2012): 575–602.

Dahrendorf, Ralf. *Class and Class Conflict in Industrial Society.* Stanford: Stanford University Press, 1959.

Daily Mail Reporter. "Goldman Sachs Chief Says 'We Do God's Work' as He Defends the Bank's Mega Profits," *Daily Mail,* November 8, 2009, accessed at www.dailymail.co.uk/news/article-1226114/Goldman-Sachs-chief-says-Gods-work-defends-banks-bumper-profits.html on May 29, 2016.

Dallaire, Roméo. *Shake Hands with the Devil: The Failure of Humanity in Rwanda.* London: Arrow, 2005.

Danto, Arthur. *Analytical Philosophy of History.* New York: Columbia University Press, 1965.

"Looking at the Future, Looking at the Present as Past." In *Mortality, Immortality: The Legacy of 20th Century Art,* edited by Miguel, A. C., Los Angeles: Getty Conservation Institute, 1999, 3–12.

Dashti-Gibson, J., P. Davis, and B. Radcliff. "On the Determinants of the Success of Economic Sanctions: An Empirical Analysis." *American Journal of Political Science* 41:2 (1997): 608–618.

David, Marcel. *La Souveraineté et les limites juridiques du pouvoir monarchique: de IXe au XVe siècle.* Paris: Dalloz, 1954.

David, Paul A. "Intellectual Property Institutions and the Panda's Thumb: Patents, Copyrights, and Trade Secrets in Economic Theory and History." In *Global Dimensions of Intellectual Property Rights in Science and Technology,* edited by Wallerstein, M.B.. Mogee M.E., and Schoen, R.A., Washington, DC: National Academy Press, 1993, 19–62.

Davidson, Donald. "Actions, Reasons, and Causes." *The Journal of Philosophy* 63:23 (1966): 685–700.

Essays on Actions and Events. New York: Oxford University Press, 1980
Davis, James. *Terms of Inquiry: On the Theory and Practice of Political Science*. Baltimore: Johns Hopkins University Press, 2005.
Threats and Promises: The Pursuit of International Influence. Baltimore: Johns Hopkins University Press, 2000.
Dayan, Daniel, and Elihu Katz. *Media Events: The Live Broadcasting of History*. Cambridge, MA: Harvard University Press, 1992.
de Certeau, Michel. *The Practice of Everyday Life*. Trans. S. Rendall. Berkeley: University of California Press, 1984.
de Franco, Chiara. "Media Power and the Rise of Emotions in International Politics." Paper presented at the Annual Convention of the International Studies Association, Atlanta, GA, 2016.
Media Power and the Transformation of War. New York: Palgrave Macmillan, 2012.
de Gaulle, Charles. *Discours et messages*, vol. 2. Paris: Plon, 1974.
de Jonge Oudraat, Chantal. "UNSCOM: Between Iraq and a Hard Place." *European Journal of International Law* 13:1 (2002): 139–152.
de Tarde, Gabriel. *The Laws of Imitation*. Trans. E.C. Parson. New York: H. Holt, 1903.
de Tocqueville, Alexis. *The Ancient Regime and the French Revolution*. Trans. S. Gilbert. London: Collins, 1971.
Democracy in America. Garden City, NY: Doubleday, 1969.
de Vries, Anthonius W. "European Union Sanctions against the Federal Republic of Yugoslavia from 1998 to 2000: A Special Exercise in Targeting." In *Smart Sanctions: Targeting Economic Statecraft*, edited by Cortright, D. and Lopez, G.A., Lanham. MD: Rowman & Littlefield, 2002, 87–108.
Debrix, François. *Re-Envisioning Peacekeeping: The United Nations and the Mobilization of Ideology*. Minneapolis: University of Minnesota Press, 1999.
Dehqanzada, Yahya A., and Ann Florini. *Secrets for Sale: How Commercial Satellite Imagery Will Change the World*. Washington, DC: Carnegie Endowment for International Peace, 2000.
Deitelhof, Nicole. "The Discursive Process of Legalization: Charting Islands of Persuasion in the ICC Case." *International Organization* 63:1 (2009): 33–65.
della Porta, Donatella, and Sidney Tarrow (eds.). *Transnational Protest and Global Activism*. Lanham, MD: Rowman & Littlefield, 2004.
"Der Teenie-Schwarm," *Frankfurter Allgemeine Sonntagszeitung* (Wirtschaft), April 24, 2016.
Descartes, René. *Discourse on Method and Meditations on First Philosophy*. Trans. D. Cress. Indianapolis: Hackett, 1980.
Meditations on First Philosophy. 2nd edn. New York: Liberal Arts Press, 1951.
Dessler, David. "What Is at Stake in the Agent/Structure Debate." *International Organization* 43:3 (1989): 441–473.
Deudney, Daniel. *Bounding Power*. Princeton: Princeton University Press, 2007.
"The Philadelphia System: Sovereignty, Arms Control, and the Balance of Power in the American States-Union, circa 1787–1861." *International Organization* 49:2 (1995): 191–228.
Dewey, John. *Democracy and Education: An Introduction to the Philosophy of Education*. New York: Macmillan, 1916.
Human Nature and Conduct: An Introduction to Social Psychology. New York: H. Holt, 1922.

The Quest for Certainty: A Study of the Relationship between Knowledge and Action. London: Allen and Unwin, 1930.

Dickstein, Morris, and Richard J. Bernstein (eds.). *The Revival of Pragmatism: New Essays on Social Thought, Law, and Culture.* Durham, NC: Duke University Press, 1999.

Diesing, Paul. *How Does Social Science Work?: Reflections on Practice.* Pittsburgh: University of Pittsburgh Press, 1991.

Dinstein, Yoram. *War, Aggression and Self-Defence,* 3rd edn. Cambridge: Cambridge University Press, 2003.

Donnelly, Elizabeth A. "Proclaiming Jubilee: The Debt and Structural Adjustment Network." In *Restructuring World Politics: Transnational Social Movements, Networks, and Norms,* edited by Khagram, S., Sikkink, K., and Riker J.V., Minneapolis: University of Minnesota Press, 2002, 155–180.

Doty, Roxanne Lynn. "Aporia: A Critical Explanation of the Agent/Structure Problem." *European Journal of International Relations* 3:3 (1997): 365–392.

Doyle, Michael W. "Kant, Liberal Legacies, and Foreign Affairs." *Philosophy and Public Affairs* 12:3 (1983): 205–235.

"Kant, Liberal Legacies, and Foreign Affairs, Part 2." *Philosophy & Public Affairs* 12:4 (1983): 323–353.

Striking First: Preemption and Prevention in International Conflict. Princeton: Princeton University Press, 2008.

Drake, William J. "Conclusion: Policies for the National and Global Information Infrastructures." In *The New Information Infrastructure: Strategies for U.S. Policy,* edited by Drake, W.J., New York: Twentieth Century Fund Press, 1995, 345–378.

(ed.). *The New Information Infrastructure: Strategies for U.S. Policy.* New York: Twentieth Century Fund Press, 1995.

Drake, William J., and Ernest J. Wilson III (eds.). *Governing Global Electronic Networks: International Perspectives on Policy and Power.* Cambridge, MA: MIT Press, 2008.

Draper, G.I.A.D. "Grotius' Place in the Development of Legal Ideas about War." In *Hugo Grotius and International Relations,* edited by Bull, H., Kingsbury, B. and Roberts, A., Oxford: Clarendon Press, 1992, 177–208.

Dray, William H. *Laws and Explanation in History.* London: Oxford University Press, 1957.

Drazen, Allan. "Political Contagion in Currency Crises." In *Currency Crises,* edited by Krugman, P., Chicago: University of Chicago Press, 2000, 47–70.

Dreyfus, Huberty, and Charles Taylor. *Retrieving Realism.* Cambridge, MA: Harvard University Press 2015.

Drezner, Daniel W. *The Sanctions Paradox: Economic Statecraft and International Relations.* Cambridge: Cambridge University Press, 1999.

Droysen, Johan Gustav. *Historik: Rekonstruktion der Ersten Vollständigen Fassung der Vorlesungen (1857), Grundriss der Historik in der Ersten Handschriftlichen (1857/1858) und in der Letzten Gedruckten Fassung (1882).* Stuttgart: Frommann-Holzboog, 1977.

Drumbl, Mark A. *Atrocity, Punishment, and International Law.* Cambridge: Cambridge University Press, 2007.

"Punishment, Postgenocide: From Guilt to Shame to *Civis* in Rwanda." *New York University Law Review* 75:5 (2000): 1221–1326.

Duby, Georges. *Le Dimanche de Bouvines, 27 juillet 1214*. Paris: Gallimard, 1973.
The Three Orders: Feudal Society Imagined. Trans. A. Goldhammer. Chicago:
University of Chicago Press, 1980.

Duchêne, François. "Europe's Role in World Peace." In *Europe Tomorrow:
Sixteen Europeans Look Ahead*, edited by Mayne, R., London: Fontana, 1972,
32–47.

Düll, Rudolf. *Das Zwölftafelgesetz: Texte, Übersetzungen und Erläuterungen*.
München: Heimeran, 1953.

Dunbar, Nicholas. *Inventing Money: The Story of Long-Term Capital Management
and the Legends Behind It*. Chichester: Wiley, 2000.

Dunlap Jr., Major General Charles J. "Lawfare Today: A Perspective," *Yale Journal
of International Affairs* 3:1 (2008): 146–154.

Dunne, Timothy. *Inventing International Society: A History of the English School*.
New York: St. Martin's Press, 1998.

Dupuy, Pierre-Marie. "A General Stocktaking of the Connections between the
Multilateral Dimension of Obligations and Codification of the Law of
Responsibility." *European Journal of International Law* 13:5 (2002):
1053–1081.

Durkheim, Émile. *The Division of Labor in Society*, New York: Free Press of Glencoe,
1964.

L'Education morale, Paris: Presses Universitaires de France, 1974.

Duvall, Raymond, and Alexander Wendt. "Institutions and International Order."
In *Global Changes and Theoretical Challenges: Approaches to World Politics for
the 1990s*, edited by Czempiel, Ernst-Otto, and Rosenau, James N. Lexington,
MA: Lexington Books, 1989: 51–73.

Dworkin, R.M. "Is Law a System of Rules?" In *The Philosophy of Law*, edited by
Dworkin, R.M., Oxford: Oxford University Press, 1977, 38–65.

Justice for Hedgehogs. Cambridge, MA: Belknap Press of Harvard University Press,
2011.

A Matter of Principle, Cambridge, MA: Harvard University Press, 1985.

Taking Rights Seriously. Cambridge, MA: Harvard University Press, 1977.

Eckerman, Ingrid. *The Bhopal Saga: Causes and Consequences of the World's Largest
Industrial Disaster*. Bhopal: Universities Press, 2005.

Edgerton, Robert B. *Sick Societies: Challenging the Myth of Primitive Harmony*.
New York: Free Press, 1992.

Edwards, Michael. *Civil Society*. Cambridge, MA: Polity Blackwell, 2004.

Ehrenfreund, Norbert. *The Nuremberg Legacy: How the Nazi War Crimes Trials
Changed the Course of History*. New York: Palgrave Macmillan, 2007.

Eichengreen, Barry. "The International Monetary Fund in the Wake of the Asian
Crisis." In *The Asian Financial Crisis and the Architecture of Global Finance*,
edited by Noble, G.W., and Ravenhill, J., Cambridge: Cambridge University
Press, 2000, 170–191.

Eichengreen, Barry, James Tobin, and Charles Wyplosz. "Two Cases for Sand in the
Wheels of International Finance." *The Economic Journal* 105:428 (1995):
162–172.

Elbe, Joachim von. "The Evolution of the Concept of the Just War in International
Law." *The American Journal of International Law* 33:4 (1939): 665–688.

Elewabadar, Mohamed. "Mens Rea – Mistake of Law and Mistake of Fact in German Criminal Law: A Survey for International Criminal Tribunals." *International Criminal Law Review* 5:2 (2005): 203–246.

Eliade, Mircea. *Images and Symbols: Studies in Religious Symbolism*. Trans. P. Mairet. Princeton: Princeton University Press, 1961.

Elliott, Kimberly Ann. "The Sanctions Glass: Half Full or Completely Empty?" *International Security* 23:1 (1998): 50–65.

Elman, Colin, and Miriam Fendius-Elman. "How Not to Be Lakatos Intolerant: Appraising Progress in IR Research." *International Studies Quarterly* 46:2 (2002): 231–262.

Elster, Jon. *The Cement of Society: A Study of Social Order, Studies in Rationality and Social Change*. Cambridge: Cambridge University Press, 1989.

"Motivations and Beliefs in Suicide Missions." In *Making Sense of Suicide Missions*, edited by Gambetta, D., Oxford: Oxford University Press, 2005, 233–258.

"Norms of Revenge." *Ethics* 100:4 (1990): 862–885.

Emirbayer, Mustafa, and Ann Mische. "What Is Agency?" *The American Journal of Sociology* 103:4 (1998): 962–1023.

Evans, Gareth J. *The Responsibility to Protect: Ending Mass Atrocity Crimes Once and for All*. Washington, DC: Brookings Institution Press, 2008.

Evans, Peter B., Harold Karan Jacobson, and Robert D. Putnam (eds.). *Double-Edged Diplomacy: International Bargaining and Domestic Politics*. Berkeley: University of California Press, 1993.

Fahrenbach, Helmut (ed.). *Wirklichkeit und Reflexion*, Festschrift für Walter Schulz. Pfullingen: Neske 1973.

Falk, Richard A. *Explorations at the Edge of Time: The Prospects for World Order*. Philadelphia: Temple University Press, 1992.

Falke, Andreas. "The EU-US Conflict over Sanctions Policy: Confronting the Hegemon." *European Foreign Affairs Review* 5:2 (2000): 139–163.

Farrall, Jeremy Matam. *United Nations Sanctions and the Rule of Law*. Cambridge: Cambridge University Press, 2007.

Farrington, John, and Anthony Bebbington (eds.). *Reluctant Partners?: Non-Governmental Organizations, the State and Sustainable Agricultural Development*. London: Routledge, 1993.

Fassbender, Bardo. "Uncertain Steps into a Post-Cold War World: The Role and Functioning of the UN Security Council after a Decade of Measures Against Iraq." *European Journal of International Law* 13:1 (2002): 273–303.

Fawthrop, Tom, and Helen Jarvis. *Getting Away with Genocide? Elusive Justice and the Khmer Rouge Tribunal*. London: Pluto Press, 2004.

Fearon, James D. "Counterfactuals and Hypothesis Testing in Political Science." *World Politics* 43:2 (1991): 169–195.

Feinberg, Richard. "The Changing Relationship between the World Bank and the International Monetary Fund." *International Organization,* 42:2 (1988): 545–560.

Feldstein, Martin S. "Refocusing the IMF." *Foreign Affairs* 77:2 (1998): 20–33.

Felice, Damiano de, and Francesco Obina. "Out of the Ivory Tower: Weaving the Theories and Practices of International Relations." *Millennium* 40:3 (2012): 431–437.

Ferencz, Benjamin B. *Defining International Aggression, the Search for World Peace: A Documentary History and Analysis*. Dobbs Ferry, NY: Oceana Publications, 1975.

Ferguson, Yale H., and Richard W. Mansbach. *Polities: Authority, Identities and Change*. Columbia, SC: University of South Carolina Press, 1996.

The Elusive Quest: Theory and International Politics. Columbia, SC: University of South Carolina Press, 1988.

Ferreira, M.J. "Hume and Imagination: Sympathy and 'the Other'." *International Philosophical Quarterly* 34 (1994): 39–57.

Fierke, Karen, and Knud Erik Joergensen (eds.). *Constructing International Relations, the Next Generation*. Armonk, NY/London: M.E. Sharpe, 2001.

Filmer, Robert. *Patriarcha and Other Political Writings*, edited by Laslett, P., Oxford: Blackwell, 1949.

Findlay, Alison. *Illegitimate Power: Bastards in Renaissance Drama*. Manchester: Manchester University Press, 1994.

Fine, Gail. *On Ideas: Aristotle's Criticism of Plato's Theory of Forms*. Oxford: Oxford University Press, 1995.

Finkielkraut, Alain. *Remembering in Vain: The Klaus Barbie Trial and Crimes against Humanity*. Trans. R. Lapidius. New York: Columbia University Press, 1992.

Finley, Moses I. *The Ancient Economy*. London: Hogarth Press, 1985.

"The Ancient Historian and His Sources." In *Ancient History: Evidence and Models*, New York: Penguin Books, 1985, 7–26.

Finley, Moses, et al. (eds.). *Economy and Society in Ancient Greece*. New York: Viking Press, 1982.

Finnemore, Martha, and Kathryn Sikkink. "International Norm Dynamics and Political Change." *International Organization* 52:4 (1998): 887–917.

Fiori, Stefano. "Adam Smith on Method: Newtonianism, History, Institutions, and the 'Invisible Hand'." *Journal of the History of Economic Thought* 34:3 (2012): 411–435.

Fischer, Fritz. *Griff nach der Weltmacht: die Kriegszielpolitik des kaiserlichen Deutschland 1914/18*. Düsseldorf: Droste, 1961.

Fischer, Markus. "Feudal Europe, 800–1300: Communal Discourse and Conflictual Practices." *International Organization* 46:2 (1992): 427–466.

Fischer-Lescano, Andreas, and Gunther Teubner. *Regime Kollisionen*. Frankfurt: Suhrkamp, 2006.

Flaumenhaft, Mera J. *The Civic Spectacle: Essays on Drama and Community*. Lanham, MD: Rowman & Littlefield, 1994.

Flavius, Josephus. *The Jewish War*. Trans. G.A. Williamson. New York: Dorset Press, 1970.

Florini, Ann (ed.). *The Right to Know: Transparency for an Open World*. New York: Columbia University Press, 2007.

Forlati, Serena. "Reactions to Nonperformance of Treaties in International Law." *Leiden Journal of International Law* 24:3 (2012): 759–70.

Foucault, Michel. *The Birth of Biopolitics*. Trans. G. Burchell. New York: Palgrave Macmillan, 2004.

Discipline and Punish: The Birth of the Prison. 2nd edn. New York: Vintage Books, 1995.

Security, Territory, Population. Houndmills: Palgrave Macmillan, 2007.

Security, Territory, Population: Lectures at the Collège de France, 1977–78.
Edited by Senellart, M. New York: Palgrave Macmillan, 2007.

Fragmenta Historicorum Graecorum. Edited by Müller, C. Cambridge: Cambridge
University Press, 2010.

Franck, Thomas M. *Fairness in International Law and Institutions.* Oxford:
Clarendon Press, 1995.

The Power of Legitimacy among Nations. Oxford: Oxford University Press, 1990.

Recourse to Force: State Action against Threats and Armed Attacks. Cambridge:
Cambridge University Press, 2002.

Frank, Joseph. *The Beginnings of the English Newspaper, 1620–1660.* Cambridge,
MA: Harvard University Press, 1961.

Franke, Ulrich, and Ralph Weber. "At the Papini Hotel – on Pragmatism in the
Study of International Relations." *European Journal of International Relations*
18:4 (2012): 669–691.

Freeman, Mark. *Necessary Evils: Amnesties and the Search for Justice.* Cambridge:
Cambridge University Press, 2009.

Freeman, R. Edward. *Strategic Management: A Stakeholder Approach.* Boston, MA:
Pitman Publishing, 1984.

Freud, Sigmund. *Group Psychology and the Analysis of the Ego.* New York:
W.W. Norton & Company, 1975.

Friedman, Milton. "Internationalization of the US Economy." Paper presented at the
Fraser Forum 1989.

"The Methodology of Positive Economics." In *Essays in Positive Economics*,
Chicago: University of Chicago Press, 1966, 3–16, 30–43.

"The Methodology of Positive Economics." In *Readings in the Philosophy of the
Social Sciences*, edited by Brodbeck, M., New York: Macmillan, 1968, 508–528.

"The Social Responsibility of Business Is to Increase Its Profits." *New York
Times Magazine*, September 13, 1970: 32–33 and 122–126.

Friedrichs, Jörg, and Friedrich Kratochwil. "On Acting and Knowing: How Pragmatism
Can Advance International Relations Research and Methodology." *International
Organization* 63:4 (2009): 701–731.

Frisch, Karl von. *The Dance Language and Orientation of Bees.* Cambridge, MA:
Harvard University Press, 1993.

Frost, Mervyn. *Ethics in International Relations: A Constitutive Theory.* Cambridge:
Cambridge University Press, 1996.

Fuchs, Christian. *Internet and Society: Social Theory in the Information Age.*
New York: Routledge, 2008.

Fukuyama, Francis. *The End of History and the Last Man*, New York: Avon Books, 1992.

Fuller, Lon L. "Positivism and Fidelity to Law: A Reply to Professor Hart." *Harvard
Law Review* 71:4 (1958): 630–672.

Fuller, Stephen. *Social Epistemology.* Bloomington: University of Indiana Press, 1992.

Gabriel, Markus. *Warum Es die Welt Nicht Gibt.* Berlin: Ullstein, 2013.

Gadamer, Hans-Georg. *Truth and Method*, 2nd edn. Edited by and trans. Joel
Weinsheimer, New York: Continuum, 2004.

Gallie, W.B. "Essentially Contested Concepts." In *The Importance of Language*,
edited by Black, M., Englewood Cliffs, NJ: Prentice-Hall, 1962.

Philosophy and the Historical Understanding, 2nd edn. New York: Schocken Books,
1968.

Galtung, Johan. "On the Effects of International Economic Sanctions, with Examples from the Case of Rhodesia." *World Politics* 19:3 (1967): 378–416.

Gambetta, Diego. "Can We Make Sense of Suicide Missions?" In *Making Sense of Suicide Missions*, edited by Gambetta, D., Oxford: Oxford University Press, 2005, 259–300.

Garfinkel, Harold. *Ethnomethodological Studies of Work*. Cambridge: Polity Press, 1984.

Garthoff, Raymond L. *Detente and Confrontation: American–Soviet Relations from Nixon to Reagan*. Washington, DC: Brookings Institution, 1994.

Gaskins, Richard. *Burdens of Proof in Modern Discourse*. New Haven: Yale University Press, 1992.

Gentili, Alberico. *De Jure Belli Libri Tres*. Classics in International Law. Oxford: Oxford University Press, 1933.

Gentner, Dedre, Keith James Holyoak, and Boicho N. Kokinov (eds.). *The Analogical Mind: Perspectives from Cognitive Science*. Cambridge, MA: MIT Press, 2001.

George, Alexander L., and Richard Smoke. *Deterrence in American Foreign Policy: Theory and Practice*. New York: Columbia University Press, 1974.

Georges, Duby. *Les Trois Ordres ou l'imaginaire du féodalisme*. Paris: Gallimard, 1978.

Georgi, Oliver. "Automatisierter Hass im Netz," *Frankfurter Allgemeine Zeitung*, May 24, 2016, accessed at www.faz.net/-gpf-8hc5h.

Gerschenkron, Alexander. *Economic Backwardness in Historical Perspective: A Book of Essays*. Cambridge MA: The Belknap Press of Harvard University Press, 1962.

Gilbert, Margaret. *On Social Facts*, London: Routledge, 1989.

Gill, Stephen. "The Global Panopticon? The Neoliberal State, Economic Life, and Democratic Surveillance." *Alternatives: Global, Local, Political* 20:1 (1995): 1–49.

(ed.). *Gramsci, Historical Materialism and International Relations*. Cambridge: Cambridge University Press, 1993.

Gilpin, Robert. "Has Modern Technology Changed International Politics?" In *The Analysis of International Politics: Essays in Honor of Harold and Margaret Sprout*, edited by Rosenau, J.N., Davis, V., and East, M.A., New York: Free Press, 1972, 166–173.

War and Change in World Politics. Cambridge: Cambridge University Press, 1981.

Gilson, Douglas. "Justice Denied," *Foreign Policy*, November 23, 2011, accessed at http://foreignpolicy.com/2011/11/23/justice-denied.

Goffman, Erving. *Behavior in Public Places: Notes on the Social Organization of Gatherings*. New York: Free Press of Glencoe, 1966.

Interaction Ritual: Essays in Face-to-Face-Behavior. Chicago: Aldine, 1974.

The Presentation of Self in Everyday Life. New York: Anchor Books, 1959.

Goldhagen, Daniel Jonah. *Hitler's Willing Executioners: Ordinary Germans and the Holocaust*. New York: Knopf, 1996.

Goldman, Wendy Z. *Inventing the Enemy: Denunciation and Terror in Stalin's Russia*. Cambridge: Cambridge University Press, 2011.

Goldsmith, Jack. *The Terror Presidency: Law and Judgment inside the Bush Administration*. New York: W.W. Norton, 2007.

Goldstein, Judith, and Robert O. Keohane (eds.). *Ideas and Foreign Policy: Beliefs, Institutions, and Political Change*. Ithaca, NY: Cornell University Press, 1993.

Goldstone, Richard. "Justice as a Tool for Peace-Making: Truth Commissions and International Criminal Tribunals." *New York University Journal of International Law and Politics* 28:3 (1996): 485–503.

Goldthorpe, John H. "The Uses of History in Sociology: A Reply." *British Journal of Sociology* 45:1 (1994): 55–77.

"The Uses of History in Sociology: Reflections on Some Recent Tendencies." *British Journal of Sociology* 42:2 (1991): 211–230.

Gordon, Joy. "A Peaceful, Silent, Deadly Remedy: The Ethics of Economic Sanctions." *Ethics and International Affairs* 13:1 (1999): 123–142.

Gowa, Joanne. "Rational Hegemons, Excludable Goods, and Small Groups: An Epitaph for Hegemonic Stability Theory?" *World Politics* 41:3 (1989): 307–324.

Gramsci, Antonio. *Selections from the Prison Notebooks of Antonio Gramsci*. Edited by Hoare, Q. and Nowell-Smith, G., London: Lawrence & Wishart, 1971.

Granovetter, Mark. "Threshold Models of Collective Behavior." *American Journal of Sociology* 83:6 (1978): 1420–1443.

Graves, Christopher. "The International Criminal Court and Individualism: An African Perspective." In *Critical Approaches to International Criminal Law: An Introduction*, edited by Schwöbel, C.E.J., Abingdon: Routledge, 2014, 221–245.

Gray, Christine D. *International Law and the Use of Force*, 2nd edn. Oxford: Oxford University Press, 2004.

Gray, John. *Black Mass: Apocalyptic Religion and the Death of Utopia*. London: Penguin, 2007.

Grotius, Hugo. *De Jure Belli Ac Pacis Libri Tres*. Trans. F.W. Kelsey. New York: Oceana, 1964 [1646].

Grzebyk, Patrycja. *Criminal Responsibility for the Crime of Aggression*. London: Routledge, 2013.

Gulick, Edward Vose. *Europe's Classical Balance of Power: A Case History of the Theory and Practice of One of the Great Concepts of European Statecraft*. New York: W.W. Norton, 1967.

Gutting, Gary (ed.). *Paradigms and Revolutions: Appraisals and Applications of Thomas Kuhn's Philosophy of Science*, Notre Dame, IN: University of Notre Dame Press, 1980.

Guzzini, Stefano. "A Reconstruction of Constructivism in International Relations." *European Journal of International Relations* 6:2 (2000): 147–182.

Haakonssen, Knud. *Natural Law and Moral Philosophy: From Grotius to the Scottish Enlightenment*. New York: Cambridge University Press, 1996.

Haan, Verena. "The Development of the Concept of Joint Criminal Enterprise at the International Criminal Tribunal for the Former Yugoslavia." *International Criminal Law Review* 5:2 (2005): 167–201.

Haas, Ernst B. "Is There a Hole in the Whole? Knowledge, Technology, Interdependence, and the Construction of International Regimes." *International Organization* 29:3 (1975): 827–876.

When Knowledge Is Power: Three Models of Change in International Organizations. Berkeley: University of California Press, 1990.

"Why Collaborate? Issue-Linkage and International Regimes." *World Politics* 32:3 (1980): 357–405.

Haas, Peter M., and Ernst B. Haas. "Pragmatic Constructivism and the Study of International Institutions." *Millennium* 32:3 (2002): 573–601.

Haass, Richard N. "Sanctioning Madness." *Foreign Affairs* 76:6 (1997): 74–85.

Haass, Richard, and Meghan L. O'Sullivan. *Honey and Vinegar: Incentives, Sanctions, and Foreign Policy.* Washington, DC: Brookings Institution Press, 2000.

Habermas, Jürgen. *Faktizität und Geltung.* Frankfurt: Suhrkamp, 1993.

Legitimationsprobleme im Spätkapitalismus. Frankfurt: Suhrkamp, 1973.

Strukturwandel der Öffentlichkeit: Untersuchungen zu einer Kategorie der bürgerlichen Gesellschaft. Berlin: Luchterhand, 1971.

"Wahrheitstheorien." In *Wirklichkeit und Reflexion, Festschrift für Walter Schulz,* edited by Fahrenbach, H., Pullingen: Neske 1973, 122–65.

Hagan, John. *Justice in the Balkans: Prosecuting War Crimes in the Hague Tribunal.* Chicago: University of Chicago Press, 2003.

Haggard, Stephen. "The Political Economy of the Philippine Debt Crisis." In *Economic Crisis and Policy Choice: The Politics of Adjustment in the Third World,* edited by Nelson, J.M., Princeton: Princeton University Press, 1990, 215–256.

"The Politics of Adjustment: Lessons from the IMF's Extended Fund Facility." In *The Politics of International Debt,* edited by Kahler, M., Ithaca, NY: Cornell University Press, 1986, 157–186.

Haggard, Stephen, and Robert R. Kaufman (eds.). *The Politics of Economic Adjustment: International Constraints, Distributive Conflicts, and the State.* Princeton: Princeton University Press, 1992.

Haggenmacher, Peter. "Grotius and Gentili: A Reassessment of Thomas E. Holland's Inaugural Lecture." In *Hugo Grotius and International Relations,* edited by Bull, H., Kingsbury, B., and Roberts, A., Oxford: Clarendon Press, 1992, 133–176.

Halbwachs, Maurice. *On Collective Memory.* Trans. L.A. Coser. Chicago: University of Chicago Press, 1992.

Halévy, Elie. *The Growth of Philosophic Radicalism.* Trans. M. Morris. London: Faber and Faber, 1972.

Hall, Rodney Bruce. "The Discursive Demolition of the Asian Development Model." *International Studies Quarterly* 47:1 (2003): 71–99.

National Collective Identity: Social Constructs and International Systems. New York: Columbia University Press, 1999.

Hamati-Ataya, Inanna. "Beyond (Post) Positivism: The Missed Promises of Systemic Pragmatism," *International Studies Quarterly* 56:2 (2012): 291–305.

Hammond, Philip. *Media, War and Postmodernity.* London: Routledge, 2007.

Handel, Michael I. "The Yom Kippur War and the Inevitability of Surprise." *International Studies Quarterly* 21:3 (1977): 461–502.

Hansen, Lene. "How Images Make World Politics: International Icons and the Case of Abu Ghraib." *Review of International Studies* 41:2 (2015): 263–288.

Hardin, Garrett. "The Tragedy of the Commons." *Science* 162 (1968): 1243–1248.

Hardin, Russell. *David Hume: Moral and Political Theorist,* Oxford–NewYork: Oxford University Press, 2007.

Hare, R.M. *The Language of Morals.* Oxford: Clarendon Press, 1972.

Hariman, Robert, and John Louis Lucaites. *No Caption Needed: Iconic Photographs, Public Culture, and Liberal Democracy*. Chicago: University of Chicago Press, 2007.

Harkin, Michael. "Potlach in Anthropology." In *International Encyclopedia of the Social & Behavioral Sciences*, edited by Smelser, N.J. and Baltes, P.B., New York: Elsevier, 2001, 11885–11889.

Harre, Rom. *Varieties of Realism: A Rationale for the Natural Sciences*. Oxford: Blackwell, 1986.

Hart, H.L.A. *The Concept of Law*. Clarendon Law Series. Oxford: Oxford University Press, 1961.

"Positivism and the Separation of Law and Morals." *Harvard Law Review* 71:4 (1958): 593–629.

Punishment and Responsibility. Oxford: Clarendon Press, 1968.

Hart, H.L.A., and Tony Honoré. *Causation in the Law*. Oxford: Clarendon Press, 1959.

Hart, Nicky. "John Goldthorpe and the Relics of Sociology." *British Journal of Sociology* 45:1 (1994): 21–30.

Harvey, David. *The Enigma of Capital: And the Crises of Capitalism*. Oxford: Oxford University Press, 2011.

Hasenclever, Andreas, Peter Mayer, and Volker Rittberger. *Theories of International Regimes*. Cambridge: Cambridge University Press, 1997.

Hasluck, Margaret Masson Hardie. *The Unwritten Law in Albania*. Cambridge: Cambridge University Press, 1954.

Hayek, Friedrich A. von. "The Use of Knowledge in Society." *American Economic Review* 35:4 (1945): 519–530.

Hayner, Priscilla B. "Fifteen Truth Commissions – 1974–1994: A Comparative Study." *Human Rights Quarterly* 16:4 (1994): 597–655.

Unspeakable Truths: Confronting State Terror and Atrocity, New York: Routledge, 2001.

Hegel, Georg Wilhelm Friedrich. *Philosophy of Right*. Trans. T.M. Knox. Oxford: Oxford University Press, 1967.

Helleiner, Eric. "Explaining the Globalization of Financial Markets: Bringing States Back In." *Review of International Political Economy* 2:2 (1995): 315–341.

Heller, Jon, Kevin. "The Taylor Sentencing Judgment: A Critical Analysis." *Journal of International Criminal Justice* 11:4 (2013): 835–855.

Hellmann, Gunther. "Pragmatism and International Relations." *International Studies Review* 11:3 (2009): 638–662.

Hempel, Carl. *Aspects of Scientific Explanation, and Other Essays in the Philosophy of Science*. New York: Free Press, 1965.

"The Function of General Laws in History." In *Aspects of Scientific Explanation*, edited by Hempel, C., New York: Free Press, 1965, 231–244.

Henham, Ralph. "Developing Contextualized Rationales for Sentencing in International Criminal Trials." *Journal of International Criminal Justice* 5:3 (2007): 757–778.

Punishment and Process in International Criminal Trials. Aldershot: Ashgate, 2005.

Henkin, Louis, and Council on Foreign Relations. *How Nations Behave: Law and Foreign Policy*. New York: Praeger, 1968.

Herodotus. *The Histories*. Trans. A. De Sélincourt. Harmondsworth: Penguin Books, 1954.

Hesse, Mary B. *Models and Analogies in Science*. Notre Dame, IN: University of Notre Dame Press, 1966.

Hexter, J.H. *Reappraisals in History*. Chicago: University of Chicago Press, 1961.

Hirschman, Albert O. *Exit, Voice, and Loyalty: Responses to Decline in Firms, Organizations, and States*. Cambridge, MA: Harvard University Press, 1970.

The Passions and the Interests. Princeton: Princeton University Press, 1977.

"The Political Economy of Import-Substituting Industrialization in Latin America." In *A Bias for Hope: Essays on Development and Latin America*, New Haven: Yale University Press, 1971, 85–123.

"The Rise and Decline of Development Economics." In *Essays in Trespassing: Economics to Politics and Beyond*. Cambridge: Cambridge University Press, 1981, 1–24.

Hirsh, Michael, and John Barry. "How We Stumbled into War." *Newsweek*, April 12, 1999.

Hirst, Paul. "The Global Economy – Myths and Realities." *International Affairs* 73:3 (1997): 409–425.

Hobbes, Thomas. *De Cive*. New York: Appleton-Century-Crofts, 1949 [1642].

Elements of Law. Oxford: Oxford University Press, 1994.

Leviathan. Edited by MacPherson, C.B. Baltimore: Penguin Books, 1968 [1651].

Leviathan. Edited by Tuck, R. Cambridge: Cambridge University Press, 1991.

Holbrooke, Richard C. *To End a War*. New York: Random House, 1998.

Hollis, Martin, and Steve Smith. *Explaining and Understanding International Relations*. New York: Oxford University Press, 1990.

Holmes, Stephen. *Passions and Constraint: On the Theory of Liberal Democracy*. Chicago: University of Chicago Press, 1995.

"Political Psychology in Hobbes's Behemoth." In *Thomas Hobbes and Political Theory*, edited by Dietz, M.G., Lawrence: University of Kansas Press, 1990.

"The Secret History of Self- Interest." In *Beyond Self-Interest*, edited by Mansbridge, J., Chicago: University of Chicago Press, 1990, 267–286.

Homer. *The Iliad*. Trans. S. Butler. Cambridge MA: Harvard University Press, 1924.

The Odyssey. Trans. A.T. Murray. Cambridge, MA: Harvard University Press, 1919.

Honneth, Axel, and Joas Hans. *Social Action and Human Nature*. Cambridge: Cambridge University Press, 1988.

Hopf, Ted. "The Logic of Habit in International Relations." *European Journal of International Relations* 16:4 (2010): 539–561.

Hopple, Gerald W. "Intelligence and Warning: Implications and Lessons of the Falkland Islands War." *World Politics* 36:3 (1984): 339–361.

Horkheimer, Max, and Theodor W. Adorno. *Dialectic of Enlightment*. London: Allen Lane, 1973.

Huband, Mark. *The Skull beneath the Skin: Africa after the Cold War*. Boulder, CO: Westview Press, 2001.

Hubbard, L. Ron. *Dianetics: The Modern Science of Mental Health*. Los Angeles: Bride Pub. Inc., 1950.

Hufbauer, Gary Clyde, Jeffrey J. Schott, and Kimberly Ann Elliott. *Economic Sanctions Reconsidered*, 2nd edn. Washington, DC: Institute for International Economics, 1990.

Hughes, Edel, William Schabas, and Ramesh Chandra Thakur (eds.). *Atrocities and International Accountability beyond Transitional Justice*. New York: United Nations University Press, 2007.

Human Rights Watch. "Rwanda: Justice after Genocide – 20 Years On." 2014. Available at www.hrw.org/news/2014/03/28/rwanda-justice-after-genocide-20-years.

Hume, David. "Dialogue Concerning Natural Religion [1799]." In *Hume on Religion*, edited by Wollheim, R., London: Fontana, 1963.

"Dialogues on Natural Religion." In *Writings on Religion*, edited by Flew, A., La Salle, IL: Open Court, 1992.

The History of England: From the Invasion of Julius Caesar to the Revolution in 1688. Indianapolis: Liberty Classics, 1983.

"The Idea of a Perfect Commonwealth." In *Essays, Moral, Political, and Literary*, edited by Miller, E.F., Indianapolis: Liberty Classics, 1985, 512–532.

An Inquiry Concerning Human Understanding. Edited by Selby-Bigge, L.A. Oxford: Clarendon, 1975.

An Inquiry Concerning the Principles of Morals. Edited by Hendel, C. Indianapolis: Bobbs-Merrill, 1957.

The Natural History of Religion. Edited by H.E. Root. London: Adam and Charles Black, 1956.

"Of Essay Writing." In *Essays, Moral, Political, and Literary*, edited by Miller, E.F., Indianapolis: Liberty Classics, 1742, 533–537.

"Of the Balance of Power." In *Essays, Moral, Political, and Literary*, edited by Miller, E.F., Indianapolis: Liberty Classics, 1985, 322–341.

"Of the Independency of Parliament." In *Essays, Moral, Political, and Literary*, edited by Miller, E.F., Indianapolis: Liberty Classics, 1985, 42–46.

"Of the Liberty of the Press." In *Essays, Moral, Political, and Literary*, edited by Miller, E.F., Indianapolis: Liberty Classics, 1985, 9–13.

"Of the Original Contract." In *Social Contract: Essays by Locke, Hume, and Rousseau*, edited by Barker, E., London: Oxford University Press, 1960, 147–168.

"On the Standards of Taste." In *Essays, Moral, Political, and Literary*, edited by Miller, E.F., Indianapolis: Liberty Classics, 1985, 222–249.

"The Parties of Great Britain." In *Essays, Moral, Political, and Literary*, edited by Miller, E.F., Indianapolis: Liberty Classics, 1985, 64–72.

"The Rise of Arts and Sciences." In *Essays, Moral, Political, and Literary*, edited by Miller, E.F., Indianapolis: Liberty Classics, 1985, 111–137.

A Treatise of Human Nature. Edited by Selby-Bigge, L.A. Oxford: Clarendon University Press, 1978.

A Treatise of Human Nature. Edited by Norton, David Fate, and Norton, Mary J. Oxford–New York: Oxford University Press, 2000.

Humphreys, Paul. "Causation in the Social Sciences: An Overview." *Synthese* 68:1 (1986): 1–12.

Hurrell, Andrew. "International Society and the Study of Regimes: A Reflective Approach." In *Regime Theory and International Relations*, edited by Rittberger, V. and Mayer, P., Oxford: Clarendon Press, 1993, 49–72.

Ignatieff, Michael. "The Elusive Goal of War Trials." *Harper's* 294:1762 (1997): 15.

Igreja, Victor, and Beatrice Dias-Lambranca. "Restorative Justice and the Role of *Magamba* Spirits in Post-Civil War Gorongosa, Central Mozambique." In *Traditional Justice and Reconciliation after Violent Conflict: Learning from African Experiences*, edited by Huyse, L. and Salter, M., Stockholm: International Institute for Democracy and Electoral Assistance, 2008, 61–84.

Ikenberry, John, G. *After Victory: Institutions, Strategic Restraint, and the Rebuilding of Order after Major Wars*. Princeton: Princeton University Press, 2001.

Independent International Commission on Kosovo. *The Kosovo Report: Conflict, International Response, Lessons Learned*. Oxford: Oxford University Press, 2004.

Ingrao, Charles W. *The Habsburg Monarchy, 1618–1815*. Cambridge: Cambridge University Press, 2000.

International Commission on Intervention and State Sovereignty. "The Responsibility to Protect." Ottawa: International Development Research Centre, 2001.

Jabbari, David. "From Criticism to Construction in Modern Critical Legal Theory." *Oxford Journal of Legal Studies* 12:4 (1992): 507–542.

Jackson, Patrick Thaddeus. *The Conduct of Inquiry in International Relations*. London–New York: Routledge, 2011.

"On the Cultural Pre-Conditions of Political Actors." Paper presented at the Annual Meeting of the American Political Science Association, Boston, MA, September 3–6, 1998.

Jackson, Patrick, and Daniel Nexon. "Relations before States: Substance, Process and the Study of World Politics." *European Journal of International Relations* 5:3 (1999): 291–327.

Jackson, Robert H. "Armed Humanitarianism." *International Journal* 48:4 (1993): 579–606.

Quasi-States: Sovereignty, International Relations, and the Third World. Cambridge: Cambridge University Press, 1990.

Jacobs, Dov. "A Narrative of Justice and the (Re)-Writing of History: Lessons Learned from WW II French Trials." In *The Hidden Histories of War Crimes Trials*, edited by Heller, K.J. and Simpson, G., Oxford: Oxford University Press, 2013, 122–136.

Jakobs, Günther. "Bürgerstrafrecht und Feindstrafrecht." *HRRS: Onlinezeitschrift für Höchstrichterliche Rechtsprechung zum Strafrecht* 3 (2004): 88–95.

Jellinek, Georg. *Die Rechtliche Natur der Staatenverträge: Ein Beitrag zur Juristischen Construction des Völkerrechts*. Vienna: A. Hölder, 1880.

Jervis, Robert. *The Logic of Images in International Relations*. New York: Columbia University Press, 1970.

System Effects: Complexity in Political and Social Life. Princeton: Princeton University Press, 1997.

"Understanding the Bush Doctrine." *Political Science Quarterly* 118:3 (2003): 365–388.

Johnston, David. *The Rhetoric of Leviathan: Thomas Hobbes and the Politics of Cultural Transformation*. Princeton: Princeton University Press, 1986.

Jonker, Gerdien. *The Topography of Remembrance: The Dead, Tradition and Collective Memory in Mesopotamia*. Leiden: Brill, 1995.

Jonsen, Albert R., and Stephen Edelston Toulmin. *The Abuse of Casuistry: A History of Moral Reasoning*. Berkeley: University of California Press, 2000.

Joseph, Jonathan. *The Social in the Global: Social Theory, Governmentality and Global Politics*. Cambridge: Cambridge University Press, 2012.

Kagan, Donald. *Thucydides: The Reinvention of History*. New York: Penguin, 2010.

Kagan, Robert. *Paradise and Power: America and Europe in a New World Order*. London: Atlantic Books, 2003.

Kahler, Miles. "External Influence, Conditionality, and the Politics of Adjustment." In *The Politics of Economic Adjustment: International Constraints, Distributive Conflicts, and the State*, edited by Haggard, S. and Kaufman, R.R., Princeton: Princeton University Press, 1992, 89–138.

(ed.). *The Politics of International Debt*. Ithaca, NY: Cornell University Press, 1986.

Kahn, Paul W. *The Reign of Law: Marbury v. Madison and the Construction of America*. New Haven: Yale University Press, 1997.

Sacred Violence: Torture, Terror, and Sovereignty. Ann Arbor: Michigan University Press, 2008.

Kant, Immanuel. *Critique of Pure Reason*. Trans. P. Guyer and A.W. Wood. Cambridge: Cambridge University Press, 1998.

Critique of the Power of Judgment. Trans. P. Guyer. Cambridge: Cambridge University Press, 2000.

Der Streit der Fakultäten. Edited by Reich, K. Hamburg: Meiner, 1959.

Kant's Political Writings. Edited by Reiss, H. Cambridge: Cambridge University Press, 2011.

Kritik der Reinen Vernunft, vol. 2. Edited by Weischedel, W. Wiesbaden: Inseln-Verlag, 1956.

The Metaphysics of Morals. Trans. M. Gregor. Cambridge: Cambridge University Press, 1991.

On the Old Saw That Might Be Right in Theory but Won't Work in Practice. Trans. E.B. Ashton. Philadelphia: University of Pennsylvania Press, 1974.

"Perpetual Peace." In *Kant's Political Writings*, edited by Reiss, H., Cambridge: Cambridge University Press, 1988.

"Perpetual Peace." In *Kant's Political Writings*, edited by Reiss, H., Cambridge: Cambridge University Press, 2011.

Perpetual Peace: A Philosophical Sketch. Cambridge: Cambridge University Press, 1970.

Prolegomena to Any Future Metaphysics That Will Be Able to Come Forward as Science. Trans. G.C. Hatfield. Cambridge: Cambridge University Press, 2004.

Werkausgabe, vol. 3. Edited by Weischedel, W. Frankfurt: Suhrkamp, 1956.

"Zum Ewigen Frieden." In *Zum Ewigen Frieden: und Auszüge Aus der Rechtslehre*, edited by Niesen, P. and Eberl, O., Berlin: Suhrkamp, 2011.

Kantorowicz, Ernst H. *The King's Two Bodies: A Study in Mediaeval Political Theology*. Princeton: Princeton University Press, 1957.

Kaplan, Morton A. "The New Great Debate: Traditionalism vs. Science in International Relations." *World Politics* 19:1 (1966): 1–20.

System and Process in International Politics. New York: Wiley, 1967.

Katzenstein, Peter J. (ed.). *The Culture of National Security: Norms and Identity in World Politics*. New York: Columbia University Press, 1996.

Katzenstein, Peter J., Robert O. Keohane, and Stephen D. Krasner. "International Organization and the Study of World Politics." *International Organization* 52:4 (1998), 645–685.

Kaufman, Robert R. "Stabilization and Adjustment in Argentina, Brazil, and Mexico." In *Economic Crisis and Policy Choice: The Politics of Adjustment in the Third World*, edited by Nelson, J.M., Princeton: Princeton University Press, 1990, 63–112.

Kay, David. "The IAEA: How Can It Be Strenghtened?" In *Nuclear Proliferation after the Cold War*, edited by Reiss, M. and Litwak, R., Washington, DC: Woodrow Wilson Center Press, 1994, 309–334.

Keck, Margaret E. "Social Equity and Environmental Politics in Brazil: Lessons from the Rubber Tappers of Acre." *Comparative Politics* 27:4 (1995): 409–424.

Keck, Otto. "Rationales Kommunikatives Handeln in den Internationalen Beziehungen: Ist eine Verbindung von Rational-Choice-Theorie und Habermas' Theorie des Kommunikativen Handelns möglich?." *Zeitschrift für Internationale Beziehungen* 2:1 (1995): 5–48.

Keen, Andrew. *The Internet Is Not the Answer*. London: Atlantic Books, 2015.

Keen, David. *Endless War? Hidden Functions of the "War on Terror"*. London: Pluto Press, 2006.

Keenan, Joseph Berry, and Brendan Francis Brown. *Crimes against International Law*. Washington, DC: Public Affairs Press, 1950.

Kelly, Donald. "The Development and Context of Bodin's Method." In *Jean Bodin: Proceedings of the International Conference on Bodin*, edited by Denzer, H., München: Beck, 1973, 105–123.

Kelman, Mark. *A Guide to Critical Legal Studies*. Cambridge, MA: Harvard University Press, 1987.

Kelsen, Hans. *General Theory of Law and State*. Trans. A. Wedberg. Cambridge. MA: Harvard University Press, 1945.

Principles of International Law, 2nd edn. Edited by Tucker, R.W. New York: Holt, 1966.

Pure Theory of the Law. Trans. M. Knight. Gloucester, MA: Peter Smith, 1989.

"Will the Judgment in the Nuremberg Trial Constitute a Precedent in International Law?" *The International Law Quarterly* 1:2 (1947): 153–171.

Kendall, Sara, and Sarah Nouwen. "Representational Practices at the International Criminal Court: The Gap between Juridified and Abstract Victimhood." *Law and Contemporary Problems* 76 (2013): 235–262.

Kennedy, David. *The Dark Side of Virtue: Reassessing International Humanitarianism*. Princeton: Princeton University Press, 2005.

"The Move to Institutions." *Cardozo Law Review* 8:5 (1987): 841–988.

"Primitive Legal Scholarship." *Harvard International Law Journal* 27:1 (1986): 1–98.

Kennedy, Duncan. *A Critique of Adjudication: Fin de Siècle*. Cambridge, MA: Harvard University Press, 1997.

"Form and Substance in Private Law Adjudication." *Harvard Law Review* 89 (1976): 1685–1778.

Keohane, Robert. *After Hegemony: Cooperation and Discord in the World Political Economy*. Princeton: Princeton University Press, 1984.

"The Analysis of International Regimes: Towards a European–American Research Program." In *Regime Theory and International Relations*, edited by Rittberger, V., and Mayer, P., Oxford: Clarendon Press, 1993, 23–45.

"The Demand for International Regimes." In *International Regimes*, edited by Krasner, S.D., Ithaca, NY: Cornell University Press, 1983, 141–172.

"International Institutions: Two Approaches." *International Studies Quarterly* 32:4 (1988): 379–396.

"Neoliberal Institutionalism: A Perspective on World Politics." In *International Institutions and State Power: Essays in International Relations Theory*, Boulder, CO: Westview Press, 1989, 1–20.

Keohane, Robert O., and Joseph S. Nye. *Power and Interdependence: World Politics in Transition*. Boston, MA: Little, Brown, 1977.

Kessler, Oliver (ed.). *Die Internationale Politische Ökonomie der Weltfinanzkrise*. Wiesbaden: Springer, 2011.

"Forum on Critical Realism," *Review of International Studies* 28:1 (2012): 187–274.

King, Gary, Robert Keohane, and Sidney Verba. *Designing Social Inquiry: Scientific Inference in Qualitative Research*. Princeton: Princeton University Press, 1994.

Kirkpatrick, David. *The Facebook Effect: The Inside Story of the Company That Is Connecting the World*. New York: Simon & Schuster, 2010.

Kirshner, Jonathan. "Review Essay: Economic Sanctions: The State of the Art." *Security Studies* 11:4 (2002): 160–179.

Kissinger, Henry. *World Order*. New York: Penguin Press, 2014.

A World Restored: Europe after Napoleon. New York: Grosset & Dunlap, 1964.

Klabbers, Jan. "The EJIL Foreword: The Transformation of International Organizations Law." *European Journal of International Law* 26:1 (2015): 9–82.

"The Redundancy of Soft Law." *Nordic Journal of International Law* 65:2 (1996): 167–182.

Klotz, Audie. *Norms in International Relations: The Struggle against Apartheid*. Ithaca, NY: Cornell University Press, 1999.

Knieper, Rolf. *Nationale Souveränität: Versuch über Ende und Anfang einer Weltordnung*. Frankfurt: Fischer, 1991.

Kopelman, Elizabeth S. "Ideology and International Law: The Dissent of the Indian Justice at the Tokyo War Crimes Trial." *New York University Journal of International Law and Politics* 23:2 (1991): 373–444.

Korhonen, Outi. "International Governance in Post-Conflict Situations." *Leiden Journal of International Law* 14:3 (2001): 495–529.

Koselleck, Reinhart. "Historia Magistra Vitae: The Dissolution of the Topos into the Perspective of a Modernized Historical Process." In *Futures Past: On the Semantics of Historical Times*, Cambridge, MA: MIT Press, 1985: 21–38.

Koskenniemi, Martti. "Carl Schmitt, Hans Morgenthau, and the Image of Law in International Relations." In *The Role of Law in International Politics: Essays in International Relations and International Law*, edited by Byers, M., Oxford: Oxford University Press, 2000, 17–34.

"Constitutionalism as Mindset: Reflections on Kantian Themes about International Law and Globalization." *Theoretical Inquiries in Law* 8:1 (2007): 9–36.

From Apology to Utopia: The Structure of International Legal Argument. Helsinki: Finnish Lawyers' Pub. Co., 1989.

"International Law in Europe: Between Tradition and Renewal." *European Journal of International Law* 16:1 (2005): 113–124.

"The Politics of International Law." *European Journal of International Law* 1:1 (1990): 4–32.

Koslowski, Rey, and Friedrich Kratochwil. "Understanding Change in International Politics: The Soviet Empire's Demise and the International System." *International Organization* 48:2 (1994): 215–247.

Kotkin, Joel. *Tribes: How Race, Religion, and Identity Determine Success in the New Global Economy*. New York: Random House, 1992.

Krasner, Stephen D. (ed.). *International Regimes*. Ithaca, NY: Cornell University Press, 1983.

Sovereignty: Organized Hypocrisy. Princeton: Princeton University Press, 1999.

"Structural Causes and Regime Consequences: Regimes and Intervening Variables." In *International Regimes*, edited by Krasner, S.D., Ithaca, NY: Cornell University Press, 1983, 1–22.

"Westphalia and All That." In *Ideas and Foreign Policy: Beliefs, Institutions, and Political Change*, edited by Goldstein, J. and Keohane, R.O., Ithaca, NY: Cornell University Press, 1993, 235–264.

Kratochwil, Friedrich. *The Humean Conception of International Relations*. Princeton: Princeton University, Center of International Studies, 1981.

"On the Notion of 'Interest' in International Relations." *International Organization* 36:1 (1982): 1–30.

"Errors Have Their Advantage," *International Organization* 38:2 (1984): 305–320.

"Regimes, Interpretation, and the 'Science' of Politics." *Millennium* 17:2 (1988): 263–284.

Rules, Norms and Decisions: On the Conditions of Practical and Legal Reasoning in International Relations and Domestic Affairs. Cambridge: Cambridge University Press, 1989.

"The Limits of Contract." *European Journal of International Law* 5:4 (1994): 465–491.

"Sovereignty as 'Dominium': Is There a Right of Humanitarian Intervention?" In *Beyond Westphalia? State Sovereignty and International Intervention*, edited by Lyons, G.M. and Mastanduno, M., Baltimore: Johns Hopkins University Press, 1995, 21–42.

"Politics, Norms and Peaceful Change." In *The Eighty Years Crisis: International Relations 1919–1999*, edited by Dunne, T., Cox, M., and Booth, K., Cambridge: Cambridge University Press, 1998, 193–218.

"Vergeßt Kant: Reflexionen zur Debatte über Ethik und Internationale Politik." In *Politische Philosophie der Internationalen Beziehungen*, edited by Chwaszcza, C. and Kersting, W., Frankfurt: Suhrkamp, 1998, 96–152.

"Constructing a New Orthodoxy? Wendt's *Social Theory of International Politics* and the Constructivist Challenge." *Millennium*, 29:1 (2000): 73–101.

"Constructivism as an Approach to Interdisciplinary Study." In *Constructing International Relations: The Next Generation*, edited by Fierke, K.M. and Joergensen, K.E., Armonk, NY–London: M.E. Sharpe, 2001, 13–35.

"History, Action and Identity: Revisiting the 'Second' Great Debate and Assessing its Importance for Social Theory." *European Journal of International Relations* 12:1 (2006): 5–29.

"Evidence, Inference and Truth as Problems of Theory Building in the Social Sciences." In *Theory and Evidence in Comparative Politics and International Relations*, edited by Lebow, R.N., and Lichbach, M., New York: Palgrave Macmillan, 2007, 25–55.

"Ten Points to Ponder about Pragmatism: Some Critical Reflections on Knowledge Generation in the Social Sciences." In *Pragmatism in International Relations*, edited by Bauer, H. and Brighi, E., London: Routledge, 2008, 11–25.

The Puzzles of Politics: Inquiries into the Genesis and Transformation of International Relations. New York: Routledge, 2011.

"Problems of Policy Design Based on Insufficient Conceptualization: The Case of Public Goods." In *Multilevel Governance of Interdependent Public Goods: Theories, Rules and Institutions for the Central Policy Challenge in the 21st Century*, edited by Petersmann, E.-U., Florence: EUI Working Paper RSCAS 2012/23, 2012, 42–61.

"Politics, Law, and the Sacred: A Conceptual Analysis." *Journal of International Relations and Development* 16:1 (2013): 1–24.

"A Guide for the Perplexed? Critical Reflections on Doing Interdisiplinary Legal Research." *Transnational Legal Theory* 5:4 (2014): 541–556.

The Status of Law in World Society: Meditations on the Role and Rule of Law. Cambridge: Cambridge University Press, 2014.

"Immanuel Kant (1724–1804): A Little Kantian 'Schwaermerei'." In *The Return of the Theorists: Dialogues with Great Thinkers in International Relations*, edited by Lebow, R.N., Schouten P., and Suganami, H., London: Palgrave Macmillan, 2015, 99–109.

"Re-reading Inter-disciplinarity by Re-reading Hume." In *The Power of Legality: Practices of International Law and their Politics*, edited by Rajkovic, N., Aalberts, T. and Gammreltoft-Hansen T., Cambridge: Cambridge University Press, 2016, 29–74.

"Practising Law: Spoudaios, Professional, Expert or 'Macher': Reflections on the Changing Nature of an Occupation." In *The Law of International Lawyers: Reading Martti Koskenniemi*, edited by Wouter, W., de Hoon, M., and Galan, A., Cambridge: Cambridge University Press, 2017, 225–264.

Kratochwil, Friedrich, and Joerg Friedrichs. "Of Acting and Knowing: How Pragmatism Can Advance International Relations Research and Methodology." *International Organization* 63:4 (2009): 701–731.

Kratochwil, Friedrich, and Rey Koslowski. "Understanding Change in International Politics: The Soviet Empire's Demise and the International System," *International Organization* 48:2 (1994): 215–248.

Kratochwil, Friedrich and Edward Mansfield (eds.). *International Organization.* New York: Harper Collins, 1994.

Kreps, David. "Corporate Culture and Economic Theory." In *Rational Perspectives on Positive Political Economy*, edited by Alt, J., and Shepsle, K., Cambridge: Cambridge University Press, 1990, 90–143.

Kress, Kenneth J. "Legal Reasoning and Coherence Theories: Dworkin's Rights Thesis, Retroactivity, and the Linear Order of Decisions." *California Law Review* 72:3 (1984): 369–402.

Krever, Tor. "International Criminal Law: An Ideology Critique." *Leiden Journal of International Law* 26:3 (2013): 701–723.

Kripke, Saul A. *Wittgenstein on Rules and Private Language: An Elementary Exposition.* Cambridge, MA: Harvard University Press, 1982.

Krugman, Paul. *The Return of Depression Economics.* New York: W.W. Norton, 1999.

Krygier, Martin. "Law as Tradition." *Law and Philosophy* 5:2 (1986): 237–262.

Kuhn, Thomas. "Logic of Discovery or Psychology of Research." In *Criticism and the Growth of Knowledge*, edited by Lakatos, I., and Musgrave, A., Cambridge: Cambridge University Press, 1970, 1–23.

The Structure of Scientific Revolutions. Chicago: University of Chicago Press, 1962.

The Structure of Scientific Revolutions, 2nd edn. Chicago: University of Chicago Press, 1970.

Kundera, Milan. *The Unbearable Lightness of Being*. New York: Harper & Row, 2005.

Kunkel, Wolfgang. *Römische Rechtsgeschichte: eine Einführung*. Köln: Böhlau-Verlag, 1956.

Kurki, Milja. *Causation in International Relations: Reclaiming Causal Analysis*. Cambridge: Cambridge University Press, 2008.

"Reflectivist and Constructivist Approaches in International Relations: More Cases of Humeanism." In *Causation in International Relations: Reclaiming Causal Analysis* (Cambridge: Cambridge University Press, 2008), 124–144.

Kurzman, Dan. *A Killing Wind: Inside Union Carbide and the Bhopal Catastrophe*. New York: McGraw-Hill Companies, 1987.

Kutz, Christopher L. "Just Disagreement: Indeterminacy and Rationality in the Rule of Law." *Yale Law Journal* 103:4 (1994): 997–1030.

Laffey, Mark, and Jutta Weldes. "Beyond Belief: Ideas and Symbolic Technologies in the Study of International Relations." *European Journal of International Relations* 3:2 (1997): 193–237.

Laidi, Zaki. *A World without Meaning: The Crisis of Meaning in International Relations*. London–New York: Routledge, 1998.

Lakatos, Imre. "Falsification and the Methodology of Scientific Research Programmes." In *Criticism and the Growth of Knowledge*, edited by Lakatos, I., and Musgrave, A., Cambridge: Cambridge University Press, 1970, 91–196.

Lakatos, Imre, and Alan Musgrave (eds.). *Criticism and the Growth of Knowledge*. Cambridge: Cambridge University Press, 1970.

Lake, David A. "Anarchy, Hierarchy, and the Variety of International Relations." *International Organization* 50:1 (1996): 1–33.

Hierarchy in International Relations. Ithaca, NY: Cornell University Press, 2009.

"Why 'Isms' Are Evil: Theory, Epistemology, and Academic Sects as Impediments to Understanding and Progress." *International Studies Quarterly* 55:2 (2011): 465–480.

Lakoff, George. *Women, Fire and Dangerous Things: What Categories Reveal about the Mind*. Chicago: University of Chicago Press, 1987.

Lakoff, George, and Mark Johnson. *Philosophy in the Flesh: The Embodied Mind and Its Challenge to Western Thought*. New York: Basic Books, 1999.

Lang, Anthony F. *Punishment, Justice and International Relations: Ethics and Order after the Cold War*. London: Routledge, 2008.

Lansing, Paul, and Julie C. King. "South Africa's Truth and Reconciliation Commission: The Conflict between Individual Justice and National Healing in the Post-Apartheid Age." *Arizona Journal of International and Comparative Law* 15:3 (1998): 753–789.

Lapid, Yosef, and Friedrich Kratochwil. "Revisiting the 'National': Toward an Identity Agenda in Neorealism?" In *The Return of Culture and Identity in IR Theory*, edited by Lapid, Y., and Kratochwil, F., Boulder, CO: Lynne Rienner, 1996, 105–128.

Lasch, Christopher. *The Culture of Narcissism: American Life in an Age of Diminishing Expectations*. New York: Norton, 1978.

Latour, Bruno, and Steve Woolgar. *Laboratory Life: The Social Construction of Scientific Facts*. London: Sage, 1979.

Layton, Samuel. "Reframing European Security: Russia's Proposal of a New European Security Architecture." *International Relations* 28:1 (2014): 25–48.

Le Prestre, Philippe G. "Environmental Learning at the World Bank." In *International Organizations and Environmental Policy*, edited by Bartlett, R.V., Kurian, P.A., and Malik, M., Westport, CT: Greenwood Press, 1995, 83–101.

Leander, Anna. "Risk and the Fabrication of Apolitical, Unaccountable Military Markets: The Case of the CIA 'Killing Program'." *Review of International Studies* 37:5 (2011): 1–16.

Lebow, Richard Ned. "The Long Peace. The End of the Cold War and the Failure of Realism." In *International Relations Theory and the End of the Cold War*, edited by Lebow, R.N. and Risse-Kappen, T., New York: Columbia University Press, 1995, 23–56.

Lebow, Richard Ned, and Robert Kelly. "Thucydides and Hegemony: Athens and the United States." *Review of International Studies* 27:4 (2001): 593–609.

Lebow, Richard Ned, and Thomas Risse-Kappen (eds.). *International Relations Theory and the End of the Cold War*. New York: Columbia University Press, 1995.

Lebow, Richard Ned, and Janice Gross Stein. "Beyond Deterrence." *Journal of Social Issues* 43:4 (1987): 5–71.

We All Lost the Cold War. Princeton: Princeton University Press, 1994.

Lebow, Richard Ned, Wulf Kantsteiner, and Claudio Fogu (eds.). *The Politics of Memory in Postwar Europe*. Durham, NC: Duke University Press, 2006.

Leibniz, Gottfried Wilhelm. "Caesarinus Fuerstenerius (1677)." In *Philosophische Schriften und Briefe, 1683–1687* (Berlin: Akademie, 1880).

Lenway, Stefany Ann. "Between War and Commerce: Economic Sanctions as a Tool of Statecraft." *International Organization* 42:2 (1988): 397–426.

Levine, Daniel J., and Alexander D. Barder. "The Closing of the American Mind: 'American School' International Relations and the State of Grand Theory." *European Journal of International Relations* 20:4 (2014): 863–888.

Levy, Jack S. "Prospect Theory, Rational Choice, and International Relations." *International Studies Quarterly* 41:1 (1997): 87–112.

Lewis, Clarence Irving. *Mind and the World-Order: Outline of a Theory of Knowledge*. New York: Dover Publications, 1956.

Lewis, W. Arthur. *Development Planning: The Essentials of Economic Policy*. London: Allen and Unwin, 1966.

Growth and Fluctuations, 1870–1913. London: Allen & Unwin, 1978.

Libicki, Martin. "The Emerging Primacy of Information." *Orbis* 40:2 (1996): 261–274.

Licht, Sonja. "The Use of Sanctions in Former Yugoslavia: Can They Assist in Conflict Resolution?" In *Economic Sanctions: Panacea or Peacebuilding in a Post-Cold War World?*, edited by Cortright, D. and Lopez, G.A., Boulder, CO: Westview Press, 1995, 153–160.

Linke, Horst Günther. "Russlands Weg in den Ersten Weltkrieg und Seine Kriegsziele 1914–1918." In *Der Erste Weltkrieg: Wirkung, Wahrnehmung, Analyse*, edited by Michalka, W., München: Piper, 1994, 54–94.

Lippmann, Walter. *The Phantom Public*. New Brunswick, NJ: Transaction Publishers, 1993.

Lipschutz, Ronnie D. "Restructuring World Politics: The Emergence of Global Civil Society." *Millennium* 21:3 (1992): 389–420.

Lipschutz, Ronnie D., and Cathleen Fogel. "'Regulation for the Rest of Us?' Global Civil Society and the Privatization of Transnational Regulation." In *The Emergence of Private Authority in Global Governance*, edited by Hall, R.B., and Biersteker, T.J., Oxford: Oxford University Press, 2002, 115–140.

Lipschutz, Ronnie D., and Judith Mayer. *Global Civil Society and Global Environmental Governance: The Politics of Nature from Place to Planet*. Albany, NY: SUNY Press, 1996.

Livingston, Donald W. *Hume's Philosophy of Common Life*. Chicago: University of Chicago Press, 1984.

Philosophical Melancholy and Delirium: Hume's Pathology of Philosophy. Chicago: Chicago University Press, 1998.

Livingston, Steven. "The CNN Effect Reconsidered (Again): Problematizing ICT and Global Governance in the CNN Effect Research Agenda." *Media, War & Conflict* 4:1 (2011): 20–36.

Lo, Bobo. *Russian Foreign Policy in the Post-Soviet Era Reality, Illusion, and Mythmaking*. Houndmills: Palgrave Macmillan, 2002.

Locke, John. *An Essay Concerning Human Understanding*. Edited by Nidditch, P.H. Oxford: Clarendon Press, 1975.

The Second Treatise of Government. Indianapolis: Bobbs-Merrill, 1960.

Two Treatises of Government. Edited by Laslett, P. Cambridge: Cambridge University Press, 1960.

Lockwood, David. "Social Integration and System Integration." In *Explorations in Social Change*, edited by Zollschan, G.K., and Hirsch, H.W., Boston, MA: Houghton Mifflin, 1964, 244–257.

Loraux, Nicole. *The Invention of Athens: The Funeral Oration in the Classical City*. Cambridge, MA: Harvard University Press, 1986.

Loughlin, Martin, and Neil Walker (eds.). *The Paradox of Constitutionalism: Constituent Power and Constitutional Form*. Oxford: Oxford University Press, 2007.

Löwith, Karl. *Weltgeschichte und Heilsgeschehen: die theologischen Voraussetzungen der Geschichtsphilosophie*. Stuttgart: Metzler, 2004.

Luhmann, Niklas. *Die Gesellschaft der Gesellschaft*. 2 vols. Frankfurt am Main: Suhrkamp, 1998.

Rechtssoziologie, vol. 2. Reinbeck: Rohwolt, 1972.

Social Systems. Trans. J. Bednarz and D. Becker. Stanford: Stanford University Press, 1995.

Lukes, Steven (ed.). *Power: Readings in Social and Political Theory*. New York: New York University Press, 1986.

Lustick, Ian S. "History, Historiography, and Political Science: Multiple Historical Records and the Problem of Selection Bias." *American Political Science Review* 90:3 (1996): 605–618.

Lyon, David. *Surveillance Studies: An Overview*. Cambridge: Polity Press, 2007.

Machiavelli, Niccolò. *The Discourses*. Edited by Crick, B. Baltimore, MD: Penguin, 1970.

The Prince. Trans. G.A. Bull. Baltimore, MD: Penguin, 1972.

Mackie, John. *The Cement of the Universe: A Study in Causation*. Oxford: Clarendon, 1988.

Macpherson, C.B. *The Political Theory of Possessive Individualism: Hobbes to Locke.* Oxford: Clarendon Press, 1962.
The Political Theory of Possessive Individualism: Hobbes to Locke. New York: Basic Books, 1977.
Madison, James. "Federalist 10: The Same Subject Continued: The Union as a Safeguard against Domestic Faction and Insurrection." In *The Federalist Papers*, edited by Rossiter, C., New York: Mentor, 1961, 77–84.
Maier, Hans. *Die ältere deutsche Staats- und Verwaltungslehre.* München: C.H. Beck, 1980.
Maitland, Frederic William. *The Constitutional History of England: A Course of Lectures Delivered.* Union, NJ: The Lawbook Exchange, 2013 [1908].
Mallinder, Louise. *Amnesty, Human Rights and Political Transitions Bridging the Peace and Justice Divide.* Oxford: Hart, 2008.
Manan, Wynard. *Statement by Mr. Wynand Malan, Deputy Chairman of the Human Rights Violations Committee of the Truth and Reconciliation Commission.* May 16, 1997. Available at www.justice.gov.za/trc/media/pr/1997/p970516a.htm.
Mandeville, Bernard. *The Fable of the Bees: Or Private Vices, Publick Benefits.* Edited by Harth, P. London: Penguin, 1989.
Mann, Michael. "In Praise of Macro-Sociology: A Reply to Goldthorpe." *British Journal of Sociology* 45:1 (1994): 37–54.
Manners, Ian. "Normative Power Europe: A Contradiction in Terms?" *Journal of Common Market Studies* 40:2 (2002): 235–258.
Mansbridge, Jane. "The Rise and Fall of Self-Interest in the Explanation of Political Life." In *Beyond Self-Interest*, edited by Mansbridge, J., Chicago: University of Chicago Press, 1990, 3–22.
Mansfield, Edward. "The Distribution of War over Time." *World Politics* 41:1 (1988): 21–51.
Manuel, Frank Edward (ed.). *Utopias and Utopian Thought.* Boston, MA: Houghton Mifflin, 1966.
Mapel, David, and Terry Nardin (eds.). *International Society: Diverse Ethical Perspectives.* Cambridge: Cambridge University Press, 1998.
March, James G., and Johan P. Olsen (eds.). *Ambiguity and Choice in Organizations.* Bergen: Universitetsforlaget, 1976.
Marchuk, Iryna. *The Fundamental Concept of Crime in International Law: A Comparative Law Analysis.* New York: Springer, 2014.
Mariniello, Triestino. *The International Criminal Court in Search of Its Purpose and Identity.* London: Routledge, 2015.
Marks, Stephen P. "Forgetting 'the Policies and Practices of the Past': Impunity in Cambodia." *Fletcher Forum of World Affairs* 18:2 (1994): 17–43.
Marks, Susan, and Clapham, Andrew. "Victims." In *Human Rights Lexicon* (Oxford: Oxford University Press, 2005), 399–411.
Martinez, Jenny S. "Understanding Mens Rea in Command Responsibility." *Journal of International Criminal Justice* 5:3 (2007): 638–664.
Marx, Karl. "German Ideology." In *The Marx–Engels Reader*, edited by Tucker, R.C., New York: W.W. Norton, 1972, 146–200.
"On the Jewish Question." In *The Marx–Engels Reader*, edited by Tucker, R.C., New York: W.W. Norton, 1978, 26–52.
"Theses on Feuerbach." In *The Marx–Engels Reader*, edited by Tucker, R.C., New York: W.W. Norton, 1972, 143–145.

Marx, Karl, and Friedrich Engels. "Manifesto of the Communist Party." In *The Marx–Engels Reader*, edited by Tucker, R.C., New York: W.W. Norton, 1978, 469–500.

Mason, Alpheus Thomas. *Harlan Fiske Stone: Pillar of the Law*. Hamden, CT: Archon Books, 1968.

Mastanduno, Michael. *Economic Containment: CoCom and the Politics of East–West Trade*. Ithaca, NY: Cornell University Press, 1992.

Masterman, Margret. "The Nature of a Paradigm." In *Criticism and the Growth of Knowledge*, edited by Lakatos, I. and Musgrave, A., Cambridge: Cambridge University Press, 1970, 59–89.

Masters, Roger D. "World Politics as a Primitive Political System." *World Politics* 16:4 (1964): 595–619.

Matheny, Albert R., and Bruce A. Williams. "Scientific Disputes and Adversary Procedures in Policy-Making: An Evaluation of the Science Court." *Law and Policy Quarterly* 3:3 (1981): 341–364.

Mathews, Jessica T. "Inspectors Had the Real WMD Clues," *Financial Times*, February 9, 2004, 15.

Maturana, Humberto R. "Biology of Cognition." Biological Computer Laboratory Research Report BCL 9.0 (Urbana: University of Illinois, 1970).

McAdams, A. James (ed.). *Transitional Justice and the Rule of Law in New Democracies*. Notre Dame, IN: University of Notre Dame Press, 1997.

McCullough, Roy L. *Coercion, Conversion and Counterinsurgency in Louis XIV's France*. Leiden: Brill, 2007.

McDougal, Myres S., and Florentino P. Feliciano. *Law and Minimum World Public Order: The Legal Regulation and International Coercion*. New Haven: Yale University Press, 1961.

McDougal, Myres, and Harold Laswell. "The Identification and Appraisal of Diverse Systems of Public Order." In *The Strategy of World Order*, edited by Falk, R.A., and Mendlovitz, S.H., New York: World Law Fund, 1966, 45–74.

McHarg, Aileen. "Reconciling Human Rights and the Public Interest: Conceptual Problems and Doctrinal Uncertainty in the Jurisprudence of the European Court of Human Rights." *The Modern Law Review* 62:5 (1999): 671–696.

McLuhan, Marshal. *Understanding Media: The Extensions of Man*. New York: McGraw Hill, 1964.

McNair, Arnold Duncan, Michael R.E. Kerr, and Robert A. MacCrindle. *The Law of the Air*. London: Stevens & Sons, 1953.

Mead, George Herbert. *Mind, Self & Society from the Standpoint of a Social Behaviorist*. Edited by Morris, C.W. Chicago: The University of Chicago Press, 1962.

Mearsheimer, John J. "The False Promise of International Institutions." *International Security* 19:3 (1994–1995): 5–49.

Mearsheimer, John J., and Stephen M. Walt. "Leaving Theory Behind: Why Simplistic Hypothesis Testing Is Bad for International Relations." *European Journal of International Relations* 19:3 (2013): 427–457.

Mégret, Frédéric. "International Criminal Justice: A Critical Research Agenda." In *Critical Approaches to International Criminal Law: An Introduction*, edited by Schwöbel, C.E.J., Abingdon: Routledge, 2014, 17–53.

Meier, Christian. *The Greek Discovery of Politics*. Trans. D. McLintock. Cambridge, MA: Harvard University Press, 1990.

Meinecke, Friedrich. *Die Idee der Staatsräson in der neueren Geschichte*. Edited by Hofer, W. München: Oldenbourg, 1960.

Meister, Robert. *After Evil: A Politics of Human Rights*. New York: Columbia University Press, 2010.

"Forgiving and Forgetting: Lincoln and the Politics of National Recovery." In *Human Rights in Political Transitions: Gettysburg to Bosnia*, edited by Hesse, C.A. and Post, R., New York: Zone Books, 1999, 135–176.

Mercer, Jonathan. "Emotional Beliefs," *International Organization* 64:1 (2010): 77–106.

Reputation and International Politics. Ithaca, NY: Cornell University Press, 1996.

Mettraux, Guénaël (ed.). *Perspectives on the Nuremberg Trial*. Oxford: Oxford University Press, 2008.

Michael, Thorsten. "Time to Get Emotional: Phronetic Reflections on the Concept of Trust," *European Journal of International Relations*, 19:4 (2012): 868–890.

Michelman, Frank I. "Justification (and Justifiability) of Law in a Contradictory World." In *Nomos XXVIII: Justification*, edited by Pennock, J.R., and Chapman, J.W., New York: New York University Press, 1986, 71–99.

Mill, John Stuart. *A System of Logic, Ratiocinative and Inductive; Being a Connected View of the Principles of Evidence and the Methods of Scientific Investigation*. London: Longmans, 1930.

Utilitarianism: Text and Criticism. Edited by Sosa, E., and Smith, J.M. Belmont: Wadsworth, 1969.

Miller, Richard. *Fact and Method: Explanation, Confirmation and Reality in the Natural and the Social Sciences*. Princeton: Princeton University Press, 1987.

Minear, Richard H. *Victors' Justice: The Tokyo War Crimes Trial*. Princeton: Princeton University Press, 1972.

Victors' Justice: The Tokyo War Crimes Trial, 2nd edn. Ann Arbor: University of Michigan Press, 2001.

Mink, Louis O. "Narrative Form as a Cognitive Instrument." In *The Writing of History: Literary Form and Historical Understanding*, edited by Canary, R.H., and Kozicki, H.. Madison: University of Wisconsin Press, 1978, 129–149.

Minow, Martha. *Between Vengeance and Forgiveness: Facing History after Genocide and Mass Violence*. Boston, MA: Beacon Press, 1998.

Mitchell, Ronald B. *Intentional Oil Pollution at Sea: Environmental Policy and Treaty Compliance*. Cambridge, MA: MIT Press, 1994.

"Sources of Transparency: Information Systems in International Regimes." *International Studies Quarterly* 42:1 (1998): 109–130.

Mitchell, W.J.T. *Cloning Terror: The War of Images, 9/11 to the Present*. Chicago: University of Chicago Press, 2011.

Mitteis, Heinrich. *Lehnrecht und Staatsgewalt: Untersuchungen zur Mittelalterlichen Verfassungsgeschichte*. Köln: Böhlau, 1974.

Momigliano, Arnaldo. "Ancient History and the Antiquarian." *Journal of the Warburg and Courtauld Institutes* 13 (1950): 285–315.

Montesquieu, Charles de Secondat. *The Spirit of the Laws*. Trans. T. Nugent. New York: Haffner, 1966.

Montgomery, Richard. "Non-Cartesian Explanations Meet the Problem of Mental Causation." *Southern Journal of Philosophy* 33:2 (1995): 221–242.

Moore, Barrington. *Social Origins of Dictatorship and Democracy: Lord and Peasant in the Making of the Modern World*. Boston, MA: Beacon Press, 1966.

Moravcsik, Andrew. "Taking Preferences Seriously: A Liberal Theory of International Politics." *International Organization* 51:4 (1997): 513–553.

"Theory Synthesis in International Relations: Real Not Metaphysical." *International Studies Review* 5:1 (2003): 131–136.

Morgenthau, Hans. *Politics among Nations*, 4th edn. New York: Knopf, 1967.

Scientific Man vs Power Politics. Chicago: University of Chicago Press, 1946.

Morozov, Evgeny. *The Net Delusion: The Dark Side of Internet Freedom*. London: Penguin, 2011.

Morton, Fried. *The Evolution of Political Society*. New York: Random House, 1967.

Mouzelis, Nicos. "In Defence of 'Grand' Historical Sociology." *British Journal of Sociology* 45:1 (1994): 31–36.

Moyn, Samuel. *The Last Utopia Human Rights in History*. Cambridge, MA: Harvard University Press, 2010.

Müller, Carl. *Fragmenta Historicorum Graecorum*. Cambridge: Cambridge University Press, 2010.

Müller, Harald. "Arguing, Bargaining and All That: Communicative Action, Rationalist Theory and the Logic of Appropriateness." *European Journal of International Relations* 10:3 (2004): 395–435.

Die Chance der Kooperation: Regime in den Internationalen Beziehungen. Darmstadt: Wissenschaftliche Buchgesellschaft, 1993.

"Spielen Hilft Nicht Immer: Die Grenzen des Rational-Choice-Ansatzes und der Platz der Theorie Kommunikativen Handelns in der Analyse Internationaler Beziehungen." *Zeitschrift für Internationale Beziehungen* 2:2 (1995): 371–391.

Murphy, Craig. *International Organization and Industrial Change: Global Governance since 1850, Europe and the International Order*. New York: Oxford University Press, 1994.

Murphy, Sean D. "Aggression, Legitimacy and the International Criminal Court." *European Journal of International Law* 20:4 (2009): 1147–1156.

Humanitarian Intervention: The United Nations in an Evolving World Order. Philadelphia: University of Pennsylvania Press, 1996.

Nagel, Thomas. *The View from Nowhere*. New York: Oxford University Press, 1986.

Nardin, Terry. *Law, Morality, and the Relations of States*. Princeton: Princeton University Press, 1983.

Nelson, Joan M. (ed.). *Economic Crisis and Policy Choice: The Politics of Adjustment in the Third World*. Princeton: Princeton University Press, 1990.

Nelson, Paul. "Agendas Accountability and Legitimacy among Transnational Networks Lobbying the Bank." In *Restructuring World Politics: Transnational Social Movements, Networks, and Norms*, edited by Khagram, S., Sikkink, K., and Riker, J.V., Minneapolis: University of Minnesota Press, 2002, 131–154.

The World Bank and Non-Governmental Organizations: The Limits of Apolitical Development. New York: St. Martin's Press, 1995.

Neumann, Iver B. *At Home with the Diplomats: Inside a European Foreign Ministry.* Ithaca, NY: Cornell University Press, 2012.

Neumann, Iver B., and Ole J. Sending. *Governing the Global Polity: Practice, Mentality, Rationality.* Ann Arbor: University of Michigan Press, 2010.

Neumann, Iver B., and Jennifer M. Welsh. "The Other in European Self-Definition: An Addendum to the Literature on International Society." *Review of International Studies* 17:4 (1991): 327–346.

Newton, Isaac. *Philosophiae Naturalis Principia Mathematica.* Trans. A. Motte. Edited by Cajori, F. Cambridge: Cambridge University Press, 1934.

Nietzsche, Friedrich. "Sittlichkeit und Verdummung." In *Morgenröte*, edited by Colli, G., and Montinari, M., Berlin: de Gruyter, 1988.

"Unzeitgemäße Betrachtungen, Zweites Stück: Vom Nutzen und Nachteil der Historie." In *Nietzche Gesamtausgabe*, vol. 1, edited by Colli, Giorgio, and Montinari, Mazzino, Muenchen-Berlin: DTV and Walter de Gruyter 1988, 243–334.

Nino, Carlos S. "The Duty to Punish Past Abuses of Human Rights Put into Context: The Case of Argentina." *Yale Law Journal* 100:8 (1991): 2619–2640.

Radical Evil on Trial. New Haven: Yale University Press, 1998.

Noonan, Harold W. *Hume.* Oxford: Oneworld Publishing, 2007.

Hume on Knowledge. Abingdon: Routledge, 1999.

Nossal, Kim Richard. "International Sanctions as International Punishment." *International Organization* 43:2 (1989): 301–322.

Nouwen, Sarah M.H. "'As You Set out for Ithaka': Practical, Epistemological, Ethical, and Existential Questions about Socio-Legal Empirical Research in Conflict." *Leiden Journal of International Law* 27:1 (2014): 227–260.

Nouwen, Sarah M.H., and W.G. Werner. "Doing Justice to the Political: The International Criminal Court in Uganda and Sudan." *European Journal of International Law* 21:4 (2011): 941–965.

"Monopolizing Global Justice: International Criminal Law as Challenge to Human Diversity." *Journal of International Criminal Justice* 13:1 (2015): 157–176.

Nye, Joseph S. *The Paradox of American Power: Why the World's Only Super Power Can't Go It Alone.* Oxford: Oxford University Press, 2002.

O'Connell, Mary Ellen. "Debating the Law of Sanctions." *European Journal of International Law* 13:1 (2002): 63–79.

"Enforcing the New International Law of the Environment." *German Yearbook of International Law* 1992 (1992): 293–332.

"The Myth of Preemptive Self-Defense." Washington, DC: American Society of International Law Task Force on Terrorism, 2002. Available at www.asil.org/taskforce/oconnell.pdf.

O'Donnell, Guillermo A., Philippe C. Schmitter, and Laurence Whitehead. *Transitions from Authoritarian Rule.* Baltimore: Johns Hopkins University Press, 1986.

O'Neill, Onora. "The Dark Side of Human Rights." In *Contemporary Debates in Political Philosophy*, edited by Christiano, T., and Christman, J., Chichester: Blackwell-Wiley, 2009, 425–436.

O'Sullivan, Meghan L. *Shrewd Sanctions: Statecraft and State Sponsors of Terrorism.* Washington, DC: Brookings Institution Press, 2003.

Oakeshott, Michael. *Rationalism in Politics and Other Essays.* Edited by Fuller, T. Indianapolis: Liberty Fund, 1991.

Obstfeld, Maurice. "Models of Currency Crises with Self-Fulfilling Features." *European Economic Review* 40:3 (1996): 1037–1047.

Ohlin, Jens David. "Three Conceptual Problems with the Doctrine of Joint Criminal Enterprise." *Journal of International Criminal Justice* 5:1 (2007): 69–90.

Onuf, Nicholas. *The Republican Legacy in International Thought*. Cambridge: Cambridge University Press, 1998.

World of Our Making: Rules and Rule in Social Theory and International Relations. Columbia: University of South Carolina Press, 1989.

Oppenheim, L. *The Future of International Law*. Oxford: Clarendon Press, 1921.

Oren, Ido. "The Subjectivity of the Democratic Peace: Changing US Perceptions of Imperial Germany." *International Security* 20:2 (1995): 147–184.

Orford, Anne. *International Authority and the Responsibility to Protect*. Cambridge: Cambridge University Press, 2011.

Osiander, Andreas. *The States System of Europe, 1640–1990: Peacemaking and the Conditions of International Stability*. Oxford: Oxford University Press, 1994.

Osiel, Mark. "The Banality of Good: Aligning Incentives against Mass Atrocity." *Columbia Law Review* 105:6 (2005): 1751–1862.

"Making Public Memory, Publicly." In *Human Rights in Political Transitions: Gettysburg to Bosnia*, edited by Hesse, C.A., and Post, R., New York: Zone Books, 1999, 217–262.

Making Sense of Mass Atrocity. Cambridge: Cambridge University Press, 2009.

Mass Atrocities, Collective Memory, and the Law. Brunswick, NJ: Transaction Books 1997.

Ostrom, Elinor. *Governing the Commons*. Cambridge: Cambridge University Press, 1990.

Otteson, James. "Adam Smith's First Market: The Development of Language." *History of Philosophy Quarterly* 19:1 (2002): 65–86.

Oxfam, and Deborah Hardoon. "Wealth: Having It All and Wanting More." Oxford: Oxfam, 2015.

Pape, Robert A. *Dying to Win: The Strategic Logic of Terrorism*. New York: Random House, 2005.

"Why Economic Sanctions Do Not Work." *International Security* 22:2 (1997): 90–136.

Park, Susan, and Antje Vetterlein (eds.). *Owning Development: Creating Policy Norms in the IMF and the World Bank*. Cambridge: Cambridge University Press, 2012.

Parmentier, Stephan, and Elmar Weitekamp. "Punishing Perpetrators or Seeking Truth for Victims: Serbian Opinions on Dealing with War Crimes." *International Criminal Law Review* 13:1 (2013): 43–62.

Parsons, Talcott. *Social System*. Glencoe: Free Press, 1951.

The Structure of Social Action. New York: Free Press, 1949.

Pasic-Chakrabarti, Sujata. "Culturing International Relations Theory: A Call for Extension." In *The Return of Culture and Identity in IR Theory*, edited by Lapid, Y., and Kratochwil, F., Boulder, CO: Lynne Rienner, 1996, 85–104.

Pasquino, Pasquale. "Political Theory, Order, and Threat." In *Political Order: Nomos XXXVIII*, edited by Shapiro, I. and Hardin, R., New York: New York University Press, 1996, 19–41.

Patomäki, Heikki. "How to Tell Better Stories about World Politics." *European Journal of International Relations* 2:1 (1996): 105–133.

Patomäki, Heikki, and Colin Wight. "After Post-Positivism? The Promises of Critical Realism." *International Studies Quarterly* 44:2 (2000): 213–237.

Paulus, Andreas. "Second Thoughts on the Crime of Aggression." *European Journal of International Law* 20:4 (2009): 1117–1128.

Pauly, Louis W. "Global Finance, Political Authority, and the Problem of Legitimation." In *The Emergence of Private Authority in Global Governance*, edited by Hall, R.B., and Biersteker, T.J., Oxford: Oxford University Press, 2002, 76–90.

Opening Financial Markets: Banking Politics on the Pacific Rim. Ithaca, NY: Cornell University Press, 1988.

Pauly, Louis W., and Simon Reich. "National Structures and Multinational Corporate Behavior: Enduring Differences in the Age of Globalization." *International Organization* 51:1 (1997): 1–30.

Pauwelyn, Joost. "Enforcement and Countermeasures in the WTO: Rules Are Rules – Toward a More Collective Approach." *American Journal of International Law* 94:2 (2000): 335–347.

"A Typology of Multilateral Treaty Obligations: Are WTO Obligations Bilateral or Collective in Nature?" *European Journal of International Law* 14:5 (2003): 907–951.

Payne, Rodger A., and Nayef H. Samhat. *Democratizing Global Politics Discourse Norms, International Regimes, and Political Community*. Albany, NY: SUNY Press, 2004.

Peevers, Charlotte. *The Politics of Justifying Force: The Suez Crisis, the Iraq War, and International Law*. Oxford: Oxford University Press, 2013.

Peirce, Charles S. *Collected Papers of Charles Sanders Peirce*. Edited by Hartshorne, C., and Weiss, P. Cambridge, MA: Harvard University Press, 1934.

Peltonen, Hannes. *International Responsibility and Grave Humanitarian Crises: Collective Provision for Human Security*. Abingdon: Routledge, 2013.

"Re-drawing Boundaries: Fuzzy Boundaries, Conceptual Spectrums, and Polity Comparison" (mimeo, 2014).

Pereira da Silva, Luiz A. "The International Financial Institutions (IFIs) and the Political Lessons from the Asian Crises of 1997–1998." *International Social Science Journal* 53:4 (2001): 551–568.

Perlmutter, David. *Photojournalism and Foreign Policy: Icons of Outrage in International Crises*. Westport, CT: Praeger, 1998.

Peskin, Victor. *International Justice in Rwanda and the Balkans: Virtual Trials and the Struggle for State Cooperation*. Cambridge: Cambridge University Press, 2008.

Peter, Matthias. "Britische Kriegsziele und Friedensvorstellungen." In *Der Erste Weltkrieg: Wirkung, Wahrnehmung, Analyse*, edited by Michalka, W., München: Piper, 1994, 95–124.

Petersmann, Ernst-Ulrich. "The WTO Constitution and Human Rights." *Journal of International Economic Law* 3:3 (2000): 19–25.

Peterson, M.J. "The Use of Analogies in Developing Outer Space Law." *International Organization* 51:2 (1997): 245–274.

Pettit, Philip. *Republicanism: A Theory of Freedom and Government*. Oxford: Oxford University Press, 1997.

Picciotto, Salomone. "Democratizing Globalism." In *The Market of the Public Domain? Global Governance and the Asymmetry of Power*, edited by Drache, D., London: Routledge, 2001, 335–359.

Pijl, Kees van der. *Nomads, Empires, States: Modes of Foreign Relations and Political Economy*. London: Pluto Press, 2007.

Transnational Classes and International Relations. London: Routledge, 1998.

Piketty, Thomas. *Capital in the Twenty First Century*. Trans. A. Goldhammer. Cambridge, MA: The Belknap Press of Harvard University Press, 2014.

Plato. "Republic." In *The Collected Dialogues Including the Letters*, edited by Hamilton, E. and Cairns, H., Princeton: Princeton University Press, 1989.

Pogge, Thomas, and Keith Horton (eds.). *Global Ethics: Seminal Essays*. 2 vols. St. Paul, MN: Paragon House 2008.

Polanyi, Karl. *The Great Transformation*. Boston, MA: Beacon Press, 1957.

Polkinghorne, David. *Narrative Knowledge and the Human Sciences*. Albany, NY: SUNY Press, 1988.

Popitz, Heinrich. *Die Normative Konstruktion von Gesellschaft*. Tübingen: Mohr, 1980.

Popkin, Margaret, and Naomi Roht-Arriaza. "Truth as Justice: Investigatory Commissions in Latin America." *Law & Social Inquiry* 20:1 (1995): 79–116.

Popper, Karl. *Conjectures and Refutations*. New York: Harper, 1957.

Conjectures and Refutations: The Growth of Scientific Knowledge. New York: Harper & Row, 1965.

The Myth of the Framework: In Defense of Science and Rationality. London: Routledge, 1994.

Objective Knowledge: An Evolutionary Approach. Oxford: Clarendon Press, 1972.

"Of Clouds and Clocks." In *Objective Knowledge*, edited by Popper, K., New York: Oxford University Press, 1972.

The Poverty of Historicism. New York: Harper & Row, 1961.

Porter, Michael E., and Mark R. Kramer. "Strategy and Society: The Link between Competitive Advantage and Corporate Social Responsibility." *Harvard Business Review* 84:12 (2006): 78–92.

Postema, Gerald J. "Public Practical Reason: Political Practice." In *Theory and Practice*, edited by Shapiro, I. and Wagner De Crew, J., New York: New York University Press, 1995, 345–385.

Powell, Robert. "Anarchy in International Relations Theory: The Neorealist–Neoliberal Debate." *International Organization* 48:2 (1994): 313–344.

Priestley, Joseph. *The History and Present State of Electricity*. 2 vols. New York: Johnson Reprint, 1966 [1767].

Przeworski, Adam. *Democracy and the Market: Political and Economic Reforms in Eastern Europe and Latin America*. Cambridge: Cambridge University Press, 1991.

Pufendorf, Samuel von. *Die Verfassung des Deutschen Reiches*. Stuttgart: H. Denzer, 1976.

Einleitung zu der Historie der Vornehmsten Reiche und Staaten, So Jetziger Zeit in Europa Sich Befinden. Frankfurt: Knoch, 1732.

Putnam, Robert D. "Diplomacy and Domestic Politics: The Logic of Two-Level Games." *International Organization* 42:3 (1988): 427–460.

Quine, Willard Van Orman. "Two Dogmas of Empiricism." In *From a Logical Point of View* (Cambridge, MA: Harvard University Press, 1953), 20–46.

Rabkin, Rhoda. "The Aylwin Government and 'Tutelary' Democracy: A Concept in Search of a Case?" *Journal of Interamerican Studies and World Affairs* 35:4 (1993): 119–194.

Rajkovic, Nikolas. *The Politics of International Law and Compliance: Serbia, Croatia and the Hague Tribunal.* New York: Routledge, 2012.

Rajkovic, Nikolas, Tanja Aalberts, and Thomas Gammreltoft-Hansen (eds.). *The Power of Lagality: Practices of International Law and their Politics.* Cambridge: Cambridge University Press, 2016.

Ramsbotham, Oliver, and Tom Woodhouse. *Humanitarian Intervention in Contemporary Conflict: A Reconceptualization.* Cambridge: Polity, 1996.

Ranke, Leopold von. "Englische Geschichte." In *Sämmtliche Werke* (Leipzig: Duncker & Humblot, 1875).

Ratner, Steven R. *The New UN Peacekeeping: Building Peace in Lands of Conflict after the Cold War.* New York: Palgrave Macmillan, 1995.

The Thin Justice of International Law: A Moral Reckoning of the Law of Nations. Oxford: Oxford University Press, 2015.

Raul, Joel R. "Comity in International Law." *Harvard International Law Journal* 32:1 (1991): 1–80.

Rawls, John. *The Law of the Peoples*, Cambridge, MA: Harvard University Press, 1999.

Political Liberalism. New York: Columbia University Press, 1993.

Raz, Joseph (ed.). *Practical Reasoning.* Oxford: Oxford University Press, 1978.

Regan, Donald H. "Glosses on Dworkin: Rights, Principles, and Policies." In *Ronald Dworkin and Contemporary Jurisprudence*, edited by Cohen, M., Totowa, NJ: Rowman & Allanheld, 1984, 119–160.

Reinhard, Hans. *Rechtsgleichheit und Selbstbestimmung der Völker in Wirtschaftlicher Hinsicht: die Praxis der Vereinten Nationen.* Berlin: Springer, 1980.

Reinisch, August. "Developing Human Rights and Humanitarian Accountability of the Security Council for the Imposition of Economic Sanctions." *American Journal of International Law* 954:1 (2001): 851–872.

Reisman, W. Michael. *Nullity and Revision: The Review and Enforcement of International Judgments and Awards.* New Haven: Yale University Press, 1971.

Rengger, Nicholas. *Just War and International Order: The Uncivil Condition in World Politics*, Cambridge: Cambridge University Press, 2013.

"On Theology and International Relations: World Politics Beyond the Empty Sky." *International Relations* 27:2 (2013): 141–157.

Rescher, Nicholas. *Process Metaphysics: An Introduction to Process Philosophy.* Albany, NY: SUNY Press, 1996.

Reus Smith, Christian. "Human Rights in a Global Oecumene," *International Affairs* 87:5 (2013): 1205–1218.

Individual Rights and the Making of the International System. Cambridge: Cambridge University Press, 2013.

(ed.). *The Politics of International Law.* Cambridge: Cambridge University Press, 2004.

Rex, John. *Key Problems of Sociological Theory*. London: Routledge & Kegan, Paul, 1961.

Rhodes, P.J. "The Atthidographers." *Studia Hellenistica* 30 (1990): 73–81.

Ricoeur, Paul. *Time and Narrative*. Trans. K. McLaughlin and D. Pellauer. 3 vols. Chicago: University of Chicago Press, 1984–1988.

Rini, Adriane. *Aristotle's Modal Proofs*. Dordrecht: Springer, 2011.

Risse, Thomas. ""Let's Argue!": Communicative Action in World Politics." *International Organization* 54:1 (2000): 1–39.

(ed.), *Governance without a State: Politics and Policies in Areas of Limited Statehood*. New York: Columbia University Press, 2011.

Risse-Kappen, Thomas (ed.). *Bringing Transnational Relations Back In: Non-State Actors, Domestic Structures, and International Institutions*. Cambridge: Cambridge University Press, 1995.

Ritchelson, Jeffrey T. "Can the Intelligence Community Keep Pace with the Threat?" In *Nuclear Proliferation after the Cold War*, edited by Reiss, M. and Litwak, R., Washington, DC: Woodrow Wilson Center Press, 1994, 291–308.

Robertson, David. "Civil Society and the WTO." *The World Economy* 23:9 (2000): 1119–1134.

Robertson, Geoffrey. *Crimes against Humanity: The Struggle for Global Justice*. London: Allen Lane, 1999.

Roeling, B.V.A. *The Tokyo Trial and Beyond*. Edited by Antonio Cassese. Cambridge: Polity Press, 1993.

Rorty, Richard. *Contingency, Irony, and Solidarity*. Cambridge: Cambridge University Press, 1989.

Philosophy and the Mirror of Nature. Princeton: Princeton University Press, 1981.

Rosecrance, Richard. "The Rise of the Virtual State." *Foreign Affairs* 75:4 (1996): 45–61.

Rosenberg, Justin. *The Empire of Civil Society: A Critique of the Realist Theory of International Relations*. London: Verso, 1994.

Rosenberg, Tina. *The Haunted Land: Facing Europe's Ghosts after Communism*. New York: Vintage Books, 1995.

Rosencranz, Armin, and David Louk. "Doe v. Unocal: Holding Corporations Liable for Human Rights Abuses on Their Watch." *Chapman Law Review* 8 (2005): 135–147.

Rosenmeyer, Thomas G. *The Art of Aeschylus*. Berkeley: University of California Press, 1982.

Rostow, W.W. *The Stages of Economic Growth: A Non-Communist Manifesto*. Cambridge: Cambridge University Press, 1960.

Rousseau, Jean-Jacques. *A Discourse on Inequality*. Edited by Cranston, M. London: Penguin Books, 1984.

"Of the Social Contract." In *The Social Contract and Other Later Political Writings*, edited by Gourevitch, V., Cambridge: Cambridge University Press, 1997.

The Social Contract and Discourse on the Origin and Foundation of Inequality among Mankind. Edited by Crocker, L.G. New York: Washington Square Press, 1971.

Röling, B.V.A., and Antonio Cassese. *The Tokyo Trial and Beyond: Reflections of a Peacemonger*. Cambridge: Polity Press, 1993.

Rowe, David M. *Manipulating the Market: Understanding Economic Sanctions, Institutional Change and Political Unity of White Rhodesia*. Ann Arbor: University of Michigan Press, 2001.

Ruggie, John G. *Constructing the World Polity: Essays on International Institutionalization*. London–New York: Routledge, 1998.

"Continuity and Transformation in the World Polity: Toward a Neorealist Synthesis." *World Politics* 35:2 (1983): 261–285.

"International Regimes, Transactions, and Change: Embedded Liberalism in the Postwar Economic Order." *International Organization* 36:2 (1982): 379–415.

Just Business: Multinational Corporations and Human Rights. New York: W.W. Norton, 2013.

(ed.). *Multilateralism Matters: The Theory and Praxis of an Institutional Form*. New York: Columbia University Press, 1993.

Winning the Peace: America and World Order in the New Era. New York: Columbia University Press, 1996.

Runciman, W.G. *The Theory of Cultural and Social Selection*. Cambridge: Cambridge University Press, 2009.

Rüsen, Jörn. *Historische Vernunft*. Göttingen: Vandenhoeck & Ruprecht, 1983.

Russett, Bruce M. *Grasping the Democratic Peace: Principles for a Post-Cold War World*. Princeton: Princeton University Press, 1993.

Ryle, Gilbert. *The Concept of Mind*. Chicago: University of Chicago Press, 1984.

Sachs, Jeffrey. *Developing Country Debt and Economic Performance*. Chicago: University of Chicago Press, 1989.

"Proposals for Reform of the Global Financial Architecture." Mimeo, December 1998.

"What We Have Learned So Far from the Asian Financial Crisis." Mimeo, January 1999.

Sack, Robert David. *Human Territoriality: Its Theory and History*. Cambridge: Cambridge University Press, 1986.

Sagar, Rahul. "Is Ideal Theory Practical?" *Review of International Studies* 37:4 (2011): 1949–1965.

Sallust. *The War with Jugurtha*. Cambridge, MA: Harvard University Press, 2013.

Samadi, David B. "Forget Self-Driving Cars: Here's How Google Plans to Change How We Live Forever," *The Observer* (Style & Design), May 14, 2015.

Santos, Boaventura de Sousa. "Law: A Map of Misreading: Toward a Postmodern Conception of Law." *Journal of Law and Society* 14:3 (1987): 279–302.

Sartori, Giovanni. "Concept Misformation in Comparative Politics." *The American Political Science Review* 64:4 (1970): 1033–1053.

Sassen, Saskia. "Global Financial Centers." *Foreign Affairs* 78:1 (1999): 75–86.

Schachter, Oscar. "International Law in Theory and Practice: General Course in Public International Law." *Recueil des Cours* 178:5 (1982): 1–395.

Schadewaldt, Wolfgang. *Die Anfänge der Geschichtsschreibung bei den Griechen: Herodot, Thukydides*. Edited by Schudoma, I. Frankfurt: Suhrkamp, 1982.

Scharpf, Fritz Wilhelm. *Demokratietheorie zwischen Utopie und Anpassung*. Konstanz: Universitätsverlag, 1970.

Schauer, Frederick F. *Playing by the Rules: A Philosophical Examination of Rule-Based Decision-Making in Law and in Life*. Oxford: Oxford University Press, 1991.

Scheffer, David J. "International Judicial Intervention." *Foreign Policy* 102 (1996): 34–51.

Scheinman, Lawrence, and Atlantic Council of the United States. *Assuring the Nuclear Non-Proliferation Safeguards System*. Washington, DC: Atlantic Council of the United States, 1992.

Schelling, Thomas. *Arms and Influence*. New Haven: Yale University Press, 1967.

The Strategy of Conflict. Cambridge, MA: Harvard University Press, 1980.

Schiff, Benjamin N. *Building the International Criminal Court*. Cambridge: Cambridge University Press, 2008.

Schiffer, Werner. *Theorien der Geschichtsschreibung und Ihre Erzähtheoretische Relevanz*. Stuttgart: Metzler, 1980.

Schliesser, Eric. "Reading Adam Smith after Darwin: On the Evolution of Propensities, Institutions, and Sentiments." *Journal of Economic Behavior and Organization* 77:1 (2011): 14–22.

Schmidt, Eric, and Jonathan Rosenberg. *How Google Works*. New York: Grand Central Publishing, 2014.

Schmidt, Siegfried (ed.). *Der Radikale Konstruktivismus*. Frankfurt: Suhrkamp, 1987.

Schmitt, Carl. *The Concept of the Political*. New Brunswick, NJ: Rutgers University Press, 1977.

The Concept of the Political. Trans. G. Schwab. Chicago: University of Chicago Press, 1996.

The Nomos of the Earth in the International Law of the Jus Publicum Europaeum. Trans. G.L. Ulmen. New York: Telos Press, 2003.

Schmitt, Michael N. "Computer Network Attack and the Use of Force in International Law: Thoughts on a Normative Framework." In *Essays on Law and War at the Fault Lines* (The Hague: T.M.C. Asser Press, 2012), 3–48.

Schoppa, Leonard J. "The Social Context in Coercive International Bargaining." *International Organization* 53:2 (1999): 307–342.

Schrijver, Nico. "The Ban on the Use of Force in the UN Charter." In *The Oxford Handbook of the Use of Force in International Law*, edited by Weller, M., Oxford: Oxford University Press, 2015, 465–487.

Schwöbel, Christine E.J. "The Comfort of International Criminal Law." *Law and Critique* 24:2 (2012): 169–191.

Scobbie, Iain. "The Invocation of Responsibility for the Breach of 'Obligations under Peremptory Norms of General International Law'." *European Journal of International Law* 13:5 (2002): 1201–1255.

Scott, James C. *Seeing Like a State: How Certain Schemes to Improve the Human Condition Have Failed*. New Haven: Yale University Press, 1998.

Seaman, Michael G. "The Athenian Expedition to Melos in 416 BC." *Historia: Zeitschrift für Alte Geschichte* 46:4 (1997): 385–418.

Searle, John. "Collective Intentions and Actions." In *Intentions in Communications*, edited by Cohen, P., Morgan, J., and Pollack, M., Cambridge, MA: MIT Press, 1990, 401–416.

The Construction of Social Reality. London: Penguin, 1995.

Intentionality: An Essay in the Philosophy of Mind. Cambridge: Cambridge University Press, 1983.

Speech Acts. Cambridge: Cambridge University Press, 1969.

Seidl-Hohenfeldern, Ignaz. "International Economic Soft Law." *Recueil des Cours* 163 (1979): 165–246.

Seligman, Adam B. *The Idea of Civil Society.* Princeton: Princeton University Press, 1992.

Sellars, Kirsten. *"Crimes against Peace" and International Law.* Cambridge: Cambridge University Press, 2013.

Sellars, Wilfred. *Science and Metaphysics.* London: Routlege and Kegan Paul, 1968.

Sen, Amartya. "Rational Fools: On the Behavioral Foundations of Economic Theory." In *Scientific Models and Men*, edited by Harris, H., London: Oxford University Press, 1987, 317–344.

Sennett, Richard. *The Fall of Public Man.* New York: Norton, 1992.

Sewell, William H. "A Theory of Structure: Duality, Agency, and Transformation." *The American Journal of Sociology* 98:1 (1992): 1–29.

Shear, Joseph K. (ed.). *Mind, Reason and Being in the World: The McDowell–Dreyfus Debate.* Abingdon: Routledge 2013.

Shklar, Judith N. *Legalism: Law, Morals, and Political Trials.* Cambridge, MA: Harvard University Press, 1986.

Shlaim, Avi. "Failures in National Intelligence Estimates: The Case of the Yom Kippur War." *World Politics* 28:3 (1976): 348–380.

Sikkink, Kathryn. "Codes of Conduct for Transnational Corporations: The Case of the WHO/UNICEF Code." *International Organization* 40:4 (1986): 815–840.

Sil, Rudra, and Peter J. Katzenstein. "Analytic Eclecticism in the Study of World Politics: Reconfiguring Problems and Mechanisms across Research Traditions." *Perspectives on Politics* 8:2 (2010): 411–431.

(eds.). *Beyond Paradigms: Analytic Eclecticism in the Study of World Politics.* New York: Palgrave Macmillan, 2010.

Simma, Bruno. "Nato, the UN and the Use of Force: Legal Aspects." *European Journal of International Law* 10:1 (1999): 1–22.

Simmel, Georg. *Conflict and the Web of Group Affiliations.* New York: Free Press, 1955.

Simmel, Georg, and Otthein Rammstedt. *Soziologie: Untersuchungen über die Formen der Vergesellschaftung.* Frankfurt am Main: Suhrkamp, 1992.

Simmonds, N.E. "Between Positivism and Idealism." *Cambridge Law Journal* 50:2 (1991): 308–329.

"Why Conventionalism Does Not Collapse into Pragmatism." *Cambridge Law Journal* 49:1 (1990): 63–79.

Simons, Geoff L. *The Scourging of Iraq: Sanctions, Law and Natural Justice*, 2nd edn. New York: St. Martin's Press, 1998.

Simpson, Gerry J. *Law, War & Crime: Iraq and the Re-Invention of International Law.* Cambridge: Polity, 2007.

Skinner, Quentin. *Reason and Rhetoric in the Philosophy of Hobbes.* Cambridge: Cambridge University Press, 1996.

Skocpol, Theda. *States and Social Revolutions: A Comparative Analysis of France, Russia, and China.* Cambridge: Cambridge University Press, 1979.

Slaughter, Anne-Marie. "A Global Community of Courts." *Harvard International Law Journal* 44:3 (2003): 191–220.

"International Law in a World of Liberal States." *European Journal of International Law* 6:4 (1995): 503–538.

"A Liberal Theory of International Law." *Proceedings of the Annual Meeting (American Society of International Law)* 94 (2000): 240–253.

"The Real New World Order." *Foreign Affairs* 76:5 (1997): 183–197.

Sloterdijk, Peter. *Die Schrecklichen Kinder der Neuzeit über das Anti-Genealogische Experiment der Moderne.* Frankfurt: Suhrkamp, 2014.

Smith, Adam. "Considerations Concerning the First Formation of Languages (1761)." In *Lectures on Rhetoric and Belles Lettres,* edited by Bryce, J.C., Oxford: Clarendon Press, 1983.

"History of Astronomy." In *Essays on Philosophical Subjects,* edited by Wightman, W.P.D., and Bryce, J.C., Oxford: Clarendon Press, 1980, 33–105.

An Inquiry into the Nature and Causes of the Wealth of Nations. Oxford: Clarendon, 1979 [1776].

"Lectures on Jurisprudence (1762/63 and 1763/64)." In *The Glasgow Edition of Works and Correspondence of Adam Smith,* edited by Meek, R.L., Raphael, D.D., and Stein, P., Oxford: Clarendon Press, 1978.

The Theory of Moral Sentiments (1759). Edited by Raphael, D.D. and Macfie, A.L. Oxford: Clarendon Press, 1976.

Smith, Anthony D. *Nationalism and Modernism: A Critical Survey of Recent Theories of Nations and Nationalism.* London: Routledge, 1998.

Nations and Nationalism in a Global Era. Cambridge: Polity Press, 1995.

Smith, R. Jeffrey, and Glenn Frankel. "Saddam's Nuclear Weapons Dream: A Lingering Nightmare," *Washington Post,* October 13, 1991, A1, A44–45.

Soafer, Abraham D. "On the Necessity of Preemption." *European Journal of International Law* 14:2 (2003): 209–226.

Sørensen, Georg. "What Kind of World Order?" *Cooperation and Conflict* 41:4 (2006): 343–363.

Sosa, Ernest (ed.). *Causation and Conditionals.* London: Oxford University Press, 1975.

Soutou, Georges-Henri. "Die Kriegsziele des Deutschen Reiches." In *Der Erste Weltkrieg: Wirkung, Wahrnehmung, Analyse,* edited by Michalka, W., München: Piper, 1994, 28–53.

L'or Et Le Sang: Les buts de guerre économiques de la première guerre mondiale. Paris: Fayard, 1989.

Spiro, David E. "The Insignificance of the Liberal Peace." *International Security* 19:2 (1994): 50–86.

Sponeck, Hans-Christof von. *A Different Kind of War: The UN Sanctions Regime in Iraq.* New York: Berghahn Books, 2006.

Sponeck, Hans von, and Denis Halliday. "The Hostage Nation," *The Guardian,* November 29, 2001, accessed at www.theguardian.com/world/2001/nov/29/iraq.comment.

Stahn, Carsten. "Accommodating Individual Criminal Responsibility and National Reconciliation: The UN Truth Commission for East Timor." *American Journal of International Law* 95:4 (2001): 952–966.

"Between 'Faith' and 'Facts': By What Standards Should We Assess International Criminal Justice?" *Leiden Journal of International Law* 25:2 (2012): 251–282.

"Judicial Review of Prosecutorial Discretion: Five Years On." In *The Emerging Practice of the International Criminal Court,* edited by Stahn, C., and Sluiter, G.R., Leiden: Martinus Nijhoff Publishers, 2009, 247–280.

"Justice Delivered or Justice Denied?: The Legacy of the Katanga Judgment." *Journal of International Criminal Justice* 12:4 (2014): 809–834.

Stallings, Barbara. "Politics and Economic Crisis: A Comparative Study of Chile, Peru, and Colombia." In *Economic Crisis and Policy Choice: The Politics of Adjustment in the Third World*, edited by Nelson, J.M., Princeton: Princeton University Press, 1990, 113–168.

Steinberger, Peter J. *The Concept of Political Judgment*. Chicago: University of Chicago Press, 1993.

Steiner, Henry J. World Peace Foundation, Harvard Law School, and Human Rights Program. *Truth Commissions: A Comparative Assessment*. Cambridge, MA: World Peace Foundation, 1997.

Stewart, James G. "The End of 'Modes of Liability' for International Crimes." *Leiden Journal of International Law* 25:1 (2012): 165–219.

Stiglitz, Joseph E. "Democratizing the International Monetary Fund and the World Bank: Governance and Accountability." *Governance* 16:1 (2003): 111–139.

Globalization and Its Discontents. London: Allen Lane, Penguin, 2002.

"Prize Lecture: Information and the Change in the Paradigm in Economics." Nobelprize.org, June 14, 2016, available at www.nobelprize.org/nobel_prizes/economic-sciences/laureates/2001/stiglitz-lecture.html.

Strange, Susan. *States and Markets*. London: Pinter, 1998.

"Towards a Theory of Transnational Empire." In *Global Changes and Theoretical Challenges: Approaches to World Politics for the 1990s*, edited by Czempiel, E.O., and Rosenau, J.N., Lexington, MA: Lexington Books, 1989, 161–176.

"Wake up, Krasner! The World Has Changed." *Review of International Political Economy* 1:2 (1994): 209–219.

Subotic, Jelena. *Hijacked Justice: Dealing with the Past in the Balkans*. Ithaca, NY: Cornell University Press, 2009.

Suganami, Hidemi. "Agents, Structures, Narratives." *European Journal of International Relations* 5:3 (1999): 365–386.

Sunstein, Cass R. *On Rumors: How Falsehoods Spread*. New York: Farrar, Strauss, Giroux, 2009.

Republic.com. Princeton: Princeton University Press, 2001.

Talbott, Strobe. *Deadly Gambits: The Reagan Administration and the Stalemate in Nuclear Arms Control*. New York: Vintage Books, 1985.

Endgame: The Inside Story of Salt II. New York: Harper & Row, 1980.

Tallgren, Immi. "Who Are 'We' in International Criminal Law? On Critics and Membership." In *Critical Approaches to International Criminal Law: An Introduction*, edited by Schwöbel, C.E.J., Abingdon: Routledge, 2014, 71–95.

Tamir, Yael. *Liberal Nationalism: Studies in Moral, Political, and Legal Philosophy*. Princeton: Princeton University Press, 1993.

Tan, Kok-Chor. *Justice, Institutions, and Luck: The Site, Ground, and Scope of Equality*. Oxford: Oxford University Press, 2012.

Tarrow, Sidney. *Power in Movement: Social Movements and Contentious Politics*. Cambridge: Cambridge University Press, 1998.

Taylor, Charles. *Modern Social Imaginaries*. Durham, NC: Duke University Press, 2004.

"Self-Interpreting Animals." In *Human Agency and Language*, edited by Taylor, C., Cambridge: Cambridge University Press, 1985, 45–76.

Sources of the Self: The Making of Modern Identity. Cambridge, MA: Harvard University Press, 1989.

Teitel, Ruti. *Globalizing Transitional Justice: Contemporary Essays*. Oxford: Oxford University Press, 2014.

Humanity's Law. Oxford–New York: Oxford University Press, 2011.

"Transitional Jurisprudence: The Role of Law in Political Transformation." *Yale Law Journal* 106 (1997): 2009–2080.

Transitional Justice. Oxford: Oxford University Press, 2000.

Teschke, Benno. *The Myth of 1648: Class, Geopolitics, and the Making of Modern International Relations*. London: Verso, 2003.

Tesón, Fernando R. *Humanitarian Intervention: An Inquiry into Law and Morality*. Dobbs Ferry, NY: Transnational Publishers, 1988.

Tetlock, Philip E., and Aaron Belkin. *Counterfactual Thought Experiments in World Politics: Logical, Methodological, and Psychological Perspectives*. Princeton: Princeton University Press, 1996.

Teubner, Gunther. *Recht als Auto-Poietisches System*. Frankfurt: Suhrkamp, 1989.

The Hague Institute for Global Justice, and Netherlands Institute of International Relations Clingendael. "Special Report on Transnational Governance and Democratic Legitimacy." 2014. Available at www.clingendael.org.

Thies, Cameron G. "Progress, History and Identity in International Relations Theory: The Case of the Idealist–Realist Debate." *European Journal of International Relations* 8:2 (2002): 147–185.

Thomas, Caroline. "The Pragmatic Case against Intervention." In *International Relations, Political Theory, and the Ethics of Intervention*, edited by Forbes, I. and Hoffman, M., London: Macmillan, 1993, 91–103.

Thompson, John B. *The Media and Modernity: A Social Theory of the Media*. Stanford: Stanford University Press, 1995.

Thucydides. *The History of the Peloponnesian War*. Trans. R.W. Livingstone. Oxford: Oxford University Press, 1960.

History of the Peloponnesian War. Trans. R. Warner. London: Penguin Books, 1972.

Tönnies, Ferdinand. *Community & Society*. East Lansing, MI: Michigan State University Press, 1957.

Tostensen, Arne, and Beate Bull. "Are Smart Sanctions Feasible?" *World Politics* 54:3 (2002): 373–403.

Totani, Yuma. "The Case against the Accused." In *Beyond Victor's Justice?: The Tokyo War Crimes Trial Revisited*, edited by McCormack, T.L.H., Simpson G.J., and Tanaka, T., Leiden: Martinus Nijhoff Publishers, 2011, 147–161.

Toulmin, Stephen. "Does the Distinction between Normal and Revolutionary Science Hold Water?" In *Criticism and the Growth of Knowledge*, edited by Lakatos, I., and Musgrave, A., Cambridge: Cambridge University Press, 1970, 39–48.

Return to Reason. Cambridge, MA: Harvard University Press, 2001.

Tuomela, Raimo. *The Philosophy of Social Practices: A Collective Acceptance View*. Cambridge: Cambridge University Press, 2007.

"What Goals Are Joint Goals?" *Theory and Decision* 28:1 (1990): 1–20.

Tuomela, Raimo, and Kaarlo Miller. "We-Intentions." *Philosophical Studies* 53:3 (1988): 367–389.

Udall, Lori. "The World Bank and Public Accountability: Has Anything Changed?" In *The Struggle for Accountability the World Bank, NGOs, and Grassroots Movements*, edited by Fox, J. and Brown, L.D., Cambridge, MA: MIT Press, 1998, 391–436.

van der Haar, Edwin. "David Hume and International Political Theory." *Review of International Studies* 34 (2008): 225–242.

van Genugten, Willem J.M., and Gerard A. de Groot (eds.). *United Nations Sanctions: Effectiveness and Effects, Especially in the Field of Human Rights, a Multi-Disciplinary Approach*. Antwerpen: Intersentia, 1999.

Vanhanen, Tatu. *The Process of Democratization: A Comparative Study of 147 States, 1980–88*. New York: Crane Russak, 1990.

Varadarajan, Radhabinod. "Pal's Dissent at the Tokyo Trials." *European Journal of International Relations*, 21:4 (2015): 793–815.

Vasilyan, Syuzanna. "Moral Power as Objectification of the Civilian/Normative EUlogy: The European Union as a Conflict-Dealer in the South Caucasus." *Journal of International Relations and Development* 17:3 (2014): 397–424.

Väyrynen, Raimo (ed.). *Globalization and Global Governance*. Lanham: Rowman & Littlefield Publishers, 1999.

Vennesson, Pascal, and Nikolas M. Rajkovic. "The Transnational Politics of Warfare Accountability: Human Rights Watch versus the Israel Defense Forces." *International Relations* 26:4 (2012): 409–429.

Ventzke, Ingo, *How Interpretation Makes Law: On Semantic Change and Normative Twists*. Oxford: Oxford University Press, 2014.

Vergil. *The Aeneid of Vergil*. Trans. Allen Mandelbaum. New York: Bantam Books, 1961.

Virilio, Paul. *War and Cinema*. London: Verso 1989.

Volk, Ulrich. *Das Problem eines Semantischen Skeptizismus: Saul Kripkes Wittgenstein-Interpretation*. Rheinfelden: Schäuble, 1988.

Voltaire. *Essai sur les Moeurs*. Paris: Imprimerie de la Societe Litteraire Typographique, 1785.

Vuori, Juha. "Constructivism and Securitization Studies." In *Handbook of Security Studies*, edited by Cavelty, M.D., and Theiery, B., London: Routledge, 2010, 52–72.

Wade, Robert. "Greening the Bank: The Struggle over the Environment, 1970–1995." In *The World Bank: Its First Half Century*, edited by Kapur, D., Lewis, J.P., and Webb, R.C., Washington, DC: Brookings Institution, 1997, 611–735.

Walker, R.B.J. *After the Globe, Before the World*. Abingdon: Routledge, 2010. *Inside/Outside: International Relations as Political Theory*. Cambridge: Cambridge University Press, 1993.

Wallerstein, Immanuel Maurice. *The Modern World System: Capitalist Agriculture and the Origins of the European World Economy in the Sixteenth Century*. New York: Academic Press, 1976.

Waltz, Kenneth N. "The Myth of National Interdependence." In *The International Corporation: A Symposium*, edited by Kindleberger, C.P., Cambridge, MA: MIT Press, 1970, 205–223. *Theory of International Politics*. Reading, MA: Addison Wesley, 1979.

Walzer, Michael. *Spheres of Justice: A Defense of Pluralism and Equality.* New York: Basic Books, 1983.

(ed.). *Toward a Global Civil Society.* Providence, RI: Berghahn Books, 1995.

Wang, Q. Edward, and Georg G. Iggers. *A Theory of Contestation.* Heidelberg–New York: Springer, 2014.

(eds.). *Turning Points in Historiography: A Cross-Cultural Perspective.* Rochester, NY: University of Rochester Press, 2002.

Wapner, Paul. "Politics beyond the State: Environmental Activism and World Civic Politics." *World Politics* 47:3 (1995): 311–340.

Watkins, John. "Against Normal Science." In *Criticism and the Growth of Knowledge*, edited by Lakatos, I., and Musgrave, A., Cambridge: Cambridge University Press, 1970, 25–38.

Weber, Max. *Aufsätze zur Wissenschaftslehre*, 5th edn. Tübingen: J.C.B. Mohr, 1985.

Gesammelte Aufsätze zur Wissenssoziologie. Tübingen: J.C.B. Mohr, 1922.

Gesammelte Aufsätze zur Wissenssoziologie. Edited by Winckelmann, J. Tübingen: J.C.B. Mohr, 1971.

"Objectivity in the Social Sciences." In *The Methodology of the Social Sciences* (New York: Free Press, 1996), 49–112.

"On the Concept of Sociology and the Meaning of Social Conduct." In *Basic Concepts in Sociology.* Trans. H.P. Secher. Secaucus, NJ: The Citadel Press, 1972, 29–58.

"Politik als Beruf." In *Gesammelte Politische Schriften* (Stuttgart: UTB, 1988), 396–451.

The Protestant Ethic and the Spirit of Capitalism. Trans. T. Parsons. London: Routledge, 1992.

Wirtschaft und Gesellschaft: Grundriss der Verstehenden Soziologie, vol 1. Edited by Winckelmann, J. Köln: Kiepenheuer & Witsch, 1964.

Weil, Prosper. "Towards Relative Normativity in International Law?" *The American Journal of International Law* 77:3 (1983): 413–442.

Weisman, Steven R. "Editorial Observer; Coming to Terms with Kosovo's 'Old' Hatreds." *New York Times*, June 12, 1999, accessed at www.nytimes.com/1999/06/12/opinion/editorial-observer-coming-to-terms-with-kosovo-s-old-hatreds.html.

Weller, Marc. "The Rambouillet Conference on Kosovo." *International Affairs* 75:2 (1999): 211–251.

Welsh, Jennifer M. (ed.). *Humanitarian Intervention and International Relations.* Oxford: Oxford University Press, 2004.

Welzel, Hans. *Das neue Bild des Strafrechtssystems: Eine Einführung in die Finale Handlungslehre.* Göttingen: Otto Schwartz, 1961.

Wenar, Leif, and Branko Milanovic. "Are Liberal People Peaceful? *Journal of Political Philosophy* 17:4 (2009): 452–486.

Wendt, Alexander. "Anarchy Is What States Make of It." *International Organization,* 46:2 (1992): 391–425.

"Collective Identity Formation and the International State." *The American Political Science Review* 88:2 (1994): 384–396.

"Driving with the Rearview Mirror: On the Rational Science of Institutional Design." *International Organization* 55:4 (2001): 1019–1049.

Quantum Mind and Social Science: Unifying Physical and Social Ontology.
  Cambridge: Cambridge University Press, 2015.
Social Theory of International Politics. Cambridge: Cambridge University Press,
  1999.
Wendt, Alexander, and Raymond Duvall. "Institutions and International Order." In
  *Global Changes and Theoretical Challenges: Approaches to World Politics for
  the 1990s,* edited by Czempiel, Ernst-Otto, and Rosenau, J.N., Lexington, MA:
  Lexington Books, 1989, 51–73.
Werner, Wouter G. "We Cannot Allow Ourselves to Imagine What It All Means:
  Documentary Practices and the International Criminal Court." *Law and
  Contemporary Problems* 76:3–4 (2013): 319–339.
Westmoreland, William C. *A Soldier Reports.* Garden City, NY: Doubleday, 1976.
Wheeler, Nicholas. *Humanitarian Intervention in International Society.* Oxford:
  Oxford University Press, 2003.
Wheeler, Nicholas, and Justin Morris. "Humanitarian Intervention and State Practice."
  In *International Society after the Cold War: Anarchy and Order Reconsidered,*
  edited by Fawn, R. and Larkins, J., New York: St. Martin's Press, 1996, 135–171.
"The Kosovo Bombing Campaign" In *The Politics of International Law,* edited by
  Reus-Smith, C., Cambridge: Cambridge University Press, 2004, 189–216.
Saving Strangers, Humanitarian Interventions in International Society. Oxford:
  Oxford University Press, 2002
White, Hayden. *The Content and the Form: Narrative Discourse and Historical
  Representation.* Baltimore: Johns Hopkins University Press, 1999.
Tropics of Discourse: Essays in Cultural Criticism. Baltimore: Johns Hopkins
  University Press, 1978.
Whitehead, Alfred N. *Process and Reality.* Chicago: University of Chicago Press,
  1981.
Widner, Jennifer. "Courts and Democracy in Post-Conflict Transitions: A Social
  Scientist's Perspective on the African Case." *The American Journal of
  International Law* 95:1 (2001): 64–75.
Wiener, Antje. *The Invisible Constitution of Politics: Contested Norms and
  International Encounters.* Cambridge: Cambridge University Press, 2008.
Willett, Thomas. "For a Broader Public Choice Analysis of the International Monetary
  Fund." In *Governing the World's Money,* edited by Andrews, D.M., Henning,
  C.R., and Pauly, L.W., Ithaca, NY: Cornell University Press, 2002, 60–78.
Towards a Broader Public Choice Analysis of the International Monetary Fund.
  Claremont, CA: Claremont Institute for Economic Policy Studies, 2002.
Williams, Bernard Arthur Owen. *Moral Luck: Philosophical Papers, 1973–1980.*
  Cambridge: Cambridge University Press, 1981.
"Persons, Character and Morality." In *Moral Luck: Philosophical Papers,
  1973–1980* (Cambridge: Cambridge University Press, 1981), 1–19.
Williams, Mary Frances. *Ethics in Thucydides: The Ancient Simplicity.* Lanham, MD:
  University Press of America, 1998.
Williams, Michael C. "Hobbes and International Relations." *International
  Organization* 50:2 (1996): 213–236.
The Realist Tradition and the Limits of International Relations. Cambridge:
  Cambridge University Press, 2005.

"Words, Images, Enemies: Securitization and International Politics." *International Studies Quarterly* 47:4 (2003): 511–531.

Wittfogel, Karl August. *Oriental Despotism: A Comparative Study of Total Power.* New Haven: Yale University Press, 1957.

Wittgenstein, Ludwig. *Philosophical Investigations.* Trans. G.E.M. Anscombe. New York: Macmillan, 1953.

Preliminary Studies for the "Philosophical Investigations" Generally Known as the Blue and Brown Books. New York: Harper & Row, 1964.

Remarks on the Foundations of Mathematics. Trans. G.E.M. Anscombe. Oxford: Basil Blackwell, 1956.

Wolf, Susan. *Meaning in Life and Why It Matters.* Princeton: Princeton University Press, 2010.

Wong, David B. "Psychological Realism and Moral Theory." In *Theory and Practice,* edited by Shapiro, I., and Wagner DeCrew, J., New York: New York University Press, 1995, 108–137.

Woods, Ngaire, and Amrita Narlikar. "Governance and the Limits of Accountability: The WTO, the IMF, and the World Bank." *International Social Science Journal* 53:170 (2001): 569–583.

Wrong, Dennis. *Problem of Order: What Unites and Divides Society.* New York: Simon and Schuster, 1994.

Yamada, Otozō. *Materials on the Trial of Former Servicemen of the Japanese Army: Charged with Manufacturing and Employing Bacteriological Weapons.* Moscow: Foreign Languages Pub. House, 1950.

Yarhi-Milo, Keren. *Knowing the Adversary: Leaders, Intelligence, and Assessment of Intentions in International Relations.* Princeton: Princeton University Press, 2014.

Yee, Albert S. "The Causal Effects of Ideas on Policies." *International Organization* 50:1 (1996): 69–108.

Young, Oran. *Compliance and Public Authority: A Theory with International Applications.* Baltimore: Johns Hopkins University Press, 1979.

"The Effectiveness of International Institutions: Hard Cases and Critical Variables." In *Governance without Government: Order and Change in World Politics,* edited by Rosenau, J.N., and Czempiel, E.-O., Cambridge: Cambridge University Press, 1992, 160–194.

(ed.). *Global Governance: Drawing Insights from the Environmental Experience.* Cambridge, MA: MIT Press, 1997.

International Governance. Ithaca, NY: Cornell, 1994.

Zalaquett, Jose. "Balancing Ethical Imperatives and Political Constraints: The Dilemma of New Democracies Confronting Past Human Rights Violations." *Hastings Law Journal* 43:6 (1991): 1425–1438.

Zanotti, Laura. *Governing Disorder: UN Peace Operations, International Security, and Democratization in the Post-Cold War Era.* University Park: Pennsylvania State University Press, 2011.

Zarakol, Ayşe. *After Defeat: How the East Learned to Live with the West,* Cambridge: Cambridge University Press, 2011.

"What Makes Terrorism Modern?: Terrorism, Legitimacy, and the International System." *Review of International Studies* 37:5 (2011): 2311–2336.

Zehfuss, Maja. "Sprachlosigkeit Schränkt Ein." *Zeitschrift für Internationale Beziehungen* 5:1 (1998): 109–137.

Zimmermann, Andreas, and Carsten Stahn. "Yugoslav Territory, United Nations Trusteeship or Sovereign State?: Reflections on the Current and Future Legal Status of Kosovo." *Nordic Journal of International Law* 70:4 (2001): 423–460.

Zips, Martin. "Empört Euch!" *Süddeutsche Zeitung*, January 23/24, 2016.

Zoller, Elisabeth. *Peacetime Unilateral Remedies: An Analysis of Countermeasures.* Dobbs Ferry, NY: Transnational Publishers, 1984.

Zollschan, G.K., and Hirsch, H.W. (eds.). *Explorations in Social Change.* Boston, MA: Houghton Mifflin, 1964.

Zolo, Danilo. *Cosmopolis: Prospects for World Governance.* Cambridge: Polity Press, 1997.

Zumbansen, Peer, and Gralf-Peter Calliess. *Rough Consensus and Running Code: A Theory of Transnational Private Law.* Oxford: Hart, 2010.

Zürn, Michael (ed.). *Globalizing Interests: Pressure Groups and Denationalization.* Albany, NY: SUNY Press, 2005.

Index

CPSIA information can be obtained
at www.ICGtesting.com
Printed in the USA
LVHW010225251022
731490LV00009B/409